A Companion to
Pirandello
Studies

A Companion to Pirandello Studies

EDITED BY

John Louis DiGaetani

FOREWORD BY

Eric Bentley

Greenwood Press

NEW YORK • WESTPORT, CONNECTICUT • LONDON

Library of Congress Cataloging-in-Publication Data

A Companion to Pirandello studies / edited by John Louis DiGaetani.
    p.   cm.
    Includes bibliographical references and index.
    ISBN 0–313–25714–0 (lib. bdg. : alk. paper)
    1. Pirandello, Luigi, 1867–1936—Criticism and interpretation.
  I. DiGaetani, John Louis, 1943–
  PQ4835.I7Z5465   1991
  853'.912—dc20   90–43377

British Library Cataloguing in Publication Data is available.

Library of Congress Catalog Card Number: 90–43377
ISBN: 0–313–25714–0

First published in 1991

Greenwood Press, 88 Post Road West, Westport, CT 06881
An imprint of Greenwood Publishing Group, Inc.

Printed in the United States of America

The paper used in this book complies with the
Permanent Paper Standard issued by the National
Information Standards Organization (Z39.48–1984).

P

In order to keep this title in print and available to the academic community, this edition was produced using digital reprint technology in a relatively short print run. This would not have been attainable using traditional methods. Although the cover has been changed from its original appearance, the text remains the same and all materials and methods used still conform to the highest book-making standards.

Dedicated to the memory

of

Theresa Rose Cavallo DiGaetani

Contents

x

Contents

Acknowledgments

I would like to thank Giuseppe and Maria Elena Albanese and Romana Cortese for their personal encouragement on this project. For professional help on this book, thanks are due to Eric Bentley, Toby Cole, and Enzo Lauretta. I would also like to thank Glauco Cambon, who encouraged me to work on this book and who unfortunately did not live to see its completion. I remember using Professor Cambon's own anthology of essays on Pirandello while I was a graduate student at the University of Wisconsin. Finally, I would like to thank Hofstra University for granting me a sabbatical leave to work on the editing of this collection.

Foreword

Eric Bentley

In the matter of Luigi Pirandello, where do things stand in 1991? We are confronted, I would say, with a two-sided situation. On the one hand, Pirandello is "hailed" by critics and scholars not just for exercising influence but for exercising an influence of the highest and most crucial kind ("seminal" influence) both on playwrights and on theatre people generally. On the other hand, he is ignored by the reading public and in the English-speaking world is not seen as the peer of such contemporaries as Joyce, Proust, Gide, Lawrence, or Mann.

Only one volume of Pirandello has been regularly available in the United States during the fifties, sixties, seventies, and eighties: the five-play collection, *Naked Masks*. One of the seven novels has still not been translated at all; the other six have been only spottily available. Of the 233 stories, though over a hundred have been published in English at one time or another, in 1991, only a handful are in print and even these are nowhere to be found in bookstores.

Many of Pirandello's writings are totally unknown to the English-speaking world. That is evident: they have not been translated into English. Does it matter? Is he perhaps one of a number of writers who are best known through a couple of masterpieces, a scattering of anthologized poems or stories? "Best known" because their other work is inferior and adds little either to one's knowledge or enjoyment? This can certainly be argued. Even in the lists of minor poetry, his poetry is minor. He is, by common consent, a major playwright, but most of the 44 plays fail to rise to the high plateau of the several masterpieces. Yet the effort to dismiss the bulk of Pirandello's works fails signally with the short stories. There is very little dross here. On the contrary, an astonishingly high average level is attained—and maintained—till the last year of the writer's life.

Then there are the novels. A rumor has gone round the world: "Pirandello, major playwright, minor novelist." This, I would think, is the greatest injustice his reputation has suffered. On what foundation? Surely a chancy one. No one of the seven volumes ever stopped the clock, as, say, *Ulysses* was to do, not to mention *A La Recherche du Temps Perdu*, or even Pirandello's own most successful plays, *Six Characters* and *Enrico IV*. Bad timing? Yet Pirandello can hardly be blamed for the fact that critics were not ready to appraise the fiction until they had decided that his major contribution was in drama. It is also true that none of the seven novels is *the* Pirandello novel, excusing the reader from any obligation to read the others. Then again, while as a playwright in the 1920s he could easily outrun most of the competition, in fiction the competition included several of the greatest writers of the past hundred years.

Perhaps the largest factor of all was the magnitude of *Six Characters* as a cultural event throughout Europe and the Americas. Everything else in Pirandello's career was overshadowed by it. And if all his other work would henceforward be underpraised, the world-famous revolutionary masterwork was overpraised, not least by the Maestro himself, who is clearly the author of the sentence, "*Six Characters* is the most original and the most powerful work of all the theatres ancient and modern in all nations," a sentence he pretended had been written by Bernard Shaw.

Rather than speculate further on the reasons why the novels have been underrated, let me report the intense, albeit somewhat secret, fascination they have exercised upon me over a period of decades. I call it secret because it is not revealed in any of the studies of Pirandello that I published down the years. The external reason for this omission was that, professionally, I was a drama critic, not a fiction critic, yet there was also an internal reason, which certainly has to do with my own interior and may have to do with Pirandello's. From the day I found an old copy of *Shoot!* on Fourth Avenue, I was hooked. (It was autographed by Pirandello, Marta Abba, and Scott Moncrieff but cost only two dollars.) No voice in modern literature had ever seemed to speak so intimately to me. I was very sad at the time, and Pirandello's seemed the only sadness to match my own: the two of us were in league against the universe. And if this sounds trivial or adolescent, I must report that deeply vital contact had been made between myself and Pirandello's novels, and it would prove permanent. At another point I read all seven of them in rapid succession (six in English and the untranslated *Suo Marito* in Italian), an experience that took me back to the reading, as a boy, of a dozen Dumas novels in a single gulp, and, more recently, to playing Mahler's nine symphonies on the hi-fi one after the other with hardly a pause. Such experiences silence the critic in me: I've enjoyed the feast so greedily, I forget my after-dinner speech. And the speech I make later will not be about the feast. I did not write about Pirandello's novels but about his plays. They are not more enthralling than the novels but they are more compact and so, for some of us, more manageable. The plays bring sharp focus on central issues, brief encounters of immense power, astonishingly simple images that stamp themselves indelibly on the mind. But it is in the fiction that Pirandello's vision of life is spread out before us, "a tale for every day in the year."

Shall we ever be able to see the work of Pirandello as a whole? Something of the sort should surely be an aim of "Pirandello studies." The primary task will be translation: we need a Collected Works, in English, to start out from. Next highest in priority is recognition of the fiction—its merit and its range. The silence of such as myself must be broken! It is bizarre that, for example, while so much has been written about *Six Characters in Search of an Author*, so little has been written about a novel that ranks with it in quality and stands close to it in theme, *One, None and a Hundred Thousand*. It is bizarre that critics who have recognized the genius that went into Chekhov's short stories, and Henry James', have either overlooked Pirandello's altogether or failed to detect and describe the genius therein.

Reverting to the two-sided situation in the matter of Luigi Pirandello, I should add that, as the work of Pirandello is more fully assimilated, even the vaunted influence of Pirandellian theatre will change. Up to now, it has been little more than the influence of a single idea: life as role playing (which, dramaturgically, has meant plays within plays *ad nauseam*). The danger is this was to see in Pirandello only a thinker or only a playmaking craftsman. Missing was the writer! Missing was literature. Translators, myself included, bear part of the blame— to the extent that we have failed to bring Pirandello's particular and peculiar style through into another language. This style *is* the man, and it *is* what carries such otherwise impossibly abstruse speeches as those of the Father in *Six Characters*.

For the English-speaking world, Luigi Pirandello remains, in 1991, *terra incognita*. Attention needs calling, most of all, to that which is the foundation of his greatness in fiction and drama alike: his language, his prose. (The turn from fiction to drama around 1920 represented, among other things, a decision to concentrate on one form of prose: conversational dialogue conceived as talked action—*azione parlata*.)

Introduction: Pirandello's Life and Work

John Louis DiGaetani

Luigi Pirandello has entered the realm of the major literary figure in several ways: He won the Nobel Prize for Literature in 1934, his plays are often staged, and they are frequently studied in colleges and universities around the world. This book was designed to improve the general understanding of this major figure by providing a series of scholarly essays about Pirandello and his writings. One of my chief goals as editor was to broaden the average reader's perspective on Pirandello, ensuring that he would be seen as a more accomplished author than simply the writer of *Six Characters in Search of an Author*, his most famous play. Thus, this reference companion includes chapters about other plays, about his novels and short stories, and even translations of several of his poems. The combination will, I hope, testify to the genuine breadth of creativity that characterizes this wonderful Italian writer.

In *A Companion to Pirandello Studies* the reader will find a structured collection of essays by some of the best-known Pirandello experts and scholars of modern drama. Using a variety of styles and topics (and not always agreeing), these writers explore different approaches to analyze significant aspects of Pirandello, including Pirandello's world, his background, his plays, his major works, his novels, his influence, and how he can be most effectively performed. Both his theatrical and nontheatrical works will be discussed here so that the reader will arrive at a clearer, better, and more comprehensive understanding of this great revolutionary in modern literature. Although the writers in this volume do not always agree (just as the editor intended), only such a variety of points of views, styles, and approaches can be expected to represent adequately the range and richness of Luigi Pirandello's literary work.

PIRANDELLO'S LIFE

Luigi Pirandello was born in Sicily in 1867 into a wealthy family. His father Stefano became quite rich from his sulphur mines, and although his relationship with his son was never completely harmonious, Luigi tried to be an obedient Sicilian son in every way he could, and the father tried to help his boy in any way he could. That he sent Luigi to Bonn, Germany, for graduate work in philology, at the father's expense, indicates an unusual and loving father, supportive despite family quarrels between father and son. For a Sicilian boy to study in Germany was certainly unusual, and graduate work in philology rather than mining, engineering, or metallurgy represented an equally unusual direction (Giudice, 8–22).

In part, the difficult relationship between father and son reflected even more disturbing relations between the son and his mother, who seems to have remained a mere shadow, and a nervous shadow at that, in the presence of the domineering and rigid Sicilian father. Perhaps because of difficulties in his relationships with both parents, Luigi Pirandello remained convinced—for most of his adult life— that all personal relationships were doomed to failure, that effective communication between people must remain very difficult and probably impossible. Simply put, this belief mirrored the internal conflicts and failures in interpersonal relationships within the Pirandello household. Certainly Stefano's rages and his doctrinaire pronouncements to other family members controlled the moods of his wife and indeed the entire family (Giudice, 18–19).

Luigi Pirandello's own marriage served largely to confirm his suspicions about the impossibility of all human intimacy. Acting the obedient Sicilian son, he married the woman his father had chosen for him. In Sicilian tradition, the father arranged the marriage, in this case with the daughter of his business partner, Calogero Portulano. The bride was Antonietta Portulano, who eventually would become insane and require hospitalization in a mental asylum—the culmination of many years of horrible conflicts and groundless accusations voiced within the family of Luigi Pirandello. Despite the presence of three children, their marriage became a mutual horror, primarily because of serious mental problems, especially paranoia, displayed by Pirandello's wife.

In addition to his traumatic experiences with her insanity, Pirandello's native and ingrained pessimism worked to focus both his theatrical and literary art not only on the dark side, the insane, but also on the novel, the innovative, the avant-garde, until finally he reached the realm of great literature—in several genres.

A comic vein also emerged in Pirandello, and many of his plays and stories remain comedies after all. The doom and gloom aspect of his personality was balanced with an ironic, if often bitter, wit. Pirandello first became famous as a playwright in Italy by writing Sicilian comedies, which indeed were often funny. *Liolà* contains much comedy, as do many of his other plays. Even his rather grim *Henry IV* has in it many comic situations—for example, the courtiers having to pretend they are living in the time of Henry IV, or the comic asides of Belcredi, who all along suspects that Henry IV is only pretending to be insane (Bassnett-McGuire, 104–10). So there is the comic Pirandello as well as the tragic Pirandello. In fact, his novel *The Late Mattia Pascal* contains the comedy of a middle-aged man's attempts to escape from his social responsibilities. In addition, Pirandello's most famous essay is titled *Umorismo*, and in it he describes the comic strain he labels as "humoristic" to distinguish it from the merely funny or silly (Bentley, 6–8). In tone, however, much of that essay seems Germanic, especially in its critical definitions and divisions. This tone is not accidental since Pirandello received so much education in Germany.

"IL VIAGGIO IN GERMANIA"

In many ways, Pirandello's writing combines Germanic philosophical rigor with Sicilian passion, perhaps because it was not usual—then or now—for a boy from Sicily to study philology and philosophy at a German university. That Pirandello's father paid for his son to go to Bonn for his Ph.D. degree indicates both sympathy and foresight on the father's part. Pirandello's advanced education in Germany may well represent the most crucial intellectual event in his life as a writer. Certainly his letters home to his family, especially to his father, indicate a highly complex reaction to living so far north, in a country so very different from rural Sicily. To his father, Luigi attempted to demonstrate just how different he found everything in Germany, from the food to the characteristic manner of furnishing a room (Pirandello, 30–50). He also found strange and different the way people responded to each other, how they talked without the rigid formality and usual game-playing of the Sicilian style. Briefly, people seemed more trusting and less suspicious of each other in Germany; they appeared more open to an honest interchange of ideas. German society also seemed less rigidly class-conscious than that in rural Sicily. All these differences caused the young Sicilian student deep concern, and they generated much confusion about himself and his proper relations to both his peers and his society. Luigi's experiences while living in Bonn finally made him question whether he wanted to return and live in Sicily for the rest of his life. Ultimately, of course, he did return to live in Italy, but significantly Luigi made Rome his home rather than his native Agrigento.

While his emotional reaction to living in Germany was mixed, Pirandello's German education aided his career in many ways. His first long piece of writing was his dissertation, which he wrote in German about the Sicilian dialect he had heard in his hometown of Agrigento. This Ph.D. dissertation, and even more its acceptance for book publication, must have developed Luigi's confidence as a writer. If he could achieve so much in German, what could he do in his native

Italian language? The fledgling writer was clearly encouraged by his experiences in Bonn.

Pirandello's philosophical education in Germany also served to structure his mind in a particular, definable way. The Hegelian philosophical concept of dialectical analysis—thesis, antithesis, and attempted synthesis—must have been drilled into the head of a philosophy and philology student at the University of Bonn since Hegel was a very popular figure during the late nineteenth century. Many of Pirandello's works employ Hegelian structure. In *Six Characters in Search of an Author*, for example, we have: thesis, the actors in rehearsal; antithesis, the characters looking for an author; synthesis, the resultant conflicts in the play. In *Henry IV*: thesis, Henry IV is insane; antithesis, Henry IV is pretending insanity; synthesis, the conflicts between the two theories. Or perhaps thesis, the sane world of the visitors; antithesis, the insane world of Henry IV; attempted synthesis, the comic conflicts in the opening scene and the tragic conflicts in the final scene. In *Liolà*: thesis, the social world of rural Sicily; antithesis, the mythic world of Liolà; synthesis, attempted resolution of these conflicts. Significantly, in Pirandello's characteristic pattern the synthesis is attempted, but it rarely succeeds in solving the problem.

Taken as a whole, however, the Hegelian format clarifies the thematic concerns in Pirandello's plays, even though the attempted synthesis usually results in conflicts and tragedy rather than any achieved harmony. This format indicates the power of German philosophical training on Pirandello's literary art. In his comedies, a synthesis sometimes occurs; more typically in his tragedies, a synthesis is attempted but is left aborted and incomplete.

While a philosophical student in Germany, Pirandello also absorbed some of the major philosophical trends that were sweeping across Germany at the time. Aside from the Hegelian dialectics already discussed, he would have studied two major figures, namely Schopenhauer and Nietzsche. Both represent mighty forces in the history of German philosophy, and both were at the height of their popularity at the turn of the century, when Pirandello was in Germany. Some of their ideas became part of Pirandello's intellectual framework. From Schopenhauer came the dark strain of pessimism that colors some of Pirandello's most famous work (Illiano, 170). Schopenhauer's classic *Studies in Pessimism* presents an image of man as doomed to isolation and unhappiness. His *The World as Will and Idea* has as its central thesis the idea that man is eternally in conflict, a being who can never find much happiness in life. It was not coincidental that Schopenhauer became the major inspiration for Richard Wagner's saddest opera, the tragic *Tristan und Isolde*. In the second act of that opera, Tristan fashions a lesson on Schopenhauer for the benefit of his lover, Isolde, and together they are doomed in consequence of their adulterous love. A devout disciple of Schopenhauer, Tristan seeks death at the end of each of the acts of Wagner's opera; finally, in Act III he succeeds with his suicide.

More positive than the gloomy Schopenhauer, Friedrich Nietzsche emphasized a hope for society in his famous *Thus Spake Zarathustra*, but society's hope depends on its refusal to restrain its Zarathustra. Profoundly antidemocratic, Nietzsche felt that any hope for the future of mankind must reside in the figure of a superman—the Zarathustra figure—who would lead humankind into a period of enlightenment. Nietzsche's political thought influenced Pirandello's thinking on social and political issues, and Nietzsche helps to explain an early attraction to Mussolini and his brand of Italian fascism. Pirandello honestly believed that Mussolini embodied the Nietzschean Zarathustra—the superman whom he felt Italy desperately needed. Once a totalitarian police state had been established in Italy, however, Pirandello came to realize the horror he had earlier embraced.

When we examine the contents of Pirandello's personal library, we must be surprised at all the German literature and philosophy it contains. Here are Goethe, Schopenhauer, Schlegel, Luther, Schiller—all the major German dramatists and philosophers printed in handsome German editions (Barbina, 144–63). Overall, the contents of his library indicate that Pirandello must have read German easily and very well. On reflection, this is not at all surprising when we recall the number of years Pirandello spent in Bonn and the amount of reading and writing he must have done as a graduate student at a German university. In fact, once he became a prominent playwright, Pirandello often felt that he was more widely appreciated in Germany than in his Italian homeland. In Berlin especially, Pirandello quickly became acclaimed as a great playwright. Max Reinhardt and other prominent German directors staged many of his plays, in some cases producing the first non-Italian productions. In addition, several German state theaters had Pirandello Festivals during the playwright's lifetime—a tribute that no Italian city paid him. Significant productions of Pirandello plays were staged in Berlin, Frankfurt, Dresden, Vienna, Hamburg, and Bonn (Cometa, 7–19). But Italian theaters and the Italian government did not respond so favorably to his art.

Pirandello even felt betrayed by his own government because Mussolini did not support his Arts Theater in Rome as strongly as promised. That theater always had major financial problems (Giudice, 169–71), and Pirandello was undoubtedly aware that more financially stable German state theaters existed at the same time. In particular, Wagner's success with the Bayreuth Festival demonstrated to many other twentieth-century dramatists the rich possibilities of theater as a national force, a powerful outlet for artistic awareness and accomplishment. Thus, while contemporary German state theaters were staging Pirandello festivals and producing many of his plays, Italian theaters seemed largely uninterested in his work.

Perhaps because of this feeling of neglect in his homeland, at the height of his fame Pirandello went into a voluntary exile. Not coincidentally, the place where he now chose to live in exile was Germany. This so-called Berlin exile occurred from 1928 to 1930, when Pirandello wrote his play *Tonight We Improvise*. In that play the character of Hinkfuss functions as a clever parody of the German director Max Reinhardt. As a whole, the play announced Pirandello's release from any simplistic or merely reactive attachment to German culture.

As we have seen, the complexity of his German/Italian connections shows up in the playwright's career as a significant literary and dramatic theme. What we have is roughly the reverse of the legendary German Italienische Reise; in this case, it is the Italian artist who goes to Germany to study and who comes away much changed, and a far better artist. Perhaps "il Viaggio in Germania," a rather unusual occurrence for an Italian artist, best describes just what happened to Luigi Pirandello.

Yet at the turn of the century, many Italian musicians and composers were going to Germany. Already a tradition had been established in which Italian singers and composers went to Northern Europe for the opera seasons—Salieri, Cherubini, Spontini, Bellini, and Verdi had all done this. In addition, Puccini premiered many of his operas outside Italy—the Metropolitan Opera in New York staged the premiere of *La Fanciulla del West* and of *Il Trittico*. The Monte Carlo Opera staged the premiere for *La Rondine*. Again, by the turn of the century, Ferruccio Busoni had become a famous teacher and composer in Berlin, and Catalani felt the influence of Wagner. A turn-of-the-century group of composers in Milan, known as the Scapigliatura, found special inspiration in the operas of Wagner (DiGaetani, 18–21). Boito's *Mefistofele*, Catalani's *La Wally*, and Puccini's *Le Villi* were products of this movement.

Given this binational artistic milieu, Pirandello's desire to experience his own "Viaggio in Germania" must be seen as a natural part of a tradition in Italian culture at a time when Germany seemed to be the home of the artistic avant-garde to many Italian artists. Pirandello's sense of German receptivity to new developments in the arts was strengthened when he saw his avant-garde plays staged much more frequently in Germany than in his native Italy. Finally, perhaps, any mixing of the cool north and the hot south would result in a complex combination in the arts. In Pirandello's case, it resulted in an enlarged conception of theater and fiction, rewarded with a Nobel Prize.

PIRANDELLO AND MUSSOLINI

Between north and south there was a political connection in Pirandello's thinking as well. Long before Hitler became the dictator of Germany, Pirandello had joined the Italian Fascist party. He said that he became a fascist long before Mussolini showed up, and this statement undoubtedly is accurate. Pirandello's political position was both antidemocratic and anticommunistic. So Mussolini's Fascist party seemed a safe alternative. Significantly, Pirandello joined very publicly at a moment when the party was in trouble, following the assassination of the socialist leader, Matteoti. However, Pirandello also had ulterior motives for joining the Fascist party, aside from his belief in many of its principles. He felt that if he helped Mussolini, Mussolini would help him. Specifically, Pirandello wanted Italy to establish a National Arts Theater, well financed by the state and run by himself (Giudice, 148–58).

In part, that did occur. Mussolini did allow a National Arts Theater, called the Teatro d'Arte, to come into existence, and he provided state funds for it. He did not, however, fund it well enough, at least according to Pirandello. Even more, Mussolini himself went to the new theater, though he was not always pleased with what he saw. As a result, the relationship between the two men became more and more strained, and Pirandello's troupe always seemed to be experiencing severe financial troubles. In 1928 the company had to disband because of financial problems, and at that time Pirandello went into voluntary exile in Germany. He had become disillusioned with fascism, or at least with Mussolini.

What Pirandello had not counted on was the totalitarian police state that Mussolini established in Italy. Pirandello did not foresee the system of state censorship which his own Zarathustra would create. Reminiscent of the power of the Austrian censors in Italy before unification which Verdi had to contend with, Mussolini's system of artistic censorship meant that Pirandello and other artists of the period could not express themselves freely. Instead, they had to deal with powerful state censors, whose approval was needed before performances of new works could be arranged. Pirandello's play *La Nuova Colonia* demonstrates his disgust with fascism in particular and with politics in general. By his own command, he denied the state its desire to turn his funeral into a statewide glorification of fascism. Instead, Pirandello's will demanded a simple and totally private funeral service (Giudice, 207), which the fascist authorities interpreted as an insult to their regime. Even so, nothing remains to show that Pirandello ever became fond of democracy. His early novel *The Old and the Young* indicates very early in his career a firm belief that the poor cannot help themselves politically and that, without leadership, the lower classes always suffer most. For Pirandello's generation of writers and artists, democracy was sometimes connected with the people who caused World War I—however unjustly that accusation now seems to us.

PIRANDELLO TODAY

Pirandello's two greatest plays, *Six Characters in Search of an Author* and *Henry IV*, have entered the canon of accepted classics of the modern stage, and they are often produced around the world. But one goal of this book is to show that, great though these two plays are, there is much more to Pirandello and his art. In addition to the plays, his fine novels, short stories, and poems also deserve attention. In all these works certain basic themes appear, and today these themes remain relevant for readers and audiences alike. *It Is So (If You Think So)* argues in favor of the subjectivity of all reality—insisting that we can never know what the objective reality is because there is no objective reality. That theme also appears in *Henry IV*, as well as in many of Pirandello's short stories and novels. *The Late Mattia Pascal* deals with the fantasy of escape from social responsibility, and the bliss that most people expect to result from such escape. That Mattia Pascal returns to an entangling family at the end of the novel, a family that he

xxvi Introduction

dreamed of escaping at the beginning, suggests something about both the nature
of reality and the possibilities for human happiness.

Those concerns are timely indeed. The theme of the search for identity—so
successfully portrayed in *Six Characters in Search of an Author* and in several
other plays—provides a poignant reminder that angst at least partly defines human
experience in our own times. Again, the continuing search for new forms in
theater and new meanings in life, as well as a pervasive belief in the extreme
difficulty of maintaining human relationships, appear in both Pirandello's work
and in contemporary literature and life. From Thomas Pynchon's novels to
Derrida's recent theories of deconstructed meaning, the search for adequate
interpretations of art and of society remains a timeless human problem. Pirandello
investigated these same concerns imaginatively and thoughtfully in his writing.

WORKS CITED

Barbina, Alfredo. *La Biblioteca di Luigi Pirandello*. Rome: Bulzoni, 1980.
Bassnett-McGuire, Susan. *Luigi Pirandello*. New York: Grove Press, 1983.
Bentley, Eric. *The Pirandello Commentaries*. Evanston, Ill.: Northwestern University
    Press, 1986.
Cometa, Michele. *Il Teatro di Pirandello in Germania*. Palermo: Novecento, 1986.
DiGaetani, John Louis. *Puccini the Thinker*. New York: Peter Lang Press, 1987.
Giudice, Gaspare. *Pirandello, a Biography*. London: Oxford University Press, 1975.
Illiano, Antonio. *Metapsichica e Letteratura in Pirandello*. Agrigento: Vallecchi, 1982.
Pirandello, Luigi. *Lettere da Bonn: 1889–1891*. Rome: Bulzoni, 1984.

Chronology

1922–1937	*Novelle per un anno* is published in 15 volumes.
1924	*Each in His Own Way* premieres in Milan; Pirandello joins the Fascist party.
1925	Pirandello's Teatro d'Arte begins in Rome with a subsidy from the Italian government.
1928	Teatro d'Arte is disbanded because of lack of funds; *La nuova colonia* premieres in Rome; Pirandello lives in Berlin until 1930.
1930	*Tonight We Improvise* premieres in Königsberg, Germany.
1934	Pirandello wins the Nobel Prize for Literature.
1936	December 10, dies in Rome.
1937	Pirandello's last play, *The Mountain Giants*, is staged in Florence.

Part One

PIRANDELLO'S WORLD

1

Pirandello and Philosophy

Gustavo Costa

In an essay published in 1935, Benedetto Croce passed a stern judgment on Pirandellian philosophy because it reflected the main features of modern irrationalism, which Croce considered antithetic to his own thought. Croce dismissed Pirandello's philosophy as a compulsive and inconclusive mental activity ("convulso inconcludente filosofare") that jeopardized the Sicilian writer's creative power (337). Needless to say, Croce, who repeatedly proved to be a very sensitive and intelligent critic, completely missed the point in Pirandello's case.

The history of Pirandellian studies shows that the best critics were not intimidated by Croce's negative attitude. On the contrary, they concentrated on the sources of Pirandello's philosophic ideas. In 1939, Franz Rauhut published a pioneering essay on the scientific components of Pirandellian thought and demonstrated the impact that two works dealing with those problems of the soul, which encompass both experimental psychology and philosophy, had on Pirandello's mind.[1] One was Alfred Binet's *Les altérations de la personnalité* (1892); the other was Giovanni Marchesini's *Le finzioni dell'anima* (1905). Three years after the Second World War, in 1948, Mathias Adank printed his doctoral dissertation, prepared at the University of Bern (Switzerland), on Pirandello's relationship with Germany. Adank stressed the relevance of German philosophers in Pirandello's education. Among these were not only great thinkers such as Schopenhauer and Nietzsche, but also a competent yet modest professor of philosophy, Theodor Lipps, who held a course on the aesthetics of comedy and tragedy at the University of Bonn during the academic year 1889–1890, when Pirandello transferred there from Rome.[2] However, Rauhut, in his fascinating book on Pirandello's youth (1964), where he reaffirmed Binet's and Marchesini's influence, did not mention at all Schopenhauer and Nietzsche (implicitly dissenting from Adank's claims). Rather, he asserted that Pirandello, in his first academic year at Bonn, could not have mastered enough German to be able to follow Lipps's lectures, whose content, however, became familiar to him later, when he read Lipps's essay on *Komik und Humor* (1898).[3] In 1966 Gösta Andersson's important monograph appeared, and a new, significant Pirandellian source was added to Binet and Marchesini: the philosophy of Gabriel Séailles.[4]

By now the times were ready for a global evaluation of Pirandello's works. It was apparent that, by emphasizing one literary genre at the expense of others, or by drawing a sharp line separating art from thought, one could not reach a full understanding of Pirandello, who cherished diversity over uniformity. This evolution of Pirandellian criticism, which marked the beginning of a new awareness of the interdependence of Pirandello's artistic and philosophic talents, had its best representative in Giovanni Macchia, author of a penetrating essay published for the first time in 1969. According to Macchia, the most prominent feature of Pirandello's *oeuvre* is the intercommunication of various genres, so that the fantastic dimension thrives on its contiguity with philosophic apothegms, moral dicta, and idiosyncratic themes, which all rebound, like rubber balls, from one Pirandellian work to the other.[5] Macchia has sanctioned Rauhut's and Andersson's views about Binet's and Séailles's influence on Pirandello, and has also pointed out the relevance of Maurice Blondel. Thus, Macchia has successfully maintained that Pirandello generously spreads sentences borrowed from Binet, Séailles, and Blondel over the most famous pages of his narrative or dramatic works (445). There is no need to stress the relevance of Macchia's considerations which have enjoyed a widespread popularity, not only because of their author's prestige, but also because Macchia was able to recycle them under various disguises. (This was an obvious proof that Pirandello's technique of rebounding rubber balls is still alive in the literary world.)[6]

The period of uncertainty, when Pirandello's critics were torn between Croce's radical attack against Pirandellian philosophy and Adriano Tilgher's self-serving praise of Pirandello, viewed as an interpreter of modern thought and an adversary of the Italian neo-idealistic school, was at last completely over. The loss of prestige that the Crocean model suffered in the late fifties and sixties created in Italy a new intellectual climate that was more suited for a better comprehension of Pirandellian philosophy. As Claudio Vicentini noted in an influential book, originally published in 1970, once the Italian critics abandoned the Crocean distinction between poetry and thought, they could identify with the strenuous tendency of Pirandellian characters to condense their dramatic situation in abstract speculations, one of the most vital components of Pirandello's art (5). A follower of Luigi Pareyson, Vicentini tried hard to achieve a full acceptance of Pirandellian philosophy. Although Croce maintained that a profound and rigorous thought could not but be systematic, Vicentini convincingly argued that this was not necessarily true, since there are great thinkers who prefer to write in aphoristic form and Pirandello belongs to such a category: his philosophy is asystematic but coherent in its inner inspiration and development. According to Vicentini, whoever wants to understand Pirandello should take into consideration the following three interconnected elements: (1) his art, accompanied by his capacity for self-criticism and nourished by philosophical considerations; (2) his poetics, which reflect his individual artistic experience and transform into theory his everyday writing activity; and (3) his philosophy, which deals with cognitive, aesthetic, and ethical problems and is rooted in every aspect of life, including his creative writing (8). From this viewpoint, the problem of Pirandellian philosophy appears to be indistinguishable from the problem of Pirandellian art, from which it can be separated only for the sake of educational needs. Not only Pirandello's essays, but also every figment of his imagination has a philosophical dimension which, of course, cannot fit the Procrustean schemes of Tilgher's interpretation, still dependent on the systematizing habit of traditional philosophers.

Various scholars debated the problem of Pirandellian thought at the thirteenth international conference, organized in 1983 by the National Center for Pirandello Studies (Centro Nazionale di Studi Pirandelliani), in Agrigento, Italy. Papers focused on Pirandellian philosophy were read by Vittorio Stella ("Pirandello e la filosofia italiana"), Salvatore Guglielmino ("Retroterra e implicazioni del saggio su *L'umorismo*"), Franca Angelini ("Pirandello e Sartre"), and Michele Cometa ("Pirandello e Lipps: due letture psicologiche dell'umorismo").[7] Perhaps the most stimulating contribution is the one by Stella who imparts a new direction to the research on the sources of Pirandellian philosophy, switching its focus from European to strictly Italian thought. Without denying the influence of non-Italian authors such as Schopenhauer, Spencer, Taine, Binet, Séailles, Nordau, Lipps, and Bergson, Stella maintains that Pirandello's mind was shaped mainly by Italian philosophers (6). One of the best sections of Stella's paper is dedicated to the problem of the relationship between Croce and Pirandello, a traditional bone of contention among Pirandello scholars.[8] Contrary to his predecessors' opinion, Stella believes that the philosophical differences separating Croce and Pirandello are more specious than real. Stella detects an idealistic bent in Pirandello, namely, a secret attraction to the new philosophy diffused in Italy by Croce and Gentile. It was under the influence of Crocean ideas that Pirandello, during his youth, came to reject, on the one hand, the positivistic tenets of the historical school, and, on the other hand, the poetics of naturalism (18). Idealistic thought continued to have a sure hold on Pirandello during his entire life. It popped up on important occasions, as appears from his two commemorative speeches on Giovanni Verga (the high point of Pirandello's career as a literary essayist), where he touches on typically Crocean views, such as the creative form, the eternity of art, and its capacity of transcending the necessities of practical life (Stella, 17). One is tempted to enlarge on this homemade Pirandello, who entertained a secret love affair with the very idealistic philosophy he openly detested.

At first sight, we are inclined to view Pirandello's flirtation with Croce's philosophy as a typically "grotesque" plot, a sardonic and paradoxical comedy in the style of Luigi Chiarelli's *La maschera e il volto* (*The Mask and the Face*). But it would be hazardous to endorse such a conclusion. In this case, we should be overcautious since many aspects of late nineteenth- and early twentieth-century Italian philosophy are still obscure, in spite of innumerable studies dealing with this subject—Eugenio Garin's *Cronache di filosofia italiana*, for example. Even some basic concepts, such as positivism and anti-positivism, frequently used in discussing Italian philosophers, including Pirandello, are to be considered unreliable tools, which can lead astray the unsuspecting scholar, who has embarked on the difficult task of drawing up a map of Italian intellectual life. What is commonly called positivistic is nothing but the self-serving and distorted image that Benedetto Croce and Giovanni Gentile, the two champions of idealism, traced to their adversaries. As Mario Dal Pra, a subtle historian of philosophy, has demonstrated, Croce and Gentile acknowledged that positivism had the great merit of disposing of the spiritual thought that prevailed in Italy at the beginning of the second half of the nineteenth century. At the same time, they blamed positivism for its alleged faults, namely, its lack of doctrinal coherence, its naive and imprecise metaphysics founded on naturalism, its excessive enthusiasm for science, and its inability to express an epistemology adequate to contemporary scientific methods (363). It is obvious that positivism was a completely different movement from the one depicted by Croce and Gentile, as appears from the revival of studies initiated after the Second World War and still in full bloom (a revival brought about by the fading away of neo-idealism and by the triumph of different trends of thought, more sympathetic to the positivistic mentality). A large number of studies were devoted to Roberto Ardigò, leader of the Italian positivists, and to other prominent representatives of the same movement, such as Ludovico Limentani, Alessandro Levi, Erminio Juvalta, and Giovanni Marchesini, author of *Le finzioni dell'anima* (The figments of the soul), a widely discussed book, which did not escape Pirandello's attention.[9]

If we look at them closely, certain polemic oppositions sanctioned in the manuals appear to be exaggerated and, in some cases, nonexistent. Despite some fundamental differences, more or less irreconcilable, the Italian philosophy of the late nineteenth and early twentieth centuries proves to be much more closely knit and homogeneous than is commonly believed. On the one hand, we have a very dynamic brand of positivism that is increasingly extending its initial, naturalistic boundaries, to reach the positions of neo-idealism and, at least in the case of Marchesini, surpassing them. On the other hand, we have the neo-idealistic polarity between the a prioristic, holistic, and abstract philosophy of Gentile, untouched by the needs of contingency, and Croce's astute compromise, founded on a complicated blend of idealistic and empirical components, which was suggested mainly by Croce's irrepressible interest in historical research. Indeed, it is impossible to foresee what kind of final picture the studies in progress will substitute for the present generalizations offered by manuals. However, it is safe to say that every thinker of the beginning of our century was more or less influenced by cultural modernism (a rather vague but indispensable term, as Michael H. Levenson observed not long ago).[10] Modernism, which transmitted its contagion even to Marxism, according to Eugene Lunn's book on Lukacs, Brecht, Benjamin, and Adorno,[11] was the common ground in which both positivists and neo-idealists thrived. From this viewpoint, we can easily explain the affinities between Croce's and Pirandello's thought, which Stella pointed out. Croce was deeply affected by modernism, which he preferred to call "irrationalism," and, notwithstanding his repeated attacks on it, he carved a place for it in his philosophy. This is the case not only of aesthetics, the focus of Stella's inquiry, but also of ethics and the concept of the individual.

In debating the Croce–Pirandello relationship, critics have overlooked an important fact: Croce's philosophy presented a paradoxical view of the individual, whose existence is affirmed and denied at the same time. As Carlo Antoni, a keen interpreter of Crocean thought, noted more than thirty years ago, Croce celebrated the individual, inasmuch as he maintained that the universal spirit is real only when it individualizes itself, becoming an historical subject. At the same time, however, Croce identified the individual with those practical needs and instincts, which he viewed as transient manifestations of the so-called vitality (one of the four categories or forms of the Spirit) (99–100). Croce was torn between the empirical view of man as a responsible maker of history and the Hegelian view of man as a mere instrument of the Spirit, which is the only entity endowed with reality (Antoni, 100).

This wavering between the universality of the Spirit and the individuality of man pervades Croce's writings. Let us consider, for instance, the *Filosofia della Pratica* (*Philosophy of the Practical*), the third volume of the *Philosophy of the Spirit*, which was originally published in 1908. In Part I, Section II, Chapter V ("Development and Progress"), Croce asserts that history "is and is not the work of individuals," since it is made by "the universal Spirit, of which individuals are manifestations and instruments" (257). In the preceding Chapter IV ("Volitional Habits and the Individuality"), Croce emphasizes the precarious state of man vis-à-vis the Spirit, specifying that the individual is not something real, a monad or a soul, created by God. It is simply the historical situation of the universal Spirit in each instant of time, and therefore all the habits created by the historical circumstances: "The individual is not a 'monad' or a 'real,' he is not a 'soul' created by God all in a moment and all of a piece; the individual is the historical situation of the universal Spirit at every instant of time, and, therefore, the sum of the habits due to the historical situations" (241). According to Croce, the individuals and the situations coincide so perfectly that it is improper to speak about the same individual in two different situations or about two different individuals in the same situation: "Those modes of conceiving and talking of one *and the same* individual in two *different* situations, or of two *different* individuals in the *same* situation, are to be avoided, because individual and situation are all one" (241). Pirandello could find in Croce further arguments

supporting the discontinuous and aleatory view of human personality, which
Binet held on the basis of completely different premises.

Pirandello, who since his early youth had adopted a radical skepticism about
religious matters, was taken aback by the metaphysical core of Crocean philosophy, where the transcendent and provident God of the Jewish-Christian tradition, despite his secular transformation into the universal Spirit, retained his
essential characteristics. Croce's religious attitude is evident when he states that
we should regard ourselves as the servants of the historical reality, which gives
life to us and knows more than we do, adding that such a reality was dimly
envisaged by the religious people under the guise of God the father and the all-
wise: "We are the children of that Reality which generates us and knows more
than we, the Reality of which religions have caught a glimpse and called it God,
father, and eternal wisdom" (242). Interpreting in his own way Vico's philosophy, Croce recognized in what he called "religious and semi-fanciful thought"
an imperfect formulation or "a confused presentiment of the truth" (258), which
obviously was deemed to coincide with his tenets.

In order to better convey the idea of the strict affinity linking his philosophy
to Christianity, Croce resorted to ritualistic expressions: "the struggles to find
the suitable employment can be expressed with the words that religion has taught
us when we were children: the 'vocation' and the special 'mission' that is allotted
to us in life, until the last giving of accounts and the words of dismissal and
repose: *Nunc dimitte servum tuum, Domine!*" (242). Croce did not hesitate to
incorporate into his thought the religious concept of Divine Providence, recalling
it from the mystic realm of transcendence to the rational realm of immanence.
He argued that history, inasmuch as it is rational, must be guided by a providential
design, which is not superimposed on individuals from above, but derives from
them and operates through them. Croce felt strongly about this idea. He was
convinced that, without it, life would be unbearable, because man, confronted
by horrible sufferings, would not have enough force to resist: "This affirmation
of Providence is not conjecture or faith, but evidence of reason. Who would feel
in him the strength of life without such intimate persuasion? Whence could he
draw resignation in sorrow, encouragement to endure? Surely what the religious
man says, with the words "Let us leave it in God's hands," is said also by the
man of reason with those other words: 'Courage, and forward'?" (258).

As I have demonstrated in another essay,[12] Pirandello obliquely attacks Crocean philosophy, condensing it in a polemic and grotesque phrase spoken by
Ciampa in *Il berretto a sonagli* (*Cap and Bells*, 1917), Act I, Scene IV: "We
are puppets, my dear Signor Fifì! The Divine Spirit enters into us and pulls the
strings. I am a puppet, you are a puppet, we are all puppets."[13] Ciampa's remark
alludes not only to Hegel, contrary to Vittorini's opinion (560), but also, first
and foremost, to Croce, who, just one year later, was ironically praised as the
homme du jour of Italian philosophy in Alberto Savinio's *Hermaphrodito* (1918)
(38). Savinio's scathing attack, involving not only Croce but also Bergson and

Unamuno, reveals the cordial dislike avant-garde writers felt for the philosophical establishment of early twentieth-century Europe. Pirandello preferred to concentrate his satire on Croce, offering in the passage from *Il berretto a sonagli*, which I have quoted above, a typical example of what Jean Spizzo calls *"confrontation spéculaire."* This is one of the most common methods by which Pirandello obtains grotesque, antitragic, and scandalous effects, amounting to a rebellion against the monstrous power of prejudice in every sector of human life.[14] In 1917 it was quite normal for a poor intellectual from southern Italy, such as Ciampa, to be under Croce's spell. The fact that Ciampa is a simple scribe does not prevent him from writing articles for a provincial newspaper, as appears from Act I, Scene IV: "Leave the journalists be! A superfluous activity, that only flourishes at night."[15] Ciampa is aware of his limitations but, at the same time, tends to attribute them to the uninspiring Sicilian town in which he resides: "And as for me, my dear Signor Fifì, to take a breath of air in a great city such as Palermo is to live for a little while! I am suffocating here! Here I cannot breathe. But the moment I step out into the streets of a city I no longer seem to be walking on the earth; I'm in paradise! Ideas come to me!" In my opinion, Ciampa is Pirandello's alter ego, or rather a negative and distorted image which the Sicilian writer had obtained of himself, while resorting to his technique of specular confrontation. It is exactly in this interplay of mirrored and more or less misleading images that the secret magic of Pirandellian art is to be found.

Pirandello caricatures himself in Ciampa, who caricatures Crocean thought, because he is no less skeptical than Pirandello himself about the power of human reason. Ciampa is a reasoner undergoing a serious crisis, who finally discovers that frenzy is more rewarding than reason, as appears from the last scene of *Il berretto a sonagli*: "Come now! Give yourself the pleasure of being mad for three months! You think it's nothing? To be insane? If only I could do it! . . . To wind the insane spring as far as it will go! To put on the madman's cap and bells and run through the streets spitting the truth into the faces of the passersby!" (48) From this point of view, Ciampa, the Crocean philosopher who converts to anti-Crocean irrationalism, appears to be the hero of a parable illustrating Pirandello's hostility toward any philosophy that claimed to possess the truth. In so doing, the Sicilian writer remained faithful to his youthful abhorrence for the ideological crisis of the fin-de-siècle culture, as appears from his essay "Arte e coscienza d'oggi" (Art and Consciousness Today, 1893).

Pirandello viewed modern consciousness as a nightmare peopled by sad, menacing ghosts, as a nocturnal and desperate battle, in which enemies are not easily distinguished from friends, while different banners make their rounds. Under such circumstances, how could it have been possible to trust the optimistic expectations of certain intellectuals?[16] More than twenty years later, in 1916, when his son Stefano was a prisoner in Austria, Pirandello expressed in a significant letter the same disenchantment with the study of philosophy: he advised

Stefano not to spend too much time reading philosophical works, since Pirandello had already read all of them and knew that they could not answer the important questions of human destiny.[17] A man holding such an unflattering opinion of philosophers was destined to remain impervious to the appeal of Croce, who was believed to have created a system of thought able to reconcile the perennial dilemma of good and evil, life and death, so much so that he identified the eulogy of life with the eulogy of death, because we can live only by dying at each moment of our existence: "In truth, there is no need to oppose a eulogy of Life with a eulogy of Death; for how could we live, if we did not die at every instant?"[18] Yet it would be unfair to ignore the anxiety Croce felt and tried to exorcise with the classical serenity of his philosophical system, founded on the balance of the fundamental forms of the Spirit (Art, Thought, Vitality, and Morality).

Although the gaps in our knowledge of early twentieth-century Italian thought are considerable and, therefore, any attempt to offer a panoramic view of it cannot but be tentative, a basic point should be kept in mind: Pirandello's philosophy is not only a reflection, more or less parodic, of ideas held by the most illustrious thinkers of his own time, but it is also an original contribution to the philosophical debate that took place in Italy. In other words, Pirandello is to be considered, along with Croce and Gentile, as one of the great interlocutors of the Italian philosophical scene. He cannot be fully evaluated without taking into account the entire range of Pirandellian writings (the critical as well as the creative ones). As far as Croce is concerned, one might reverse Stella's position, according to which Crocean thought exerted a profound impact on Pirandello, by showing that Pirandellian philosophy, partly because of its affinity to Croce's views, contributed to a basic development of Crocean philosophy: namely, its reorientation toward Vitality, through an acrimonious discussion kept alive in an incessant flow of narrative, dramatic, critical, and journalistic writings.

It is a well-known fact that, in the last stage of his intellectual career, Croce increasingly focused on the multiplicity of irrational forces characterizing our interior life, namely, our humors, appetites, instincts, needs, affections, desires, and passions. He considered these forces to be manifestations of the so-called Vitality (the most elementary and brutish among the four categories of the Spirit) (Antoni, 228). This development of Croce's philosophy was certainly due both to his practical and intellectual experiences. Among the practical, the tragedy of the Second World War and the concomitant regression to barbarism of highly civilized nations are certainly to be reckoned with, while the intellectual are to be found in the writings that afforded food for thought. Historians of philosophy pointed out the importance of Gentile's works, particularly his *Filosofia dell'arte* (*The Philosophy of Art*, 1931), stressing the centrality of feeling and sensuality in spiritual life.[19] One might also be tempted to take into consideration the influence of psychoanalysis, which did not escape Croce's attention. (A case in point would be Silvio Tissi's *La psicanalisi scienza dell'io* [1929], containing an evaluation of Pirandello).[20] However, it would be naive to disregard the role that Pirandellian vitalism had in Croce's reconsideration of the relevance of irrational motivations in human society. Nobody in Italy had launched a more formidable attack than Pirandello against the bastion of logic, in order to promote the triumph of vitalism over rationalism, as appears from a typical passage of Pirandello's *L'umorismo* (*On Humor*, 1908): man is endowed with "a certain devilish little machine," namely, logic, "a kind of filter pump that connects the brain to the heart," and enables the brain "to pump the emotions from the heart and to extract ideas from them."[21] For Pirandello, the mistake of logicians is that they believe we can have "an absolute idea or conception of life," while we can simply entertain a "feeling" of it, "depending on the times, the circumstances, and luck." (140) It is worthy of note that the above quoted passage had its origin in *Il fu Mattia Pascal* (*The Late Mattia Pascal*, 1904) and bounced to other Pirandellian writings, such as "Cronache stravaganti: La fiera della sapienza" (Eccentric chronicles: The wisdom fair, 1906), *Suo marito* (Her husband, 1911), and *Ma non è una cosa seria* (It Is Not Serious, 1919).[22] This is not a purely philological consideration, but a proof, on the one hand, of Pirandello's doctrinal consistency and, on the other hand, of his tenacity in hammering his ideas again and again for the profit of the intellectual community of his times.

Pirandello made *feeling* the pivot of his philosophy, and, by doing so, he adopted the anti-intellectual tradition of Western thought, represented by authors such as Pascal, Schopenhauer, and Bergson, all of whom are quoted in Pirandellian writings.[23] The same tradition produced modern existentialism, a movement that numbers among his precursors Dostoevski, whose impact on Pirandello cannot be emphasized enough. The Sicilian writer quotes Dostoevski in *L'umorismo*, where he maintains that the comic, namely, the "perception of the opposite," should not be confused with humor, namely, the "feeling of the opposite," which constitutes a much more complex state of mind: "Another illustration: 'Oh sir, my dear sir! Perhaps all this seems *ludicrous* to you as it does to others; perhaps I am only burdening you with the stupid and trivial details of my domestic life, but it is not a laughing matter to me, because I feel it all . . .'." Then Pirandello comments on this passage from *Crime and Punishment* in the following way: "This outcry is precisely the painful and exasperated protest of a humoristic character against someone who, right there before him, dwells on an initial superficial perception of his situation and only succeeds in seeing its comic side" (113).

There is no doubt that Dostoevski is to be viewed as an inspirer of Pirandello's irrationalism, despite the fact that the name of the Russian narrator appears only once in *L'umorismo*. This work, in which Pirandello cites a plethora of Italian and non-Italian authors, is founded on romantic irony, or the reversed sublimity of Jean Paul Richter, as well as on Dostoevski's paradoxical and tragic vision of human destiny. Pirandello ignored Dostoevski's political and religious preoccupations, which the Sicilian writer could not share. In this way, the Russian novelist became a formidable witness of the crisis of modern culture, and, as such, a writer germane to Pirandello, who regarded Dostoevski as a master of artistic and philosophic truths. Pirandello's reverence for Dostoevski, the author of *The Double*, is also proved by the fact that the theme of the double is essential to Pirandellian art, as Jean-Michel Gardair has convincingly demonstrated.[24] What this means on the level of the history of Italian philosophy during the first half of the twentieth century is that Pirandello was not alone in his strenuous battle against neo-idealistic thought.

NOTES

1. F. Rauhut, "Wissenschaftliche Quellen von Gedanken Luigi Pirandellos," *Romanische Forschungen*, 53 (1939):185–205.

2. M. Adank, *Luigi Pirandello e i suoi rapporti col mondo tedesco* (Aarau: Druckereigenossenschaft, 1948), 68–70, 79, 87 and *passim*.

3. F. Rauhut, *Der junge Pirandello, oder das Werden eines existentiellen Geistes* (München: C. H. Beck, 1964), 38, 44–45, 407–408 and *passim*.

4. G. Andersson, *Arte e teoria: Studi sulla poetica del giovane Luigi Pirandello* (Stockholm: Almqvist & Wiksell, 1966), 142–224 and *passim*; G. Andersson, "Il saggista Pirandello, lettore di Gabriel Séailles," in *Pirandello saggista* (Palermo: Palumbo, 1982), 303–19.

5. G. Macchia, "Luigi Pirandello," in *Storia della letteratura italiana*, eds. E. Cecchi and N. Sapegno, IX, *Il Novecento* (Milan: Garzanti, 1969), 444–45.

6. The same passage also appears in G. Macchia, "Introduzione a Pirandello narratore," in L. Pirandello, *Tutti i romanzi*, eds. G. Macchia and M. Costanzo, 4th ed. (Milan: Mondadori, 1981), I, XIII; G. Macchia, *Pirandello o la stanza della tortura* (Milan: Mondadori, 1981), 27. This book was awarded the Pirandello Prize by a committee chaired by Raul Radice: see "Premi Pirandello a Bona, Macchia e a Luca Ronconi," *Corriere della Sera*, November 1, 1981:21.

7. See *Pirandello e la cultura del suo tempo*, eds. S. Milioto and E. Scrivano (Milan: Mursia, 1984), 5–30, 143–56, 273–84, and 303–16.

8. I will mention only the most significant studies on the topic: D. Vittorini, "Benedetto Croce e Luigi Pirandello," in *Benedetto Croce*, ed. F. Flora (Milan: Malfasi, 1953), 555–65; V. Fazio Allmayer, "Il problema Pirandello," *Belfagor*, 12 (1957):18–34; O. Borrello, "Il pensiero estetico di Pirandello," *Letterature moderne*, 11 (1961):634–53; D. Della Terza, "Luigi Pirandello e la ricerca della distanza umoristica," in *Studi in memoria di Luigi Russo* (Pisa: Nistri-Lischi, 1974), 405–22; S. Monti, *Pirandello*. Storia della critica, 31 (Palermo: Palumbo, 1974), 14–15 and *passim*; A. Illiano, *Introduzione alla critica pirandelliana: Saggi e rassegne*, Quaderni veronesi di varia letteratura e umanità, 10 (Verona: Fiorini, 1976), 38–45; A. Asor Rosa, "Pirandello saggista fra soggettivismo e oggettivismo," in *Pirandello saggista*, 11–21; E. Bonora, "Pirandello studioso di Dante," in ibid., 89–102; P. Cudini, "Pirandello e Croce: a proposito di Dante," in ibid., 103–14; E. G. Caserta, "Croce, Pirandello e il concetto di umorismo," *Canadian Journal of Italian Studies*, V. 6, Nos. 22–23 (1983):103–10.

9. M. Dal Pra, "Il positivismo critico di Giovanni Marchesini," *Rivista critica di storia della filosofia*, 37, No. 4 (October-December 1982):363–364. On the debate about *Le finzioni dell'anima*, see G. Lanaro, "La critica alle *Finzioni dell'anima* nella cultura italiana del primo novecento," in ibid., 430–42.

10. M. H. Levenson, *A Genealogy of Modernism: A Study of English Literary Doctrine 1908–1922* (Cambridge: Cambridge University Press, 1984), vii. The composite character of Croce's philosophy, which appears as a sort of compromise between positivism and Gentile's thought, did not escape the attention of U. Spirito, "La filosofia," in U. Spirito, A. Volpicelli, and L. Volpicelli, *Benedetto Croce* (Rome: Anonima Romana Editoriale, 1929), 7–26.

11. E. Lunn, *Marxism and Modernism: An Historical Study of Lukacs, Brecht, Benjamin, and Adorno* (Berkeley: University of California Press, 1982). See also the review that Stephen Zelnick dedicated to Lunn's book in *Journal of Aesthetics and Art Criticism*, 43, No. 4 (Summer 1985):408–409. I believe that the concept of modernism can help us to go beyond the dichotomy positivism/anti-positivism, which continues to monopolize the attention of Pirandellian scholars, as appears from U. Schulz-Buschhaus, "*L'umorismo*: L'anti-retorica e l'anti-sintesi di un secondo realismo," in *Pirandello saggista*, 77 and *passim*.

12. G. Costa, "Self and Representation in Pirandello's *Henry IV*," *Modern Language Studies*, 11, No. 3 (Fall 1981):16–17.

13. L. Pirandello, *Cap and Bells and Man, Beast and Virtue*, trans. N. A. Bailey and R. W. Oliver (New York: Performing Arts Journal Publications, 1983), 27.

14. J. Spizzo, "Pirandello: théâtre du reflet, théâtre du conflit," in *Lectures pirandelliennes*. Centre de recherche de l'Université de Paris VIII—Vincennes, Groupe Cultures, idéologies et sociétés des XIX et XX siècles,' Section italien, II (Abbeville: F. Paillart, 1978), 175–232.

15. Pirandello, *Cap and Bells*, p. 27.

16. L. Pirandello, *Saggi, poesie, scritti vari*, ed. M. Lo Vecchio-Musti. *Opere di Luigi Pirandello, VI* (Milan: Mondadori, 1960), 880.

17. L. Pirandello, "Lettere al figlio Stefano," *Almanacco letterario Bompiani*, 1938:41. On Pirandello's correspondence with his son Stefano, see also "Un inedito di Pirandello," *Corriere della Sera*, December 1, 1984:19.

18. B. Croce, *Philosophy of the Practical: Economic and Ethic*, trans. D. Ainslie (London: Macmillan, 1913), p. 252.

19. G. Gentile, *The Philosophy of Art*, trans. G. Gullace (Ithaca-London: Cornell University Press, 1972), 155–79. Gentile describes love as a "vehement and mighty force which seems to spring from the womb of nature and to carry all away with the devastating fury of a hurricane," and asserts that "the love of the sexes can . . . generate the most powerful mutual attraction and the swiftest and most complete unity, whenever minor differences drop out of sight and two souls meet face to face in the feeling of their fundamental unity" (ibid., 161 and 163).

20. An absolutely negative opinion on Tissi was expressed by M. David, *Letteratura e psicanalisi* (Milan: Mursia, 1967), 166. A more favorable attitude is to be found in L. Russo, "Pirandello e la psicoanalisi," in *Pirandello e la cultura*, 33–37. For the Croce–Freud relationship, see D. Coli, *Croce, Laterza e la cultura europea* (Bologna: Il Mulino, 1983), 86–92.

21. L. Pirandello, *On Humor*, trans. A. Illiano and D. P. Testa, *Studies in Comparative Literature*, 58 (Chapel Hill: University of North Carolina Press, 1974), 139.

22. See Pirandello, *Tutti i romanzi*, I, 628 and the corresponding note on 1050. In addition to the texts quoted by Macchia and Costanzo, see also "Cronache stravaganti: La fiera della sapienza" (originally published in *Gazzetta del Popolo*, January 10, 1906), in S. Zappulla Muscarà, "Archetipi e rari del Pirandello saggista," in *Pirandello saggista*,

393–94. New insights on Pirandello's way of writing can be gathered from the autograph manuscript of *Il fu Mattia Pascal* which I have discovered in the Houghton Library of Harvard University: see P. Mauri, "Così nacque il fu Mattia," *Repubblica*, December 5, 1986:24–25.

    23. See G. Faggin and M. L. Falorni, "Sentimento," in *Enciclopedia filosofica*, V (1967), cols. 1277–84.

    24. J. M. Gardair, *Pirandello e il suo doppio*, Presentazione di G. Macchia (Rome: Abete, 1977). Gardair does not mention Dostoevski's *The Double* which was translated into Italian in 1925 and 1933: see A.M.V. Guarnieri Ortolani, *Saggio sulla fortuna di Dostoevskij in Italia* (Padua: CEDAM, 1947), 115 and 117. *The Double* was translated very early into German by L. A. Hauff (1889), when Pirandello was at the University of Bonn: see *Gesamtverzeichnis des deutschsprachigen Schriftums (G. V.), 1700–1910*, 30 (1981), p. 135; *The British Library General Catalogue of Printed Books to 1975*, 86 (1981), 161. Another German translation (by Frida Ichak) appeared in 1909: see *Gesamtverzeichnis*, 30 (1981), 135. Dostoevski's novel was also translated into French in 1906: see *Catalogue général des livres imprimés de la Bibliothèque Nationale: Auteurs*, 41 (1910), col. 604. On *The Double* see K. Miller, *Doubles: Studies in Literary History* (Oxford: Oxford University Press, 1985), 130–36.

WORKS CITED

Adank, Mathias. *Luigi Pirandello e i suoi rapporti col mondo tedesco: Inauguraldissertation der Philosophischen Fakultät I der Universität Bern zur Erlangung der Doktorwürde*. Aarau: Druckereigenossenschaft Aarau, 1948.

Andersson, Gösta. *Arte e teoria: Studi sulla poetica del giovane Luigi Pirandello*. Stockholm: Almquist & Wiksell, 1966.

———. "Il saggista Pirandello, lettore di Gabriel Séailles." *Pirandello saggista*. Palermo: Palumbo, 1982. 303-19.

Antoni, Carlo. *Commento a Croce*. Venice: Neri Pozza, 1955.

Asor Rosa, Alberto. "Pirandello fra soggettivismo e oggettivismo." *Pirandello saggista*, 11–21.

Bonora, Ettore. "Pirandello studioso di Dante." *Pirandello saggista*, 89–102.

Borrello, Oreste. "Il pensiero estetico di Pirandello." *Letterature moderne* 11 (1961):634–53.

Caserta, Ernesto G. "Croce, Pirandello e il concetto di umorismo." *Canadian Journal of Italian Studies* 6, No. 22-23 (1983):103–10.

Coli, Daniela. *Croce, Laterza e la cultura europea*. Bologna: Il Mulino, 1983.

Costa, Gustavo. "Pirandello e la filosofia." *Pirandello 1986: Atti del Simposio internazionale (Università di California, Berkeley, 13–15 marzo 1986)*. Eds. Gian Paolo Biasin and Nicolas J. Perella. Rome: Bulzoni, 1987. 149–64.

———. "Self and Representation in Pirandello's *Henry IV*." *Modern Language Studies* 11, No. 3 (Fall 1981):16–24.

Croce, Benedetto. "Luigi Pirandello." *La letteratura della nuova Italia: Saggi critici*. Vol. VI. Bari: Laterza, 1974. 335–52.

———. *Philosophy of the Practical: Economic and Ethic*. Trans. Douglas Ainslie. London: Macmillan, 1913.

Cudini, Piero. "Pirandello e Croce: a proposito di Dante." *Pirandello saggista*, 103–14.

Dal Pra, Mario. "Il positivismo critico di Giovanni Marchesini." *Rivista critica di storia della filosofia* 37, No. 4 (October-December 1982):363–86.

David, Michel. *Letteratura e psicanalisi*. Civiltà letteraria del Novecento: Saggi, 10. Milan: Mursia, 1967.

della Terza, Dante. "Luigi Pirandello e la ricerca della distanza umoristica." *Studi in memoria di Luigi Russo*. Pisa: Nistri-Lischi, 1974. 405–22.

Faggin, Giuseppe, and Maria Luisa Falorni. "Sentimento." *Enciclopedia filosofica*. 2nd ed. Florence: Sansoni, 1967. Vol. V, cols. 1277–84.

Fazio Allmayer, Vito. "Il problema Pirandello." *Belfagor* 12, No. 1 (January 31, 1957):18–34.

Gardair, Jean-Michel. *Pirandello e il suo doppio*. Ed. Giulio Ferroni. L'evento teatrale: Sezione "Saggi," 3. Rome: Edizioni Abete, 1977.

Garin, Eugenio. *Cronache di filosofia italiana, 1900/1943*. Bari: Laterza, 1966.

Gentile, Giovanni. *The Philosophy of Art*. Trans. Giovanni Gullace. Ithaca and London: Cornell University Press, 1972.

Guarnieri Ortolani, Anna M. V. *Saggio sulla fortuna di Dostoevskij in Italia*. Università di Padova: Pubblicazioni della Facoltà di Lettere e Filosofia, 24. Padova: CEDAM, 1947.

Illiano, Antonio. *Introduzione alla critica pirandelliana: Saggi e rassegne*. Quaderni veronesi di varia letteratura e umanità, 10. Verona: Fiorini, 1976.

Lanaro, Giorgio. "La critica alle *Finzioni dell'anima* nella cultura italiana del primo Novecento." *Rivista critica di storia della filosofia* 37, 430–42.

Levenson, Michael H. *A Genealogy of Modernism: A Study of English Literary Doctrine 1908–1922*. Cambridge: Cambridge University Press, 1984.

Lunn, Eugene. *Marxism and Modernism: An Historical Study of Lukács, Brecht, Benjamin and Adorno*. Berkeley: University of California Press, 1982.

Macchia, Giovanni. "Luigi Pirandello." *Storia della letteratura italiana*. Eds. Emilio Cecchi and Natalino Sapegno. Vol. IX: *Il Novecento*. Milan: Garzanti, 1969. 439–92.

———. *Pirandello o la stanza della tortura*. Milan: Mondadori, 1981.

Mauri, Paolo. "Così nacque il fu Mattia." *Repubblica*, December 5, 1986:24–25.

Milioto, Stefano, and Enzo Scrivano, eds. *Pirandello e la cultura del suo tempo*. Collana di saggi e documentazioni del Centro Nazionale di Studi Pirandelliani, 9. Milan: Mursia, 1984.

Miller, Karl. *Doubles: Studies in Literary History*. Oxford: Clarendon Press, 1985.

Monti, Silvana. *Pirandello*. Storia della critica, 31. Palermo: Palumbo, 1974.

Pirandello, Luigi. *Cap and Bells and Man, Beast and Virtue: Two Plays*. New York City: Performing Arts Journal Publications, 1983.

———. "Un inedito di Luigi Pirandello." *Corriere della Sera*, December 1, 1984:19.

———. "Lettere al figlio Stefano." *Almanacco letterario Bompiani* 1938:32–45.

———. *On Humor*. Trans. Antonio Illiano and Daniel P. Testa. University of North Carolina Studies in Comparative Literature, 58. Chapel Hill: University of North Carolina Press, 1974.

———. *Saggi, poesie, scritti varii*. Ed. Manlio Lo Vecchio-Musti. Opere di Luigi Pirandello, VI. Milan: Mondadori, 1960.

———. *Tutti i romanzi*. Eds. Giovanni Macchia and Mario Costanzo. 4th ed. Milan: Mondadori, 1981.

"Premi Pirandello a Bona, Macchia e a Luca Ronconi." *Corriere della Sera*, November 1, 1981:21.

Rauhut, Franz. *Der junge Pirandello, oder das Werden eines existentiellen Geistes.* München: C. H. Beck, 1964.

———. "Wissenschaftliche Quellen von Gedanken Luigi Pirandellos." *Romanische Forschungen*, 53 (1939):185–205.

Russo, Luigi. "Pirandello e la psicoanalisi." *Pirandello e la cultura del suo tempo*, 31–54.

Savinio, Alberto. *Hermaphrodito.* Turin: Einaudi, 1974.

Schulz-Buschhaus, Ulrich. "*L'umorismo*: l'anti-retorica e l'antisintesi di un secondo realismo." *Pirandello saggista*, 77–86.

Spirito, Ugo, and Arnaldo and Luigi Volpicelli. *Benedetto Croce: La filosofia, L'estetica e la critica letteraria, La storiografia, La teoria del diritto, La scienza economica, La politica.* Rome: Anonima Romana Editoriale, 1929.

Spizzo, Jean. "Pirandello: théâtre du reflet, théâtre du conflit." *Lectures pirandelliennes.* Centre de recherche de l'Université de Paris VIII—Vincennes, Groupe "Cultures, idéologies et sociétés des XIX et XX siècles," Section italien, II. Abbeville: F. Paillart, 1978. 175–232.

Stella, Vittorio. "Pirandello e la filosofia italiana." *Pirandello e la cultura del suo tempo*, 5–30.

Vicentini, Claudio. *L'estetica di Pirandello.* Saggi di estetica e di poetica, 11. Milan: Mursia, 1970.

Vittorini, Domenico. "Benedetto Croce e Luigi Pirandello." *Benedetto Croce.* Ed. Francesco Flora. Milan: Malfasi, 1953. 555–65.

2

Pirandello's Philosophy and Philosophers

Daniela Bini

"I have never taken upon myself any philosophical responsibility. I have always intended to make art, not philosophy," Pirandello once said in an interview.[1] He was probably discouraged and oppressed by the many voluminous treatises that Benedetto Croce, the Italian leading philosopher, was constantly producing. In 1916 to his son Stefano, prisoner of the Austrians, he in fact wrote not to "waste too much time on books of philosophy which say very little.[2] In another interview he commented: "In Italy there is a trend started by some critics to see in my work a philosophical content that is not there, I assure you."[3] He would certainly not have liked to be placed in the category of philosophers who "are and will always be idlers . . . a family of sick people who, by profession, spread gloom among mankind" (*Saggi*, 896). Their most recent accomplishment, Pirandello continues, is to have reduced earth to an incommensurably small atom, a ridiculous spinning-top thrown around the sun. At the same time they have reduced man to the level of any other living creature without any purpose but serving nature's course just as animals and plants do.

This might seem a discouraging start for a study of Pirandello's philosophy. Yet his critical attitude must be seen as part of a broader and more complex philosophical discourse. With his violent polemic, Pirandello was giving the final blow to an idea of philosophy on which Western thought had rested for two thousand years: philosophy as order, as systematic thought, responding to the eternal human quest for stability, certainty, and meaning. Plato had started it—Pirandello would in fact begin with throwing him out of his ideal Republic (*Saggi*, 896)—and two thousand years later Hegel had given it the most elaborate and impressive form. If idealism in Italy was synonymous with Croce, Pirandello's polemic was directed mainly against him and accordingly against two thousand years of metaphysics.[4]

"Arte e coscienza d'oggi" is the essay, written in 1893 when Pirandello was only twenty-six, that offers a detailed exposition of his ideas on philosophy and especially on modern philosophy. Here he writes: "The old laws having collapsed, the new ones not yet established, it is natural that the concept of the relativity of everything has widened so that . . . nobody is any longer able to establish a fixed, unshakable point" (*Saggi*, 900). With the collapse of objective truths, of the belief in a certain and absolute reality, there follows the crisis of language; objective, abstract terms have lost their meaning, with the loss of a common ground. From this, he continues, stems our intellectual malaise.

Vicentini, to whom Pirandellian criticism owes one of the most serious and detailed studies ever written on Pirandello, accurately examines all the early writings, mainly poems and letters, and finds there the whole of Pirandello's pessimistic philosophy. In a letter written to his sister Lina in 1886 he examines this loss of direction, ideals, and values with a lucid mind, but also with dramatic intensity (15–18). It calls to mind a seemingly desperate letter written by another young philosopher and artist. Later (in 1906) Carlo Michelstaedter expressed to his sister Paula the same anxieties caused by a human and a social crisis, "when all ties seem to get loose . . . the paths of existence are no longer drawn toward a culminating point, but they are all confused and disappearing."[5] Perhaps Carlo had not read *Il fu Mattia Pascal*, which had come out only two years earlier. Yet the words that Paleari, philosopher and believer in spiritualism, speaks to Adriano Meis, who is in bed recovering from his eye operation, strike the same note. We are living now without any lights, he says; they have all been put out. "Darkness and confusion! All the big lanterns have been blown out. Which way are we to turn?"[6] The tone is, of course, much lighter than Carlo's; here Pirandello is playing with a serious subject in his characteristic fashion, that of the humorist who in every experience discovers two opposite faces. The big lanterns are metaphors for human ideals, absolutes, laws. We will come back to Paleari's wisdom later.

Pirandello's statements about philosophy should be read in the context of contemporary thought. In the Preface to his book on Pirandello, Vicentini points out the necessity of abandoning the "idealistic identification of philosophy and systems" if we want to penetrate into the world of Pirandello (7). He claims to have learned this lesson from Luigi Pareyson, but credit must also be given to Leopardi who first taught it.

The Weak Thought of Gianni Vattimo's school, which through Gadamer and Pareyson goes back to Sartre, Heidegger, and Nietzsche, has suggested the theory that the only possible philosophy left to man is that which constantly questions itself, totally aware of the precariousness of each statement as of the weakness and limitations of his tool: thought. "The thought of truth that is the only possible philosophical thinking," says Vattimo, "is not the thought that sets foundations, as Metaphysics has always believed; on the contrary it is that which, exhibiting the caducity and mortality precisely as being does, knocks down the foundations'' (*Il Pensiero Debole*, 23).

At the turn of the century, another phenomenon took place that altered the rational constructions of the human mind; the irrational, which two thousand years of rationalism had relegated to the fringe of the human mind, entered the realm of philosophy and scientific study, acquiring a respectable status.

Pirandello could not have written philosophical treatises—boring pages without life he would have considered them—yet his philosophy is coherently and clearly elaborated in his essays and may be even better in his artistic production. As Vattimo says, the borderline between philosophy and art has disappeared. Philosophical statements can often be made through art much more forcefully, since it uses as a vehicle the synthetic power of imagination. This, as Leopardi says, is much more effective than sheer, cold reasoning.[7] At the same time, speaking in strictly philosophical terms and having learned Heidegger's lesson, "the work of art can be an actual realization ('messa in opera') of the truth, because truth is no longer a metaphorically stable structure, but an event."[8]

Over and over Pirandello claimed his total lack of interest in philosophical texts. After many studies, scholars are more or less in agreement with Pirandello's claim. "Psychoanalysis was in the air just as relativism and Freud and Einstein acted upon the artists even from a distance," wrote Russo.[9] Yet the debate on Pirandello's own philosophy has always been alive, and many attempts are still being made fit him into a school of thought. Again the "systematic fallacy," if I may call it so, is lurking. We are still trapped in our Aristotelian past, our language, our thoughts. When we use the word "philosophy," there appears before our eyes a neat construction where every piece fits, and all together form a logical, harmonious whole, where our anxieties disappear and we can rest for a while. But we will not find anything of the sort in Pirandello. The rationalism of our classical tradition, based on the assumption of an outside objective reality, before being systematically dismissed by Nietzsche and Heidegger, had already been called into question by Ivan Karamazov.

ADRIANO TILGHER, BENEDETTO CROCE, AND INTERPRETATION

It was Adriano Tilgher who in 1922, in his long study on contemporary theater, created the image of Pirandello as philosopher. In this study Tilgher was developing his own philosophy and saw it enacted in Pirandello's works. The core of Tilgher's thought is the contrast life–form—life representing continuous movement, freedom, and change, close to the Bergsonian idea, and form being man's intellectual creations and abstractions that try to fix life. Thus, although form is born from the human necessity to clarify and give life a meaning, it is doomed to kill it, thus failing in the attempt. In Tilgher's view the history of modern philosophy from Kant on is based on this dualism. Tilgher used his reflection as the basis for his aesthetics, where form coincides with the artistic product.

Pirandello, even before expressing the main points of his philosophy in his plays, had already elaborated them in his famous essay *On Humor*. What interests us here are his thoughts on life and form. "Life," he writes, "is a continual flux which we try to stop, to fix in stable and determined forms, both inside and outside ourselves, because we are already fixed forms. . . . The forms in which we seek . . . to fix in ourselves this constant flux are the concepts, the ideals with which we would like consistently to comply, all the fictions we create for ourselves, the conditions, the state in which we tend to stabilize ourselves."[10] But inside us, he continued, life goes on "indistinct under the barriers and beyond the limits we impose" (*On Humor*, 137). He returns to this idea in his notes (*Foglietti*) where he states that one cannot be in the abstract. "Being must happen, must create its own appearance to itself: the world. The World is the activity of being, it is appearance, illusion to which being itself grants the value of reality" (*Saggi*, 1275).[11] And in another note: "Life is being that wants itself. [It is Being] which gives itself a form. It is the infinite which becomes finite. In every form there is a purpose, thus an end. Every form is death" (*Saggi*, 1275).

Tilgher's theoretical pages on Pirandello which, having been written by a philosopher, endowed Pirandello with a sound intellectual status, could not but impress him. For a while Pirandello considered Tilgher his spokesman, but the close relationship did not last. Too many basic differences—politics first of all—divided the two writers. Furthermore, Tilgher was a systematic thinker who needed a theory in which to organize his ideas, the precise thing Pirandello was constantly opposing.

The image of Pirandello as philosopher was shattered by the philosopher par excellence, Benedetto Croce, who labeled Pirandello's ideas "compulsive, inconclusive philosophizing."[12] According to Croce, Pirandello's pseudo-philosophizing was destroying every artistic attempt. It was again Croce's philosophy of the "distinct," the same that had relegated most of Leopardi's works to a non-artistic limbo, that was now performing the same operation on Pirandello's. For Croce, reason and imagination were distinct faculties, and accordingly so were philosophy and art. A philosophical poet was to him a contradiction in terms, a hybrid. The polemic between the two intellectual giants was long-standing and has been well documented in many studies.[13] It is mainly against this Crocean distinction that Pirandello raised his criticism. Croce had, in fact, excluded altogether the presence of thought as reflection in the artistic activity. Pirandello, whose theory of humor is founded on such a presence, could not accept Croce's statement that would place his entire production outside the realm of art. As Vicentini pointed in out *L'estetica di Pirandello*, the polemic reached a dead end. Beyond the aesthetic contrast there was a much more profound opposition. Croce's optimistic vision was still supported by a blind faith in the power of the Hegelian spirit, endowed with a synthetical capability to create systems. Pirandello's pessimism issued from a world of chaos where the spirit in nothing but a manmade phantom.

Since Tilgher's study and the polemic with Croce, Pirandello's philosophical ideas have been amply studied, as have the influences and relations with major currents of thought. Analogies have been made with Greek thought, Pascal, Leopardi, Bergson, and Schopenhauer as well as with the contemporary psychological theories of Binet, Freud, Séailles, and Nordau. Other analogies have been formed with the existentialism of Jaspers and Heidegger, with naturalism, as well as with expressionism and surrealism.[14] The multiplicity of possible approaches to reading Pirandello is the very proof of his protean personality, constantly changing and assuming different forms—this, in the hope (as he often repeated) of escaping the fate of being tied to any one.[15]

For those critics who refused to admit the presence of any philosophy in Pirandello, reason could be found in his negative remarks about this discipline. Like Leopardi, Pirandello attacks rational thought because it unhinges all fictions and myths created by man and makes them crumble at his feet, plunging him into darkness. Yet Pirandello's polemic against reason, like Leopardi's, was motivated precisely by his total dependence on it. Reason could not be dismissed, because it is that which makes man what he is, what differentiates him from all other living things. Reason is the core of man's essence and cannot be rejected. That it is also the cause of human unhappiness is a different matter. This only reveals a sad truth: that suffering is man's destiny, and that in the universe he does not occupy a special place; neither does nature worry about him more that about all its other creatures, as Leopardi well taught us. Both Pirandello and Leopardi have a pessimistic philosophy, but a philosophy, nevertheless, whose foundations are fixed in that very destructive reason that causes so much suffering. Man's destiny and moral end are the discovery of reason. Man, however, has another attribute that distinguishes him from other living beings: his imagination which, by creating fictions, allows him to escape from reality. What must be emphasized, though, is that the creations of the imagination have their *raison d'être*, their necessary start in the negativity of reality. That is to say, there would be no fiction if reality were not finite, limited, thus insufficient. The negative element is the propeller of a dialectical movement that creates positivity.

HIS PHILOSOPHY

If we now go back to the essay cited at the beginning, "Arte e coscienza d'oggi," we will be able to find the starting point of Pirandello's philosophical reflections. He wrote it at the age of twenty-six, and it can be called his "Storia del genere umano."[16] As Leopardi had done, Pirandello traces the history of humankind, from the happy beginning of its "naive" state, as Schiller would say, to the desperation of his present alienation. In the beginning there was man in the center of the universe. Nature was made to serve him, to satisfy his desires and needs. The stars were shedding their light to brighten man's nights, and the gods were created to take care of people and to ease that dark moment they called death. But "a curse on Copernicus," exclaims Mattia Pascal, for destroying this magnificent construction, throwing man with his earth in a miniscule place in the infinite space, taking away from him all his prestige and power. And a curse on all the scientists and philosophers who followed him in his destructive operation. Illusions were gone, and with them, says Pirandello echoing Leopardi, went happiness. Rationalism had destroyed them (*Mattia Pascal*, 2).[17]

It is in this light that the passage quoted at the beginning of this study should be examined. Philosophers are cursed because they spread gloom by destroying the creation of human imagination. Unfortunately, however, as Leopardi had said more than once, destruction of the illusions does not bring about the removal of those human needs that create them. Man continues to ask questions, but there is no science or philosophy able to answer them. He finds himself "lost in . . . an immense labyrinth surrounded in every direction by an impenetrable mystery" (*Saggi*, 900).

If we examine a few notes Pirandello took at the end of his life for the autobiographical story "Information on My Involuntary Sojourn on Earth," we find Pirandello's *vision du monde* completely unchanged. "Earth seems to be made for men, but it is not true. Man, ruler of the earth? Ants, roaches, bacteria. . . . Man the ugliest among the animals. The craziest, the unhappiest. No certainties. And he pretends to judge! No possibility of knowing what and how things are and he wants to say they are so and so" (*Saggi*, 1103). After forty years life's mystery stands still in all its overpowering darkness. Human tragedy is existential, not historical, or better it is also historical, but because it is necessarily inherent in man's essence. "Men," Leopardi had said, "are miserable by necessity, yet determined to think themselves miserable by accident" (*Pensicri*, 71), and Pirandello would have agreed.

The last years of the nineteenth century and the first of the twentieth were years of reflection on existential problems. By then Pirandello's philosophy was fully established and would never change. In "Rinunzia" written for *La Critica* in 1896, he continues the discussion he had begun in "Arte e coscienza d'oggi." Here, in particular, he attacks the popular positivism and the myths of science. The occasion was the discovery of X-rays. Roengten had presented his study in 1895, an event Pirandello uses as an incentive to tackle once more the issue of scientific knowledge. "Which answers have science and modern philosophy given to man with their discoveries?" asks Pirandello. Rather than offering answers, they imply the supreme renunciation, surrender before the mystery of life. "Don't we call nature today what we in the past more poetically called God?" The scientific definition of nature "as a symbol of mechanical connection" does not help us to understand it any better (*Saggi*, 1056). What the new scientific method lacks is the ethical perspective on life that is reduced to mere mechanical laws. Leopardi called it "il senso dell'animo" (the sentiment of the soul), which in spite of all mechanistic explanations continues to ask questions about meaning. "Science extracts life and almost destroys it in order to anatomize it" (*Saggi*, 1058). "We," continues Pirandello, repeating an idea very dear to him and often reiterated by his characters, "will never be able to have a precise notion of life; but only a feeling, thus mutable and variable" (*Saggi*, 1059). Later on in his *Foglietti* he was to write: "we don't have an absolute idea of life, but a mutable, variable sentiment" (*Saggi*, 1269). In the intense movement of life we must suspend judgment. Pirandello is afraid that simply to think of this intense feeling will end it (*Saggi*, 1272). The dichotomy between life and thought has been established and, never to be resolved, will trouble Pirandello to the end. Serafino Gubbio will represent one choice and Moscarda the opposite, yet the two poles of the dichotomy will never be mediated. Pirandello's entire artistic production takes its initial inspiration from here. All his characters will come to life in order to represent this eternal conflict.

ON HUMOR

Pirandello's long essay *On Humor*, written in 1908, has rightly been called the true manifesto of his philosophy. Yet we must do justice to the first of Pirandello's philosophers: to Mattia Pascal, father of humor, the real inspirer of the essay.[18] Had not Pirandello said more than once that his characters often would knock on the door of his study and force their way in? Mattia, in fact, is humor in action; the theoretical elaboration of this philosophy will follow his performance. (This performance will be examined later with that of the other philosophers.)

In *On Humor* Pirandello returns to the idea that life cannot be known and that man can only have a feeling for it. This opposition between life and knowledge can be connected with the dichotomy life–form we have already examined and that Tilgher had exalted as Pirandello's great intuition. The connection will appear evident as the examination of Pirandello's various texts progresses. Man needs concepts, ideas, abstractions in order to make sense of life, just as he needs a form, an appearance in order to acquire an identity for himself and others.

Man embodies the contrast between life, which is senseless, and the need to make sense of it. Man's constant attempts are all bound to fail. "In certain moments of turmoil, all these fictitious forms are hit by the flux and collapse miserably under its thrust" (*On Humor*, 137). If we place this statement next to the one we examined earlier about *being* and *becoming*, the connection will emerge clearly. "One cannot be in the abstract. It is necessary for being to happen. It must create its own appearance to itself: the world" (*Saggi*, 1275). And we can now continue: "The world is the activity of being, an appearance, an illusion to which being gives the proof of reality" (1275). Although "without a form, being does not live," "being kills itself in every form." "Here is the eternal contradiction" (1276).

The cold and dry logic of this statement acquires dramatic force in the story "The Trap," which epitomizes Pirandello's philosophy. The main character, the speaker, is also the spokesman of this universal message. His bitterness and his caustic remarks are caused by his discovery of the contradiction of human existence. We need to have a reality, to fix our being in a form that others can recognize and to which they can relate. But what does that operation mean? "If not but arresting in us the perpetual vital movement," asks our character, "to turn us into miserable, stagnant ponds, whereas life is continual incandescent . . . flux" (*Novelle*, I, 682). It is poetry that comes to rescue the philosopher at this point. Since the contradiction, the paradox, of life cannot be resolved through reason, it can only be represented through imagination. "Life is wind, life is sea, life is fire, not earth that solidifies and takes upon itself a form." As Nietzsche had said, man experiences the world through the creation of metaphors.[19]

It is interesting now to examine the second part of the story "The Trap." There the imaginative tone collapses, but it is nevertheless the logical development of the philosophical argument treated in the first part. If man must, for the simple fact of being born as an individual, enter this trap, that is, his peculiar form, woman here is seen as the personification of it. The trap takes on a sexual significance that lowers the tone of the story; the language becomes coarse and loses the poetical élan that it had in the first part. This change is certainly not accidental.

Pirandello, since early age and because of childhood experiences, had a very complex attitude toward sexuality and the mysterious, unrestrainable, and powerful maternal instinct.[20] His constant returning to the issue shows a compulsive need to understand, coupled, I believe, with an unconscious or possibly conscious feeling of envy. Women in his fiction represent nature, instinct, the irrational, procreation, thus real life. There is an ambiguous air about them, which was caused perhaps by Pirandello's inability to arrive at their essence. Men, on the other hand, represent spirit, reason, philosophical inquiry, and in "The Trap" this double dichotomy is spelled out. Le Spera in *The New Colony* is the noblest of all his female characters. At the end of the play she triumphs over humankind, by virtue of her maternal instinct, her total commitment to life. When the island, shaken by the earthquake, plunges into the sea with all its inhabitants, La Spera stands alone on a rock embracing her child, symbol of the continuation of life. Yet the ambivalent feelings Pirandello has toward this character are apparent in his making her a prostitute, a class of women for whom he had the lowest opinion.

The creativity that man was denied by nature in this world he acquires in the world of art. In Pirandello's words women seem to be excluded from artistic creativity. The only exception, as far as I know, is Silvia Roncella in *Suo Marito*. Yet there is an explanation for her existence. In Silvia Roncella, Pirandello was experimenting with something new: the woman artist, thus a contradiction in terms, an individual who has in herself two contradictory essences—the female instinct to create life and the male need to create art. Pirandello's goal is to show that fiction kills life. It happens when Silvia's child dies in order to let her spiritual creation live. Her play, in fact, is a great success. With this message, however, we are again plunged into the labyrinth of Pirandello's feelings. Must women be only mothers? Is art the exclusive prerogative of men? Is it inferior to life? At times it seems that Pirandello wants to convince us of the contrary. Man wants his revenge on woman. Art continues nature's work, he said through the mouth of Dr. Fileno. "Man, the writer, will die, the instrument of the creation; but his creature will never die" (*Novelle*, I, 177). Art transcends life, and we are tempted to extend Pirandello's formula and conclude that art is superior to life, as man is to woman.

Although this discussion has digressed somewhat from the central concern of these pages, "The Trap" is an exceptional story because in it Pirandello succeeded in representing that complex analogy between the two levels of reality that he tried to explain in his essays but was not able to compress in a unified whole. Fiction allows him to do just that.

The process of knowing, that is, of establishing a cognitive relation between subject and object, becomes a process of creating images, ideas that cannot but be subjective. This relativistic view of the world is a main source of inspiration to Pirandello. Most of his plots and characters reflect it.

In an article published in *Marzocco* in 1896, Pirandello wants to assure his public that he is not a follower of Berkeley's *esse est percipi* philosophy and that "the world is not only the idea I can form of it. . . . The World exists for itself . . . and in my representation I must try to realize it, as much as possible . . . seeing it as it sees itself . . . feeling it as it feels itself (Vicentini, 34–35). We could call this the moral imperative that everyone must live by, yet it remains as illusion. Life, in fact, constantly shows us how elusive it is, because the individual is determined in his contacts with others by his own makeup, feelings, and needs. These inevitably affect our own interpretation of reality.

In *On Humor* Pirandello insists on the mistakes we make "in good faith" in seeing ourselves and others, and on how always "in good faith" we act and live (which is the same thing) (*On Humor*, 132).[21] It is at this point that the humorist performs his task. Through reflection he realizes the spontaneous fiction each of us creates and takes it apart, bringing out the opposite side of it and giving birth to the sentiment of the opposite.[22]

Pirandello's language becomes somewhat confused or at least ambiguous at this point. The word *sentimento* has two meanings, as it did in Leopardi. On the one hand it is feeling as opposite to reason; on the other hand it is consciousness. Pirandello often repeats that man is the only living creature that *feels* himself live. The tree does not. Echoing Paleari, he tells us that "from its standpoint, the earth, the sun, the air . . . are not things [the tree] differs from. Man, instead, is given at birth the sad privilege of feeling himself alive, with the true illusions that result from it: that of taking this inner feeling, changeable and varying, as something that really exists outside himself" (*On Humor*, 140). Thus, the word "sentiment" is used in Schiller's sense: as the opposite of naive. Sentiment is the discovery of the "other," of the principle of dialectics. It is a complex entity made out of feeling and reason.

When Pirandello then explains that the masks we make of ourselves, or of others, that the forms we fix the outside world in, are the creation of our "sentiment," he is trying to tell us that this operation, prompted by feeling, is performed by reason for the sake of feeling. The contradictory essence of human nature manifests itself in all its power. It is man's feeling that needs order, meaning, sense (which seeks to be rationalized, justified) thus, feeling commits an act of violence against itself. Man is a hybrid creature made up of two opposite elements whose task is to trouble and torture him.

The beautiful page on "Logic" can help us to follow Pirandello's argument with the help of a very effective metaphor. It is worthwhile to underline the fact that Pirandello resorts to metaphor when he must mediate reason and feeling. Only art, in fact, far from trying to make sense of the contradictions of life, can represent them alive. Logic is "a certain devilish little machine" that nature gave men, but that "for the sake of their well-being, men should have left to rust without ever using"—"a kind of filter pump that connects the brain to the heart" (*On Humor*, 139). It is the same devilish machine described by Magnasco in the play *It's Nothing Serious*. If we read *heart* as *feeling, instinct, life* and *brain* as *concept, ideas, reason*, we can well see that the function of this pump is to connect two opposites, to rationalize life—task, we already know, that is doomed to fail. The pump acts as a filter through which emotions pass in order to be "purified" "cooled," "idealized." This operation, however, as Leopardi also clearly saw, presents man with all the evils of the world "on a pharmacy shelf all nicely labelled with the word Poison over skull and bones" (*On Humor*, 139).

In what follows, Pirandello creates another metaphor to explain the "sentiment" of life, proving what was said above: the necessity of resorting to the imagination in order to give body to an opposition. Sentiment is that spark which Prometheus stole from the sun to give to man, and it corresponds precisely to the little lamp of Signor Anselmo; even the words he uses to describe it are the same (Mattia Pascal, 155). Pirandello, who in the novel seems to smile at the elaborate "lanternosophy" of Mr. Paleari, makes it his own in the essay, for, after all, it is a philosophy of doubts, of questions, of hypothesis. The mystery, the darkness outside ourselves that is created by the little lamp man lights inside himself, that is our sentiment or self-consciousness, could also be our own creation and not exist in itself. Once our light is put out, there will be no "frightening shadow" around us.

It is a long passage, structured through questions. No statement is made. It is built on hypotheses and "maybes." Its structure is extremely convoluted, and Pirandello's purpose is—it seems clear—to overwhelm the reader, losing him in his syntax—just as he is lost in the universe. Pirandello, the humorist, is at work here through an analytical process that could go on indefinitely. The humorist, in fact, is now working on Prometheus who then realizes that Zeus is nothing but a shadow created by his light. If he were to put his light out, Zeus would disappear. But he will not do it—"he knows not, wants not and cannot," says Pirandello—and the shadow remains "terrifying and tyrannical for all men who fail to realize the faithful deception" (*On Humor*, 141). In his presumptuous superiority the humorist has not freed man from his shadows. Prometheus will forever help man to keep his spark alive.

The end of Chapter V of *On Humor* is a masterpiece of imaginative genius, which cannot but prove what the text suggests: the greatness of the human mind, specifically Pirandello's. Picking up a thread Mattia Pascal had left, he calls Copernicus one of the greatest humorists because he dismantled the image of the universe man had created. In his hands the earth becomes a tiny ball, a grain of sand thrown at random in the universe, and man becomes just a little worm. The discovery of the telescope gave man's grandiose pretensions the final blow. If, in fact, "the eye looks from below through the smaller lens and sees as big all that nature had providentially wanted for us to see small," our soul, says Pirandello, looks "from the larger lens," and earth and man sink together "with all our glories and greatness" (*On Humor*, 142). When man performs such an operation he is acting as a humorist, he is seeing things in one way and in the opposite at the same time. "Every feeling, every thought . . . that arises in the humorist immediately splits into its contrary, every affirmative into a negative, which finally ends up assuming the same value as the affirmative" (*On Humor*, 125). Dr. Post, alias Dr. Fileno, will make of this procedure a whole philosophy: the Philosophy from Afar. He has learned to distance himself from the present, he has renounced life, and passes time "secluded like a hermit amidst his books of history and philosophy."[23]

Yet the work of the humorist never ceases. Each statement generates its opposite. After seeing earth and men as small as dots, the humorist asks, echoing the more dramatic but identical question Leopardi had asked: "But is man really as small as he looks when seen through an inverted telescope? If he understands and conceives of the infinite greatness of the universe, how, then, can one say that man is small?" (*On Humor*, 142).[24] But, as we saw earlier, the chain of self-defeating argument never stops, and the next step is that if then man "feels big and a humorist finds out, he may end up like Gulliver, a giant in Lilliput and a toy in the hands of the giants of Brobdingnag" (142).

Dr. Post, the inventor of the Philosophy from Afar, becomes Dr. Fileno in the story "The Tragedy of a Character." With him we definitely enter the realm of fiction led by a character who explains to us the basic principles of aesthetics.

"Art is life not reasoning. It is a living idea," wrote Pirandello late in his life (*Saggi*, 1259). Was he here deliberately making up an oxymoron? Is this statement a contradiction in terms? After having drastically separated life from form, he was saying that art is the idea that has life. How, then, was he using the word "form"? Was he contradicting himself or did he want to be paradoxical? Here Pirandello tried to say that art is a superior activity that has the power to represent life as it is, in its flux. It is still a theoretical statement that can leave us puzzled. Yet if we listen to Dr. Fileno, Pirandello's artistic creation, and to his metaphorical language, this apparently contradictory discourse will reveal itself in all its clarity. "We [characters] are living beings, more alive than those

who breathe and wear clothes. Less real, perhaps, but more alive! One is born
into life in so many different ways . . . nature avails herself of . . . human fantasy
in order to pursue her work of creation."[25] As we saw when discussing the issue
of creation, Pirandello, through Fileno, is proclaiming the immortality of art.
Men, writers, will die, but characters will live forever.

Pirandello takes a major leap here. In the chaos of life, amid the absurdities
and limits of existence, there stands human imagination, the creative function
that not only competes with nature's creation but surpasses it. In an enlightening
page, Pirandello further clarifies this major point. "Imagination," wrote Pirandello at the end of his life, "shows us the constant correspondence between
nature and thought, the perpetual motion from one to the other, and it seems to
resolve, without our ever becoming aware of it, the insoluble problem of the
relation between spirit and body. . . . The mystery of creation is the mystery of
life" (*Saggi*, 1266). The religious tone is confirmed by other passages where
the artist/Christ analogy is openly made. Many years before in "Teatro nuovo
e teatro vecchio" Pirandello had tried to explain this superior work of artistic
creation with the language of religion, and his explanation ended with an open
identification of Christ with the real artist (*Saggi*, 234). In the same essay
Pirandello brings into his discussion on aesthetics the ethical aspect of art.
Hamlet's existential question *to be or not to be*, says Pirandello, to give an
example of his idea, has been fixed on his lips forever; it is the problem of
man's essence that will never be resolved, represented alive, eternally present,
to all generations of men. This perfect form, although it has not helped men to
resolve the existential crisis, has placated his soul with its beauty and universal
meaning (*Saggi*, 236).

"HIS HUMORIST PHILOSOPHERS"

Pirandello's philosophers are all men, since, as we have seen before, for
Pirandello reason is basically male. Of course, since Pirandello has taught us
the impossibility of a drastic separation between faculties and the presence of
the most various entangled elements, we should approach his philosophers with
caution. The "beast" that lies inside is bound to emerge at times. In fact, the
man who is more vulnerable to the power of feelings and passion is often the
one who will resort to reflection and philosophy. Such is the case with Viola/
Gala as with many others.

In "A Warning on the Scruples of the Imagination," an appendix to *Il fu
Mattia Pascal*, Pirandello wrote: "Isn't it perhaps true that man never reasons
so passionately (or so wrongly—not that that changes anything—) as when he
is suffering? He wants to arrive at the root of his sufferings, he wants to discover
who causes them, and whether they are deserved" (*Mattia Pascal*, 247).

Mattia Pascal/Adriano Meis embodies better than all other Pirandellian characters the real dilemma of man's existence. The intolerableness of an oppressive
family situation and a strong need of freedom and fate give Mattia the chance

to disappear from the world forever and to be born anew as Adriano Meis, a free being, having cut off all those threads that connected him to the outside world. Outside of life he observes and judges it, but he soon realizes the absurdity of his state, or better his nonstate. Absolute freedom is nonsense since freedom is defined by its limits, namely, the presence of the other who negates it. Adriano soon understands that absolute freedom coincides with the negation of life.

There is a beautiful passage in the novel where Adriano, who is enjoying the new self his fantasy has created, which he can form and change at his pleasure, reflects on this fact and realizes that "nothing can be invented without some kind of roots in reality." Life, as he would repeat in the "Warning," is much more unpredictable and fantastic than fantasy. "How many things substantial, minute, unimaginable our invented product needs before it can become again that very reality from which it was born. How many threads bind our invention to the complicated tangle of life, threads we have severed to make our creation a thing apart!" (*Mattia Pascal*, 88). Mattia is reflecting on his creation, that is, Adriano Meis, and is discovering the necessity for it to be rooted in real life. Yet there is also a metanarrative level on which we can read this passage. Pirandello is questioning the very process of artistic creation—not only Adriano Meis as a new identity created by Mattia Pascal, but also Adriano Meis as fictional character invented by Pirandello the artist.

"Now what was I if not an invented man? A walking invention who wanted and, for that matter, was forced to remain apart, even when thrust into reality" (*Mattia Pascal* 88). The "threads" Adriano has severed could be tied only to his fantasy. But the crisis begins as soon as Adriano tries to build his new persona. Since he had no legal identity, he could have no home. He could have no friends since "friendship means confiding," and Adriano could not confide his past to anyone (101). So he had to be content with the sole company of his own self. "Yet . . . to tell the truth, I was afraid that I would no longer be satisfied or happy alone with my own company" (102). Besides had he not acquired a new appearance "for others"? "If everything I had imagined and constructed concerning Adriano Meis was of no use for other people, to whom was it useful? Me? But I could believe it, if at all, only when others believed it, too" (*Mattia Pascal*, 102). Adriano realizes that it is impossible to live in unlimited freedom. So he throws himself into crowded streets and cafés and observes the life that passes by. "But life—observed this way, as if by an outside spectator—seemed shapeless and aimless; I felt lost in the jostling crowds" (102). Adriano Meis can thus exist only outside of life. This artificial construction will fall apart as soon as feelings overcome reason, making their way through the puppet. Adriano falls in love. Life pulls him in again, shattering the fiction Mattia had created. Having erased Adriano, Mattia has little left to do. Society had canceled him even as Mattia and his return from the beyond are not accepted. He will then—his life over—lock himself up in the library, among books that tell about life, and write his autobiography. That is, he will write, register on the page that life which he can no longer experience.

The opposition between living and reflecting, action and contemplation, can only be acknowledged, but it can never be resolved, for it has at its root the eternal opposition of life and form. In order to understand life man must stop it; he must step out of it. Thus, what he has before him is no longer life but a corpse. This is what Cosmo Laurentano in *I vecchi e i giovani* (*The Old and the Young*) decided to do. In the heat of major historical changes, which will bring about the unification of Italy, Don Cosmo retires from life in the company of his books as the other Sicilian nobleman, the Prince Salina, will do. Through this exceptional character who seldom appears in the novel and does not act, Pirandello makes his most revealing comments on philosophy. "Don Cosmo was so abstract and solitary a spirit that the life of the world could not succeed in penetrating his conscience . . . and often . . . from the frozen peak of his stoical indifference, he let fall like an avalanche the most naked of truths.[26] The linguistic richness of this passage suffices to convey the full range of meanings. It reveals its tragic essence which consists in a self-defeating task. In order to understand the world the philosopher removes himself from it, creating around himself a wasteland. His reason has frozen all life around him. The judgments he makes and the truths he discovers come down on us like solid blocks of ice. The metaphor of snow and avalanche conveys dramatically the image of power, coldness, and death, which make up the essence of philosophy.

Pirandello, however, has not finished surprising us. Immediately after the metaphor just examined, Capolino, commenting on Don Cosmo's books by Romagnosi, Rosmini, Hegel, and Kant, asks a rhetorical question. "Philosophy, eh?" (*The Old*, I, 74). Cosmo's reply leaves Capolino in dismay. "Poetry!" he responds, and he proceeds to explain to his puzzled interlocutor. "Yes, [poetry], for study, my dear sir, there is little or nothing; what there is is enjoyment of the grandeur of the human intellect, which on a hypothesis, that is to say on a cloud . . . builds up castles, pinnacles and towers: all these various systems of philosophy, my dear *avvocato*, . . . seem to me . . . do you know what they seem to me? churches, chapels, shrines, temple of different styles poised in the . . . " (74). Philosophical systems, religions, and sciences are all human fictions created by man for his comfort, just like poetry, another product of man's fantasy. "Breathe," Don Cosmo continues, "and the whole structure collapses; breathe, and all these castle which tower like mountains crumble, because there is nothing inside them; a void, my dear sir . . . a void and the silence of mystery" (74). The only voice that could still speak a word in this universal silence is that of Leopardi's Great Wild Rooster: "thus this stupendous and frightening mystery of universal existence, before it can be declared or understood, will vanish and be lost."[27]

These philosophers who have "understood the game" have inside themselves a "frolicsome little devil" who amuses himself "by representing to us outside ourselves, as reality, what a moment later he himself reveals to us as our own illusion, laughing at us for the efforts we have made to secure it" (II, 360). But the little devil reveals itself yet a greater humorist for he also laughs at us, as in Cosmo's case, "for not having had the sense to delude ourselves, since outside these illusions there is no other reality" (II, 360). The conclusion, therefore, is that man never wins, whether he believes in them or not, but the believer is certainly less miserable.

Don Cosmo Laurentano shares with his other Sicilian friend, the Prince Salina, his love for and attraction to the sky. It is an old *topos* that through Dante goes back to the Greeks—the *topos* of the contemplative life. The two noble Sicilians also share it with all Pirandello's philosophers. In the physical and metaphysical night that surrounds him, Cosmo (and his name is *à propos*) "fixed his gaze upon a few stars, nailheads of the mystery" as he calls them, "that appeared in a clear patch of sky, among the ragged clouds" (II, 363).

The sight of the starry sky helps Berecche (the protagonist of "Berecche e la guerra") to detach himself from life, to cool his emotions by placing everything in perspective. It is at night that the *"vis philosophica* manifests itself." Life is suspended in sleep—a taste of death Leopardi calls it. Darkness hides everything; noise ceases; and far in the distance burn eternal fireflies. Berecche, who has learned his lesson from Dr. Fileno, can even place himself on one of them, and from there he watches the miniscule earth that swarms with billions of little ants. "Is there anyone who thinks that time does not exist in the heavens? That everything plunges into the abyss and vanishes in this endless tenebrous void? And that on this little grain, tomorrow, in a thousand years, there will be no longer anything or very little will be about said this war that now appears to us formidable and immense?" (*Novelle*, II, 749).

Berecche can reach an objective view of the world around him through his philosophical detachment. Yet, as Leopardi had often repeated, the reasons of philosophers, though true, cannot really answer our deep questions. Dr. Fileno's telescope cannot help for very long. Man is caught in this life, Berecche in his big war, and the idea that in a thousand years only a few sentences will record it in a history book does not help him. On the contrary, it infuriates him. There are millions of big tragedies in those million little lives, each of which demands full attention and consideration because it is the only one each of us has and all that we have. Unfortunately, Pirandello's philosophers know, as does Bernardo Sopo, that in the "deepest bottom of the darkness he felt inside which neither the light of science nor that of faith could succeed in eliminating, an indefinable anxiety was palpitating. The anxiety of an unknown awaiting him that something had to be done which was never what he was gong to do" (*Novelle*, II, 591). Bernardo Sopo can analyze clearly his feelings and arrive at the only possible conclusion. The need for an answer, a goal, constitutes the essence of human nature. Yet it can never be fulfilled. Life has no purpose but to continue indefinitely.

The philosopher's detachment from life is, however, what makes him not only unable to live, but also, in the end, unable to understand the life he set out to study. This is what the Fat Man shows to the Philosopher in the short play, *All'uscita* (At the Gate). The philosopher is here continuing Cosmo Laurentano's speech that tombs, like churches, are constructions that man builds for himself to house a feeling which, in order to live, has no need of housing. His philosophical virtue must, however, withdraw before the common sense of the Fat Man, symbol of life, who has actually understood much better than the philosopher the thoughts and actions of his wife and her lover. Similarly Judge D'Andrea in *La patente* (*the License*), whose daily work is to judge life, having lost touch with it, in the abstraction of his airy reflections, cannot understand natural human actions. His inability to live is shown right at the beginning, through his physical description: "With a shoulder higher than the other one he would walk crooked . . ." (*Novelle*, I, 512). He cannot easily move through life. Furthermore, he lives secluded and so "he could not have seen too many things . . . but certainly he must have thought of many and when thinking is the saddest, at night" (512). Once more the contraposition of life–thought, living–knowing, is established from the start. At night, Judge D'Andrea gazing up at the stars reflects on proportions, relations, numbers, and the result is the awareness that nothing can be known. His nocturnal speculations do not help him at all with his job as judge. Doubts, questions remain unaltered and often become bigger. It is, instead, Chiarchiaro, poor, boorish, unpolished Chiarchiaro who, after having tried in vain to convince D'Andrea that he wants to go on with the trial and to lose it, explodes: "It seems to me, Mr. Judge, that you do not understand anything." D'Andrea is ready to agree with him, fully aware of his detachment from reality. The learned judge, the scholar who studies hundreds of books, must be taught the simplest lesson of life by the ignorant, simple man.

This theme also appears in the novel *Shoot!* Before becoming a cameraman, Serafino Gubbio had studied philosophy and literature since he had "the worm of philosophy gnawing [his] brain.[28] What he has learned from philosophy, says Serafino with sarcasm, is "to draw back with an instinctive shudder from reality. . . . I took now at everything, myself included, as from a distance" (*Shoot!*, 48).

Giacomo de Benedetti called *Shoot!* the most autobiographical of Pirandello's novels, where the identification between author and character is more than suggested (275). His profession, cameraman, is therefore a very natural expression of his personality, insofar as it requires precisely this very objectivity, coldness, abstraction. No feelings must accompany the shooting of a movie. Serafino must only be "a hand that turns a handle" (58). This consideration, however, does not please Serafino, who can foresee the day in which even his being a hand will no longer be needed, and his place will be taken up by a machine. Man creates the machines that will supplant him. "Zeus's last bomb" will demonstrate more dramatically precisely this phenomenon.[29]

Throughout the novel Serafino repeats the truths already discovered by Pirandello's philosophers: that animals have all they need to live content, whereas men were given a superfluous something that constantly torments them and whose activity is the creation of an artificial world. "A world that has meaning and value for them alone, and yet one with which they themselves cannot ever be content, so that without pause they keep on frantically arranging and rearranging it" (*Shoot!*, 14). "On this earth man is destined to fare ill, because he has in him more than is sufficient for him to fare well, that is to say in peace and contentment. And that it is indeed an excess, for life on earth, this element which man has within him . . . is proved by the fact that it . . . never succeeds in finding rest in anything" (15–16). But if Serafino has completely lost touch with life, Simone Pau, his friend, is a philosopher who has not. The death of his artist friend, the violin player, who significantly has no name—he represents, in fact, pure disinterested art that can no longer speak to the ear of modern man—prompts him to a beautiful monologue, where the philosophical truth goes hand in hand with human emotions, or better it is at their service.[30] A few people are kneeling near the body of the dead friend praying. Outside of the room Simone talks to Serafino.

A man has died. . . . And five people, in there, have gone on their knees round him to pray to someone, to something, which they believe to be outside and over everything . . . a sentiment of theirs which rises independent of their judgment and invokes the same pity which they hope to receive themselves, and it brings them comfort and peace. Well, people must act like that. You and I who cannot . . . are a pair of fools. Because in saying these stupid things I am now saying, we are doing the same thing, on our feet, uncomfortably, with only this result for our trouble, that we derive from it neither comfort nor peace. (*Shoot!*, 149)

Tolerance and consideration are what Simone is advocating here. "We must be compassionate toward the beast which is inside us," he had said shortly before (146). "There is nothing to be known beyond that which . . . is represented . . . in actions" (150), and "they are all stupid in the same way . . . life is all a mass of stupidity always, because it never comes to an end" (150). Simone teaches a lesson of tolerance and humility to Serafino, whose job is shooting actions, and to us all, who constantly perform and judge actions.

Serafino feels comforted. Philosophy, he thinks, is like religion: "it always comforts even when it is desperate, because it is born from the need to overcome a torment" (150). Even when it does not succeed in overcoming it, philosophy still comforts us because it takes the torment outside our soul in order to examine it. And this is already a relief.

The chapter ends with another monologue, this one by Serafino who questions his profession. If being a cameraman consisted in recording human actions as they occur spontaneously, namely, life as it naturally unfolds, he could be happy with his profession. But movies are made by actors who fake actions, who pretend to be what they are not.

Here Pirandello is bringing out in the open an issue very close to his heart: that of the competition between cinema and theater, which to him would translate into the opposition between science, seen in its industrial, mechanical form, and art. The issue is complex and will not be examined here. What is relevant to our discourse, however, is Pirandello's belief in the higher value of art precisely because of its ability to represent life as it unfolds.

But what is the difference between actors and men? Are they not all playing a part? Don't they all have a fixed role to perform? When Serafino thinks of the pathetic scene played by Aldo Nuti who tries to camouflage his shame and pain through rhetoric, he once more reflects on the core of the existential puzzle.

Who is he? Ah, if each one of us could for an instant tear himself away from that metaphorical ideal which our countless fictions, conscious and unconscious . . . lead us inevitably to form of ourselves; he would at once perceive that this he is another, another who has nothing or little in common with himself; and that the true he is the one that is crying his misdeeds aloud within him; the intimate being, often doomed for the whole of our lives to remain unknown to us! (Shoot!, 193)

It is the metaphor of ourselves which we try to preserve, at any cost.

"Life cannot be explained through logic" (200). We continue to make the same mistake in trying to do just that because there is no logic in life, and we cannot adapt it to an artificial abstraction. It is always "at the very moment when logic, striving against passion, thinks that it has secured the victory, passion with a sudden lunge snatches it back" (200) just as the earth shakes suddenly off her back thousands of man-made buildings. Serafino picks up this discussion again a little later, emphasizing the absurdity of placing life before us as "an object of study." "It is absurd," he continues, "because when set before one like that [it] inevitably loses all its real consistency and becomes an abstraction, void of meaning and value" (226). And how can you explain life when by doing that you have just killed it? "The most you can do now is to dissect it" (224). At the end of the novel the opposition of life–thought, action–contemplation finds an extreme and atrocious metaphor. Serafino will be filming a double killing. His machine will thus act as the wonderous weapon that it is: the eye that observes and tries to stop life. And he will stop it, indeed. "That machine had in its maw the life of a man; I had given it that life to eat to the very last" (Shoot!, 332).

Aldo Nuti is probably the most tragic of the characters in this novel. He is trapped in his role of the betrayed jealous lover to such an extent that his apparent rebellion at the end, his will to end his life and that of his beloved, will fit perfectly into this very role. His suicidal action takes the dramatic connotation of the act of a religious fanatic. Like the first Christians, he willingly throws himself in the ring to be torn to pieces and devoured by the tiger.

Serafino is thus filming a double killing; he is actually killing life twice. Aldo Nuti murders Nestoroff with a rifle, a man-made machine just like Serafino's camera, and will be killed by the tiger. It could seem that justice is restored with this violent act of nature. Yet Pirandello's polemic against the murderous act of observing and recording life is not over. His final indictment against it is Serafino's shooting that very scene of slaughter and the final killing of the tiger which, once it has performed its role in the movie, can be dismissed. In the end only the machine and the film are left. The life they recorded has been destroyed forever.

Lamberto Laudisi is perhaps the most successful of Pirandello's philosophers. Faithful to himself from beginning to end, he keeps himself out of the action, observes it, and comments on it. At the beginning, of *Così è (se vi pare)* [It Is So (If You Think So)] in the second scene of Act I, he presents his philosophy. His sarcasm about people's curiosity is justified by its being useless, he says, wasted energy. "What can we really know about other people?"[31] We are what and how they see us, each one in his own way. This is the message that the veiled woman at the end of the play has for us all. "I am she whom you believe me to be" (*Naked Masks*, 138). The whole play pivots on that principle: that we cannot know the truth and that there is no one truth for all, but thousands, millions as many as there are people seeking it. The veiled woman of *It Is So (If You Think So)* is both the second wife of Signor Ponza and the daughter of Signora Frola. "How is it possible?" asks the Prefect. Is Pirandello telling us that the principle of non-contradiction at the basis of Western logic is no longer holding? Can A and non-A be both at the same time? Leopardi had already answered this question affirmatively, thus stating that contradiction is the essence of life. Pirandello, without ever questioning or dwelling on the existence of a reality out there, has only one certainty,—that is, the impossibility of knowing, or at least of arriving at, the exclusive possession of that reality.

The veiled woman is two different persons for those around her, because they want her to be so. But she could have been a thousand others as her brother Vitelangelo Moscarda will show us. And what is she to herself? "For myself," she replies to the amazed public, once more speaking in unison with Moscarda, "I am nobody" (*Naked Masks*, 138).

Contrary to what might first appear, the core of the issue here is not gnostic, but ethical. What Laudisi/Pirandello wants to tell us is that we must respect what others see and feel, even when it does not agree with what we see and feel.[32] This is what Signor Ponza and Signora Frola show us. Each of them has his beliefs and convictions; nevertheless, they respect those of others, in this particular case, each other, although they are different. What difference does it make where the truth lies? Ponza and Frola live intensely in their beliefs; they are as real to them as their sufferings are real. Nothing else matters, save the possession of an hypothetical objective truth which in its abstract form would destroy every emotion, every life.

The tragedy of Ponza and Frola consists in the violence that has been inflicted on them by the community that wants to invade the privacy of their most intimate life. The only truth that matters, Laudisi proclaims, instead, is in the minds of those two, which he can enter only "through what they say to [him] of themselves" (*Naked Masks*, 97). The lost documents, papers of their past that the community is eagerly seeking, do not count because the two individuals themselves have canceled, annulled them "in their own souls." "She has created for him and he for her, a world of fancy which has all the earmarks of reality itself . . . and this world of fancy, this reality of theirs, no document can possibly destroy, because the air they breathe is of that world'' (98).

In the interview *Conversando con Pirandello* published in *Messaggero della domenica* in 1919, Pirandello called his last novel *One, None, and a Hundred Thousand* ''the complete synthesis of all [I] had done and source of what [I am] going to do in the future.[33] Three years later in another interview, for *Epoca*, he called it the novel of ''the decomposition of personality.''[34] *One, None, and a Hundred Thousand* summarizes and clarifies Pirandello's philosophy through a long exercise of self-analyses. In the same interview Pirandello is concerned with dissipating the image of his negative thought. He wants to correct a misunderstanding. ''It is we who create reality, I say; and it is indispensable that it be this way. But woe to those who stop only at one reality. One ends up with atrophy, suffocation, death. It is necessary, instead, constantly to change and vary an illusion'' (Vicentini, 221).

The novel is a mosaic of pieces taken from everything Pirandello wrote. From Vicentini's accurate list we can see that there are basic ideas that go as far back as twenty years. ''The crisis of identity,'' as Gioanola calls it, that began with *The Late Mattia Pascal* has reached its conclusion.[35] Vitalangelo Moscarda is the natural son of Stefano Giogli, the philosopher/psychoanalyst—the short story ''Stefano Giogli uno e due'' was written in 1909. He introduces himself at the start as an inept, ''a typical anti-hero of Twentieth Century literature like Svevo's Zeno or Musil's Man without Qualities.[36]

The novel has neither a real plot nor action. It is a long psychoanalytic session in which patient and analyst are one and the same. Between them is a mirror that has ''the effect of expropriating him who looks in it.'' It is the medium that separates ''life from conscience,'' ''the one who lives from him who watches living.''[37] Laudisi's brief monologue in front of the mirror at the beginning of Act II, Scene 3, of *It Is So (If You Think So)* serves as an entrance into Pirandello's last novel. Before the mirror Laudisi had asked his image who of the two was mad; before the mirror Moscarda discovers his own madness.

The theme of madness was a constant companion of Pirandello's life and art. Although as a literary *topos* the theme is at least as ancient as Erasmus' *Folly*, Pirandello was personally and emotionally involved with a clinical case: that of his wife. He was to discover that the borderline between normality and pathology is very fine and that madness is generally the outburst of the beast that hides in all of us. That beast is our real self, the only part of us that is not constructed and is, by nature, true and sincere. He who speaks the truth is often considered mad by society, because, by so doing, he violates social conventions, showing their hypocrisy and falsity. By attributing the label of madness to those who attempt to disrupt it, society preserves itself and its order. This is what Ciampa wants from Mrs. Fiorica. She has spoken a painful truth that has threatened the social order. By agreeing to be locked up in an insane asylum she will restore it. In *Il berretto a sonagli* (*Cap and Bells*), the identification between madness and truth is complete. Ciampa spells it out for us: "It is very easy to act as a mad person. I'll teach you how. It's enough that you start shouting the truth in the face of everybody and everybody will consider you mad" (*Novelle*, II, 404).

Moscarda tells us from the start that he belongs to "the race of those who remain on land" ("della razza di chi rimane a terra"), to use Montale's powerful metaphor, to the race, that is, of contemplative beings, those who observe and do not live.[38] He, in fact, though married, fails to procreate; life has withdrawn from him; his world is that of thought. "I was prone to fall, at any word said to me, at the sight of a housefly buzzing about, into depths of reflection and pondering that left me with a hollow feeling inside."[39] "I could certainly see farther than [those who had passed me on the way] but go—where was there to go?" (*One*, 16).[40] This is probably why he is so outraged by his wife's comment that the right side of his nose hangs down lower than the left side. How could that have escaped him in so many years? The mirror becomes the means of Moscarda's self-analysis, a metaphor for conscience, as Biasin has well shown. And conscience, as self-knowledge, Biasin continues, quoting Pirandello, coincides with madness. "But it was precisely because I possessed this accurate-mirroring consciousness that I was mad" (142).[41] This is madness that is caused by an excess of logic, that devilish machine, that nasty little pump that cools off any feeling.

Moscarda analyzes himself before the mirror of his conscience and soon arrives at axiomatic conclusions:

1. That I was not to others what up to then I had believed that I was to myself; 2. That I could not see myself living; 3. That not being able to see myself living, I remained a stranger to myself, that is, one whom others believed they saw and knew, each after his own fashion, but not I (*One*, 41).

Four more points follow, all logically connected—the logical connection is pivotal in this novel—in what could be called Pirandello's *summa philosophica*. Book one ends shortly thereafter with a proposal: to try "to find out who I was, at least, to those close to me . . . and to amuse myself by maliciously decomposing the 'I that I was to them'," (42).

Throughout the novel, Moscarda has the attitude of a lecturer. He distances himself from the others who have the silly "presumption" to believe that "reality as it is for you, ought to be and is the same for all others "(49). Using the inductive method that the culture of his time had taught him, he takes his readers step by step from the particular to the general, establishing an analogy between inner and outer nature. What man does to his own nature and that of others—that is, camouflaging it by fabricating masks—he does to nature outside, when he builds forms, that is, buildings, cities, which should house his need for order. City is to nature what society is to man. The violence of city on nature is beautifully expressed by the image of the timid tendrils of grass—they have a relevant place in much of Pirandello's work. While growing in the middle of the square's pavement, they are gently trying "to take possession of the earth

5

again'' (*One*, 74). The novel is also an indictment of modern civilization. Nature, as Pirandello had said before, at times amuses itself in "knocking down all our ingenious constructions. Cyclones, earthquakes. But man does not give up. He rebuilds" (75). It is the only way he has to know the world. This is why he builds himself too, "like a house." "We can only know that to which we succeed in giving form" (75). Consequently, I cannot "recognize myself in that form which you confer upon me, nor you yourself in that which I confer upon you" (75–76). Yet, as Cosmo Laurentano told us—and he had learned it from Leopardi—the most tragic conclusion is that "there is no reality beyond" those forms (76).

Moscarda plans to destroy all those forms of himself which the others have constructed and first of all that of the usurer, the falsest of all. His fight, however, is not only against those particular forms but against form *tout cours*. "Everything was now comprised in the horror of being locked within the prison of any form whatsoever" (*One*, 215). The conclusion of the novel is, therefore, the only one possible. Having destroyed one by one the forms of himself, nothing remains except life in its pure, natural state: the state of continuous flux in which man and nature are indistinct and indistinguishable. "No conclusion" is the title of the last chapter because life, Pirandello repeated *ad infinitum*, does not conclude. "I am dying every instant, and being born anew and without memories; alive and whole, no longer in myself, but in everything outside" (*One*, 268).

Biasin is surely correct not to place much emphasis on Pirandello's pantheism. The end of the novel, he says, "should rather be considered as an indication, a metaphor of something other than and different from contemporary society."[42] I may add that the annulment into nature is the logical conclusion of a logical process that is the most logical enemy of logic: Pirandello could not but take it to its final step. It is a negative end that should be used as an extreme, paradoxical model—a lesson to be kept in mind, a fiction that might help us to compensate for the alienation and rhetoric, as Michelstaedter would say, of our times. It is the artistic metaphor that can express the logically inexpressible, the only medium that can give body to the paradox of life.

Existentialism is not easily defined. Philosophers and writers of different ilk have equally been labeled existentialist. If one were looking for a single word to describe the philosophy of Pirandello, it would with all due caution be just that.

The similarities between the elements of Pirandello's thought, as they have been developed in this essay, and the standard definitions of existentialism offered in the *Encyclopedia of Philosophy* are indeed striking. "Concepts are necessarily inadequate attempts to grasp individual existence, which always evades complete conceptualization," writes Alasdair MacIntyre, and, he continues, "Order is a deceptive mask that the universe, especially the social universe, wears. The individual thus confronts the universe with no rational scheme by means of which he can hope to master it. Reason will only lead him to formulate generalizations that will, if he relies upon them, let him down.[43] These principles in their generality can well be used for most of twentieth-century thought—for Kafka, Svevo, Musil, Montale, Sartre, and Camus, the writers of the crisis of the self. The entry "existentialism" concludes with a remark that brings us back into the heart of Pirandello's thought. Commenting on the fact that all major existentialist philosophers "have also made large contributions to imaginative literature," MacIntyre concludes that "the content of existentialist philosophy makes it clear that dramatic dialogue whether in plays or in the novel is probably a form of expression more consistent with the author's intentions than deductive argument would be" (149). And Pirandello would once more have agreed. This statement brings us back to the beginning of this study, to the discussion about philosophy and literature and the disappearance of a boundary between them. Philosophy exists only as literature, as poetry, Cosmo Laurentano told us, for the world out there is unknown and man can only invent an interpretation of it.

Nietzsche said that the task of the *Übermensch* does not consist in "unmasking and dissolving human errors, but in seeing them as the very source of the wealth that . . . gives flavor, color, being to the world."[44] The postmodern man, says Vattimo, echoing Nietzsche in *All-Too-Human*, is he who having abandoned the certainties of metaphysics "is able to appreciate the multiplicity of appearances as such."[45] In contemporary hermeneutics Pirandello's forms have acquired the full philosophical status that the Platonic Ideas or the Hegelian Spirit had in the past. After all, they too were manmade forms. The only difference is that today their maker has not only the courage, but also the pride to admit that they are fiction, that they are his own creations.

NOTES

1. All citations of Pirandello's untranslated work will be made from *Opera di Luigi Pirandello* in six volumes (Milan: Mondadori, 1960). The volumes are: *Novelle per un anno*, I, II, which will be quoted as *Novelle*, I, II; *Tutti i romanzi*, I, II, quoted as *Romanzi*, I, II; *Maschere nude*, I, II, as *MN*, I, II; and *Saggi poesie scritti varii* as *Saggi*. The reference is here in *Saggi*, 1259. The translation is mine.

2. The quote is taken from Gustavo Costa, "Pirandello e la filosofia" in *Pirandello 1986, Acts of the International Symposium, University of California, Berkeley*, March 13–15, 1986. Rome: Bulzoni, 1987, 149–64, 159.

3. The interview was quoted in Leonardo Sciascia's *Pirandello e la Sicilia* (Caltanissetta-Rome: Salvatore Sciascia, 1968), 103.

4. I do not want to give the impression that the whole of Italian idealism can be reduced to Croce. Giovanni Gentile was also an outstanding philosophical figure with a well-designed system. He was never, however, a major voice in the public debate with Pirandello, who instead had many heated exchanges with Croce.

5. Carlo Michelstaedter, *Epistolario* (Milan: Adelpi, 1983), 158. The credit of pointing out the similarities between Pirandello and Michelstaedter goes to Carlo Salinari, *Miti e coscienza del Decadentismo* (Milan: Feltrinelli, 1960), 274.

6. Luigi Pirandello, *The Late Mattia Pascal*, trans. by William Weaver (New York: Doubleday & Co., 1964), 157. Hereafter the book will be referred to as *Mattia Pascal*.

7. As Costa points out, the strict relationship between art and philosophy in Pirandello was first studied in detail by Giovanni Macchia in *Storia della litteratura italiana*, ed. by E. Cecchi and N. Sapegno, IX: *Il Novecento* (Milan: Garzanti, 1969), 444–45. Costa, 150.

8. Gianni Vattimo, *La fine della modernità* (Milan: Garzanti, 1985), 84. Vattimo recognizes the credit of his ideas to Heidegger. His conception of art is connected to his ontological distinction between being and happening. Credit must be given to J. Lacan and his followers for the development of the lingusitic implication of this discourse. The impossibility of establishing a connection between signifier and signified, which coincides with impossibility of dominating and transforming reality, is used by Lacan, however, as the very means to state the omnipotence of the signifier. On the topic see Franco Rella's "Il discredito della ragione" in *Crisi della ragione* edited by Aldo Gargani (Torino: Einaudi, 1979), 147–77. Lacan's discovery is not too far from Leopardi's dichotomy reason–imagination. When reason discovers the nothingness of reality, the illusions created by imagination acquire full credit and power.

9. Luigi Russo, in his study "Pirandello e la psicanalisi," sees no direct contact between Freud and Pirandello. The playwright had in fact claimed never to have concerned himself with psychoanalysis—of course, he had read *Les altérations de la personnalité* by Alfred Binet which came out in 1902. Binet acted as the intermediary between Freud and Pirandello. *Pirandello e la cultura del suo tempo*, ed. by S. Milioto and E. Scrivano (Milan: Mursia, 1984), 37–49. On Pirandello and Freud see also Robert S. Dombroski, "Pirandello e Freud: le dimensioni conoscitive dell'umorismo," *Pirandello Saggista* (Palermo: Palumbo, 1982), 59–67.

10. L. Pirandello, *On Humor*, trans. by A. Illiano and D. P. Testa (Chapel Hill: University of North Carolina Press, 1974), 137. From now on it will be cited directly in the text.

11. The translation is mine, as it will be with the other quotes from Pirandello and from Italian scholars unless otherwise stated. In this theory Pirandello was influenced by Alfred Binet's *Les altérations de la personnalité* and by Giovanni Marchesini's *Le finzioni dell'anima*. He mentions these two texts in his essay. Vicentini has examined the sources in detail, identifying the ideas Pirandello took. Another text that made an impact on him was *Segni dei tempi*, published in 1892, where the author, Gaetano Negri, discusses Binet's book. For a detailed analysis of the issue, see Vicentini, 40–48. Renato Barilli in his outstanding recent study on Pirandello gives Gösta Andersson the credit he deserves for having pointed out the similarities between Pirandello and another French philosopher, Gabriel Séailles, especially with regard to his aesthetics. What Barilli wants to show is a similar trajectory taken by Pirandello and Bergson who was a disciple of Séailles. See *Pirandello. Una rivoluziona culturale* (Milan: Mursia, 1986), 280–89. The book by Gösta Andersson was *Art e teoria. Studi sulla poetica del giovane Pirandello* (Stockholm: Almquist & Wiksell, 1966).

12. Benedetto Croce, "Luigi Pirandello," *La letteratura della Nuova Italia. Saggi critici* VI (Bari: Laterza, 1974), Paperback 13, p. 337. The quote was taken from Gustavo Costa, "Pirandello e la filosofia," 149.

13. Salinari, Giudice, Vicentini, and more recently Vittorio Stella and Gustavo Costa have discussed and analyzed the Croce/Pirandello relationship at length. Whereas the previous studies have always focused on the differences between the two, Stella (and

Costa seems to be in agreement) tends to minimize those divergencies and finds in Pirandello a tendency toward idealism. Costa develops Stella's hint and also focuses his attention on Croce's "incessant torment which was tossing beyond the Olimpian facade of his philosophical system" (Costa, 160). Vittorio Stella, "Pirandello e la filosofia italiana," *Pirandello e la cultura del suo tempo*, 5–30. The major attacks against Croce are in the essay "Arte e scienza" now published in *Saggi* 163–79). For a complete bibliography on this issue, see Vicentini, 126.

14. Many of the interpretations mentioned can be found in the rich volume of the collected papers given at the Thirteenth International Conference on Pirandello (December 1983)—*Pirandello e la cultura del suo tempo* (mentioned above,)— in especially, L. Russo and M. Cometa on Pirandello and psychoanalysis (31–54, 303–26); S. Campailla on Pirandello and *verismo* (87–102); J. Thomas on Pirandello and surrealism (157–74). The relation with existentialism was examined by F. Angelini (273–84). Many recent studies underline the various analogies; among these studies are Sciacca's *L'estetismo, Kirkegaard, Pirandello* (Milan: Marzorati, 1974) which points out the line extending from Greek thought, Pascal, Leopardi, Schopenhauer, and Bergson. More on psychoanalysis: C. Donati's *La solitudine allo specchio—Luigi Pirandello* (Rome: Lucarini, 1980); R. Dombreski's study already quoted; and P. Puppa, *Dalle parti di Pirandello* (Rome: Bulzoni, 1987). On the same topic is E. Gioanola's exciting book *Pirandello, la follia* (Genoa: Il melangolo, 1983) which takes as a point of departure R. D. Laing's famous *The Divided Self* (New York: Penguin Books, 1960). Psychology and anthropology are also used in E. Ferrario's *L'occhio di Mattia Pascal. Poetica e estetica in Pirandello* (Rome: Bulzoni, 1978). G. Corsinovi wrote *Pirandello e l'Espressionismo* (Genoa: Tilgher, 1979) and R. Barilli in the volume already cited (see note 11) wrote on Pirandello and existentialism. He sees Pirandello as an influence on Camus and as a follower of what he calls spiritualist positivism after Séailles and Binet. More on Pirandello and existentialism, especially on Jaspers and Heidegger, is in "Il pensiero tedesco degli anni 20" by J. Thomas in *Pirandello e la Germania* (Palermo: Palumbo, 1984), 7–32, and of Sartre in Halina Sawecka's "L'opposition pirandellienne forme—vie et la dialectique sartrienne êtreparaître," *Pirandello: Poetica e presenza* (Rome: Bulzoni, 1987), 291–304.

15. If we really feel the need of a label for Pirandello's philosophy, we could borrow Asor Rosa's "critical positivism" or Schulz-Buschhaus's "heterodox rationalism." In fact, Pirandello rejects the religious or mythological aspect of positivism—the giver of objective and final truth—but maintains its reflexive and analytical aspect. The terms in their vagueness would be harmless enough. A. Asor Rosa, "Pirandello fra soggettivismo e oggettivismo," and U. Schulz-Buschhaus, "L'umorismo: l'anti-retorica e l'anti-sintesi di un secondo realismo." In *Pirandello saggista* (11–21; 77–86).

16. The title of the first of Giacomo Leopardi's *Operette morali*. It was Gösta Andersson who pointed out the connection between "Arte e coscienza d'oggi" and the reading of *Degenerazione* by Max Nordau (Milan: Dumolard, 1893) which was published in Berlin the year before with the title *Entartung*. Yet, as Vicentini points out, Pirandello accepts only the destructive part of this positivistic text, that is, the demolition of all metaphysics, but nothing of its positive part, that is, the faith in the sciences. Vicentini, 41–42.

17. Pirandello's writings contain many references to Leopardi. Here Pirandello had in mind the moral dialogue in "The Copernicus" in G. Leopardi, *Operette morali—Essays and Dialogues*, trans. by G. Cecchetti (Berkeley: University of California Press, 1982), 416–41.

18. Salvatore Guglielmino has recently done a comparative analysis of the two texts to bring out the many identical elements. See "Retroterra e implicazioni del Saggio su 'L'umorismo' " in *Pirandello e la culture del suo tempo*, 143–55. It must also be remembered that a stimulus to the writing of the essay came from the reading of *Komik und Humor. Eine psychologisch-ästhetische Untersuchung* written by Theodor Lipps in 1898. Pirandello also had a chance to attend Lipps's lectures on the same subject when he was a student in Bonn in the winter of 1889–1890. Pirandello, however, did not agree with Lipps's Hegelian aesthetics; he quotes Lipps in his essay only to criticize him. The reading of Lipps's essay mainly helped Pirandello to clarify his own ideas. Michele Cometa with a comparative analysis of the two texts has recently shown that the part that gave Pirandello more stimuli was the section on the essence of humor where he found a definition of the "feeling of the opposite." "Pirandello e Lipps: Due letture psicologiche dell'umorismo" in *Pirandello e la cultura del suo tempo*, 310.

19. Here, however, what comes to mind is the metaphorical language of Heraclitus, the philosopher of the flux, who identified life with fire. Analogies could also be found with Parmenides whose philosophy pivots on the opposition life–thought, being–becoming. A helpful study of Heraclitus and Parmenides is in G. S. Kirk and J. E. Raven, *The Presocratic Philosophers* (Cambridge University Press, 1969). 182–215, 263–85.

20. His first encounter with sexuality was intertwined with that of death and prohibition. Pressed by the curiosity to see a corpse, as a child he once entered the morgue where besides finding the corpse he wanted to see, he witnessed, unseen, an act of sexual intercourse. He experienced another psychological shock when he discovered that his father was cheating on his wife with his cousin. They would meet on Sunday morning in the church, where one day young Luigi went to catch them, and spat at the woman. Gaspare Giudice, *Pirandello. A Biography* (London: Oxford University Press, 1975), 10, 18.

21. Again the importance that the book by Giovanni Marchesini, *Le finzioni dell' anima* (1904), had for Pirandello in those years should be underlined. Marchesini was a disciple of Ardigò who attempted to save positivism by opening it up to new intellectual currents. See the helpful article "La critica alle *Finiono dell'anima* nella cultura italiana del primo Novecento" by G. Lanaro in *Rivista critica della Storia della filosofia* 37, 4 (October-December 1982), 430–42.

22. Pirandello calls it "il sentimento del contrario." I prefer the translation *sentiment* to that of *feeling* chosen by Illiano-Testa, for it has in itself the connotation of conscience.

23. "Da Lontano" was published in the political-military journal *La preparazione* in 1909 (*Saggi*, 1064–75). Removing oneself from life in order not to be hurt by it any longer is what many of Pirandello's characters do. One of the most successful is Memmo Viola alias Leone Gala of *The Rules of the Game*. The only contact he maintains with life, a very concrete one, indeed, is through his hobby, cooking, which he does every day in the company of his friend/butler/philosopher.

24. G. Leopardi, *Zibaldone*, 2 vols. in *Tutte le opere a cura di Francesco Flora* (Milan: Mondadori, 1937), I, 301.

25. Luigi Pirandello, *Short Stories*, trans. by Frederick May (London: Oxford University Press, 1965), 99.

26. The Old and the Young, 2 vols., trans. by C. K. Scott-Moncrieff (New York: E. P. Dutton., 1928), I, 73. Hereafter the novel will be cited as *The Old*.

27. Leopardi, *Operette morali*—Essays and Dialogues, 379. Don Cosmo Laurentano's character acquires yet more force by having an antagonist in the person of Lando Lau-

rentano. (The echo of Cosmos and Land, heaven and earth, although it might be accidental, cannot pass unnoticed.) Lando is a man of action, and, although he had a well-stocked library, as he read "he was irresistibly led on to translate all that he read into action, into living reality" (II, 63). But when he read about historical facts "he would feel an indescribable sense of discomfort at seeing, reduced to words, what had once upon a time been life; reduced to ten or twenty lines of print, uniformly arranged one after another, in precise order, what had been a disordered movement, stir and turmoil. He would fling the book from him in a fit of disgust" (II, 64). He could not help comparing the real voices and deeds of people with those "artificial compositions, a fixed life, stereotyped in unalterable forms, logical contradictions, mental architectures . . . away with them all! Movement, life not thoughts!" (II, 64)

28. Luigi Pirandello, *Shoot!*, trans. by C. K. Scott-Moncrieff (London: Chatto & Windus 1927), 48. The next references will be in the text.

29. The expression was borrowed from Gian Paolo Biasin's masterly essay. It is the title of a chapter of Svevo in his *Literary Diseases* (Austin-London: University of Texas Press, 1975), 63.

30. The character of the violin player is highly symbolic. He never speaks, and in the story he has renounced any contact with the world and has put away his violin. He will play only once, for the tiger, and the scene will be very moving. Here Pirandello is openly attacking the so-called civilization, the mechanization of society which no longer has room for the artist. It is clear that to Pirandello art represents the natural, speaks to the heart of life, to its genuine core. Thus, Serafino assents to play only for the tiger, symbol of the most uncorrupt nature. Pirandello will develop this thesis in his last play, *The Giants of the Mountain*, where art will literally, not only figuratively, be torn to pieces by modern men.

31. Luigi Pirandello, *Naked Masks. Five Plays*, edited by Eric Bentley (New York: E. P. Dutton., 1952), 68 (hereafter *Naked Masks*).

32. Laudisi: "All I am saying is that you should show some respect for what other people see and feel, even though it be the exact opposite of what you see and feel" (*Naked Masks*), 71.

33. The interview is quoted in Vicentini, 220.

34. Also quoted in Vicentini, 221. As in the essay on humor, Vicentini pointed out the influence of Binet in regard to this idea of the decomposition of personality. In his enlightening book, previously mentioned (note 14), P. Gioanola studies this very aspect of Pirandello's philosophy using as a basis for it Laing's *The Divided Self*. Speaking of Pirandello's expertise in self-analysis, Gioanola considers him "one of the great writers of the nineteen hundreds who, independent of Freud, has offered the most intense definition of the unconscious" (136).

35. The Crisis of Identity: from *The Late Mattia Pascal* to *One, None, and a Hundred Thousand*" is the title of the third chapter in his book (79).

36. Biasin's *Literary Diseases*, 123.

37. Gioanola, 109. For a detailed treatment of the semantic and metaphoric implications of the mirror see Biasin, 101–108.

38. The verse is from "Falsetto" in Eugenio Montale's *Tutte le poesie* (Milan: Mondadori, 1977), 23.

39. Luigi Pirandello, *One, None, and a Hundred Thousand*, trans. by Samuel Putnam (New York: E. P. Dutton., 1933), 15. Hereafter it will be referred as *One*.

40. The Italian is more incisive: "maandare, non sapevo dove andare"—I did *not know* where to go). *Romanzi*, II, 741.

41. Biasin, 110. Eugène Minkowski, in the 1930s, was the first to study schizoid phenomena in terms of detachment from the regular flux of life. "Contrary to the idea of traditional psychiatry which considered any psychotic condition as the result of reduced or defective reasoning faculties, [Minkowski] was proposing an interpretation of madness as pure reasoning." This interesting analysis is in Gioanola's book. Gioanola also points out Minkowski's influence on Laing (Gioanola, 123).

42. Biasin, 126. He points out that a similar position is found in Renato Barilli's outstanding book, *La line Svevo-Pirandello* (Milan: Mursia, 1972), 220–26. In his intelligent essay "Irrazionalismo ed emancipazione" J. Thomas rightly considers the positive myth of the dissolution into nature as one of the fictitious constructions man creates for his own needs. The essay is in *Pirandello e la cultura del suo tempo* (157–74), 174.

43. Alasdair MacIntyre, "Existentialism," in *The Encyclopedia of Philosophy*, 8 vols., Paul Edwards ed., vols. 3, 4 (New York: Macmillan, 1967), 147.

44. In Vattimo, *La fine della modernità*, 177.

45. Vattimo, *Al di là del soggetto. Nietzsche, Heidegger e l'ermeneutica* (Milan: Feltrinelli, 1981), 49.

WORKS CITED

Andersson, Gösta. *Arte e teoria. Studi sulla poetica del giovane Pirandello*. Stockholm: Almquist & Wiksell 1966.

Angelini, Franca. "Pirandello e Sartre." *Pirandello e la cultura del suo tempo*. Milano: Mursia, 1984, 273–84.

Asor Rosa, Alberto. "Pirandello fra soggettivismo e oggettivismo." *Pirandello saggista*. Palermo: Palumbo, 1982. 11–21.

Barilli, Renato. *La linea Svevo-Pirandello*. Milano: Mursia, 1972.

———. *Pirandello. Una rivoluzione culturale*. Milano: Mursia, 1986.

Biasin, Gian Paolo. *Literary Diseases*. Austin: University of Texas Press, 1975.

Campailla, Sergio. "Il verismo e Pirandello." *Pirandello e la cultura del suo tempo*. Milano: Mursia, 1984. 87–102.

Cicotta, Strong M. "L'esistenzialismo nelle novelle di Pirandello" in *Le Novelle di Pirandello*. Atti del 6° Convegno di Studi Pirandelliani (Agrigento: Edizioni del Centro nazionale di Studi pirandelliani, 1980). 103–17.

Cometa, Michele. "Pirandello e Lipps: Due letture psicologiche dell'umorismo." *Pirandello e la culture del suo tempo*. Milano: Mursia, 1984. 303–326.

Corsinovi, Graziella. *Pirandello e l'Espressionismo*. Genova: Tilgher, 1979.

Costa, Gustavo. "Pirandello e la filosofia," *Pirandello 1986*. Roma: Bulzoni. 1987. 149–164.

Croce, Benedetto. "Luigi Pirandello." *La Letteratura della Nuova Italia. Saggi critici* VI. Bari: Laterza, 1974.

De Benedetti, Giacomo. *Il Romanzo del Novecento*. Milano: Garzanti, 1971.

Dombroski, Robert S. "Pirandello e Freud: le dimensioni conoscitive dell'umorismo." *Pirandello Saggista*. Palermo: Palumbo, 1982. 59–67.

Donati, C. *La solitudine allo specchio–Luigi Pirandello*. Roma: Lucarini, 1980.

Ferrario, E. *L'occhio di Mattia Pascal. Poetica e estetica in Pirandello*. Roma: Bulzoni, 1978.

Gioanola, Elio. *Pirandello, la follia*. Genova: Il melangolo, 1983.

Giudice, Gaspare. *Pirandello. A Biography*. London: Oxford University Press, 1975.

Guglielmino, Salvatore. "Retroterra e implicazioni del saggio su L'umorismo." *Pirandello e la cultura del suo tempo*. Milano: Mursia, 1984. 143–155.

Kirt, G. S., and J. E. Raven. *The Presocratic Philosophers*. Cambridge University Press, 1969.

Laing, R. D. *The Divided Self*. New York: Penguin Books, 1960.

Lanaro, G. "La critica alle *Finzioni dell'anima* nella cultura italiana del primo Novecento." *Revista critica della Storia della filosofia* 37, 4 (1982): 430–42.

Leopardi, Giacomo. *Operette morali—Essays and Dialogues*. Trans. G. Cecchetti. Berkeley: University of California Press, 1982.

———. *Pensieri*. Trans. W. S. Di Piero. Louisiana State University Press, 1981.

———. *Zibaldone*. Ed. Francesco Flora. 2 vols. Milano: Mondadori, 1937.

Macchia, Giovanni. *Storia della letteratura italiana*. Ed. E. Cecchi and N. Sapegno. IX: *Il Novecento*. Milano: Garzanti, 1969.

MacIntyre, Alasdair. "Existentialism." *The Encyclopedia of Philosophy*. Ed. Paul Edwards. 8 vols. New York: Macmillian, 1967.

Michelstaedter, Carlo. *Epistolario*. Milano: Adelphi, 1983.

Montale, Eugenio. *Tutta le poesie*. Milano: Mondadori, 1977.

Nordau, Max. *Degenerazione*. Milano: Dumolard, 1893.

Pirandello, Luigi. *The Late Mattia Pascal*. Trans. William Weaver. New York: Doubleday, 1964.

———. *Naked Masks. Five Plays*. Ed. Eric Bentley. New York: E. P. Dutton, 1952.

———. *The Old and the Young*. Trans. C K. Scott-Moncrieff. 2 vols. New York: E. P. Dutton, 1928.

———. *One, None, and a Hundred Thousand*. Trans. Samuel Putnam. New York: E. P. Dutton, 1933.

———. *On Humor*. Trans. Illiano and D. P. Testa. Chapel Hill: University of North Carolina Press 1974. 137.

———. *Opera di Luigi Pirandello*. 6 vols. Milano: Mondadori, 1960.

———. *Shoot!* Trans. C. K. Scott-Moncrieff. London: Chatto & Windus, 1927.

Possiedi, Paolo. "Il topos della contemplazione del firm amento nelle *Novelle per un anno di Pirandello*." *Italica* 65, 1 (1988): 1–18.

Puppa, Paolo. *Dalle parti di Pirandello*. Roma: Bulzoni, 1987.

Rella, Franco. "Il discredito della ragione." *Crisi della ragione*. Ed. Aldo Gargani. Torino: Einaudi, 1979.

Rovatti, Pier Aldo. *Il pensiero debole*. Milano: Feltrinelli, 1983.

Russo, Luigi. "Pirandello e la psicanalisi." *Pirandello e la cultura del suo tempo*. Ed. S. Milioto and E. Scrivano. Milano: Mursia, 1984. 31–54.

Salinari, Carlo. *Miti e coscienza del Decadentismo*. Milano: Feltrinelli, 1960.

Sawecka, Halina. "L'opposition pirandellienne forme—vie et la dialectique sartrienne être-paraître." *Pirandello: Poetica e presenza*. Ed. P. D. Giovanelli. Roma: Bulzoni, 1987. 291–304.

Schulz-Buschhaus, Ulrich. "L'umorismo: l'anti-retorica e l'anti-sintesi di un secondo realismo." *Pirandello: Poetica e presenza*. Ed. P. D. Giovanelli. Roma: Bulzoni, 1987. 77–86.

Sciacca, M. F. *L'estetismo, Kirkegaard, Pirandello*. Milano: Marzorati, 1974.

Sciascia, Leonardo. *Pirandello e la Sicilia*. Caltanissetta-Roma: Salvatore Sciascia, 1968.

Stella, Vittorio. "Pirandello e la filosofia italiana." *Pirandello e la cultura del suo tempo*. Milano: Mursia, 1984. 5–30.

Thomas, Johannes. "Il pensiero tedesco degli anni 20." *Pirandello e la Germania*. Palermo: Palumbo, 1984.

—————. "Irrazionalismo ed emancipazione." *Pirandello e la cultura del suo tempo*. Milano: Mursia, 1984. 157–76.

Vattimo, Gianni. *Al di là del soggetto. Nietzsche, Heidegger e l'ermeneutica*. Milano: Feltrinelli, 1981.

—————. *Il pensiero debole*. Milano: Feltrinelli, 1983.

—————. *La fine della modernità*. Milano: Garzanti, 1985.

Vicentini, Claudio. *L'estetica di Pirandello*. Milano: Mursia, 1970–1985.

3

Reluctant Pilgrim: Pirandello's Journey Toward the Modern Stage

Jana O'Keefe Bazzoni

Appearance and reality, mask and face, form and life, gaming, disguise, ambiguity, irony, the problem of identity, the nature of illusion, madness, life as a play, relativity, multiplicity of personality, the break of aesthetic distance, the participatory audience, the mirror—any one of these themes and techniques may come immediately to mind on hearing the term *pirandellismo*, Pirandellism.

This Pirandellian legacy has been widely acknowledged and assessed. Virtually all of the modern theater is post-Pirandellian in some sense, and perhaps theater since the 1960s is even more so. Particularly because Pirandello's ideas regarding the function and relationships of the various theater artists to the text has such contemporary significance, it is important to acknowledge another less frequently studied Pirandellian legacy to the modern stage: Pirandello's written record of his own search for an understanding of the nature of theater, culminating in his acknowledgment of a new theatrical imperative and his demand for a renewal of the stage. In a series of works published between 1899 and 1918 as well as in two late essays on the theater written in 1934 and 1935, Pirandello documents his conflicts with the drama and stage of his time as well as his suggestions for change. These writings on the theater bracket the period during which Pirandello wrote his most famous plays, plays that continue Pirandello's theoretical argument in practical, dramatic form.

In the discussion that follows, I will examine these articles and essays regarding the theater in an attempt to trace the evolution of Pirandello's theater theory and assess its contribution to his gradual transformation from a writer of narrative into a writer for the theater. The discussion assumes familiarity with Pirandello's major plays and often relies on direct quotations and paraphrases from the theatrical theory under examination in a descriptive rather than an interpretative fashion in the hope that the reader will come to a clearer understanding of Pirandello's development as a dramatist and will reflect anew on corresponding ideas as they occur in the plays themselves.

Pirandello came into prominence as a playwright relatively late in life, in his fifties, after a literary career as a writer of short stories and novels. Although many of Pirandello's friends were playwrights, producers, or critics, he deliberately avoided contact with the theater and maintained both a physical and emotional distance from the theater world by attending few plays and by ignoring his colleagues' theater talk (Giudice, 104). Always a very private and independent man, Pirandello had a distrust for the theater and for actors, very public and collaborative entities.[1] Yet the theater had intrigued him since his youth, when he had made several unsuccessful attempts to have plays produced (Giudice, 32, 52).

This early lack of theatrical success no doubt contributed to his apparent dislike and distrust of the theater world and perhaps underlies some of the disdainful comments he makes in articles on theater about theater professionals. No doubt, too, that the actor's world, so apparently dependent on ingenuity, chance, and the presence of an audience, was incomprehensible to Pirandello, a writer who epitomized the image of the solitary, desk-bound playwright which Pirandello's contemporaries, the futurists, so disdained in their Synthetic Theatre Manifesto.[2] There were, of course, other reasons for Pirandello's neglect of the theater: the demands of his teaching job and the particular situation of his family life in the period before 1919 (Nardelli, 165). There was also in Pirandello an acute sense of vulnerability as a writer for the stage where his work would be at the mercy of actors and producers, directors, and the audience.[3]

When Pirandello began to write for the theater again, it was with an obviously ambivalent attitude toward actors and the entire production process. In fact, Giudice suggests that his motives were as much financial as artistic and that the possibility of reaching a larger audience with his ideas was a factor (107–108). A reading of his theater theory written prior to *Sei personaggi in cerca d'autore* (*Six Characters in Search of an Author*) suggests an additional reason: Pirandello's struggle with each of the elements of the theatrical process—character/actor/text/director/audience—and his growing need to bring his own conflicts into their natural and inevitable forum, the stage.

Pirandello, the literary man, had published theater theory as early as 1899 and had begun to articulate in a journalistic forum what he had not yet been able to do as a playwright. In the 1899 piece, "L'azione parlata" (Spoken Action), Pirandello writes that "Every descriptive narrative device should be abolished on the stage."[4] Playwrights must use words born of character and not imposed by the author's personal style, "spoken action, . . . words, expressions, phrases not invented but born when the writer has immersed himself in his creation to the point where he feels as his character does and wants what his character wants'' (1015–16). Because, says Pirandello, and here he makes a point central to his theater theory: "The drama does not make the characters but rather these make the drama. And before anything else we must have the people, alive, free, agents.'' Pirandello argues that character must take precedence over all other elements of drama and that as characters must speak in their own voices, not that of their author; all artificially imposed language and all descriptive, narrative techniques must be banned.

In 1908, his long and very important essay, *L'umorismo*, (*"On Humor"*) appeared, and in the same year, another essay, entitled *Illustratori, attori e traduttori*, (*Illustrators, Actors* and *Translators*) was published. It is in *L'umorismo* that we get Pirandello's description of the kind of writer he describes as a humorist: "He sees the world, if not exactly naked, in shirt sleeves, so to speak. . . . '' (*Opere*, 158). Blessed, or perhaps cursed with a reflective state of mind, the humorist writer sees life as a constant contradiction and operates with a "feeling of the opposite" which leads him to decompose his characters, showing their "incongruities,'' rather than represent character as coherent and consistent. This kind of writer's role is to tear away the masks and illusions man makes and remind us of the harsh reality of the unknown, of the human predicament. The humorist writer must show the contradictions in his characters, simultaneous realities in conflict. Pirandello's structural factor will be a stripping away, an unmasking. Rather than an accumulating of facts, there is to be a peeling away of illusions and a juxtaposition of contrasting "truths.'' The character at the center of the drama will of organic necessity be shown in *all* his aspects, all his contradictions, through the structural (destructural) characteristic peculiar to the kind of writer who looks on tragedy and comedy simultaneously, the one in constant shadow of the other—"the humorist observes both the body and its shadow, and sometimes pays more attention to the shadow than to the body.'' (160).

Although *L'umorismo* is not an essay on the theater and Pirandello is not specifically referring to the dramatic writer, I have included a discussion of the essay here because it is basic to Pirandello's poetics; his description of the humorist writer's attitude toward character has an application in the drama as well as to the narrative. The double vision of the humorist writer (and Pirandello is, of course, defining his own outlook) has a significant impact on the structural element of Pirandello's drama, in particular, the theater trilogy. This structure will not be simple, concise, direct (a synthesis), but rather will be "disorganized, unravelled and whimsical"—digressive, rather than constructive or composed.

The other essay of 1908, *Illustratori, attori e traduttori*, concerns the specific problem of transferring the writer's work onto the stage in performance. The processes of illustrating an article, translating into another language, or transferring a written work to the stage are analogous, says Pirandello in this essay, and they are equally unsatisfactory for the writer and his work of art. Pirandello dwells on aspects of the actor's work more than on the work of the illustrator or translator—an indication, perhaps, of the greater subconscious importance for him of the writer/actor/stage relationship.

In *Illustratori, attori e traduttori*, Pirandello's prescription for the actor is analogous to his advice to the writer in *L'azione parlata*: the actor, too, must immerse himself in the character, must reconceive the character according to his own imagination, so that the character comes to life "alive and active not only within him but become with him and in him body and spirit" (216). But, says Pirandello, in the very process, as the actor assumes the role, there is a conflict with the writer's work. From the vast possibility of details offered by the character, the writer combines, concentrates, and unifies character—makes it "less real, but more true." The actor does the opposite: in giving the character material substance, the actor makes the character "less true, but more real," a "fictitious and conventional stage materiality," "adulterated substance" in an "artificial, illusionary space." "Once the transfer from one spirit [the writer] to another [the actor] is accomplished, changes are inevitable." A translation, at best a good one, is the result.

Pirandello credits superior actors who can rethink a play or character and improve on it, but he says that in such cases, the result becomes the true "original," not the inferior stuff from which the performance was made. On the question of whether or not actors are competent to judge plays (a question of interest to Pirandello's contemporaries), Pirandello says no: "The actor doesn't know how to recognize artistic merits in a play because he is only looking for a good part, and if he finds it the play is good and if not, it is bad" (222). Once again, however, Pirandello recognizes common ground in the work of the writer and actor: like the writer, the actor must experience the character for himself. Although the process is analogous, the results are not since the actor will inevitably transform the character. For Pirandello at this point, the problem cannot be solved by writing with a particular actor in mind. When writers through "sad necessity" write with a particular actor in mind, they are enslaved by the physical and artistic realities of the actor for whom they are writing and no longer can have the character at the center, but have instead the actor's own stage persona, a particular physical presence.

Having acknowledged the necessity of the actor as the agent of a character's transference to the stage, Pirandello concludes that actors are an unfortunate necessity whose method of work, physical presence, and psychic difference from the author are insurmountable barriers for him. Pirandello's essay shows a certain begrudging respect for superior actors but does not yet see a way to share the stage. He also does not yet think of himself as a playwright and clearly pities those who are faced with that dilemma. Yet, the very beginning of the essay affords us a glimpse of those famous six characters:

Let's imagine for a moment that these characters . . . emerge from the book alive before us, in our room, and they start speaking with their own voices and moving and performing their action without any descriptive or narrative support from the book. Nothing to be amazed at! This is exactly what dramatic art must do (*Opere*, 213–14).

The development of this notion first appears in Pirandello's narratives, the 1911 novel *Suo marito* (*Her Husband*), the short story, "La tragedia di un personaggio," ("Tragedy of a Character"), and the 1915 story "Colloquio coi personaggi" ("Conversation with Characters")[5] and does not appear in the full realized stage version until 1921.

The 1918 essay *Teatro e letteratura*, (*Theatre and Literature*) reworks much of the 1908 essay, often incorporating whole paragraphs verbatim from the earlier piece. The main addition is directed at those "gentlemen theater professionals" who continue to cling to realism. Pirandello remarks that those who attempt to reproduce everyday life on stage as though it is knowable by a piling up of dates and facts are "voluntary martyrs to an absurd system, to an aberration of theory . . . to which gentlemen theater professionals reveal themselves bound" (*Opere*, 1021). By 1918, Pirandello was a spokesman for the "new theater" typified by such grotesque plays as Luigi Chiarelli's *La maschera e il volto* (*The Mask and the Face*, 1916) and Pirandello's own *Così è (se vi pare)* (*It Is So [If You Think So]*, 1917). But even after the success of that play (in which the facts cannot be known and all versions of a family's story are "true"), Pirandello had not fully committed himself to writing for the theater. Although he wrote to his son Stefano in 1917 outlining the idea for a work to involve characters who have been abandoned by their author,[6] by 1919 he was about to abandon the theater, and by 1920 he was writing that he hoped the play would be the last phase of what he referred to as "this theatrical parenthesis."[7] Ironically, it was the beginning of his success in the theater as well as the prolongation of the parenthesis that was to last the rest of his life. Had Pirandello reconciled for himself the author/character/stage relationship? He had not; rather, he had brought the dilemma that had been piecing itself together in his theoretical and practical work to present itself directly on the stage, offering a critique and challenge to realism's subject matter, structural techniques, acting style, and scenic design.

As Pirandello increasingly became a theater practitioner, his ideas about those "unfortunate necessities," the actors, such as those he'd pictured in *Sei personaggi*, were to undergo change. He began to work with actors more directly, even reversing his opinions about writing with actors in mind by writing plays specifically for Ruggero Ruggeri and later for Marta Abba. He now invited the actors' collaboration and enjoyed a degree of acceptance in the theatrical community which working in collaboration with actors and technicians brought him. Yet in 1922, the year *Enrico IV* (*Henry IV*) was produced and *Sei personaggi* became an international success after the Piteoff production in Paris, Pirandello was still uncomfortable with the theatrical processing of his art into theater. In a 1922 interview, Pirandello described his continued horror over the rehearsal and performance process: "When I've written a play, when it's finished, alive or dead, as it is, from my hands, when my part in the creation is finished, then the actors cut, fix, criticize. . . . If you were to be at the rehearsals of one of my works, you'd realize that for me it's torturous.''[8]

Despite the torture of the rehearsal and production process, or perhaps because of it, Pirandello took on a new theatrical role: that of producer and director with his own company, the Teatro d'Arte. During his years as a director, he traveled in Italy and abroad and lived in the company of actors and other theater practitioners, making their life his own. In several plays written during the twenties and early thirties, he explored the *work* of actors (the theater trilogy), the actor's *dilemma* (*Trovarsi* [*To Find Oneself*]) and *Questa sera si recita a soggetto*, [*Tonight We Improvise*]), and the actor's *social function* (*I Giganti della montagna* [*The Mountain Giants*]).

In his 1924 essay on Eleanora Duse, "Piu che un'attrice," ("More Than an Actress"), Pirandello uses his theories on the actor's method to analyze that great actress's career and acknowledges her superior powers in the early portion of her career while critiquing her later career in which he believed that her acting had become all feeling and no reflection, all personality. This idea would resurface in *Questa sera si recita a soggetto* and in *I Giganti.*[9]

The last two pieces of theater theory we will explore were written in 1934 and 1935, well after the period of Pirandello's international success and near the end of his life when most of his writing was finished, when he had become *Somebody* as his play of 1933, *Quando si è qualcuno* (*When One Is Somebody*), attests. Pirandello had become a Nobel Prize winner and a kind of figurehead for the Italian theater in a nation consciously attempting to create an image of international importance for itself under Mussolini's leadership.

In October 1934 the Alexander Volta Foundation Congress, an international theater meeting, was convened in Rome. In his opening address to the conference, Pirandello spoke of the need to recognize the link between the daily life of the audience and the theater: "Theater is a prolongation of daily life, which is in itself theatrical, it is a form of life itself: we are all actors, and if the theaters were abolished or abandoned, theater would continue in life insuppressible; and the very nature of things would appear as spectacle (*Opere*, 1037).'' Of course, he had already expressed this viewpoint in the theater trilogy, especially in *Ciascuno a suo modo* (*Each in His Own Way*, 1924) with its deliberately multiplaned simultaneity, its melange of "real"-life characters mirrored by actors on stage interspersed with actors as audience who mix and perform among actual spectators who are themselves expected to act. He expressed his belief in the importance of theater's unique function: "Of all the other performances which can momentarily enter into the life of people, it is the one that recapitulates and reflects moral values most intimately: the theater is what lasts" (1041). And,

The theater offers what might properly be called a public trial of human actions as they truly are, in that pure and everlasting reality which the imagination of poets creates as an example and warning for our commonplace and confused natural life—a trial both free and human, which spurs the consciences of the judges themselves to an ever loftier and more rigorous moral life (1041).

In the Volta speech, Pirandello also addressed the question of the director's role, a question he had first raised briefly in the 1929 essay "*Se il film parlante abolira il teatro*" (Whether the talking picture will abolish the theater) and at some length in the same year in *Questa sera si recita a soggetto*. As Pirandello said:

It is to be hoped that the question debated now for some time—whether the theater is to offer a spectacle in which the work of art, the poet's creation, is as one of many elements in the hands of and at the command of the director, equal to the scenic apparatus, the play of lights, and the actors, or if instead, all of these elements, together with the unifying work of the director (who has sole creative responsibility for the production only) should rather be used to give life to the work of art that includes them all and without which each of them, for themselves, night after night, would have no reason for being: that life, I mean, which is inviolable because it is complete in every aspect, as every work of art must be, and that therefore must not be changed arbitrarily or tampered with by the director (1041).

In *Questa sera si recita a soggetto* Pirandello had dealt, in typically dialectical fashion, with the question of the director-dominated stage. Drawing on his own experience both as a director and as an observer of the work of directors such as Piscator and Reinhardt, Pirandello created the third of his theater-in-the-theater plays which both critiques the total theater concept and simultaneously uses it.[10] Although he indicts some of the egomaniacal attitudes of modern directors in the grotesque figure of Hinkfuss, he also uses Hinkfuss to mouth Pirandellian theater theory and to affirm it: that in order to live, dramatic art must be continually renewed, through the artists of the stage—director, actors, scenic artists, and technicians—together with the audience, whatever the cost of the struggle.

The last theater theory in essay form, written in 1935, appeared as the 1936 introduction to Silvio D'Amico's *Storia del teatre italiano* (*History of the Italian Theatre*).[11] Typically, Pirandello borrows from himself by quoting segments of his 1934 Volta address regarding the nature and purpose of the theatrical occasion. Much of the essay is Pirandello's explanation of the development of the *commedia dell'arte* from its earliest to its later form. He credits the author/actors of the *commedia* with the evolution of the famous *commedia* characters. When they lose their identities as authors and become actors themselves, working "as it were in the warm breath of the audience" away from "the isolation of their solitary desk," they create in a new way and "in the company of others." These are authors whose purpose is no longer to create art: "the transitory, impassioned life of the Theater must have taken such full possession of them that the only interest left to them was that of the spectacle itself—a complete absorption in the quality of the performance and communication with the audience."

Pirandello himself had traveled quite a distance from his own desk, even in this essay addressing "professors of literary history" in tones he once reserved for "gentlemen theater professionals." In what is perhaps the most important, provocative, and controversial point he makes in the essay, one with great significance for the current theater situation, Pirandello discusses the necessity for a "revitalizing spirit" for the Italian theater.

The Theater is not archaeology. Unwillingness to take up old works, to modernize and streamline them for fresh production, betrays indifference, not praiseworthy caution. The Theater welcomes such modernization and has profited by it throughout those ages when it was most alive. The original text remains intact for anyone who may want to read it at home, for his own edification; those who want to be entertained by it will go the Theater, where it will be put on for them rid of those portions that have lost their freshness, brought up to date where its language is outworn, readapted to the tastes of today.

Why is this legitimate?

Because in the Theater a work of art is no longer the work of the writer (which, after all, can always be preserved in some other way), but an act of life, realized on the stage from one moment to the next, with the cooperation of audience that must find satisfaction in it (27–28).

In his theater theory, both that published in essays or articles and that played out in his dramas, Pirandello documented his own evolving ideas about the nature of the theater experience. He put the problems of his own life and times and the dilemmas of the theater world on the stage. He offered his audience the opportunity to act in judgment over beings like themselves and over the form in which those beings were presented as witnesses to the trials of life, particularly the life of the theater. As a playwright, Pirandello was able to demonstrate in clear and precise terms his thoughts and feelings, his own doubts, images, mysteries, and struggles. Imagine, intuited, invented, his theater is a reflection of his times and our own and is a true "original" of undoubted universal significance.[12]

NOTES

1. See, for example, the account of the 1916 production of *Liolà* with the Angelo Musco Company, in Giudice, 108–109.

2. In that Manifesto, the futurists announced: "We have an unconquerable repugnance for work written at the desk, a priori, without considering the place which it's going to be presented." In *Marinetti e il futurismo*, ed., and with an Introduction by Luciano de Maria (Milan: Mondadori Editore, 1973), 168.

3. Giudice makes a case for Pirandello's particularly sensitive attitude toward the audience through his readings of Pirandello's letters to his son, Stefano, regarding audience reactions. See 107 (letter of July 11, 1916) and 111 (letter of June 29, 1917). Nardelli,

on the other hand, claims Pirandello was not at all concerned about audience reaction, (179).

4. *Opere di Luigi Pirandello*, Vol. 6: *Saggi, poesie e scritti varii* (Milan: Mondadori Editor, 1960), 1015.

5. Claudio Vicentini, *L'estetica di Pirandello* (Milan: Mursia, 1970), 167–71.

6. The work was to be a novel. See Giudice, 111; Vicentini, 171.

7. Vicentini, 179. The notion of "parenthesis" had been used privately, at least as early as 1917, as noted by Giudice, quoting from a letter to Stefano (April 18, 1917), 111.

8. "Una visita a Luigi Pirandello," in *Tempo*, March 9, 1922. Cited in Vincentini, 180.

9. "Piu che un attrice," appears to have been published first in English translation in *Century Magazine*, June 1924, under the title "Eleanora Duse: Actress Supreme." Eric Bentley reprinted the essay, under the title "Eleanora Duse," in *The Theory of the Modern Stage* (Middlesex, England and Baltimore: Penguin Books, 1970 ed.), 158–69.

10. Many writers on Pirandello's works have commented on the influence of these directors on Pirandello's work and theory as well as on his attitude as expressed in the Hinkfuss character. Two examples are Renate Matthaei, *Luigi Pirandello*, translated by Simon and Erika Young (New York: Frederick Ungar Publishing Co., 1973), and Lucio Lugnani, *Pirandello: letteratura e teatro* (Florence: La Nuova Italia, 1970). Their conclusions differ regarding Pirandello's intentions: Mattaei thinks the play is "one long attack on Reinhardt" (149), but Lugnani says that, although Hinkfuss is drawn with intentional irony, the theories are to be taken seriously and as possibly valid (148–70).

11. Quotations from Pirandello's "Introduzione al teatro italiano" in the following discussion are taken from the translation by Anne Paolucci, in *The Genius of The Italian Theatre*, edited by Eric Bentley (New York: New American Library, 1964), 11–29.

12. In an essay not discussed here, *Teatro nuovo e teatro vecchio*, (New theater and old theater), 1923, Pirandello makes the point that those who create anew, by heeding their own artistic intentions, are "new theater" no matter what period of chronological time their works reflect. In this sense, "new theater" exists in every age and yet is bound by none; it is both original and timeless. In *Saggi*, 227–43.

WORKS CITED

Bentley, Eric. *The Theory of the Modern Stage*. Middlesex, England and Baltimore: Penguin Books, 1970.

Giudice, Gaspare. *Pirandello, A Biography*. Trans. Alastair Hamilton. London: Oxford University Press, 1975.

Lugnani, Lucio. *Pirandello: letteratura e teatro*. Florence: La Nuova Italia, 1970.

Marinetti, Filippo Tommaso. *Marinetti e il futurismo*. Ed. Luciano De Maria. Milan: Mondadori, 1973.

Matthaei, Renate. *Luigi Pirandello*. Trans. Simon and Erika Young. Florence: La Nuova Italia, 1970.

Nardelli, Federico V. *Vita segreta di Pirandello*. Rome: Vito Bianco, 1962.

Pirandello, Luigi. "Introduction to the Italian Theater." Trans. Anne Paolucci. *The*

Genius of the Italian Theater. Ed. Eric Bentley. New York: New American Library, 1964.

————. *Opere di Luigi Pirandello, Saggi, poesie e scritti varii*. Milan: Mondadori, 1960.

Vicentini, Claudio. *L'estetica di Pirandello*. Milan: Mursia, 1970.

4

Woman or Mother? Feminine Conditions in Pirandello's Theater

Mary Ann Frese Witt

Women as objects of desire, scorn, fear, as victims or as traps; conflicts arising over pregnancy and female identity—these lie at the very heart of Pirandello's dramatic plots. The triangular basis of a number of plays (old man–young woman–young man; husband–wife–lover) might place Pirandello squarely in the tradition of both classical and *boulevard* comedy were it not for the absence of, or at least the lack of emphasis on, romantic love. For Pirandello there can be no comic resolution, no affirmation of eros, fertility, or even delight in seeing the duper duped, because these have become the very sources of the problems that he explores in their agonizing and endless labyrinths. Even *Liolà*, long hailed as a life-affirming, sun-drenched masterpiece, poses, as we will see, social and psychological questions that undermine its comic surface. Pirandello's humorism often subverts a classically comic situation, engaging the reader or spectator in a *sentimento del contrario*. In *Think It Over, Giacomino*, for example, we have what could be, in Harry Levin's terms, a classical conflict between "killjoy" and "playboy," centered, naturally, on the possession of a woman. In this play, however, it is the old man (normally the killjoy) who must persuade the young man (normally the playboy) to fulfill his role as lover. In addition, the woman in question is valued not as an object or a subject of erotic desire but primarily in her role as mother of a child, a condition not infrequent in Pirandello's works.

"Non è una donna, è una madre,"[1] (She's not a woman, she's a mother) says the Father of his wife in *Six Characters in Search of an Author*. The statement is revealing in that not only this character but also the playwright himself appears to view the other gender as a series of categories, or dramatic roles, roles defined not by the character herself but by others' views of her. We are privileged to witness the Father's sense of himself as both *man* and *father*, and indeed his agonizing consciousness (like that of other male characters such as "Enrico IV" and Leone Gala) of the fact that a man in his life plays many parts. Pirandello's female characters often play one or more roles assigned to them by the absent but controlling author and by the male characters in their lives. These roles can be defined broadly as those of *madre/moglie/figlia/donna* (mother/wife/daughter/ woman.) The *figliastra*, the stepdaughter, struggles against this categorization. Here I would like to examine some major examples of what I take to be the two primary categories, those of *mother* and *woman*, and to attempt to redefine the nature of the female in Pirandello's theater.

Pirandello's veneration of motherhood, along with his fascination–repulsion toward pregnancy, surely stem in part from his upbringing in what his biographer Giudice terms "atavistic Muslim-Catholic Sicily" (27) with its taxonomy of women and girls as Virgin, Mother, or Dishonored, as well as his deep attachment to his own mother and his distrust of his father. The formative episode between Luigi's father Stefano and his niece—Stefano made the girl pregnant and arranged for her to marry a man who would legitimize her unborn child—no doubt served as a model for many of the dramatist's situations. Pirandello's conflicts with his father, leading to a final acceptance of authority, may, as Giudice suggests (10), have prepared him for his later commitment to fascism. Certainly his attitudes toward motherhood agree with fascist ideology on the subject, in part no doubt because both have their origins in the same "atavistic" values. In the development of Pirandello's aesthetics and thought, as in early fascist ideology, we witness a curious combination of a revolutionary, modernist critique of bourgeois institutions such as marriage and the family with an attachment to the most traditional archetypes.
  "La madre è una costruzione irreducible" (the mother is an irreducible construction), says Baldovino in *The Pleasure of Honesty* (IV, 602). The fascist critic Ascanio Zapponi interprets this phrase to mean that on this "instinctive" as opposed to "intellectual" basis, in conformity with fascist ideology, one can begin to construct (107). Baldovino makes this remark just after delivering a most Pirandellian speech on the "construction" of one's personality in various situations. About to step into his new role as husband of his friend Fabbio's pregnant mistress Agata in order to keep her "honest," Baldovino curiously asks if there is a mother involved and upon hearing that there is makes the remark quoted above. The stage directions for Agata's mother, Signora Maddalena, describe her as: "fifty two years old . . . full of passion for her daughter, she only sees through her eyes" (IV, 584). If our "constructions," as Baldovino maintains, are masks that hide our most intimate feelings—what we are for ourselves as opposed to what we are for others—then it appears that maternity

is the one construction in which social role and intimate feelings coincide, a role so all-consuming that it eclipses all others. Paternity, as Baldovino himself will show, can be intellectually constructed, whereas maternity need only be instinctively accepted. *The Pleasure of Honesty* has been seen as Pirandello's optimistic comedy in which love triumphs over reason,[2] but in fact the real triumph is not that of love but of maternity. At the beginning of the third act, Maddalena says of her daughter that she is now nothing but a mother (IV, 635) and at the end of the play, when Agata has chosen to follow him and leave her lover, Baldovino says to his wife: "con la maternità, l'amante doveva morire. Ecco, voi non siete piu altro che madre" (with maternity, the lover [in you] had to die. Now you are nothing but a mother, IV, 644). The play's happy ending thus allows Agata to assume her "irreducible" maternal state and Baldovino to "construct" his paternal one. The biological father, as often in Pirandello, can be dispensed with.

Several Pirandellian situations postulate a variation on the cuckold theme, with a man donning the mask of paternity for another man's child or children. *Think it over Giacomino* is perhaps the prototype; others include *All for the Good; Man, Beast, and Virtue, The Life I Gave You* (although offstage), and *Liolà*.

Critics from Gramsci to Bentley and beyond appear to have accepted at face value Pirandello's claims in his letter to his son Stefano that *Liolà*, written as a summer vacation diversion, is "full of songs and sunshine and is so light-hearted that it doesn't seem like one of my works at all." Yet as Susan Bassnett-McGuire points out, the plot of *Liolà* is basically that of Machiavelli's *La Mandragola* (a comedy to be sure, but scarcely "light-hearted"). She maintains that, while Liolà may be pro-life, he is profoundly antifeminist, a stance that sours his proclamations of sun and song (136–41). I would argue that the question of feminism or antifeminism doesn't even enter the picture. Rather, what makes it impossible (at least now) to read *Liolà* as a primarily light-hearted comedy is the fact that the play makes sense only within the Sicilian codes that Pirandello establishes as parameters and that even within these codes Liolà's primary project is to rob women of all dignity and autonomy. For example, Liolà prides himself on his "generous offer" to marry Tuzza, and he justifies his own promiscuity, which results in several pregnancies, with a folksy formulation of the most traditional double standard: "Everyone knows how my children were born!—Girls who went astray. [*Ragazzotte di fuorivia.*] It's bad to force a well-guarded gate, but he who travels on an open and beaten road . . . " (V, 681). Liolà also justifies his activities by generously offering to raise the children he has fathered, but of course what he does is to let his mother handle the work while he plays with them. Thus, his women are denied the only status that in the Sicilian code could give them dignity, that is, maternity. And Liolà has the best of both worlds! In a sense he is indeed the product of his author's summer fantasies—a male mother.[3] Creative and fecund both as poet and progenitor, he enjoys the "irreducible" state of motherhood without what Pirandello sees as its bestial, instinctive, limiting aspects—functions divided between the natural mothers and the grandmother.

The treatment of maternity and woman in this play is also developed in the comparison of the "good" woman Mita with the "bad" woman Tuzza, both of whom attempt to deceive Uncle Simone into believing that their children, fathered by Liolà, are his. Acting on her own behalf, with her mother, Tuzza attempts to defend her interests and fails. Mita, on the other hand, submissive and docile, does exactly what Liolà tells her to do and succeeds. As in classical comedy, Liolà the playboy outsmarts Uncle Simone the killjoy (fathering a child on his wife), and yet the happy ending is deeply troubled. Tuzza's desperate attempt to kill Liolà out of jealousy and revenge anticipates Enrico IV's successful stabbing. If Liolà seemed to challenge the stifling moral and social order of the Sicilian village in his defiance of the institutions of marriage and property, that order is firmly reestablished in the end. The unwed Tuzza is the dishonored woman, unhappily married Mita the honored mother, and Liolà the happy father–mother, having expropriated the maternal rights of the dishonored girls. The purported champion of "nature" against "society," Liolà has in the end affirmed the necessity of hypocrisy and trickery for the maintenance of the social order.

Motherhood triumphant and legitimized rather than love triumphant thus constitutes the outcome of both of these early Pirandellian "comedies." Maternity is perhaps more properly the stuff of comedy in *Man, Beast, and Virtue* (1922), whose situation constitutes a farcical variation of those in *Liolà* and *The Pleasure of Honesty*. Here a lover must desire that his mistress's husband perform his conjugal duties so that the child she is carrying will appear to be his and her "honor" thus preserved. Whereas Agata actually chooses her husband over her lover (evolving, as we have seen, from *amante* to *madre*), Signora Perella, like Mita, submissively follows her lover's plan to deceive her husband. She thus assumes several roles, dependent on the two men's perceptions of her. In his attempt to seduce Captain Perella to make love to his wife, Paolino at one point brings out a makeup kit to paint a "horrible mask" on his beloved. He explains his reasons for doing so in terms of his perception of the role that the captain will assign to his wife. "Non ti vuole madre! E tu la darai a lui, codesta maschera, alla sua bestialità!" (He doesn't want you as a mother. You must wear this mask to appeal to his bestiality!, IV, 717). Paolino soon finds, however, that he has misjudged his audience. Upon seeing his wife, the captain roars with laughter, because she is playing the wrong role. He explains to Paolino: "Benissimo, sì ... Se fosse una ... lei m'intende! Come moglie, no ... e buffa!" (Yes, she looks great ... If she were a ... you know what I mean. But as my wife, no ... she looks ridiculous, IV, 721). In a later conversation the captain makes clear that the distinction between the categories of wife and woman is in his mind a clear one. "Come c'entrano adesso le mogli, scusi? Noi stiamo parlando delle donne ... " (What do wives have to do with the subject? We're talking about women), he says to Paolino, who argues in defense of his own interests that there *are* times when a husband should treat his wife like a woman.

Signora Perella is thus *moglie* to the captain, *donna* to Paolino, *madre* to her son, and, finally, thanks to an extraordinary love potion administered to her husband, a dignified *madre* in the social order. Her modest and "virtuous" nature, praised by Paolino, along with her expectant state, gives her yet another role in her lover's eyes. As Pirandello tells us in the stage directions, she sits in the moonlight in the pose of "Ecce Ancilla Domini" while Paolino holds out a lily in the position of the angel making the annunciation, the latter proclaiming "Oh santa mia!" (IV, 730). Elevated from *donna* to *Madonna*, finally secure as *madre*, Signora Perella appears to exist only as she is painted, perceived, or taken by lover or husband. A comic model of one of Pirandello's basic female types, she is as she is desired and, for herself, no one.

More than in any other play, motherhood is presented in *La vita che ti diedi* (*The Life I Gave You*) with its almost entirely female cast and its ostensibly female concerns. The action of this play that has been called a tragedy is, however, dominated by an absent male—the dead son of the main character Donn'Anna. The central problem is that of *allontanamento*—the changing and distancing of the fundamental mother–child tie. The primary situation, Donn'Anna's reaction to the death of her son, appears as the extreme form of the secondary, "normal" situation of her sister Donna Fiorina who finds her young adult children, returned after a year at school, transformed into "other people" and no longer really hers. In fact, as Donn'Anna remarks, her son was already "dead" to her when he defied her by leaving home. The life she desperately attempts to preserve is his life as he was before he left home, a life she seeks to preserve in his room. "Io voglio quella sua stanza la com'ere; che stia la viva, viva della vita che io le do, ad attendere il suo ritorno." (I want his room to be as it was, alive with the life I give it, waiting for his return).

With no realistic cause attributed to it, the son's actual death seems to be somehow a logical outgrowth of his "death" to his mother. Her desperate attempt to keep her son "alive" includes enticing Lucia, the married woman who carries his child, to come to her villa and stay in her son's room. By keeping Lucia with her while she gives birth to her son's child, Donn'Anna will gain a daughter, while the "life she gave" will be given back to her. This scheme is complicated when Lucia's own mother Francesca, referred to as "l'altra madre," comes to reclaim her daughter and to convince her to go back to her other children. Donn'Anna at last realizes the folly of her scheme—her role as mother is finished; Lucia, not she, will be the mother. "Sarai tu la madre allora; non piu io! . . . Lo riavrai tu, la, mio figlio—piccolo com'era—mio— . . . e io ora, muojo, muojo veramente qua" . . . *E piangera, piangera come non avra mai pianto* . . . (You will be the mother, not I! You'll have my son as he was when he was little— . . . and I am now really dying, dying here . . . *And she cries as she has never cried before*, IV, 498). Like Signora Morli, Lucia cannot remain "una e due" and will reassume the maternal role. The resolution of this "tragedy" is not unlike that of Pirandello's comedies in that the young woman ends by reaccepting her assigned roles of *fliglia* and *madre*, obeying her mother by returning to her husband while carrying the lover's child. Here, however, the protagonist Donn'Anna also assumes a new role, transforming herself from *madre* to *mater dolorosa*, which means for her a kind of death in life. Having lived entirely in the irreducible construction of motherhood, she "dies" when she no longer exists in that capacity. She foresees a similar destiny for Lucia: "Vai, vai, figlia,—vai nella tua vita— . . . povera carne macerata anche tu.—La morte e ben questa." (Go daughter, go into your life . . . poor broken flesh like mine.— This is what death is.) The mother's lot is to "break her body" (as Pirandello says elsewhere), giving life only to move toward a status of death in life when her children—whether by death or *allontanamento*—are no longer hers.

The figure of *mater dolorosa*, sometimes a "widow" of both husband and son, was a familiar one on the European scene following World War I. In the interest of glorifying sacrifice to the *patria* as well as in what seemed to be a fanatic fervor to increase the Italian birth rate, Mussolini, in the early years of his fascist government as well as throughout the regime, attempted to raise to a level of almost mystical veneration the images of both the young mother and the sacrificing mother (see DeGrand, Macciocchi, and Caldwell). In 1923, the year in which *La Vita che ti diedi* was written, the first congress of fascist women was held. As recounted by Maria Antonietta Macciocchi, both Mussolini's discourse and that of the fascist women themselves portray the Duce as not only the Super Male, Husband, and Lover of all women, but also in some mystical sense both father and mother of their children. In the words of the Marchesa di Casagrande's address to the Duce: "Esse (le madri) li hanno allevati (i figli) ma voi li avete ispirati; avete posto con la vostra anima nei loro cuori non una fiaccola ma un rogo vivo . . . Sono vostri soldati, fiori purissimi della primavera italica . . . Per il nostro amore . . . auspice il Duce, siamo convenute da tutte le terre che piu hanno udito il ruggito del leone di San Marco, per gettare la semenza che dovra germinare i fiori della nuova Primavera." (The mothers raised the children, but you inspired their birth; you placed in their soul not a torch but a living fire . . . They are your soldiers, the purest flowers of the Italian spring . . . Out of our love . . . under the auspices of the Duce, we have convened here from all the lands that have heard the roar of the lion of Saint Mark, to sow the seed from which will sprout the flowers of the new spring.) (Macciocchi, 41–42). Sacrifice and reproduction, the roles assigned to women in *The Life I Gave You*, are here glorified through bombastic rhetoric and erotico-mystical devotion to the Duce. Macciocchi theorizes that what fascist discourse really implies is the castration of all Italian males except for the Duce—he alone will be the *Maschio-Marito*, the real father, as the Marchesa states, of the sons of the new Italy. Certainly the "giorno della fede," December 22, 1935, when Mussolini asked Italian women to give him their wedding bands to help support his Abyssinian campaign, must have had something of the aura of a mystical mass marriage.

(Pirandello contributed his Nobel Prize medal to the campaign.) The man for all women—Pirandello appears to have written around that time a story with that title ("L'Uomo di tutte le donne") concerning a man whom all women find irresistible, a man who has fathered most of his friends' children.[4]

It would be impossible here to discuss at any length the thorny question of the extent of Pirandello's commitment and artistic relationship to fascism, but his preoccupation with the reproductive and sacrificial functions of women, their "irreducible" roles as mother, at least, seems to coincide with images upheld by the regime. *The Life I Gave You* is also remarkable for its absence of fathers. Not a word is said about Donn'Anna's husband, who presumably fathered the son she has lost; neither the children of her sister Donna Fiorina nor Lucia appear to have a father. The only father discussed, but more as son and lover than as father, is the great absent one, the sacrificed son whom his mother hopes to see reborn in Lucia. Perhaps the women praying to the Virgin at the opening of the play ("Mater Christi, Mater Divinae Gratiae, Mater purissima," IV, 451) indicate that the primary relationship is that between mother and child and that the mother–son relationship in particular in some sense recapitulates the model of the Virgin Mother and Christ. The official father (the presumed case of Lucia's husband here and a major theme in the comedies discussed above as in *Think it Over Giacomino*) often plays the role of St. Joseph in Pirandello. Presumably a nonbeliever in the Christian God, but profoundly influenced by Catholic culture, did Pirandello transfer his ambivalent feelings about his own father to a veneration of the Father of the new sons of Italy, the one who could transform Italian mothers into Madonnas, in a new secular trinity?

The state of maternity becomes even more idealized in Pirandello's late "myth plays." *The New Colony*, in particular, recounts the transformation of prostitute to Madonna. With her new ideal of loving one man, the father of her child, but looking after and caring for all in the utopian community, the prostitute La Spera discovers the "miracle" of milk returning to her breasts while becoming a "queen and saint," "transfigured." She is also an object of value in the community: until a shipment of women arrives, her lover Currao's power over the others comes from the fact that he "owns" her. When Currao eventually wants to leave her to marry a young virgin, and to take his son, La Spera resists mightily. If Currao really cared for him, she reasons, he would give him to his mother, because only a mother can give him real love (V, 1153). In the end, it would seem that La Spera has become not only Madonna but Mother Earth. When Currao attempts to take the child by force, La Spera grasps him in a "mother's desperate embrace," the earth trembles, the island and its inhabitants sink into the sea, and La Spera remains alone on a rock, nursing her child upon the waters! The "irreducible construction" alone survives the attempts to construct new men in a new society. It is on this rock, Pirandello seems to imply, that such attempts can begin anew.

More could be said about mothers and maternity in Pirandello's drama: the

metaphorical value of the maternal villa or palace in *Each in His Own Way,
Henry IV*, and *The Life I Gave You*; the mother–son relation in *Each in His Own
Way*; the mother–daughter relation in *Tonight We Improvise*; the suffering mother
in *The Other Son*; and of course the mother figure in *Six Characters*, to mention
a few. Roberto Alonge (1978) has discussed at some length mother figures and
what he calls "the problematic of Mother Earth" in the late plays, arguing that
Pirandello's vision coincides with the fascist dream of a return to a precapitalist,
agrarian society. My analysis intends to show that the preoccupation with maternity, while it takes different forms, is central to Pirandello's theater from
beginning to end. I would, however, like to explore here a different facet of
Pirandello's fascination with maternity, not so much in his dramatic works as
in his dramatic theory: his particular use of the traditional metaphor of maternity
as artistic creation.

"Si pensi che il mistero d'ogni nascita artistica e il mistero stesso d'ogni
nascita naturale; non cosa che si possa apposta fabbricare ma che deve natural-
mente nascere" writes Pirandello in 1934.[5] (The mystery of every artistic birth
is the same mystery as that of natural birth; it is not something that you can
make on purpose but something that must be born naturally.) Arguing against
art as a form of conscious propaganda, he does *not*, as some of his commentators
believe, take a stance in favor of "pure" art. Theater, for example, is for him
the form that most intimately mirrors contemporary moral values (VI, 1007).
The birth metaphor as used here implies a primitive concept of the reproductive
process. There seems to be no possibility of intentionality, and there is no mention
of a father. Artistic birth, it would seem, simply flowers as the mysterious result
of the influences ("germs") that enter the artist's mind, influences that are
inevitably tied to the social fabric but that will not result in *conscious* propagation.

Pirandello had already developed the birth metaphor more extensively in the
preface to *Six Characters* where he used the same words: "Il mistero della
creazione artistica e il mistero stesso della nascita naturale." Just as a woman,
in his view, cannot decide to become a mother, but one day finds herself a
mother, "Cosi un artista, vivendo, accoglie in se tanti germi della vita, e non
puo mai dire come e perche, a un certo momento, uno di questi germi vitali gli
si inserisca nella fantasia per divenire anch'esso una creatura viva in un piano
di vita superiore alla volubile esistenza quotidiana" (I, 36). (Thus an artist, by
living, lets into himself so many germs of life, and he can never say how or
why, at a certain moment, one of these vital germs inserts itself in his fantasy
to become a living creature, living on a plane superior to that of inconstant daily
existence.) The allegorical figure "Fantasia," introduced previously as Pirandello's servant, here joins the birth metaphor to appear as an egg, or perhaps a
womb. If the "germs" come from outside, they come from no particular source
and are appropriated by the artist, so that the process of artistic birth now appears
as a kind of parthenogenesis.

The problem of the Six Characters as posed in this preface and in the novella
entitled *La Tragedia di un personaggio* appears to be, in the terms of this

metaphor, that they are searching for a maternal space—a womb—in order to be artistically born, and thus come to eternal life. Dr. Fileno, the character–protagonist in "La Tragedia," explains with an example. "Mi dica lei chi era Sancho Panza! Mi dica lei chi era Don Abbondio! Eppure vivono eterni perche— vivi germi—ebbero la ventura di trovare una matrice feconda, una fantasia che li seppe allevare e nutrire per l'eternita," (I, 821). (Tell me, who was Sancho Panza! Who was Don Abbondio! And yet they have eternal life because as living germs they had the good fortune to find a fertile womb, a fantasy that was able to raise and nurture them for eternity), words that are repeated by the Father to the director in the play. The metaphor now makes the character seem either an Aristotelian *homunculus* or an embryo somehow formed elsewhere and the author a kind of male surrogate mother. Dr. Fileno asks Pirandello-as-author to "ri-prendermi e darmi la vita che quell'imbecile non ha saputo darmi" (1:77) (take me back and give me the life that that imbecile [his previous author] was unable to give me). Is the search for an author thus prompted by the fear of *allontan-amento* (the problem of *The Life I Gave You*) and the desire for a return to a blissful pre-birth or pre-Oedipal state? A character's eternal life, it would seem, must be sought through a kind of regression/rebirth through a male mother.

It is clear that if the process of artistic creation is described in metaphorical terms taken from female processes, an author for Pirandello can only be male. Careful to distinguish between lofty, immortal artistic birth and lowly, mortal carnal birth, Pirandello reinforces this distinction in the preface with his de-scription of the character of the Mother. Unlike the other characters, the Mother is not in search of an author because she has no spirituality and thus no con-sciousness of being a character. Living entirely by instinct, she is entirely passive and carnal: "quasi un ciocco di carne compiutamente viva in tutte le sue fun-ziomni di procreare, allatare, curare e amare la sua prole, senza punto bisongo percio di far agire il cervello" (almost a block of flesh complete in its functions of giving birth, nursing, caring for and living its offspring without having to use the brain at all, IV, 42). The author thus succeeds in expropriating the birth process from its lowly female context to endow it with the mental and spiritual capacities proper to the male. It is no wonder that Liolà, the male mother, was also a poet. Seen in this light, Pirandello's obsession with maternity may signify not so much an interest in women and mothers per se as a kind of womb envy, or a preoccupation with the metaphorical value of the low form of birth for the high. In any case, as we have seen, motherhood provides Pirandello's female characters with a fundamental role in society, as in the dramatic text.

In contrast to the irreducible mothers, women who appear as *donna* in Pir-andello's drama seem shifting, illusory, unstable, and theatrical. As traditional Pirandellian criticism points out, the plays written with roles for Marta Abba, from about 1924 on, present beautiful, mysterious, solitary, often lost and vic-timized, but fascinating creatures. These may appear to be "strong" female roles—as indeed from the point of view of an actress they undoubtedly are—

but what has not been sufficiently pointed out is the fact that Pirandello's concerns with role and identity or with the theater as metaphor for life are quite gender specific. The veiled woman who appears at the end of *Così è (se vi pare) (Right You Are, If You Think You Are)* is not, as has been often supposed, an allegory for the illusiveness of truth but rather a figure of the mobility of female identity, subject as it is to the perceptions of those whose roles give them a more solid grounding: in this case the mother and the husband. In this reading, it is clear that Lina/Giulia Ponza can be both Signora Frola's daughter and Signor Ponza's second wife, for like an actress she can play her assigned parts of both *figlia* and *moglie* while being, for herself, no one. The figure of the woman without a proper identity who plays the parts assigned by what we might call her "authors" will become even more prominent in the Marta Abba plays, but the antecedents are to be found throughout the early Pirandello.

The Sicilian comedy *Il Berretto a Sonagli (Cap and Bells)*, written in 1918, is a case in point. The first part of this play takes place in an entirely female world in which women, organized by the jealous wife Beatrice, actually seem to be controlling the plot. It soon becomes clear, however, that the action is really dominated by the great absent one, Beatrice's husband, the bank president. When Beatrice tries to engage Ciampa, the humble employee whom Beatrice's husband has cuckolded, on her side, Ciampa opts to maintain appearance, "honor," and the patriarchal order. To do otherwise would be to acquiesce to female plotting and thus to anarchy. Ciampa gets his way by invoking the old Sicilian code—he could kill both his wife and Beatrice's husband and get away with it. Beatrice, in order to save her husband's life, consents to play the role that Ciampa assigns her: she will feign madness to the point of allowing herself to be sent to an asylum in order to discredit the accusations she has made. Ciampa, one of Pirandello's great roles for the *attore brilliante* Musco, understands at a level beyond the grasp of the other (primarily female) characters the nature of social hypocrisy and the inevitability of theatrical "masking" in life. In a manner consistent with Pirandello's later male protagonists, however, Ciampa *chooses* not only the role he himself will play, but also the "mad" mask that Beatrice will don. While it is true that Beatrice acquiesces in the choice that Ciampa has made for her, she does so under the control of the absent one—out of duty to her husband, whose life Ciampa now controls. We thus have a paradoxical, humoristic situation in which a husband/lover and cuckolded husband act in collusion against the wronged wife. (Ciampa's wife, it should be noted, appears on stage only briefly and seems entirely under the control of her husband and her lover.) The hypocrisy of the patriarchal social order is exposed, yet it must be maintained, not torn apart by female plotting. Ciampa will be satisfied with the appearance of keeping his wife under lock and key and by manipulating the Sicilian code to his own advantage.

The much later "theatrical" play *Questa Sera si recita a soggetto (Tonight We Improvise)* (1930) plays, with some variations, on the theme of female roles. In the play within the play, or the subject of the proposed improvising, we have as in *Cap and Bells* an initially all-female world presented: in this case a mother and four daughters attempt to control their own style of life in opposition to prevailing Sicilian codes. Here it is an absent father, in conjunction with the codes, who dominates. One of the daughters, Mommina, because of her father's death and a scandalous affair with a singer, feels obliged to marry a jealous Sicilian in order to protect the family honor. Mommina, who would have become an opera singer, is virtually imprisoned by her husband. Determined to confine her entirely to the role of mother, the husband attempts to control her very thoughts (IV, 277). Mommina's attempt to leave her prison in imagination by performing an imaginary *Trovatore* for her daughters results in her death. In Pirandello's theatrical labyrinth, the actress who plays the role of Mommina is also supposed to have a heart attack and die. Here the woman appears as victimized by roles in both life and art.

As if extending the truncated role of Signora Ponza, the actress Delia Morello in *Each in His Own Way* first appears to the audience wearing a thick veil. Delia, it soon becomes apparent, is ready to accept her role as "written" either by Diego or Francesco or, in the end, by Michele Rocca. In Delia Pirandello creates not a new type of woman but a new incarnation of his vision of woman: woman as actress, or the condition of actress as metonymical with the nature of woman. Several of Pirandello's female characters recall in one form or another Signora Ponza's final words. Ersilia in *Vestire gli ignudi (To Clothe the Naked)*, who is in a sense searching for both a veil and an author, confesses that she has never had the strength to be anything. Tuda's last words in *Diana e la Tuda* are "Io che ora sono cosi: niente . . . piu niente . . . " (Now I am nothing . . . nothing at all, IV, 443). The unknown woman in *Come tu mi vuoi (As You Desire Me)* puts herself into the hands of Boffi saying, "—non conosco piu nulla e non mi conosco . . . un corpo senza nome in attesa che qualcuno se lo prenda!'' (I don't know anything; I don't know myself. I'm a nameless body waiting for someone to take it! IV, 942–43). The lack of existential identity expressed by these characters posits woman as enigma for herself as for others, driving men to speculate about this enigma and to try to capture it in a comprehensible and controlled way. Ersilia is offered a role by each of her former lovers as well as by her writer. The unknown woman, using the picture of Cia as model, dresses herself to play the part. Again like a more developed Signora Ponza, she is revealed in the end to exist only in the roles created for her by others. By virtue of the fact that her only choices appear to be Bruno's wife or Salter's mistress, she remains *l'ignota*, her only identity that of a relative being.[6]

What we might call the Signora Ponza syndrome, or the relativity of female identity, is evident even and perhaps especially in what at least one critic has seen as Pirandello's feminist play, *Trovarsi (To Find Oneself)*, 1932.[7] On one level the plot does indeed concern a gifted, intelligent, beautiful woman (the play is dedicated to Marta Abba) who renounces marriage to the man she loves in order to continue her acting career. On closer look, however, we are dealing not with a liberation from bourgeois marriage (the capricious young Swedish artist Elj is anything but a Sicilian husband), but the failure of a woman to realize herself sexually on the one hand and the profession of actress as a metonymical with the non-identity of woman as individual on the other.

The first act of *To Find Oneself*, like that of *Each in His Own Way*, presents the secondary characters' discussion of the actress. What is Donata Genzi's true nature, what is she like as a woman, and indeed can an actress have a life as a woman? The dialogue again picks up the words of Signora Ponza's self-definition: "LA MARCHESA BOVENO. Be' sara pure in qualche modo, nella vita; e si potra dir come! Tranne che per voi una 'vera' attrice non sia piu una donna! (Well, she must be some way in life, and we'll be able to say how! Unless, as you think, a 'true' actress is no longer a woman!) SALÒ: Una no; ecco: tante donne! E per se, forse, nessuna. (*A* woman no; *many* women! And for herself, perhaps, no one," V, 904). Salò maintains that a life as *donna*, which seems to imply for all the characters a love life, is excluded by the "abnegation" which the condition of actress implies: "negare se stessa, la propria vita, la propria persona, per *dar*si tutta e *dar*la tutta ai personaggi che rappresenta" (to deny one's self, one's own life and person to *give* oneself entirely and *give* it entirely to the characters one plays." Donata's very name contains the duality which discussion about her person has prompted: *donna/data*, the woman/the given one.

Once Donata the actress has made her entrance, the discussion continues, now with the added dimension of Donata's own narcissistic speculations. "How can you know what I really am," she asks the other characters, "if I don't know myself?" To play different roles on the stage, return to one's dressing room, take off the makeup, and be unable to "find oneself"—Donata postulates the problem to be solved, but in a way that is neither philosophical nor strictly dramatic. Pirandello seems to have invented a particular style for her alone.

As Donata says: "Cose a cui si pensa senza volerlo, quasi di nascosto da noi stessi . . . sogni . . . pena di non essere . . . come dei fiori che non han potuto sbocciare . . . —ecco, finche si resta cosi, certo non si ha nulla; ma si ha almeno questa pienezza di liberta . . . '' (things we think about without wanting to, as if hidden from ourselves . . . dreams . . . pain of nonbeing . . . like flowers that were unable to bud . . . —as long as things stay like that we have nothing, but at least we have this fullness of freedom . . . , V, 914). These sentence fragments, held together by ellipses and sometimes accompanied by protests of inability to express herself, typify Donata's long "speeches" throughout the play. Here Pirandello almost seems to be attempting his own version of *l'écriture feminine*, a writing that seems to emanate from the subconscious without consciously imposed grammatical and syntactical structures. Donata, one might say, does not "think like a man."

Donata's attempt to "find herself" is performed almost as an experiment but an experiment incited by a capricious, unmediated act. To the fullness of freedom as mere potential, Donata opposes the notion of "throwing oneself" into life and accordingly throws herself on the next man she finds, the young Swedish-

Italian aristocrat–sailor–painter Elj. The end of the first act, then, finds both Elj and Donata ready to leave the villa of Donata's friends, a closed space that has been dominated by social interaction and narcissistic speculation, to "throw themselves" into a boat on a stormy, dangerous sea.

As the second act opens, Elj has saved Donata from drowning, brought her to his house, and the two have become lovers. Renée Moliterno points out the "surprising" (for its time and for Pirandello) nature of the dialogue between Elj and Donata in its reference to sexual intimacy.[8] "You thought too much of yourself," Donata tells her lover the morning after, adding that that is perhaps simply in the nature of men. Donata's attempt to be a woman rather than an actress has then failed on one important count. When Elj tells her how he loves the gestures she uses with him, Donata realizes that these are the same gestures she is famous for on the stage. Her awareness that the woman/actress dichotomy is more complex than she had thought prompts another meditation in what we now recognize as the Donata style:

> Sai, è . . . è per forza così . . . perche io sono stata sempre vera . . . sempre vera . . . ma non per me . . . ho vissuto sempre come di la da me stessa; e ora voglio essere 'qua'— 'io'—'io'—avere una vita mia, per me . . . devo trovarmi! (You know, it's . . . of course it's this way . . . because I have always been true . . . always true . . . but not for me . . . I've always lived as if above myself; and now I want to be 'here'—'I'—'I'—to have my own life, for me . . . I have to find myself!) (V, 931)

Elj asks Donata to be his wife, but the capricious young man who lost his mother at an early age, whose primary desire is to return to the sea that he envisages as a woman, and whose uncle, when he comes to speak with Donata, treats him like a spoiled child, seems to be seeking a mother as well as a lover and in any case a woman who will tolerate his capriciousness. Unable to decide on the marriage, at the end of the second act, Donata, with the advice and help of Elj's uncle, sets up another experiment. She will return to the theater to allow Elj to see her on the stage.

The play thus has a dialectical structure: the first act concerns the actress who desires to be a woman; the second act the woman who still desires to be the actress; the third act sets up and accomplishes the synthesis of actress/woman. The synthesis, however, does not resolve the tensions between the two modes of being and on one level appears to separate them even further. Elj cannot tolerate seeing Donata on the stage using the gestures of intimacy that he desires for himself alone (making a spectacle of herself, giving herself to the public). He walks out of her life, vowing to return to the sea. Donata must choose, it would seem, between being an actress and being a woman. On another level, however, what Donata discovers upon returning to the stage is that being a woman and being an actress are one and the same, or that acting is the quintessential mode of being a woman. When Giviero congratulates her for her triumphant performance as actress, she corrects him: "Ancora dite dell'attrice?

No! no! Io me son sentita felice come donna! come donna! Felice di potere ancora amare! Questa era la mia vittoria! . . . mi sono liberata!'' (Do you still speak of the actress? No! no! I felt happy as a woman! As a woman! Happy to still be able to love! That was my victory! . . . I have freed myself!) (V, 962).

In her attempt to love as a woman, it would seem that Donata discovered that loving is also a form of acting, and back on stage she rediscovers that acting is a form of loving. Donata says in a visionary trance: ''Io posso avere tutto l'amore che voglio—e darlo!—io, tutto l'amore! e a me l'amore di tutti!'' (I can have all the love I want—and give it—I, all the love! And for me the love of all!'') (V, 967). Donata's fundamental narcissism affirms itself in the process of ''finding'' herself, as does her Pirandellian awareness that the self cannot be found because it is after all nothing but a series of creations or constructions. The play ends with her words: ''Vero e soltanto che bisogna crearsi, creare! E allora soltanto, ci si trova.'' (The only truth is that one must create oneself, create! Only then does one find oneself.) (V, 968). The original dichotomy is bridged as the figure of Donata no longer seeks to be *donna* or *data* but resolves itself as *donna data*, the given woman, the woman offered to the public as *tante donne*, many women. While it is true that the actress, unlike other women, can in a sense liberate herself from the anguish of being ''for herself, no one,'' it is also true that as a player of roles or a wearer of masks created by men, existing only in the myriad forms perceived in the mirror of the audience, the condition of actress is a heightened, condensed, artistic representation of what it means, in the Pirandellian world, to be a woman.[9]

It might be objected that what I have postulated as the feminine condition, or more properly the condition of *donna*, woman, in Pirandello's theater is quite simply the human condition which for Pirandello is by definition theatrical. This is in a sense true, but I would argue that the feminine condition represents (paradoxically, since the female for Pirandello as for many other male writers is not Man but Other) at once the most radical and the purest form of Pirandellian theatricality. This would explain why so many of Pirandello's characters are women. The helplessness experienced before the awareness that the self does not exist; the acceptance of the fact that facets of self can be found only by playing the roles created by others—such intuitions are endemic to Pirandello's women. Men, in Pirandello's theater, are not infected by the Signora Ponza syndrome. ''Henry IV'' loses his name, but not, entirely, his sense of self, for he chooses his roles and manipulates the other characters in his fake medieval world. The difference between a title such as *As You Desire Me* and *Henry IV* is symptomatic. Both imply a loss of ''real'' identity and the adoption of a theatrical one, but whereas the man assumes his persona, the woman exists only ''as wanted.''

The one way for a woman in this Pirandellian world to escape the condition of relativity is to assume her instinctive destiny, the irreducible construction of motherhood. This condition, however, is also part of a social code, and its security depends on the willingness of a man to play the part of (not necessarily to be) the father. The fundamental relation between a mother and her "creatures" appears to be one that men both admire and envy. Pirandello, as we have seen, appropriates the state of motherhood by incorporating it into his metaphor for artistic creation Be relegating the domain of the instinctual and the carnal to women, the male mother gives birth to and nourishes spiritual children, combining the best of both worlds. Pirandello's veneration of *Madre/Madonna*, as well as his portrayal of women as relative being, coincide with the fascist discourse of the period, while bearing the unique stamp of the conservative Sicilian who became a radical modernist.

NOTES

1. All translations, unless otherwise noted, are my own.
2. By, among others, Renate Matthaei, 70.
3. Roberto Alonge is, to my knowledge, the only commentator to have pointed out this characteristic of Liolà, whom he calls "l'unico uomo-madre di tutto il teatro pirandelliano" (1986:94). Alonge gives examples of the types listed in his title (mothers, whores, sex slaves, and men alone), concluding that Pirandello's work is essentially reactionary, patriarchal, and "maschilista" (109).
4. The fragments of this novella, which was to appear in the fifteenth volume of *Novelle per un anno*, published in 1937, appear in 6:1052–53.
5. "Discorso al Convegno 'Volta' Sul teatro drammatico" (Rome, October 1934, published 1935) in 6:1004.
6. Susan Sontag, in directing *Come tu mi vuoi* for the Teatro Stabile di Torino in 1980–1981, gave the play a feminist interpretation, explained and critiqued by Jennifer Stone. In Stone's reading, the story of the unknown woman is "an anatomy of power and powerlessness, which is not always gender specific" (44). I read the text of the play certainly not as a feminist statement, but as quite gender specific, especially in the light of Pirandello's other female figures.
7. Susan Bassett-McGuire, for example, maintains that "Donata's refusal to allow her love for Elj to become the centre of her life is a strong statement about a woman's need for personal freedom" and that this "startlingly advanced attitude" does not square with fascist ideology at all (126). For Roberto Alonge, on the other hand, Donata's long-maintained virginity and her inability to assert her rights to sexual pleasure with Elj show how she is "completely submissive to masculine ideology" (1978:216).
8. "Par ce manque de participation," Moliterno maintains, "la femme est réduite a n'être qu'un objet de plaisir et cette dégradation est ressentie avec d'autant plus d'acuité par Donata qui a consacré toute sa vie, jusqu'alors, a une lucide et inlassable recherche de son être" (134).
9. It is interesting to note that Pirandello refers to the feminist movement of his day as a "construction" and a "masquerade." The piece called "Feminismo," first published in *La Preparazione* in February 1909, consists of a series of vignettes on a certain "Doctor Paolo Post," who seems to adopt the *filosofia del lontano* to various situations. His daughter, a feminist, appears briefly as a caricature with huge glasses distorting and "confusing" her eyes, and a masculine, guttural voice. Post explains that feminism is an "ideal construction" for our days—a balloon that will fly, lose air, and then burst. The so-called prejudices decried by the emancipation reclaimed for feminists are nothing

but a "sdegnosa mascherata del bisogno fisiologico" (an indignant mask of the phys-
iological need), or the desire of woman for a husband (6:1027–31).

WORKS CITED

Alonge, Roberto. "Subalternità e masochismo della donna nell'ultimo teatro Pirandel-
    liano." In *Struttura e ideologia nel teatro italiano fra '500 e '900*. Torino:
    Stampatori, 1978. 200–233.
——. "Madri, puttane, schiave sessuali e uomini soli." *Studi Pirandelliani, dal testo
    al sottotesto*. Bologna: Pitagora, 1986. 90–110.
Bassnett-McGuire, Susan. *Luigi Pirandello*. New York: Grove Press, 1983.
Caldwell, Lesley. "Reproducers of the Nation: Women and the Family in Fascist Policy."
    In David Forgacs, ed. *Rethinking Italian Fascism: Capitalism, Populism, and
    Culture*. London: Lawrence & Wishart, 1986. 110–41.
De Grand, Alexander. "Women under Italian Fascism." *Historical Journal* 19/4
    (1976):947–68.
Giudice, Gaspare. *Pirandello: A Biography*. Trans. Alastair Hamilton. New York: Oxford
    University Press, 1975. 27.
Kelly, A. "Una rivaluazione della maternità nelle protagoniste Pirandelliane." *Le Ragioni
    critiche* 6/21 (1976):169–75.
Levin, Harry. *Playboys and Killjoys: An Essay on the Theory and Practice of Comedy*.
    New York: Oxford University Press, 1987.
Macciocchi, Maria Antonietta. *La Donna 'Nera': Consenso femminile e fascismo*. Milano:
    Feltrinelli, 1977.
Matthaei, Renate. *Luigi Pirandello*. Trans. S. and E. Young. New York: Frederick Ungar,
    1973.
Moliterno, Renée. "Asservissement ou libération des femmes dans le théâtre de Piran-
    dello." In J. Nicolas, ed. *Hommage à Louise Cohen: Langue et littérature ital-
    iennes*. Paris: Belles Lettres, 1982. 121–40.
Montante, M. "The Woman in the Plays of Luigi Pirandello and Paul Claudel." *Claudel
    Studies* 7/2 (1980):38–47.
Oldcorn, Anthony. "Pirandello o del candore?" *Modern Language Notes* 42/1
    (1976):139–49.
Pirandello, Luigi. *Opere*. 6 vols. Milano: Mondadori, 1960.
Stone, Jennifer. "Beyond Desire: A Critique of Susan Sontag's Production of Pirandello's
    Come tu mi vuoi." *Yearbook of the British Pirandello Society* 1 Bristol (1981):19–
    25.

5

Pirandello's Literary Uses of Theosophical Notions

Antonio Illiano

Pirandello's use of theosophy extends from *Il fu Mattia Pascal* to his major plays and is a literary phenomenon that sheds critical light on both the genesis and composition of the works.

Theosophy is both a mystical wisdom-religion and a speculative system. As a wisdom-religion, it has been rooted from time immemorial in the history of humankind and in the origins of religious beliefs and practices. As a speculative system with both religious and philosophical implications, however, theosophy can be traced back to Plato and to such early mystical movements and esoteric doctrines as Orphism and pre-Christian gnosticism.

The name, which means divine wisdom and not wisdom of God, is generally attributed to the second-century philosopher Ammonius Saccas, whose disciple, Plotinus, was the formulator of the doctrine of neo-Platonism.[1] In this doctrine man is conceived as potentially divine, for he can achieve a mystical union with the One, the embodiment of the supreme sphere of being, through contemplation and self-purification. Within this context, Plotinus also suggested a theory of the education of the soul through reincarnation. The embodied human soul, immersed in matter and unable to abide completely in the universal soul, can be overwhelmed by sensual desire. Yet the soul can rise from that fallen state and bring back the experience of what it has suffered and learned, thus understanding how blessed it is to reside in the intelligible world of pure forms.

In the following centuries, with the growing opposition of more orthodox doctrines, theosophical speculation declined considerably, only to reemerge, under varying guises and forms, in the writings of medieval and Renaissance mystics from Meister Eckhart to Giordano Bruno and Jacob Böhme. The Renaissance also witnessed a flowering of experimentations into alchemy, occultism, and Hermeticism. Since the Renaissance, traces and trends of theosophical thinking may be detected in the course of Western thought, particularly in some aspects and movements of the history of literature and philosophy in the eighteenth and nineteenth centuries.[2]

A new and, to some extent, controversial chapter in the history of theosophical speculation opened in 1875 with the foundation in New York of a Theosophical Society, which was committed, on the one hand, to the traditionally theosophical investigation of the mysterious powers of nature and, on the other, to the more philanthropic endeavors of establishing a universal brotherhood of humanity and promoting the comparative study of religion, science, and philosophy. The teachings of the Society, which exhibited a definite propensity toward Oriental mysticism while remaining indebted to Western theosophical and philosophical traditions as well, were eventually compounded and set forth, along dogmatic and often intricate lines, by Helene P. Blavatsky, the principal founder of the Society, in *The Secret Doctrine* (1888), the first and most influential reference work of modern theosophy.

An underlying tenet of the newly restored wisdom-religion was, in fact, the fundamental belief in a secret doctrine or esoteric message which, throughout the centuries, had allegedly been the claim to possession by an elite group of masters adept in mysticism and occultism. This esoteric message, along with other facts and factors such as the eccentric and often sharply conflicting personalities of the founders, was perhaps among the leading causes of the peaceful recognition of the theosophic credo. As the new adepts began to spread the word, however, the esoteric trend began to take hold as well, and a series of popular books and manuals helped to carry the message to the general public. In spite of its controversial nature, the Theosophical Society did eventually become a sort of cultural phenomenon of international importance for the history of religious and philosophical thinking in the late nineteenth and early twentieth centuries.[3]

In literature this wave of theosophical interest lent new credence to the old and well-rooted Western tradition of spiritualistic and occultistic concerns, evolving from the Holy Grail to Novalis, Poe, James, and other modern writers. Pirandello became interested in this trend around the turn of the century, perhaps in Capuana's circle in Rome. It must again be noted, however, that there is a great deal of difference between spiritism (or spiritualism) and theosophy, which was conceived and lived essentially as a doctrine and a system of thought. Theosophists themselves have rightfully and repeatedly disclaimed any true or serious connection with spiritism, especially when this phenomenon is interpreted only in terms of the seance, which for many years degenerated to the level of widespread social and semisuperstitious practices. Pirandello was aware of the difference between spiritism and theosophy. While polemically motivated against spiritism—the scene of the seance in *Il fu Mattia Pascal* works both as a structural device and as a topical parody of the misguided adepts whose fanatic credulity is easily manipulated by fraud. Pirandello's inquisitive mind was predictably intrigued by the philosophical and psychological tenets of the theosophical school. Its publications were readily available to him in the French translations of such primary texts and guides as Helene P. Blavatsky's *The Secret Doctrine* and the *Key to Theosophy* (1889), Annie Besant's *Death and After* (1893), *Karma* (1895), *Man and His Bodies* (1896), and Charles W. Leadbeater's *The Astral Plane* (1895). These books, together with the work of the French theosophist Dr. Théophile Pascal, form the bulk of Anselmo Paleari's collection.[4]

Following the main dictates of traditional theosophical speculation, modern theosophy postulates the existence of one eternal and inscrutable principle, the root of all. This being, with the help of a semihierarchical trinity (which also ordains the dialectical function of life–form, positive–negative, the two opposite but inextricable attributes of all existence), cyclically issues the universe by way of seven modifications of atomic and molecular substance which appear as stratified in several coexistent planes or levels of being. A plane is not a geographic or cosmographic dimension, but a state, a condition, a stage, and a principle of universal life in both its macrocosmic and microcosmic forms. It follows that the principles are actually consubstantial, even though the sevenfold stratification is the compound of a higher spiritual triad and a lower quaternary of physical elements.

The seven principles constitute the ladder of evolution that promotes and regulates the progress of the individual from the lower to the higher stages. The evolution is achieved through a complex system of purgatorial purifications and cyclical reincarnations. The first and lowest principle is the physical body, built of material molecules and provided with a purely physical consciousness. The second principle, the etheric double or astral man (also called phantom), is the exact counterpart of the physical body. It belongs to it, and though separable from it, cannot move too far from it and is perceptible only to clairvoyants. It is the vehicle of *Prana*, the third principle, and principle of life and vitality, the force that makes all that is share in the unchanging source of universal life. *Prana*, joined to *Kama*, the fourth principle, becomes the breath of life. *Kama* is the desire body, the principle of all feelings, emotions, and passions, good and bad, that constitute man's sentient and sensual nature.

After death, as the physical body and its double, with the departure of life-energy, are left to decay, the desire body will persist for a time in a special dimension called *Kama-loca*, a sort of Hades or limbo. This region is populated by a wide range of "shells" or shades wandering about until all traces of human passions have dissolved and, in those cases where the earthly links are more deep-rooted and deep-felt, constantly pleading for the resolution of their emotional plight. Of particular interest in this region are also the spectres of the so-called elementaries or spooks, the unsavory specimens of the lowest and foulest human type, who are magnetically drawn to all scenes and whirlpools of terrestrial depravity by their animal instinct, cunning, and lack of conscience. Madama

Pace appears to be an original emissary of such a crowd. The Six Characters may be seen as shades or shells from this purgatory, whence they emerge periodically to enact or reenact their unfulfilled feelings, incarnated passions, and vital yearning for artistic realization. Here are the shells of suicides, tormented by their own unlived experiences and forced, like the late Mattia Pascal, to await their second deaths.

The fifth principle, *Manas*, from Sanskrit *man*, the root of "to think," is the universal thinking principle, the mind, the power of intelligence and reason that constitutes in man the primary force of evolution from the lower to the higher planes.[5] *Manas* achieves evolution as the vehicle of the higher spiritual planes and the incarnating Ego behind the fleeting human persona that gives the illusion of temporal existence. It is this principle, the real "I," the enduring individuality repeatedly clothing itself in transient personalities, which, after each incarnation, reviews and stores the experience acquired, drawing from it the appropriate amount of knowledge and registering the levels of growth toward divine wisdom.

The law that regulates the necessary process of gradual purification through repeated reincarnations is called *Karma*, the law of cause and, according to which effect, every action produces results and is subject to retribution. The principle or norm that guides the cosmic chain of evolution and, on the human level, assures the development of freedom with responsibility is the precept that "as a man soweth, so shall he also reap." This is what makes perfection possible, for thought and knowledge are the most influential factors in the production of causes, and the mentality of one life is the result of thinking in the past lives. (It may be incidentally noted here that what people generally recognize as "genius" is not merely an arbitrary phenomenon but the product of the long creative work of the past and the compounded knowledge acquired through the centuries—a process that is bound to continue in the future.)

The working of the karmic law is a cardinal factor in the development of self-knowledge in all human beings at a stage of advanced intelligence and perception. This is precisely the stage reached by Mattia Pascal, a genial character whose charismatic nature is consistently attuned to his enterprising quest for self-knowledge through a forcibly stepped-up pace of *maturazione* that would normally require several lives.[6] Indeed, *Il fu Mattia Pascal* can be regarded as the first, and perhaps the most sophisticated, *Bildungsroman* of the twentieth century. The name itself suggests a convergence of the names of Blaise Pascal, whose thoughts on human personality Pirandello knew, and Dr. Théophile Pascal, the French theosophist whose book on the seven principles pointed, with the Socratic epigraph *connais-toi* printed on the title page, to the complexities of the problem of man's self-determination.

Mattia Pascal/Adriano Meis is constantly reflecting on, or confronting himself with, the wisdom of his decisions and the value of the outcome of his actions. His evident limitations and character defects—impressionability, caution, shrewdness, tendency to pretend and compromise, recrimination, rationalization, selfishness, and so on—are often connected with, or dictated by, his deep-seated need for self-analysis. Inevitably, this trend leads to traumatic insights and painful utterances of self-recognition such as the one tersely recorded at the beginning of the chapter on reincarnation:

Folle! Come mi ero illuso che potesse vivere un tronco reciso dalle sue radici? Eppure, eppure, ecco, ricordavo l'altro viaggio, quello da Alenga a Torino: m'ero stimato felice, allo stesso modo allora. Folle! La liberazione! dicevo . . . M'era parsa quella la liberazione! . . . Mi pareva, a ripensarci, addirittura inverosimile la leggerezza concui, due anni addictro, m'ero gettato fuori d'ogni legge, alla ventura. E mi rivedevo nei primi giorni, beato nell'incoscienza, or piuttosto nella follia . . . Cominciavo gia ad accorgermi.

. What a fool! How could I have deluded myself into believing that a trunk can live when cut off from its roots? And yet, I remembered now the other journey, the one from Alenga to Turin. Then, too, I had believed myself happy in the same way. What a fool! Liberation. I said then . . . *That* had seemed a liberation! . . . Thinking back, it seemed unbelievable the foolhardiness with which, two years back, I had thrown myself out of every law haphazardly. And again, in the first days, blissful in my unawareness, or rather madness, . . . I was now beginning to realize . . .

Here the protagonist is not only questioning the soundness of his original plan but is finally waking up to his own fundamental ignorance of himself. However, it is too late to change. The experiment, once begun, has proceeded regularly according to its own inner logic and is by now irreversible: the chain of incarnations is now open and progressing.

Shortly after his arrival in Pisa, Mattia Pascal/Adriano Meis, by now caught in his own scheme, not knowing what to do, as he puts it, and hoping to find some distraction from so many problems, decides to take the two "dead" out for a stroll. It is worth noting that in the revised edition (1918) the author should have felt obliged to add a few touches and bring into the open a new active principle that was not so readily discernible in the original edition: "Il meglio era non dar confidenza a nessuno dei due. O bianco campanile, tu potevi pendere da una parte; io, tra quei due, ne di quà ne di là." The reader has by now acquired a reasonably clear understanding as to who the two "dead" are, or think they are; but who is this new "I" stuck between them, resolved to ignore them and unable to lean to either side? Is it a third fleeting personality suddenly emerging, or is it rather the thinking principle, the noumenal sense of individuality that has been implicitly operative from the beginning and explicitly suggested by such revealing elements as Mattia Pascal's features, particularly his beard and squinting eye, and by other hints such as the names Pascal-Meis, both closely connected with philosophical thinking?[7] Or is it possibly a transitory form of non-personality that will soon have to settle for the shell of what once was Mattia Pascal? The protagonist himself does not know. Whatever the case may be, the late Mattia Pascal, after his unusual journeying, is back in the limbo of *Kama-loca*, still alive but unable to live—a true outsider. All he can do now is to take Pellegrinotto's advice and turn writer, a choice warranted by his talent and apprenticeship as a librarian, reader, and intellectual. This may also imply that his writing is of a kind of report-memoir drafted while he was still in *Kama-loca*, a ledger-record of experience for safekeeping and possible future use. After all, if we choose to overlook the projected eventuality of a continuing education through rebirth, what is left worth existing for, for the late Mattia Pascal?

Pirandello has compressed the modern scheme of theosophical reincarnation into a short span of human existence. This genial and ingenious application—in addition to providing unity, structural coherence, and dramatic tension for his narrative—allows Pirandello to realize or stabilize what constitutes one of the essential trends and patterns in the psychological configuration of his fictional and dramatic characters: what might be called the Tantalus syndrome, a chronic condition of existential incompleteness, yearning without attaining, ontological suspension.

The first significant dramatization of this predicament is in *All'uscita* (1926), a striking one-act play staged at the back gate of a cemetery, and packed with action and symbolism. The dead are seen as "quelle apparenze che si diedero in vita," that is, just as they imagined or deluded themselves to be while still alive. After emerging through the gate, they wander off in a state of dismay and uncertainty, presumably toward their place or condition in the purgatory of *Kamaloca*, where they will sooner or later dissolve and disappear as they purge themselves free of their human attachments. The author captures two of these unlikely ghosts as they, in their bewilderment, linger "at the exit" and engage in a conversation about their past and present condition: the skinny and bold figure of a philosopher still reasoning and rationalizing about the existential need that compels human beings to give an objective reality to their emotions and ideas; and a fat man, who bewails the loss of his pleasure in living and being alive, and who feels like a beggar in front of a door that has been slammed in his face—the door to his former human life, which he had learned to accept with all its miseries and predicaments, including his wife's unfaithfulness. He is awaiting her arrival, for, as he rightly predicts, she will be murdered by her lover at the first shriek of her malignant laughter. Her bloody shadow does in fact appear and, sneering at her husband's with unbearable laughter, begins to retell the gruesome details of her violent end. A fourth apparition, the child with a pomegranate, emerges through the gate. The murdered woman helps him eat the fruit, and the child vanishes as his last wish is fulfilled. The woman breaks into tears as she finally realizes her own unfulfilled motherhood. This act seems to dispel the fat man's guilts or resentments, as he too disappears leaving his cane to fall noisily to the ground. The murdered women, frightened, turns to stare at the empty space beside her, but the philosopher motions to her to look instead at three massive aspects of real life as they approach from the fields: a peasant man and woman, a donkey bearing a load of hay, and a little girl. As if seeing the terrible gaze of the murdered woman fixed on her, the little girl hides her face in her hands while the old donkey sniffs at the scattered peelings of the pomegranate, first lifting and then dropping some of them. The peasant picks up the cane and drives the donkey forward. The group moves on, and the murdered woman, stretching out her arms in despair, runs after the little girl. Only the shadow of the philosopher remains, still reasoning.

The play was originally published with the subtitle *mistero profano*, probably because it was conceived as a purely symbolical (and not religious) tale of the human condition. The murdered woman's blood (heightened sexuality, misguided or twisted from its natural purpose, leads to violent death) and evil laughter (aberrant and destructive frustration) are appeased through the feeding of the child by the woman in a characteristic scene that unfolds with the suggestive intensity of a ritual and marks the major turning point in the rapid and forceful development of this mystery play. The ritual evolves around the unifying symbol of the pomegranate, a central figuration that signals and objectifies the converging predicaments of the "appearances." The pomegranate, the symbol of fecundity, is by extension the feeling of life itself that the philosopher indicates as the condition that determines our need for self-delusion (which would not be necessary in a hypothetical state of nonbeing). The sense of being alive is in fact what the fat man regrets losing; what the child craves, for it was prematurely taken away from him; and what the murdered woman felt in the violent passion of her "burning" blood.

With respect to the woman, clearly the most troubled and restless, the appearance of the child with the pomegranate has special significance and far-reaching implications. Her immediate and deeply empathic recognition of the child's need leads the "repressed" mother to help him with bursts of morbidly condescending care which the playwright deliberately emphasizes in order to provide the scene with an explicitly artful and slightly grotesque ritual. The philosopher, who is aware of her painful awakening, points out to her the only possible way to redemption: the oncoming peasant family with the donkey, a sort of bucolic group symbolizing clean and basic family life where needs are easily satisfied through the more normal processes of natural existence. (The donkey sniffs, attempts to nibble on, but refuses to eat the peelings of the pomegranate left on the ground.) The murdered woman runs after the little girl, presumably to reassure her of her true feeling and to relearn the value of natural emotion in order to gain release as soon as possible from her purgatorial condition and eventually hope for reincarnation (in the distant future) in a family setting similar to that of the little girl. The function of the group of peasants is not merely to create a structural polarity as "massive figures" contrasting with the "appearances," but to introduce a sort of visual morality scene for the sake of the murdered woman's redemption. In any case, it seems likely that she too has found a way of vanishing out of *Kama-loca*, thus indicating that the essential trend of emotion is toward movement and evolution, whereas reason is inevitably committed to a static role of analytic reflection.

Pirandello has successfully blended some of the basic concepts of theosophy with his relativistic perception of reality and human psychology. This blending is achieved partly through the application of a network of symbols that may indeed present some problems in terms of stage presentation and interpretation of the seemingly sketchy but masterfully orchestrated concentration of dialogues and stage directions. In an atmosphere of heightened emotionalism, the "appearances" tend to evoke and confess their troubles with keen and compelling voices. This exasperated need for self-analysis is the direct result of their search for either evasion or self-realization, a sort of subliminal anxiety and uncertainty that ties them to their former human condition. The habit of indulging in piecemeal, choked-up, and often self-depreciating confession is not merely a matter of technique. Already in such an early play as *All'uscita*, Pirandello's major characters are conceived and portrayed as locked in and consumed by a deep-seated feeling of their own existential incompleteness.

What is a matter of technique, and one not readily detectable as part of the inner workings of the playwright's developing system of dramatic characterization, is the inherently theosophical stratification of the "appearances" on three different levels of consciousness and being: a subtle device that will eventually contribute to the genial definition of the independent character on the purely artistic level. In *All'uscita*, the boy with a pomegranate lives as an expression of the vital principle or life instinct that is necessary to all other levels of human existence; the fat man lives on the purely emotional level, whereas the murdered woman is a more complex figuration of the emotional and animal nature of human life. The philosopher lives on a mental plane but close to the emotional level: at this point Pirandello abandons the theosophical ladder of progress toward spiritual bliss and reaches a stage of rationalizing impasse that the philosopher himself seems willing to accept and perpetuate as the inevitable outcome of his own mystifying logic. The philosopher is the perfect candidate for everlasting isolation, another typical example in a coherent line of outsiders that, through Laudisi, leads directly to the lucid and tragic isolation of Enrico IV. Finally, the peasant family can be viewed as an example of untroubled existence and natural balance to be placed between the two early stages (physical and vital) of the theosophical evolution. Nonetheless, as it was noted earlier, the group seems to fulfill more consistently the purpose of staging an exemplary scene for the murdered woman's benefit.

The Six Characters, constantly yearning for the stage of completion and purification, also live on three different theosophical levels of consciousness: the two children exemplify purely physical existence; the Mother and the Son exist on a purely emotional level; the Stepdaughter and the Father are at different stages of development between the emotional and the mental planes. Accordingly, at the end of their tearful performance, they will separate. The gunshot will signal the end of the bourgeois plot and their violent return to different regions of the artistic limbo of the unrealized, the limbo from which they will be magnetically attracted to the door of any idle author or to any real or potential stage. The two children will presumably return to their state of unconscious innocence; the Stepdaughter, leaving the stage with the shrieking laughter of a completed but still unfulfilled vengeance, will presumably sink close to the sorriest unredeemed; the Father, Mother, and Son are left as a group, on a stage lighted in green and then in blue, perhaps sharing a mystical hope for redemption through religious experience.

To still another level, that of pure instinct, belongs the seventh character, the spook of Madama Pace, the grotesque portrayal of a sense of peace and harmony that will never be realized, for it is not sought in earnest. Her flashy dress and vulgar behavior are in tune with her hybrid jargon, which is not merely the trademark of her international and intercultural profession but the true indicator and measure of her lack of perception and moral conscience; she is a character so grossly vulgar as to shock even the actors. (It is perhaps no coincidence that the clumsy mixture of Spanish and Italian was equally offensive to Mattia Pascal who, as a true man of intelligence, can learn or relearn a language as well as experience the kind of trance or clairvoyance that allows him to find and play out a winning streak while the cacophonic Spaniard, a born loser, remains in his blindly obtuse sense of confusion.)

The pathetic apparitions or ghosts of *All'uscita* have naturally developed into full-fledged theatrical creations. Each character identifies with an emotion while all of them actualize a new concept that they all recognize as the essence of their being: the fulfillment of artistic autonomy. The phantoms have shed all traces of their theosophical genesis and have finally attained the new and original Pirandellian status of artistic concepts, true, alive, and permanent.

In the complex world of *Six Characters*, Pirandello is poetically able to achieve a syncretic interplay of elements in which all diversity is miraculously translated into aesthetic unity. He is not interested in the occult or parapsychological phenomena as such. Rather, he is inclined to make use of any source of knowledge that will lend philosophical, narrative, and structural support to the complex cosmos of his artistic vision. In Pirandello's creative experience, the artist could never be reduced to a medium. (In fact, for any great writer this concept would amount to a restrictive and meaningless redefinition of true genius.) The artist, however, can act or react as a medium for the purpose of achieving true aesthetic synthesis.

NOTES

1. Plotinus, *The Descent of the Soul into the Body*, vii. For the analogous views of other Church Fathers such as St. Gregory and St. Jerome, see J. Head and S. L. Cranston, eds., *Reincarnation: An East-West Anthology* (New York, 1961).

2. See Auguste Viatte, *Les sources occultes du Romantisme:Illuminisme-Théosophie* (1770–1820), 2 vols. (Paris, 1928).

3. *Anthologie littéraire de l'occultisme*, eds. R. Amadon and R. Kanters (Paris, 1950).

4. These titles are mentioned in *Il fu Mattia Pascal* (Chap. x) as part of Anselmo Paleari's theosophical library.

5. These are the two levels above *Manas*: *Atma*, the universal spirit and a radiation of the absolute; and *Buddhi*, the soul, a vehicle of the universal spirit.

6. The idea of *maturazione* is already in the story of *Notizie del mondo* (1901): those

who are incapable of "ripening" for another life are condemned to return to earth until they find the right "exit."

7. Angelo Camillo de Meis (1817–1891) was an anti-positivist scientist and thinker.

WORKS CITED

Besant, Annie W. *Death—and After?* London: Theosophical Publishing Society, 1893.
————. *Karma*. London: Theosophical Publishing Society, 1895.
Blavatsky, Helene P. *The Secret Doctrine: The Synthesis of Science, Religion, and Philosophy*. London: Theosophical Publishing Society; New York: W. Q. Judge, 1888.
————. *The Key to Theosophy*. London: Theosophical Publishing Society, 1889.
————. *Collected Writings*. 1st [American] ed. Los Angeles: Philosophical Research Society, 1950–1958.
Capuana, Luigi. *Spiritismo*. Catania: Giannotta, 1884.
Leadbeater, Charles W. *The Astral Plane, Its Scenery, Inhabitants and Phenomena*. London: Theosophical Publishing Society, 1895.
Pascal, Théophile. *Les sept principes de l'homme, ou sa constitution d'après la théosophie*. Paris: Chamuel, 1895.
Pirandello, Luigi. *Maschere nude*. Milan: Mondadori, 1958.
————. *Tutti i romanzi*. Milan: Mondadori, 1973.

6

Medical Ethics in the Plays of Luigi Pirandello

Angela Belli

Luigi Pirandello, Italy's foremost modern dramatist, was born in Chaos. Literally. The site, located near Girgenti (Agrigento) on the southern coast of Sicily, well deserved its name at the moment of Pirandello's birth, for on that day, June 28, 1867, it was the scene of a raging cholera epidemic. Yet nothing of the local disorder could give any hint of the global turbulence that the youngest inhabitant of Chaos was to create in the theaters of the world. In 1934 he was awarded the Nobel Prize for Literature. The citation focused on "his bold and brilliant renovation of the drama and the stage." And a "renovation" is precisely what he accomplished. His achievement was to synthesize bold dramatic technique with startling thematic content in a manner never before seen but to be seen much afterward. Considered the most seminal playwright of our era, Pirandello created the ethos from which emerged the dramatic art of our time. He foreshadowed the current preoccupation in the theater with such themes as illusion versus reality, existential anguish, the disintegration of personality, and the isolation of modern man.

Pirandello himself considered the biographical facts of his life of little consequence, but a consideration of them reveals how frequently the private man and the artist fused in him. As a child he enjoyed every advantage provided by a well-to-do family. His father was a successful businessman, the owner of a sulfur mine. Despite pressure to become a lawyer, he nonetheless showed a preference for literature from his teens. Expelled from the University of Rome for an act of insubordination, he eventually earned his doctorate at the University of Bonn in 1891 with a dissertation written in German on the dialect of his native region. In 1894 he dutifully agreed to marry the daughter of his father's business associate, a wealthy sulfur merchant. The marriage provided him with the financial independence that enabled him to live in Rome and to pursue his interests as a writer of fiction. His social life in the capital in the company of fellow artists was intellectually stimulating.

In 1903 his financial security collapsed. A disastrous landslide forced the closing of the mine in which the fortunes of his father and his wife were invested. Finding himself suddenly poor with a young family to support, Pirandello was obliged to rely on an oppressive teaching position for a living. His wife's mental collapse added further anxiety to his mental life. Her illness took the form of a persecution mania accompanied by fits of jealousy during which she would accuse her husband of duplicity and repeated infidelity. Pirandello tolerated her accusations with infinite patience for some fifteen years until it became necessary to confine her to an institution. During these years he found himself confronting a double self—his real self and the self created out of his wife's imagination. The author's keen interest in psychology, his fascination with the theory of the subconscious personality, and his preoccupation with the conflict between illusion and reality all reflect events in his life. While Pirandello had gained recognition for his poetry, short stories, and novels, it was not until he wrote his major works for the stage that he attracted worldwide attention. With the premiere of *Six Characters in Search of an Author* in 1921, he was recognized as an important innovator in the theater. His masterpiece *Henry IV* brought him international acclaim.

Apart from Pirandello's absorption in the aesthetic issue of the dichotomy between reality and artistic truth, it is his distinctly modern view of man and his place in the universe that continues to command wide interest. Man as depicted in Pirandello's theater is man out of harmony with his world, man unsustained by the values that once supported his antecedents. Those few characters who occasionally display something of a positive attitude toward life do so at the price of having abandoned all hope of order and having resigned themselves to an irrational universe. Often accused of creating a non-dramatic or "cerebral" theater, Pirandello nonetheless had a profound influence on the work of Eugene O'Neill, Jean Anouilh, Jean Genet, Samuel Beckett, and Eugene Ionesco. While handling the broad abstract questions, the Italian dramatist set his characters in familiar settings and dramatized ordinary experience. Frequently he fixed his attention on matters of specific concern in personal relations. In so doing, he was drawn to an area of inquiry that has only recently begun to absorb current playwrights—the interaction of patients and physicians in the face of catastrophic illness and death. The questions raised in the dramas are those of our time, complicated even more by the rapid advance of twentieth-century technology. To find such questions at the heart of the dramatic conflict in current plays often surprises; to find them in Pirandellian drama astonishes, particularly when we consider that the dramatist pre-dated the technology. That he was able to analyze the issues at all was due precisely to his capacity to reduce a human situation to its essential meaning. That he was drawn to situations occurring most frequently in the world of medicine was due, undoubtedly, to personal experience.

Certainly such is the case with his study of madness in his greatest creation, *Henry IV*. In the newness of his dramaturgy, or, as it seemed to some, the chaos of it, he delighted in confronting his audience with subject matter that was confusing, unsettling, and even terrifying. He exposed them to issues that would not intrude upon the general consciousness for decades to come, material that was totally new, notably in terms of its unique treatment. Although Sophocles presented a study of madness in what is probably his earliest extant play, the *Ajax*, his dramatic conception differs from that of Pirandello as the classical world differs from the modern.

In late 1912 Pirandello completed one of his earliest pieces for the theater, a one-act play entitled *The Doctor's Duty*. In submitting the work to a renowned drama critic of the day, he commented that the dramatic situation invoked "a deep ethical problem" (Ragusa, 64). From our vantage point, it is clear that the problem Pirandello explored is a major one confronting the medical profession in our time—that is, the matter of providing life-sustaining treatment for the competent patient who, for diverse reasons, has expressed the wish to be allowed to die with dignity. This is exactly the issue on which Brian Clark's play *Whose Life Is It Anyway?* (1978) turns. In that recent work the hero's dilemma is complicated by his physician's access to advanced means that now makes it possible to prolong life beyond all previous expectations, certainly those of 1912, the date of Pirandello's work. Yet in some fundamental ways, specifically in the way each character relates to his physician in his life-death struggle, the heroes of both plays have much in common. The dramatic conflict at the core of both works is between the rights of patients and the rights of professionals.

The setting and plot of the Italian drama are typical of Pirandello's art. In a city of southern Italy a man recovering from a gunshot wound is being held under house arrest. Maintaining a vigil outside his bedroom, his anxious wife and cynical mother-in-law await the doctor and the lawyer. The tale that emerges is one of violence and passion. The convalescent, Tommaso Corsi, has bungled a suicide attempt following his murder of a friend who had discovered him in the act of adultery with his wife. Protesting innocence, Corsi defends himself by maintaining that it was he who was seduced by the wife and that he killed the husband only after the latter fired the first shot, the weapon apparently having changed hands in the confusion. Horrified at the sight of the corpse on the floor and the unfaithful wife jumping out the window, Corsi turned the gun on himself. The struggle that follows is between the doctor who fights to save him and the patient who, determined to die, resists his efforts.

In recounting his role in the event, the doctor, Lecci, displays all the pride of a physician whose training and skills enable him to achieve his goal:

The real trouble . . . came from an accumulation of complications, one more serious than the next and all of them quite unforeseen. I was forced to improvise remedies that were

quite often opposed to each other, and all so risky that, believe me, they'd have discouraged and stopped anyone else in my place. If I'd allowed myself for a moment to
hesitate or doubt even slightly, good-by! I can tell you that I've never in my whole career
had a satisfaction to equal this one (70).

In a departure from scientific terminology, he labels his achievement a
"miracle."

Part of the miracle is the transformation that occurs in Corsi. Having passed
the crisis, he now has a new appreciation for life, taking pleasure even in the
ordinary, familiar objects in his house. His renewed vision extends beyond his
confining walls. In his delirium he had fancied that the green blanket that covered
him was a field of green grass. The peace of an imagined countryside filled him
with hope, hope for a new beginning. In his lucid moments he begins to believe
that he can make a new start for himself in a simple pastoral existence with his
forgiving wife at his side. All that is required is a month in the country. In this
frame of mind he greets Cimetta, the lawyer. Cimetta's grim task is to remind
Corsi that he faces trial for murder, and the case for the prosecution rests on
solid ground. Cimetta sums it up: On the charge of adultery, Corsi is guilty.
Instead of being punished by the wronged husband, Corsi killed him. He then
tried to kill himself, an act that implicitly confirms his guilt and enables him to
escape punishment, since it was unsuccessful. If this were not enough, the victim
was an assistant district attorney.

In the absence of a death penalty in Italy, Corsi faces certain life imprisonment.
His sudden realization of the truth of his situation plunges him into despair and
brings us to the heart of the dramatic conflict. Corsi's dream has been of a free
existence where he can regain his self-esteem. He looks forward to working and
building a future for his family. Instead, he faces a life of confinement and
disgrace, a life he describes as one of "enforced, brutish idleness." His sense
of honor suffers at the thought of the shame his innocent wife and children will
endure. Lashing out at Lecci, he questions the doctor's right to save his life
only to reserve him for an intolerable existence in prison. In response to the
argument that he must pay for his crime, Corsi argues that his aborted suicide
followed a judgmental decision to punish himself, even more than the law would
have. The doctor's intervention prevented him from exercising control over his
own fate. Lecci's response is to cite the moral obligation of the physician to
preserve life. It is, as the play's title reminds us, his duty. In assuming the moral
agency for his patient, Lecci is acting to promote Corsi's well-being as seen
from his professional standpoint. What he fails to acknowledge is the autonomy
of his patient as a value in any physician-patient transaction. While he preserves
Corsi's life, he exposes him to the justice of those who would deprive that life
of any meaning.

His breath restored, Corsi faces the loss of his personhood and its accompanying feelings of worth and dignity. Corsi's argument hinges on the key factor
in current debate relating to life-sustaining treatment, namely, the quality of the

life to be preserved. Whether the patient is a paraplegic facing life on a respirator or a man immobilized forever within prison walls, the nature of his existence is so severely restricted as to raise questions about the distinction between life and death. The President's Commission for the Study of Ethical Problems in Medicine, which was convened within recent years for the specific purpose of studying ethical issues, concurred that decisions regarding life-sustaining treatment rest ultimately with the competent patient and recognize him as the pivotal decision-maker regarding his self-determination and encourage that sense of worth which Corsi longs for. In 1912 Pirandello reached the same conclusion. His drama ends with his hero determining his own fate. His argument concluded, Corsi, enraged, rips the bandages from his wound. Lecci moves instinctively to save him, only to be checked by the dying man's threatening cry and his own sudden recognition that he does not, in fact, have the right to interfere with his patient's wishes. For a physician, even a fictional one, to reach that conclusion long before the problem was to be examined by a presidential commission is testimony to Pirandello's genius for isolating the crucial issues in human relations.

In his masterpiece *Henry IV* Pirandello created a psychological drama in which an audience witnesses the inevitable propulsion of a mentally ill individual toward a criminal act. The plot deals with the misfortune of a wealthy aristocrat who, some twenty years prior to the play's opening, had suffered an accident, while amusing himself and his friends at a historical pageant. Impersonating the eleventh-century German emperor, Henry IV, he had fallen from his horse and sustained a severe blow to the head. Upon awakening, he began to act his role in earnest, manifesting all the symptoms of madness to the startled company. Included in the group were the lady he loved, Matilda, acting the part of Matilda of Tuscany, an enemy of the emperor's, as well as the Baron Tito Belcredi, his rival for Matilda's love.

His loving sister immediately rejects the thought of confining Henry (who is not known by any other name in the play) to an institution. She prefers to nurture the illusion which is his only source of happiness. Accordingly, she arranges for him to live in a solitary villa where her concern and her wealth succeed in reconstructing the royal residence of the German emperor. One salon is decorated to resemble the throne room. Servants are hired to impersonate various personalities in the historical figure's life. Each detail must be authentic, each participant must take his role seriously, and a requirement for employment is a thorough familiarity with the historical facts. Such accuracy is essential, for the peculiar nature of Henry's illness is that, while he is out of touch with present reality, he is sharply aware of the historical time in which he lives. Well versed in the facts regarding the political intrigues and personal relationships that constituted the world of the man whose identity he has assumed, he will tolerate no blunder on the part of the players surrounding him.

One day the son of Henry's sister arrives to fulfill his mother's dying wish that he care for his uncle who, she sensed, is close to a cure. The nephew is accompanied by a psychiatrist, Dr. Dionysus Genoni, one of many physicians who have examined Henry. The middle-aged Matilda is also there. In the intervening years she has been married and widowed, and she arrives with her beautiful daughter Frida, the living image of her former self. Completing the group is Belcredi, who has succeeded at last in becoming Matilda's lover. All follow the directives of the physician, who has diagnosed Henry's case as one of ordinary madness. Confident of a cure, Genoni proposes a unique shock treatment that consists of suddenly confronting Henry with both Matilda and her daughter dressed as the eleventh-century Matilda of Tuscany. Seeing mother and daughter as one will, he believes, restore to the patient the lost consciousness of distance and time. What Genoni does not know is that some twelve years after the accident Henry experienced a spontaneous cure of sorts and that he can be quite lucid. He has continued to play his role out of choice. Confronting contemporary life proved too painful when he became aware of the rapid passage of time and the total futility of regaining what he had lost. He characterizes himself as a hungry wolf arrived at a banquet that has been cleared away. His reaction is to retreat into the illusion that has become a refuge from a frustrating reality. He has, in short, accepted the fantasy as truth. Henry, prompted by the visitors' intrusion, reveals his true state to his "counselors." The audience discovers, moreover, that the fateful accident was the work of Belcredi. Wishing his rival out of the way, he pricked his horse from behind and caused the animal to rear. Just as we accept Henry's return to normalcy and prepare ourselves for a quick resolution of the dramatic action, the hero calmly turns to a "monk," newly arrived to take up his duties, and proceeds to dictate his memoirs, the memoirs of Henry IV!

When Henry suddenly comes upon Matilda and Frida, in costume, he is terrified. Past and present blur in one confused image. For one instant the panic-stricken man fears that he is mad once more. Only the arrival of the others confirms that he is the victim of an ill-conceived scheme. In a rage he seizes Frida, who seems the living embodiment of the life he lost, and claims her as his own. Belcredi rushes forward to free the girl, only to face a sword-wielding avenger. In one instant Henry obliterates twenty years of passivity and runs through the man who robbed him of a meaningful existence. As the physician shouts a defensive "I told you so!" to the horrified onlookers, the curtain descends on the trembling hero gathering his servants about him as if for protection. He is resolved now to remain imprisoned within the sanctuary of illusion.

While some ethical issues have become muddled by advancing technology, it is the increased awareness of the complexity of human personality which has confounded many psychological issues. Definitions of mental illness, the effective and proper treatment of the mentally ill, the quality of life in dehumanizing institutions—all are matters that pose dilemmas for professionals, frequently dividing their judgment. Pirandello's accomplishment was to ponder similar matters in the theater. *Henry IV* is, in effect, an attack on traditional definitions of madness. The playwriter's credo was the relative nature of truth. He focused his art on the illusory nature of reality by writing plays in which conflict arose from the tension between the rational and the irrational, the conscious and the subconscious in human affairs. Every scene in *Henry IV* raises questions regarding the consciousness of the hero's actions. Henry continually slips in and out of the role he has assumed. One can never be sure if he is, in truth, insane since the fundamental question "What is insanity?" must first be examined. When Henry informs his servants of his assumed madness, one of them comments, "I wish I had known that it was not true." Henry surprises us with the response, conveyed in a tone of anguish, according to the stage directions, "Does it appear to you that it is not true?" (305). Such thematic content was new and perplexing. And, in some plays, notably *Six Characters in Search of an Author*, Pirandello gleefully confused the issues further by challenging the nature of the illusion created by the dramatic art itself.

The havoc that Pirandello caused in the theater with his unique explorations anticipated by some forty years the disorder in evidence at an international convention of psychiatrists when the participants considered the case of a living individual who shared much in common with the fictional Henry IV. The deliberations received much attention in Rome in 1961 and were considered of sufficient interest to be reported in a New York newspaper. The account reads as follows:

Rome, Sept. 13—An Italian who is convinced he is the reincarnation of an ancient Egyptian nobleman has baffled delegates to an international convention here on psychoneurotic illness. Baron Ricardo Ricciardelli says: "I am the reincarnation of a high dignitary of the court of Amenophus IV, the great pharaoh. In my former life I committed a horrible crime and now a curse follows me. In order to find peace I must get rid of my fortune."

His children, fearful of losing their inheritance, produced their father's diary in court in an attempt to prove him mentally unbalanced. The judge merely ruled that Baron Ricciardelli might no longer administer his business affairs and huge agricultural estate. The Baron will not be committed to a mental institution.

Baron Ricciardelli once was confined to a clinic. He spent all his time there studying books on Pharaonic dynasties and came out more convinced than ever of his reincarnation.

In Italy a man can think he is anybody, so long as he does no harm.

Some psychiatrists at the convention are astonished by the judge's decision not to put the Baron in a mental institution.

"However, there is much we do not understand about inheritance and inherited complexes," one delegate commented.

An international convention for the study of genetics and hereditary characteristics in man is meeting in Rome at the same time. A geneticist commented:

"We do not overlook the fact that Buddhists believe in reincarnation and Buddha himself felt he must give away his family fortune before he could find peace. Nobody at this convention is going to say Buddha was mentally unbalanced, and neither are the international psychiatrists in their convention and neither is the judge who heard Baron Ricciardelli's case" (Ebener, 29).

If the psychiatrists at an international convention in 1961 could not agree on a definition of madness or the need for institutionalization, we could hardly expect their predecessors to do so in 1921 when psychiatry as a discipline was a relative newcomer to the medical school curriculum. Henry's psychiatrist is baffled by his patient. He cannot understand his lucid madness. He is mystified by the reasoned account that Henry gives of his frequent hallucinations: "Phantoms in general are nothing more than trifling disorders of the spirit: images we cannot contain within the bounds of sleep. They reveal themselves even when we are awake, and they frighten us" (301). What Dr. Genoni fails to grasp is the extent to which fiction has become the source of both truth and happiness for Henry. His patient understands his physician's inadequacy as he admonishes him, "I am not a madman according to your way of thinking" (310).

The physician's way is the way of scientific dogmatism. He remains detached from his patient while applying the rules of logic in devising a cure. In representing the scientific community, Dr. Genoni articulates the objective medical tradition. What he lacks is the perspective of the artist with its imaginative faculty that would enable him to glimpse the irrational and illusory nature of Henry's universe. Thus, the clinical empathy considered vital in establishing a satisfactory physician-patient relationship, particularly in cases of mental illness, never develops. Dr. Genoni's narrow vision causes him to err in providing effective treatment. Truly believing his patient to be insane, he nonetheless expects him to react in a most reasonable way to the shock he receives. The blunder is devastating.

Genoni takes as his model the god of the Deists whose sole relation with man consisted of setting his world in motion like a giant clock. The Doctor, too, wishes to set a clock in motion. His clock is his patient. He reveals his goal: "We may hope to set him going again, like a watch which has stopped at a certain hour . . . just as if we had our watches in our hands and were waiting for that other watch to go again.—A shake—so—and let's hope it'll tell the time again after its long stop" (295). The metaphor of the divine clockmaker, central to the thinking of the Deists, for whom reason was the touchstone to moral validity, suits Pirandello's character as well, for it reveals much about the physician's lofty self-image, his faith in rationalism, and his perception of his patient as object.

From a certain perspective, however, Genoni is closer in identity to a Greek deity. Dionysus, celebrated as the god of wine and revelry, is also associated with madness. In the process of perfecting the art of wine-making, he sampled the new brew without moderation (contrary to the Greek ideal) and apparently went quite mad. The madness was viewed as the vengeance of Hera on Dionysus for being the illegitimate offspring of her philandering husband, Zeus. As a result of his affliction, Dionysus was obliged to wander about in search of a cure. Upon being cured, he journeyed throughout the world bestowing the precious elixir on mortals. Madness, which now became an infallible weapon for him, accompanied him wherever he appeared. Consequently, his cult was dreaded in Greece. The worship of Dionysus raises some interesting questions regarding the primitive view of intoxication as a form of madness, while revealing the confusion surrounding the nature of madness since earliest times. By acting as a Dionysus, Genoni further complicates his patient's life and precipitates the catastrophic ending of the drama. Referring to the travesty that was designed to cure him, Henry recalls to our mind the god when he informs his physician, "Do you know, Doctor, that for a moment you ran the risk of making me mad again?" (309).

In the physician's failure to achieve a meaningful therapeutic relationship with the hero of the drama, in his incapacity to comprehend the complexity of his patient's mental state and the fragility of his emotions, Pirandello exposes a major problem existing between physicians and patients in current medical practice. He also indicates where the solution may be found—in the only reality where Henry can exist, in the realm of the intersubjective, where caring human relationships have the power to heal.

A recent and popular subject of scientific investigation has involved individuals who have experienced a form of clinically defined death and who have been resuscitated by means of advanced technology that is applied routinely in our modern medical settings. The noted psychiatrist Elisabeth Kübler-Ross has provided the major impetus to the movement. Her interviews with an increasingly available number of subjects have produced some findings which, though not scientifically proven, nevertheless pose some intriguing questions regarding the nature of life and death. In the process, a number of unresolved theological questions of concern are also raised. The psychological trauma for the patient is frequently of such magnitude as to alter significantly his perception of reality. For the most part the event has a positive effect, with the individual gaining new courage and losing his fear of death.

Long before Kübler-Ross and the advances in resuscitative techniques were gaining wide attention, Pirandello was turning his attention to the emotional state of the subject and the moral dilemma produced in such a situation. In his play *Lazzaro*, which is a modern reworking of the New Testament account of the man who died and was restored to life by Christ, Pirandello seized the opportunity to examine the conflict between medical technology and traditional Christian thinking, placing under his microscope the elusive relationship between man and God. The Lazarus figure of the drama, Diego Spina, is a religious formalist who is obsessed with thoughts of death and who constantly practices sacrifices and self-mortification as a means of gaining rewards and avoiding punishment in the afterlife. A crisis occurs when, upon being struck by an automobile and pronounced dead at the scene, he is resuscitated by means of an injection of adrenalin to the heart. The medical facts are withheld from him by his physician, Dr. Gionni, who knows of his distrust of science and his uncompromising belief that only God can bring the dead back to life. Despite efforts to the contrary, he learns the truth by chance and suffers a predictable trauma. Instantly, he surmises that since he has no recollection of his death, there is no life beyond earth, and since he, the most pious of men, did not see God, there is no God. Questioning the existence of the soul, he plunges into an existential abyss.

In this drama Pirandello presents what was to his audience an extraordinary event, though it is actually a preview of what has now become a daily event. True, he cannot be expected to have the medical knowledge to create a physician who convinces us with his expertise. Compared to current techniques, an injection of adrenalin appears almost crude and wholly inadequate. But he does anticipate Kübler-Ross's findings regarding the psychological impact of the event on the participant, and he does present a convincing portrait of an individual whose view of reality is completely altered.

Prior to his moral crisis, Diego had erred in viewing God as an abstraction existing beyond his present reality. In so doing, he denied the vitality and joy of life. When struck by the automobile, his vital functions ceased. But his death, in fact, was the joyless existence he had been leading. After his physical death, a transformed Diego is led by his seminarian son to believe in a God who is at one with the soul existing within himself. Rejecting the dichotomy of body and soul, he comes to view life as an external present. Death is simply a moment during which the spirit is renewed in a glimpse of the whole of existence.

Like many patients of Kübler-Ross, Pirandello's hero overcomes his fear of death, and, despite parting company at times with traditional Christian thinking, renews what are essentially religious values; he also savors the joy of life with new intensity. The miracle that recalls him to life is due directly to medical intervention. Diego's doctor, however, reconciles the traditional with the modern account by affirming that he serves simply as an instrument of God, who works His will through the miracles of science.

Pirandello's personal interests aside, we can account for the artist's early probings in areas of current concern by recalling Erich Fromm's comment in a lecture: "I think there is no such thing as medical ethics. There are only universal ethics applied to specific human situations." In exploring the dramatic world Pirandello has created, we sense the wide scope of his art. And we recognize as our guide a broad, philosophic, humanistic conscience.

WORKS CITED

Clark, Brian. *Whose Life Is It Anyway?* New York: Avon, 1978.
Ebener, Charlotte. "Baron's 'Reincarnation' Has Doctors Up in the Air." *New York Post* (September 13, 1961): 29.
Pirandello, Luigi. *The Doctor's Duty.* Trans. William Murray. In *Pirandello's One-Act Plays.* New York: Funk and Wagnalls, 1970.
————. *Henry IV.* Ed. Anthony Caputi. Trans. Edward Storer. In *Modern Plays.* New York: W. W. Norton, 1966.
Ragusa, Olga. *Pirandello: An Approach to His Theater.* Edinburgh: Edinburgh University Press, 1980.

Part Two

BACKGROUND INFORMATION

7

Pirandello: The Sicilian Experience

George Bernstein

Pirandello is a child of Sicilian culture in many respects, even though he spent most of his life outside that tormented island. The family life out of which he came was marked by a father whose powerful presence inspired both fear and respect and who risked his life on more than one occasion. When Luigi Pirandello became a young man who had begun to acquire a literary reputation, he was still the son who would submit to his father's will in the crucial matter of choosing a wife. The regional dialect around his home in Agrigento was one he not only learned but also employed in some of his writing. Sometimes he translated from standard Italian into dialect, and on other occasions from the dialect to the standard. In the University of Bonn, his dissertation topic was the dialect of Agrigento. In many ways he carried his identification with the island culture throughout his life.

Scholars in history and the social sciences as well as literary observers have interpreted that Sicilian culture in their own fashion. Historians have often done research in Sicilian villages and cities, while writers about literature have often used that literature itself as the source for their view of island mores. The general consensus is that the historical past has led Sicilians to place enormous stock in their sense of honor and respect and to be extremely vigilant about their women for fear of loss of honor by the women, a loss touching the family as a whole. If honor is stained, and this need not occur in the sexual domain alone, there must be a way of avenging oneself.

The desire for revenge is but one major aspect of the larger cultural dimension of the need to follow form. Much of how people live is determined by their understanding of the proper form to be followed in human relationships. Within that world are such matters as greeting people in the right way, respecting women, and recognizing the inviolability of property. Tension both in Sicilian culture and in Pirandello's work often derives from the boundaries of form having been violated by sexual passion, envy, the desire for independence, and other feelings that threaten the traditional way of life.

SICILY AND PIRANDELLO

The Sicilian novelist and essayist Leonardo Sciascia has reflected on the relationship between Sicily and Pirandello for many years. Perhaps the most important of his works on this question is *Pirandello e la Sicilia* in which Sciascia views Sicily as a historical essayist who reaches back to the time of the ancient Greek settlements, through the Arab conquests, and into the centuries of Spanish domination. In the essay on Girgenti (Agrigento) he uses the Spanish historian Américo Castro's masterwork, *La realidad histórica de España*. Castro argues that Spain, rather than a nation, is a way of being. Sciascia contends that Sicily is also a way of being, *un modo di essere*. One important aspect of that being was to develop a critical and analytical way of looking at things and at the same time not to want to change life's most basic conditions. There was also an exaggerated individualism in which a "virile exaltation would play an important role." (16). The conquests that Sicilians endured for so many centuries would turn them away from believing that collective, organized protest made any sense.

The first chapter of Federico Vittore Nardelli's biography of Pirandello is entitled *La Patria*. Nardelli, like Sciascia, devotes attention to the Greek beginnings, though much more sparingly. Like numerous others who have written about Pirandello's Sicily, he portrays Girgenti (Agrigento) partially through descriptions provided by Pirandello in his writing. Both Nardelli and Sciascia believe some Sicilian traits can be traced back to the Arab period, perhaps most of all jealousy and a "poisoned melancholy" (Nardelli, 4–5).

Gaspare Giudice's biography, *Luigi Pirandello*, provides an introduction in the first chapter entitled *La Sicilia*. In this case too, the author believes that the creation of a setting for Pirandello's life is in the past, but the roots of Pirandello are in midcentury, in the "circumstances and destiny of his childhood and those of his cultural education" (2). Part of Pirandello's conditioning, according to Giudice, was the family experience with midcentury political upheavals that contributed to Sicily's continued semicolonial status within a united Italy. The family's predisposition toward Garibaldism and anti-Bourbonism can be seen in some of Pirandello's writings, perhaps especially in the 1913 novel *I Vecchi e i giovani*. The Sicily depicted by the biographer is one of disappointment in political activity and an antipathy toward the state.

Along with Sicily and its values, Giudice presents the father as the towering figure of authority, one to whom the son Luigi would acquiesce in some very crucial ways in the course of his life. According to Giudice, the son would continue into manhood as a person of extreme sensibility to whom a feeling of ambiguity was natural. His audacity would be demonstrated in the world of literature; the father's, in contrast, would occur in confronting enemies and family in everyday life.

Giudice says he depended to a considerable degree on Pirandello's own writings as sources. Much of what Giudice writes is based on "an intuition fundamentally born from the reading of the work, with an understanding of it as continuous autobiography" (553). Nardelli's biography leans toward the hagiographic, although it has the advantage, as Giudice notes, of the author's having spoken at length with Pirandello himself.

Monique LeRoux in her article "De la sicilianité: Sciascia lecteur de Pirandello" is interested in both Sciascia and Pirandello. When, for example, she quotes Sciascia from *Le Parrochie di Regalpetra*, his words might apply almost equally to Pirandello: "All my books are one. It is a book on Sicily which touches all the sensitive points of past and present, and which is articulated as the history of the perpetual defeat of reason, and of those who personally were carried off and destroyed in that defeat." For LeRoux, Sciascia has created a Pirandellian world (178).

Giuseppe Padellaro in his *Trittico siciliano* avoids historical context and instead paints a psychological portrait composed of a series of aphorisms about Sicilian life. So, for example, he writes that the only thing that can make a Sicilian forget "decline in the recent past is a tender word . . . from the family . . . and revenge" (71). Perhaps Padellaro's interpretation is simplified, but a fair amount of literature in the social sciences reinforces in prodigious detail the points he makes so pithily.

Bonaventura Tecchi, in his article "Pirandello siciliano ed europeo," writes from the point of view of an Italian scholar who has researched German romanticism. Tecchi argues that it was not necessary for Pirandello to go to Germany to be influenced by romantic melancholy and irony because it was already present in Leopardi. However, Pirandello lacks the German romantic faith in the ultimate unity of things in the universe. According to Tecchi, Pirandello was convinced that things were disintegrating and that there was no ultimate clarification (80). At the same time, Tecchi sees Pirandello as a typical representative of an age of crisis. The first earthquake in the series was the French Revolution. Pirandello, then, is participating in a "literature of crisis" that existed in Italy and in other societies. Tecchi is one of many scholars who seeks to establish connections between the major political upheavals of the last third of the eighteenth century and some new directions in literature. Tecchi argues that the traditional concepts of the self (*Io*) were challenged in German romanticism by such devices as playing with the mirror, by employing it to suggest the precariousness of the self, of the multiplicity of images, of the unreliability of self-perception and perception of others. History and literary criticism blend in Tecchi to portray Pirandello as a figure of crisis.

The literature on Pirandello's relationship to Sicily often stresses one or both of two themes: first, the powerful effect of historical circumstances on the outlook and behavior of the family and, second, the complex relationship of form, illusion, and self-delusion. The two themes are present in his work.

ASPECTS OF SICILIAN CULTURE

Historically Sicilians have believed that they had to look after their own interests and that their own interests could rather easily and seriously conflict with those of another. Others would pursue theirs to one's own detriment. Therefore, a world of clever defenses had to be erected, and one had to develop *furberia* (cunning) and to avoid appearing gullible. A person did not wish to be called a fool, but perhaps even more important, no one would want to be maneuvered into a disadvantageous position. A person had to be constantly on the alert to the menace presented by the *furberia* of others. In a world of what appeared to be limited resources and wealth, people had to see to it that their own property not be stolen by others. The property might be land, the family home, or, for example, a wife or daughter (Schneider and Schneider, 82–86). At the same time, if a person were not personally involved, it was possible to admire the guile and stratagems of others.

It might be argued, as Sciascia states in his novel *Mafia Vendetta*, that "the family is the Sicilian's State" (95). In Italian and Sicilian history there is a long-standing antagonism between the government and Sicilians who see themselves as invariably exploited by the outsider. In previous centuries, there were many outsiders and conquerors, among them Arabs, Normans, the Hohenstaufen, the Angevins, and the Aragonese. In addition, various Spanish administrations ruled for more than four hundred years (Smith, 115–70).

It is perhaps no wonder that the Sicilians developed a whole series of social and psychological defenses, among which was what a character in Lampedusa's *Il Gattopardo* saw as a "terrifying insularity of mind." A profound sense of the need for self-defense grew over the centuries, and since military defense had proved fruitless, other forms were more pervasive, more deeply rooted, and often more subtle.

If Sicilians decided that they should not allow their fate to be determined by intruders, they had to protect what they already had and needed to keep. It was out of this complex interplay of conquest and reactions to it, and the impoverishment of land and people, that a code of honor emerged as one of the most important elements of a culture of self-defense. Men who were heads of families, somewhat analogous to states responsible for territorial protection and aggression, believed it imperative that they protect their patrimonies. They made a claim for the respect of others, and underlying this claim was the understanding that an assault on family rights and prerogatives should be met with swift retaliation. If there were disputes over land, grazing, and water rights, they would be seen not only as economic conflicts, but also as conflicts where family honor was at stake. Action, sometimes overt and swift, at other times subtle and slow, would be taken if the family saw its honor threatened. Insults might range from something serious, as one's daughter or wife being raped, or being a lover outside the bonds of matrimony, to something as seemingly innocuous as who would offer an aperitif to whom at a bar (Schneider, 1–24).

Warding off aggression meant, perhaps more than anything else, seeing that the honor of the family's women was protected. Male family members were responsible for the women's honor, and good fathers had to see to it that their daughter's virginity was preserved until marriage. Woman's nature was seen as being in conflict with the interests and reputation of the family (Garbaccia, 4–6). Young women had to be kept in a kind of semiseclusion so that they would learn modesty (Pitt-Rivers). If a daughter lost her virginity before marriage, it was a stain on the family's honor. The family had failed because for the most part the girl's complicity was assumed and, as a result, the general interests of the entire family subverted (Schneider and Schneider, 86–89).

Honor, maintained and lost, in sexual and other matters, is often a concern in Pirandello's writings. In *La Giara* there is the honor of the craftsman Zi'Dima, who sees his masterwork insulted by the landowner. In *Il berreto a sonagli* an older employee of the household has a wife who has had an affair with the master of the house, and the old man devises an ingenious revenge without resorting to murder. In *Il realtà del sogno* the father, in keeping with Sicilian mores, is "more jealous than a tiger . . . " and has "inculcated . . . in his daughters . . . a dread of men" (Novelle per un anno II, 655). In *Il buon cuore* a seventeen year old is not supposed to tell anyone she is pregnant. In the story "*Zia Michelina*" a fortyish woman is accused not so much of sexually dishonoring herself but of wanting to take advantage financially of someone much younger than she.

These are all variations of the same basic theme: honor must be protected. If it is lost, the center of one's self in Sicilian society is irreparably damaged. Therefore, it is imperative to fight for one's honor when it is threatened and to attempt to recover some of it when it has already been stained. If it has been attacked, there is more than one way to deal with it, depending partly on the social and economic circumstances of the persons offended. One may respond with rage as does the daughter in *Sei Personaggi* and not quite be able to find the appropriate channel for revenge. Or it may be the husband Ciampi in *Il berretto a sonagli* who, with a guile made crystal-clear to others, offers his recipe for revenge. Resentment, rage, revenge, and honor intertwine in Sicilian culture and in some of Pirandello's work as well.

FAMILY LIFE OF LUIGI PIRANDELLO

In many traditional families, the father has often been portrayed as a distant figure with awesome power. Luigi Pirandello was no stranger to that situation. Stefano Pirandello, the playwright's father, could stand up for his own rights and at the same time prove an intimidating presence to both wife and children.

Within a Sicilian context, the father had more than his fair share of macho courage. Federico Vittore Nardelli reports this in a particularly dramatic incident (16–17).

Stefano Pirandello had rented a sulfur mine that promised to be profitable, and so he was quickly approached by Cola Camizzi, capo of the Agrigento mafia, who expected to take his fair share of whatever might be earned. In the course of their first conversation, Gamizzi touched Stefano Pirandello on the buttocks. The latter quickly turned, smacked the mafioso, and proceeded to pummel him in the face, leaving him swollen with bruises. Stefano Pirandello then left, but Camizzi caught up with him. Armed with two weapons, the mafioso fired and wounded his challenger. Stefano Pirandello looked as though he might be finished off, but a servant present picked up the larger weapon, which Camizzi had put down when he expected to finish off his enemy with a revolver, and slammed Camizzi on the head. The mafioso staggered away while Pirandello fired after him. Camizzi was given a seven-year jail sentence, and, because the father threatened to kill him if he returned, he stayed away from Agrigento.

The father could not permit his person to be treated contemptuously by someone with power who wished to show his superiority. Midnineteenth-century Sicilian culture was often ruled by mafiosi and to challenge even that small-scale gesture by Camizzi was to invite serious trouble. But the sense of honor and inviolability in Pirandello's father turned out to be stronger than that in the mafioso.

As a child, adolescent, and young man, Pirandello had a difficult relationship with his father. Running a mine was no easy task in the mid-nineteenth century (Sonnino, 349–51). The son would demonstrate to himself and to others that he did not want to compete in the more gross, demanding, and cruel world of hard, physical labor in the mines (Ambroise, 14–30). However, the son would not escape the world of demanding social and psychological relationships. Seeing himself as a person who desperately needed to communicate with others, he reached out to his parents, but apparently they did not respond with the human contact he sought. When Pirandello as an adult referred to the spiritual life of the writer, such a view could be seen as evolving partly out of his life as an author, but it might also be seen in part as how he believed himself to be different from his father.

Gaspare Giudice believes that the relationship between husband and wife in *L'esclusa* (1893) is a portrait of Pirandello's mother and father. It is worth quoting not only because of its significance for Pirandello's life but also because it casts light on some aspects of Sicilian culture at that time and later:

... It was impossible to reason with him. ... For many years she had learnt to judge every sorrow, every grief, not on its own terms, but in terms of the rage it would arouse in her husband. ... Sometimes all that was needed for the entire house to be plunged into mourning was that an object should be spoilt or broken—not even an object of any great value, but simply an object which could not be immediately replaced ... You had

to see him . . . when the object was broken. He regarded it as a lack of respect not for the object, which was relatively valueless, but for himself. . . .
In so many years of marriage she had managed to mollify him a little, by treating him gently, by forgiving him offences which were not always slight, but without infringing on her own dignity and without making her forgiveness weigh on him. But still he would sometimes fly into a rage over a mere trifle . . . and since nobody dared breathe a word, he would sink into a black, silent fury for weeks on end. . . . He suspected that many things were kept hidden from him—and if he ever found out that something *had*, even if it were years later, he would give vent to his accumulated irritation without even thinking that he was being unjust and that everything had been done simply so as not to vex him (Sciascia, *Pirandello e la Sicilia*, 60–61).

One might study this passage as a psychological portrait of Pirandello's family, but also view it as a picture of Sicilian life. The father as a figure of absolute authority is presented here. To the outside world, the husband-father would have to see that he not be mocked either in deeds or in words (Bell, 90–95). That tradition was a terribly complicated one, as many of Pirandello's stories testify. The proper form, the protection of form, and the insistence that it be observed are frequent themes in Italian literature, reflecting the deep fear that a flaunting of conventions is a threat not only to the stability and security of the family, but to the foundations of human society. The forms, therefore, are not simply forms. There is no fundamental distinction between life and form. Pirandello's father challenging the mafioso was part of that basic cultural pattern. At the same time, psychological reality threatens the power of form. The conflict between the two is often present. In *Il berretto a sonagli* the injured person carries form to the farthest point, insisting that someone be committed to a mental institution to protect his name and honor. Face-saving was crucial (Simione, xxxi–xxxiv).

The desire for proper form was part of Pirandello's family life, both the one he came from and the one he created. But that deep need for propriety was often threatened by terrible passions, not all of them sexual. The possible relationships between form and passion would become even more complicated by Pirandello's need for openness, at least in his writing. He sought a certain kind of honesty. The search was perhaps doomed to failure in his family situation and in the context of Sicilian traditions.

The forces of rage and evasion also existed in the family he helped create with Antonietta Portulano, the daughter of his father's business partner. His wife would later become a psychopathic paranoid, not only providing disturbing sources for his creative work but also making part of his life a domestic horror.

A childhood friend, Antonio De Gobernatis, relates some of the conversation he had with Luigi Pirandello about his marriage:

> . . . Putting his hand on my shoulder, he told me he was getting married. I thought he was joking . . .
>
> 'Do you know her?', he asked me candidly.

'No. Do you?'

'No. I'm going to Porto Empedocle to meet her' (Giudice, 163).

In this rather terse exchange we have many aspects of traditional engagement and marriage before the mid-twentieth century (Maraspini, 136–96). Pirandello did not appear to resent the fact that his father had sought to arrange the marriage. This situation occurred in many countries. When his father presented the name of Antonietta Portulano as a prospect, the son had been to the University of Palermo and of Bonn, had begun to establish a reputation for himself as a man of letters, had lived in Rome, and had had his doctoral thesis accepted. Geographically and to a much lesser extent psychologically, he had moved away from Agrigento and Sicily, but he still accepted the traditional authority of the father in arranging the marriage. If it was not a love marriage, the pair might in the course of time come to love one another or at least have some affection for one another. In any case, the focus in the arranged marriage was the continuation of the institution of marriage itself and the assertion of traditional customs (Maraspini, 171).

The two concerned families arranged to meet. Pirandello's friend De Gobernatis reports that when Pirandello spoke to him about the encounter, the latter thought Antonietta Portulano "suitable to be a wife" (Giudice, 57). This statement might be read to mean that she would be the kind of wife that a young Sicilian husband would wish to have: proper, submissive, and providing at least the appearance of being willing to learn from her husband. But she also came from a family of terribly jealous and watchful people. She had a father who would indulge in paroxysms of rage. Apparently, when she was out walking with young friends, if she simply looked to one side or the other, he would explode. If one kept one's eyes forward, then one affirmed one's innocence, and a glance to either side was a seduction, a provocation. So Antonietta Portulano brought to her marriage her experience with family rage. Pirandello had already experienced it in his own family, but now something new would be added: her traditional fear of seduction and adultery, of betrayal, and of soiling the family name which played such a role in Sicilian life. Some of Pirandello's work would contain echoes of his wife's own pathological paranoia. In her madness she often accused him of flirtations and infidelity. In the terrors of her mind she created situations similar to those Pirandello created in the world of art. Rage and jealousy occurred in both his life and his art, as well as in Sicilian culture.

SICILY IN PIRANDELLO'S LITERARY WORK

One important example of the Sicilian influence in Pirandello is his translation into Sicilian dialect of a number of his works, or in some cases from dialect into standard Italian. The original *Pensaci, Giacominu* became *Pensaci, Giacomino* at the Teatro Nazionale in July, 1916. *Liolà* was given in dialect in the

Teatro Argentino in Rome in November 1916. *Il Berretto a sonagli* was translated into dialect and also given in the same theater on June 27, 1917. This was soon followed by *La Giara* in dialect at the Teatro Nazionale in July 1917. *La patente* was staged in dialect in the Teatro Argentino in February 1919.

Although we should not exaggerate Pirandello's commitment to translations from and into dialect, the activity requires explanation. Pirandello must have felt some need to reach back into his roots, to ensure that the original speech patterns he had heard as a child and youth would not be lost. The use of dialect may also have been another way of attempting to present a reality that he considered authentic. The Sicily that he experienced and that he portrayed was almost never idealized. A romantic journalist paying attention to the dialect might very well have related it to such things as the beauty of the moon, the seductive odor of summer blossoms, and the power of romantic emotions expressed by Sicilians. But for the most part, Pirandello's fascination with the island, in dialect or standard Italian, was with the torment and disappointments that were inevitable. He would not avoid the squalid and the illusory (Fido, 554–555). The use of dialect would not be a means of romanticizing Sicilian life, but of showing the harsher aspects of reality.

Pirandello used the Sicilian experience in his first novel, *L'esclusa* (1908). The protagonist, Marta Ayala, suffers ostracism from her husband, her father, and others in the community where she lives. She is innocent of any moral lapse, but later, ironically, she will find respectability again, even though she committed adultery. Douglas Radcliff-Umstead observes that portions of this novel present the Sicilian need for "dialectical demonstration of their point of view" (130–31). One must prove in the course of time that one was right, even if that demonstration should occur years after the event. But that dialectical component is accompanied by the need for revenge. Early in the novel, Marta Ayala's husband insists that a duel must be fought to protect his honor. There is an interplay of a certain kind of Sicilian logic in argument, and the need to vindicate oneself through action. It is probably no accident that the region of Agrigento is historically a center of mafia activity. The notion of *omertà* and other aspects of the mafia code are more extreme examples of the ethic already present in much of the society. Honor must be salvaged when it has been threatened, and one must inspire respect (Blok, 172–173).

A situation can begin as a love relationship and become transformed into one in which saving face, that is, protecting one's sense of honor, becomes crucial (Ragusa, 77–78). In *Il berretto a sonagli*, the furious Beatrice feels she must avenge herself against her husband and his mistress. That wild thirst for revenge is challenged by the old clerk, Ciampa, who wishes to protect his honor since it is his young wife, Nina, who is the master's playmate.

What are the alternatives as Ciampa presents them? He lays them out to the astonishment of others in the room:

. . . I say—with the greatest calm in the world—that this evening, or tomorrow, when my wife returns to the house, I will split her head open with an ax. And I will not kill her alone for that would merely give pleasure to the Signora. I must also kill him, the cavaliere. I'm forced to. I have no choice . . .

The others cry out that it is madness, and this inspires Ciampa to present an alternative with Sicilian *furberia* to the mistress of the house:

I gone crazy? No, pardon me, you're the one who's gone crazy. Your brother recognizes it, the commissioner recognizes it . . . Your mama, everyone! And therefore you're crazy! If you're crazy, you must go to the insane asylum! It's simple!

Others do not quite understand why, and Ciampa explains:

. . . Don't you see that this is the only way? For her! For the president! For everyone! Don't you see that she's made her husband ridiculous, and now she must make amends before the entire province? If you say: "She's *insane!*" everything's finished, everyone understands. Insane, she must be cared for and cured. Only that way will I be freed from the necessity of vengeance (*Sicilian Comedies* 46–48).

Although almost all cultures of the world frown on adultery, the response within particular cultures has varied from condescending social distance to revenge through murder. In *Il berretto a sonagli* Pirandello portrays one real possibility: killing the adulterous partner as well as the lover. In this play and in other works of his, honor must be satisfied. In his works, as in the world of Sicily, an insult that is public or in danger of becoming a public matter must be dealt with. When Pirandello's father was touched by the local mafia boss, there was quick retaliation for the public insult: a physical beating and shooting. Honor could be satisfied in a visible, physical form. In *Il berretto* the threat of murder is but one possible answer to honor stained. The plot leads to something more refined, and also quite consistent with the Sicilian moral code. If, in a sense, the public face is everything, then a means must be found to protect it. If a presentation of reality is offered to the world by someone who is insane, then the accusation itself can be shown to be insane. Ciampa's honor is protected, and it is possible to continue to pretend that nothing has happened as far as the life of the community is concerned. In the perennial conflict between reality and appearance, the choice is made for appearance. Form will conquer.

When Pirandello wrote about the struggle between appearance and reality and the need to wear masks, he worked not only as a creative person who had found his central concern, but also as a Sicilian who expressed the torments of life on the island. That larger context of troubles included the terrible insularity of Sicilian experiences, and perhaps a permanent sense of insecurity that made so much of the fear of having one's things (*roba*) lost (LeRoux, 173). Among the "things" that might be lost was one's wife. If there was such a danger—particularly through the threat of adultery—one had to act to protect not only the property, but also matters like public face, a sense of honor, and the rightness of appearances.

In this powerful world of appearances and the need to sustain them, there is nevertheless a desire to escape them. The author and some of his characters seem to suffer from much the same dilemma. On the one hand, there is the knowledge and experience that have come from life on the island, testifying to the great force of the cultural tradition. Yet there is also the desire to escape the pain of such confinement. In some important respects, Pirandello himself managed to do so. He fled to Bonn, found his home in Rome, and later traveled to many countries where his plays were performed. He also acquired international fame, which may also constitute a way of leaving the region one comes from. At the same time, Sicily is a way of life not easily escaped. Often his characters are people who realize that a horrible game is being played, that they are caught in some net, that they must try to escape. If they can, they believe they will not be characters, not those with masks imposed by their culture, but persons with a freedom they had not had before. The desire to flee from being a character created from the outside is a theme underlying some of Pirandello's work. Emanuele Licastro puts it this way:

The visible struggle of the majority of Pirandello's protagonists . . . is against roles or positions in society, positions which may become roles. The character who wrestles with his role wants to change from a player of a part into a person. A role is alienating because it is only a fragment of the totality of a human being; a role denies man his authenticity (54).

The "authenticity" that Licastro suggests people long for is indeed a deep desire of the Sicilians and others in Pirandello's world, and to some degree in the world of the Sicilians themselves. Both the case of the artistic creation and the real world present enormous obstacles. If Beatrice in *Il berretto* cries out, "Mi libero! Mi libero! Mi libero!," her efforts will lead her to a mental institution. Not only will she not have her revenge, but she will lose for a time whatever security came from the social role that she played in her husband's social class and in the home in which the play is acted out. She is worse off at the end. As Olga Ragusa has said in reference not only to this play but also to *Liolà* and *La giara*, "the margin of freedom that can be won is minimal" (83).

Rage, vengeance, illusions, and deceptions almost always emerge victorious in the world created by Pirandello. All these elements can be interpreted as crucial to Sicilian life. They were not what Pirandello might have wished as central passions of the island, but he sought to depict reality rather than romanticize it.

It was an island he never quite escaped, even in death. In his will he asked that he be returned to where he was born if any of his ashes were still left:

Burn me. As soon as my body has been burned the ashes must be thrown to the winds, for I want nothing, not even my ashes to remain. But if this cannot be done the funeral urn must be taken to Sicily and walled into some rough stone near Agrigento, where I was born (Giudice, 546).

Although his first choice was to return to the universe, his second was to return to the region of his birth, childhood, youth, and early adulthood. His experiences with his family and with his art would all finally lead him back to where he began.

WORKS CITED

Alvaro, Corrado. "Prefazione." *Novelle per un anno*, Luigi Pirandello. Milan: Arnoldo Mondadori, 1975. 6–41.

Ambroise, Claude. *Invito alla lettura di Sciascia*. Milan: Mursia, 1988.

Bell, Rudolph. *Fate and Honor, Family and Village: Demographic and Cultural Changes in Rural Italy since 1800*. Chicago: University of Chicago Press, 1979.

Blok, Anton. *The Mafia of an Italian Village 1860–1960. A Study of Violent Peasant Entrepreneurs*. New York: Harper Torchbooks, 1975.

Fido, Franco. "Una novella 'siciliana' di Pirandello e i suoi rapporti col verismo." *Atti del Congresso Internazionale di Studi Pirandelliani. 2–5 Ottobre 1961*. n.p.p.: Le Monnier, 1961. 553–58.

Garbaccia, Donna R. *From Sicily to Elizabeth Street. Housing and Social Change Among Italian Immigrants, 1880–1930*. Albany: State University of New York Press, 1984.

Giudice, Gaspare. *Luigi Pirandello*. Turin: UTET, 1963.

LeRoux, Monique. "De la sicilianité: Sciascia lecteur de Pirandello." *Revue de littérature comparée*. No. 2 (April-June 1985): 171–78.

Licastro, Emanuele. "Pirandello: Conversation with Sicily." *Canadian Journal of Italian Studies*, Vol. 6, Nos. 22–23 (1983):52–59.

Maraspini, A. L. *The Study of an Italian Village*. Paris: Mouton, 1968.

Nardelli, Federico Vittore. *Vita segreta di Pirandello*. Rome: Vito Bianco Editore, 1962.

Padellaro, Giuseppe. *Trittico siciliano. Verga, Pirandello, Quasimodo*. Milan: Rizzoli Editore, 1969.

Pirandello, Luigi. *Il berretto a sonagli, la giara, il piacere dell'onestà*. ed. Corrado Simioni. Milan: Arnoldo Mondadori, 1987.

———. *Naked Masks. Five Plays by Luigi Pirandello*. Ed. Eric Bentley. New York: E. P. Dutton, 1952.

———. *Novelle per un anno*. 2 vols. Milan: Arnoldo Mondadori, 1975.

———. *Novelle per un anno. La giara*. Milan: Arnoldo Mondadori, 1987.

———. *Novelle per un anno. L'uomo solo*. Ed. Corrado Simioni. Milan: Arnoldo Mondadori, 1970.

———. *I vecchi e i giovani*. Ed. Corrado Simioni. Milan: Arnoldo Mondadori, 1987.

Pitt-Rivers, J., ed. *Mediterranean Countrymen: Essays in the Social Anthropology of the Mediterranean*. Paris: Mouton, 1963.

Radcliff-Umstead, Douglas. *The Mirror of Our Anguish: A Study of Luigi Pirandello's Narrative Writings*. Rutherford, N.J.: Farleigh Dickinson University Press, 1978.

Ragusa, Olga. *Luigi Pirandello. An Approach to His Theater*. Edinburgh: Edinburgh University Press, 1978.

———. "Introduction." *Sicilian Comedies. Cap and Bells and Man. Beast and Virtue*. By Luigi Pirandello. New York: Performing Arts Journal Publications, 1983. 7–16.

Schneider, Jane. "Of Vigilance and Virgins: Honor, Shame and Access to Resources in Mediterranean Societies." *Ethnology*, Vol. 10 (1971):1–24.

———, and Peter Schneider. *Culture and Political Economy in Western Sicily*. New York: Academic Press, 1976.

Sciascia, Leonardo. *La corda pazza. Scrittori e cose della Sicilia*. Turin: Giulio Einaudi Editore, 1970.

———. *Mafia Vendetta*. New York: Viking, 1968.

———. *Pirandello e la Sicilia*. Caltanissetta: Salvatore Sciascia Editore, 1968.

Simione, Corrado. "Introduzione." *Il berretto a sonagli, la giara, il piacere dell onestà*. By Luigi Pirandello. Ed. Corrado Simione. Milan: Arnoldo Mondadore, 1987. viii–xxii.

Smith, Denis Mack. *A History of Sicily. Medieval Sicily 800–1713*. New York: Viking, 1968.

———. *A History of Sicily. Modern Sicily after 1713*. New York: Viking, 1968.

Sonnino, Sidney. *I contadini in Sicilia*. Florence: Vallecchi Editore, 1925.

Tecchi, Bonaventura. "Pirandello siciliano ed europeo." *Atti del Congresso Internazionale di Studi Pirandelliani. 2–5 Ottobre 1961*. n.p.p.: Le Monnier, 1961. 77–91.

8

Pirandello and Surrealism

Vincenzo Bollettino

This study traces the relationship between Pirandello's recurrent themes in his works: the evocation of dreams, the return to innocence, the eternal struggle between content and form, the vibrant contact with the pristine forces of life, and the iconoclastic element in the language and the theoretical postulates of the French surrealists. The study focuses on three plays: *Six Characters in Search of an Author*, *Henry IV*, and *Trovarsi*, which will be examined within the framework of André Breton's two surrealist manifestos—those of 1924 and 1930.

Pirandello had published most of his major works by 1921, while surrealism as a theoretical school did not truly come about until 1924 with the publication of the first surrealist manifesto of André Breton. Nevertheless, this first surrealist manifesto was the result of years of work beginning in 1917 with Soupault and continuing with Aragon. Thus, it is possible to seek a relationship between Pirandello's work and surrealism without any violation of historical chronology.

The major problem with the study of Pirandello's work is not so much tracing its similarities and dissimilarities with French surrealists as it is determining in what definitive way it is linked with their constructive theoretical application of poetics and how much of that theory was already present in Pirandello's works prior to the publication of the first surrealist manifesto of 1924. The dates of publication of *Six Characters* and *Henry IV* seem to sustain the thesis of a few Italian critics who wish to affirm that Luigi Pirandello did indeed invent surrealism, or if not, that he had at least anticipated many of its precepts (de Castris 195). Our concern, however, is to find in Pirandello's works an approach and

a way of seeing reality that are parallel to that of surrealism without asserting a
causative influence.

One aspect common both to Pirandello and to surrealism is what Domenico
Vittorini has succinctly termed "l'umanità Pirandelliana" (9). Pirandello is intimately concerned with the suffering man, especially modern man, whose intellectual and emotional sense of time and space have been attacked by the two
major forces of the twentieth century: rationalism and capitalism. Pirandello and
the surrealists see man as a being bereft of a past and, so, nostalgic for it.
Centuries of rational conditioning of his being deprived him of imagination.
Pirandello sees modern man as a pessimist, living in complete loneliness, fully
aware that he is not wanted by and does not belong to the society in which he
lives. Man is at the mercy of oppressive and arbitrary forces and institutions.
His life is stupid, and his efforts are aimless and futile. Pirandello also regards
the sad condition of his fellow man with a deep sense of guilt and condemns
established values and morality. This new view of man causes Pirandello to
delve into a reality that had never before surfaced in Italian, or, for that matter,
European literature. At a later time the works of Eliot, Faulkner, Joyce, and
Henry Miller will also attest to the disappearance of utopias and the nineteenth-
century notion of the perfectibility of man. Literature begins to reveal an individual struggling blindly, surrounded by decay and prone to perversion, disease,
drug addiction, sadism, thwarted obsessions, and maladjustment. He is resentful,
given to dreams, and lives in hollow obeisance.

Surrealism's new humanism calls for the liberation of man from false institutions. It teaches him to look at reality with a dreaming mind capable of fusing
contraries, the real with the unreal. For the surrealist in search of the new man,
reason is an obstacle to spontaneity. Logical reasoning based on deduction is
anathema. Rational language itself is considered to be a hindrance to the release
of those automatic inner thoughts that pertain to the realm of dreams. Surrealism
denies the rules of logical syntax as well as those at the lexical level while
negating those canons that separate the creative arts into genres. Ideally, the
inner thought is to flow onto the white page without any obstacle or thoughtful
direction whatsoever. Literature becomes dramatically transformed, as does the
image of man himself. Radicalism in all levels of societal structures, as well as
in the objective reality, as preached by the status quo of middle-class society,
becomes supreme. The surrealists profoundly believe in the possibility of creating
a new, unlimited man, the sort of universal man the Renaissance had envisioned,
but without the classical model for his behavior and aspirations. The surrealist
sees man as an utterly free being who totally rejects the old values based on
reason and realism, choosing instead, as Anna Balakian states, "the infinite
expansion of reality as a substitute for the previously accepted dichotomy between
the real and the imaginary" (14). The call for social protest is explicit in both
surrealist manifestos.

Surrealism does not succumb to the bleak nihilism of its counterpart, dadaism,
which even refuses the use of language. It aligns itself ideologically to the

objective of the Communist party in its desire to accomplish, through a radical change in the basic social and philosophical structures, the liberation of humanity. Breton's adherence to the Communist party, however, was shortlived and counterproductive, for he soon realized that mere social transformation would not necessarily lead to a change in mentality. Pirandello also believes that, once the exterior limitations based on differences in time and space were eliminated and the dichotomy between the real and the imaginary shortened, a new humanism would foster a superior kind of reality capable of reconciling disparities.

The surrealists, as well as Pirandello, are romantic in the extreme. They assume an antinaturalist attitude, opposing the naturalists' repression of imagination, the standardization imposed by the commercial interests of the ruling class, and the subsequent regimentation that had reached a point of absolute monotony. The romanticism of the surrealist is not, however, that of a Shelley. In the words of René Crevel, "it is the leaping of imagination, triumphant over reality, over relative values, smashing the bars of Reason's cage" (3).

Pirandello's mode of applying surrealist technique departs from the general surrealist stream. In the creative process particularly, the pure surrealist refuses to accept the logical aspects of language ruled by syntax. Rather, he combines words according to inner emotional need. Furthermore, he refuses to use capital letters or follow the orthographic signs, placing words on the page so that they can elicit automatic meanings or revelations in the mind of the reader. The spoken word now becomes as important as the visible word because, to the surrealist poet, previously unheard-of combinations allude to possibilities not within the reach of the sequential, logical mind. In poetry, the expected poetic devices of meter, stanzas, or rhyme are all "hindrances" to the free flow of thought, to be eschewed in favor of free verse and irrational imagery. The traditional metaphor typically fused concrete things with abstract attributes. The surrealist prefers an automatic metaphor that, arising from the subconscious, manages to fuse things that reason would never allow. The literary text in surrealist thinking actually is closer to a perfect psychological document than to literature, for literary activity, by its very nature, casts an emotional aspect on a concrete, rational base.

Both the surrealists and Pirandello place great importance on the word, for only the word is endowed with the means to penetrate that absolute reality denied to us by reason. This super-reality is not to be found, as Breton explained in his first manifesto of 1924, in the beyond. It is not simply a product of fantasy and imagination, although imagination is a means to reach it. It is, in fact, hidden in the very relationship between man and things. To bring out the new, the magical, or the surreal the artist must first destroy, distort, and then rearrange the object, revealing different perspectives simultaneously. Picasso's whole concept of cubist art emphasizes the deformation of reality. Quite naturally, the emancipation of the object from conditioned reality underscored both the physical reality of the object and seeing it. Pirandello also came to realize that the important thing on stage was not so much the choice of theme, actor, or objects, but rather the position of the actors and the objects vis-à-vis one another and the spectators viewing them. The principal purpose was to destroy the conventional value of the object and to replace it with one capable of estranging the usual common denominator of perception. Pirandello's art becomes art when the spectator is able to establish an intimate relationship between the action on stage and his own inner world, as well as the spatial and temporal correspondences of people and objects. Such a moment was to Breton "the aesthetic absolute, the most to be envied and extolled" (*Surrealism,* 175).

Surrealists essentially believe that reality is divided into two basic parts: visible reality, based on reason and verifiable through our senses, and an inner reality revealed through dreams. Surrealists place learned behavior, logic, traditions, obedience to laws, and the preservation of order as seen by the dominant group of society in the external sphere. In it man feels secure and protected by the common bonds that exist between him and the current form of government. There is, however, a second reality that the surrealist equates with intuition, imagination, mysticism, and the irrational behavior based on dreams and hallucinations. As Freud did before them, the surrealists attribute greater value to this inner world than to the external one. Indeed, Breton gave Freud ample credit for his work on dream interpretation since he himself had been a student of psychiatry in 1912. He foresaw the ultimate fusion of the two realities into one sort of absolute reality which he called surreality:

Je crois à la résolution future de ces deux états, en apparence si contradictoires, que sont le rêve et la réalité, en une sorte de réalité-absolue, de surréalité, si l'on peut ainsi dire.[1]

I believe in the future resolution of those two states, in appearance so contradictory, of dreams and reality, in a kind of absolute reality, of Superrealism, if one can call it such (Breton, 24).

It should be clarified that the absolute for Breton is not to be found in a metaphysical realm but within human experience. It can be reached only by those who are able to fuse contraries, that is, the real with the unreal. To Pirandello the surreality contained within reality, the dream as it lives in everyday events, and the interior desire clashing with exterior obstacles are all part of the passionate energy of life which to the surrealists were part of the *merveilleux.*

Pirandello's *Six Characters, Henry IV,* and *Trovarsi* are built on the exact dichotomy expressed by the French surrealists. However, Pirandello's disturbing distortions of reality appeared on stage with the *Six Characters* and *Henry IV* between 1919 and 1921. These two works not only made clear all his previous conventional qualities. They also changed the artist's conception of the world in Europe and in America. Previous European theater became obsolete and dead. Pirandello wrote both plays in 1921, the first in three weeks and the second in two weeks without a pause, without connecting or changing anything. A major precept of surrealism was to be that the creative process would have to function automatically and with no interference whatsoever from any aspect of society, logical reasoning, or traditions. Breton defines surrealism this way:

Automatisme psychique pur par lequel on se propose d'exprimer, soit verbalement, soit par écrit, soit de toute autre manière, le fonctionnement réel de la pensée. Dictée de la pensée, en l'absence de tout contrôle exercé par la raison, en dehors de toute préoccupation esthétique ou morale.

"Strict psychic automatism by which one proposes to express either verbally or in writing or in any other manner, the actual functioning of thought. Dictated outside of all aesthetic or moral preoccupation" (Breton, 40).

At the beginning of *Six Characters*, the actors and the Manager are immersed in a rehearsal of another play, *Mixing it Up* (*Il gioco delle parti*). The tranquility and order of the external events are soon put to flight with the appearance of the Six Characters asking for an author who would listen to their drama. The play is based entirely on this duality—one normal and familiar, the other abnormal and hostile. For Pirandello, as for the surrealists, the two are part of the same reality. The Father in *Six Characters* explains to the Manager:

I say that to reverse the ordinary process may well be considered a madness: that is, to create situations, in order that they may appear true. But permit me to observe that if this be madness, it is the sole raison d'être of your profession, gentlemen.[2]

The two realities present in Pirandello's work as well as in the theoretical aspirations of French surrealism are multifaceted and variable. To the reality controlled by a mechanical clock and shared by all within given circumstances belongs the realm of reason, intelligence, practicality, measured actions, and behavior, and habitual and learned language which, frozen by repetitive usage, has been rendered inauthentic. The unreal world, dreamlike or absurd, opposes that world which conforms to the social reality of reason and order. It heralds erratic, inexplicable, iconoclastic, and revolutionary behavior. The sudden and peculiar appearance of the Six Characters shatters forever the stable, orderly world of the Manager and the actors to the point that the real and the unreal fuse to reveal a sudden and psychic super-reality which the French surrealists called the "absolute" and Pirandello the "third dimension" in the creative process of a work of art. For both, art ceased to be seen as a source of mere aesthetic entertainment and pleasure and became instead a new instrument of metaphysical knowledge. Pirandello's new mission is to give life to the fantastic characters on the stage and to use the instrument of human fantasy in order to pursue its high creative purpose. But to do that, Pirandello first has to envelop everyone in the theater, including the Manager and actors, by filling their minds with doubts and terror and then by attacking the old solid certainties: truth, beauty, justice, reality, virtue, family, motherhood, freedom, and law. Actors, playwright, spectators, and characters are forced to reexamine everything.

These two Pirandellian plays express a sudden mistrust in the values that had sustained Western civilization since the Greeks and the Romans. Indeed, in the years immediately following World War I, most avant-garde young writers appeared rebellious, extremely radical, and morally scandalous. They joined the extreme left or the extreme right, almost indiscriminately. Pirandello, Marinetti, and Céline went right. Picasso, Breton, Mayakovsky, and Meyerhold went left. To stay in the center was to face artistic death and oblivion as well as political persecution from both parties. Both extremist movements were then inchoate explosions of a similar hatred of the middle class, democratic parliamentary world which, to them, was responsible for mass killings, persecutions, immoral behavior, and the destruction of genuine artistic endeavors. But while French surrealists looked to a theoretical experimentation with language to create their super-reality, Pirandello only had to look a bit deeper into Sicilian reality, which in itself was surreal. That was life as he had known it, real life behind the painted scenery. Pirandello knew that Sicily is a notoriously and astoundingly improbable island where outlandish and terrifying things happen every day, everywhere, to everyone as a matter of course—the kind of things novelists everywhere must painstakingly invent. Apparently, all a Sicilian writer had to do was to record life as observed in the home, at the cafes, or in the marketplaces in order to show that surrealism in these parts of the world was reality. Pirandello takes the mere theoretical dualism which is at the base (or reality versus unreality in French surrealism) one step further by creating a dichotomy between the reality of the actor and that of the character. In French surrealism one considers a mere dream, an unattainable desire:

C'est ainsi que je m'encourageais a une audacieuse tentative. Je résolus de fixer le rêve et d'en connaître le secret . . . n'est-il pas possible de dompter cette chimére attrayante et redoubtable, d'imposer un règle à ces espirits de nuits que se jouent de notre raison? . . . De ce moment, je m'applique à chercher le sens de mes rêves.

Thus it was that I urged myself to embark upon an audacious initiative. I resolved to capture the dream and to plumb its secret. . . . Was it not possible to tame this charming and redoubtable chimera, to impose order upon these spirits of the night which make sport of our reason? . . . From that moment on I set myself to seek out the meaning of my dreams.[3] (Nerval, 2).

In Pirandello a search born of an intimate need to reveal the making of a work of art also occurs, which follows the same building code of the external, well-ordered, and established society. For the surrealist, the irrational world becomes the link between the two realities whose relationship is grasped solely by the mind. The more remote the relationship between the two, the stronger the resulting link. But for Pirandello it is the encounter of two very different actions that shatters ordinary behavior. For Pirandello, as it will be later for Artaud (once himself a surrealist), the theater is the double of life. There is life within a book, as there is life in every other object that inhabits the earth. "One is born to life in many forms, in many shapes, as tree, or as stone, as water, as butterfly, or as woman. So one may also be born a character in a play" explains the father in *Six Characters*. Pirandello feels that the theater should no longer act as a sedative for the sentimental needs of a complacent audience. Rather, it should stimulate them to see the wonder of things and to participate ecstatically in the search for "the absolute," just as for the surrealists twentieth-century reality could no longer be viewed or captured through nineteenth-century language and literary techniques.

But even as the Six Characters cannot gain vital existence unless their creator permits them to act out their drama, so the sense of wonder of the absolute cannot be grasped unless the artist is able to fuse contrary realities to the point of revealing a third dimension. "If this miraculous empathy can occur at all," states Anna Balakian, "it is because all men at some time or another are subject to the profound need of deviating from the circuit of the orderly connection between things, and the greatest revelation that can come to them is to discover that they are not hermetically sealed within it" (*Surrealism*, 176).

Whereas the surrealists merely desire to escape from the conventions of everyday occurrences in life in search of a dreamlike world, Pirandello states emphatically that the world itself is inescapable until one confronts the basic absurdity of life. Even then, however, Pirandello's protagonist finds himself unable to escape from oppression, from chaos. The protagonist has lost entirely the ability to represent himself, to act, to tell his side of the story. He is completely aware of the disintegration that surrounds every human action; he has an indescribable desire to reintegrate his being, but he fails. Every time he attempts an escape he is caught and placed again in a form. "She is here" explains the father in *Six Characters*, "to catch me, fix me, and hold me eternally in the stocks for that one fleeting and shameful moment of my life. She can't give it up! And you, sir, cannot either fairly spare me it" (Bentley, 224). Pirandello clearly shows that the essence of things knows no definite form. The characters in a work of art have no definite characteristics; they are fluid. Characteristic traits are but momentary reactions due to certain circumstances that change soon after and provoke correspondingly new reactions. But for characters to exist they must have a form that gives reason to their existence. At first the Six Characters are refused by the Manager and laughed at by the actors because they have no visible form. They have a vital drama to enact, but because they are so radical in the presentation of their existential events, the Manager only accepts them as possible characters in a play that would have to submit to the rules and regulations of the theater and the expectations of the spectators. Two of the protagonists are conscious of the need for a form and therefore for a chance to be given the breath of life by the Manager: the Father and the Stepdaughter. They are eager and full of energy, ready to become part of a fixed artistic form. Pirandello, however, refuses to grant them the most intense expression that would allow them to be born independently of the mind of the author. To Pirandello, the highest gift that a work of art can bestow is individual freedom from conformity together with one's natural reflexes. A character becomes such when he is no longer the same, but becomes other and acts his drama forever. While the surrealist pretended to populate the world of the subconscious through the help of the irrational metaphor, Pirandello goes on to say on stage and not in theory that the fact of life is that man is confronted with the impossibility of ever being fully himself and, therefore, the corrosion of his illusory personality is inevitable. The artist is only able to capture certain moments in the life of a character which he must arbitrarily fix in time and space as so many isolated images of a suddenly stopped reel of film. Such is the only possible reality of a Lear, a Don Quixote, a Don Juan, or a Tartuffe.

The sense of absurdity that invades practically all Pirandello's works is never the force in surrealist thinking. Breton, in fact, fervently believed that a supreme point of reference could reconcile opposites. Indeed, the surrealist poet determined to direct his energies toward the realization of that supreme reality by insulting reason for the benefit of spontaneity, logic for the benefit of the lyric, and everyday reality for a sense of the marvelous. But Pirandello, overwhelmed by the ridiculousness of reality, strives to create an impression of the absurd by revolutionizing dramatic techniques: the play within a play, the use of the double, the mind of the author in the play, the nudity of the stage, the multiple use of space and the fragmentation of time, the presentation of the creative process in stages, the degree of vital force in a character that separates him from another, and the use of a language that never reaches the receiver for it carries no message. These new methods make the world appear upside down: the Father almost commits incest; the family unity is shattered by misunderstandings; the Manager no longer directs the play but becomes a character in a second play about to be performed. The chaotic world of the play is further convoluted by the fact that there is no unity in space, time, speech, or theme.

But what, in fact, separates Pirandello from surrealism in the use of these techniques is that, while the surrealist writer expects to fuse these contraries automatically, in Pirandello there is a deep awareness that the creative image is not caused by hallucination or induced by drugs, but is an exact reflection of life itself. For Pirandello the world is abysmally illogical and confused. The surrealist ignores the given world order in hopes of divining the magical event. Pirandello finds no route for escape. In effect, he uses absurd situations on stage to depict an absurd reality. Pirandello's works depict man's plight on a social, historical, philosophical, and creative level, whereas the surrealist writer avoids the direct mention of any emotional aspect. Pirandello's themes are love, death, misery, incommunicability, loneliness, isolation, absurdity. Sentimental expression is taboo in surrealistic thinking, for that hinders the essential revelation. Surrealism prefers to use dreams to induce a trancelike state capable of heralding inner creative reality. But Pirandello does not use any vague means of achieving artistic gratification. His theater, poetry, and narrative deal with a reality so intense as to seem surreal. Pain as envisioned by the Sicilian writer is not the suffering of an individual, but rather the anguish that involves all of humanity.

A surrealist writer would be baffled to learn that many of Pirandello's plots came from local stories he read in the morning paper or that his friends mailed to him regularly. Pirandello's own family experiences were yet another source. One cannot take too lightly that Pirandello's wife was mad. She was beautiful and intelligent, but she suffered from a persecution mania that grew worse as she got older. She truly believed that her husband was unfaithful to her and that he intended to poison her. She interpreted his every word, act, gesture, and decision as further proof of his murderous design. Yet she behaved so lucidly and cunningly that Pirandello was baffled and confused. She even accused her husband of having an incestuous affair with their sixteen-year-old daughter, who had to be sent away to placate her mother's demented mind. Pirandello himself was to admit later that his wife's mental illness had served as a prism through which the most banal and colorless events became tangles of seemingly logical but contradictory versions of the same reality, as in *Six Characters* and *Henry IV*. Hence, Pirandello had no need to search for impossible dreams through the alchemy of sound and colors that were, in the words of Rimbaud, capable of making us see the other side of reality.

If *Six Characters* is a technical *tour de force* wherein Pirandello exposes most of the concepts that link him with surrealism—the search for the absolute, the transformation of reality, the negation of reason, and the radical use of language, image, and space—*Henry IV* is technically more conventional but contains all of Pirandello's themes. Many consider the play to be his best. It is a drama of madness, true and feigned, and its contrast with reality, which appears to be only a different kind of madness. At the same time it is a spectacular drama in which Pirandello succeeds in creating a good plot, believable sentiments, and recognizable characters.

The main character in *Henry IV* stands alone, as in classical theater. He is Henry IV, the medieval German monarch who was humiliated by Pope Gregory VII in 1077 for his refusal to recognize both the Pope himself and the dictate that a king must be sanctioned by Rome. As do all Pirandellian beings, Henry IV thinks and questions and is therefore subject to doubts and suffering. Surrealism stresses doubt and the eventual revolt against reason, logic, and bourgeois attitudes. The group in *Henry IV* (part of that external, logical reality shared conventionally by many) is composed of three servants, all paid to perform as confidants of Henry IV, and two visitors. This external world is ruled by reason and science and, in fact, has as its authoritative speaker the doctor, an object of Henry's ridicule.

In *Henry IV*, Pirandello goes one step beyond the so-called dual reality of the surrealists by fragmenting reality into multiple planes, each with its own space and time. The play is, in fact, an attempt to appreciate reality on the basis of its many probable levels. At one point the demented protagonist becomes the only logical person in the play, while the others' reality assumes the appearance of a mask. Either through suspension, tension, or direct involvement, the audience participates in the play, thus adding another side, another point of view to the already varied vision. Each character plays three roles, and each role has its own use of space and time. The three levels present in the play move through a recurrent process of identification-alienation-identification. By moving continuously from identification to alienation, and back to identification, it becomes evident that Pirandello is presenting reality as a play of mirrors that reflect a space and time inaccessible to the spectator or reader. This is clearly not a matter of the dichotomy of reality. For Pirandello, as for the surrealists, truth resides in the psychological actualism captured by language.

In *Henry IV*, Pirandello takes language more seriously than ever. Indeed, words are the only true reality for his protagonist. It is through words and costumes that Henry IV is relegated to medieval times. Aragon claimed throughout his life that language was his only possible reality, and Pirandello shows in this play that there is no thought beyond words. Henry IV must rely on his medieval mask, the only concrete reality not only for him but also for the others who consider him. Pirandello seems to claim that if a thing cannot be expressed then it is not. Verbal images are therefore the only basis for creativity.

Although Pirandello never says so explicitly, it is altogether likely that he too feels that the artificiality of bourgeois manners and attitude is born of their excessive familiarity with the objects of their world. Breton warns the modern reader of the peril of familiarity much as the Russian formalists had done two decades earlier, for it leads to a sterility of the mind. Ironically, the others see the world of the demented Henry IV as highly orderly because it is fixed forever in the time and place of a past historical event. To the spectator, however, this world is of value precisely because it is unknown, unfamiliar, and therefore destined to be repeated. But for Pirandello's characters this world is not only unknown, but also difficult to explain because of a lack of exact words. For Henry IV himself reality is not what he is but what he could have been if his society had not cheated him and if he too could have worn a mask. Society itself never takes off its mask for fear of not being able to accept the grotesqueness of reality. Henry IV is forever frozen in time, while life is constantly changing beyond the mere meaning of words. The visitors in the play show change through the different costumes they wear as they play different parts, but Henry IV always remains in his regal suit. Henry IV is also fully aware that the changes the others undergo because of circumstances make them slaves of time, while he is permitted to see the movement of things as through a prism. He is privy to that eternal struggle between form and content which the seventeenth-century Mexican playwright, Sor Juana Ines de la Cruz, expressed in the metaphor of water in a glass: to feel its essence, it must be in a glass, but that very form strangles it. Nonetheless, without the glass the water cannot achieve a form and therefore we would have no consciousness of it.

Let us now move to a discussion of those techniques used by Pirandello and later taken as part of the surrealist creative apparatus. First, Pirandello makes ample use of "polarity"—that is, the presentation of two elements fundamentally opposed to each other by their very nature. For example, the setting of *Six Characters*, together with the author and manager, actors and characters, are mutually exclusive of one another. Henry IV, in speech, thoughts, space, and time, clashes with the visitors who consider him demented. With the use of polarity and ambiguity Pirandello creates powerful juxtapositions to shock the reader or spectator. Surrealism, too, clearly brings together irrational juxtapositions (rain–sun, woman–child, sea–mountain) in order to create a double vision capable of undercutting both the unified, objective view of realism and the philosophy of positivism.

Another element frequently used by Pirandello is the notion of the "double." Each of his characters has two or more opposite aspects. The Father in *Six Characters* is seen not only as a good man, concerned for the happiness of his wife, but concurrently as a corruptor of minors and destroyer of family ties and morality. For Pirandello the theater becomes the double of life in a necessary and cruel relationship. Pirandello's definition of the drama as a combination of comic and tragic aspects of a given reality is also tied to his notion of the double. For the surrealists, later on, language will become the double of reality, especially that language that fuses the contrary aspects of reality. Pirandello actually intends to force an active participation on the part of the spectator who, because of the obvious lack of a clear-cut message in Pirandello's plays, becomes the messenger of the play.

The most common and brilliantly used element in a Pirandellian play is the "collage"—that is, the presentation on stage of scenes, characters, historical periods, and past events to create a kaleidoscopic perspective of reality. These multiple and simultaneous elements are tied together only by the subjective feelings of each of the protagonists. The pictures hanging in *Henry IV*, the fall suffered by the protagonist in the past, and the changing of costumes, together with the changing of language and gestures, all contribute to a fragmented view of reality.

Both *Six Characters in Search of an Author* and *Henry IV* move by analogy. The acts and scenes move toward one another illogically; the characters are separated by time and space into groups of two, three, and four which are pulled together only to be quickly divided and transformed analogically. The solitary villa in *Henry IV* becomes a castle at Goslar. Donna Matilda Spina becomes the Marchioness who had given hospitality to Pope Gregory VII who had excommunicated Henry IV. Frida her daughter is the Marchioness when young. The Doctor is Dionysius Genoni, but also the Monsignor who interceded for Henry IV to Pope Gregory.

Of all the plays Pirandello wrote, *Trovarsi* is perhaps the one that comes closest to the surrealistic poetics. The play was performed for the first time in 1932 with great success. One will recall that this is the date of publication of Breton's second surrealist manifesto in which the French poet stressed the importance (1) of the search for lyrical purity in poetry and (2) of the struggle to evade reason, which inhibits reality and obscures the *merveilleux* in it. In *Trovarsi* Pirandello has one of his characters explain the following notion:

"To paint the way I would want . . . things the way they appear at certain moments . . . the explosion, the residue of all common events that have reduced life, nature . . . as a worthless coin, valueless. I do not understand; it is as if one yearned to feel humiliated, fall under the same sky that befriends one with the same stars. Ha, I am choking. Did it ever happen to you, without knowing why or how, that suddenly you were seeing life, things with new eyes . . . everything pulsates, with breath of light—and you stood up with your soul wide opened by an extraordinary sense of stupor" (141–42).

There is no doubt whatsoever that there is a close affinity in thought and language between Breton's surrealistic views, as expressed in his manifestoes of 1924 and 1930, and Pirandello's ideas. However, I would caution against the too hasty view that the closeness is due to the influence of one author on the other. The fact is that both Breton and Pirandello derive their aesthetic views from a common source: Bergson's *"élan vital"* and the extremes of idealism that preached the search for the vital in the subconscious. But while with the French surrealist Bergson's intuition culminates in the triumph of the chaotic and surreal expression, in Pirandello it never actually reaches this automatism of association. His presence in the creative process is constant. Rather than associating two fundamentally unrelated things, Pirandello intentionally substitutes the usual line of reasoning with the unusual. The surrealists would never permit us to perceive the plan at work.

Elj, the protagonist of *Trovarsi*, desires novelty both as a refusal to enslave his mind and spirit to the routine and as a means of evading that mystical reality which the Fascist party created in Italy. Indeed, shortly after joining the Fascist party in a period of nationalistic euphoria, Pirandello recognizes the shortfalls of the regime, among them, the opposition of the party to the intellectual thinking of the time. In 1934 Pirandello openly attacked the fascist government for its indifference to the arts and called for total freedom in artistic creation.

But for the French surrealists love is the crystal that communicates with "the absolute." Love is the point at which reality and the *merveilleux* are reconciled. For Aragon "L'amour est un état de confusion du réel et du merveilleux" (Aragon, 250). For Pirandello, love is merely a temporary evasion of a harsher, fragmented reality that imprisons the character in a labyrinthine structure. Love, childhood memories of the Sicily of the past, freedom from the tumults of war, and nostalgia for the simplicity of nature become Pirandello's provisional consolation for the grotesqueness of contemporary reality. Yet his protagonists know all too well that the temporary disassociation from reality through love, dreams, and the irrational associations prescribed by the surrealists cannot alter the determinant relationship with reason, morality, and conditioned behavior. Indeed, the dramatic attraction of Pirandello's protagonists lies exactly in their knowledge of the impossibility of evading reality.

While the surrealists fuse contraries in an absolute, the dialectic view of reality is never resolved in Pirandello. Pirandello's protagonists in *Trovarsi* see the reality of man's condition as a constant fragmentation and alienation from the poetic visions of childhood dreams, from the fleeting sense of fullness and security that love and intimacy with nature provide. Life for these characters is a constant search, a continuous making and remaking so as not to cease existing. They desire a moment of repose in which there is no change of masks or roles, when one is simply part of the totality of life with no awareness. "One cannot live like that . . . as if on vacation? Without having the need to create anything. . . . and stay close to me, with your eyes closed if you wish to live—Do you wish to find yourself? But one has to find himself in life, at times, without looking for anything" (*Trovarsi*, 150), explains Elj the protagonist of *Trovarsi* ("to find oneself"). Donata, the actress, reveals the eternal drama of Pirandello's protagonists:

As you know it is like that by nature because I was true to life—always true—but not to myself—I have lived there far away always by myself; and now I want to be here–I–I–I want to have a life that I can call mine, all mine–I have to find myself! (Translation mine, *Trovarsi*, 145).

Donata never reaches the absolute. The deep sense of futility that results from the impossibility of escape from a fixed mask is constant in Pirandello's plays. The only way to overcome that is through a personal and spiritual descent into the realm of nothingness, a difficult but not altogether impossible task.

For the surrealists, love as the frenzied primitivism of uncontrolled sexual instincts is a way to deny the ethical and moral efficacies of the bourgeoisie. Conversely, love is also a means of achieving greater heights, of sublimating the sordidness of everyday life. It is, in fact, the entrance into the world of the absolute where contraries fuse.

Pirandello sees love as the moving force that sustains and nourishes the hopes for an evasion from an everlasting fixed form. The surrealists know it as that spark that ignites a hedonistic and voluptuous life that is not, by the way, averse to crime. The works of Robert Desnos and Louis Aragon abound in examples of a free love capable of rejuvenating through desire.

To fulfill his desire, Louis Aragon transforms the show window of a cane store into a world of wonders:

The canes were gently swaying to and fro, like kelp. I hadn't yet recovered from this spell when I noticed a form swimming between the various strata of the display. She was slightly smaller than the average woman but in no way impressed one as dwarflike. Rather, her diminutiveness seemed the optical effect or distance, yet this apparition was directly inside the window. Her hair had come undone, her fingers occasionally grasped the canes. I would have taken her for a siren, in the most literal sense of the word, for it seemed to me that the lower portion of this charming specter, who was naked to the girdle which she wore at hip level, tapered into a dress of steel or scales or perhaps rose petals;—"The ideal!" was all I could exclaim in my confusion (Aragon, 28–30).

In Pirandello's plays even desire is unattainable. In fact, one senses in *Trovarsi* a world devoid of imagination, dreams, and desires. All that Donata is allowed

to hope for is, perhaps, the possibility of closing her eyes to the fragmented
world of the exterior while looking for her real life.

In surrealism imagination motivated by desire reigns supreme. Through imagination man realizes his dreams, his essence. In the words of Alphonse Louis
Constant:

Imagination, in effect, is like the soul's eye; therein forms are outlined and preserved;
thereby we behold the reflection of the invisible world; it is the glass of vision and the
apparatus of magical life (Levi, 60–61).

But Pirandello sees no way out of the prison in which his protagonists suffer
both physically and spiritually. Reality as seen by others and created by language
and circumstances is a thick wall against which it is impossible to struggle. For
the surrealist writer imagination illuminates reality and provides man with the
key to the world of freedom. Because the world of imagination is the route to
super-reality, it is the surrealists' objective to inculcate in man the powers and
the means of imagination that most men ignore. Surrealism negates reason, the
natural enemy of the imagination, for it is an obstacle in the quest for the absolute.
"There is no solution outside love" says Andre Breton. Love is the point where
reality and the marvelous achieve a certain reconciliation. "Love is a state of
confusion of the real and the wondrous." It is the spiritualization of the physical
and the objectivation of the subjective. Existence and essence come together in
love.

But in *Trovarsi*, in *Six Characters*, and in *Henry IV*, there is a dialectical
tension that remains unresolved, a profound antithesis that finds no outlet. The
result is tragic. All that Pirandello's characters have is time, yet they desire the
eternal. Their mental projections reach the infinite but are unable to overcome
time and the effects of diversity.

Even in the vision of woman Pirandello and surrealism differ markedly. The
surrealists sing of woman and consider her the miracle of nature:

Yet, woman, you supplant all form. I was on the verge of forgetting this abandon, and
even the black nonchalances you like, when you reappear and everything withers in your
footsteps toward night I irretrievably lose all memory of day—charming substitute, you
are the synopsis of a world of wonders, of the natural world, and it is you who are reborn
when I close my eyes. You are the wall and its breach. You are the horizon and the
immediate presence. The ladder and the iron rings. Total eclipse. Light. Miracle (Aragon,
207–208).

The woman in the surrealist mind attracts and provokes. Indeed, she is the most
marvelous thing that exists, a mystery that enchants man. Because she is the
mirror of the absolute, woman can always be the bridge between internal reality
and super-reality.

For Pirandello woman is also a bridge, but not between the here and the beyond. Rather, she is a link to the original, pristine life where all is silence in the depth of the sea:

If you think about it silence is natural to the fish. Yes the silence we have lost because we screamed so as to let everyone know of our tragedy in having remained outside of our real, essential being. . . . The woman is all water. She belongs there. All her body is but the contours of the sea not of the earth (*Trovarsi*, 151).

While *l'amour fou* or *l'amour sublime* preached by the surrealists is anything but self-sacrificial, nevertheless it is understood to be only a means to achieving *le merveilleux*. In this respect carnal love is fused with spiritual love to form an essentially religious experience. According to Breton, "The surrealists gave an almost sacred character to the erotic embrace, to copulation, to sexual beauty and mystery in woman, to the liberating powers of orgasm, and discuss these questions freely and openly" (Balakian, 83–84).

Erotic love for the surrealists is not sinful. They feel no compunction about describing the effects of love in the most candid terms. In Pirandello there is no worship of woman as an image of religious passion. She is, rather, the mystical element that leads man to meditation and silence. She leads him to the state of impassivity, free from all ideas, which are nothing other than a reflection of a world fragmented by time. Woman is the entrance to the sea, the realm of life in nothingness. This is not the nothingness so easily associated with French existentialist thinking. It is the reverse, a universe of the spirit in which everything communicates freely with everything else, transcending limitations.

Pirandello does not fit the automatic writing format of surrealism. He shares neither the surrealist views on the nature of love and literary creation nor their scandalous zeal. Yet the Italian playwright does share with them the need to find new ways of approaching the theater as an art form. Surrealists seek to explore the recently discovered world of Freud, just as Pirandello tries to capture the true nature of man in the complexities of twentieth-century economic, social, political, and artistic thought. Like the surrealists, Pirandello also believes in the word's power to fuse the real with the unreal, the present with the past. Both Pirandello and the surrealists shun reason as the ultimate medium of gaining access to the essence of things, favoring, instead, fantasy and imagination. Both negate rhetorical and traditional language, searching, instead, for a more authentic expression that would serve their reality—and spiritual needs.

NOTES

1. André Breton, *Manifeste du surréalisme* (Paris: Jean-Jacques Pauvert, 1972), p. 24.

2. Eric Bentley, ed., *Naked Masks: Five Plays by Luigi Pirandello* (New York: E. P. Dutton, 1952), p. 216.

3. Gérard de Nerval, *Aurelia ou le rêve et la vie* (Paris: Lettres Modernes, 1965), p. 2.

WORKS CITED

Aragon, Louis. *Le Paysan de Paris*. Paris: Gallimard, 1926.

Balakian, Anna. *André Breton, Magus of Surrealism*. New York: Oxford University Press, 1971.

————. *Surrealism, the Road to the Absolute*. New York: E. P. Dutton, 1970.

Bentley, Eric, ed. *Naked Masks: Five Plays by Luigi Pirandello*. New York: E. P. Dutton, 1952.

Breton, André. *Manifeste du surréalisme*. Paris: Jean-Jacques Pauvert, 1972.

Crevel, René. *L'Esprit contre la raison*. Marseille: Cahiers du Sud, 1927.

de Castris, Arcangelo Leone. *Storia di Pirandello*. Bari: Editori Laterza, 1986.

Levi, Eliphas. *Dogme et rituel de la haute magie*. Paris: Germer Baillère, 1956.

Nerval, Gérard de. *Aurelia ou le Rêve et la vie*. Paris: Lettres Modernes, 1965.

Pirandello, Luigi. *Maschere Nude*. Milan: Arnoldo Mondadori Editore, 1955.

Vittorini, Domenico. *The Drama of Luigi Pirandello*. New York: Dover Publications, 1957.

9

Setting the Scene:
Theater in Italy
Before Pirandello

Jennifer Lorch

In 1924 a group of literary and theater people asked Luigi Pirandello if he would join them as a figurehead in an ambitious theatrical enterprise. They wished to establish an art theater in Rome that would be a multiple venture: plays, dance, concerts, and exhibitions were to take place in the one venue. The center was also to provide a home for a theatrical company that would also tour in Italy and abroad as well as provide a season of plays in Rome. The funding for the venture was to be mixed. The original members put in 5,000 lire each and formed a joint stock company, but they also expected both private and public enterprise to contribute generously. It is a measure of Pirandello's enthusiasm for the project that, though in the first instance he put in the same sum as everyone else, he later sank further funds in the venture and agreed from the outset to direct the theatrical company without remuneration.[1]

The Teatro d'Arte group received sufficient funds to enable it to transform the Teatro Odescalchi, where Podrecca had shown his famous puppet company before beginning his world tour in 1924, into an intimate, well-furbished theater. On April 3 of the following year the theater opened with two one-act plays, one by Pirandello himself, *La sagra del signore della nave*, the other by Lord Dunsany, *The Gods of the Mountain*. The reviews were favorable, complimenting both the refurbished theater and the theatrical direction and performances.[2] The King was not present, but the government was represented by Benito Mussolini, who had ensured that the national government had made its financial contribution and who had also assisted the fund-raising activities. On April 3, 1925, it seemed that Italy had both an art theater and the beginnings of a new national theater.

Part of the agreement with the government was that the Teatro d'Arte company would travel as a national company when abroad.

Luigi Pirandello was fifty-seven when the Teatro d'Arte opened. The next three years of his life were to be consumed in a frenetic and obsessive activity aimed at fostering the theatrical company in Italy and, more particularly, abroad. Ten years before, he had been a largely unacknowledged playwright. It was as a man of letters that he had first gained recognition: as a poet, short story writer, realist, avant-garde novelist, and essayist. By 1924 he was an internationally acclaimed dramatist, but not an experienced theater practitioner. His experience in theater was limited to seeing his plays staged and attending some of the rehearsals. What induced the man of letters and dramatist to become a man of the theater and devote so much of his time and money to this theatrical venture? The answers probably lie in both historical and psychological analysis. This chapter will concentrate on the historical in an attempt to unravel why a highly gifted dramatist with no theatrical background should find it necessary to engage in the physicality of theater-making in order to satisfy his dramaturgical aspirations.

The story goes back to the traditions of theater-making in Italy both before and after Unification. It concerns the structure of theatrical companies and the constitution of theater audiences, the economic effects of Unification on theater, the political hopes of those who saw in theater a means of "making the Italians,"[3] and at the turn of the century the development of art theaters in other European capitals. Finally, in the few years before the establishment of the Teatro d'Arte, Italian theater would involve the aims and aspirations of a newly formed political party of a strongly nationalist persuasion, the Fascist party.

THE STRUCTURE OF THEATRICAL COMPANIES

The structure of professional Italian theatrical companies during the nineteenth century was a hierarchical one based on the concept of "role." "Il ruolo è la caratteristica centrale, il perno, sia della struttura della compagnia che del sistema di produzione-spettacolo nel teatro di tradizione." (The role is the central characteristic, the pivot, of both the structure of the company and the system of show production in traditional theater, Palombi, 53). The idea that an actor "is a role" rather than "plays a part" was a characteristic of *commedia dell'arte* companies which are conventionally taken to have originated in the mid-sixteenth century since the first extant contract for a theatrical company is dated 1545. The notion of "role," however, probably goes back even further since the most likely origin of the *commedia dell'arte* characters are the stock characters already existing in popular theater.[4] Nineteenth-century theatrical organization, however, also owed much to Carlo Goldoni's concept of "character." In his attempts during the mid-eighteenth century to create a social drama that sought to reinstate the classical concept of comedy as a means of reforming society through laughter, rather than merely entertaining an audience, Goldoni worked with talented actors from the *commedia dell'arte* tradition. For Golinetti, one of his chief actors, for instance, who played the role of Pantalone, Goldoni wrote the part of Momolo cortesan, basing the character of Momolo on what he knew of Golinetti's character.[5] In this way Goldoni gradually built up a number of plays where the parts were fully written and based on the major psychological traits and physical characteristics of the actors and actresses in his company who had previously been used to playing the masked *commedia dell'arte* roles. In the complex relationship between "role," "part," and "repertory" inherent in nineteenth-century Italian theater, type-casting of this kind was an important additional factor.

The "role" was both a category of parts and a hierarchical grade in the company. As a category of parts, young actors and actresses, whether *figli d'arte*, that is, born into actors' families, or *dilettanti*, talented amateurs who wanted to turn professional, would be guided in their choice of role by the company's director. He or she in turn would be influenced when allocating parts by characteristics that the particular aspiring actor exhibited.

A company's status would be determined largely by its size.[6] A company *di prima categoria* would expect to have the following roles: *primo attore* (leading man) and *prima attrice* (leading lady); *brillante* (comic actor) and *caratteristica* (character actor); *madre* (mother); *primo attore giovane* (juvenile lead) and *prima attrice giovane* (young female lead); *seconda donna* (second actress); *promiscuo* (an actor able to take various roles); and several *generici*, that is, bit-part players who had not yet established themselves in roles. The *primo generico*, however, was usually considered to be a minor role. Below the *generici* were the *comparse*, that is, the non-speaking roles. Among the named roles there were further distinctions: the most sought-after positions were those of *primo attore* and *prima attrice*, and even here there was a further refinement. It was possible to be *primo attore assoluto*, which meant that the leading actor of this status could define his terms with relation to the company's repertoire.[7]

In addition to the "roles" and *generici*, companies of good repute would have a team of stage hands and technical staff: the *direttore di scena* (stage manager), the *trovarobe* (property person), the *amministratore* (treasurer), the *segretario* (secretary). The *suggeritore* (prompter) requires individual mention. He held special power within a company; he had the whole script while the individual actors tended to be given only their parts. Many actors learned their parts by listening to the prompter who spoke the whole play in a loud whisper even during the public performances. Often the actors took on his inflections, interpretations, and even gestures or, in striving to hear the prompter, lost control of the characterization they were attempting to communicate.[8] Then there were the stage hands—*machinisti*—who were responsible for the curtain and scene shifting.

In a well-financed company of good repute, the task of each member of the company was clearly defined by contract. Within the hierarchical system there was a respect for the skills of others. In smaller companies the necessities of getting the show on made the hierarchical system less rigid. Technicians would take minor parts, and actors would help to shift scenery. An average second-rank company would have about eleven to twelve members.

At the head of each company was the *capocomico*. As the name implies, this person was the chief actor, but frequently combined the work of administrative and financial head of the company with the role of the leading actor or actress. The tasks of the *capocomico* were both diverse and diffuse. He or she was financially and artistically responsible for the company. This meant raising money, ensuring that bills were paid, finding and renting the performance spaces, known as *piazze* for the tour, establishing the repertoire, allocating the parts, directing the play, and training the actors. In large first-category companies, some of these tasks would be allocated to the administrator; in smaller, less well-established companies, the *capocomici* would have to do everything themselves.[9] The *capocomici* gave their names to their companies; hence, the Compagnia Rossi had Ernesto Rossi as its *capocomico*, and the Compagnia Salvini had Tommaso Salvini as its *capocomico*.

The great majority of theatrical companies were self-financing and itinerant, two further characteristics that had remained unchanged since at least the sixteenth century. Before the construction of the railways, this meant horse-pulled wagons. Since the company depended on box office takings for its livelihood, the relationship between audience, critics, theatrical repertoire, and innovation was one of delicate checks and balances. A sense of mission felt by a number of leading theatrical practitioners to make known, for instance, innovatory texts from other countries, or to revive plays that had not been presented for some time on an Italian stage was tempered by a knowledge of what a particular critic might praise and what a particular audience would appreciate. As Cesare Molinari has clarified, "Il pubblico veniva identificato, tout court, con il cliente." ("The public came to be identified, *tout court*, with the client" Molinari, 49.) Salvini wrote in his memoirs that Italian theatergoers could be divided into two kinds, "i dotti e i buon gustai" (the well-educated and those there for a good time, Salvini, 185–86). Some stability of financial returns was ensured by the *abbonamento* system, which is still in practice in Italy today. Theater seats could be booked in advance for the whole season, guaranteeing that the company has some estimate of the minimum it could expect from that particular run of performances. Theater seats were held in such high esteem with Neapolitan society, for instance, that a permanent theater seat was sometimes part of a bride's dowry (Salvini, 157).

Actors' or technicians' contracts with a company would be from one to three years. After a season of playing, touring from one *piazza* (performance space) to another, the company would return to base, the members would disperse, and the *capocomico* would begin again the task of putting together another company for the following season, which could, of course, include members of the former company.

Such, then, was the life of the actor in nineteenth-century Italy. Of no fixed abode, frequently on the road, living in temporary lodgings with cooking facilities, accompanied by their spouses who were usually company members themselves, the children attending the local schools until they too became part of the professional company, using their own idiomatic language, nineteenth-century actors, like their forebears, lived in an enclosed world that revolved entirely around their art.[10] With daily performances in the evening and rehearsals during the day, except when traveling, there was no time for other interests or relaxation. Acting was not a job or career (though there was a career structure in the hierarchy of roles). It was a way of life, a commitment, similar to that made by members of a religious community. This life-style continued well into the twentieth century, as is well illustrated by Claudia Palombi's book *Il gergo del teatro*. Palombi interviewed a number of retired elderly actors and actresses now living in the actors' retirement home in Bologna. All except one had participated in the role system, and all had stories to tell about the itinerant life of the actor.

Before Unification, however, a few companies enjoyed outside financial support. These were the royal companies supported by the ruling houses of Turin, Milan, Parma, and Naples, and they enjoyed a monopoly (known as *il privilegio*) in their respective cities. Because of the prestige of these companies, the higher and guaranteed stipends, and the possibility of staying in one place for at least part of the year, places in these companies were much sought after. Opinions regarding the artistic merit varied, however. At the age of sixteen, Tommaso Salvini, who had spent an intense and fruitful season in Gustavo Modena's company building up his repertoire, took a three-year contract with the Compagnia Reale de' Fiorentini in Naples (from which he was later released) with the double role of *primo e secondo amoroso* (first and second lover)—roles that were dropped in later companies—and a stipend that would increase each year. Tommaso Salvini's opinion of the Royal Company in Naples, as related in his memoirs, supports the notion that subsidy causes art to stagnate. The actors had been for a long time in the one company, they seemed intimidated by the tastes of the audience who had no enthusiasm for new material and had themselves become so indigenous that they would not have been able to appear on stages farther north without being severely criticized for accent and gestures (67–69). Some fifteen years later, Salvini, now a well-known leading actor, returned to the company as a leading actor with responsibility for direction to find little had changed, except that everyone had gotten much older. It was basically the same company as before. To vary things, some actors changed roles. As part of Salvini's contract that he should choose the season's opening play, he selected Voltaire's *Zaire*. There was no suitable set, he was told. So he chose *The Harpist*, but the leading lady did not yet know her part. He chose *Orestes*; the actor who was to play Pilades was ill. Finally, Salvini agreed to act in whatever play the company was willing to stage, and as a result, he, known best as tragedian, found himself obliged to open the season playing Lord Bonfil in Goldoni's comedy *Pamela*, with the second actress in the leading role (Salvini, 159–60).

If the Compagnia de' Fiorentini based in Naples and supported by the Bourbon government had become insular, the northern companies' short-lived attempts at creating *teatri stabili* (fixed repertory theaters), based in Turin, Milan, and Parma and supported by their respective governments, were much more successful attempts at state subsidy of theater. The Reale Compagnia Sarda, supported by the House of Savoy, in particular, gained a high reputation that was in later, harder times, to be nostalgically remembered. This enterprise remained in people's minds as an outstanding example of how the state might support and encourage theater of quality.[11]

THE THEATER AND UNIFICATION

Unification in 1860 had a marked effect on Italian theater. After the euphoria of the political statement of unification, the long, hard task of creating a nation-state, of "making Italians," in the much quoted phrase of Massimo d'Azeglio, had to begin. During the Risorgimento period, historical dramas such as Pellico's *Francesca da Rimini* and Niccolini's *Nabucco* provided covert allusions to freedom which some deemed to be a suitable means of stirring patriotic feeling.[12] The debate now turned to the function of theater in the construction of a new nation-state. Cesare Trevisani's report on the state of dramatic literature over the twenty-year period prior to 1867, commissioned by the minister Berti, stresses the importance of the contribution of drama in raising national morale.[13] Trevisani advocated a theater that was accessible to the people. A theater that is a theater of pure delight, a show of luxury, is not fulfilling its role within society, he argued. Much of Trevisani's report is an analysis of plays written in the last twenty years. Although he has praise for tragedies, he is firm in his view that it is social comedy that is now required for an educational program toward a sense of national unity. Trevisani's report points to a need to look for and encourage new playwrights who can deliver the right kind of play for a newly emergent nation. This had also been the view of the governments of Turin and Florence. In both capitals competitions were organized in an effort to seek new and suitable dramatic talent (Ferrone, 19–21).

If some ministers and government officials accorded to theater a role in creating a nation-state of enlightened bourgeois, the financial decisions with regard to theater made that aspiration a practical impossibility. With the fall of separate royal houses, with the exception of the house of Savoy which became the Italian monarchy, the new state appropriated the theaters of the former principalities. As an interim measure, while it was deciding what to do, the new Italian government (now based temporarily in Florence) paid out subsidies in 1863 to theaters in Milan, Naples, Turin, Parma, Piacenza, Modena, Pontremoli, Borgo San Dominico, Borgataro, and Massa. However, as theater was thought to favor the few rather than benefit all, it was proposed to abolish all national subsidy to theater. In 1866 the Home Office (Ministero degli Affari Interni) under Chiaves presented a bill that would cede the use of state-supported theaters to municipal authority. There had been general agreement at the beginning of the new era on the principle that central government was to administer the general interests of the nation, while local authorities were to respond to local needs. Theater was designated a local need that would receive financial support from the newly created municipalities. The fabric of those theatrical buildings that had passed to the state on Unification would be maintained by the state until they passed to the ownership of private individuals or to a municipality, who would thenceforth be responsible for them. There was then the question of whether the municipalities should be obliged or encouraged to support theater and the arts within their jurisdiction. Those who defended the idea of voluntary support won the day. Hence, in some places theater received no subsidy at all.[14]

At the same time, the privilege and therefore the monopoly were removed from the former royal theaters, which meant that other groups could act in those cities. With the ban on competition removed, an increasing number of theater groups and theater buildings came into being. In 1873 Enrico Rosmini made the total 940 in 699 towns (579–87), a little less than the official census in 1870 (Molinari, 36), but still a huge increase in what had been in use in the 1840s and 1850s. Theaters were categorized into first, second, and third category. Of Rosmini's 940, 881 were in the third category. The size of theater varied from the thirty-seater Teatro Dante at Vellano to the 30,000 arena at Milan.

At this time two characteristics began to surface that would remain constants of Italian theater well into the twentieth century. The first was the *mattatore* actor, and the second statements and complaints about the state of Italian theater, its organization, its actors, and its plays.

It is difficult to pinpoint with precision the date when the term *mattatore* was used in Italy to refer to a particular kind of theatrical star. The word comes from the Spanish word *matador* and was used to refer to a person who excelled in a particular activity. When referring to actors, it was used to describe those who so outshone their colleagues that the whole production was geared to demonstrate their talents. This sometimes meant adapting the text to cut minor parts or lessening the parts of other characters in order to allow the audience to see more of the actor or actress they had come to see. On other occasions a *capocomico* would gather around himself a group of lesser actors whom he could pay less and whose mediocrity would allow him to shine all the more. The cult of the *mattatore* actor was also linked to the tendency to tour abroad. The cult was begun by Ernesto Rossi and Adelaide Ristori when they went to Paris with the Reale Sarda Company in 1855 and continued well into the twentieth century. A trip to Paris with a prestigious company, to the city where Italian *commedia dell'arte* troupes had been so well received in the seventeenth century and Goldoni in the eighteenth, was a very different undertaking, however, from the later trips of Ernesto Rossi and Tommaso Salvini.[15] Tommaso Salvini's first major tour was to South America in 1871 at the invitation of an impresario and businessman, Signor Pestalardo, and the tour marked a turning point in his development. His memoirs indicate that the company that he gathered together for the purpose was composed of actors who were no more than adequate. It is significant that from this time onward in the memoirs, Salvini, who previously had described some actors at length, mentioned the performances and abilities of his colleagues less and less. When assembling a company to accompany him to the United States, Salvini said "Sarebbe tedioso il nominare gli altri, giàcche questi due soli (Isolaina Piamonte and Alessandro Salvini) erano sufficienti a dar fama di buona a una compagnia. (It would be boring to name the others; these two [Isolaina Piamonte and Alessandro Salvini] were sufficient to give a good reputation to a company, 278).

Before the late 1860s and early 1870s, a *capocomico* was regarded as *primus inter pares*, but during the early years of Unification the *capocomico* was the star and other actors received minimal credit. At the same time, the responsibilities of the *capocomico* became increasingly onerous with the removal of subsidies and no state support for theater. Despite Salvini's statement that actors did not work on a commercial basis, the best analysis of this situation is an economic one. With no financial support at home, with increasing competition due to the free market, the leading actor made himself (or herself) a product to be sold at the highest rate to the highest bidder. Only through the earnings of the *capocomici* abroad could the rest of the troupe survive.

In 1880 Salvini received what he considered to be a most strange invitation. The American owner of theaters in Boston asked him to come to America and act in Italian with his American company. After much misgiving Salvini agreed, and a successful collaboration took place. Salvini's trip to New York marked the beginning of a new stage in the *mattatore* actor. It was now made clear, if clarification had been needed, that it was the actor, not the company, that was the attraction. The different acting styles of the *mattatore* and the foreign company helped to foster the concept of difference on which the *mattatore* system thrived.

International acclaim for its actors helped to foster the image of Italy and Italians as a nation of culture, but it did little to help Italians construct their country. So often were the most famous actors abroad, Italians themselves saw little of them, thus repeating a pattern that had become established when the best troupes from the late sixteenth to the eighteenth centuries established their reputation in Paris, Bavaria, and Russia.

DRAMATIC TEXTS

The poor quality of supporting actors, some of whom often did not know their lines, was a recurrent lament about Italian theater during the late nineteenth and the early twentieth centuries. Another concerned the quality of dramatic texts in Italian. Between Carlo Goldoni, whose last major Italian play *Il ventaglio* was produced in Paris in 1763, and Gabriele d'Annunzio, whose first major play was first presented in Rome in 1901, no major Italian dramatists would warrant a place in a history of European drama. Giacometti, Nota, Torelli, Ferrari, Giacosa, Praga, to name but a few, all produced well-made plays that were consolidatory rather than innovative, their content reflective of the social processes rather than a radical questioning of them. Some plays seemed to presage the longed-for revival that nevertheless failed to materialize. Achille Torelli's *I mariti*[16] was one of these and caused a flutter of excitement. It was heralded by Luigi Capuana as a truly national play (93–94). It seemed to satisfy all the requirements put forward by Cesare Trevisani in his report on theater. Its theme concerned the gradual process of change. Fabio Regoli, the male protagonist, aristocratic on his mother's side, middle class on his father's, combines the courteous civility of the upper classes, demonstrably lacking in the more obviously aristocratic characters, with the solid virtues of the bourgeoisie. It is his ideas that are endorsed in the play, and it is he who has a creative influence over the other characters. For Fabio, education supplants rank as a man's most prized possession. Love is not romantic evasion but deep care supported by hard work and making money to provide for wife and family. Husband and wife, in their separate spheres with different tasks, are linked in a joint enterprise of providing education and happiness for their children.

Fabio is the new man. He combines inner rectitude and hard work with successful self presentation. A lawyer in a country that needs an all-embracing legal system, he is classically educated and respects the past (at the end of the play he is seen consulting sixteenth-century documents), but he looks to the future. In his flighty young wife, Emma, he perceives the seeds of seriousness that are to develop in his loving and solicitous presence. Masculine and feminine roles are clearly divided and defined: action in the public world for the man, child bearing and child rearing for the woman—a sharing of responsibilities for the construction of the new order. All these themes make the play quietly cohere with the prevailing ideology. Furthermore, the play is set in Naples, a number of the characters are Neapolitan, while the play is written in Tuscan by a Neapolitan, thus bridging the north/south divide. It was awarded first prize in the Florentine competition set up to discover and foster rising dramatists.[17]

It shows something of Torelli's sense of theater and dramatic tact that Fabio, who bears the major themes of the play, is one of the lesser characters in terms of speeches and stage time allotted to him. In fact, the play's form was innovative and also caught the critic's eye. Both Capuana and Costetti observe that there is no central action around which the rest of the characters are grouped, but rather "quattro [azioni], tutte di fronte con ammirabile arditezza non slegate, e non disordinate, ma strette da una catena d'oro che fa le ceci dell'antica unità" (Four actions of the same importance, not separate or lacking in order, but held together as on a golden chain which stands in the old unity, Capuana, 95). The play was presented by one of the best companies of the period, the Bellotti-Bon Company. Luigi Bellotti-Bon, a comic actor, had been part of the Campagnia Reale Sarda in 1855 and in the following year had performed with members of the company in Paris, Berlin, and Dresden. Luigi Bellotti-Bon and his colleagues had been acclaimed abroad, but he had become increasingly conscious of the lack of a good modern Italian repertoire. In 1859, with a banker's financial assistance, he had formed his own company, determined to build a repertoire of Italian plays. By 1865 he had control of three companies and had encouraged no fewer than seventy-eight works. His reputation and efforts were such that some critics attribute the theatrical revival of the 1860s to him. But the revival was short-lived. Achille Torelli produced no other play to match the success of *I mariti*, and Bellotti-Bon was himself the victim of his own ambitions for theater. Harassed by debts and commitments he could see no way of fulfilling, he took his life in 1883.[18] Other playwrights such as Guisepe Giacosa, whose well-acclaimed *Tristi amori* gave temporary hopes that Italy had its Ibsen, and Marco Praga, whose social comedies contained some excellent parts for women, gave short-lived hope that the turning point had come.

It was, therefore, not only the structure of theater companies and economic conditions that lay at the base of the problems of Italian theater in the last decades of the nineteenth century. The search for and failure to find dramatic genius was symptomatic of a particular attitude to theater that ran counter to past achievements. At a time when the energies of the governing group were directed to establishing a standard Italian language and a national educational system, it was difficult to credit with importance the two major Italian traditions, improvised theater and dialect theater, which had come together in *commedia dell'arte* performance. As Gian Luigi Beccaria puts it, Italian is a language "vissuta per secoli più sulla carta, sui libri voglio dire, che non in bocca della gente. Una lingua più scritta che parlata. Una grande lingua d'elite modellata sul latino, e tale rimasta da Dante a Manzoni" ([a language] which for centuries has lived more on paper, I mean in books, than as a spoken language. A language more written then spoken. A great language of an elite, modeled on Latin and remaining like that from Dante to Manzoni, 13). From the 1860s this "lingua più scritta che parlata" was meant to become both the everyday and literary language of the nation. But it would take a long time for the literary language to become a spoken language and even longer for a dramatist to cast successfully this spoken literary language into theatrical dialogue. Italy's problems of theater were then in part linked with the much larger language problem. Theatrical talent there was, but in Cesare Trivisani's opinion the fact that there were better dialect writers than Italian writers of theater called for regret rather than celebration because "col loro lusinghiero successo ritardano, non volendo, il grande beneficio della completa unificazione." (With their flattering success they hold up, without intending to, the great benefit of unification, 180).

For centuries improvisation had been a talent that Italians had been proud of and that had been much admired by foreigners. Adriano Valeriani in his funeral oration for her in 1570 praised Vincenza Armani, one of Italy's earliest known actresses, for her capacity to improvise (135). When Mrs. Piozzi toured in Italy, one experience that impressed her was hearing women improvise poetry (Piozzi, 161–63). The ability to create without a fully written out script was a distinguishing feature of the *commedia dell'arte*. This skill was beginning to fascinate non-Italian Europeans during the second half of the nineteenth century and was more fully explored at the beginning of the twentieth century. George Sand in the midnineteenth century, and later her son Maurice, set a fashion that was to develop with Vachtangoff in Moscow and Gordon Craig in Italy. Their experiments with improvisational methods led them to believe that they were discovering the pure roots of theater. Late nineteenth-century Italians took a different view. The following quotation from a lecture, "Carlo Gozzi e la fiabi" by Matilde Serao clarifies that view well:

la risurrezione della commedia dell'arte, anche menomata, anche ridotta a brevissime manifestazione, anche messa li solo per bisogno scenico e per contrasto morale, non può non essere giudicato un atto di annichilimento letterario, da parte di un autore. La Commedia dell'Arte e la improvisazione capricciosa di cervelli comici che non vogliono chinarsi a seguire il pensiero dell'altro, dell'autore; e il libito di chi appare sulle scene e sovra una vecchia trama sbiadita cerca mettere i colori di una recitazione naturale; e la sostituzione della coscienza personale dell'attore a quella certamente più elevata e più nobile dell'autore. Non un passo indietro, nella via dell'arte, ma certo, ma mille passi indietro!"

. . . the revival of the *commedia dell'arte,* however minimal, even if reduced to a very brief appearance, or inserted merely for theatrical effect and moral contrast, can only be deemed an act of literary destruction from an author's perspective. *Commedia dell'arte* is the wayward improvisation by bright actors who have no desire to follow the thoughts of another, that is, the thoughts of the author; it is the whim of those who appear on stage and seek to cover over an old and faded plot with the illusory colors of natural acting: it is the substitution of the personal consciousness of the actor for the certainly higher and nobler consciousness of the author. Not just one step backwards along the path of art, but most assuredly, a thousand steps backwards! (256).

Pirandello himself is the heir to such assumptions. One of his best plays, *Sei personaggi in cerca d'autore* (*Six characters in Search of an Author*) is built on the dichotomy between the play as fixed literary form, creation of the author, and the play as performance, creation of the actor.

In the absence of major contemporary Italian texts, Italian *capocomici* were always on the lookout for new plays from abroad. In listing his vast repertoire of some eighty plays, which he sent to Cesare Dondini in Naples in 1862, Ernesto Rossi listed "una quantità di commedie e drami tradotti dal francese" (a number of comedies and dramas translated from French, 156) which amounted to over a quarter of his repertoire, in addition to major tragedies by Shakespeare, Corneille, and Schiller. The social comedy, therefore, that Cesare Trevisani thought the appropriate dramatic form to foster cohesive thoughts in the minds of Italian theatergoers, whom he saw as an untapped pool of people to be molded into citizens of the new state, came largely from France. That so many of the play texts were not Italian continued to be a constant source of concern for Italians of the late nineteenth and early twentieth centuries, a concern that was voiced satirically by Pirandello in *Sei personaggi in cerca d'autore* when he has the *capocomico* say:

Che vuole che le faccia io se dalla Francia non viene più una buona commedia, e ci siamo ridotti a mettere in scena commedie di Pirandello, che chi l'intende è bravo, fatte apposta di maniera che nè attori nè pubblico nè restino mai contenti.

What do you expect me to do if the French haven't got any more good plays to send us, and we're reduced to putting on plays by Pirandello? Anyone who can understand those plays is a better man than I am, made as they are so to annoy actors, critics, and audience alike! (75).

It was not until 1916, with the presentation of Luigi Chiarelli's *La maschera e il volto* (*The Mask and the Face*), that a new dramatic movement began to surface in Italy. With this play, Antonelli's *L'uomo che incontro sè stesso*, Rosso di San Secondo's *Marionette che passione!* . . . , and some of the early Pirandello plays, new voices began to be heard, voices that had both a radical edge and had explored different theatrical techniques and methods of presenting characters and ideas.

EARLY TWENTIETH-CENTURY ATTEMPTS AT THEATRICAL REFORM

By the end of the nineteenth century, mounting criticism of Italian theater from within Italy led to a number of attempts to foster a different kind of theater. Criticism centered on the nomadic way of life characteristic of Italian theatrical companies and on the multifarious nature of the work of the *capocomico*. The remedy, it was thought, therefore lay in *teatri stabili* and directors, people who had artistic responsibility for staging the play without being actors and business-people as well.

The first of these attempts at regeneration and reform was Domenico Lanza's Teatro d'Arte, established in Milan in 1898. This was an early attempt in the new era to run a *teatro stabile*, that is, a non-touring repertory theater that catered to the tastes of the local public. Lanza, a theater critic of *La Stampa* and later of the *Gazzetta del Popolo*, attracted a nucleus of well-known actors, and his venture was well supported during its short life by the Turinese intelligentsia. The theater opened with an Italian tragedy, Pietro Cossa's *I Borgia*, and included in its repertoire Italian and foreign classics alongside contemporary plays. Lanza wanted to present what he considered good drama that dealt with moral and spiritual problems. Ibsen figured prominently. The theater had one year's intense but costly life and then closed its doors. The company, however, had achieved its success as it had intended to do. Without leaving the city it had become well known in other parts of Italy (Camilleri, 18–22).

Another serious attempt to avoid the excesses of a self-contained theatrical system came with Edoardo Boutet's Stabile Romana at the Teatro Argentina. Silvio d'Amico, a leading theater critic of the first half of the twentieth century, saw in Boutet the first person seriously to attempt to rescue theater not only from the wretchedness of its nomadic life, but also from the tyranny of the *capocomico* (472). Plays at the Teatro Argentina were performed in their entirety, not adapted to suit actors' whims. Discipline in the company was intense; attention was paid to correct costume, appropriate sets, and lighting; the actors knew their parts. Improvisation, "entrances," "exits"—any theatrical trick to gain audience appreciation—were abolished in favor of a clean and clear presentation of classical and modern plays. The theater opened with *Julius Caesar* on December 29, 1905, and was followed by Goldini's *Il ventaglio* (*The Fan*) and later Hauptman's *The Weavers*. Classics and new foreign plays continued to fill the repertoire. After nearly a year, however, tension grew between the leading actor, Ferruccio Garavaglia, who was well liked by the public, and the disciplinarian Edoardo Boutet, who was determined that Garavaglia should not become a *mattatore* actor. Giacinta Pezzana, who had been the leading lady in Lanza's Teatro d'Arte, was also part of the Stabile Romana. Her letters to Sibilia Alerama testify to some of the problems experienced by the theater. In June 1906, Boutet found it necessary to initiate a tour of major Italian cities. This gained him and the company acclaim, but Giacinta Pezzana gives an inside view in a letter to her friend that suggests that Boutet's ambitious idealism and Garavaglia's egoism were destroying the company.

Ho scoperto a che ora aspira il Boutet: a provare che se egli fu capace di creare una Compagnia Stabile che viaggia: se seppe far saltar fuori trecentomila franchi di fondo allo scopo; se giunse a scoprire che vi fu un autore francese che scrisse un "Giorgio Dantini" (come dicono qui) e la scrisse "or sono molti anni," ha poi anche la potenza, non solo di ridurre la Pezzana alle condizioni d'una comicuccia da sei lire al giorno pagandola 30, ma di esaurire le 300 000 mila lire in pochi mesi portano la Stabile in Città di provincia che rendono 120 lire al giorno, per una compagnia che, con le spese di viaggio e tasporti, viene a costare 500. . . . Agli sforzi del genio di Boutet, si uniscono quelli di Garavaglia, che aggirandosi nella cerchia del suo Io, lo aiuta con tutte le sue sforze a compiere l'opera di distruzione.[19]

I've now discovered what Boutet is aiming at: he wants to prove that if he was capable of creating a traveling repertory company, if he knew how to raise three hundred francs for the purpose, if he managed to discover that there was a French author who wrote a "Giorgio Dantini"—as they say here—and he wrote it "many years ago," he also has the power not only to reduce Pezzana to the conditions of a cheap little 6 lire a day actress by paying her 30, but also of exhausting the 300,000 thousand lira in a few months by taking the repertory theater to provincial cities that yield 120 lira a day, for a company which, with traveling and transport expenses costs about 500 lira a day . . . To Boutet's brilliant efforts add those of Garavalgia, who revolving in the circle of his own ego, helps him with all his strengths to complete this work of destruction.

Of all the attempts to establish a *teatro stabile*, the Stabile Romana was the longest lasting. A succession of directors assumed the task of maintaining the repertory theater in Rome. In 1918 Viriglio Talli, who directed Pirandello's *Così e (se vi pare)* (*Right You Are [If You Think So]*), took it on, spending a season in Rome and then taking the company on tour. The company was called Drammatica Compagnia di Roma per il Teatro Argentina, but this also folded in 1920.

Another attempt to provide a *teatro stabile* was the Teatro Manzoni in Milan directed by the playwright and theater critic Marco Praga. Praga's program was less ambitious than either Lanza's or Boutet's. He presented drawing room comedies in realistic settings. In one, for instance, they used a real Carpaccio painting. The first play to be staged by the company was Torelli's *I mariti* which was well received by the Milanese audience. During the 1913 season, Praga staged a Pirandello play, which, however, was not well received. Significantly, Pirandello was to attribute its failure to the acting which, he claimed, distorted the emphasis he had given to the play.[20]

These three attempts to provide repertory theater in major cities all had certain characteristics in common. With the exception of the actor Cesare Dondini who took over the Argentina in 1913, the creators and directors of these theaters were all men of letters, playwrights, or critics rather than men of the theater. All were working in opposition to what they saw as decadent theatrical traditions, and all aimed to provide a theatrical experience for a large number of people in well-established theaters. Other approaches to reform involved smaller ventures, where, since a smaller audience was the target, greater experimentation could take place. Among these were Enzo Ferrieri's Teatro del Convegno, Enrico Cavacchioli's Teatro della piccola Canobbiana, Gualtiero Tumiati's Teatro della Sala Azzurra, and Anton Giulio Bragaglia's Teatro degli Indipendenti in Rome. This last was the closest to what would now be seen as an avant-garde experimental workshop.

ELEANORA DUSE AND GABRIELE D'ANNUNZIO

When the poet D'Annunzio and the actress Eleanora Duse began their much discussed relationship in 1897, it might have seemed that another way forward for theater was about to be born. From 1879 when she played in a stage version of Zola's *Thérèse Raquin*, Eleonara Duse was recognized as Italy's finest actress. D'Annunzio was Italy's finest poet. The combination of such talents would surely regenerate Italian theater in ways never glimpsed by earnest, less imaginative reformers.

D'Annunzio's dream of a Festival Theater built on the shores of Lake Albano to the south of Rome embodied the idea of theater as ceremonial and pure, and was very different in its conception from any of the attempts to provide good repertory theater in urban centers. For D'Annunzio, theater had little or nothing to do with social drama. It was the realization of poetic images in historically accurate settings that would tap the spiritual resources of the nation and create a national drama. Other reformers sought to correct and discipline the Italian actor; Eleanora Duse herself was later to say that in order to change Italian theater it was necessary for all contemporary Italian actors to die of the plague.[21] D'An-

nunzio saw the actor as a means to his end, as one element of his poetic vision
that included settings, lighting, music, and poetry. The actors—and D'Annunzio's plays required large casts—were used choreographically. There was no
place in his theater for the detailed, deliberately restrained, but continuous flow
of movement that was characteristic of Eleanora Duse's style. Her attempts at
the poetic tragedy of Shakespeare with Arrigo Boito had been largely unsuccessful. Her major successes had been in the dramas of Ibsen. As extant pho-
tographs show, her style in D'Annunzio's plays changed: she became grandiose,
statuesque, and had no opportunity to use the acting style she had carefully
developed which conveyed emotion through the small gesture.[22]

D'Annunzio, who had no practical experience of theater, provided impressive
poetic spectacles combined with extreme historical accuracy, leading to enormous
expense. The main reasons why D'Annunzio's theatrical vision did not last longer
than it did lay in two areas. One is simply financial: D'Annunzio's directorial
style was enormously expensive. Historical accuracy costs. *Francesa da Rimini*,
financed by Eleanora Duse, was said to have cost 400,000 lire. The second cause
lay in the problem of style. Not only were actors required to act against their
own style; the whole conception of theater was alien to the preconceptions not
only of actors, but also of theater audiences and critics. The intense mood that
D'Annunzio was trying to create on stage both to amaze the eye and to touch
the innermost soul caused ironic laughter as well as wild applause, as a sentence
from Domenico Oliva's review of *Francesca da Rimini* shows:

The contrasts were so many and so intense, the wild applause of some of the ladies and
gentlemen in the audience was so mingled with the disapproval, the ironic laughter, the
whistling that echoed round the elegant auditorium that one must conclude that the opinion
of the public was decidedly uncertain (Barker and Bassnett, 12).

A number of attempts at theatrical reform in the early twentieth century were
Italian responses to an Italian situation. Lanza, Boutet, and Praga may have
differed about which texts they wanted to stage, how they wanted to do them,
and their relationship with their local public. Their activities made it clear,
however, that all three were concerned to reform the practice of Italian theater,
to remedy what they saw as a lack of discipline and shoddy presentation. Their
reform stressed the importance of the play text, but it was also actor centered.
D'Annunzio's vision on the other hand, like Gordon Craig's a little later, saw
the actor as but one of a number of components that included lighting, music,
costumes, and scenery, all of which, in D'Annunzio's case, was to serve, and
to be subordinate to, the word of the creator, the poet. In his experimentation,
which aimed not to reform but to offer something quite other than conventional
realist theater, his vision was European. His far-reaching ideal of a theater for
the people needs to be seen in the light of other experiments with performance
space during the last decade of the nineteenth century. As Susan Bassnett has
pointed out, "Duse and D'Annunzio, in expressing their ambition for a modern
Greek-style theatre, were following a clear line of development that was running

throughout Europe" (124). Romain Rolland in France, Wagner at Bayreuth, and Strindberg in Östergotland were but three examples of this trend to create a people's theater.

Pirandello admired Eleanora Duse and disliked D'Annunzio. He attended the first night of *Francesca da Rimini* and wrote later:

I doubt whether I ever suffered so much inside a theatre as I suffered at the first production that Duse gave at the Costanzi in Rome of D'Annunzio's *Francesca da Rimini*. The art of the great actress seemed to be hampered, oppressed; crushed even by the gorgeous trappings of D'Annunzio's heroine; just as the action of the tragedy itself is hampered, oppressed, crushed by the tremendous panoply of rhetoric that D'Annunzio's ponderous erudition thrusts upon it.[23]

Pirandello shared with D'Annunzio the notion of the primacy of the word of the poet, but he considered D'Annunzio's texts superficial, larded with superimposed symbolism, and written in decidedly untheatrical language. Though later in life, specifically when he was considering the survival of live theater in competition with cinema and other mass entertainment, Pirandello would return to consider the function of theater for the masses, in his earlier theatrical career and up to the time when he established the Teatro d'Arte in Rome, his points of comparison are with other European art theaters in Europe[24] and with *teatri stabili* in Italy, not with the D'Annunzian vision. The plan presented to Mussolini for establishing the Teatro D'Arte, taken from a project set up by Lamberto Picasso who was to be the leading actor in his company (Alberti, 126–30), shows Pirandello conscious both of the Italian theater's past and of contemporary developments in Europe. He intended to provide for a small discerning Roman public a good repertory theater that would provide well-presented stagings of new Italian and European plays, combined with some touring that would give the theater and company both a national and international status.

From the consideration of the antecedents to his theater and drama, it is now possible to locate Pirandello within an Italian and European theater context. In Italy he is one of the reformers, nearly all of whom, like him, were original men of letters rather than theater practitioners. His plays developed from the social realist drama of the nineteenth century that Trevisani thought so important for the creation of a new nation-state. His major innovation in those plays was to provide both a radical critique of the social fabric and later of the realist form itself. The major distinction is to be found in the quality of his plays. The Teatro d'Arte was short-lived; it was disbanded in the summer of 1928. Pirandello's plays, on the other hand, lived on to be a major influence on European drama.

NOTES

1. Pirandello's involvement with the Teatro d'arte is fully documented in Alessandro d'Amico and Alessandro Tinterri, *Pirandello capocomico* (Palermo: Sellerio, 1987). See

also A. Richard Sogliuzzo, *Luigi Pirandello, Director* (Metuchen, N.J., and London: Scarecrow Press, 1982).

2. See, in particular, Corrado Alvaro in *Il Risorgimento*, 3.IV.1925, now in Corrado Alvaro, *Cronache e scritti teatrali*, ed. Alfredo Barbina (Rome: Abete, 1976), 76–86; Silvio D'Amico in *L'Idea Nazionale* 4.IV.1925, now in Silvio d'Amico, *Cronache del Teatro* (Bari: Laterza, 1963), I, 490–96; and Adriano Tilgher in *Il Mondo*, 4.IV,1925, now in Adriano Tilgher, *Il problema centrale* (Cronache teatrali, 1914–1926) (Genova: Edizioni del Teatro Stabile di Genova, 1973), 355–341.

3. Massimo d'Azeglio had said at the period of Unification: "We have made Italy, now we must make Italians." See Martin Clark, *Modern Italy, 1871–1982* (London and New York: Longman, 1984), 30 and *passim*.

4. This is the view of Ferdinando Taviani in a recent major work. Ferdinando Taviani and Mirella Schino, *Il segreto della Commedia dell'Arte* (Firenze: Usher, 1982).

5. Carlo Goldoni, *Tutte le opere*, ed. Giuseppe Ortolani (Milan: Mondadori, 1935), I, 184–86.

6. For information concerning Italian theatrical companies, see Claudia Palombi, *passim*; and Cesare Molinari, *L'attrice divina: Eleanora Duse nel teatro italiano fra i due secoli* (Roma: Bulzoni, 1985), 36–55.

7. In his memoirs Ernesto Rossi explained that when he was offered a contract with the Compagnia Reale Sarda in 1852 it was for *primo attore* only, and not *primo attore assoluto* which would have carried with it the right to choose his parts; Ernesto Rossi, *Quarant'anni di vita artistica* (Firenze: Niccolai, 1877), 60.

8. Ernesto Rossi was eloquent on the importance of knowing the part well so that a strained memory did not impede a full projection of the character; Ernesto Rossi, pp. 200–201. Luigi Pirandello also had strong views about the damage that a prompter's interpretation could do to the communication of the play; see Dario Niccodemi, *Tempo passato* (Milano: Treves, 1929) 82–88.

9. See Tommaso Salvini's memoirs for a description of the problems of the *capocomico*; Tommaso Salvini, Ricordi, *Anecdoti ed Impressioni* (Milano: Fratelli Dumolard, 1895), 175–83.

10. This way of life is evoked with attractive nostalgia by Carlo Tamberlani, *Pirandello nel Teatro che c'era* (Roma: Bulzoni, 1982), 165–76.

11. For further information about the Compagnia Real Sarda, see Lamberto Sanguinetti, *La compagnia reale sarda (1820–1855)* (Bologna: Cappelli, 1963).

12. For further information about theater during the Risorgimento, see Federico Doglio, "Dal Romanticismo al Risorgimento" in *Il teatro tragico italiano* (Bologna: Guanda, 1960), cixl–clxiv; and Federico Doglio, ed., *Teatro e Risorgimento* (Bologna: Cappelli, 1972).

13. See Cesare Trevisani, *Delle condizioni della letteratura drammatica italiana nell'ultimo decennio* (Firenze: Bettini, 1867) on this topic.

14. Enrico Rosmini, *La Legislazione e la Giurisprudenza dei Teatri* (Milano: F. Manini, 1872–1873). Chapter 7 deals with government grants and state legislation for theater.

15. For a graphic account of the hazards of the long voyages involved in such tours, see Salvini, 249–57.

16. Achille Torelli's play *I mariti* was staged at the Niccolini Theater in Florence in 1867 and was very well received; see Luigi Capuana, "Achille Torelli" in *Teatro italiano contemporaneo* (Palermo: Luigi Pedone Lecuriel, 1872), 92–112; and Siro Ferrone, *Il teatro di Verga* (Rome: Bulzoni, 1972), 22.

17. Achille Torelli, *I mariti* is now in *Teatro italiano*, ed. Eligio Possenti (Milano: La Nuova Accademia, 1962), IV, 103–98.

18. See the entry in *Enciclopedia del Teatro* (Roma: Casa Editrici Le Maschere, 1954), II, 2144–21.

19. Giacinta Pezzana to Sibilla Alerama, Gramsci Institute, Rome.

20. Luigi Pirandello, in his "Lettera alla protagonista," preface to *Se non cosi* (Milan: Treves., 1917), ix–xii. See Olga Ragusa, *Luigi Pirandello* (Edinburgh: Edinburgh University Press, 1980), 65–66.

21. Silvio d'Amico, "Dal capocomico al regista" in *Cinquant'anni di teatro in Italia*, ed. Giulio Pascuvio (Rome: Bestetti, 1954), 21.

22. Susan Bassnett, "Eleanora Duse" in John Stokes, Michael Booth, and Susan Bassnett, *Bernhardt, Terry, Duse, the Actress in Her Time* (Cambridge: Cambridge University Press, 1988), 141–45.

23. Luigi Pirandello, "Eleanora Duse" in *The Theory of the Modern Stage*, ed. Eric Bentley (Harmondsworth: Penguin Books, 1968), 165–66.

24. Clive Barker and Susan Bassnett, "Locating Pirandello in the European Theatre Context," *The Yearbook of the British Pirandello Society*, 5 (1985), 1–19.

WORKS CITED

Alberti, A. C. *Il teatro nel fascismo*. Rome: Bulzoni, 1974.

Alvaro, Corrado. *Cronache e scritti teatrali*. Ed. Alfredo Barbina. Rome: Abete, 1976.

Barker, Clive, and Bassnett, Susan. "Locating Pirandello in the European Theatre Context." *The Yearbook of the British Pirandello Society*, 5 (1985), 1–19.

Beccaria, Gian Luigi. *Italiano antico e nuovo*. Milan: Garzanti, 1988.

Camilleri, Andrea. *I teatri stabili in Italia (1898–1918)*. Bologna: Cappelli, 1959.

Capuana, Luigi. *Teatro italiano contemporaneo*. Palermo: Luigi Pedone Lecuriel, 1872.

Clark, Martin. *Modern Italy, 1871–1982*. London and New York: Longman, 1984.

D'Amico, Alessandro, and Tinterri, Alessandro. *Pirandello capocomico*. Palermo: Sellerio, 1987.

D'Amico, Silvio. *Cronache del teatro*. Ed. E. Ferdinando Palmieri and Sandro d'Amico. Bari: Laterza, 1963.

———. "Dal Capocomico al regista" in *Cinquant'anni di teatro in Italia*. Ed. Giulio Pascuvio. Rome: Bestetti, 1954.

Doglio, Federico. *Il teatro tragico italiano*. Bologna: Guanda, 1960.

———. *Teatro e Risorgimento*. Bologna: Cappelli, 1972. *Enciclopedia del Teatro*, II. Rome: Casa Editrice Le Maschere, 1954.

Ferrone, Siro. *Il teatro di Verga*. Rome: Bulzoni, 1972.

Goldoni, Carlo. *Tutte le opere*, I. Ed. Giuseppe Ortolani. Milan: Mondadori, 1935.

Molinari, Cesare. *L'attrice divina: Eleanora Duse nel teatro italiano fra i due secoli*. Rome: Bulzoni, 1985.

Niccodemi, Dario. *Tempo passato*. Milan: Treves, 1929.

Palombi, Claudia. *Il gergo del teatro*. Rome: Bulzoni, 1986.

Pezzana, Giacinta. Letters to Sibilla Aleramo, Gramsci Institute, Rome.

Piozzi, Hester Lynch. *Observations and Reflections Made in the Course of a Journey through France, Italy, and Germany*. Ed. Herbert Barrows. Ann Arbor: University of Michigan, 1968.

Pirandello, Luigi. "Eleanora Duse" In *The Theory of the Modern Stage*. Ed. Eric Bentley. Harmondsworth: Penguin Books, 1968.

————. *Maschere nude*, I. Milan: Mondadori, 1958.

————. *Se non così*. Milan: Treves, 1917.

Ragusa, Olga. *Pirandello*. Edinburgh: Edinburgh University Press, 1980.

Rosmini, Enrico. *La legislazione e la giurisprudenza dei teatri*. Milan: F. Manini, 1872–1873.

Rossi, Ernesto, *Quarant'anni di vita artistica*. Florence: Niccolai, 1887.

Salvini, Tommaso. *Ricordi, anecdoti ed impressioni*. Milan: Fratelli Dumolard, 1895.

Sanguinetti, Lamberto. *La compagnia real sarda (1820–1855)*. Bologna: Cappelli, 1963.

Serao, Matilde. "Carlo Gozzi e la fiaba." *La vita italiana nel Settecento, conferenze tenute a Firenze nel 1895*. Milan: Treves, 1896.

Sogliuzzo, Richard. *Luigi Pirandello, Director*. Metuchen, N.J., and London: Scarecrow Press, 1982.

Tamberlani, Carlo. *Pirandello nel "Teatro che c'era."* Rome: Bulzoni, 1982.

Taviani, Ferdinando, and Schino, Mirella. *Il segreto della commedia dell'arte*. Florence: Usher, 1982.

Tilgher, Adriano. *Il problema centrale (Cronache teatrali 1914–1926)*. Genoa: Teatro Stabile di Genoa, 1973.

Torelli, Achille, "I mariti" in *Teatro italiano*, IV. Ed. Eligio Possenti. Milan: La Nuova Accademia, 1962.

Trevisani, Cesare. *Delle condizioni della letterature drammatica italiana nell'ultimo decennio*. Florence: Bettini, 1867.

Valeriano, Adriano. "Oratione in morte della divina Signora Vincenza Armani, comica eccellentissima." Verona, 1570.

10

The Hidden Image in Pirandello and Shakespeare

Matthew N. Proser

> In certain moments of inner silence, in which our soul strips itself of all its
> habitual fictions and our eyes become sharper and more piercing, we see
> ourselves in life, and life itself, as if in a barren and disquieting nakedness;
> we are seized by a strange impression, as if, in a flash, we could clearly
> perceive a reality different from the one that we normally perceive, a reality
> living beyond the reach of human vision, outside the forms of human reason.
>
> Luigi Pirandello, *On Humor* (138)

Shakespeare's consciousness of the remarkable capacity of the human mind to
shape a believable fiction not only in dramas, but also in human relations themselves (to Elizabethans so much like plays) is sharply caught in his bittersweet
Sonnet 138.

> When my love swears that she is made of truth,
> I do believe her though I know she lies,
> That she might think me some untutored youth,
> Unlearnèd in the world's false subtleties.
> Thus vainly thinking that she thinks me young,
> Although she knows my days are past the best,
> Simply I credit her false-speaking tongue;
> On both sides thus is simple truth suppressed.
> But wherefore says she not she is unjust?
> And wherefore say not I that I am old?
> O, love's best habit is in seeming trust,

And age in love loves not to have years told.
Therefore I lie with her, and she with me,
And in our faults by lies we flattered be. (*The Sonnets*, 138)

Operating in Sonnet 138 is a fiction that "lies like truth" because each of the participants accepts the other's false guise in order to defend his own. The poet, who sees himself as aging, is happy to accept the fantasy that he is young and to "credit" his lady's flattering acquiescence to this delusion even when he knows she lies. Their fictions enable them to love. Equally, he will credit her honesty, a virtue she herself knows she sadly lacks, although he recognizes that she is dishonest just as she does. His false "youth" and her false "honesty" (with all its sexually allusive innuendo) are a currency passed between them that makes the bargainers marketable for each other and for themselves. For the sake of love, they become creatures other than they are. Shakespeare's subtle, wry, and rueful language creates a little scene of lovers in bed trying to plump up the pillows of desirability, as if sex were not really a blind instinct that could extract satisfaction out of a variety of encounters, aesthetic or unaesthetic, moral or immoral, as the case may be. Notwithstanding "love's best habit "(both repeated act and costume)—which is "seeming trust"—actually works. The lovers may feel guilty, but their mutual fiction brings them together nonetheless. Theirs may be a union forged out of flattery and self-delusion, and their awareness of this may lace their pleasure with wormwood; but does blind Cupid really care if his arrow is not tipped with gold?

The lovers in Shakespeare's sonnet create a theater out of their own desires, and the play's the thing, even if the sad truth crouches by the side of the bed like a silent dog. Reflected on in this way, the situation in Sonnet 138 takes on a Pirandellian cast: truth is overcome by the masks and fictions life requires for its survival. Human creatures cannot function without self-deluding intervals of amateur theatricals, and humans need to function at least as much as they need to know themselves.

A partial analogy might be seen in Pirandello's greatest tragedy, *Henry IV*. "Henry" explains to Marchioness Matilda Spina why it is that in representing the Holy Roman Emperor he so ridiculously paints his cheeks like a clown and dyes his hair only in the front:

But we all of us cling tight to our conceptions of ourselves, just as he who is growing old dyes his hair. What does it matter that this dyed hair of mine isn't a reality for you, if it *is* to some extent, for me?—you, you, my Lady, certainly don't dye your hair to deceive the others, nor even yourself; but only to cheat your own image a little before the looking-glass. I do it for a joke! You do it seriously! But I assure you that you too, Madam, are in masquerade, though it be in all seriousness. I am not speaking of the venerable crown on your brows or the ducal mantle. I am speaking only of the memory you wish to fix in yourself of . . . the fading image of your youth! (*Henry IV*, 519)

Both the mad "Henry" and sane Donna Matilda are in masquerade; both try to cheat the mirror of the true image of themselves. Donna Matilda makes herself up and dyes her hair "seriously," while "Henry" rouges himself like a marionette and lets the true gray of his hair show at the back of his blonde-fronted head. But both know the truth inwardly; and they know that the world knows it too. Nevertheless, they choose the masquerade, the fiction, and act themselves out in the theater of their own eyes. And convince themselves! She preserves her lost youth in a mind that recognizes she is aging but cannot accept the truth. He preserves a false image of youthful realness that protects an aging, vulnerable creature "all gray, inside." As in the case of Shakespeare's Sonnet 138, the truth pays the piper while the figures live out their lives knowing of truth's existence, but refusing to let it be.

A central metaphor in both Shakespeare and Pirandello that expresses the relationship between the self and its guises is that of the mirror. The notion is ubiquitous in Shakespeare, but is most memorable in *Hamlet* and *Richard II*. It occurs in Pirandello's *It Is So (If You Think So)*[1] when the play's *raisonneur*, Laudisi, addresses himself in self-mocking soliloquy before a looking-glass on the mantel. He points his finger at his image in the mirror and smiles so that his reflection smiles:

> . . . As for me, I say that here, right in front of you, I can see myself with my eyes and touch myself with my fingers. But what are you for other people? What are you in their eyes? An image, my dear sir, just an image in the glass! (*It Is So*, Act 2, p. 102)

Those survivors of an earthquake, Ponza and his mother-in-law, Signora Frola, turn their mirrors outward creating contradictory versions of the mysterious wife/daughter whose true identity remains hidden even after the play's conclusion. They use every effort to deflect the gaze of their inquisitive neighbors away from the meaning of the wife/daughter shared in some mysterious and contradictory manner between them. By means of accusations and demonstrations of humiliated frailty they attempt to defend themselves from the wrenching emotional anguish attached to the veiled, exposed, but never fully identified figure who appears at the end, a figure who claims to be two contrary people at the same time: Ponza's second wife, and the daughter of Signora Frola, the mother of his first. Importuning the group of sensation-seekers pestering her, the veiled figure cries that she is *both* the daughter of Signora Frola *and* the second wife of Ponza, but as for herself, "I am nobody!" But the real point underlying this statement is uttered slightly earlier when she says: "What else do you want of me, after this, ladies and gentlemen? There is a misfortune here, as you can see, which must stay hidden: otherwise the remedy which our compassion has found cannot avail" (*It Is So*, Act 3, pp. 137–38). The inner image of truth in Pirandello, whatever its internal or external guises, as Eric Bentley has instructed us, remains "concealed, *concealed*, CONCEALED!" (4).

   Such is not the case in Shakespeare's *Richard II*. Here Richard's inner image
of truth is ultimately concealed neither from the deposed king nor from those
around him. Here the mirror is an instrumentality as well as a metaphor. In the
deposition scene, when the king calls for a looking-glass and holds it before his
face, he sees the difference between what the glass shows and his own true
condition, and the contrast brings him to a truthful insight about himself which
he himself is courageous enough to face in the presence of court:

> Give me the glass, and therein will I read.
> No deeper wrinkles yet? Hath Sorrow struck
> So many blows upon this face of mine,
> And made no deeper wounds? O, flatt'ring glass!
> Like to my followers in prosperity,
> Thou dost beguile me. . . . (*Richard II*, IV.i.275–80)

   What Richard begins to perceive is that he can no longer hide from the pain
of his situation by theatrical self-demonstrations and poetic self-dramatizations
that try to deflect the gaze of others away from his inner sense of failure,
humiliation, and shame, and toward what he even here partially strives to project
as a heart-rending image of his victimized state. Nor can he deflect his own eyes
from self-scrutiny. As he increasingly recognizes his own complicity in his fall,
he also increasingly feels his anguish and guilt with an unvarnished clarity. When
he melodramatically shatters the mirror, ironically, he also shatters the theatrically false image he has previously attempted to project and he begins to move
inward toward a new identity. To Henry Bolingbroke's remark, "The shadow
of your sorrow hath destroyed/The shadow of your face," Richard replies,

>   Say that again.
> "The shadow of my sorrow"? Ha, let's see.
> 'Tis very true, my grief lies all within,
> And these external manners of laments
> Are merely shadows to the unseen grief
> That swells with silence in the tortured soul.
> There lies the substance. . . . (IV.1. 291–98)

   Unlike the case of Ponza and Signora Frola, moral and existential reality lies
in the open acknowledgment of suffering and its clarifying *exposure*. Inside
himself, Richard sees the true image of his nakedness, and the painful public
exposure leads to his new stage of self-confrontation and self-acceptance: "I
wasted time, and now doth time waste me . . . " (V.v.49). In Shakespeare, the
compassion that Pirandello requires for his central, suffering characters—a compassion that respects the defenses and self-protective fictions they build around
themselves in order to survive (Bentley, 4–5)—is not enough. It is the acknowledgment of responsibility that legitimizes compassion and distinguishes emotional self-awareness from emotional self-indulgence.

The case of *Hamlet* is equally illuminating in its use of mirrors and related images. Two key instances will serve to illustrate. The first is indirect and concerns Hamlet's harsh chastisement of his mother in the closet scene, where he "wags" his tongue in "noise so rude" against Gertrude's conduct in marrying Claudius and holds the "counterfeit presentments" of his two contrasting fathers like mirrors before her eyes. In his cruel, even brutal characterizations, she sees an image of herself:

> O Hamlet, speak no more.
> Thou turn'st mine eyes into my very soul,
> And there I see such black and grained spots
> As will not leave their tinct. (III.iv.89–92)

Hamlet's language is a verbal mirror that magnifies and reflects back the venality of Gertrude's conduct inescapably. His vehemence and passion, whetted by his anguish, shape an image of her own guilt that forces her eyes away from the self-protective status she has as queen and mother and the self-deluding sensuality that life with Claudius has reawakened in her so that she, like Richard, is forced to look inside and acknowledge the exposed truth of her own culpability. Hamlet asks:

> What devil was't
> That thus hath cozened you at hoodman-blind?
> Eyes without feeling, feeling without sight,
> Ears without hands or eyes, smelling sans all . . .
> • • • • • • • • • •
> O Shame, where is thy blush? (III.iv.77–83)

Hamlet's unsparing words expose Gertrude and force her to recognize her own unthinking sensuality. But what is real in her misconduct appears not as the effects of a "life force," as Pirandello would seem to have it in his characters, but is, instead, embodied in specific, individual human acts and actions, concrete and unintellectualized. Such acts impinge on the lives of others and those of all society, and therefore create a moral, social, and political entanglement, so that the acts themselves are more important than any philosophical notion about them. Pirandello's stance is at once more speculative, indulgent, and antisocial. It is Shakespeare's absorption in concrete actions and in the words that incite, accompany, or are the consequences of action—an absorption which, indeed, sees that words themselves *are* actions—that gives his plays their extraordinary immediacy and moral impact, and these are the essence of his drama.

The second "mirror" illustration from Shakespeare may be found in Hamlet's famous advice to the actors with its reference to the traditional Renaissance metaphor of the mirror as an image of the stage:

> Suit the action to the word, the
> word to the action, with this special observance, that

you o'erstep not the modesty of nature, For anything
so o'erdone is from the purpose of playing, whose
end, both at the first and now, was and is, to hold,
as 'twere, the mirror up to nature; to show virtue
her own feature, scorn her own image, and the very
age and body of the time his form and pressure. (III.ii.18–25)

One may dispute Shakespeare's definition of the word "nature," but whether it is to be interpreted as God's created world and the creatures in it or is defined as the ideal principles and idealized forms that lie behind appearances, the mirror itself turns outward, shaping an image of reality the audience can recognize as true. For this reason words and actions must be matched by the responsible actor: a neglect of nature's modesty makes nature herself unrecognizable and thus valueless to the perceiver, the audience. Once again, moral responsibility is a keynote. The value to the perceiver is implied by Hamlet's use of "The Murder of Gonzago," the "mousetrap" with which Hamlet snares the conscience of the king so that he reveals himself. Despite the formalities and conventions of the old-style rhetoric and gestures displayed by Player King and Queen, the new king recognizes an accurate reflection of himself and the truth of the murder he has committed and rises crying, "Giving me some light. Away!", attempting to obliterate the scene (III.ii.275). His reaction implies the further purpose of playing. The aim of playing above and beyond the accurate portrayal of "nature" is to bring the audience (in "The Mousetrap" Claudius, but in *Hamlet* us) to an admission of the truth as it exists inside us. We are all guilty players sitting at a play, as Maynard Mack implies in his remarkable and well-known piece, "The World of *Hamlet*."[2] The potential moral impact of drama is demonstrated when Claudius at prayer, stung by his most recent theatrical experience, considers the nature of his crimes but realizes he cannot give up the benefits he has won by them. He does not change, but at least he acknowledges his evil and accepts responsibility for his own possible damnation: "My words fly up, my thoughts remain below./Words without thoughts never to heaven go" (III.iii.97–98).

Like Hamlet, who speaks for Shakespeare's Renaissance notions, Pirandello also had a theory of representation which he expounds as *umorismo*. "Reflection" plays an important part in Pirandello's views too. His use of the word is rather different from that implied by Hamlet's "mirror up to nature," but it is equally revealing as to dramatic art's potential processes and goals:

. . . the work of art is created by the free movement of inner life which organizes the ideas and images into harmonious form, in which all the elements correspond with one another and with the generating idea that coordinates them. Reflection does not remain inactive, of course, during the conception and during the execution of the work of art; it is present at the birth and throughout the development of the work, follows its progressive phases and derives pleasure from it, and brings all the various elements together, coordinating and comparing them. Consciousness does not illuminate the whole realm of the spirit; particularly in a creative artist consciousness is not an inner light distinct from thought, which might allow the will to draw from it images and ideas as if from a rich source. Consciousness, in short, is not a creative power, but an inner mirror in which thought contemplates itself. One could say rather that consciousness is thought which sees itself watching over what it does spontaneously. As a rule, in the moment of artistic conception, reflection is almost a form of feeling. While the work is slowly taking shape, reflection criticizes it, not coldly and without feeling, as an impartial judge would do in analyzing it, but suddenly, thanks to the impression that it receives from the work (*On Humor* 112).

Pirandello's view of the creative process is substantially a romantic one, focusing as it does on notions of organic unity akin to those of Schlegel and Coleridge. We can even detect tenuous connections with Coleridge's view of the Secondary Imagination in the almost intuitive function of "reflection." This conscious aspect, though not the creative power itself (as *is* the intuitive Secondary Imagination) is nevertheless like a mirror that reflects back on what is inwardly created to criticize it, but "spontaneously," like "a form of feeling." The critical element in "reflection"; that is, its mirroring aspect is what makes possible the humoristic capacity that Pirandello calls "the feeling of the opposite," differentiating this from the impact of comedy, irony, or satire, which can only achieve a colder "perception of the opposite." Reflection's mirroring capacity has a conscious, an intellectual, and an intuitive aspect. Reflection spontaneously penetrates surfaces so as to reveal the opposite at the core.

Every feeling, every thought, or every impulse that arises in the humorist immediately splits into its contrary: every affirmative into a negative, which finally ends up assuming the same value as the affirmative. At times perhaps, the humorist can pretend to have only one feeling; meanwhile, inside him, the other feeling speaks to him, a feeling that at first seems to lack the courage to expose itself; it speaks to him and begins to advance . . . (*On Humor*, 125).

For Pirandello, however, the most important point about the humoristic sensibility is that despite its capacity to "disassemble" the constructions we form in life and see through them, it has the ability during "the ridiculousness of the discovery" to see "the serious and painful side . . . and, instead of feeling disdain," will in its very laughter "feel compassion" (*On Humor*, 132). On the other hand, the function of humorism is to penetrate surfaces and pull away masks. It can identify with those victimized by society like Ponza, Signora Frola, Henry, or Ersilia in *Naked* and wish their secrets to remain concealed, but it is also compelled to strip off the hypocritical costumes society's self-righteous meddlers wear to cover their own shame. Reflection "sees in everything an illusory or feigned or fictitious construction of our emotions and disassembles and unmakes it with a keen, subtle and detailed analysis" (*On Humor*, 141). Humorism can both identify with the inner nakedness of the vulnerable while despising the cloth that disguises society itself. As Pirandello says, quoting

Carlyle, " 'Society is founded upon cloth,' " and he continues, " . . . cloth is
. . . something that *composes* and *conceals*, two things which humor cannot
stand" (*On Humor*, 144). Thus, humorism's knife is double edged: with one
side it cuts away the masks that conceal society's true face; with the other it
defends vulnerable souls set off from society so that their secrets and suffering
can continue to remain concealed. Humorism means at one and the same time
to shame the shameless and to clothe the naked (*vestire gli ignudi*).

Humorism's two diametrically opposed impulses—to expose society, on the
one side, and to protect the vulnerable on the other—reveal a typically romantic
posture. Pirandello sees his victims, his Ponzas, Henrys, Ersilias, and perhaps
even his Baldovino of *The Pleasure of Honesty*, as units separated from society,
superior to it in sensitivity and intellect, and inwardly isolated from it. Society—
the gossips in *It Is So*, the actors and director in *Six Characters*, the meddling
Matilda Spina and Belcredi and Dr. Dionysus Genoni in *Henry IV*, the audience
in *Each In His Own Way*—is organized by a herd instinct that dictates to its
members their thoughts, opinions, ways of acting, and most of all their feelings.
The vulnerable—Henry, the Six Characters, Ersilia—are all wounded. At the
same time, they are implicit rebels, though not political ones. Their conduct is
often illicit or perverse in relation to society's mores. Witness Henry, who during
his reign of madness has consorted with prostitutes; or the Father in *Six Characters*, who at Madama Pace's establishment almost has relations with his stepdaughter; or Ersilia, who passionately acquiesces to her employer, Grotti, the
Italian Consul at Smyrna, allowing his toddling daughter to fall off the roof as
they cohabit there, and who later, rejected by her own fiancé, dresses herself
like a whore and goes out to solicit on a park bench. Pirandello's sympathies
are magnetized by those who fulfill proscribed impulses and *act them out*, even
to their shame. His corollary mission is to *startle the bourgeois*, who feels the
same instincts but covers them up as if they did not exist inside him.

The division in the functions of humorism—to strip away and to conceal—is
aesthetically rendered in the split that typically exists in Pirandello's plays between the figures representing society, who form a kind of audience to the play's
inner action, and the actors of that inner drama, who so often arrive from another
place, are dressed or made up strangely and mysteriously, seem to be hiding
something from their pasts, and who are thus carefully set off from the social
group (Bentley, 29). Eric Bentley's example is *It Is So*, but this division is true
in other of the plays as well, most notably *Henry IV* and especially *Each In His
Own Way*, where the audience in the play really *is* an audience at a theatrical
production. The social audience implies the "form" to which the mysterious
strangers cannot easily adhere, but who must do so to protect themselves because
at some point in the past, "life" welled up inside them in all its amoral vitality
and shamed them in their own eyes and those of others.

This characteristically Pirandellian division would appear to have biographical
roots, and indeed it can be seen in the gap Pirandello himself apparently felt
between his "life" on the one hand and his "art" on the other: " '*O si scrive*

o si vive'—either you write or live" (Bentley quoting Pirandello, 93). Key elements in Pirandello's early life and upbringing must have precipitated the splitting that can be seen in various aspects of his life and production.[3] Undoubtedly one of these was his violent, easily enraged Sicilian father, Stefano, who during the year of Pirandello's birth slapped Cola Camizzi, "the head and terror of the mafia of Agrigento" (Pirandello's hometown) who had approached him to extort money in a particularly insulting way. According to Pirandello's biographer, Gaspare Giudice, Stefano attempted to finish this altercation by striking Cola "in the face until he fell to the ground, his eyes, mouth, and cheeks swollen with bruises." When Cola came back with a gun, Stefano, lacking time to pull out his own, was shot twice, having hollered " 'Shoot, you swine!' " A servant managed to club Cola, but Stefano, with two bullet wounds in his chest, lurched after Cola as "he staggered away." Then "Pirandello followed him for twenty paces, firing the six shots in his revolver, before he fainted for loss of blood" (Giudice, 5–6).

This is hardly the ordinary kind of detail one expects in the biography of a literary figure. In his account of Pirandello's life, Giudice implies that at home Stefano flew into rages over trifles and that Pirandello's mother had to build the family's life around their fear of the father's rage (9). In this alone one could prophesy the beginning of a crack in Pirandello's sensibility. When he had grown up Pirandello may have publicly admired his father's republican patriotism, but, according to Giudice, his art served as both a release valve and as a disguise for his underlying fear and distrust of this vibrant, but frightening man (9).[4] One result of his father's volatile personality was a rebelliousness that grew in Pirandello during his adolescence. This was later "to be strictly repressed and to reappear in countless forms of disguise, in the shape of antitheses, outrages, or anarchy in his writing" (Giudice, 10), all evidence of Pirandello's inner division.

It is manifest, then, that at least some part of Pirandello's typical "raving man," his "Henry," or Baldovino, or the Father in *Six Characters*, is owed to his frustrating and overpowering image of his father, just as this frantic creature surely represents aspects of himself which he at moments questioned as "insane" or "degenerate" (Giudice, 55). The rage and rebelliousness provoked in the young Pirandello seem to have lasted him all his life and served as fuel to drive the engine of his art. The uncontrollable rages of his dictatorial father must have created dangerous feelings in the child Pirandello and a desire for a world that he *could* control. This longing appears in his love of marionettes as a little boy, puppets that he worked in his own little theater, both writing and producing vehicles for them (Giudice, 12), thus anticipating in miniature what was to be his life's greatest work—the writing of dramas. In these, he captures the threat and puzzle of his early Sicilian family life in the context of a theater within a theater (*Six Characters*, *Tonight We Improvise*, *Henry IV*), a play within a play (see Bentley, 61).

Alastair Hamilton's rather brief and limited English translation of Giudice's biography has little to say about Pirandello's mother. She suffered silently, placated the father, and occasionally intervened between the father and the son. Pirandello noted that he had difficulties with his mother, but it is hard to tell what these were. Pertinent, however, to Pirandello's creative process was his relationship to another female figure, Maria Stella, a maid in the house. It was Maria Stella who taught Pirandello at a young age to believe in ghosts (Giudice, 7), and just as the marionette theater served as a youthful model for what was to become his most significant life's work and his central metaphor in it, so ghosts, which Maria Stella taught him "could appear at any moment of the day or night and say what they have to say" (7), became a central element in *how* Pirandello wrote plays, as well as impetus behind the ghostlike characters who actually participate in some of them (e.g., the Six Characters or the Wife/Daughter in *It Is So*).

Notably, Shakespeare's ghosts, however vividly they are delineated, remain well within the conventions of Elizabethan dramatic convention. Whether we are referring to the ghost of Julius Ceasar, the ghost of Old King Hamlet, or Banquo's ghost, it is clear that these spirits come from the other world for very specific reasons (to raise conscience, guilt, or revenge or all three) and then go back to it. But Pirandello's "ghost" characters arrive as puzzles from some other place on earth, their purposes are ambiguous or dumbfounding, and their status does not imply an overarching spiritual world that interpenetrates our material one. These "ghost" characters derive from impressions arising in Pirandello's mind in the isolation of his study, and their appearance was evidently so sharp and compelling to him that it competed with reality itself. Clearly, they are projections of certain deeper and more instinctual aspects of his personality which another part of his mind contemplates and reshapes—just as he describes the process in *Umorismo*. For instance, elsewhere he writes in relation to his stories: " ' . . . I think I could remain from morning to night here in my study at the beck and call of the characters of my stories who are struggling within me. Each wants to come to life before the others. They all have a particular misfortune which they want to bring to light. . . . ' " Again he writes that " ' . . . sometimes my mind is so split and dazed that it rebels against this double or triple uprising and shouts in exasperation that the characters must either appear slowly, one at a time, or must go straight back to limbo, the three of them!' " (Giudice, 118).[5]

These Pirandellian characters are like the ghosts that Maria Stella taught "could appear at any moment of the day or night and say what they have to say" (Giudice, 7). And Pirandello's struggles to control them are like reenactments of the struggles he must have had restraining his passions against his father or his futile efforts to *control* his father. Most important is the way the characters arise out of him, aspects of his own psychological life that precede plot because they come with their own stories to him: " 'They all have a particular misfortune which they want to bring to light' " (Giudice, 118). But this strange process, or at least Pirandello's description of it, is connected with his mother and her death. Pirandello mourned her deeply, and this event in addition to his son's having gone to fight in World War I and his wife's violent periods of madness, caused intense feelings of isolation and loneliness. In this state, writes Giudice, "he resorted to the hermetic chamber of visions and the consoling evocation of his dead mother. Thus, Pirandello's mother turned into one of the vivid characters with whom he discussed his most intimate problems." This was the period "when he yielded most to his strange dealings with creatures of his imagination" (92–93).[6]

Once again, as in the case of his relationship with his father, this process of evoking characters and its connection to his mother and her death shows a kind of dissociative split. Pirandello separates himself from the real world and is accosted by "characters" who importune him for attention as if from another dimension, but they are clearly part of his own psyche and play an important part in his imaginative processes. They well out of him and are projections of his own feelings and conflicts—embodiments of his own instincts, desires, passions, and repressions, as are his dreams. Indeed, Eric Bentley writes, quoting Pirandello, that *It Is So* was born from " 'the frightening image' in a dream of 'a deep courtyard with no exit' " (28). Thus, although Roger Oliver is surely correct in seeing throughout Pirandello's work the "Sicilian" themes of "honor, jealousy, and revenge, as well as the sudden eruption of passion" (153), it can be offered that these themes are something more than ethnic manifestations. Whatever their geographic or nationalistic connections and however melodramatic may be their rendering, Bentley is correct in believing that Pirandello was "possessed" by "elemental family relationships" (61) and that they in their ghostlike representations are his true subject.

This elemental quality extends to many of Pirandello's most important figures, and his setting off of the Ponzas and Frolas, the Six Characters, even Henry himself, or Signora Moreno and Baron Nuti of *Each In His Own Way* (whose final crime-ridden embrace reenacts the conclusion of the *commedia a chiave* about them), suggests their special and more primal nature in relation to the brittle figures who observe them. Bentley understands such elemental figures as archetypes, "human beings stripped of the accretions of civilization" (35), and finds the key to them in family relationships.[7] This separation between the observers and the observed (to use terms from *Hamlet*) suffuses some of Pirandello's productions with a voyeuristic aspect that becomes clear in theatrical presentation, as for instance, in the recent revivals of Robert Brustein's productions of *It Is So* and *Six Characters* at the American Repertory Theater in Boston in the spring of 1988. This voyeuristic effect can be clearly seen, to take one example, when the actors in *Six Characters* observe the Father's attempted seduction of the Stepdaughter, or, for another, in the Father's earlier observations of his stepdaughter as a schoolgirl. The voyeurism not only illustrates the split detected in Pirandello's artistic processes and their representations on the stage; it also links up with Bentley's notion that the concealed image that lies below the visible archetypes and their actions is an image of the primal scene: "His plays hinge on scenes that have the quality of haunting fantasies, like the 'primal

scene' of psychoanalysis'' (48). Again, the primal scene (whether actually
viewed or fantasized), is a voyeuristic experience, or at least the best-known of
these is: that of the child seeing his parents make love.

Interestingly, Giudice recounts an incident taken from Nardelli's biography
of Pirandello that relates directly to these notions of voyeurism, primal scenes,
and incest. It appears that when Pirandello was yet a boy his curiosity about
what a corpse was like led him to sneak into a tower that was used as a morgue.
In the darkness he saw a body of a man with its feet sticking up with large shoes
on them. Then he heard a rustling sound, ''strange, continuous:''

Luigi peered through the twilight and gradually perceived two bodies, a woman and a
man, entwined together and performing a slow, strange, uninterrupted motion, as though
they were rocking, impelled by a spasm or regulated by a spring. They held each other
tightly and the woman's skirts were raised. The starched frill, rubbing between the two
bodies, produced that unforgettable rustle. Luigi watched them (10).

Giudice acknowledges this incident as one of the crucial episodes in Pirandello's childhood (10). In it we see a potential germ for a number of the features
here detected in Pirandello's work: the voyeuristic sexual interest, the vestiges
of the primal scene, the split between the ''audience'' and the ''characters,''
the illicit element in Pirandellian love, and the connection between love and
what the novelist Leonardo Sciascia called '' 'the smell of death' '' in some of
Pirandello's plays (10). But we must add with Giudice that ''we can hardly say
that episode alone—the encounter of an adventurous and precocious child in a
dark hall with a double spectacle of horror—determined the subsequent behavior
of the man and the writer. The boy's disappointment with his relationship with
his father may have been more important. But what is certain is that Pirandello's
life appears to be the consequence of a period of traumas, and the episode of
the morgue assumes a symbolic value'' (10–11).

But, it must be added that it assumes a *vitally* symbolic value, because the
experience in the morgue could have awakened the boy's inner fantasies concerning his own parents. Such fantasies were ever more importunate to rise to
the surface in periods of despair (which seem to have been persistent with
Pirandello) loaded as they were with sexualized aggressive feelings caught in
the image of death—of static, inert, decomposition framing the motion of carnal,
entangled, and living bodies.

The psychoanalyst Charles Kligerman points out that during Pirandello's youth
(age thirteen), Pirandello's father had an affair with an old sweetheart whom he
met in the convent parlor of an ''obliging abbess who was actually an aunt of
both lovers''(!) and that Pirandello came there one day, confronted the cousin,
and spat in her face, but that he did not expose his father when he saw ''his
shiny black shoes protruding from under the hem'' of a curtain behind which
he was hiding'' (740). We can see any number of disturbing yet illuminating
interconnections that would determine Pirandello's fantasies: the shoes of the

dead man the child Pirandello saw in the morgue framing the bodies in intercourse and the shiny, black shoes of the guilty father; the violent and taboo feelings generated by both incidents; the link Kligerman finds between this affair of Pirandello's father and Pirandello's own sexual feelings for his daughter, Lietta— father-daughter incest, according to Kligerman, being a theme in any number of Pirandello's plays; and the germ for Madama Pace in Pirandello's own relative, the abbess (738–43). In short, the potent voyeuristic moments in Pirandello's youth seem key determinants for the divisions in his life and art, as well as between them.

Here it is important to notice Bentley's reminder that by "fantasies" Freud meant the " 'psychic facades constructed to bar the way to memories of primal scenes" (Bentley, 61). In the letter to Fliess of May 2, 1897, from which Bentley quotes, Freud wrote regarding the structure of hysteria:

Everything goes back to the reproduction of scenes. Some can be obtained directly, others always by way of fantasies set up in front of them. . . . They are protective structures, sublimations of the facts, embellishments of them, and at the same time serve for self-relief (Freud, 239).[8]

Once again, in a later letter to Fliess, that of May 25, 1897, Freud emphasizes that "Fantasies arise from an unconscious combination of things experienced and heard, according to certain tendencies. These tendencies are toward making inaccessible the memory from which the symptoms have emerged or might emerge" (Freud, 247). From this standpoint, fantasies are "protective fictions" (239) meant to mask taboo memories and impulses. If this is true, it can then be hypothesized that the split detected at every level in Pirandello's artistic theory, process, and practice derives, at least in part from the danger that impulses connected with the primal scene might be detected or break through, thus exposing it and all its shameful implications. According to Kligerman, the blatant father-daughter incest almost enacted between the Father and the Stepdaughter at Madama Pace's in *Six Characters* is "a screen for the infantile primal-scene fantasy, the wish of the jealous child to interrupt his parents while they are having intercourse" (740–41). From a Freudian viewpoint, Pirandello's desire to protect his vulnerable souls, those who conceal some inviolable inner mystery, actually appears to be an unconscious desire to mask his own shamefully incestuous and aggressive impulses from the world and himself. Its corollary would be his desire to expose and ridicule the maligning and superficial "audience" surrounding the primal characters (or people in real life like them), thus showing that they too, after all, are no better than he. If he is masked, then so are they: " . . . you too, Madam, are in masquerade . . . " (*Henry IV*, Act I).

A scene in Shakespeare that likewise reflects this danger that an image of the primal scene might emerge along with its attendant recognition of the hidden impulses underneath it is, once again, *Hamlet*'s interview in the Queen's closet. To begin with, the scene is virtually always played around and *on* the Queen's marriage bed. Second, as both Gilbert Murray in *Hamlet And Orestes* and Theodore Litz in *Madness And Myth In Hamlet* (51–58) have pointed out, Hamlet's anger contains matricidal impulses derived from his jealously of his uncle, not only from his disgust with his mother's conduct. Thus viewed, there is an Oresteian dynamic to the closet scene that masks the underlying Oedipal suggestiveness.[9] From this angle, Hamlet's cruelty to his mother—his verbal thrashing of her with all its shocking sexual allusiveness—is first of all an expression of his matricidally jealous rage. In addition, his "speaking daggers" to her is actually an inverted image of the sex act from which the aggressive element has, in its extremity, detached itself and turned against the threatening object in active defense against the self's own real underlying impulses. As Jones remarks in his explanation of why Hamlet fails to take revenge: "killing his mother's husband would be equivalent to committing the original sin himself, which would if anything be even more guilty. So of the two impossible alternatives he adopts the passive solution of letting the incest continue vicariously, but at the same time provoking destruction at the king's hand" (103). Or to put the case another way, Hamlet cannot exact his revenge without risking a recognition of his own incestuous motives; or without experiencing his own true impulses; or without facing the threat of enacting the primal scene himself.

T. S. Eliot complained that Hamlet lacked a sufficient "objective equivalent to his feelings" to justify the amount of passion engendered in him (100). The foregoing analysis would seem to argue rather forcibly against such a point of view. Jones's account, if nothing else, gives sufficient cause for all the passion in Hamlet, his creator, and the audience too. On the other hand, Eliot tantalizingly adds that this lack of sufficient cause for what he characterizes as passion "in excess of the facts as they appear" is essentially "a prolongation of the bafflement of his creator in the face of his artistic problem" (101). Or to put the matter less negatively, the sense of mystery and confusion that characterizes typical responses to *Hamlet* is a function of Shakespeare's inability to isolate and render a reasonable cause within himself for his play's anguished distress. The question now arises: did this situation come about because Shakespeare, like Pirandello, could not face the truth of his own instinctual feelings and their incestuous implications?

Of course, it is as difficult to answer this question categorically for Shakespeare as it is for Pirandello. From a Freudian point of view, the most self-evident answer must be "yes" because in both cases the hidden image is unconscious in the first place and must be kept that way. But Shakespeare on his part seems to have come very close to recognition since Hamlet himself uses the word "incestuous" explicitly of his mother in Act I ("post with such dexterity to incestuous sheets" ii. 156–57) and against his new father in Act V ("thou incestuous, murderous, damned Dane" ii.326). Hamlet appears singularly repelled by the notion of incest and feels corrupted by it: "O that this too, too sullied flesh would melt . . . "(I.11.129). Pirandello also comes very close to exposing the image. Kligerman notices that, although the father-daughter incest masks *Six Characters'* mother-son incest, there is nevertheless an image of the more dangerous sort of incest in the relationship between the Mother and the older son, and even a rather primitive image of sibling rivalry and wishfulfilling murder and suicide in the deaths of the two younger children. "The father and daughter are most strikingly portrayed, but as Pirandello proceeds toward his deeper unconscious, the characters become more nebulous, until the little boy and girl become wraithful pantomimists" (742–43). Still Kligerman notices early in his essay (735–36), and later (743), that in the Preface to *Six Characters* Pirandello explicitly rejects any biographical or psychological explanation for his play by saying that the Father " 'derives from causes, and is suffered and lived for reasons that have nothing to do with the drama of my personal existence . . .' " (Kligerman, 736). This disavowal, then, must stand for Pirandello's official repudiation of the dangerous mother-son primal scene as a factor in his creative process, in the face of the surprising degree to which his own *umorismo* threatens to expose it.

As to Shakespeare, in the final analysis he addresses the sense of guilt, shame, and inner corruption quite differently from Pirandello. The clearest indication of this is seen in the way Shakespeare continues his tragedy. The voyage to England in fact witnesses the detachment of the son from the mother (rather than the restoration of the mother to the son as in *Six Characters*). Only after the voyage does Hamlet return to Denmark to carry out his duty by killing Claudius, albeit at the very last possible moment and almost by default, since he himself and his mother are already dying. In short, Hamlet appears to achieve the necessary distinction between *his* own impulses and the reality of *Claudius's* real crimes, if somewhat belatedly, thus erasing the division between the observers and the observed. The final carrying of Hamlet to the parapet for the rites of a soldier suggests his ultimate reintegration into society, not a final exclusion from it, as would seem to be the case in Pirandello's *Six Characters*.

Thus, although each playwright would appear to feel guilt and shame for proscribed impulses, it appears that Shakespeare regards sinful passions as ultimately forgivable. There is ample evidence of this in all his plays.[10] Shakespeare persistently understands the passions as capable of being integrated within a larger social context. For Shakespeare, the natural state of humankind *is* its frailty, so that when Hamlet accuses his mother of this flaw in the very first act of his play, we should not be surprised that the experience he undergoes leads him to a comprehension of his own. It is the acceptance of his own corrupt state achieved in the graveyard that stands for Shakespeare's acceptance of the inescapable truth of our most frightening and bestial instincts. To allude again to Sonnet 138: despite the truth displayed of human carnality and mutually accepted self-deception, the sonnet's image remains one of the reciprocity of shared experience, even if a rueful one. Shakespeare's classical notion of humankind's basic gregariousness suggests that humans are not fully human without their social links.[11] In Shakespeare, tragic figures like Richard II, Hamlet, Lear, and, in his way, Antony, confront the truth of their own human venality with an achieved sense of personal responsibility, thus effecting spiritual growth.

Pirandello's intuitions seem by and large more frightening and more isolating than Shakespeare's, and this is no doubt due to the violent and voyeuristic aspects of his youthful experience. His vision of life is brilliant, wary, and self-defensive. It seeks to preserve the inviolability of the human heart within the context of the human masquerade and a naked universe. The conclusions of his great plays reveal, to repeat a platitude, that human beings cannot survive without their masks: the veiled Daughter/Wife in *It Is So*, Henry in *Henry IV*, Amelia Moreno and Baron Nuti of *Each In His Own Way*, and the Characters in their tragedy—particularly the Father—remain mysteriously locked away from a broader, more embracing social contact, as if there were an irremediable gap between the individual and society. Out of this gap materializes, so to speak, the innovative creative genius galvanized by Pirandello's crueler and more vengeful impulses, which are manifested so clearly in the themes and actions of his plays, and which effect a breach between feeling and reality. Kligerman mentions that Pirandello's passions "seem to feed on hatred rather than love" (742). In life, says Giudice, Pirandello managed to resolve his differences with his family; it was in his art that he "felt an irresistible urge to protest and an anarchistic desire to break with everything, as if out of malice" (67). As Tilgher is quoted as having written of *Better Think Twice About It*, many of Pirandello's plays are full of " 'a bitter, open, lucidly logical violence' " (Giudice, 137, quoting Tilgher).

Like the boy's suicide in *Six Characters*, whether it really took place or not, or whatever its plane of reality, it is clear that human suffering reigns as life's overriding principle in Pirandello's art, a thing experienced so deeply and so completely that *it* alone stands as the unassailable fact of human existence, whatever its metaphysical condition. Those who love in Pirandello's plays are typically tainted by perversity, cruelty, secrets, madness, crime, or death, and the stain seems to be uneradicable. This is true for the Father in *Six Characters*, or Ponza, or Ersilia, or Baron Nuti and Amelia, or even the Husband in *The Man with a Flower in His Mouth*. The image of the lovers in the morgue would seem to haunt Pirandello's plays. To adapt a statement by the Leading Man in *Tonight We Improvise*, Pirandellian characters cry out their passion, "that passion that leads to crime" (*Tonight*, 181). Or as Pirandello himself put it, " 'We have within ourselves every possibility, and suddenly, unexpectedly, the thief or the lunatic can jump out of any one of us . . . ' " (Giudice, 119).

The anarchy and antisocial alienation at the core of Pirandello's work is the shadow of that breach of trust he must have felt between himself and his family—and all that his family represented to him psychologically, socially, and existentially. His plays are at one and the same time attempts to reconstitute and punish that family in the fragmenting mirror of his own disillusionment and shame. Notwithstanding, he succeeds in shaping brilliant, moving, and intellectually provocative patternings—indeed, patterns that anticipate and stimulate a variety of forms of dramatic modernism. From a Freudian standpoint, the heightened reality he gives the representatives of those family figures is an intensification characteristic of a fantasy meant to mask the threatening primary image. "Seldom has a man described so vividly the confrontation with his own unconscious and subsequent rejection of it" (Kligerman, 743). However, from an aesthetic and experiential point of view, the impact of that fantasy is like the maniacal laughter of the Stepdaughter as she flees up the theater aisle at the startling conclusion of *Six Characters*. Despite our horror and the impulse to run away, her laughter tells us everything.

NOTES

1. Or as *Così è (si vi pare)* is now more often translated as *Right You Are (If You Think You Are)*.

2. "And lastly there are ourselves, an audience watching all these audiences who are also players. Where, it may suddenly occur to us to ask, does the playing end? Which *are* the guilty creatures sitting at a play?" (Mack, 246).

3. It is not without interest that Pirandello's best novel, and his most popular one, *The Late Mattia Pascal*, concerns a young man in trouble with women and plagued by a bad marriage, who allows his village to believe that a body found in a stream and thought be a suicide is actually his. He leaves for Monte Carlo, cuts off his hair and beard, adopts the name Adriano Meis, and develops a whole new identity. Here is dissociation indeed!

4. Giudice goes so far as to suggest that "even Pirandello's belated commitment to fascism may originate from these unresolved conflicts and from a final acceptance of external authority" (9–10). However this may be, according to Giudice (6), all his life Pirandello felt incapable of communicating with his father, and this psychological barrier continued to grow between them despite his father's role in choosing him a wife and his support of him during his period as a student in Rome and Bonn, not to mention after his marriage to Antonietta Portulano.

5. The first quotation comes from a letter to Luigi Natoli of May 28, 1904; the second comes from "A Character in Distress," 1911. One might question the degree to which we are to take all this literally; on the other hand, it is clear Giudice does. Interestingly, the stories came out of the experience he called *Conversations With Characters*. This whole vaguely spiritualistic enterprise in which his prospective characters come to him in their ghostlike hauntings surely lays part of the aesthetic groundwork for *Six Characters In Search Of An Author* and other of his plays.

6. Again he writes that " '. . . sometimes my mind is so split and dazed that it rebels against this double or triple uprising and shouts in exasperation that the characters must either appear slowly, one at a time, or must go straight back to limbo, the three of them!' " (Giudice, 118).

7. This is manifest in *It Is So* and *Six Characters*, but family relationships with their inevitable Oedipal reverberations can also be felt in the interconnections of the key characters in plays like *Tonight We Improvise*, *The Pleasure of Honesty*, *Naked*, and even *Henry IV*. Moreover, love in these plays is always connected with feelings that are either violent or illicit or both, and the upshot is ordinarily tragic: Henry's murder of

Belcredi in *Henry IV*, the drowning of the little sister and the suicide of her brother, in *Six Characters*, and the suicide of Ersilia in *Naked* to name a few.

8. Freud adds: "Their accidental origin is perhaps masturbation fantasies. A second important piece of insight tells me that the psychic structures which, in hysteria, are affected by repression are not in reality memories—since one indulges in memory without a motive—but impulses that derive from primal scenes" (Freud, 239). This shift from real memories to impulses is what Masson criticizes in his revisionist discussion of Freud's views on his "seduction theory." See Jeffrey Moussaieff Masson, *The Assault On Truth: Freud's Suppression of the Seduction Theory* (New York: Farrar, Straus and Giroux, 1984).

9. It is useful to remember that the Orestes story contains a third figure in addition to Orestes and Clytemnestra—the Queen's paramour, Aegisthus. Claudius plays this role. Hamlet's jealously is rooted, according to Ernest Jones's implications, in his desire to take Claudius's place not only on his father's throne, but also in his bed, the very bed where Claudius, the play's Aegisthus figure, has also taken Hamlet's fantasized place.

10. A good example of such restorative motifs is the reconciliation of Lear and his Cordelia (a relation fraught with Freudian possibilities). Another example is the rebellious first Thane of Cawdor who is reintegrated with his community by the very manner in which he enacts his death: " . . . very frankly he confessed his treasons,/Implored your Highness' pardon and set forth/A deep repentance: nothing in his life/Became him like the leaving it . . . "(*Macbeth* I.iv.4–8).

11. Thus in *As You Like It*, it is the virtues of hospitality, comraderie, gentleness, sharing, and pity, among others, that are held aloft by Duke Senior to Orlando to demonstrate that all things are not "savage" in the Forest of Arden (II.vii). Equally, on the tragic side, when the isolated Macbeth lists the experiences of old age that his tyranny has lost him, he mentions "honor, love, obedience, troops of friends" (V.iii.25).

WORKS CITED

Bentley, Eric. "Pirandello and Modern Comedy," "Right You Are," "Enrico IV," "Six Characters in Search of an Author," and "Gaspare Guiduce's Biography," in *The Pirandello Commentaries*. Evanston, Ill.: Northwestern University Press, 1986, 1–7, 25–35, 43–56, 57–77, 91–95, respectively.
Eliot, T. S. "Hamlet and His Problems." In *The Sacred Wood*. London: Methuen & Co., Ltd., 1932, 95–103.
Freud, Sigmund. *The Complete Letters of Sigmund Freud to Wilhelm Fliess*. Ed. and trans. Jeffrey Moussaieff Masson. Cambridge, Mass.: Harvard University Press, 1985.
Giudice, Gaspare. *Pirandello: A Biography*. Trans. Alastair Hamilton. London: Oxford University Press, 1975.
Jones, Ernest. *Hamlet and Oedipus*. New York: Doubleday & Co., 1949.
Kligerman, Charles. "A Psychoanalytic Study of Pirandello's *Six Characters in Search of an Author*." *Journal of the American Psychoanalytic Association* 10 (October, 1962): 731–44.
Litz, Theodore. *Madness and Myth in Hamlet*. New York: Basic Books, 1975.
Mack, Maynard. "The World of Hamlet." In Shakespeare's *Hamlet*, ed. Edward Hubler. New York: New American Library (Signet), 1963, 234–256.

Murray, Gilbert. *Hamlet and Orestes: A Study in Traditional Types*. New York: Oxford University Press, 1914.

Oliver, Roger W. *Dreams of Passion: The Theater of Luigi Pirandello*. New York: New York University Press, 1979.

Pirandello, Luigi. *Each In His Own Way And Two Other Plays* (*The Pleasure of Honesty* and *Naked*). Trans. Arthur Livingston. New York: E. P. Dutton, 1923.

————. *Henry IV*. Trans. Edward Storer. In Block and Shedd, *Masters Of Modern Drama*. New York: Random House, 1962, 510–531.

————. *It Is So!* (*If You Think So*). Trans. Arthur Livingston. *Naked Masks: Five Plays By Luigi Pirandello*. Ed. Eric Bentley. New York: E. P. Dutton, 1952.

————. *The Late Mattia Pascal*. Trans. William Weaver. Hygiene, Colorado: Eridanos Press, 1987.

————. *On Humor*. Introduced, translated, and annotated by Antonio Illiano and Daniel P. Testa. Number 58 of University of North Carolina Studies in Comparative Literature. Chapel Hill: University of North Carolina Press, n.d.

————. *Tonight We Improvise*. In *Collected Plays*. Vol. I., ed. Robert Riety. New York: Riverrun Press, 1987.

Shakespeare, William. *The Sonnets*. Ed. William Burto. New York: New American Library (Signet), 1964.

————. *The Tragedy of Hamlet Prince of Denmark*. Ed. Edward Hubler. New York: New American Library (Signet), 1963.

————. *The Tragedy of Richard II*. Ed. Kenneth Muir. New York: New American Library (Signet), 1963.

Part Three

PIRANDELLO'S PLAYS

11

Ambiguity in
Six Characters in Search
of an Author

Gaspare Giudice

Translation by Jana O'Keefe Bazzoni*

In a letter to his son Stefano, Pirandello alluded to his play, *Right You Are* as "a great deviltry."[1] However, the real devils of vision and of dissociation would truly break loose in Pirandello, and even exceed the metaphor, while he worked on *Six Characters*. Corrado Alvaro suspected as much when he declared that Pirandello often reaches great art through unknown and unusual roads.[2] *Six Characters* is a work that the critics would have done well to treat with more caution. For a greater understanding of its values, critics should have sought different methods. To date, they have found only one-sided meanings and have established the play's rational boundaries. As early as the day after the opening of *Six Characters* in Milan, the critic Renato Simoni could offer an interpretation (which is a kind of compendium of earlier interpretations following the Roman opening): "In *Six Characters* there is anguish . . . the impotence of the artist in finding the fullness of form . . . of expression; . . . and it is not only the artist who lacks the power of expression but all of us who cannot represent others with precision and who cannot give others a true sense of ourselves" (52). This is clearly rationally oriented criticism of a kind least likely to illuminate a work rooted in barely confinable psychic forces. We have read numerous pages of those critics who have attempted to master the work: all of them use a rational scheme in which the work is captured only partially and not for long. Critics either echo one another's point of view, repeating, with little variation, what

*This chapter originally appeared in the Italian journal *Il Paragone* (1961).

others have already said, or they propose diametrically opposed interpretations—all of which demonstrates that one can enter and leave this work through various doors and traps.

Let us look at a few examples. According to Piero Gobetti, "the fundamental motif of this work is the antinomy of creation, the discrepancy between truth and its transfiguration in art" (72). According to Luigi Tonelli, in *Six Characters* "we find the contrast between life that tries to erupt, over any barrier, against any law, and art which constricts, limits, and rigidifies" (228). For Gerardo Guerrieri, the work signifies that "art is a rigid abstraction, confronted by an uncontainable human mutability" (250). On the opposite front, according to G. B. Angioletti, the thesis is that "the pure creations of fantasy are 'truer' than living people (53); for others, *Six Characters* "demonstrates that life is reality, while art with its form, kills reality, and therefore kills life" (Pompeati, 641).

G. A. Borghese has a more valid glimpse of a process of *ad infinitum* in the work, when he explains: "How can man, tormented by his inconsistency, find serenity in the *ne varietur* of artistic creation? Here is the tragedy: Art in turn projects itself into life, that which is fantasy becomes real; the tumultuous river of mutability engulfs that illusion of reality" (229). Borghese approaches an understanding that any part of this Pirandellian play can be dissected and that from that point we can initiate whichever critical interpretation we may consider appropriate.

Even in *Six Characters*, Adriano Tilgher found a pretext for one of his critical inventories of Pirandellianism, reducing the "'process of consciousness'" projected on the stage to that "through which the turmoil of the phantoms germinating from the author's fantasy, vibrating with life but still confused and dark, still partially chaotic and unrealized, attempts to compose itself into a perfect and harmonious synthesis" (237). Even today, *Six Characters* commands admiration, despite its inability to generate a clear critical perception of itself. Up to now there have only been inaccurate methods of evaluation.

Several reasons may be cited for rejecting a too rigid and schematically intellectual interpretation of *Six Characters*; these reasons compel us to search out and define the causes of the basic and structural ambiguity that we detect in the work and in its genesis: ambiguity not in the sense of failed poetic clarity, but rather in the sense of a crystallized poetry of ambiguity. To avoid abstraction, let us start our discussion with an analysis of some of the most significant speeches from the play. As support we can then add some of the author's autobiographical, theoretical-poetic testimony, which will reveal a genesis for the play that is pre-logical at its roots. Let's consider first one of the Father's lines at the beginning of the play:

The Father: I'm sorry that you laugh this way because we carry in ourselves, I repeat, a painful drama, as you no doubt can deduce from this woman, veiled in black.

[Translator's note: Except where noted, all excerpts quoted are my translations. I have translated the lines from the play literally. The play appears in a full

English translation by Eric Bentley, in *The Great Playwrights*, Volume II (Garden City, N.Y.: Doubleday, 1970), pp. 117–155].

The play's first ambiguity is in the double awareness of the *character*: a creature conditioned simultaneously by its nature as a living thing, a being in life, and as creature of the intellect, of the imagination, self-conscious by nature. In almost every line spoken by the characters, we find this double explanation, which is undoubtedly equivocal in terms of the traditional concept of the unified character, who is not divisible into a double personality. This is especially true if the two personalities must rediscover one another: one on the immediate plane of reality and the other on an intellectual plane, as *thought* between aesthetic subject matter and fantasy.

This speech helps us understand the suspect language spoken by the Father throughout—the constant imbalance, so intellectually "humoristic," born of introspection and of the reflective intersection of the character's physical, true, humanly suffering image (the human moment) with its own intellectual image. If we look into the sentence, we uncover a precise syntactic correspondence that is both cause and effect of such figurative dissonance. The human character and that which we for convenience's sake will call "intellect" do not coincide, and indeed must not coincide, but instead are distinctly focused in two different ways. Such dissociation (which nevertheless remains in poetical equilibrium) coincides with the syntactic division of the sentence into parts, which, respectively, express the instinctive and immediate zone of the character and that which reflects a more abstract self-consciousness.

The liaison between the two parts is the word "as" (Italian: *come*), which suddenly and clearly distinguishes between the two moments of the character. The first part is formed by a rather rapid succession of terms that have emotional significance: "I'm sorry," "that you laugh," "a painful drama," which are uttered in the rhythm of brief propositions and act as an emotional stimulus. The second part is more calmly illustrative and demonstrative ("as you can no doubt deduce from this woman, veiled in black"). Note the prominence of the verb *argomentare* (to deduce) used at exactly the right point to suggest the character's duality. The structure of the Father's sentences always expresses this double presence: of a human figure, actually and physiologically conditioned, and of a character intellectually self-sufficient and detached, implicitly ironic with respect to his own condition, who becomes a kind of "character's advocate" and guide of his own human adventure.

Similarly, the Stepdaughter:

Then, ladies and gentlemen, permit me. Although orphaned only two months ago, watch how I sing and how I dance.

The Stepdaughter doubles her own pain and anger, exacerbating them, on the one hand, in a wholly feminine, disrespectful, danced exhibitionism—while at the same time offering herself for a different kind of attention in a speech that is syntactically explicit, clear, and exhaustive. Use of the word "although" (*benche*), conceding, narrating, "only" (*appena*), which tones down any dramatizing, the "how" (*come*) I sing and "how" (*come*) I dance, which accentuate the sense of a request for attention from an unsympathetic audience—all are grammatical elements that have a poetic function and reveal the character's double "anima."

Although the characters' own passion and scorn remain intact, they are objectified and knowingly presented as entertainment. The subject matter and the writer's hypothesis of freedom of the imagination provide double strands that are interwoven in an immediate and inseparable opposition in every one of the characters' speeches. This is Pirandello's highly Romantic sense of irony. In *On Humor*, we read:

Another meaning, we said, a philosophical one, was given to the word "irony" in Germany. Friedrich Schlegel and Ludwig Tieck derived it directly from Fichte's subjective idealism, though it ultimately stems from the whole post-Kantean idealistic and romantic movement. The Self, the only true reality, Hegel explained, can laugh at the vain appearance of the universe; since it can create this appearance, it can also abolish it. The Self can choose not to take its own creation seriously, hence irony—a force which, according to Tieck, enables the poet to dominate his subject matter and because of which, says Friedrich Schlegel, the subject matter turns into a perpetual parody, a transcendental farce (6–7).

A similar "force," though obscure and removed to the unconscious level, presides at the birth of *Six Characters in Search of an Author*.

Analogously and equally fluctuating is the play's point of intersection between the physical space, in which the miserable and pathetic tale realistically occurs, the "theatrical" space in which the story is represented scenically, and the space of the memory to which the characters go to draw the reasons for their actions in an absolute dimension. We find here, too, a hermeneutics of a grammatical type within the bounds of the dialogue. The device used is that of simplified syntactic oppositions: it is the alternation, in the same sentence, of a present tense verb, which indicates an event that is happening or is about to happen *hic et nunc*, and of a demonstrative adjective that removes the scene to a space of a different quality, an imagined space: "*I am* trembling gentlemen, trembling to live it, *that* scene;" and in the character's reevaluation of the place where the events happened and will happen, the opposition of the demonstratives, here-that: "the room . . . *here* the shop window for cloaks . . . ; and in front of the window, *that* table with the pale blue envelope with one hundred lire in it;" in the imperfect alternated with the present: "But you men *should turn away*: I'm almost naked . . . *I don't blush anymore*. But I assure you that he was very pale, very pale at *that* moment!"

Another ambiguity concerns the temporal element. There is a continuous interweaving of the past, present, and the future in a temporal "continuum," but it appears to be simply a figurative solution. More than anything else, it is a *mental* description of a situation as tormenting as it is aesthetically fleeting. The figures have lost any temporal stability. Here are the Mother's famous lines:

No, it's happening now, it happens always! My torment is not pretence, sir! I am alive and present, always, in every moment of my torment, which renews itself, alive and present always. But those little ones there, have you heard them speak? They can no longer speak, sir! They cling to me still to keep my torment alive and present in me: but they, for themselves, don't exist, they don't exist anymore! And this one (indicates the Stepdaughter), sir, she ran away, she fled from me and she is ruined, ruined . . . If I see her here before me now it is again for this, only for this, always, always to renew for me always, alive and present the torment that I suffered for her too!

Here, without fail, every past tense corresponds to the future and is used to described what will be; the present tense is used to indicate what occurred and what will occur. The Stepdaughter is "ruined" because she will be ruined; the two little ones "cling" to the Mother because they will cling to the Mother. The Mother in effect doesn't embrace anyone; the little ones are for her "those little ones there"; the daughter isn't there, she has run away, and what remains is the torment: her actual presence is and is not.

But in the Mother's speech, there may still be a residue of implied logical conventionality. Thus, the speech could be interpreted as follows: since I am a "character," here is what happens to me, here is my terrible fate, *mater dolorosa* for all eternity. The interchangeability of tenses—present, past, and future— could then have an identifiable reason in a traditional idealistic aesthetic determined by a nontemporality of the artistic character's passion of pain. But such an attempt to "rationalize" the temporal ambiguity present in the speech cannot prove valid because, in fact, the images of the present, past, and future do not merge in Pirandello's drama. Rather, they set themselves in juxtaposition to one another and remain distinct. The realistic element of the Pirandellian scene obstructs and impedes any channeling of temporal and extratemporal motifs into one absolute stream. In a new way, Pirandello succeeds in depicting temporal plurality through these figures of dissociated contemporaneity. One thinks of the decomposition of figures on one plane such as those found in many of Picasso's canvasses. No one would deny that great art has been achieved, but neither could one deny the presence of intellectual artifice, of a new convention, which is combined with aesthetic intuition. Analogically, the aesthetic interventions used by futurists and cubists (by Picasso himself) rely on the abstract and intellectual, on the artificial, to give us, in a figurative sense, the intuition of spatial and temporal synthesis. There is a point at which the intuition of the artist cannot give us the findings of a discovery made, far from the senses, by scientists: we can reach Einstein's fourth dimension only by way of a blind alley of abstract formulas that cannot be traveled by a simple aesthetic abbreviation.

The false, equivocal perpetuity that Pirandello attributes to his characters, becomes—unknown to the author—a mocking, cruel, and impious leveling, a

pillory of the concepts of the absolute and of eternity handed down since Plato
and the basis of that idealistic aesthetic of which Pirandello was an outspoken
adherent. Absoluteness, as a characteristic attribute of works of art, was embodied in one component of the work, in the *character*. The absolute and eternal
character, detached in a way from the work of which he is a part, was a myth
of the romantic aesthetic. Pirandello, following De Sanctis and G. A. Cesareo,
often declared his belief in such a myth; but without quite realizing it, in *Six
Characters*, he mocks, contradictorily, that very absolute essence that he proposes for the character.[3] Clearly, an *absolute* cannot be more humiliated that it
is in Pirandello's play. It is embarrassed and ridiculed at the very foundation of
the drama.

The character lives, is born alive, cannot die, and yet begs to be brought to
life; and despite all attempts to save his own noble, lofty, independent dignity,
the character is debased by finding it necessary to defend his own contradictory
essence against the base stupidity of a foolish acting troupe. What can it matter,
the final exit, the final apotheosis of the characters in the midst of the artificial
lights of the stage, when the characters have undergone all the humiliation of
the shameful event?

Is there a catharsis, a paradise after purgatory? It is clear that Pirandello, much
as he wants to demonstrate the strength of his theoretical convictions regarding
the absolutes of art and of character, is careful instead to inflict purgatory on
art rather than consign it to paradise. The eternity of the characters and of art
tends to make its home in limbo. But not all of this is so clear in the work.
Nothing is clear in *Six Characters*; everything can be overturned, except, naturally, the result, the completed drama, entitled *Six Characters in Search of an
Author*. The meanings of the play navigate in ambiguity, and it is precisely
multivalence which is the play's predominant characteristic.

Note another logical application of ambiguity, caused by the dynamic inter-
secting of different planes of meaning given to the same object, resulting in the
absence of any single distinct entity, *and without the intervention of a metaphorical process*, from fact to symbol, from false to true, for a *here* to an
elsewhere and vice versa. Such an intersection of different projections of the
same object is most precisely identifiable in the Stepdaughter's monologue. (The
Stepdaughter speaks to the Little Girl who will soon drown herself in the fountain:
"My poor little love, you look bewildered . . . ") The immediate real object, the
first perception, is that of the "stage": "Who knows where you think you are!
We're on a stage, dear!" But a stage "is a place where they play at being
serious." "It is a place for acting out a play. And we'll act out a play. Seriously,
for real, you know." Up to this point, the cross reference is between play
(*commedia*) and doing it seriously (*far sul serio*), between the stage and the
implied realistic-metaphysical life of the characters.

But it is still vague, needing an object designed to act as a pendulum, able
to change its nature, to pass, in the brief period of the pendulum from a realistic-
immediate meaning to one that is objective-expressive. Here the object is "the

fountain." The fountain is a stage prop, is false. "It's false, of course." But the Little Girl plays "in a real fountain, beautiful, big, green, with bamboo trees to give shade." The sense of ambiguity (nonmetaphorical) is born from that feigned hyphen between the presentation of the prop fountain, an element of the stage, and the spontaneous birth of the imaginary fact of the real fountain, a union effected by a completely incoherent sentence: "But perhaps, child, you'd rather have a pretend fountain than a real one, to play with, hm? But no, it may be a game for others, not for you, unfortunately, for you're real, my darling, and you are actually playing in a real fountain . . ." We are not dealing here with a logical passage but with a simple, gratuitous affirmation of an artificial rapport between the two objects, giving them opposite meanings (pretend fountain = real fountain). The Little Girl likes a false fountain more than a real one, but hers is not a game: the false fountain is a real one (just as the Little Girl is a real little girl and not a false one, regardless of her artificial presence on the stage). The lack of a logical or metaphorical medium is imitated and finally rendered ambiguous by a mobilization of emotions, from the affectionate tone, from the caressing use of diminutives, from the devastating immediacy of a speech addressed to a four-year-old child who is about to die.

The fragmentation of the syntax corresponds to the incoherence of the plot's logic. The usual Pirandellian dramatic model is even further broken up into very short phrases that call into play all the possible forms of punctuation, with a prevalence of exclamation points and question marks. Meanwhile, commas are not used except to bind the repeated vocative complements, and they reappear in their normal syntactic use only at the end of the speech, when the discussion becomes descriptive of memory and reevocation. In such a breathless scheme, there is room for only a very few subordinate conjunctions. The arrangement of the sentences is therefore paratactical and structurally alogical and in itself facilitates pretense and illusion of a subtle oratory.

Certainly, the Stepdaughter's monologue, which continues in the scornful, bitter reprimand of the Boy, is one of the high points of the play, even as it is the scene most open to sentimental effects. But a strong, continuous "emotional charge" runs throughout the multiple symbolic possibilities of Pirandello's masterpiece. We don't know whether in and of itself this is of great value, but it is certainly essential to protect that degree of dramatic tension without which this great intellectual drama would fall into pure abstraction.

Pirandello made the leap into the irrational when he led us to a, so to speak, three-dimensional condition of temporal and spatial *disorder*. But it is exactly that, disorder and equivocation. The step out of time and space doesn't take place in one clear image that at a certain point succeeds in creating within itself an absolute, logical integration. On the contrary, the leap outside of the traditional concept of temporal and causal succession isn't at all definitive. Rather, the play rebounds continuously between symbolic significance and physical reality, from the subject of art as absolver of the limitations of the physical to a demonstration of the power of the senses and of blood relationships, and vice versa from a story of real life and of testimony in defense of Pirandellian theories to an idealistic *fixation* or, if you wish, *figurative* fixation in the Auerbachian sense.

Up to this point, we have considered some of the dissonances and contradictions within the microcosm of the single speech. If we now consider a sequence of dialogue, we will see all the more clearly the signs of the disintegration of logical authenticity. The thread that seems to connect the discourse of one character to that of the others is for the most part only an apparent one or almost purely casual. One frequent effect is of that of *humor*, typically of oneiric *nonsense* as at times in Kafka. To Croce's puritan rationalism this effect appeared to be the result of an involuntary farce, and certainly not as transcendental farce (as in effect it is).[4] That particular emphasis on diction, on the spasmodic movement of the period, that lack of the literary dexterity that almost always marks Pirandello's phrasing of sentences, here becomes, in the light of such a *humor*, an opportune moment for caricature and ambiguous wordplay. Words are somehow dissonant with respect to their obvious meaning.

The false path between premise and consequence, which we considered above in the Stepdaughter's speech, is present at almost every moment of the play. The individual entrances, the personal resentments, the equivocations, the solitary pursuit of their own motives which contradict those of the others, and the continual alternation, with little distance between them, of the two opposite dimensions, of the immediate truth and of the absolute, do not coexist on the hard, deaf boards of the stage. The characters take refuge from one another, and with grotesque effect. As evidence, consider the scene that follows the miraculous appearance of Madame Pace.

The Father: Look! Look!

Stepdaughter: Here she is! Here she is!

The Father: It is she! What did I tell you? Here she is. (beaming)

The Director: But what kinds of tricks are these?

The Leading Man: But what's going on here?

The Juvenile: Where did she come from?

The Leading Lady: This is a magician's trick!

The Father: (Overriding protests)

But excuse me! Why do you want to destroy, in the name of ordinary truth, this prodigy
    of a reality which is born, evoked, attracted, formed by the stage itself and has more
    right to live here than you because it is more true than you are? Which actress among
    you will play Madame Pace? Good. Madame Pace is that lady. But let's concede
    that the actress who will play her will be less real than she, who is here in person!
    Look: my daughter recognized her and immediately went to her! Wait and see, wait
    and see the scene! (Hesitating, the Director and the actors, who had backed off with
    a frightened scream, climb back on stage. But the scene between the Stepdaughter
    and Madame Pace will have started *sottovoce*, very softly.)

The Director: So?

The Leading Man: What's she saying?

The Leading Lady: You can't hear anything like that.

Juvenile: Louder! Louder!

Stepdaughter: Louder, oh sure. What do you mean, louder? These are not things which one can say out loud. I could speak loudly about them to embarrass him (indicating the Father) to get revenge! But for Madame it is different, it means prison!

The Director: Oh, beautiful. It's like that, is it? But here you have to make yourselves understood, my dear lady.

Even the various explanatory interventions ("Nature serves as an instrument of our human imagination"), the defense of one thing or another ("whoever has the fate to be born as a living character"), the usual Pirandellian grafting onto the dramatic life of the individual characters ("and how can we understand one another . . . "; "each of us, understand, believes himself to be 'one' but it is not true: he is many, sir") are not insisted on in this play, as in most of Pirandello's works. They appear and disappear without provoking obstructions and pauses in the work.

Pirandello's theories of relativism, whether those of life and form or of man at the mirror, which at one time or another have each been the theses and the structural frames of entire plays, are limited here to brief appearances. They present a moment's relief without in the least affecting the instability and the dynamic movement of the work. The play does not proceed according to a plan foreseeable or foreseen by the author: it is a snake that bites its own tail—not without masochistic enjoyment.

The outcome is the same, and the crises of meanings become more peremptory if we move from a symptomatic analysis toward a deeper study; if from an investigation of the particulars—the individual speech, the individual sequence— we push toward the discovery of the breadth of values in the work. Here it is expedient to call on four Pirandellian exegetes, Adriano Tilgher, Mario Apollonio, Silvio D'Amico, and Eugenio Levi, all four of whom have told us what *Six Characters in Search of an Author* means. From their responses, which of necessity we will cite in synthesis, it will be easy to see that the work eludes *in its entirety* even a cautious attempt at critical identification. We see how the individual critical opinions find some means to extricate themselves, one after the other, from a tangent whose point of escape remains disguised and unknown.

Adriano Tilgher begins his essay by saying: "In *Six Characters in Search of an Author*, we see dialectic itself in action, the dialectic of the formation of truth and of illusion, which is the same"; and he ends: "*Six Characters* is the drama of possibility hoping in vain for the act in which it is being; potentiality longing in vain for the definition of form" (183–84). Mario Apollonio states, "The drama's mediated theatrical event presents the insufficiency of social justice and the multiplicity of appearances of each human entity: the 'central problem' is repeated here as well, in the Father's often repeated words; but its center is in theatricality itself, which is unable to concretize the images of art" (348).

Silvio D'Amico does not even refer to the play's "theatricality," although it is indeed an important element of Pirandello's work. D'Amico seeks instead an intimate and complex meaning in the play:

Here is the tragedy of incommunicability between men: the impossibility for every human being, of coming out of himself, or that which he believes to his own self, to show himself to another in his own reality. Therefore if showing the emptiness of one's own mask to the mirror signifies the inability to live any longer, the tragedy of man is always precisely this, that to delude himself in order to live, man has no recourse but to entrust himself to his mask, as others (or he himself) have fashioned it (193).

Eugenio Levi, certainly an enlightened critic, begins by saying that critics have gone astray "in seeking the meaning of the play in the discord between conception and expression, between what the poet sought to accomplish and what he accomplished in fact." Then he too finds meanings in the work: "Of first and most immediate significance is the 'humorization' of the *characters*, and of the traditional passive role of the persona; a second meaning of the work consists in the characters' coming to find themselves in contrast no longer with actors as actors but with actors as men"; from which it follows that "the inconsistency of human life is felt all the more, the more the six characters insist upon their reality, which is an *imaginary reality*."

"The third and last, the most hidden and bitter sense of the work is that the only way for us to transform ourselves from nonconclusion to conclusion, from unreal to real is to lose our humanity" (166 ff). Not even Levi, though following an acute interpretive path, abandons the idea of an underlying thesis for the work, a kind of high and painful moral that Pirandello might have wanted to propose in his fable, a thesis that might restore rational boundaries, as the critic has done.

In the triple ramification of Levi's judgment (especially if accompanied by those of Tilgher, Apollonio, D'Amico, and the other critics mentioned at the beginning of this chapter) we can discover how a critic sufficiently skillful at syllogisms can draw meanings of the play one from another, even one within another. This "rosary" of interpretations can be told in reverse, because the play authorizes us to proceed in a direction the inverse of Levi's: to discover, first, that man, in order to transform himself from unreal to real, must lose his very humanity, transform himself into a persona "naked mask that remains," and second, that the author wanted to make such an unhappy revelation from a humoristic point of view. But all four judges defend only one interpretation of the work and exclude all the dynamic withdrawal, reappearance, and contradiction of words, meanings, and symbols.

It's like attempting to discern a shape from boiling matter—a futile operation, particularly for a work born in endless flux. *Six Characters* is a work whose characteristic trait seems to be the rejection of every ascertainable boundary.[5]

Though we remain convinced of the inevitable failure of such analysis, some understanding of the structure of the play can be gleaned by considering the circumstances of its birth. We can immediately acknowledge that the origin of *Six Characters* is different from that of almost all the rest of Pirandello's theatre. This play is found on a plane of the writer's most secret being. In other plays by Pirandello it is always possible to discern a precise design, a dramaturgical development, an underlying theme.

Nowhere else do we find such changing boundaries between different and often opposite meanings and values (the false, the apparent, the certain, the true). In *Six Characters*, everything seems pointed toward a problematic end: no specific author's intention holds a definitive line, and meanings rebound one after the other as in a game of mirrors, or they open one within another like boxes in a Chinese game. The critic must assimilate the concept of equivocation and search for its origins. *Six Characters* seems to be nourished by ambiguity at its source, on a plane below consciousness. But how was this work born as it was born? We are concerned with only one of all the dramas by Pirandello. Why does this one have such a configuration, while the others are so different? The response must be sought in the exceptional process from which the work was born. If Pirandello usually wrote his plays in sole command, on this occasion he relied to a large extent on dictation, under the direction of a vision.

Pirandello usually controlled, corrected, and more systematically reduced the unconscious solicitation of inspiration to a rational dimension, one more literary and more intentionally moralistic, more traditionally theatrical. This time he limited himself to *assisting* and to making sure that the values of the *vision* prevailed in the theatrical record that he was writing of it. Such a concession to the most intimate and most particular psychological truth or nontruth was the work's greatest merit. Nowhere else in the Pirandellian intuition will we find such fecundity of values. Such riches are never found when the writer believes he can realign the immediate stimuli of his poetic conscious onto the adjusted tracks of an idea, a thesis, an organized work.

In this abundance of values, ambiguity and equivocation represent the original force of the drama, its contemporary feeling, its finding itself, in full strength, in a culture that sought to represent man to himself as one who exists on this side of all the traditional patterns and prejudices, and thus on this side of an optimistic and too intelligible self-consciousness. Western man (the product of Western civilization) could not in all sincerity see himself by this time except in a transitory and equivocal labyrinth of consciousness.

One instrument especially adapted and designed to explain, with virginal sincerity, such a serious attack of conscience was born of psychoanalytic experience, the dictation of the unconscious, in those years of surrealist poetry and art. But for Pirandello, at least in 1921, there was a very indirect adaptation to contemporary European literature: he was able to live the European experience within a distinctly personal experience linked to his own particular psychological structure. Within this structure, by way of an unconscious self-generation, *Six Characters* becomes a *summa* of all the novelty and contemporaneousness of Pirandello.

Pirandello himself provides us with the earliest information regarding the birth of the work. In the Preface to the 1925 edition of *Six Characters*, after having stated in advance that all the explanations he could give in an attempt to clarify the play's meanings were a posteriori and didn't have much to do with its birth, he acknowledges having written the work in submission to a series of solicitations that were of an involuntary and irrational nature: "*unconsciously* I had the impression that some of [the characters] needed to be fully realized artistically, others less so"; "unconsciously [I] found the way to resolve it by means of the new perspective of the play"; and it seemed to him "the way in which I actually obtained it, a miracle." "The fact is," he adds,

that the play was really conceived in one of those spontaneous illuminations of the imagination when by a miracle all the elements of the mind answer each other's call and work in divine accord. No human brain, working in the cold, however stirred up it might be, could ever have succeeded in penetrating far enough, could ever have been in a position to satisfy all the exigencies of the play's form. Therefore the reasons which I will give to clarify the values of the play must not be thought of as intentions that I conceived beforehand when I prepared myself for the job and which I now undertake to defend, but only as discoveries which I have been able to make afterwards in tranquillity. [In *Naked Masks* (New York: E. P. Dutton., 1952), p. 368, translation by Eric Bentley.]

All of which tells us rather explicitly that Pirandello found himself in a passive state while writing this work. But there is other evidence of that.

Above all a minor but, from a Freudian viewpoint, very symptomatic proof occurs. We all know how much Pirandello the writer enjoyed using certain odd and extravagant words that can be found scattered on his page like stones from a strange flood. Regarding idiosyncratic use of the language, Giacomo Debenedetti observed, "The movement of Pirandello's prose, clear, conversational, and accelerated, halts for the sudden importance of a single word which penetrates the recitation and becomes self-entangled. (Recall, for instance, in the short story collection *One Day*, the sudden stops called for in the course of reading by an orchestra of 'calvi inteschiati' (skull-like bald men), or by 'un incalcinare di semi perche non involpassero' (a calcification of seeds to prevent their overgrowth), etc.) (Debenedetti, 284).

At a certain point in *Six Characters*, Pirandello falls unconsciously into a self-critical lapse that comically contradicts his literary enjoyment of such "overstudied and bookish" terms (Alvaro, 35). The Director says to the Stepdaughter, "your little brother went back to school and wandered like a ghost, hiding himself behind doors to contemplate a plan in which—how did you say it?" and the Stepdaughter: "sucking himself up, sucking everything up!" [si dissuga, signore, si dissuga tutto!] To which the Director replies, "I've never heard such a word! All right then, '*growing only in the eyes*' is that right?" The Stepdaughter: "Yes,

sir . . . '' Without doubt this rather exhilarating exchange of dialogue is unconsciously derived because in all of his literary career Pirandello never gave a sign
of having second thoughts in regard to his own choice of words.[6]

But this is still a minor episode that could legitimately be considered an
oversight. More important internal evidence of the automatism of vision is found
in two speeches: one made by the Father, and another, a more illuminating one,
by the Stepdaughter while they are telling the Director of their visits to the *author*
who doesn't want to give them the artistic life they desire: The Father,

When characters are alive, really alive before their author, the author doesn't do more
than follow the words and actions they propose to him; and he must want them as they
want to be. Otherwise, watch out. When a character is born, he immediately acquires
such an independence, even of his own author.

The Stepdaughter (coming forward as though in a trance),

It's true. I, too, I too, sir, went to tempt him, many times, in the melancholy of his
study, at twilight when, slumped in an armchair, he couldn't make himself rise to turn
on the light and he allowed darkness to enter the room and in that darkness we hovered
and came to tempt him.

We have the impression that we are face to face with an actual biographical
event: the author's actual practice with his characters, a habit of which we have
other confirmation. In 1915 Pirandello devoted two short stories, written in the
form of a diary, to his ''Conversations with Characters.'' (It should be stressed
that one of these characters is the author's own mother who appears to him just
after her death.)[7]

And it happened that as I went near for the first time, to the corner of the room where
the phantoms began to come alive, I found one I hadn't expected: spirit only since
yesterday.—But how, Mamma, you, here?

In the other story, the unsummoned presence of the characters is introduced
as follows:

In the darkness which came slowly and wearily after those long, sultry summer afternoons
which invaded the room little by little . . . for some days now I felt I was no longer alone.
Something hovered in that darkness, in a corner of my room. Phantoms in the darkness
which followed sympathetically my anxiety, my ravings, my outbursts, all my passion
from which perhaps they were born or were beginning to be born. They watched me,
they spied on me. They would have watched me so much that in the end, of necessity,
I would have turned toward them.

In either instance, the physical sensation of the dialogue between the writer
and character is unsettling. In ''Secret Notebook'' we read: ''The beauty of it

is this . . . (the novel) played itself out before me, but as though I wasn't there, as though it didn't depend on me."[8] We could use yet other examples of direct testimony by the author regarding his *visions*.[9] Given the literary development and amplification of the *vision*, the biographical roots remain perplexing. But here perhaps the Jung of *Psychological Types* can help us. He speaks of an archaic manner in which images appear when "the inner image is easily projected into space as a visual or auditory hallucination without being a pathological phenomenon." He tells us that "concretism of thought and feeling is archaic," and that "Such fantasies belong to the category of psychic automatic experiences. . . . Naturally these latter can occur only as the result of a relative dissociation of the psyche, since their occurrence presupposes the withdrawal of an essential sum of energy from conscious control with a corresponding activation of unconscious material."[10]

For *Six Characters*, the automatic nature of the vision seems undeniable (since we have Pirandello's own testimony in support). A nearly immediate transcription of this vision appears in the work in an extremely extended, supratemporal (or equivocally temporal) flux that unravels itself in a fluid interweaving with other dictated matter, words, games, desires, and intellectual references. More precisely, the *vision* is repeated in an *invented* structure that remains inextricably combined and conditioned by that vision.

For Pirandello this was a literary, theatrical solution that was only at the last set into a formula, after having been enacted on a deep and autonomous field of direct literary influences. The problem of fitting into a particular current of romantic or postromantic tradition of visionary literature (as indeed is the case for some of the last short stories) does not exist for *Six Characters*.

With all of this in mind, we can better understand the origins of Pirandello's theoretical arguments regarding art, appreciate their true significance, and recognize that only apparently, and by happenstance, do they appear to be fashioned after an idealistic aesthetic. "Art is an idea come to life, and in becoming, the idea *creates a body of images* in which it is clothed." "While the work of art is composed in the spirit, reflection assists at the birth and upbringing, follows its successive phases and enjoys, judges and criticises them; reflection *sometimes may also prevent the creatures' birth*." "The mystery of creation is the mystery of life itself. . . . The spirit doesn't know its origins or where it will end." "An image is already a living thing . . . its work [of the imagination] is spontaneous as is every living action."[11] The magician-poet, Cotrone, in *The Mountain Giants* says:

All we have to do is imagine and our imagination instantly takes on life, by itself. Just so long as something is quite alive within us it will be represented spontaneously and unaided, by virtue of its very life. It's the free appearance of every necessary birth. At the most, we help along the birth some how.

[Act III, *The Mountain Giants*, trans., Marta Abba. (New York: Crown Publishers, Inc., 1958), p. 88.]

And again (in "Secret Notebook"):

The boundaries of our personal, conscious memory are not absolute boundaries. On the other side of that line there are memories, perceptions, rationales. What we know of ourselves is but a part of what we are. . . . In the moment of creation doesn't the artist perhaps succeed in knowing, even without being conscious of it, many many things which in the normal state of consciousness, when the flame of inspiration is extinguished, he knows no longer? Doesn't he discover in himself, at that moment, perceptions, arguments, states of mind that are truly beyond the relative limits of his normal and conscious existence? The spirit becomes body, the body becomes spirit. . . . Feeling, desire, ideas themselves are no longer something abstract but create a body which enlivens and reveals them. (Alvaro in *Almanacco letterario Bompiani*, 9).

Pirandello persists in talking of "body," of the objective incarnation of art, and certainly not in the name of naturalism, which he criticized in theory and excluded at least from his own most often expressed poetics.

The alogical, dreamlike fabric, expressive of the ambiguity at the base of *Six Characters*, is the result of the faithful, engaged transcription of the dictates of the unconscious. Near the beginning of the play, we find a line spoken by the Father: " . . . the author who created us, alive, no longer wanted or was no longer able materially to put us into the world of art. And this was truly a crime, sir, because whoever has the fate to be born a living character can even laugh at death . . . " In these words, we find the initial mechanism that triggers the action of this play, a mechanism that is only understandable and justifiable oneirically. It represents a completely illogical point of departure on which a whole construction is based. It would be arbitrary, precisely because its foundation is illogical, to draw ensuing inferences and unequivocal theories or unambiguous theses. (Instead, critics have done nothing else, and they have found themselves at a considerable disadvantage: remember the contradictions and defects of logic that Tilgher finds in *Six Characters*.)[12] The character who knows himself to have been born artistically alive asserts aloud his claim to a life in art: he is a kind of dramatized tautology. Nothing could be more absurd than such a claim, and yet it is necessary in order to continue the dream: it's just as while dreaming, we claim to know whether we are dreaming or awake, and once we assure ourselves that we are awake, we can continue to dream. Upon such a visionary base, the drama develops, with concretized beings of various symbolisms and various degrees of life that react to the swift change of stimuli.

Notable also is the appearance in this work of the *subliminal* deepening of Pirandellian moralism: those omnipresent sexual inhibitions of his create the dramatic contrasts between Father and Stepdaughter, the contradictory presence of the paradise lost of chastity and the Stepdaughter's flagrant disregard for that loss, set against the torment of the Father's remorse and shame for an irreversible sexual incident.

Equally clear is the organization of the unconscious *vision* on the stage, in the theatrical treatment. Madame Pace is almost a supplement of the vision: the shock of her appearance is provoked precisely by her being an apparition of a secondary plane. The first vision is that of the Six Characters; from this the Pirandellian drama is born, a blend of vision and artifice; then on the plane of the play, and precisely on that of the stage, the new vision appears, sudden and upsetting. Madame Pace is evoked, by way of a dreamlike medium, through the presence of the other Characters.

Pirandello himself was surprised by the logical disorder of this work and in the Preface tried to identify some of the connecting strands. But Pirandello's explanation as critic of his own work cannot satisfy us anymore than those of other critics. What is of interest, however, is a sharper focus on those sentences of Pirandello's which show us implicitly a certain surprise on the part of the author, confronted with the apparent confusion of the work:

In my work, the presentation of the drama involving the six characters seems tumultuous and never proceeds in an orderly fashion; there is no logical development, no linking of events. It's very true. Even if I had really tried, I could not have found a more disorderly, extravagant, complicated and arbitrary method of representing the drama in which the six characters are involved.

We can add that not only "the drama in which the six characters are involved," but also the play about their drama came to light in a very particular way. Pirandello's desire to find order in the chaos is evasive and, finally, unjustified. Born of a vision, *Six Characters* cannot be rediscovered except in a recognition of its ambiguity. Each expression of the unconscious possesses many possible meanings; each gradually assumes control over logical concepts, material objects, persons, and things and uses these as free, dynamically inclined, and multidirectional instruments of their own symbolic references. It is precisely in this free and multiple capture of reality, a reflection of the depth of the artist's being, that *Six Characters* truly reveals the author's intimate and multifaceted relationship with the life of society and with history.

In this work we find that extra measure of truth that we look for in vain in other contemporary works of art. Not many have known how to say as well as Pirandello does in this work that truth is, in itself, ambiguous and elusive at its very roots.

NOTES

1. Letter of April 18, 1917, in *Almanacco letterario Bompiani 1938—XVI* (Milan, 1938), 43.

2. C. Alvaro, Preface to *Novelle per un anno* (Milan, 1957–1958), 35. Piovene also spoke of "an art half blind, half voluntary," in *Almanacco letterario Bompiani*, 81.

3. In the essay cited, *On Humor*, at 61–62, Pirandello refers to De Sanctis and G. A. Cesareo in order to reinforce his own belief in the autonomy of the character: ("The poet does not have to select anything, because that creature is free, autonomous, independent

of the poet himself." [Casareo]). But, as he will explain elsewhere, for Pirandello, the character's autonomy is also a personal, autobiographical fact.

4. "The dialogue between the six characters and the actors is so void of subject that here and there, certainly against the author's intention, it assumes a tone more in keeping with a farce than with tragedy." In *Letteratura della nuova Italia* (Bari, 1940), vol. VI, Croce, too, gives us an explanation of this work: *Six Characters* is "a drama in which Pirandello attempts to present nothing less than the future of artistic work . . . they (the six characters) are a reality which changes and the actors' reality is a fixed reality," 366.

5. We have cited many critics and could cite many more, though perhaps less authoritative ones. However, they all, without exception, arrive at checkmate. The point of view of Luigi Ferrante, a Marxist critic, is the following: "In this play, one finds a problem: not the scheme of a paradoxical agnosticism, the play concerns the objectivity of human relations and the crisis of this objectivity. This play's thesis concerns the crisis of the individual as the end of precarious social relationships, ill adapted to nourish moral dialogue, a crisis that collides with the objectivity of the ethical world, of its norms and imprisons the human being in weakness, misery and mistakes, without giving him a chance to free himself." Ferrante, *Pirandello* (Florence, 1958), 116.

6. Of significance is the list of "notes for better writing" which we find on an undated page of the "Taccuino Segreto di Luigi Pirandello" ("Secret Notebook . . . ") remarked on by C. Alvaro in *Almanacco letterario Bompiani* (1938). There are twenty-nine examples of strictly Tuscan idomatic expressions.

7. In the appendix of the Mondadori edition of *Novelle per un anno* (Milan, 1957–1958), 1126–31.

8. Pages from "Secret Notebook," collected by C. Alvaro in *Nuova Antologia* (Rome: January 1934), 6–7.

9. One should remember, for example, the words Pirandello spoke during a conference held in Buenos Aires: "this was my dream: in it I saw a deep courtyard, without exit and from this frightful image *Right You Are (If You Think You Are)* was born." And, again, according to Pirandello, the idea for *Henry IV* was born when he saw an old English print, which represented a cavalcade of knights and their ladies (*Almanacco letterario Bompiani*, cit.). And in a letter to Luigi Natoli (1897). " . . . the characters of my stories surround me. Each of them wants to come to life before the next."

10. C. G. Jung, *Psychological Types* (New York: Harcourt, Brace & Co., Inc., 1926), 554, 524–25, and 574. From Jung, we can cite some other very pertinent observations: "The image has the psychological character of a fastasy-presentation, and never the quasi-real character of hallucination, i.e. it never takes the place of reality, and its character of 'inner' image always distinguishes it from sensuous reality. As a rule, it lacks all projection into space, although in exceptional cases it can also appear to a certain extent externalized. Such a mode of appearance must be termed *archaic* . . . "(554) " . . . introverted thinking shows a dangerous tendency to coerce facts into the shape of its image, or by ignoring them altogether, to unfold its fantasy image in freedom. In such a case, it will be possible for the presented idea to deny its origin from the dim archaic image. There will cling to it a certain mythological character that we are prone to interpret as 'originality' . . . " (481–82). "Concretism of thought and feeling is archaic. Compulsion and inability for self-control (being carried away) are also archaic. That condition in which the psychological functions are fused or merged one into the other (vs. Differentiation) is archaic—the fusion, for instance, or thinking with feeling, feeling with sensation, or feeling with intuition. Furthermore, the coalescence of parts of a function

..., ambitendency, and ambivalency, i.e. the state of fusion with its counterpart, e.g. positive with negative feeling, is also archaic" (524–25). We know, in fact, that Pirandello's theory is based on the concept of the "feeling of the opposite."

11. "Taccuino Segreto di Luigi Pirandello", 9, 10, 13 (*Almanacco letterario Bompiani*, cit.). These theoretical propositions can also be illustrated from a passage in *On Humor* (37): "The artist must feel his work as—so to speak—it feels itself, and must want it as it wants itself." Or from Pirandello's Preface to *Six Characters*: "I can only say that without having wanted to find them, I found myself looking at those six characters in front of me, so alive I could touch them, so alive that I could hear them breathe, these characters that are now on the stage."

12. After having enunciated what the meanings of this play should be, Tilgher accuses Pirandello of being incoherent: "But that which should be the central motif of the play, and that which in effect dominates the work in the entire first act, doesn't find adequate development in the second and third acts, in which we do not see the characters passing from a lower to a higher plane; we do not see them proceeding from confusion to order, from chaos to artistic cosmos." And he adds: "What universal meaning could one draw from the fact that a theatre professional is not capable of developing, synthesizing an idea outlined and abandoned there—to bring to full expression characters in whom life is not yet fully expressed?" (183–84). These are the inevitable delusions of anyone who examines the play in a too pedantically logical way.

WORKS CITED

Almanacco letterario Bompiani. Milan: Mondadori, 1938.

Alvaro, Corrado. *Nuova Antologia*, January 1934, 6–10.

Angioletti, Giovanni Batista. *Luigi Pirandello narratore e drammaturgo.* Turin: Edizioni Radio Italiana, 1958.

Appollonio, Mario. *Storia del teatro italiano*, Vol. IV. Florence: G. C. Sansoni, 1950.

Borghese, G. A. *Tempo di edificare.* Milan: Garzanti, 1928.

Croce, Benedetto. *Letteratura della nuova Italia*, Vol. VI. Bari: G. Laterza e figli, 1940.

D'Amico, Silvio. *Storia del teatro drammatico*, IV. Milan: Garzanti, 1958.

Debenedetti, Giacomo. *Saggi critici—Nuova serie.* Milan: Mondadori, 1955.

Ferrante, Luigi. *Pirandello.* Florence: Parenti, 1958.

Gobetti, Piero. *Opera critica.* Turin: Baretti, 1927.

Guerrieri, Gerardo. *Dizionario letterario delle opere e dei personaggi.* Milan: Bompiani, 1948.

Jung, C. G. *Psychological Types.* New York: Harcourt, Brace and Co., 1926.

Levi, Eugenio. *Il comico di carattere da Teofrasto a Pirandello.* Turin: G. Einaudi, 1959.

Pirandello, Luigi. *On Humor.* Translated by Antonio Illiano and Daniel P. Testa. Chapel Hill: University of North Carolina Press, 1974.

———. *Opere di Luigi Pirandello, Novelle per un anno.* Milan: Mondadori, 1957–1958.

Pompeati, A. *Storia della letteratura italiana*, Vol. IV. Turin: Unione tipografico-editrice torinese, 1950.

Simoni, Renato. *Trent'anni di cronaca drammatica*, Vol. I. Torino: Società editrice torinese, 1951–1960.

Tilgher, Adriano. *Studi sul teatro contemporaneo.* Rome: Libreria di scienze e lettere, 1923.

Tonelli, Luigi. *Il teatro contemporaneo italiano.* Milan: Bompiani, 1936.

12

Pirandello's *Six Characters* and Surrealism

Anna Balakian

An affinity has often been seen between the theater of Pirandello and the surrealist mode because both adhere to such notions as the "absurd," the unconventional, the iconoclastic, and the shocking to stir the receivers of the created work. Let us examine these elements from the angle of Pirandello's *Six Characters in Search of an Author* as well as of the surrealists' position, to determine the nature of affiliations and of differences.

Undeniably, his reception in Paris had much to do with Pirandello's subsequent fame. He wrote *Six Characters* in 1921, but it was not until the play was presented in Paris in 1923 that notoriety was accompanied by sincere curiosity and serious appraisal. Apparently, the influence of innovations is more dramatic when it crosses national frontiers than within a national literature. This phenomenon is manifest in the way Europeans embraced Edgar Allen Poe, for instance, in the nineteenth century, and in the twentieth century in the way Albert Camus was received in the United States or Faulkner in the Soviet Union.

Curiously, France, the country historically noted for generating avant-gardism in poetry and painting, was rather slow in its renovation of theater. In the first two decades of this century, we see artists and poets adapt to a new world of relativism brought about by advances in physics and mathematics which distributed the three-dimensional perception of the cosmos, and by experimentations in psychiatry that let down the barriers between the conscious and the unconscious. In response, the avant-garde brought about radical changes in aesthetics such as cubism, which took place in Paris whether its perpetrators were French or whether they came from other countries to practice their art in Paris. But theatrically the only innovators identified with the avant-garde were those who were attracted to the applications of Grand Guignol Theater by Alfred Jarry and to Apollinaire's feeble attempt at experimental theater in 1918 in his play *Les Mamelles de Tirésias*. Apollinaire had been truly avant-garde as a poet, breaking the rules of prosody, playing havoc with time perceptions, and simulating simultaneity. In contrast, in his play he was serving an ideology rather than theater as a genre. In the wake of World War I, he had a message to offer rather than a new form: he deemed his plea to repopulate France to be a universal concern, relating his protagonist not to a particular society but to the universe as a whole in terms of the human power to produce 40,049 children in one day. Therefore, his theatrical presentation took on the semblance of a universal stage setting transportable from one continent to another. When he qualified his vista as "surrealist" in the introduction of his play, thus using that label for the first time to distinguish a form of art, the word would have a great reception. But his caricature of the burgeoning feminist woman of his time and his benign ridicule of humanity as a whole were still expressed within the normal stage we are accustomed to. He maintained a clear division between audience and stage, between actors and viewers, with the clear understanding that everyone involved in bringing the text to performance was subservient to the author of the text. The truth is that his play neither supports nor demonstrates his long introduction about the needs of the new theater; his second play, *Couleur du Temps*, is even more conventional.

While profound changes were taking place in poetic discourse in terms of renovation of the image and the representation of reality in painting and poetry, theater remained the same. The most popular, prolific, and durable theater was still that of the boulevards' romantic boudoir triangles, the psychological plays of Ibsen and of his followers, or the social theater of François de Curel or Henri Brieux, or even the surviving naturalist theater of Henri Becque. All of these works may have developed fresh insights on humanity and society, but they did not offer fresh, unpredictable forms of representation in the script or new presentations on the stage.

When, therefore, Pirandello burst on the scene, only Louis Aragon in France, a very young pre-surrealist, had questioned the general idea of the changing concept of beauty in the arts in a little satirical novel, *Anicet*. He had derided all the experimentations of the moment called "modern" as pretentious and shallow; he had challenged all the so-called innovators including Picasso, Charlie Chaplin, Cocteau, the Dadas, and even his dear friend André Breton under very thin disguises.

None of these early avant-gardes had raised the disturbing issues that were to be central both to Pirandello and the surrealists, namely, how the notion of beauty had changed in the modern world, what relativism had done to the definition of reality, what artists could expect of their art in terms of their own survival, in terms of its survival as intended by its author, and in terms of the fading barriers between reality and illusion. Finally, although in the past so much theory of the arts had concentrated on the effect of the work of art on the reader or viewer, was it not time to observe the effect of the viewer or reader on the work itself?: How can we understand each other if into the words which I speak I put the sense and the value of things as I understand them within myself while at the same time whoever is listening to them inevitably assumes them to have the sense and value that they have for him? (Father, *Six Characters*, Act I) [translation mine]

The question is particularly pertinent to both Pirandello and the surrealists and, as we will see, in quite different ways. When *Six Characters* hit Paris, surrealism was not yet officially declared, although André Breton and his colleagues were pondering what artistic forms their revolution was to promote. Dada had made its official arrival in Paris in 1920 but had identified with no special art form; collage and theatrical improvisations were fragmentary and meant to be executed or performed before randomly selected audiences. Neither the authors nor the viewers took these shows as dramatic structures. What interested the Dadas and the rising coterie of surrealism in the dramatic form was dialogue, which was viewed as a form of linguistic ping-pong with no special consequence for dramatic action: two streams of thought, two soliloquies interrupting each other rather than responding logically to each other, their incongruities often revealing underlying hostilities in the interlocutors.

Even after Breton's official Manifesto established certain basic principles for surrealism, the series of playlets written by Breton, Soupault, Aragon, Desnos, Tzara, and even the more extensively structured plays of Roger Vitrac were deemed extensions of poetry to illustrate perceptions such as the power of love at first sight, the impact of chance meetings, the melding of dream and the wakeful states, the capacity of language to trigger the imagination of the spectator, the need for the individual to break through the constriction of social institutions and to demonstrate that in the modern world beauty had to be convulsive, explosive, unpredictable, or not at all. In that particular context the "absurd" is something sublime and devoutly to be wished; it is a resource of the imagination. But the dramatic works of the first generations of surrealists were only blueprints for a new form of poetic discourse rather than finished dramatic works. These fragmentary efforts made it obvious that the dynamism of theater would be difficult to convey through the medium of the existing theater unless there first occurred a massive transfiguration of the structure and function of stagecraft, willed or encouraged by the author. The surrealists did not probe or even evoke the questions that touch theater art integrally. In fact, these issues were totally ignored as they would be by people who are unversed; these people, however, were supremely versed and thereby knew what they were destroying, as was the case with Pirandello. In relation to the spectators, what the surrealists hoped to do was to raise the level of imaginative power, but they did not have in mind any specific creation regarding the interplay between author and producer, or actor and audience, at least not until Antonin Artaud's *The Theater and Its Double*, which proposed theatrical devices affecting audience behavior.

But Artaud's treatise, which he really did not implement, is posterior to *Six Characters*, which contains both thesis and praxis within a single work.

When we look at *Six Characters* from the point of view of this cursory description of the salient characteristics of fragmental surrealist plays, the differences are jarring. First, Pirandello came to his rebellion as a theatrical craftsman who had mastered conventional theater. He was a professional who wanted to break the rules and not an amateur who knew no better. The impact of the aberration of form becomes much more notable when it is willed and when the rejection or negation carries the weight of new values. Pirandello's flaunting of the rules had affirmative intentions. When in the beginning of the play he has the Director telling his crew that they have to use Pirandello's plays because there is a sudden dearth of plays coming from Paris, he is expressing Pirandello's exasperation with the state of the theater. A few minutes later the characters are telling the Director the reason for their orphaned state: "He [the author] abandoned us in a fit of depression, of disgust for the ordinary theater as the public knows it and likes it," . . . is the way the Stepdaughter explains why the characters were abandoned.

Pirandello dissects the theater to find out what ails it. He wants to break down the barriers between generator, director, performer, and receiver (audience). In contrast, the surrealists wanted to break down the divisions between the genres; for them theater was nothing more than an oral poem. In poetry the surrealist effects are essentially dependent on rapid, unexpected sparks of recognition and revelation, but the all-in-one-piece impact of a poem or a painting has so far proved inaccessible to the longer time span and larger space of the dramatic piece. The *sine qua non* of a poem, whether written or oral, is its ability to manipulate words. The cult of language, no matter in what genre, is the mark of surrealist writing: automatically eruptible, analogically contrived and hallucinatory in its repercussions. Pirandello sometimes found language to be a veritable barrier to the search for truth, and he denigrates the artist's dependence on it as a crutch in his inability to get to the core of human problems: "Words, words . . . the consolation of finding a word" is said in derision.

For the surrealist there is no discrete separation between the poetic and the dramatic forms. Poetry includes all the others, which the surrealists are ready to mutate or even mutilate if they can thereby enhance the power of poetry and extend its domain. Pirandello wants to break down the rules the better to preserve the theater. What does he do in *Six Characters* in his effort to strengthen what he considers to be a debilitated form? He is questioning the problem of survival and reality. The first premise is that the work has more chance of survival than its author. "Man, the writer . . . the instrument of creation will die. But what is created by him will never die" (Father, Act I). This thought had already been the matrix of the symbolist aesthetics. But once the work attains its independence from the author, it is in turn prone to mutability because it will have to combat and resist other factors endangering its integrity as it gets to mean different things to successive audiences. But unlike the late twentieth-century Derridian "différance'' which relates to the privileged reader's inclinations to change the meaning of a text, that of the theater performance is more vulnerable. It is subjected to a triple tier of interpretation because it has to go through the process of its theatricalization in the hands first of the director, second of the actors, and only finally of the audience.

So, in truth the fate of this created reality (which is presumably ''fixed'') is as precarious as that of the human one. If human reality is ephemeral because of the impact of time, which turns today's reality into a yesterday no more substantial than an illusion, the theatrical reality that we call illusion and that at first glance seems impermeable to the ravages of human time, is just as vulnerable because of the future impact of rethinking on the part of producers, performers, and the changing responses of succeeding audiences. On the contrary, the variability of interpretation in the case of the surrealist author or painter is a cause not of fear but of exhilaration, an indication of the richness of the work. What Dali called ''the delirium of interpretation'' was an inherent goal of surrealist poetics. In fact, the palimpsestic character of surrealist discourse is part of the scheme. ''Donner à voir'' in Eluard's words and ''faire voir'' in Breton's are sheer invitations to receive not the perception of the creator of the work but the energy generated by the vision for uses other than the creator's. The astonishment of the Six Characters at being represented in ways they do not recognize would be deemed puerile by the surrealists.

In the case of *Six Characters*, the question of viability becomes even more complicated because at a certain junction reality intervenes to destroy illusion. Or in other words a real-life event—the actual drowning of a little girl and the suicide of the boy—brings art and reality into collision, violating the created reality of the fixed characters. They cannot be represented if they no longer exist. The play is pulverized before the very eyes of those who want to perform it. However relative truth may be and however dependent reality may be on point of view, these become totally academic problems as soon as the created reality disintegrates. The conclusion of the problematics of the creative process, which is the center of Pirandello's preoccupation, is a state of nihilism. It takes on a more concrete form in the idiotic laughter with which the play ends in the definitive version of the script. This is not the laughter of effervescence we sometimes meet in surrealist expression.

Surrealism forestalls the frustrations of art by its preliminary pronouncement that life is more important than art. Art is only a means of making life richer, more enjoyable. This philosophy is a safety valve against nihilism. The surrealists, who considered the sheer power of living in high gear a more satisfactory occupation than writing or painting, could not worry too much about the state of art. On the contrary, Pirandello starts in *Six Characters* by expressing his dissatisfaction with the theater of his time, picks some of the trite dramatic themes of the day (the infidelity of the Mother, the incestuous leanings of the Father, the disengagement of the Son from daily life, the prostitution of the Stepdaughter because of economic necessity), and he uses a banal plot as a vehicle for his meditation on the metaphor which theater becomes for life's problems. They emerge from these situations that have become graver in a world trying to adapt to a relativist point of view. Where the short view of the march of time might suggest that psychology was beginning to make us understand each other better than in the past, the long view that Pirandello perceived was that when truth became a relative concept, interrelationships between humans became even more impossible than under the absolute code of yore. "We think we understand one another. But we never really understand." Understanding of each other's character was never a high priority for the surrealists; instead, they reversed the mystery of human personality. What held the group together were their tropism toward certain objects, landscapes, and people, the visions they shared, the paintings to which they were drawn, and the artists they admired in mutual and sometimes illogical unison.

The primordial process of theater was and always has been the representation of life, and the creation of illusion has been only a means of reinforcing that reality. The indeterminacy of reality in the modern world made the normal process of creating that no longer reliable. Pirandello leaves us with the picture of the artist finding his art inadequate and revealing the quagmire through the deterioration of the medium. To his viewers the image of the disintegration of theater became a source of new freedom for the art. By letting the audience share his secret, Pirandello revealed to himself as well as to the adept viewer an infinite number of new channels open to theater.

Pirandello's efforts at philosophizing were expressed in the discourse of his play, but the form in which this discourse was couched proved to have more substantive value and more impact on the future of theater than the content of that discourse. He had unwittingly liberated the structure of theater for the rest of the century. A seeming informality in stage-craft opened the possibilities of audience involvement; plot irresolution became acceptable, and the curtain separating illusion from reality vanished. If the freedom of the characters from their author's intentions was already an impudent step, an even more far-reaching break in the definitive version of the play occurred when Pirandello's stage directions bid the characters to burst into the arena of the audience.

Among the surrealists who had no more faith in the theater than in the novel, the only erstwhile surrealist with sustained interest in the theater was Artaud, whose existence as an actor and sometime playwright prevailed longer than his adherence to surrealism. When in his theoretical work in drama Artaud used the metaphor of the plague, he was only reinforcing Pirandello's earlier notion of the importance of audience participation. But in Artaud's case it became a greater social than philosophical phenomenon, and neither the course of his tragic life nor his unsustained qualifications as a playwright made it possible for him to achieve an *oeuvre*.

Pirandello's philosophy and aesthetics are very closely linked together. He mingles his sense of the precariousness of life with the perilous state of art. Actually, in the last analysis the Six Characters are not so much in search of an author as of a performance, which Pirandello determines to be the essential character of theater itself. It has often been pointed out that the Characters lack the cohesion to become performable because the author has abandoned them. But in reality there is an element of rebellion on the part of the Characters against their author:

> When a character is born he immediately acquires an independence. . . . Even of his own author. That everyone can imagine him in a whole host of situations which his author never thought of placing him. He can even imagine acquiring sometimes a significance that the author never dreamed of giving him.

But performance is the essential character of theater. The play ceases to exist if not performed at all; therefore, it is more precarious than poetry or the novel. If indeed the author had scrapped the trivial material, then the Characters' second and more theater-related problem was caused by the fact that they would cease to exist no matter how good or bad their script might be unless a director and performers were to be found—and only then could they seek the judgment of the audience. Otherwise, their independence would serve no purpose, and they would be the embodiments of imperfect drafts of a work of art drifting weightlessly and reaching no one. If then a play is not a play unless it is performed, neither is it performable if its author has aborted it.

By deconstructing the mechanism of theater, Pirandello was able to demonstrate which of the elements were trappings and which were the essentials. By having the author challenged by the producer (or in the more appropriate French word the "réalisateur"), Pirandello launched in Europe the era of the great impresarios who gave their own imprints to a play and even in some cases managed to give cohesion to some loosely constructed ones. In a subsequent age, which did not produce great drama, the permissibility practiced by this new breed of directors made it possible for playwrights such as Thornton Wilder to endow drama with a certain contrived informality, giving the director more opportunity to exercise his own creativity.

The surrealists did not care specifically for the destiny of the theater. Their basic hypothesis was that a liberated mind could energize any form of writing as well as any of the other media of the arts, which were like instruments whereby man could demonstrate his psychic liberation and heightened imagination, or derive through his work a better understanding of his own mettle.

The questions Pirandello asked about the creative process were not as novel as the renovations of the craft that he put thereby into motion. Those who observed his feat were impelled toward a freer concept of theater, which in turn opened up a larger vista for dramatic representation.

In an age deeply stricken with the sense of mortality, the most fragile of the arts became the most representative of the "brave new world," whose bravura masked some muffled sobs and whose laughter suggested a feeble effort to distance from itself the impending void. Beyond the tower of despair, Pirandello had superposed the reverberations of the Stepdaughter's hysterical laughter to the earlier and more conventional sobbing with which he had originally ended his play. But neither the sobbing nor the ironic laughter is compatible with the philosophy of surrealism, which emphasizes the immediacy of life as a multi-dimensional and ever renewable reality to be espoused.

It it true that many midcentury unconventional dramatists such as Arrabal, Ionesco, Henri Pichette, and Yacine Katab were labeled neo-surrealist. Generally, however, that was a journalistic perception based on the assumption that any extravaganza in the arts is tinged with the "surrealistic." A very small number of playwrights in the era following that of the peak both of surrealism and of Pirandello would truly qualify as surrealists, although few are totally untouched by the spirit of surrealism. Those who in effect followed faithfully the surrealist line have not attained universal recognition and have emerged in countries whose literature still remains largely unfamiliar to the world at large. (But that is another issue deserving, and not getting, sufficient critical attention!) The real filiation of the noted men of the theater of the late twentieth century is with Pirandello.

A truer perspective would suggest, then, that Pirandello and the surrealists shared a moment in the history of the arts but followed parallel rather than converging paths in their spectacular irreverence for the traditional.

13

"The Delusion of Mutual Understanding": Structure, Language, and Meaning in *Six Characters*

Umberto Mariani

Pirandello's *Six Characters* reveals itself from the outset as thematically much more complex than his earlier masterpieces and far more original in form vis-à-vis the bourgeois theater of the turn of the century. We recognize, for instance, that this is the first of a group of plays (including *Each in His Own Way*, *Tonight We Improvise*, and, possibly, *The Mountain Giants*) in which Pirandello deals with the art of the theater. The theme of the nature of artistic creation, of the relationship between art and everyday reality, which his previous plays touched on only incidentally, is explored here for the first time. The staging of a play, and even the process of its creation, is put on stage. The themes, the plots, all the familiar conventions (including the use of the scenic space) of the bourgeois theater—still employed, albeit with subversive intent, in *It Is So*—are utterly rejected. *Six Characters* is a revolutionary play and was thus perceived when it was first performed on May 10, 1921, at the Valle Theater in Rome, and later in Milan and Paris.

The concept of such a play had been evolving in Pirandello's mind for a long time. In the Preface to the play, he describes the birth of the characters from the author's imagination:

For many years now . . . a nimble little servant . . . called imagination . . . has been in the employment of my art . . . ; she enjoys bringing home, for me to derive stories and novels and plays from, the most disgruntled characters in the world . . . entangled in strange situations from which they cannot find a way out, thwarted in their dreams, cheated in their hopes—with whom, in short, it is often painful to deal.[1]

In an earlier short story, he had revealed the process by which the characters evolve in the author's mind, acquiring vitality and autonomy:

> It has been an old custom of mine to give audience every Sunday morning to the characters of my future stories. Five hours, from 8:00 am. to 1:00 pm.
> I almost always find myself in bad company.
> I do not know why the world's most discontented people usually come to these receptions of mine, or people afflicted by strange illnesses, or tangled up in the strangest sort of affairs, and it is really painful to deal with them.
> I listen to them with great forbearance; I question them quite kindly; I take note of their names and the situation each one is in; I register their feelings and their aspirations. But I must add that, unfortunately for me, I am not easily satisfied. Forbearance, kindness, yes; but I do not like being conned. I want to delve deeply into their souls through a long and subtle inquiry.[2]

Finally, when through that process they had become "alive to the point that you could touch them, so alive that you could feel their breathing" (36)—when, that is, their drama had acquired sufficient solidity, and truth—then Pirandello would begin to give it form in a short story, novel, or play.

One such group of characters, born of the author's imagination and developed to the point of being charged with a kind of independent life, although, not having been given definitive artistic form, they are unfinished, in flux, is the group of six about whom Pirandello wrote to his son Stefano in 1917:

> six characters involved in a terrible drama or tragedy who are following me everywhere because they want to get into a novel; a real obsession; but I say No, no, to them, that it is useless, that they do not interest me, that nothing interests me anymore, and they show me their wounds and I chase them away.[3]

Although they have not yet received definitive artistic form, they already have a drama, a drama that makes them dramatic characters:

> To exist, every creature of the imagination, every artistic character, must have his drama, the drama in which and thanks to which he is a character. His drama is a character's *raison d'être*, his vital function, essential to his existence (40).

The Six Characters' ruling passion is that drama; it colors their vision of reality, conditions their thoughts and their behavior, torments them, enslaves them, obsesses them—turns them, that is, into dramatic characters.

Unfortunately, the drama in which they *think* they are characters too closely resembles in plot and spirit certain late nineteenth-century romantic plays, especially the bourgeois theater of the turn of the century. A wealthy, self-styled intellectual makes the gesture of reaching out for "normalcy" by marrying an ordinary woman. A son is born, and the father immediately delivers him to a healthy country nurse to raise while the mother, unoccupied in the large house, seems more able to communicate with the husband's down-to-earth secretary than with the husband himself. The husband, noticing their affinity, decides to rid himself of his wife by favoring their union. The two set up house in another part of town; soon a daughter is born, and years later a son and another daughter. The Father keeps an eye on the new family for a while. Occasionally he meets the older Stepdaughter on her way home from school and presses some little present on her, which arouses suspicion in the parents, who move away leaving no trace behind. Unfortunately, the secretary dies and poverty takes his place. The Mother brings the family back and takes in sewing jobs for a Madame Pace, who behind her atelier runs a secret house of prostitution. Every time the Stepdaughter, now eighteen, comes to deliver her mother's work, Madame Pace complains about the quality of the work and cuts the payment, while trying to make her understand that both complaints and pay cuts would cease if she would lend herself to Madame's other business. The daughter agrees in order to save her mother constant humiliation. And one day one of Madam Pace's clients is the now fiftyish Father; his attempts to undress the Stepdaughter are interrupted by the Mother, whose suspicions about her daughter's fate have brought her to the atelier to put an end to the sordid trafficking. The Father, having thus rediscovered the little family, takes them out of the squalor of their rented room and brings them home. Here, however, the first son, now twenty-two, decides to treat the Mother he has never known and the bastards who have invaded his home "with frowning indifference" and the Father, the author of such surprises, "with reserved anger" (55). The one who suffers most intensely from this rejection is the Mother, and the intensity of her suffering is felt by the two younger children as if through physical contact; they clutch her hands constantly without uttering a word, observing everything with wide eyes. Finally, the intensity of the gnawing torment they sense in their mother overcomes them. The girl drowns herself in the garden fountain, and the boy shoots himself. While the mother continues to pursue her first son from room to room, "her arms stretched out to him" (116), imploring understanding, the older daughter leaves to become a streetwalker.

Although the Characters call this "a sorrowful drama" on various occasions, their author has evidently seen it for what it is, something of an old-fashioned tearjerker, material typical of the bourgeois theater, the kind of literature that Pirandello rejected from the very beginning of his career as a playwright. (To the Father who suspects that perhaps the author has rejected them because of the Stepdaughter's importunity ["Perhaps it was because of you; because of your inordinate insistence, your inordinate excesses!"] she says: "Most certainly not! He made me the way I am! I think instead he was disgusted, angry with the theater, with the way the public sees it and likes it" (106). Therefore, no matter how often and insistently they have come back to their sessions with the author, trying to persuade him ("What we are doing before you, we have done again and again before him, trying to convince him, in the melancholy of that study of his, at dusk, when, slouched in his easy chair, he could not make up his mind to turn the light switch on and he let the dark invade the room, a darkness terming with us who came to tempt him . . . What scenes we came to propose to him!'') (105–106), the author has decided not to write a story or a novel or a play about them, not to set down in a text, give definitive form to these characters and to their drama (''The author who created us, live, did not want to, or physically could not bring us into the world of art'') (58).

They resent that denial, because the definitive artistic form would have meant not just the gift of life, but also immortality (''It was a real crime, because he who has the good fortune to be born a live character can laugh even at death, he will never die! The man, the writer, the tool of creation will die; his creature will never die! And to live forever one does not require extraordinary gifts, one needn't perform miracles. Who was Sancho Panza? Who was Don Abbondio? Yet they live forever, because—live seeds—they had the good fortune to find a fertile matrix, an imagination that was able to raise and nourish them, give them eternal life!'') (58–59). They must instead be content with having been made live characters. But they are characters, not people, and a character is a creature of the imagination, a form of communication that lives only in the act of communicating. (''We as characters have no other reality outside this illusion. . . . What for you is an illusion to create, for us is our only reality'') (102–103).

In order to live, therefore, these characters, rejected by their creator and thus deprived of a desirable immortal life, are in search of any occasion to communicate, that is, to live, even if only for a moment—a compromise, to be sure, with immortality, but certainly better than nothingness (''We want to live, sir, . . . if only for a moment''). Paying a visit to a company engaged in a stage rehearsal might just do the trick; if they were allowed to act out the play they carry inside, they would live that moment; and when they realize that the prompter might put down their parts in shorthand, they even begin to think that the director might take the place of the author, put together a script, give them definitive artistic form, and with it the immortality their creator denied them.

But they must soon realize that without definitive artistic form it is nearly impossible for them to communicate—that is, to live, even for just a moment. In the absence of a script, they are almost unable to communicate their drama, to develop their play for their audience; they can do it only in fragments, and primarily through narrative rather than dramatic scenes. Even the two dramatic scenes they try to put together are not successful: the seduction scene, constantly interrupted by external distractions, seems to the characters to lose all its dramatic power when the actors give their unsatisfactory performance; and the final scene, which is extremely short, produces chaos and rejection, instead of understanding and acceptance, and puts an end to the characters' illusion that they might get some help from this theatrical company in solving their problem.

Dramatic art is uniquely subject to betrayals along the winding path that leads from the initial inspiration to the artist's text, to a director's interpretation, to that of his company, and finally to the audience's perception, when the poetic text actually exists. Imagine then when that text is absent. Thus, the disappointment of the Six Characters when they see themselves so poorly interpreted by the actors is enormous. ("Do you think it is possible to live before a mirror that does not stop at freezing us in the image of our expression but sends it back to us as an unrecognizable distortion?") (113). The very nature of this particular theatrical company further complicates things. It is a company accustomed to perform the conventional, sentimental, romantic, simplistic plays of the turn-of-the-century bourgeois theater ("Is it my fault if we do not get any more good comedies from France?") (53), a company that cannot even begin to understand the new "Pirandellian" theater:

and we must stage the comedies of Pirandello whom nobody understands, purposely written to leave actors, critics, public always dissatisfied? Yes, a cook's cap! And beat those eggs? Do you think that you have nothing in your hands besides those eggs you are beating? No! You must portray the shell of the eggs you are beating! . . . That is, the empty form of reason without the content of blind instinct. You are reason, your wife the instincts, in a game of divided roles, wherein you who are acting your role are willfully playing the puppet of yourself. Understand? *The leading actor* (opening his arms): No, I don't. *The Director*: Neither do I! (53)

Thus, on the one hand, director and actors become interested in the family drama of the Six Characters—"I assure you that all this interests me very, very much. I feel that there is material here for a beautiful play," the director says, (75)—since it is the very stuff of turn-of-the-century, bourgeois, sentimental theater; but on the other hand they will never understand the complex nature of these "characters" or the problems they embody as "characters." The actors will even mistake them for "persons" who, having lived their strange story in real life, now want to put it on the stage for some hidden exhibitionistic or financial reason.

For the theatrical company, the different natures of the characters, their differing consciousness of being "characters" and not persons, or of having a role in their play, will remain a mystery. While "the Father and the Stepdaughter . . . more than the others are aware of being characters" (40), not persons, creatures of art in search of the moments of life that they can have only by communicating, the Mother has no awareness of acting a role. She lives and suffers it as a person in real life would, the way the creature of art she is not aware of being must; she lives "the eternal moment" (99) each time she is compelled to act the play with her family; for her it is always the first time. While the suffering of the Characters who are aware of being characters seems somewhat diminished thanks to their cathartic awareness, hers is as urgent as that of a real person. The Father and the Stepdaughter, conscious of the fact that, as characters, they live only by communicating, "obviously are more forthcoming and lead and almost drag along the dead weight of the others" (39). In contrast, the Mother "does not care at all about living . . . she has no doubt whatsoever about being alive; nor has the need to ask herself how and why she is alive ever crossed her mind. She has no consciousness of being a character since she is never, not even for a second, detached from her 'role', she is not aware of having a 'role' . . . she lives in a continuity of feeling that knows no interruption, thus she cannot become aware of the nature of her life, that is, of her being a character'' (41–42). The nature of the two children whose hands she is clasping is very similar to hers; they experience through that contact her own unsettling emotions. Instead, the Son keeps denying that he is a character, that he has a drama: the others might, but he does not, for he has no role to play in their drama. The author did not assign him one, and he will not play one. (''I have no role in it and do not want to have any; you know that I am not cut out to figure here among you! . . . my feelings cannot produce any action on my part . . . I am an unrealized character dramatically, and I feel uneasy, downright ill in their company'') (73–74). The Six Characters, that is, are different. (''Apparently not all six characters have reached the same degree of evolution'').

As characters in their turn-of-the-century sentimental family melodrama, they were rejected by their creator, who did not cast their story in definitive artistic form. But while rejecting them as characters in that tearful bourgeois play, he cast them in another play, a deeper, more modern play, the play of the rejected characters in search of an author, whose real drama is the need and the difficulty of human communication. Each according to his degree of awareness, the Six are conscious of being rejected characters in search of an author, but they must not discover that this, and not their cheap family drama, is their real drama. Even as they are in desperate search of their author and feeling deeply the deprivation inflicted on them, they must continue to believe that the drama that makes them characters, creatures of art, potentially capable of achieving immortality, is the family drama that did not get written and that they want to act out. If they were to discover that the drama which makes them immortal is instead their search for an author, and that the definitive artistic form they are seeking has been granted them in this ''other'' play, they would stop worrying about rejection. They would stop searching for their author, they would cease to exist as characters in this play, and this play would no longer exist.

Instead, conscious of both rejection and search—but unconscious that their real drama consists precisely in this situation—the Six Characters live this drama with the passion with which any authentic character must live his drama (''the drama in which and thanks to which he is a character'') (40). *And it is in the passionate experience of this drama in which they do not know that they are characters*—the drama of being rejected characters, unwilling to be deprived of the most powerful form of communication, of definitive artistic form and ultimately of immortality—*and not in the presentation of their family drama, that they develop and express the complex Pirandellian themes of this play.*

The language of the play reflects the distinction between the two dramatizations. Being an old-fashioned, turn-of-century melodrama, the family drama is presented in the familiar naturalistic language of the bourgeois theater. When the characters are revealing the background of their family drama, their individual passions, their part in the drama, and acting out the two scenes they succeed in staging, they use this language consistently and insist on "realistic" staging:

The Stepdaughter: O Lord sir, she told me what you already know: that mother's work was badly done again; that she had wasted the material; and that I must be understanding if I wanted her to go on helping us in our poverty.... No, no, my dear sir! He must tell me what he told me: "Well, let's get rid of this nice little frock immediately, then!" And I, with all that mourning in my heart, only two months old, went there, see?, behind that screen, and with these fingers that were shaking with shame, with revulsion, I unhooked my petticoat, my gown.

The Director and his actors too, accustomed as they are to bourgeois comedies or French romantic dramas, speak the same naturalistic language:

The Director: What can I do if no good comedy comes from France any more, and we are reduced to staging Pirandello's plays, which nobody understands, purposely written to leave actors, critics, and public eternally dissatisfied?

But the language of the play alters when the Six Characters interrupt the presentation of their family drama and take on the role of "Pirandellian" characters in search of understanding from their uncomprehending audience (the Director and his actors). They become characters trying to explain their essence as creations of art imagined by their author and rejected, cast into the limbo of formlessness, deprived of an immortality they feel is their due, despairing, like Dante's souls in limbo who "without hope live in desire," of ever obtaining the immortality of art. Fired by this passion, as soon as they assume this role, their language rises to new levels of conceptual coherence, capable of expressing the awareness of the artist, the mystery of artistic creation, and the problems of its genesis, of its translation into formal expression, of its communication to an audience:

You know very well that life is full of endless absurdities which, shamelessly needn't even look probable because they are real ... and that it might really be folly to try to do the contrary; that is, to try to create probable ones which would look real; but ... if this be folly, it is also the only reason for your craft ... to create ... live beings, more alive than those who breathe and wear clothes! Less real, perhaps, but truer ... Nobody knows better than you that nature uses human imagination as a tool to carry on its creative work on a higher level ... Aren't you accustomed to seeing up there, alive, confronting each other, the characters created by the author? ... Believe us, we are truly six characters, and extremely interesting ones! Although lost ... in the sense that the author who created us, live, did not want to, or physically could not, bring us into the world of art.

It is a language capable of dealing with complex problems of poetics and aesthetics with clarity and force. To the Director who interjects: "I would like to know when a character has ever been seen stepping out of his role and

defending it, pushing it, explaining it, the way you are doing?'' The Father
replies that a ''live character'' possesses autonomy, vitality, an expressive life
of his own:

You have never seen it because authors usually do not disclose the laborious process of
creation. Yet if the characters are alive, really live before their author, he does nothing
but observe the words, the gestures, they propose to him; he must want them the way
they want themselves to be; he must! When a character is born, he immediately acquires
such independence even from his author that he can be imagined by everybody in situations
in which his author never thought of putting him, and take on a significance, at times,
that his author never dreamed of giving him! . . . So why wonder about us? Think of the
bad luck of a character born alive, as I said, of the imagination of an author, who then
wanted to deny him life, and tell me if this character, left thus, alive and deprived of
life, has no business doing what we are doing before you now, after having done it again
and again, believe us, before him in order to convince him, to push him—now myself,
now the girl, now that miserable mother . . . (105).

A character is endowed, the Father asserts, with a permanence that people whose
reality is in constant flux cannot enjoy. The reality of the character consists only
in the illusion created by the work of art; he lives only in the crucial moment
of communication.

It is only as we reflect on the text that we realize how effectively this language
deals with complex aesthetic questions, because as it is spoken by the characters
it demonstrates the dynamism, the immediacy, the vivid imagery of animated
conversation. The conceptual discourse is punctuated by frequent exclamations
(''Right! Quite so! to living beings, more alive than those who breathe and wear
clothes! Less real, perhaps, but truer! We share the same opinion!'') ellipses
(''But, but! You just said'' . . . ''But if you really can change from one day to
the next . . . '') rhetorical questions (''But what do you really mean to say?''
''But those two children, have you heard them speak?'') and by numerous
interjections and vocatives (''Eh,'' ''sir,'' ''Yessir,'' ''see,'' ''please,'' ''I beg
you,'' ''nothing, sir,'' ''just so, sir,'' ''no, what on earth are you saying, sir,'').
These devices produce the feeling of immediacy proper to lively dialogue, as
do the frequent interruptions in the flow of the speech by parenthetical expressions
(''a man—I am not saying you, necessarily—a man in general, may be nobody'').
The speech of the Mother, the most instinctual of the Six Characters, who must,
however, express the difficult idea of the eternal actuality of her torment, is
broken into very short sentences, explosive fragments of thought expressed
almost exclusively through exclamations, a sequence of short, sharp cries of
grief.

Although these might at first appear mere rhetorical devices, their effect is in
fact highly dramatic. Pirandello's extraordinary stylistic inventiveness makes the
difference between the static, absent discourse that deadens so many twentieth-
century plays[4] and a dramatic interaction full of color, energy, and magnificently
eloquent characters.

Another important Pirandellian technique that keeps the development of these themes from abstraction is the pervasive use of images, references, and examples that are immediate and concrete. Thus the Father's statement "We are in search of an author" expresses the characters' sense of their lack of definitive artistic form and their quest for it.

The Mother as well, speaking about her "torment which renews itself, alive and present, always," gives concreteness to its reality by calling the attention of her audience to its concrete consequences, in the silence and staring eyes of the two children who clutch her hands and share her torment through that contact: "But those two little ones, have you heard them speak? They can no longer speak, sir! They still keep clutching my hands, to keep my torment alive and present; but they in themselves no longer exist." The language of the Son, too, exemplifies the concrete imagery that pervades all the "conceptual" passages of this play. For instance, to tell the Director that it is impossible to communicate with exactitude, without falsification, the essence of an artistic character, he shouts at him: "But haven't you understood yet that you cannot perform this play? We are not inside you, and your actors are looking at us from the outside." And to explain the revulsion that seizes the dramatic characters and their author when they see themselves betrayed by the interpretation of a poor theatrical company, he uses the familiar image of a mirror in a novel way: "Would you find it possible to live before a mirror which, besides freezing us in the image of our own appearance, sends it back to us with a grimace that is an unrecognizable distortion of ourselves?"

We have, then, two types of languages: the familiar, naturalistic language in which the characters present their family drama, and the conceptual language in which the characters define their essence as creations of art and live their roles as characters in search of an author. Yet we find the transition between one and the other almost imperceptible. In vivid immediacy and inventive power, the conceptual language matches and indeed surpasses the other. The Six Characters in search of an author live their quest for life, if not immortality, as forcefully and as passionately as the Six Characters who play out their family melodrama. The search for communication and for life is more imperative, truer to life, than the naturalistic play within the play. And it is, as we have noted, when the characters live their "role" as characters, aware of the possibility of definitive artistic form, aggrieved at not having achieved it, searching for a way to communicate their drama, rather than in the presentation of the family drama itself, that the new themes of the Pirandellian theater are developed.

Pirandello himself in the famous Preface gives us the essence of the major themes: "the delusion of mutual understanding, irremediably based on the empty abstraction of words; the multiple personality of every individual, deriving from all the possibilities of being present in each one of us; and finally the inherent, tragic conflict between life that constantly moves and changes, and form which fixes it immutably" (38). Beneath these themes lies the larger, inclusive one of the human need for communication and the difficulty, if not the impossibility, of satisfying it. To convey one's own individual human reality is rendered difficult both by the inescapable subjectivity of one's own perception of oneself and the reality around one, and by the very nature of language itself. "But this is where the root of all evil lies, in words. . . . We think we understand each other, but we never do" (65), complains the Father at the conclusion of a long dispute with his Stepdaughter and the Director in which this idea is developed, arising from the attempt by each character to promote his own view of the events.

This is a difficulty that not even communication through achieved artistic form can escape. The creation of imagination, the "live character," might have "the good fortune of finding," besides a creator, "a fertile matrix, an imagination able to raise and nourish him, make him live forever"—bring him, that is, from the original conception to the definitive formal stage not impoverished, diminished, frozen, but richly and fully realized, so that his betrayal by future interpreters will be more difficult. Yet inevitably that definitive artistic form would be subject to endless interpretive betrayals in the moment of communication, since each interpreter brings to it a whole world of ideas and feelings, a sensibility which is his and never exactly that of the author. Language is always tied to the subjectivity of the communicants. And drama is more than any other art form at the mercy of this subjectivity, given the series of interpreters it must go through, from author to director, to actors, to audience. The Six Characters, unable to hide their disappointment at the interpretation of their drama by the theatrical company, clearly understand this.

In addition to their complaints about the interpretive shortcomings of the actors, the Six Characters are also aware that the definitive artistic form they pursue so intelligently and persistently will never succeed in rendering wholly the multiplicity of the individual, nor the flow, the dynamic pulse of real life; art will tend to freeze, to contract, to simplify life. At the very moment we think we have succeeded in capturing life, it is already evolving into something different. This truth Pirandello had found in Vico: "I cling to the belief that I am always the same; yet the constant accession and decession of things that flow into and out of me make me different at every moment. More or less in the way in which movement that seems straight is subject to constant distortions."[5] The reality the artist has created is defined, finished, unchanging, while everyday reality is in continual flux—not to be captured, in this sense, by artistic form or by any form in which life may be frozen. Yet life itself, to escape the solitude of inarticulate chaos, is condemned to organize itself, to seek a form, by which it then feels imprisoned or limited, and against which (like the Father contesting the role of seducer in which he is cast by the Stepdaughter) it eventually tries to rebel.

Man is always dissatisfied with these limitations, but in his irrepressible need to communicate and be understood, he accepts as inevitable the need for a crystallizing form, however inadequate, as the only means by which to reveal himself to others. This is the central dramatic experience of these six Pirandellian characters, developed in all the encounters between them and the members of the theatrical company: to be "In search of an author," of definitive artistic form, as a necessary means to communication. And if definitive artistic form is not available, a compromise is certainly better than nothing: if not the immortality of the characters of the great masterpieces, at least the compromise of living even "only for a moment" in the actors they chance upon—aware, after all, that even definitive artistic form would have been a compromise with elusive reality.

By using dramatic characters *as* characters, Pirandello explores on another level a basic theme of his work: the fundamental human need to communicate and the difficulty of satisfying it. For, however impoverished a human life may be without communication, the life of a character is literally entirely dependent on it: in a character the need to communicate is as imperious as the human urge to live.

NOTES

1. Luigi Pirandello, *Maschere nude*, I (Milano: Mondadori, 1978), 34. Hereafter the number of the page in parentheses in the text will refer to this edition. All translations are mine.

2. Luigi Pirandello, *Novelle per un anno*, I (Milano: Mondadori, 1985) [translation mine].

3. *Almanacco litterario Bompiani 1938* (Milano: Bompiani, 1938), 43 [translation mine].

4. Beginning early in the century with the many "discussion plays" by George Bernard Shaw; see, for example, the dream sequence from the third act of *Man and Superman* (1901), often produced as a separate play, *Don Juan in Hell*.

5. Giambattista Vico, *Opere* (Milano: Ricciardi, 1953), 281 [translation mine].

WORKS CITED

Almanacco litterario Bompiani 1938. Milano: Bompiani, 1938.
Pirandello, Luigi. *Maschere Nude*. Milano: Mondadori, 1978.
———. *Novelle per un Anno*. Milano: Mondadori, 1985.
Vico, Giambattista. *Opere*. Milano: Ricciardi, 1953.

14

Six Characters in Search of an Author and Its Critique of Traditional Theater: Mimesis and Metamimesis

Emanuele Licastro

Whether one believes in the spirit of the time or in coincidence, Pirandello's *Six Characters in Search of an Author* appeared in 1921 and Joyce's *Ulysses* in 1922. The closeness of the appearances is significant enough to make us think of historical succession, be it necessary or casual. What *Ulysses* is to fiction, *Six Characters* is to theater.[1] The two works are watersheds between mimesis and metamimesis in the history of art, though neither watershed should be viewed as a complete break with the past—either as a breakdown of the older mimetic mode of preceding artists or as a breakthrough by more modern, more self-conscious ones.

Fiction as mimesis has been analyzed by many critics. The classic instance is by Erich Auerbach for whom mimesis *qua* mimesis is a positive critical and artistic judgment, the subtitle of his book being *tout court*, *The Representation of Reality in Western Literature*, not "The Artistic Representation. . . ." The pre-modern work of art, which was viewed as an effort at representing reality, in the twentieth century changes into the representation of a representation, the mimesis of a mimesis. The content of mimesis is no longer reality per se but the process of representation itself. Earlier, the artist was conscious mainly of the reality he wished to present; now he is conscious primarily of the reality of his work. Hence, "the meaning of a work of art consists in the telling of itself, in speaking to us about its own existence" (Todorov, 49). On the one hand Auerbach's mimesis, on the other Todorov's mimesis of mimesis; on the one hand the Mona Lisa, on the other her mustache. Of course, it is not, and it could not be, that at a certain moment the artist became self-conscious in respect to his work. It is at least partially true—the formalists' claim—that, as B. M. Eikhenbaum has it, "The creation of new artistic forms is not an act of representation, but of discovery, because these forms are hidden in the forms of preceding periods" (quoted in Medvedev and Bakhtin, 162).

Numberless instances show how mimetic artists were aware of their mimesis or of artists who played with their medium. The viewer of the Arnolfini portrait may be reminded of Van Eyk, but we cannot look at Parmigianino's self-portrait without being acutely aware of the painter consciously playing with the mirror, that he is holding a mirror up to a mirror and not up to nature. We cannot look at *Las Meninas* without thinking that the real king of this universe is the artist himself. But, if anything, the mimetic and the metamimetic modes in the literary sphere, especially the narrational, one of the categories of being human, has attracted more interest and critical analysis than the visual. It has not been difficult to detect in the past the narrator's self-consciousness of his role as narrator, his awareness of the would-be reader, and his mindfulness of the medium. Since *Don Quixote*, the novel as a genre has been openly and relentlessly filled with hints of metamimesis, as many scholars from diverse schools of criticism have amply commented on. However, less noticed has been a similarity between that novel's metamimetic aspects and modern metamimesis: as Cervantes with his thrusts and parries was fighting the preceding verse "narrative" of "superstructured" knighthood in the name of the prosaic and realistic bourgeoisie, modern metamimeticists, certainly the pioneers, with their own thrusts and parries fought—and some are still fighting—the preceding novels of the superstructured bourgeoisie in the name of the underground or unstructured man. Nonmimetic authorial presence and intervention are evident, though not always and not always to the same degree, throughout the history of the novel. Besides Cervantes, some of the more significant authors we might note are Richardson, Sterne, and Diderot.

The development of theater also moves from mimesis to metamimesis, and the change is not sudden. In drama we can discover metamimetic elements before the twentieth century. In many dramas, playwrights played with actors (who instead of playing a role remained characters or even actors), with plots (by mixing different planes of reality), with the play (which engendered a new play within itself), and with the script (by pretending not to have one and by improvising one, as in the *commedia dell'arte*). The *locus classicus* of metamimesis in theater is the play-within-a-play performed in Elsinore Castle. Also universal is the rhythmic chant which starts, "All the world's a stage . . . " whose message, centuries ago, Sancho—as he informs us—had already "heard many times before" (Cervantes, 580; pt. 2, ch. 3).

Lope de Vega's *Lo fingido verdadero* is another example of self-conscious theater: in the play-within-a-play, actors become themselves and act their own lives. At the end of the first act, an actor tells the audience he has been playing the role of king only for a short time and not very satisfactorily; in the second act, two actors playing the lovers elope in the play *and* in life; the third act ends with a real martyrdom (in the outer play) of a pagan actor who converted to

Christianity while reciting (in the inner play) the lines of a Christian martyr (Newberry, 14–15).

In the development of drama we must also consider that mimetic theater was achieved very slowly (not like the novel), theater being a conversion from ritual, where the audience participated in the drama, to the self-contained play. This transformation occurred both in ancient Greece from religious or social ritual into classic tragedy and comedy, and in Europe from medieval Mystery Cycles and Morality Plays into Renaissance drama (Righter, 45), when the play became the thing.

When regarding the development of mimesis into metamimesis, the critic is subject to two tendencies. First is the tendency to project the present into the past and to decode its works with modern critical analyses based on theories of interpretation, themselves born of the necessity to approach and understand modern metamimetic expressions. Unchecked, this tendency may give the incomplete impression that what remains alive and worthwhile of the past is only what can react to and substantiate later conceptions of art. For example, over-enthusiastic scholars "nurtured on Pirandello and imbued with Jean Anouilh" through the "inevitable evocation" of the Sicilian playwright may call an eighteenth-century playwright a "half-way Pirandello" (Nelson, 77).[2]

The second tendency consists in experiencing the present in terms of the past, which may give a restricted view of the present, as if it were a distortion of the past. At times it is a matter of psychological attitude, and critics will go out of their way to find a precedent for the new, so that the prior text becomes a precedent because of the modern achievement. For example, in spite of his admiring and perceptive analysis of Ibsen's plays, Raymond Williams feels compelled to state that "The phrase which [Pirandello's six] characters bring with them is the echo of Ibsen's description of his aim, fifty years earlier, 'the perfect illusion of reality' " (157). The point to be made is that with Ibsen we have exactly and only a wishful description, while in Pirandello we see a theatricalization rendered. The echo comes not from Ibsen but from the splash made by Pirandello. For another example: the more historically conscious George Steiner, touched by Kleist's characters—"most awake when they enter the stuff of dreams"—doesn't turn Pirandello into an echo but writes instead that "From the *Prinz von Homburg* there is only a short step to Pirandello" (227). An echo gives the impression of something insubstantial, unimportant; a step, especially a short step, is something necessary, willful, causal.

Perhaps the Spanish playwright Azorín struck the right note on the subject of Pirandellian antecedents. In 1924, a year after the first Spanish production of *Six Characters*, in his article "Los seis personages y el autor"—an analysis of Calderón's play *El gran teatro del mundo*, a play he thinks "analogous" to Pirandello's *Six Characters*—he warns us that "what is only recollection shouldn't be considered novelty" (quoted in Newberry, 102). It is Pirandello who reminds him of Calderón.

When the non-mimetic mode became the dominant aesthetic trend, some

critics, convinced that mimesis is synonymous with art, grumblingly accepted—
or dismissed—the new mode as "experimental," waiting for and expecting, as
it were, the real thing to arrive. Others bewailed the end of mimesis: hence, the
long pseudodebate on the death of the novel—and its facetious corollary version,
the death of the reader—until the new novel inspired new forms of literary
criticism.

Theater critics also had to find unprecedented viewpoints for approaching the
nonmimetic drama, which are necessarily grounded on theatricality, that is, on
the medium. The theater of the absurd, as Martin Esslin named it,

tends towards a radical devaluation of language, towards a poetry that is to emerge from
the concrete and objectified images of the stage itself. . . . [It] is part of the "anti-library"
movement of our time, which has found its expression in abstract painting, with its
rejection of "literary" element in pictures; or in the "new novel" in France, with its
reliance on the description of objects and its rejection of empathy and anthropomorphism
(1961, xxi).

The conceptual basis of what Lionel Abel calls metatheater are the two tenets
that the world is a stage and that life is a dream; its psychological necessity
is the unavoidable self-consciousness of the author and the autonomous, self-
conscious character. Abel starts metatheater with *Hamlet*, and he ends—he must
end—his central chapter—"Hamlet, quod demonstrandum erat"—by recalling
Pirandello: "Certainly Hamlet is one of the first characters to be free of his
author's contrivances. Some three hundred years later six characters would visit
a playwright, who has not invented them, and according to his own testimony,
ask him to be their author" (58). In his next chapter, Abel writes that *Six
Characters* is "perhaps the most original play-within-a-play written in this century" (62). Even if one disagrees with Abel's theory that tragedy has evolved
into metatheater, *Six Characters* remains no less important in the history of
theater. In fact, Walter Kerr presents a different historical analysis:

The evolution of a freshly self-conscious drama from *Hamlet* to Pirandello leads, sus-
piciously, to something very like comedy or at least to a crossbreed in which comedy
figures very importantly. Much of Pirandello is impertinently light, gracefully mocking,
in tone, rather as though it were the comedy in *Hamlet*—the comedy *of* Hamlet—that
has been pursued all the while, leaving tragic undertones as a somewhat ambiguous
residue. . . . Self-consciousness has made us essentially comic (271–72; 273).

Although this is not the place to discuss the different views of the evolution
of the theater, we are suggesting that no matter which view is adopted, Pirandello
remains an unavoidable bridge to be crossed in order to delineate a meaningful
history of drama. For example, Francis Fergusson states: "Shaw as theater artist
seems to have been feeling for something which Pirandello achieved" (198).
Raymond Williams: "When they advance into the theater, these six characters
in search of an author, . . . the central assumption of the naturalistic habit in

drama has at once been finally realized and finally questioned'' (157). Oscar Büdel sees Pirandello's originality "in the fact that he imposed upon the art form of theatre itself those principles of analytic decomposition which Ibsen was still content to apply to human psychology" (80). Martin Esslin: ''Pirandello more than any other playwright has been responsible for a revolution in man's attitude to the world that is comparable to the revolution caused by Einstein's discovery'' (1969, 49). Eric Bentley ends one of his analyses of *Six Characters* with: "whether or not [Pirandello] convinces us of his general view of things, whether indeed, as the years pass, his philosophy as such retains any interest, he has created a living image which can never die—the image of man as and of life as the game of role playing" (192).

These reminders—whose contents I do not totally share—are not meant as testimonials or as defense, for Pirandello is loquacious and demonstrative enough. Rather, they are intended as a stimulus for looking at his work and reminding ourselves of its importance. Critics have commented on Pirandello's ideas, philosophy, meaning, message—aesthetic, psychological, and social— and they have shown how this content gets expressed through the use of the theater. The present chapter will be limited—as far as it is possible—to his well-known uses of self-conscious theater.

Among the various "seeds," "echoes," "precedents," "anticipations," and "recollections"[3] that can be pointed at (some have been mentioned above), two particular ones should be underlined. One, commented on by many scholars, is the *commedia dell'arte*; from this Italian tradition it was not strange or difficult for Pirandello to envision actors playing unwritten roles, or persons become personages by the simple act of donning a mask.

The other antecedent, not noticed by scholars, is also represented by an Italian tradition: it is the Baroque whose exuberant excrescence of inventiveness, whose sheer theatricality and illusionism, surrounded Pirandello in Rome, the city of his choice. "It was in Italy . . . that this preoccupation with the nature of illusion became most striking" in the seventeenth century (Righter, 205). During that same period when the spirit gave flesh to illusion and self-delusion in *Hamlet* and to the questioning of reality in *Don Quixote*, Bernini, master of Roman High Baroque, was himself playing at mixing reality and illusion in an overwhelming theatrical performance, worthy not only of Pirandello but of every possible stage trick of the twentieth century. The "scenic prank" of 1637—as Richard Bernheimer calls it—is recounted both in an eyewitness letter to the Duke of Modena and later by Bernini himself in a letter to his friend Chantelou:

When the curtain had fallen, one saw on the stage a flock of people partly real and partly only feigned, who had come in great number to see the comedy.'' The crowd on the stage was seated in a "second auditorium" and . . . there were, in fact, "two theaters." And now Bernini proceeded to strengthen the sense of illusion by inserting two middlemen, themselves spectators of a kind, who saw what the audience beheld, and proclaimed the reality of the two rival theaters. "Upon the scene there were two braggarts [played, so

Chantelou asserts, by Bernini himself and his brother] who pretended to draw, paper and
pencil in hand, one with his face toward the real, the other toward the fictitious audience.''
After working in silence for some time, they fell into conversation and came to realize
that the group that each of them beheld was deemed illusory by the other; it being their
unavowed intent to impair the spectator's awareness of himself and to involve him in a
presumably delightful confusion of realities (quoted in Bernheimer, 243).

One experiences the same kind of sparkling inventiveness in Pirandello—so
much so that the danger of his art, one critic suggests, consists in his becoming
"victim of his own invention" (Chiaromonte, 173). Pirandello displays the same
kind of preoccupation with the "sense of illusion," the same convergence of
the "real" and the "fictitious," and the same involvement of the spectator in
a "confusion of realities" in many of his theatrical works, especially in *Six
Characters*. For, ultimately, whether mimetic or metamimetic, art, aside from
its ludic component, is a grasp at reality with the underlying fear that it is
illusion. One critic quite simply speaks of metamimesis as a "new reality"
(Scholes, 269). Yet if it is a new reality, isn't there ever more room for suspicion,
doubt, even more fear than before that it could, it might be, an illusion? And
in such a quandary shall we not cry out (with the Director) the last line of *Six
Characters* and ask for "at least a small light to see where to put [our] feet"?
(Pirandello, 116; May, 69).[4]

Although many instances of real or supposed antecedents to parts of *Six
Characters* have been pointed out, Pirandello was interested in the metamimetic
mode of representation long before he composed this play.

In the "Second Foreword (philosophical) by Way of Being an Apology" to
his novel *The Late Mattia Pascal* (1904), the protagonist-narrator, who is discussing how to write his autobiographical novel, says: "Before, when the earth
didn't turn. . . . '' His interlocutor, Don Eligio, interrupts him: "Come now! The
earth has always turned?" To which Mattia Pascal retorts: "No, that's not true.
Man didn't know it, and therefore it was as if it didn't turn" (2). The exchange
posits the question of reality and the duality of illusion and reality. Later, on
the next page, Mattia Pascal makes fun of past realistic representation, citing
such examples to be rejected as, "The Count rose betimes, at exactly half past
eight" (3). This sentence reminds us of the other sentence, "The Marquise went
out at five," which Paul Valéry once declared he would never have used in a
novel (Breton, 7). The ridicule that Mattia Pascal—and Paul Valéry—express
for this kind of writing is intended to show the weakness of mimetic art. In the
"Second Foreword" Pirandello presents the problem of man in relation to the
universe and of the artist in relation to his art. These two problems then converge
into one, and Pirandello's vision is embodied in the antinomies of reality-illusion,
art-life, form-flux, time-timelessness.

Another page from *The Late Mattia Pascal* is even more specifically pertinent
to *Six Characters* and to theater in general. One character speaking of a performance of *Orestes* in a puppet theater asks: "If at the climax of the play, just

when the marionette who is playing Orestes is about to avenge his father's death and kill his mother and Aegisthus, suppose there were a little hole torn in the paper sky of the scenery. What would happen?'' (139) Mattia Pascal ''sighs'':

Lucky marionettes . . . over whose wooden heads the false sky has no holes! No anguish or perplexity, no hesitations, obstacles, shadows, pity—nothing! And they can go right on with their play and enjoy it, they can love, they can respect themselves never suffering from dizziness or fainting fits, because for their stature and their actions that sky is a proportionate roof (140).

With his hole Pirandello helps to burst the bubble containing Western civilization as it stood at the end of nineteenth century with its belief in the wholeness of the individual. As Christianity had deflated the classical vision and as the Renaissance, the medieval, so self-consciousness demythologized the proud romantic-realistic-positivistic age. Pirandello's hole happens, independently, at the same time—*The Interpretation of Dreams* is published in 1899; *Three Essays on the Theory of Sexuality* in 1905—as Freud's demystification of the centuries-old idea and belief in the logical, and therefore totally explicable, persons who, in the words of Pirandello, ''can go right on with their play and enjoy it, they can love, they can respect themselves never suffering from dizziness or fainting fits'' (*Mattia Pascal*, 140). In the last year of his life Pirandello remarked: ''Nietzsche said the Greeks raised white statues against the dark chaos to hide it. Those times are finished. I tear them down to reveal it'' (Giudice, 544). What the subconscious does to the conscious personality, Pirandello's hole in the sky and his tearing down of statues do to theater. Orestes—no longer a white statue— staring at the rent paper sky represents the self-conscious playwright dealing with characters also conscious of themselves. In this pregnant metaphor, Pirandello expresses the kind of plays that will later be defined as metatheater, among other things. With his hole Pirandello is painting mustaches on Sophocles' statues.

Cubism has often been mentioned in regard to Pirandello's theater, and it is a perceptive comparison, for it gives a visual image to Pirandellian fragmentation of the individual.[5] However, for a visual image of the novelty of his metamimetic techniques, the comparison should be made with Cézanne: both for his startling reclamation of the fundamental medium of painting, the canvas, and for his flattening of perspective into the surface smoothness—and roughness—of *Mount Sainte-Victoire*, those Ravenna mosaics whose suppression of depth abolish time, whose timeless figures (Frank, 27–28) are de-naturalized into eternal artistic form. Reality, turned into the artifice of reality, becomes the artifice of eternity. Pirandello in *Six Characters* rescues the centuries-old mimetic stage by abolishing the pretense of the fourth wall, and in doing so converts the stage from a pseudonatural space into formal artistic space; he too flattens the realistic person-characters into timeless characters. The comparison is even more appropriate because just as Cézanne as a pioneer of metamimetic painting still worked with the shapes of nature—his pictures (as against abstract art) containing the shimmer of "natural objects" (Frank, 28) which they deny—so, in *Six Characters*, Pirandello appears to work with the mimetic materials of story, plot, and person which he too ultimately rejects.

The Characters who in 1921 went in search of an author were first conceived and rejected some ten years before when Pirandello wrote two entries in his notebook. In one, a man is going to a bordello, but

He couldn't see himself as the others saw him: A passerby like any other, unknown, tall, big, well-dressed, around fifty, among so many other unknown passersby, more or less well-dressed. He knew himself. . . . In contrast to the appearance he felt obliged to assume—of a middle age man—he felt screaming inside him the grotesque and shameful desire which would soon push him through the door . . . (*Saggi*, 1257).

On reading this entry, we can easily note such typical Pirandellian themes as life within as opposed to form without, what one is and what one is expected to be, the I and the others. If Pirandello had accepted those characters as they were, he would have fallen within the mimetic representation of reality—well told or not—as it had been done for centuries in the Western world. It would have been a pathetic or bathetic tale. In the other entry we read:

The case of the mother. But just think about it. Her shame before the legitimate son: Not to be able to look at him, for to be able to look at him it is necessary for her to annihilate the life of her other children, who are the children of her sorrow and shame, of another life where he cannot enter (*Saggi*, 1257–58).

Pirandello's refusal to present their pains within the frame of their life story— *la commedia da fare* (the play to be made)—was the master stroke that allowed for a meta-story (the play actually made) and for meta-feelings (the Characters' self-conscious desire to act them out). These six figures frozen at birth haunted their conceiver; they were a challenge, a puzzle, a Gordian knot. In 1911 Pirandello was still obsessed with self-conscious characters, and in the short story *La tragedia di un personaggio* (*The Tragedy of a Character*) he seems to have found the solution to his problem: a character presents himself to Pirandello because he is not happy with the story his own creator has forced on him; he would like Pirandello to make him come alive in a different story, one worthy of the depth of his philosophy. The short story consists of the story about a character wanting to live. The characters are also mentioned in a letter of 1916 to his son (Nardelli, 161) and again in a letter of 1917: "It's such a strange thing, so sad, so sad: Six characters in search of an author. . . . " (*Sipario*, 32).

Many analyses in many languages and from different schools of literary and dramatic criticism successfully explore *Six Characters*, the first by Pirandello himself who in his Preface to the final version offers his own brilliant exegesis. My own remarks are limited to the metamimetic use of the medium itself— stage, actors, plot, acts, props, spectators—in the making of the play.

All agree that the play-within-a-play is the foundation of *Six Characters*. However, Pirandello's use of the old metaphor is new. In fact, traditionally, "with respect to the spectator . . . the outer play . . . is an associative device ('How can people who are looking at a play be unreal?'); . . . the play within a play itself . . . is dissociative ('Like me, those onstage spectators are looking at a play, something unreal')" (Nelson, 115). So, traditionally, we identify with the outer play and distance ourselves from the inner—but not so with *Six Characters*. In Elsinore Castle we are with the court looking at a fiction; in Pirandello's play we are constantly aware of fiction. For not only are we aware of the fictive nature of the inner play (as it has always been the case traditionally), but we are also made aware of the unreality of the outer play (as traditionally was not the case). In Pirandello's play the audience obviously cannot "associate," cannot experience an unreflective identification with characters *qua* characters in search of an author. What up to now, in the history of theater was to be considered the real—that is, mimesis of life—Pirandello has placed in the *locus* of unreality, the inner play. Here, in the inner play, Pirandello places that mimeticized life represented by past theater, especially the theater just preceding him, the bourgeois drama. It is as if what was considered real and true is put in quotation marks, these being the outer play. Pirandello seems to have perceived—as some later philosophers and scientists would have it—that "truth is a device for disquotation" (Putnam, XIV). Pirandello quotes the content of that "scène à l'italienne" which for Roland Barthes represents "the locus of [the] lie . . . [for] the western theatre of the last few centuries" (82).

The story to be performed, in fact, includes children and stepchildren, marriage and broken marriage, cuckoldry and a primal scene, Oedipal and Electra triangles, sex, incest, prostitution, a child taken from his mother, maternal love, children who deny their mother and father, Lolitaism, the pistol, and death by suicide and accident. The past and present motives of Western literature are the ingredients of the story Pirandello rejects—even as he uses them as elements of collage in a cubist painting (Sypher, 269)—and relegates to the "fictitious" mimeticism of the nonbelievable inner play. It is not believed by the spectator who cannot associate with the outer play either since he has just witnessed the Characters' entrance as characters—personages—and is presented with their efforts to become persons, acting out their roles.

The main scene of *Six Characters*—it is the most elaborated, is situated in the middle of the play, is played in part twice, and is set apart and entitled "The Scene"—is at the intersection of the inner and outer plays. The spectator may be at a loss to distinguish between them. It is the scene at Madame Pace's brothel; the part repeated is the encounter between the Father and the Stepdaughter, first reenacted by themselves and then performed by the actors. The audience is prevented from identifying with the mimetic quality of the reenacted scene, even though the two Characters at this very moment are intensely (re)living their life: because, ultimately, they are *only repeating* their encounter for the sake of the actors and the Director, and because they are interrupted with comic remarks by one of the actresses—"Young Actress (*interrupting*): Oh, let's be careful! Those are our hats!" (90; translation May, 43). In addition, in order to emphasize that the scene is a scene, Pirandello places the Director in the auditorium with the spectators so that he may get a better overall view. At the end the audience is not given a moment to linger and empathize mimetically. The Director will intervene metamimetically, "*interrupting, turning to the Prompter in the box and climbing back on the stage*): Stop! Don't write that last line, leave it out" (91; 44).

When the Leading Lady and the Leading Actor perform the same scene, they are interrupted by the Father and the Stepdaughter who cannot recognize themselves in the performance or the brothel in the scenery. This intersection of the inner and outer play—actually, these rehearsals—again points to the fact that the work's main quest or inquest is "How can reality be represented?" That is, Pirandello presents the self-conscious treatment of theatrical devices, devices of expression that are not to be naively considered a hindrance but an unavoidable necessity.

Pirandello demonstrates this necessity in a very important moment: when Characters and actors come on stage for the second part[6] of the play. Convinced that the scene in the brothel cannot be performed without Madame Pace, the Father prepares the scenery in order to "evoke" her on stage. Critics quote Pirandello's belief that a character from the world of art has a life of its own, independent of its author, and that characters visited him and begged and at times tried to force him—the Father and Stepdaughter, for example—to tell their stories. We may go one step further. With the appearance of Madame Pace, not the characters but the play itself takes over its own performance. It is the theatrical medium that comes to possess a life of its own, for Madame Pace's appearance— she is the seventh character—is not necessary for the story of the Six Characters. Her actions in regard to the story have been narrated; the Director, the actors, and the audience already know what has happened. With her evocation on stage, the scene which the Director, the Father, and the Stepdaughter are preparing and the Actors and the audience are prepared to see—the reenactment of the encounter between the Father and the Stepdaughter—will not happen now because it is interrupted by what does happen: the meeting of the Stepdaughter and Madame Pace. This is the only surprise scene of *Six Characters*—after the initial appearance of the Characters themselves. In fact, all the other scenes are slowly and consciously prepared, and the audience gets prepared for them too. Although the audience also knows the content of this scene, it is not prepared for the scene itself. The surprise verges not on the mimesis of life but on theatrical action itself, an action necessitated by the genre's devices.

The same necessity of the medium which brings about Madame Pace's appearance prevents the disappearance of one of the Six Characters: when the Son, "resolutely and fiercely" declares he is not going "to play anything" (109; 62), the Stepdaughter yells at him to leave. Despite wanting to, he "stands there as if tied down by a mysterious power," unable to reach the staircase (110; 62).

The artist cannot use the medium arbitrarily; its exigencies must be respected. The theatricality of the play requires the presence of Madame Pace and of the Son. Of course, these remarks do not deny that view according to which the two Characters are forced to act because no one can avoid his destiny.

If the audience misses the clash between inner and outer play expressed in terms of theater, it cannot miss it in terms of debate: for Pirandello openly discusses the self-consciousness of the medium and the supposedly unmediated mimeticism of action. In the first part of the play, as soon as the Director "begin[s] to be really interested" and urges the Father, "Let's hear it! Let's hear it!" (64; 15), the Son "ironically" comments "Yes, now we'll hear an excerpt of philosophy" and accuses the Father of using "phrases." Soon after, the Stepdaughter interrupts the Father with the line: "Here one doesn't narrate!" (65; 17) The Son and the Stepdaughter are objecting to the Father's effort to justify his behavior. However, when the Father and the Stepdaughter—of the six they are the most interested in the play—each delivers a speech, the Director jumps in with: "But all of this is narration" and the Son echoes: "But, yes, literature!" (69; 21) To the Father's answer: "What literature! This is life, sir! Passion!" the Director declares: "Maybe! But it is not actable." Later he urges: "Let's come to the facts, the facts. These are discussions" (71; 24). The contrast of the inner and outer play is evident: the Son and the Stepdaughter are using "narrative" symbolically as justification. The Director, who belongs to the outer play, is speaking of the medium—narrative doesn't belong on stage.

The same contrast can be noticed in the reactions of the Director and the Mother to the scene at Madame Pace's. "It is significant," writes Olga Ragusa, "that the scene [the Stepdaughter] cannot wait to act is judged damaging to her reputation by both the Mother and the [Director], the two guardians of propriety in the play" (*Luigi Pirandello*, 148–149). We would add that one is the realistic guardian in the inner play, while the other is the guardian of the medium in the outer play. The Mother is worried about her daughter's respectability, the Director about the play and the censors.

Sentimentalism is the most subtle danger in mimetic art because it may be confused with sentiment. At times it is almost impossible to separate them— witness Oscar Wilde's laughter at Little Nell. Especially subtle is the sentimentalism that too easily envelops children. In the inner play there is one such sentimental moment, and Pirandello desentimentalizes it with the intervention of the outer play. Toward the end of the play it must be decided how to combine two scenes—one in the house, the other in the garden—into one since the Director deems it "impossible" to have them in different places. The Stepdaughter, who would prefer to have the scene played outside, recalls her little sister's joy in the garden. Her description is filled with many saccharine clichés: baby talk, little flowers, embracing amorous and innocent little arms, purity close to the "contaminated body" of a prostitute, prostitution forced by poverty, and sleeping four in a bed. It is possible, even probable, that many spectators will feel some "pity" for all this bathos; they will be taken in by the inner play. In fact,

Pirandello succeeded in taking in the leading Italian literary critic and philosopher of his time, Benedetto Croce, who didn't like the play but liked this soliloquy very much—"There are words that move [us] to profound pity"—and he regretted Pirandello "didn't want . . . to give life to this story" (4; 332). Which is the story Pirandello emphatically rejects, since he is aiming at something different. In fact, the stage direction at the end of the Stepdaughter's lines reads: "In so saying, torn by memory, she bursts out in a long, desperate cry. . . . Everyone is deeply moved. The Director approaches her, almost paternally, and comforts her: We'll have the garden. Don't worry. You'll see. You'll be very pleased. We'll combine the scenes in the garden" (107; 60).

The comfort the Director will bring is not related to the Stepdaughter's suffering, since his consoling words belong to the outer play: If the spectator—won over like everyone else on the stage—feels that the words of the Stepdaughter are sincere and are to be taken at face value, then the Director's remark besides being cruel is so defining as to appear almost comical. If the spectator remains unmoved, believing that her words are not sincere and that the Stepdaughter is merely using them to seduce—she is, after all, a prostitute—the Director into playing the scene as she wishes, then both the Stepdaughter's words and the Director's consoling response belong to the outer play, while the sentimental reaction of all the others onstage comes from the inner play. If the description is felt to be both sincere *and* useful in convincing the Director to build the garden, then both audience and people onstage remain in the inner play, the Director continues to belong, as always, to the outer play, while the Stepdaughter is in both, "living" in the inner and "acting" in the outer. Whatever the interpretation, at this moment the two plays touch and give off sparks. In one line and one gesture—the Director's—the rejection of the would-be-play and the heightening of the metamimetic medium are represented.

Immediately after delivering his consoling line, the Director calls (by name!) a stage hand and yells: "Ehi, lower down some backdrops with trees. Two small cypresses here in front of the fountain." (107; 61) He will also ask for a "bit of sky," and to the Electrician a "bit of lunar atmosphere . . . blue." The spectator forgets those feelings aroused by the inner play and is absorbed by the stage paraphernalia. The theater tricks are constantly brought to the spectator's attention; the action of *Six Characters*, after all, is turning the story of the rejected Characters into a play. In fact, the author they are in search of is not any author but a playwright. Otherwise, why would they come to a theater? It should not be forgotten that the author who rejected them was a novelist or a short story writer, the author of those entries years before.

Not only does *Six Characters* consist of discussions and rehearsals of scenes of a play to be made, but it is also a long interruption of the discussion and rehearsal of another play. In the final version of *Six Characters* Pirandello enlarged the rehearsal time of *Il giuoco delle parti* at the beginning, and at the end he added some lines that are a clear reminder of the first scene. The last words the Director tells the actors are: "Go, go! What else do you want to do now! It's too late to start the rehearsal again. We'll do it this evening" (116; 69). *Six Characters* can be viewed as a play-within-a-play within a play. This latter is a mimetic play: it is already made. It has author, script, and actors ready to perform. The innermost play is yet to be made (the *commedia da fare* of the subtitle); it will become another mimetic play, a substitute for the one interrupted. It has Characters but not yet an author, script or actors. The play in between (what we have been calling the outer play) consists in the attempt to give the Characters an author, script, and actors. In Pirandellian terminology: The first play—*Il giuoco delle parti*—is already "form"; the third—the play to be made— is incipient "form," or life about to be made form. The second—consisting of the title's search—represents a state of flux, the anguish of spontaneous life resisting that form to which it is forever and unavoidably condemned. But in *Six Characters* life doesn't yield to form. The Characters want to act their own parts; they don't allow them to be mimeticized. They don't yield to the actors. Their story doesn't become a plot, since "Actors and characters . . . cannot simultaneously occupy the same stage" (Ragusa, 1980, 159).

The less we are interested in theater, the more we will think that "The plot of the play within the play contains the essential drama, for the rest is comic badinage . . . and a great deal of discussion." So writes Kligerman (732) while proposing a psychoanalytic view. Granted that such an interpretation is meaningful and insightful, the drama the psychoanalyst is speaking of has been told (and hidden; "in every disclosure there is also concealment," as Martin Heidegger warns) many times before. What makes *Six Characters* original and new is the theatrical "badinage." The play asks: How to tell (and hide) the story *now*, now that we very well know that it is the same old "essential" story— now that Orestes knows he is Orestes, now that Sophocles knows he is Sophocles and he is creating not life, not even an imitation of life, but a play.

The struggle to present reality by means of the medium and not by mirroring it is also evident in the conclusion. After the Girl is (supposed to be) drowned and the body of the Boy (who commits suicide) is carried off behind the backdrop by all except the Father and the Director, all the Actors come back on stage, some screaming "reality" and others "pretense." Here too the inner play and the outer overlap, for the opinion is not divided between the Father—"Reality, reality"—and the members of the Company. Some of the Actors believe with the Father that what has happened is real.

No matter now many stage tricks, theater props, and discussions on art, the symbiotic contrast of content and medium is always present in *Six Characters*. With this contrast in mind it seems easier to understand two points that continue to appear puzzling. Critics have assumed and commented on the namelessness of the Characters, and they are reminded of another nameless Pirandellian character, Henry IV. But the latter instance is not the same. Instead of listing the character's name, Pirandello intentionally gives his assumed name in parentheses preceded by an ellipsis: " . . . (Enrico IV)". However, the Six Characters are not nameless; they are listed as the Father, the Mother, and so on, because that is the way roles are assigned for a new play. A director may say Orestes or Hamlet, but for a new play he will express himself as the Director in *Six Characters*: "You'll be the Mother," (81; 33) "You, the Son," "You, miss, of course the Stepdaughter" (81; 34). As soon as the play-within-a-play is ready, the names will become available. In fact, Pirandello has already named the Characters: within the inner play, within their story, they call each other by their names. The Stepdaughter calls the Girl "Rosetta," (111; 64), and there is a moment when the Characters even defend their own names. After assigning the role of the Mother, the Director observes: "It is necessary to find a name for her," and to the Father's suggestion: "Amalia," he answers: "But this is the name of your wife. We wouldn't really want to call her with her real name!" And the Father: "Why not, excuse me? If that's her name . . . " (81; 33). The argument ends with the Director conceding: " . . . if you want Amalia, it will be Amalia" (81; 34). Of course, the script will never be written; they will continue to be Characters, so they will not be able to use their names.

The members of the Company are also listed according to their roles; yet when it is necessary they use names. The Director calls the Stage Manager (51; 3) and a Stage Hand (107; 61) by name. So both the Characters and the members of the Company have names, but they can use them only within their own separate circles. They remain separate because the Characters' story is not performed. Only in a mimetic story will names be listed in the *dramatis personae*.

The parallel presence of the two plays is held until the last moments of *Six Characters*: there appear the Father, the Mother, and the Son, then the Stepdaughter who, with a mocking laugh, will run away. The Boy and the Girl are not present. Why? One can, of course, agree that the last scene represents the reunion of the original nuclear family and that the presence of the two children is therefore not required. But neither is the Stepdaughter's running away required: the audience already knows of her departure just as it knows the children have died. So why is there a final appearance of the Stepdaughter but not of the children?[7] This is the other question that continues to puzzle many critics. I would like to suggest that the children's absence in the last scene is yet another element that underlines the colliding presence of the two, inner and outer, plays. The children do not appear because they belong only to the inner play. The audience, by the children's absence, is reminded that they are part only of the mimetic would-be-play, which never was and never will be. The other four Characters also belong only to the inner play, but they are different because their rehearsals were—partly, awkwardly, badly—imitated (or intended to be imitated) by the Actors. The children don't have counterparts among the members of the Company. And without actors there can be no performance; without a medium, and awareness of the medium, there can be no reality in art.

Even when the Characters and the Company more or less reach an agreement on how to play a scene or choose a name, it is always a struggle. It is impossible for the two groups to comprehend each other. On the stage they remain separate. Yet, like parallel lines in a non-Euclidian universe, at an unspecifiable point the two plays combine. Pirandello planned another integral element of the theatrical medium, the audience. While the Characters and the Company members are aware of their own and the others' point of view, they cannot combine them since they have binary vision. The audience, helped by being "dissociated" both from the inner and the outer play, is able to see bi-optically, producing a stereoscopic image that will combine the two plays into a new modern depth perspective, whose vanishing point seems not to be as far as the eye can see but, within, as far as our mind's eye can fathom. Just as the modern author can no longer pretend to mirror nature without being aware of the mirror (no longer Parmigianino's, crystalline, seductive, and convex but a different one, rough and hard with an asymmetrical surface), so the audience—the reader, the viewer—will also be aware of both. *Six Characters* is the first, clearest, and most exemplary instance of this stereoscopic image in modern theater.

NOTES

1. See M. T. Reynolds for "connections" between Joyce and Pirandello, "the two giants of modernism" (59). She presents a detailed bibliography on the subject.

2. Among the books that present in-depth treatment of the earlier use of theatricality— the role of the audience, actor, script improvisation, and the play-within-a-play—we can cite Anne Righter's on the English drama, from the Middle Ages to Shakespeare; Robert Nelson's which, after a chapter on Shakespeare, deals with the French theater from Rotrou to Anouilh; and Wilma Newberry's on "the Pirandellian mode in Spanish literature" from Cervantes to Sastre.

3. In regard to *Six Characters'* originality, I would like to recall the question of the originality of another work-within-a-work, Fellini's *8 1/2*. Christian Metz writes: "*8 1/2* with its 'film within the film' belongs to the category of works of art that are divided and doubled, thus reflecting on themselves. . . . Alain Virmaux has shown that, although mirror construction in the cinematographic domain is not an invention of Fellini's since it is found already in various earlier films . . . the author if *8 1/2* is nevertheless the first to construct his *whole* film, and to order *all* his elements, according to the repeating mirror image. In fact the precursors of *8 1/2* only partially deserve to be called 'mirror-construction' works, because in them the 'film within the film' was only a marginal or picturesque device, . . . at times a simple 'trick' of the script-writer's, . . . at best a fragmentary construction . . . lending perspective to only part of the film's substance, the rest being presented directly, and not through reflection" [italics in the original, 228–29].

4. I am translating and citing the final version of *Six Characters*. For the reader's convenience, I also cite page references to Frederick May's English translation. On the difficulty of finding in the United States a readily available English translation of the play in its final version, see Ragusa, " 'Six Characters.' "

5. For example, Wylie Sypher writes, "Pirandello invites us to examine the texture of his drama exactly as a cubist invites us to examine the contrasting textures of his painting, the very invitation raising doubt about holding the mirror up to nature" (293); also, "Pirandello, like Picasso, was seeking a 'way beyond art' and, like the [contemporary] scientists, accepted reality as a continual transformation where fiction impinges on fact, where art intersects life" (295).

6. The play is not divided into acts—after all, the play has not been written. The first interruption happens so that the Director and the Father can go backstage to discuss the action of the play; the curtain remains raised. The second interruption is the lowering of the curtain by mistake.

7. If not the living children, at least their corpses could have been made to appear and disappear in a play of light.

WORKS CITED

Abel, Lionel. *Metatheatre*. New York: Hill and Wang, 1953.

Auerbach, Erich. *Mimesis*. Garden City, N.Y.: Doubleday, 1957.

Barthes, Roland. *Empire of Signs*. Trans. Richard Howard. New York: Hill and Wang, 1982.

Bentley, Eric. *The Life of the Drama*. New York: Atheneum, 1967.

Bernheimer, Richard. "Theatrum Mundi." *The Art Bulletin* 38 (1956): 225–47.

Breton, André. "Manifesto of Surrealism (1924)." *Manifestoes of Surrealism*. Trans. Richard Seaver and Helen R. Lane. Ann Arbor, Mich.: The University Press, 1969. 1–47.

Büdel, Oscar. *Pirandello*. New York: Hillary, 1966.

Cervantes, Miguel d. *Don Quixote*. Trans. Samuel Putnam. New York: Viking, 1949.

Chiaromonte, Nicola. "The Ceremonial Theater of Jean Genet." Trans. Alastair Hamilton. *Tempo Presente*, November 1966. Rpt. in *The Worm of Consciousness and Other Essays*. New York, London: Harcourt Brace Jovanovich, 1976. 160–82.

Croce, Benedetto. "Luigi Pirandello." *La Letteratura Italiana*. Vol. 4. Bari: Laterza, 1963. 326–33. 4 vols. 1963.

Esslin, Martin. "Pirandello: Master of the Naked Masks." *New York Times*, June 25, 1967, Sec. 2:1 + . Rpt. in *Reflections*. Garden City, N.Y.: Doubleday, 1969. 49–57.

———. *The Theatre of the Absurd*. Garden City, N.Y.: Doubleday, 1961.

Fergusson, Francis. *The Idea of Theatre*. Garden City, N.Y.: Doubleday, 1949.

Frank, Joseph. *The Widening Gyre*. Bloomington, Ind.: Indiana University Press, 1963.

Giudice, Gaspare. *Luigi Pirandello*. Torino: UTET, 1963.

Kerr, Walter. *Tragedy and Comedy*. New York: Simon and Schuster, 1967.

Kligerman, Charles. "A Psychoanalytic Study of Pirandello's *Six Characters in Search of an Author*." *Journal of the American Psychoanalytic Association* 10 (1962): 731–44.

Medvedev, P. N., and M. M. Bakhtin. *The Formal Method of Literary Scholarship*. Trans. Albert J. Wehrle. Baltimore: Johns Hopkins University Press, 1978.

Metz, Christian. *Film Language. A Semiotics of the Cinema*. Trans. Michael Taylor. New York: Oxford University Press, 1974.

Nardelli, Federico V. *Vita segreta di Luigi Pirandello*. Rome: V. Bianco, 1962.

Nelson, Robert J. *Play Within a Play*. New Haven, Conn.: Yale University Press, 1959.

Newberry, Wilma. *The Pirandellian Mode in Spanish Literature*. Albany, N.Y.: SUNY Press, 1973.

Pirandello, Luigi. *The Late Mattia Pascal*. Trans. William Weaver. Garden City, N.Y.: Doubleday, 1964.

———. "*Letter* to son." *Sipario* 7, 80 (1952):32.

———. *Saggi*. Milan: Mondadori, 1965.

————. *Sei personaggi in cerca d'autore*. Maschere Nude. Vol. 1. Milan: Mondadori, 1967. 2 vols.

————. *Six Characters in Search of an Author*. Trans. Frederick May. London: William Heinemann Ltd., 1954.

Putnam, Hilary. *Realism and Reason*. Cambridge, New York: Cambridge University Press, 1983.

Ragusa, Olga. *Luigi Pirandello*. Edinburgh: Edinburgh University Press, 1980.

————. " 'Six Characters,' 1921–1925 and Beyond." Eds. Biasin and Perella. *Pirandello 1986*. Rome: Bulzoni, 1987. 19–30.

Reynolds, Mary T. "Joyce and Pirandello." *Review of National Literatures* (Pirandello) 14 (1987): 58–78.

Righter, Anne. *Shakespeare and the Idea of the Play*. London: Chatto and Windus, 1964.

Scholes, Robert. "On Realism and Genre." *Novel* 2 (1969) 269–271.

Steiner, George. *The Death of Tragedy*. New York: Hill and Wang, 1961.

Sypher, Wylie. *Roccoco to Cubism in Art and Literature*. New York: Vintage Books, 1960.

Todorov, Tzvetan. *Littérature et signification*. Paris: Larousee, 1967.

Williams, Raymond. *Drama from Ibsen to Brecht*. New York: Oxford University Press, 1969.

15

On *Henry IV*

Maurice Valency

In the arts, in general, the nineteenth century may be said to end with the death
of Victor Hugo in 1885; thereafter, in poetry, painting, and music, the new era
was ushered in with considerable fanfare. In the theater the rupture with tradition
was less abrupt, and the changing state of affairs became fully apparent only
after the end of the First World War. Then quite suddenly, as it seemed, the
decline of realism was accelerated, and the logical principle relaxed its age-long
hold on the drama. In Paris, by 1925, a play such as Cocteau's *Les Mariés de
la Tour Eiffel* could find an audience, and the way was open for every sort of
dramatic experiment provided the necessary management could be found. Pirandello experimented a little with futurism. He wrote the scenario for a futurist
pantomime called *Salamandra*, performed in 1928 under Prampolini. Two years
before that Pirandello's company produced Marinetti's *Vulcani* in Florence. But
Six Characters had carried him as far into the irrational as he cared to go. His
next play dealt with madness, but Pirandello's approach was eminently sane.

Henry IV is without doubt the most poignant of Pirandello's plays, and in
some respects the most personal. *Quando si è qualcuno* (*When Someone Is
Somebody*) affords an unhappy glimpse of the author trapped by success; but
success is easier to bear than failure, and in *Henry IV* there is surely some
aftertaste of the disastrous reception of *Six Characters* in Rome. In 1921 Pi-

Source: From *The End of the World: An Introduction to Contemporary Drama* by Maurice Valency.
Copyright © 1980 by Oxford University Press, Inc. Reprinted by permission.

randello was fifty-four. He had had little joy in his life. *Six Characters* was the best he had done in the theater, his most original effort, and it had been rejected in Rome with jeers and insults. He had long cherished the conviction that the Italian press was arrayed against him and the "new drama" he represented. Now he was certain of it. Success came to him soon thereafter, unexpectedly and in full measure. It rescued him from despair and from poverty, and provided him with impregnable defenses; but it came too late to restore his genial spirits. After the initial rejection of *Six Characters* there were no more light-hearted stories, and it was irony rather than humor that colored his plays.

Henry IV was in some sense the fruit of despair. He began writing it immediately after the first performance of *Six Characters*, and went at it furiously. In four months it was finished. He distilled into it all the bitterness with which a lifetime of misfortune had inspired him, and all the scorn and indignation of an unforgiving nature. It was a magnificent act of revenge, and it was the high point of his genius. He never wrote better, or as well.

In all probability, had *Six Characters* been gratefully received he would not have been capable of writing *Henry IV*. And afterward, when his talent was recognized and applauded, he had no need to reach so high. *Henry IV* marks both the pinnacle of his effort and the beginning of his decline as an artist. He was to write twenty plays after it. But after it there was no more madness, and there were no more masterpieces.

All art tends to self-portraiture. The temptation to see in the hero of *Henry IV* a likeness of the author is well-nigh irresistible, but it is best to resist it. There are no doubt some analogies. As for a likeness—if there is a likeness, it is exaggerated and romanticized out of all semblance to its subject. Pirandello had an example of madness vividly before his eyes from the early years of his marriage to Antonietta until two years before the composition of this play; he himself, however, was sorely afflicted with sanity. As an acute and sensitive observer of the lunacies of others, it is true, he could hardly escape some breath of contagion. Such are the psychic hazards of the profession. Doubtless when he wrote he had himself in mind; but the degree in which he identified himself with his characters must remain a matter of conjecture. Between himself and his characters he invariably interposed an intermediary. In his stories the narrator does not lose sight of himself for a moment, nor we of him.

In his youth, we are told, the man who in the play becomes *Henry IV* was often carried away emotionally, yet always, so to speak, in cold blood:

Belcredi: I don't mean to say that he was only pretending to be carried away like that. No, on the contrary, he was often really excited. But I am ready to swear, doctor, that no sooner did he feel himself carried away like that, then he would catch sight of himself in the very act, so. And I think this happened to him more and more often. What's more, I'm sure it annoyed him. Every so often he'd get into a perfect fury with himself. It was comical.

Donna Matilde: That's true.

Belcredi: (To Donna Matilde) And Why? (To the doctor) I think because that sudden clarity of perception made him feel, suddenly, a stranger to his own feelings, so that they seemed to him—not feigned—he was in fact sincere—but like something to which he had to give, then and there, the value of—what shall I say—an intellectual act—something artificial he did in order to compensate for the warmth of heart which he lacked. And then he would improvise, exaggerate, he would let himself go, you understand, in order to lose sight of himself again. That made him seem unstable, fatuous, and even sometimes—why not admit it—sometimes even ridiculous.

In *Henry IV* the protagonist is nameless. At twenty-seven he was a studious young man of uncertain temper, hopelessly enamored of the beautiful Matilda Spina, at that time a girl of nineteen. Matilda made him suffer. One day he took part in a ceremonial pageant in which the young people of the town costumed themselves as historical figures. He chose to represent the Emperor Henry IV, the penitent of Canossa, whose history he had diligently studied in preparation for the pageant. Matilda was costumed as the Countess Matilda of Tuscany, his enemy, in whose castle Pope Gregory was installed at the time of the Emperor's humiliation. In the course of the cavalcade, someone prodded the Emperor's horse from behind. The horse reared. The rider suffered a fall and hurt his head. When he recovered consciousness, he had regressed mentally in time 800 years. He believed now that he was really Henry IV, and for twenty years he remained suspended in time between January 1076—the date of Henry's excommunication—and the time of his pilgrimage to Canossa in January of the following year.

When the play opens he is still playing the madman, but he is no longer mad. It is fully eight years since he recovered his wits, and he has taken mischievous pleasure in continuing the role to which his accident consigned him twenty years before. At that time a wealthy sister contrived to surround him with the trappings of his delusion—the ancient castle, which he took to be Goslar, the costumes, and the imperial retinue. Thus, he has lived out an elaborate masquerade, forcing all those who approach him to act out their assigned parts as characters in his fantasy, an artificial reality he constructed for himself within the less satisfactory reality that was the work of others. But now, after eight years, he is weary of the game. He would like to conclude his performance and to rejoin the rest of the world.

There are difficulties. The reality of the outer world has a formal rigidity which does not yield readily to the wishes of the individual. In fantasy Henry IV was permitted to take interesting liberties with time. He has in fact taken twenty years to live through some days or weeks of history. Thus, in fantasy, he is still a young man of twenty-seven. But while his mind was obedient to his wish, his body was synchronized with other rhythms. In twenty years his body has aged twenty years. He is forty-seven.

There are those who, at forty-seven, refuse to accept middle age; but Henry IV is not mad. He is entirely aware of his temporal situation and is disposed to poke fun at his pretense. His makeup is deliberately clownish. He has made up his face in a caricature of youth, just as he has made his sanity into a caricature of madness.

Unexpectedly an opportunity is presented for him to escape from his dream. His sister is now dead; but before her death she had suspected that her brother was coming to his senses. His nephew, Di Nolli, has brought a group of friends to visit the madman, among them a psychiatrist. There is Henry's former flame, Donna Matilda, now a widow; and her daughter Frida, who is engaged to Di Nolli; and Belcredi, an old friend, who is now Matilda's lover. The doctor has devised a plan. He proposes to shock Henry out of his delusion by forcing his mind back to the moment of his trauma, and then plunging it suddenly into the present time-current, thus forcing a readjustment of his sense of time. The means are at hand. There is a life-size portrait of Matilda in her masquerade costume hanging in the throne room of the castle alongside the portrait of the Emperor. The doctor proposes to bring these portraits to life by having Frida impersonate the Countess Matilda in the costume her mother wore on the day of the pageant, while Di Nolli impersonates Henry IV. At a suitable moment, both these figures will step out of their frames, and, confronted with two Countess Matildas, one at nineteen and the other at thirty-nine, Henry will have to reset his inner clock-mechanism back twenty years to the time of his fall, and forward 800 years to the present.

The plan works perfectly. The pretended madman is shocked into an admission of sanity. But it is not clear to him, as matters stand, whether the sanity is preferable to madness. In the end he chooses madness, and in a momentary fit of excitement—which may well have been simulated, an act of the intellect, as Belcredi put it at the outset—he runs a sword through Belcredi, whom he holds responsible for his misfortune, and thus condemns himself to play out his part for the rest of his days.

Unlike *Six Characters in Search of an Author*, *Henry IV* is a well-made play, logically conceived and provided with all the traditional apparatus of the genre— a proper exposition, a sequential complication, climax, and denouement, and a full complement of surprises. But while this form is conventional, the idea is strikingly original, and the texture extraordinarily rich and dense. *Six Characters* is full of ambiguities. In comparison *Henry IV* is straightforward and unequivocal. What is said of the relations of madness and sanity, life and form, reality and unreality, constitutes a precise and compendious statement of Pirandello's attitude toward life at the high point of his career. The play is, in this sense, definitive.

Like *Il giuoco delle parti* (*The Rules of the Game*), which in some ways it resembles, *Henry IV* is a play of jokes, a *scena delle beffe*. The practical joke that Belcredi played on his friend and rival, by goading his horse into throwing him, cost Henry twenty years of his life. He repays the jest twenty years later with a trick that costs Belcredi his life. But while this action provides the framework of the play, it is not the source of its dramatic energy. That depends on other motifs. Among them is the theme of alienation, the theme that gives tragic color to the novel, *The Late Mattia Pascal*. Mattia Pascal escapes from his world by pretending to commit suicide. When he tries to return to his former life, he finds the way barred by time and change. Similarly, Henry escapes—in this case into the past—and he too finds it impossible to readjust his life:

I open my eyes, little by little, and at first I don't know if I am awake or asleep; but yes, I am awake; I touch this thing and that: I can see things clearly once again. . . . Ah, as he says (He points to Belcredi) off with it, off with it now, this mask! this prison! Let's open the windows: let's breathe the air! Let's go, let's run out! (Then, stopping suddenly) Where? to do what? to have people pointing me out, secretly, as Henry IV, not as I am here, but walking arm in arm with you, among my old friends?

For the sane, reality is a house of detention as closely guarded as an asylum for lunatics. The penalty for escape is alienation but there is no other way to achieve wisdom. In *Henry IV* the hero has gained, through madness, insights that sane people lack and do well to avoid. He has discovered the fragility of the structure on which the everyday world is based, and has tested for himself the gossamer that holds it together. From his own experience he knows that madness offers an alternative reality, no more irrational or inconsequential than the reality of normal people and, for all but practical purposes, of equal validity. It is for this reason, Henry says, that madness inspires terror in those who are not normally accounted mad:

Because to find yourself before a madman, do you know what that means? To find yourself before one who can topple from its foundations everything that you have built up in yourself and around yourself, your logic, the logic of all your constructions! Well, what do you expect? They construct without logic, these blessed creatures, the madmen. Or with a logic of their own that flies in the air like a feather. . . . You say, this is not possible, but for them everything is possible.—But, you say, it's not true. And why? Because it doesn't seem true to you, to you, to you, and to a hundred thousand others. Ah, friends! You should see what seems true instead to those hundred thousand others who are not called madmen, and what a spectacle they make of themselves with their agreements, their flowers of logic!

There is reason, certainly, to believe that *Henry IV* affords a closer look at the author than any of his other plays; but, it may be repeated, it would be a mistake to insist on its autobiographical character. Those who might enjoy seeing in *Henry IV* a self-portrait of the author will find there, obviously, a Pirandello magnified to imperial proportions; and the likeness will reflect chiefly those aspects of the author's personality that clamored for exhibition at this time. It could not represent the whole man, for the reason, as Pirandello so often pointed out, that the whole man cannot be represented. If, in any case, the singular character of his hero does in some way represent the character of the author, then what we are invited to see is the case of the unfortunate man who, by a sudden stroke of fortune, had been condemned, eighteen years before, to spend

his life in the company of a madwoman and a throng of imaginary beings in a
world of his own devising, and who was now afforded a chance to escape into
a more normal reality.

But, in truth, it was not the fall of his father's fortunes that condemned
Pirandello to a world of fantasy. He had freely chosen this world for himself
from the time when his brother Innocenzo agreed to substitute for him in his
military service so as to leave him free to pursue a literary career in Rome. The
tragedy of *Henry IV* may well have a more general implication than one is usually
inclined to see in it. It might reasonably be said to exemplify the predicament
of those who abstract themselves—like Leone Gala—from the world of men in
order to live in the world of art, the ideal world where the Will to Live is not
operative, and where nothing changes and nothing dies. This world has the
permanence of history. It is fully lived out and formed, and is therefore dead
and relatively harmless. But it also has its terrors. Henry IV tells the Abbot of
Cluny, that is to say, the doctor,

I believe, Monsignor, that phantasms, in general, are at bottom none other than little
fragments of spirit: images that one does not succeed in containing within the kingdom
of dreams: they reveal themselves also during waking hours, by day; and they are frightening. I am always so frightened when by night I see them before me—so many disordered
images, laughing, dismounted from their horses.

For Pirandello, also, there was something frightening about the writer's profession. More than once he feared that he would go mad. But *Henry IV* is not a
study of madness. Henry is not mad. It is a study of sanity. In this play the
madman belongs to the type of the Wise Fool, a familiar character who, under
cover of his cap and bells, is permitted to utter truths that are normally not
spoken. Henry is a superb *raisoneur*. He also has the advantage—like Ibsen's
Dr. Relling in *The Wild Duck* and Dr. Stockman in *An Enemy of the People*—
of being a bit unbalanced, just enough to add salt to his utterance. He is excep-
tionally convincing precisely because his credibility is in question and he is, as
a character, entirely ambiguous. He tells Bertoldo, his retainer,

It suits everyone, you understand? It suits everyone to make the world believe that certain
people are mad in order to have an excuse for shutting them up. You know why? Because
you cannot bear to listen to them. What did I say about those people who have just left?
That the one is a whore, the other a dirty libertine, the other a quack. . . . But it's not
true! No one can believe that! Yet they all stand there listening, terrified. Well, now—
I'd like to know why they are afraid if it's not true.—You can never take anything
seriously that a madman says! All the same they stand there, listening like that, with
their eyes glazed with fear—. Why? Tell me, you tell me—why?

Before *Henry IV* was finished, Pirandello must have realized that he was
engaged on his masterpiece. But he had not yet fully recovered from the shock
of the opening of *Six Characters* in May, and he badly needed reassurance. In

the summer of 1921 he sent a summary of his plot to Ruggeri with a covering letter. " . . . without false modesty I may say that the subject is worthy of you and of the power of your art. But before setting to work, I should like you to tell me what you think, whether you like it and approve it." Ruggeri liked it very much, and Pirandello went on to finish it. Meanwhile, in September, Niccodemi presented *Six Characters* in Milan. Pirandello was much encouraged.

Henry IV opened at the Teatro Manzoni in Milan on February 24, 1922 before an appreciative audience that hardly knew what to make of the play but heartily applauded Ruggeri's performance. Pirandello was elated. He wrote to his daughter Lietta, now newly married and living in Chile, "*Enrico IV* is a triumph, a real triumph. Ruggeri gave a magnificent performance, and the play was repeated every evening during the company's stay in Milan, with superabundant marks of public enthusiasm. It has been the greatest success I have had so far; the daily papers of Turin, Rome, Venice, Genoa, Florence, Naples and Sicily have all devoted two columns to the event." Six months later Palmarini presented the play in Rome, with equal success.

The press was, in fact, extremely respectful; but the critics had reservations. There had been a good deal of applause. Ruggeri's performance was, by all accounts, spectacular. The critics, however, were unable to distinguish the play from the performance, and they preferred to withhold a final judgment. Silvio d'Amico declared it a masterpiece. For the rest, the Italian press was unanimous in praise of *Henry IV* only after the success of *Six Characters in Search of an Author* in Paris the following year.

In the fall of 1923 *Henry IV* was produced in New York, together with *Six Characters* and *As Before, Better than Before*. The following year it was performed in Warsaw and in Athens, and in 1925 Pirandello's own company presented it in repertory in London. Two years later *Henry IV* had been played in most of the great cities of Europe, bringing confusion and controversy wherever it was seen. In 1934 Pirandello was awarded the Nobel Prize. Then it became a classic and was chewed over extensively in seminars.

16

Henry IV—
The Tragic Humorist

Susan Bassnett

Luigi Pirandello is generally considered one of the great seminal dramatists of the twentieth century, ranked alongside Ibsen, Strindberg, Chekhov, and Brecht. Plays like *Six Characters in Search of an Author* and *Henry IV* have been widely translated and produced frequently by both professionals and amateurs. Outside Italy, it is perhaps less widely known that Pirandello was also a gifted prose writer, producing no less than 7 novels and 14 collections of short stories, together with a substantial body of critical essays and theoretical writings. If we add to these his 6 collections of poetry, and the total of 16 one-act plays and 27 full-length plays, the true size of his literary output begins to appear.

In spite of the popularity of some of his plays, not very much of the great body of Pirandellian texts has been translated into English. As a result, a curious distinction has arisen between the Pirandello familiar to Italian readers and the Pirandello known to English-speaking readers. The Italian Pirandello comes across as a witty, cynical writer, deeply concerned with the problem of fragmented personality and the ironies of multiple identity, whereas the English Pirandello emerges as altogether more serious, more intellectual or "cerebral" as he has often been described. And, of course, in English Pirandello is regarded primarily as a dramatist, which is a somewhat restrictive view since the links between his prose works and his theater works are an essential clue in our understanding of his work as a whole.

Pirandello began writing for the theater as early as 1898, when he wrote the one act play *L'epilogo* (The Epilogue) that was published but not produced. It was not until 1910 that a Pirandello play was staged, when Nino Martoglio directed two one-act plays and Pirandello began to write full-length pieces. Throughout his life he was to write short stories and novels alongside plays, however, and a considerable number of his plays are based on earlier prose works. In his essay *Spoken Action* (L'azione parlata) written in 1899, Pirandello emphasized the close relationship between prose narrative and theater, and argued that for what he called the "miracle" of theater to occur, a new language had to be developed:

a language that is itself spoken action, a living language that moves, the expression of immediacy, at one with action, the single phrase that must belong uniquely to a given character in a given situation: words, expressions, phrases that are not invented but are born when the author is fully at one with his creation so as to feel what it feels and want what it wants.[1]

Critics and biographers have made much of the fact that the bulk of Pirandello's theater output stems from the period after his wife Antonietta had been put into a nursing home because of her mental illness. This illness took the form of manifestations of pathological jealousy, and in 1918, when Pirandello's eldest son Stefano came back from the First World War, the family decided to have Antonietta committed. Whatever the connection between this occurrence and Pirandello's writing for the theater, the fact remains that the theme of jealousy runs as a leitmotif throughout Pirandello's work and was obviously a human predicament that he found compellingly significant.

Approaching the theater of Pirandello, it becomes immediately obvious that there are no easy labels to attach to this work. Some of his plays, notably the theater-in-the-theater trilogy, show his ability to experiment with theater form, while others conform to the well-made three-act play of the naturalist theater tradition but deal with the theme of multiplicity in human relationships and the tragedy of man's search for a universally recognized identity. Time and again Pirandello explores themes that were to recur later in the century in the theater of the absurd and the theater of cruelty. The fact that it is impossible to label Pirandello clearly is a nicely ironic touch that he would himself have liked, for in all his work he was concerned primarily with the idea of the impossibility of truth. Again and again his writings illustrate the idea of relativity, of a many-sidedness that denies the existence of a single absolute. Even language, the instrument of man's daily communication, is inadequate. As the Father says in *Six Characters in Search of an Author*:

Don't you see that the whole trouble lies here? In words. Each of us has within him a whole world of things, each one has his own special world. And how can we ever come to an understanding if I put into the words I utter the sense and value of things as *I* see them.

Nor is identity a unique fact. In *Right You Are (If You Think So)* Signora Ponza, the mystery lady that the Neighbors in the play seek to explain, refuses any single definition of her relationship to the man claiming to be her husband and the woman claiming to be her mother and says simply, "I am whoever you believe me to be." Pirandello acknowledges the impossibility of single definitions or simple solutions and offers us a vision of the world in which nothing is ever certain.

The titles of many of his plays further illustrate Pirandello's tendency to make us think twice about our notions of security. *Così è (se vi pare), Right You Are (If You Think So), Ciascuno a suo modo (Each in His Own Way), Come prima, meglio di prima (As Before, Better Than Before), O di uno o di nessuno (Either Someone's or No-one's), Non si sa come (You Don't Know How), Sogno, ma forse no (A Dream, But Perhaps It Isn't)*—all these play titles are enigmas, deliberately ambiguous in their construction. And the titles reveal another significant Pirandellian element—humor, a feature that, unfortunately, does not always come across so clearly in English translation but that is a lynch pin in all his works.

If we consider for a moment what Pirandello means by *humor*, various difficulties arise. Clearly, he does not mean "comedy" as such, for his themes are all too often suffering, death, and human misery. Pirandello belonged to an age of de-structuring, to the world of cubism and Dada, the world in which ideal order had ceased to be the concern of art. In place of an image of ideal order, art in the early twentieth century substituted an image of fragmentation, of a whole broken into myriad particles, an image that mirrors the splitting of the atom and the theory of relativity in the scientific world. In Italy, the Futurist Manifesto of 1910 had proclaimed the destruction of the past: "Sweeping the whole field of art clean of all themes and subjects, which have been used in the past. Alleviate all attempts at originality however daring, however violent."[2]

In such a world, humor derives from the clash between the desire for fixity and stability and the impossibility of achieving that goal. Life, as Pirandello says in his essay *On Humor* published in 1908, is like a vast river that continually overflows its banks and cannot be controlled. All man can do is to create illusory safeguards in art and life as a way of dealing with the inexorability of that great tide: "Concepts and ideals by means of which we hope to give coherent enduring shape to all the fictions we create for ourselves, to the conditions and the state in which we tend to settle down and establish ourselves."[3] In *Tonight We Improvise*, Hinkfuss, the director whose speeches show close links to *On Humor*, explains the paradox that is life: "Life must obey two necessities, both opposites, which prevent it from either lasting consistency or constant motion. If life were always in motion, it would never be consistent: if it were always consistent, it would not long move. And life must be consistent in motion."

The irony of this problem takes on another dimension when we come to the question of the relations between life as both consistency *and* motion and art.

For the world of art is a means of freezing and fixing within the frame of form. Every time we pick up a novel, the characters do the same thing, though our perceptions may alter. But the problem here, the "humor," is that the work of art has immortality and "lives" forever precisely because it is not life.

It is easy to see why Pirandello increasingly came to write for the theater, since theater is the ultimate paradox: the play is a fixed work of art brought to life by human beings who assume roles, and, although the text is *fixed*, the *process* of performing that text ensures that it will never be the same twice. It moves and is fixed; theater, in other words, is a mirror-life.

The other great irony about the life/theater dichotomy is that theater, no matter how moving or realistic or surreal or unintelligible, is made up of signs. When an actor wears a crown, he is a king in the world of the play since the crown carries the sign-value of kingliness, and we accept that sign without questioning whether or not the crown is really made of gold. Similarly, when an actor dies, we accept the sign of death in the playing, but if an actor *did* die on stage, this would cease immediately to be theater and become life. Fascinated by this multilayered nature of theater, Pirandello played with the possibilities the medium had to offer. Erving Goffman, a sociologist rather than a theater specialist, has prepared a neat resume of Pirandello's various experiments in his book *Frame Analysis*. Goffman suggests that Pirandello used three main formats to explore the issues of motion versus fixity, appearance versus reality. In the first type of theater, "the traditional respect for the projected characters is sustained." Into this category belong the plays that follow the traditional naturalistic format. In the second category are those plays like *Six Characters*, where "the conventional performer-character line is attacked but the attacks stop at the stage-line." So *Six Characters* is still a three-act play, in spite of the various devices used to give the impression of breaking the form, and it is in the third category that Pirandello breaches the line between onstage and auditorium, in plays such as *Tonight We Improvise* and *The Mountain Giants*.

Considerable attention has been given to Pirandello's experiments with theater form. Indeed, his reputation is largely that of an innovative dramatist, but of all his plays the one that stands out in terms of emphasis on a single character is *Henry IV*. This is the most frequently performed play by Pirandello in English, and has frequently been compared to *Hamlet*. Discussing Henry IV, the Czech director Vaclav Hudecek describes Henry as the epitome of twentieth-century man: "The desire to take one's bearings in this absurd world, ceaseless efforts to draw up the map of oneself and the mental dispersion resulting from the conglomerate of these confused sentiments characterize the man of the second half of the XXth century. All this can be found in Henry."[4]

The first production of *Henry IV* (*Enrico IV*) took place on February 24, 1922, at the Teatro Manzoni in Milan. Ruggero Ruggeri played Henry, and this was to remain one of his most successful roles for years to come. The only other contemporary actors who achieved a similar success with the role were Lamberto Picasso and Leonardo Bragaglia. Each played Henry with different emphasis:

Ruggeri focused on what he saw as an essential lyricism in the role, whereas Picasso stressed the bitterness and terse irony of the character.[5] Writing to the director Virgilio Talli, Silvio d'Amico described the play as: "quite fantastic. Absolutely unlike anything that has been seen in the theatre before, and there is no doubt that it is a work of major importance."[6]

  The success of the play in Italy, combined with the international reputation that Pirandello had so suddenly acquired following the scandalous *Six Characters* in 1921, meant that *Henry IV* was translated into English shortly after its Italian premiere. Edward Storer's version was published in 1923, and the first U.S. production, retitled *The Living Mask*, was presented at the 44th Street Theater in New York on January 24, 1924. Stark Young's review of the first night criticized the actors for their excessive sentimentality but stressed the importance of the play as a milestone not only in the Pirandello's development as a dramatist, but also in world theater.

Nothing in town is to compare to Pirandello's *Henry IV*—well or badly done—as worth seeing. If there is a tendency in many of his plays to think, talk, analyze, without embodying these processes in dramatic moulds that carry and give them living substance— and I think that is one of Pirandello's dangers, his plays too often when all is said and done boil down too much to single ideas—this fault cannot be laid on *Henry IV*. In this play Pirandello has discovered a story, a visual image, and a character that completely embody and reveal the underlying idea. This drama has a fantastic and high-spirited range in the spirit of the Italian comedy tradition; it also has a kind of Shakespearean complexity and variety; and in the second act, at least, something like a poetry of intellectual beauty.[7]

  London had to wait a year longer for the play to arrive, but in compensation it was first performed in Britain by Pirandello's own company with Ruggero Ruggeri in the title role. The company toured with four plays (*Six Characters*, *Henry IV*, *Right You Are*, and *Naked*). *Henry IV* was by far the most popular, judging by the enthusiastic response of reviewers. *The Times* on June 19, 1925, also raised the comparison with Shakespeare, and *The Manchester Guardian* reviewer, one day later, pointed out that, despite his own inadequate Italian, the play was obviously a great work: "no one of ordinary sensitiveness could miss the fact that Pirandello has put on the stage a great tragic figure and found a great actor to make it live for us."[8]

  The plot of *Henry IV* is, as reviewers noted, straightforward. Some twenty years before the action begins, a group of young Italian aristocrats had staged a masquerade—each guest had elected to come as a famous historical character. One of these young men had chosen to come as the Emperor Henry IV, carefully studying the background to his role to ensure greater authenticity. During the masquerade he had fallen from his horse, hit his head, and, as a result of the cerebral damage caused by the fall, had awakened suffering from the delusion that he was indeed Henry IV. Being of a sufficiently wealthy background for private nursing to be arranged, the young man was shut away in a country villa instead of an asylum. In order to humor his delusion, the villa was decorated to look like a medieval castle, with successive servants and nurses dressed in costumes of the time of Henry IV.

The play starts with a joke. The latest in a series of servants, Bertoldo has just arrived at the villa in the wrong costume, having confused his Henries and believing he has come to the court of Henry IV of France. His arrival provides a means of filling in the details of Henry's madness for the audience, and shortly after this introduction, visitors are announced. The young Marquis di Nolli, Henry's nephew, his fiancee Frida, her mother Matilda, and her mother's lover, Belcredi, have come to visit Henry, bringing with them a psychiatrist. The servants insist that they dress up before meeting Henry, and as they prepare to be received into his presence, further details come to light. We learn that there was once something between Matilda and Henry at the time of the masquerade, in which both she and Belcredi were involved, and we learn also that Belcredi views Henry's madness with a certain cynicism. Their uneasiness as they wait for Henry creates a sense of tension, and when he does finally appear, toward the end of Act I, his entrance comes as a shock. For Henry is now nearly fifty years old, pallid and with greying hair, but he has dyed parts of his hair yellow and is heavily made up in an attempt to hide the ravages of time. He looks, in short, the perfect picture of a madman. In the scene that follows, however, his madness is more difficult to pin down, and he seems at times to be playing with his distinguished visitors, making them more ill at ease than ever.

Act II begins with the Visitors discussing their impression of Henry. The Doctor talks in learned terms about madness, but neither Matilda nor Belcredi, for different reasons, is convinced that he is mad at all. The Doctor devises a plan which, he hopes, will cure Henry by jolting him into the twentieth century. Matilda's daughter, Frida, who looks now as her Mother did twenty years before, is to dress up in her costume. There are two life-size portraits in the room, one of Henry and one of Matilda at the time of the masquerade. Frida and Di Nolli will stand in front of the portraits, and when Henry appears Frida will step down out of the frame, as it were. This plan, according to the Doctor, will shock Henry into an awareness of normal time.

While the visitors are offstage preparing for this moment of truth, Henry reveals to his group retainers that he is not mad at all. Some years previously he had found his madness "cured," but he has gone on living as Henry IV because he has chosen to do so. The sane Henry reflects bitterly on the irony of madness—madmen "construct with logic," they live apart from the terror that sane people face, the terror of knowing that nothing in life can ever be fixed and that time destroys everything. Henry achieves tragic stature in this second act, in contrast to the shallowness of the retainers who do not understand the profundity of what he says to them.

The crisis comes in Act III, a brief act that moves at a rapid pace. Frida plays her part and steps out of the picture frame, and Henry is goaded into telling the visitors about his years of madness and sanity, how he has lived twenty years shut away in a masquerade that has become his reality. This is my life, he tells them, but even as he does so he is forced to recognize the inevitability of the passing of time. No longer able to recognize the aging Matilda, he seizes Frida in a sudden vain attempt to hold on to the love of his imagination. Belcredi intervenes, shouting that Henry is not mad and cannot hide behind a mask of madness. In a wild gesture of retaliation, Henry stabs him. This gesture confirms everyone's belief that he is mad, and the play ends with Henry condemned to live out the rest of his life as Henry IV, trapped forever in the guise of a madman. "Here together . . . forever" are the last words of the play. Henry has stepped out of his role for an instant, but his action in that split second of time has forced him back into it, permanently.

When Henry first appears, he talks about life in terms that recall *L'umorismo*, where Pirandello discusses the flux that moves forever beneath the bounds man imposes in an attempt to order his consciousness and construct a personality for himself. Henry warns of the dangers of not resigning oneself to what is, and of the need to cling to something in a moving universe:

There's not much you can say: we're all fixed in all good faith in a splendid concept of what we are. However, Monsignor, while you're standing there so firmly, holding on tight with both hands to your sacred robes, something is slipping away out of the sleeves, slipping slithering like a serpent . . . something you don't even notice. *Life*, Monsignor!

Since Henry is talking to the Doctor in disguise, this speech is especially ironic and meaningful on various levels: life slips away, consumed by time, while man clings to his own illusion, his own mask of false security, his "borrowed robes" of faith. Here, the Doctor is disguised visibly as Monsignor Ugo de Cluny, from the eleventh century. It is even more ironical that at this point both characters and audience believe Henry to be mad, and imagine that he is unaware of the Doctor's "real" identity. The notion of Henry acting a part has still not become relevant, although Di Nolli and Belcredi did comment earlier on how madness has turned Henry into a great actor—he has become, with madness, a magnificent, terrifying actor.

The levels of disguise operating in this speech are numerous. The play is being performed by actors, therefore persons in assumed roles; the retainers and visitors are disguised in eleventh-century costume; Henry is in costume and is playing the role of a madman; and finally, the disguise to which Henry refers is the existential disguise man assumes for security, a notice to which he returns again and again. He is repeating the same facts as expressed by R. D. Laing when he states that "a man without a mask is indeed very rare. One even doubts the possibility of such a man. Everyone in some measure wears a mask."[9]

The madman as prophet, the fool speaking truths, is by no means an original idea. Like the Fool in *King Lear*, or like Lear in his real madness and Edgar in his feigned madness, Henry is beyond social conventions and can say what he likes. When he is on stage, he dominates the scene and the others seem cowed before him. His madness, real or not, gives him a power over the "normal"

world because, since he is not subject to its laws, he is the personification of
what man most fears—unpredictable and inexplicable action. On the other hand,
as Laing says, unpredictable actions are not grounds for declaring someone to
be insane, and he admits that many people regarded as normal are deeply psychotic. He also mentions the relativity within madness:

I am aware that the man who is said to be deluded may be in his delusion telling me the
truth, and this in no equivocal or metaphorical sense, but quite literally, and that the
cracked mind of the schizophrenic may *let in* light which does not enter the intact minds
of many sane people whose minds are closed.

Again, like the Fool in *King Lear*, Henry is called Henry IV throughout, and
we never learn whether this was in fact his name before the accident. Pirandello
does not alter his name according to whether or not he is playing a role, as in
the case of the actors in *Questa sera si recita* . . . where the stage directions
alternate between referring to them as members of the company or as characters
in the play. Henry begins and ends the play as Henry. He is cut off from life
in the twentieth century, and therefore his name in that period is as meaningless
as all the other details of the century that he rejects, such as clothes, cigarettes,
or electric light.

   The relativity of madness is the pivotal point of the whole play and from this
various other aspects of relativity are touched on. In this respect, *Henry IV*
provides almost a resume of the principal themes of Pirandello's theater—the
relativity of perception and of language, the relativity of freedom, existence seen
as imprisonment in itself, the notion of life as a game wherein each person plays
an assigned role. The first scene of the play, which serves as a comic vehicle
to provide the audience with details of Henry's situation, immediately introduces
some of these themes. When Bertoldo discovers that he has read up on the wrong
time period, like an actor learning the wrong part, he asks the others who he is
supposed to be in the eleventh-century court where they play their roles. Landolfo
replies: "And you can comfort yourself with the fact that we don't know who
we are either. He's Arialdo; he's Ordulfo; I'm Landolfo . . . That's what he calls
us. We're used to it now. But who are we? Names of that time period." The
retainers exist only as names and have no place in history, no part other than
what Henry determines they will play. They exist because of Henry and for him;
he alone has a notion of who they are, because, as Landolfo says, he has at
least labeled them with names. In assuming these roles, they have sacrificed not
only any identity they may have had in the twentieth century, but because they
do not believe in what they are doing, they also treat the whole thing as a joke
and do not even live as people in the eleventh century. Just as the Spectators in
Each in His Own Way were characterized and named by their opinions, so these
retainers have lost everything except the names given to them by a man they
believe is mad.

   Landolfo explains further that they are puppets, to be manipulated by Henry:

We're like this, without anyone to give us a clue or give us a scene to play. How shall I put it? The form is there, but without any content. We're worse off than the real privy counsellors of Henry IV because, true, no one gave them a part to play either, but at least they didn't know they were supposed to be playing one. They played a part because they played it. Only it wasn't a part, it was their life.

This speech takes us back to *Questa sera si recita*, where the actors claim that they must live their roles or be nothing. The four retainers, superficially comic though they appear to be, are trapped in an even more tragic situation than Henry or Giovanni who play their roles with a kind of conviction. The retainers' role-playing is without direction or purpose, and they are entirely at the whim of a madman. If we extend this situation onto a more universal level, the retainers can be seen as a man and the madman in control is chance, or god. Gloucester's words in *King Lear* (IV,i) apply to this play with the same existential force of all time:

> 'Tis the time's plague, when madmen lead the blind.

While the retainers exist only as names chosen by Henry, he possesses an awareness of the relativity of identity beyond that of any other character in the play. In Act II, when the Visitors leave, Henry cries out bitterly against the relativity of language itself, the meaninglessness of names and labels:

What do they succeed in imposing? Words! Words that everyone understands and repeats in his own way. But then, that's how so-called public opinion is formed. But woe betide the man who finds himself branded with one of these words some day, that everyone repeats, like "madman" for example.

In Act I, Henry reminds the Visitors of the importance of knowing who they are, over and above the labels they bear:

"I feel the spirit of the times and the majesty of whoever knows how to be what he ought to be: a Pope!"

Henry then continues, reminding them that chance can destroy even the apparent security of Popes:

I tell you that tomorrow the roles could be reversed. And what would you do then? Would you by any chance laugh at a Pope dressed as a prisoner?—No.—We'd be even. Today I'm wearing the mask of a penitent; tomorrow he'd be wearing that of a prisoner. But woe betide the person who doesn't know how to wear his mask, be it that of a king or of a Pope.

The roles can be changed without warning, and only those who manage to keep on playing their parts can have some relief from the processes of change and subsequent pain. But even this relief is illusory, as demonstrated by Henry himself, who continues to play his role and remains trapped in that role forever. His escape into his own world of "madness' is seen to be another form of imprisonment. Henry may be free from many of the restraints that confine people in the "sane" world, such as social convention, consecutive time, and coexistence with others, but he is just as subject to the passing of time and is confined in the world of his own creating. Belcredi sums up the position of all humankind, mad or sane:

This is the illusion: that we'll go out of life through a door in front of us. It isn't true. If you begin to die as soon as you're born, then whoever started first is ahead of us all. And old father Adam is the youngest of the lot.

In this dark vision, the madman has a special place, for the madman is free to follow any pattern or nonpattern he chooses. And in this freedom to separate themselves from the need to have fixed beliefs and forms, madmen come closer to the essence of life itself.

If life is inconstancy and motion, as Pirandello reiterates in play after play, and man is constantly striving to create a niche for himself beyond that movement, then the madman, unaware of his "privilege," is the one with the insight into what being alive means. In a universe of motion, the madness is to strive for fixity, not to live out a life of formless movement. In *On Humor* Pirandello tells us that:

The collective consciousness, the soul of the race of which we are a part lives within each of us; and the ways in which others judge and feel and act pressure us subconsciously. In society, masks, disguises and pretence control operations—the more habitual they become, the less we are aware of them; and in the same way, we mask our real self, pretending to be other than we are, adopting a dual, even a manifold "persona".

In such a context, the "sane" man is the more mad since he lives out a daily delusion that constancy is possible. The irony of the play is in the realizations: those declared by some to be "mad" because they do not conform to the social norms are less "mad" than those who believe in the existence of absolutes, but whatever their state of madness or sanity, all men are condemned to exist in a world of motion and time, from which even illusion is no valid escape. Moreover, since illusion is itself formless, man seeks stability through an indefinable abstract, the ultimate absurdity.

Walter Starkie uses a musical image to describe the structure of this play: "Like a theme ever recurring through the mazes of orchestration of a symphony, the idea of distance and time is repeated again and again in this play" (184). This seems to be an excellent image, but I would also add the themes of art as fixity and life as motion, the relative freedom of the madman and the artist, and the notion of what the individual sees and how he translates that visual experience into a highly personal understanding. Time and history are crucial, but so also is the problem of perception, the idea of life itself as madness, the impossibility of ever judging sanity by other than purely relative means. Henry is supposedly mad in Act I, declares himself sane in Act II, commits a "mad" gesture in Act III, where, it must be noted, the stage directions are deliberately ambiguous, and Henry is described as laughing like a madman. But Henry is consistent in his real or feigned madness. The truths he speaks in Act I when we all believe he is mad are reiterated in Act II when he "proves" his sanity by admitting that he knows he is playing a role and living in another time period. He changes moods abruptly, moves about in time, and physically he moves rapidly round the stage, going from person to person in Act I. In Acts II and III he moves in and out of apparent sanity; his moods seem more controlled, his movements are less pronounced, but his cynicism and sufferings are constantly present.

As the play progresses, it becomes increasingly clear that we are being shown that language, perception, and finally reality are all relative, and that the great problem facing man is how to communicate with his fellows. Henry, the madman, must follow up his words with actions to prove their "truth" to the others, so he has to show the four retainers how he can act and construct scenes before they believe he is "cured," and in the final act he communicates by committing a violent action, murder, which ironically "proves" to the others only that their beliefs are confirmed and he is mad after all. His final gesture, the murder of Belcredi, is inevitable because on one level it is his last desperate attempt to show that his role is real and not a game and cannot be dismissed as easily as the others presume, and on another level it is the action of a man trapped into a corner and forced to react. The world he has been keeping himself from has finally caught up with him, and like Leone Gala in the *Rules of the Game* he is forced to recognize that he cannot exist in isolation, in his own private dream world.

The Visitors are real, their attempts to "cure" him do happen, and he can no longer insist on closing himself in the eleventh century to escape. At the conclusion of the play, the realization of how this reality has trapped him forever forcibly in a role he previously played of his own free will is emphasized by the stage directions, and by Henry's words:

Yes, now . . . inevitably . . . (gathers his retainers round him, as if to shield himself,) here together, here together . . . forever!

Others have broken his safe world of illusion and destroyed it, and he is caught in his own game, condemned to play it forever. The parallels with Leone Gala are quite clear: the one sought a world without emotion, a rational world, the other sought a world of unconfined movement, and both tried to keep complete control. Both ultimately share the same fate: immobility. The warning is plain; society may be represented by the petty, unpleasant characters who come to visit Henry, but they have not tried to define the world they live in. Matilda is condemned to being a jealous, unhappy, middle-aged woman, and the Doctor is condemned to being a phony who puts his trust in inadequate laws of science. They have no choice, no matter how they may try to forget. But Henry is finally condemned to being the mad Emperor because he tried consciously to play a role and create an illusion to save himself pain. No one can escape in the end, and the fake world of recreated history is as inadequate as the makeup Matilda wears to disguise her age.

The disguise motif, so crucial to the play, moves from being comic in the first scene to the tragic moments at the end of the play, when Henry realizes that he will never be able to take off his costume. When the three retainers meet Bertoldo, who is erroneously wearing sixteenth-century costume, and one of the lackeys lights up a cigarette, the whole notion of costume becomes farcical. Later, when Matilda, the Doctor, and Belcredi are forced to dress up in order to meet Henry, they do so with a mixture of amusement and uneasiness and when Frida, the living portrait, appears wearing her mother's costume, she can only comment on its size and how uncomfortably it fits her. For Henry alone the costume he wears is real because he has chosen to wear it and made it his. By the end of the play, he has been reduced to the same fate as all other men, forced to wear his costume, his disguise, regardless of his will. The one moment of instinct, when he broke the ordered world of recreated life, when he cheated (in a sense) and performed an unscripted act, leads to his downfall. His own personality erupted through the character of Henry IV to make him commit an act that the Emperor never conceived. As he gathers his retainers about him, the fear of this improvised action, the knowledge that he has broken out of his role, that he is doomed to remain Henry IV forever suddenly touches him and appalls him. Yet even in this final tragic moment, the bitter irony that characterizes the play is apparent. Henry has "proved" his madness, and Belcredi (the only one who knew that, as the stage directions indicate, the action was provoked by the life of his own pretense) is dead. Henceforth, the Visitors will have no doubts about Henry's madness, and the last vestiges of communication, the game he was able to play with them for so long, will no longer exist.

Henry IV is therefore a play that takes us into the heart of Pirandello's vision of the world. It is a play about the relativity of madness, and the question of what constitutes the boundaries of madness is a recurrent theme in twentieth-century art, especially in the theater.

In *Madness and Civilization*, Michel Foucault comments that "The ultimate language of madness is that of reason, but the language of reason enveloped in the prestige of the image, limited to the locus of appearance which the image defines" (95). Madness is therefore the point of overflow, the moment when all supposed boundaries of reason are swept away. By choosing to write a play about madness, Pirandello found a way of exploring the ideas set out in *On Humor*. A close analysis of the play reveals with what bitter irony he deals with the plight of one man as a metaphor for the plight of all humankind. Henry's predicament is a sign of man's predicament, caught between structures and definitions in a world over which he has no control. It is a vision of the world that is at the same time humorous and tragic. If we laugh at Henry's absurdities, it is because the pain is too great for tears.

NOTES

1. Luigi Pirandello, *L'azione parlata* (*Spoken Action*) (1899) translated by Susan Bassnett, *in Saggi, Poesie, Scritti varii* (Milan: Mondadori, 1960).
2. See *Manifesto of the Futurist Painters* (Umberto Boccioni, Carlo Carra, Luigi Russolo, Giacome Salla, Gino Severini), in Umberto Apollonio, ed., *Futurist Manifestos* (New York: Farrar, Straus & Giroux, 1971).
3. Luigi Pirandello. *On Humor* (L'Umorismo) (1980), in *Saggi, Poesi, Scritti varii* (Milan: Mondadori, 1960).
4. Vaclav Hudecek "On *Henry IV*," *ITI World Theatre*, 16, No. 4 (1967): 1.
5. Leonardo Bragaglia, *Interpreti Pirandelliani* (Rome: Trevi, 1969), 169–78.
6. Silvio D'Amico, letter to Virgilio Talli, December 13, 1921, translated by Susan Bassnett and Jennifer Lorch (forthcoming).
7. Stark Young, review of January 22, 1924, reprinted in *Immortal Shadows* (New York: Scribner's, 1948).
8. Review in *The Manchester Guardian*, June 20, 1925.
9. R. D. Laing, *The Divided Self* (London: Penguin Books, 1965), 95.

WORKS CITED

Appollonio, Umberto, ed. *Futurist Manifestos*. New York: Farrar, Straus & Giroux, 1971.

Bragaglia, Leonardo. *Interpreti Pirandelliani*. Rome: Trevi, 1969.

Foucault, Michel. *Madness and Civilization*. London: Tavistock, 1964.

Goffman, Erving. *Frame Analysis: An Essay on the Organization of Experience*. London: Penguin, 1974.

Hudecek, Vaclav,"On *Henry IV*," *ITI World Theatre* 16, No. 4 (1967): 1–10.

Laing, R. D. *The Divided Self*. London: Penguin, 1965.

Pirandello, Luigi. *Saggi, Poesie, Scritti Varii*. Milan: Mondadori, 1960.

Starkie, Walter. *Luigi Pirandello 1867–1936*. Berkeley: University of California Press, 1967.

Young, Stark. *Immortal Shadows*. New York: Scribner's, 1948.

17

Tonight We Improvise:
Spectacle and Tragedy

Olga Ragusa

Tonight We Improvise [Questa sera si recita a soggetto], which has been called
"possibly the most unjustly neglected major play in modern times" (Bassnett–
McGuire, 101), is one of Pirandello's later works—written, that is, and performed almost ten years after the affirmation of his worldwide reputation.

It had its premier in Germany, the center of theatrical experimentation in the
1920s and early 1930s, where in 1925 Pirandello had witnessed Max Reinhardt's
production of *Six Characters*, an important moment in the evolution of his
thinking about that play, which together with other reasons led to the significant
revision of its first version.[1] From German reviews published at that time, reviews
of the performances of the Teatro d'Arte's tour in fourteen different cities, it
appears that the plays (*Six Characters*, *The Pleasure of Honesty*, *Right You Are
[If You Think So]*, and *Henry IV*) as directed by Pirandello himself in the original
Italian were experienced as so different from the German versions already known
by the public as to be judged almost unrecognizable. Pirandello found this
encounter with his own work through the dis-forming and re-forming lens of a
different acting tradition and a different conception of staging and directing to
be so stimulating that when a few years later, disgusted by developments in
Italy, he decided to leave his country for a time, he chose Berlin as his residence.
It was there that he worked on the film version of three of his plays (a project
that did not come to fruition), attended the theater almost nightly, and wrote
Tonight We Improvise (whose only fixed character, as we will see, Doctor
Hinkfuss, took his name from Pirandello's landlord, Hinckfuss).

Of course, Pirandello's was not so much a flight as a return to Germany. As in his earlier university years, he had carried the knowledge of his native dialect with him (which then became the subject of his dissertation). Now he came armed—sustained and weighed down—by forty years of literary and theatrical practice, by a cast of characters in the hundreds, who embodied his views on life and had as yet often found only temporary location in stories and plays already written, and by the continuous reflection on his art. The most important documents on art, such as the essay *On Humor*, go back to his first contacts with German philosophy and literature. The heritage of romanticism, and specifically the discovery of romantic irony,[2] had nourished both the innovations of his own theater and those of the German stage with which he now became closely associated.[3] We will expect to find many of the strands of remembered past and freshly experienced present entwined in an original and meaningful statement about life, art, and theater in *Tonight We Improvise*. Even at the distance of fifty years, this statement remains puzzling in its complexity and its unresolved, "living," apparent contradictions.

The title of the play, whether in Italian or English or other languages into which it has been translated, refers to a type of theater, *commedia dell'arte*, which rose to great popularity in the sixteenth and seventeenth centuries but had been completely replaced on the legitimate stage by the nineteenth. The creation of actors, of tightly knit acting companies in which the "art," the know-how, was handed down from father to son, from mother to daughter, *commedia dell'arte* constitutes Italy's greatest contribution to the European comic tradition. With its scenarios, its masks, and its repertories of lines, it is recalled in the introductory note to *Tonight We Improvise* (p. 226).[4] Its inner dynamics for the actor, the strains it puts on the actor, are illustrated by the Character Actress when she objects that she cannot "pretend" to slap the Old Comic Actor. She must actually slap him, because in the absence of a written part, "it must all come from here (and she makes a gesture from the stomach upward)" (238– 39). The company called on to perform in *Tonight We Improvise* is not accustomed to acting in this manner, and its rebellion off and onstage in Part I results from its encounter in a devalued setting (that of a play without a script) of the principle of *immedesimarsi*, to identify with, which Pirandello postulates elsewhere as the very key to artistic creation.[5]

Whereas in a conventional play we might have expected to speak of characters with names and fully rounded make-believe identities and personalities, we have instead been speaking of actors designated only by their roles. Like the *commedia dell'arte* style of recitation, insistence on the dichotomy between actor and character is a novelty in *Tonight We Improvise*, although this one, too, is not an absolute one in the Pirandello *corpus*. The reader or the spectator turns to the "Cast of Characters" for *Six Characters*, *Each in His Own Way*, and *The Mountain Giants* and finds that in all three cases a distinction is being made— even typographically—between two groups: between the "Characters of the play to be made" and the "Actors of the company" in the first instance, between "Characters fixed in the role of the play on stage" and "Temporary, occasional characters in the theater lobby'' in the second, and between the ''Characters in the Countess's company'' and the ''Scaglionati,'' characters who act for the magician Cotrone (among whom are puppets, apparitions, and even an angel) in the third. In each case, although the distinction is specific to the particular play, the contrast is one of essence. It is the very being, the ontological status, of the opposed groups that is at issue. In *Tonight We Improvise* the fact of the distinction, which it took Pirandello so much effort in *Six Characters* to establish and demonstrate in an easily perceivable fashion, is taken as a given. So much so that the division into groups has disappeared. The Character Actress, the Old Comic Actor, the Leading Actor, and the Leading Actress not only *play* the roles assigned to them, but they *have become* those roles: they *are* Signora Ignazia, Sampognetta, Rico Verri, Mommina. This fusion between actor and character for the duration of a performance is usual in the accepted illusion of reality on stage, but in Pirandello the experience for the spectator is destabilizing because it is forced on his consciousness. In *Tonight We Improvise* the process by which a character is created on stage (not in its author's imagination as in the Preface to *Six Characters*) is made visible as the actors begin to be introduced to the audience physically, in their bodily consistency (not as printed marks on a page). But they insist on being presented instead as the characters they are playing, the characters they are ''making'' life and blood.

The characters are ''introduced'': the very use of the expression implies that there is someone to do the introducing, a kind of master of ceremonies, who is distinct from the actors or actors-turned-characters. Such a one is Doctor Hinkfuss, whose name is the only one appearing on the manifesto that announces the performance. Such would also be the voice of the author in narrative. We come to another characteristic of *Tonight We Improvise*, another novelty for reader and spectator: the narrative quality of the play, the blurring of the lines between storytelling and story-acted-out. Both drama and narrative are representational forms, and the techniques of the one are often found in the other. It should come as no surprise that in a writer as prolific as Pirandello in both genres there should be instances of confusion between them, an instinctive, spontaneous slipping in and out of what is in theory separate. But because drama and literary criticism have in the heyday of theater rarely been entrusted to the same person, it took some time for the process by which this occurs to be pinpointed and analyzed.[6] As in *Each in His Own Way* (whose revised edition was subsequent to the premier of *Tonight We Improvise*) so in *Tonight We Improvise* the play begins with a description, which then quickly turns into an acted-out demonstration, of circumstances prior to the action on stage. The stage is set, as it were, but it is not the traditional stage with its missing fourth wall. The focus, instead, is on the audience: on why they are there, on what their expectations are, on what the reactions of the critics will probably be, on the hubbub and excitement, the self-satisfaction and the fault-finding of the public as it looks forward to and is at the same time distrustful of what the evening will bring. Once Hinkfuss enters the theater, he takes over, quelling the tumult with his authority. But the narrator's

voice is back at the end of the Intermezzo when the stage directions expand into
a multifaceted commentary on Hinkfuss's novel way of making theater, a built-
in vindication of Pirandello's own "improvised" play (267–68). The stage directions, in other words, which are normally atypical in Pirandello because they
go well beyond telling an actor where to stand and what to do, here reveal their
origin in the narrator's point of view. Pirandello did not stop being a storyteller
when he took up drama. In his lifelong quest for ever more direct and effective
communication, his storytelling grew into drama; it did not replace it.

The presence of a narrative dimension and its impact on the play may be more
easily perceived by the reader than the spectator of *Tonight We Improvise*. But
no one can miss the exploitation of theatrical media other than the stage, and
together with the radical enlargement of acting space, it is indeed the most
striking novelty of this play.

As soon as the actors have been introduced and, breaking through the formality
Hinkfuss wishes to impose on them, have been given an essay on their instant
ability to "be" their roles, we have a break, a five-minute interval for the
preparation of the first diversion Hinkfuss has promised. " 'It will be well at
the beginning,' he must have thought, 'to suggest Sicily with a little religious
procession' " (247), say the stage directions at this point, incidentally giving
the contents of a character's mind in true narrative fashion. As had already
happened in *The Festival of the Lord of Our Ship* (first performed in Rome by
the Teatro d'Arte in 1925), a procession moves from the entrance door to the
auditorium, by way of the central aisle, up to the stage, where the portal of an
ancient church is just visible off-center. The chanting of the worshipers arriving
merges with the sound of church bells and the barely perceptible resonance of
organ music in the church. With the disappearance of the last villager into the
church and the fading out of the sacred music, another part of the stage setting
lights up. The transition is instantaneous: the long white wall of the building
running from left to right becomes transparent, and wild jazz music issues forth
from the interior of a cabaret. The first real scene, in the conventional sense of
the word, now takes place: the practical joke played on Sampognetta by one of
the customers of the cabaret, the revelation of the mutual feeling of compassion
that links Sampognetta and the Chanteuse, and the arrival, on the street outside,
of Signora Ignazia, her daughters, and their admirers on the way to the opera.
The group around Sampognetta and the one around Signora Ignazia clash in a
second conventional scene, which dramatizes the antagonism between the townspeople and these outsiders. Hinkfuss puts an end to the scene, calling for the
stage to be cleared.

What follows is a radical and unheralded redirection of the play. There is no
lowering of the curtain, no printed indication of the beginning of a new act, no
hint that the next scene will not be played out against a conventional stage
setting, the make-believe street (the destined meeting place in so much drama)
of the scenes just concluded. The story line continues uninterrupted, but it is
now played where one would not have expected to find it: a new acting space

has been empowered. Offstage a gramophone plays the end of the first act of a familiar Italian opera, and on the white wall on stage, which has been turned into a screen, a film of the performance is being projected. Signora Ignazia and her party have arrived at the opera—late as usual and amid the loud and indignant remonstrances of the rest of the audience. They make their way to their box, and instantly the various audiences—the make-believe audience at the opera, the "real" audience in the theater, and the really real audience watching *Tonight We Improvise*—are no longer separate, for *their* box is at the same time *the* box that had been left empty from the beginning and is now lit up "by a special warm light coming one knows not from where" (254), the suggestive light of the supernatural. As Hinkfuss had promised, the time has come for the public to participate in the action—another novelty in this play with respect to traditional theater.

Considerable discussion has arisen about this point. The degree of audience participation envisaged by Pirandello in this and others of his plays has seemed tame indeed in comparison with some of the more extreme developments in the theater intended to wrest control from the author.[7] But it is not my purpose here to bemoan the fact that Pirandello did not write a different play from the one he wrote, that his iconoclasm had its limits, and that he remained faithful to his conception of the artist's commitment to the creation of an organic work of art.[8]

Given this disclaimer, this rejection of erecting what came afterward (or in the work of others) as a critical measuring rod by which to judge (negatively) what came before, it is now necessary to examine closely exactly what role Pirandello assigned to the public in the action as written out and in his reasoning about Hinkfuss's margin of improvisation in the Intermezzo. From the moment Signora Ignazia and her followers arrive at the opera through to the end of the Intermezzo, there is no return to a conventionally set stage. Rather, there is a continuous flow of events involving both the characters and the audience: the "real" audience in the play and the really real audience watching the performance of the play in the theater. The business at the opera (changing seats, trading insults with other spectators) takes place in the box, which occupies its normal place in the hall. When shortly thereafter Hinkfuss announces the end of the act, Verri, Signora Ignazia, and the others heave a sigh of relief and troop out into the foyer. At Hinkfuss's invitation, "that part of the audience whose habit is to leave the hall between one act and the next" (257) does likewise, so that they can continue to enjoy the spectacle "those blessed people" will continue making of themselves. Five short scenes, played simultaneously in different parts of the lobby, now take place: Nenè, Totina, Sarelli, and Pomarici make straight for the refreshments stand, teasing and gossiping; Dorina and Nardi walk up and down, exchanging views on the encounter with Sampognetta; they join the others at the bar where the conversation becomes general; over to one side, Verri and Mommina argue unhappily: she defending herself and her family, he attacking their shameless behavior; Signora Ignazia, seated on a bench together with two of the other young men, makes a fool of herself with her excessive hatred of

Sicily and her silly admiration for the continental way of life. The spectators crowd around the various groups, watching and eavesdropping, gathering impressions. Meanwhile, for those who have remained in the auditorium, Hinkfuss creates a sixth scene. A miniature airfield in perspective appears on the stage, suggested by the fact that the young men are aviators: a tiny house, the officers' club, a few tiny planes scattered on the field, the buzzing sound of an invisible airplane, stars in the sky, and "the sensation of limitless space" (267). Nothing else happens on stage except the construction of this picture.

But Pirandello also airs the possibility that at any one particular performance no one will choose to remain seated during the intermission, and that the time at Hinkfuss's disposal might permit the creation of an additional scene or two. For those cases he suggests alternatives: Hinkfuss can postpone the construction of the airfield until the audience returns to the auditorium; he can regulate the raising and the lowering of the curtain or the switching on and off of the lights differently; he can disappear into the wings, step down into the audience, or address the public from the stage. What matters above all, as the stage directions spell out, is that Hinkfuss remain aware of the reactions of the spectators. He is to be alert to just how much they can take "of these things which, if they are not actually superfluous, are still an extra" (267–68), and to be ready to cut short the full range of "wonders" that the well-equipped stage would enable him to produce. In this respect, then, the public can actively influence (participate in) the performance of a play, not retrospectively in revisions of the text, but in the very act of its being staged. For the purpose at hand, however, Pirandello assumes that there will be simultaneity between the five scenes in the foyer and the illusionistic scene on stage. Thus, he can move to the last part of the Intermezzo, which enacts a moment of life in the theater already familiar in Pirandello's work through the Choral Interludes of *Each in His Own Way*.[9] The make-believe spectators, the represented audience, who—in another departure from convention—have not been segregated from the actors/characters during the simulated intermission, come back to their seats. Hinkfuss quizzes them on what they have learned in the lobby.[10] Their information is relayed by the Gentleman in the Orchestra and the Young Spectator, but it is scoffed at by Hinkfuss, who believes that Sampognetta's love for the Chanteuse and Verri's nervousness, stretched to the breaking point, had been self-evident from the beginning.[11] In this manner the gap in the story-being-told, between the first act at the opera and the return home of Signora Ignazia, her daughters, and their escorts at the end of their evening out, is closed. Part III follows immediately as the curtain rises on La Croce's parlor.

So far it is the theatrical aspects of *Tonight We Improvise* that have been privileged: the uncovering of the mechanisms of performance in the case of a special kind of play (an improvised play) and the characteristics in this respect of the particular play under discussion. This level of *Tonight We Improvise* might be called the frame around the picture, the larger enclosure that holds the lit-up stage, the darkened seating area, and other, even more subsidiary, areas in the theater. It is time to turn to what lies at the center: the pretext without which there would have been no play, whether improvised or fully (if that is ever possible) written out. This inner play has by and large been judged to be the least interesting, most old-fashioned, and unsophisticated in its harking back to the popular taste for melodrama in the nineteenth and early twentieth centuries, especially as exemplified in Italy by the success of opera in large cities and small towns alike.

It is well known that *Tonight We Improvise*, like others of Pirandello's plays, had an antecedent in his narrative universe: the short story " 'Leonora, addio!' " (first published in 1910).[12] Hinkfuss brings the text on stage with him, rolled up like a bundle of papers, degraded to the level of scenario, which he describes as "a trifle" (*robetta*) (233). It is of so little consequence to the entertainment being prepared that its author was not even named in the advertisements and playbills of the performance. The story is not about the professional making of theater, but it is at least in part about the passion for opera as escape from a humdrum existence "in a dusty town in the interior of Sicily."[13] More significantly, however, it is about jealousy, a theme familiar in Pirandello's theater as far back as *The Vise* (*La morsa*, 1898). "It represents," says Hinkfuss of the story (in a splendid instance of Pirandellian self-commentary, of which we can quote only a fragment), "a case of the most terrible kind of jealousy, jealousy for which there is no cure because it is jealousy of what is past" (234). The characters are those with whom we are already acquainted: the La Croce family and the young army officers[14] who gather about them. They are attracted by the four good-looking, fun-loving daughters of the "only hospitable family" in town and by their mother, who is ready to accept their fast behavior as an affront to "the island's savages" (570) and a fine example of what is acceptable in the more progressive milieu of the Continent.[15] But from the first line of the story the focus is on Verri (who incidentally, is also the first of the actors to rebel in Part I of the play). The Sicilian Verri is impressed and amused by his uninhibited fellow officers, but he cannot light-heartedly join in their antics. Where for them there is no tomorrow, for him there is serious commitment. When he falls in love with Mommina, the most sensible of the sisters, the most ready to sacrifice herself for her family, and perhaps the most Sicilian in her innate reserve, he decides to marry her in spite of her mother's opposition (she would prefer an "easier" husband for her daughter) and in spite of the townspeople's derision of his foolishness. He is determined to save Mommina from the temptations of her environment. To silence all possible criticism, he segregates her from all contacts by locking her up in an apartment at the top of a tall building, from which nothing can be seen except the sky and the distant sea.

Part III of *Tonight We Improvise* takes us from the enlarged and varied acting space of Part II and the Intermezzo to the customary drawing-room setting in Pirandello of a conventionally furnished suite of rooms visible in perspective on stage. Signora Ignazia's party has just returned from the opera, and one of the typical scenes alluded to in the story is in progress: "When the theatre was closed, there would be a dance academy at the La Croces', with lessons in flirtation and acting'' (569). A departure from the short story is the introduction of Signora Ignazia's sudden toothache, a circumstance that adds the spice of broad comedy at this point. All the more jarring will be the change in mood brought about by Verri's return from the drugstore and his discovery that, in spite of her promises, Mommina has been drawn into the mock rendition of a scene from *Trovatore* (ludicrously intended to deaden Signora Ignazia's pain). The singing and dancing, the play-acting, masquerading, the laughter, and the bursts of applause, punctuated by Signora Ignazia's stabs of pain, her cries and exclamations, her fidgeting and sighing, are replaced by a sudden moment of silence as Verri, ''stunned by the abyss his rage opens in front of him'' (278), hurls himself against Pomarici, who has been playing the piano, and throws him to the ground. From this point on, until the end of the play, there is no further room for levity. Passion—the passion of the Shakespearean ''two boards and a passion,'' drama stripped of every ornament and concentrated exclusively on man's capacity for suffering—has made its entry. The tug-of-war between Hinkfuss and the actors will continue, and instances of the difficulties of theatrical improvisation will reoccur, but the actors strengthened and elevated, freed by their realization that the story is in them and is triumphantly in them, run Hinkfuss and his tinsel stage effects out of the theater, recovering it for drama made by words alone.[16]

The drama is articulated in two capital scenes: Sampognetta's death and Mommina's. The one has been judged the stuff melodrama is made of;[17] the other is the materialization—the coming to external form—of the implicit. The one is an addition to the short story; the other is the repetition, the working out into a staged action, of what was already there. Both share intensity, the intensity with which they must be played and which must reflect itself on the audience so that its impact can survive the disruptions engendered by the particular, ''improvised,'' manner of production of the evening. The two scenes have been prepared for unobtrusively by the Gentleman in the Orchestra and the Young Spectator when they focused on the feelings of Sampognetta and Verri as the source from which the rest of the dramatized plot develops. The second of the two scenes ends in immovable silence: the presence of death registered in the absolute stillness not only of the inert body on the floor, but also in the surviving family members crowded about it. ''Tableau'' (310), say the stage directions tersely, and it is the signal for the moment of silence that memorializes the dead. There follows the ebbing back of life: Hinkfuss running down the central aisle, ecstatic at the effect; the actors and actresses, no longer in their roles, commenting on their achievement; a new pact struck with the director (henceforth there will be written parts); and finally the conciliatory *captatio benevolentiae*, the old valediction to the audience of comedy: '' . . . the public may wish to forgive us'' (311), and Hinkfuss's bow.

But how can an audience—and to a lesser extent perhaps a reader[18]—be expected to remain fixed on tragedy when the mounting tension, the growing "terror" of its coming to pass, is constantly undercut? No sooner does Verri cry out his "reason"[19] and make his plea for his right to be different than "spontaneously coming out of his role" he addresses Mommina "with the exasperation of the Leading Actor forced into saying what he doesn't want to say" (280); and the distracting bickering among the actors starts again. Sampognetta, "death on his face, his bloodstained hands clutching his stomach pierced by a knife, his vest and trousers likewise bloodstained" (282), cannot even make his entrance. It is only after a long digression that involves Hinkfuss and everyone else (in and out of role) that he is able to deliver his blood-chilling lines—no longer in direct address but in what turns out to be much more effective, retrospective narrative:

And Death should have entered with me, made its appearance here amid the shameless carousing of this household: Death in its drunkenness, as it had been established, drunk with wine that had become blood. And I should have spoken, yes, I know, I should have been the first to speak to everyone's horror—I—taking courage from the wine and the blood, holding on to this woman—thus!—and I should have spoken senseless, disjointed, terrible words, for that wife, for those daughters of mine, and even for these young men, because I had to show them that, if I appeared to be a fool, it was because they were bad, a bad wife, bad daughters, bad friends. (286).

The case of Mommina's scene is somewhat different. Its preparation is more extended: Sampognetta's, after all, figures as an afterthought for which Hinkfuss alone took credit; Mommina's was the climax of the story from the beginning. The tension has mounted. Once set up, the scene is permitted to play through in its entirety. The disruption that follows, which constitutes the ending of *Tonight We Improvise*, substituting, as we have seen, the accommodation of comedy for the inevitable defeat of tragedy, has a more drastic effect: it reflects back on the whole play and raises the doubt that the inner story was indeed only a pretext.

In the letter Pirandello wrote to Salvini, making recommendations about the Italian production of the play, he appears to come down unequivocally on the side of pretext. "It is not possible," he writes in answer to Salvini's suggestion that Hinkfuss be kept out of the finale, "that he should not come back. The tragic effect must be achieved fully with Mommina's death and the arrival of her husband with her mother and sisters. It is natural that Hinkfuss should break it when he expresses his satisfaction. That final tragic scene cannot be an end in itself. We have to get to the conclusion of that whole experiment at 'improvisation.' "

But Pirandello's statement and the interpretations to which it has given rise must now be seen in perspective. It is no doubt appropriate at one level. It reflects the emphasis on theatrical experimentation in Pirandello's immediate surroundings at the time, his undoubted bedazzlement by productions that could rely on a full range of theatrical machinery, his desire to participate in a kind of theater that no longer depended on the use of words alone. However, it overlooks a much wider context, a much longer apprenticeship, which it was not Pirandello's place to recall because he had lived it but which cannot be overlooked by whoever approaches the later Pirandello today. The apprenticeship began with the elaboration of a view of the meaning of life in the declining years of the nineteenth century and its uninterrupted exemplification in a gallery of characters caught in their highest distress: Ciampa, Chiarchiaro, Ponza, Leone Gala, Martino Lori, Enrico IV, Ersilia, Tuda, and others. The reader or spectator who comes to one of the later works, such as *Tonight We Improvise*, unfamiliar with the earlier ones (except possibly *Six Characters*, *Cosí è [se vi pare]*, and *Enrico IV*), will be deprived of the density of references necessary to treat the inner story with respect. He will lack the key to what had become a shorthand: Pirandello's achieved personal self-expression. In order to restore the balance, he will have to reopen for himself the perspective that leads backward from the glitter and the glamor that characterized the entertainment style of the 1930s to the harsh contours of Sicilian life in a far-off island and in the distance of time.

REVIEW OF CRITICAL LITERATURE

A particular work in an author's *oeuvre*, as in this case *Tonight We Improvise*, must be considered both in the continuity of its author's literary career and as an artifact that stands complete and separate, to be reacted to, judged, enjoyed, or rejected on its own. In reconstructing the critical life of a play, this double focus becomes strikingly obvious. The public's first contact with a play written and intended for production is in the theater, and it is in that arena that its survival or disappearance is often decreed. But by the time *Tonight We Improvise* was written, Pirandello was sufficiently well known to insure that the play would receive and continue to receive attention regardless of its success on stage. Its critical literature thus includes both theatrical and literary studies, and the fact that it has not been frequently produced cannot be taken as the sole reason for its relative neglect in comparison with others of Pirandello's works.

The earliest reactions to the play are found in reviews of its first productions: in German translation at the Neues Schauspielhaus in Königsberg (1929) and at the Lessing-Theater in Berlin (1930), and in the original Italian at the Teatro Carignano in Turin, followed by performances in Milan and Rome (1930). The relevant bibliography can be found in Barbina and Donati, whose indices are analytical, giving entries under each separate work of Pirandello's; Bragaglia is similarly valuable for the early and later production and reception history.

Because Tilgher's seminal work on Pirandello preceded *Tonight We Improvise*, the play does not appear in the critic's elaboration of a conceptual framework: the conflict between form and life, to explain Pirandello's "philosophy" of art and life. This formulation, however, persisted for many years in Pirandello criticism and can be found applied to *Tonight We Improvise* in later studies.

Pirandello himself joined *Tonight We Improvise* together with *Six Characters* and *Each in His Own Way* in 1933 when he published the first volume of the definitive edition of his plays. He called the three ''a trilogy of the theatre within the theatre,'' in spite of the fact that they had been written independently of one another and at different times within a lapse of almost ten years. In retrospect, he had discovered that they had a theme in common: the dramatization of theatrical life itself. In the three plays, he wrote, ''are represented all possible conflicts of the complex of elements that constitute theater.'' Pirandello's statement was widely reproduced (for instance, in Eric Bentley's edition of *Naked Masks*) and has been used self-reflexively as perhaps the most popular key for analyzing *Tonight We Improvise*, in which as a consequence the theatrical elements of the play are given pride of place.

Pirandello studies, as distinct from reviews and other occasional evidence of interest in the man and his work, can be dated from the 1961 International Congress held in Venice on the twenty-fifth anniversary of his death. The *Atti* of that meeting set out the main categories under which his work has been studied since. Although no paper dealt exclusively with *Tonight We Improvise*, contributions on Pirandello's place in world drama and on various aspects of his theater were an important step in the direction of a better focus on critical problems that would eventually be brought to bear on *Tonight We Improvise* as well.

Roberto Alonge has shown how the progress of Pirandello criticism was inhibited after World War II when the later Pirandello, specifically his theatrical production after 1924, the year in which he joined the Fascist party, was rejected. Mario Baratto, for instance, mentions only *Questa sera si recita a soggetto* among those plays, and only because he is able to interpret it reductively in line with Gramsci's preference for ''popular'' literature, as ''a return to (Pirandello's) Sicilian origins.''

It was only with the 1976 meeting of the Centro Nazionale di Studi Pirandelliani at Agrigento, dedicated to the trilogy, that the study of *Tonight We Improvise* came into its own. The expected completion of the new *Maschere nude* edition, under the direction of Sandro d'Amico, will finally make available—fifty years and more after the premiere of *Tonight We Improvise*—an authoritative edition of the text with critical apparatus, comparable and perhaps superior to the one that already exists in French.

NOTES

1. See Ragusa, ''*Six Characters.*''
2. Muecke gives this capsule definition: ''Romantic Irony—the irony of the fully-conscious artist whose art is the ironical presentation of the ironic position of the fully-conscious artist'' (20).
3. For an initial orientation regarding Pirandello's extensive contacts with Germany, see Adank and Büdel. For an excellent survey of the situation as it affects *Tonight We Improvise*, see Bouissy, 1472–85.
4. Since the volume of the critical edition of *Maschere nude* slated to include *Questa sera si recita a soggetto* has not yet been published, references in this chapter are to the

standard edition listed under Works Cited. Translations throughout are the present writer's, although there are two translations of the play into English: see under Works Cited.

5. For some instances, see Ragusa, *Luigi Pirandello*, by referring to the entry *"immedesimarsi"* in the Index.

6. See Jansen, "Struttura narrativa," for an analysis with regard to the stage directions.

7. Calendoli is one of the several critics who has investigated this aspect of Pirandello's place in modern drama.

8. See Ragusa, *Luigi Pirandello*. " 'And the real miracle,' says Cotrone in *The Mountain Giants*, 'will never be the representation itself (i.e., the performance of the play), but always the fantasy of the poet in which those characters were born living . . . ' " In Pirandello's conception fantasy, or better, imagination, is a life-giving force similar to nature in its overwhelming drive to creation (self-realization). Metaphors of birth, gestation, survival, and death recur time and again in his remarks on the psychology of literary invention. Indeed, nowhere has the organic metaphor, so deeply embedded in the aesthetics of romanticism, been developed more fully than in the work of Pirandello. In the midst of a totally pessimistic view of life which cannot remove its gaze from the inevitability of death, Pirandello has triumphantly affirmed the immortality of the work of art: "All that lives, by the fact itself that it lives, has form, and for that very reason must die; except the work of art which lives forever precisely because it is form" (Preface to *Six Characters*) (168).

9. The Choral Interludes were already part of the first version of *Each in His Own Way* (1924), but with respect to audience participation *Tonight We Improvise* represents a radical development. The audience in the earlier play is portrayed on stage, like any other scene in the play; in *Tonight We Improvise*, it has been moved to the hall of the theater itself.

10. Ostensibly for the benefit of the rest of the audience, but no doubt also because Pirandello was extremely interested in the problem of *dispositio* (the arrangement of the subject matter into acts and scenes). See Ragusa, *Luigi Pirandello*, 156, where the same concern of Pirandello's is discussed with reference to *Six Characters*.

11. Here we have one of those sudden implied juxtapositions of opposites that occur in Pirandello: two methods of exposition are contrasted, the naturalistic and the psychological. The audience spokesmen have been raised on naturalistic drama; Hinkfuss has passed beyond it. "For the naturalists," Pirandello writes in " 'Appunti' editi dall'autore," "a thought can be written down insofar as it can be described, that is, insofar as it issues into an action, a spoken word. For the psychologists, it has value even before it has reached the outer world, before it has a perceptible life outside the character that thinks or feels it. . . . Basically, the psychologists display an effort that for the naturalists is only preliminary. They tell us the first 'whys'; the naturalists study them as much as the psychologists, they seek them out, ponder them, and present the effects of those 'whys' to the reader" (1210).

12. Bouissy mentions some other antecedents, "une série d'images obsessionel les parvenues à leur suprême degré d'évidence plastique" (1489), the earliest one of which goes back to 1897.

13. Hinkfuss's amplified variant reads: " . . . in a city of the interior of Sicily, where (as you know) passions are strong, smoulder deep down; and then flare up violently . . . " (234).

14. Not aviators as in the play. It is interesting to note that, in order to avoid censorship

in Italy at the time of the play's premiere there, Pirandello suggested a further change in the young men's occupation: "Why don't you turn them into young mining engineers sent by a Belgian company owning mines in Sicily," he wrote to Guido Salvmi, the director for the Turin production. "They should wear some kind of 'uniform': blue or khaki jackets or something like that, as long as it is colorful. In that case, Dr. Hinkfuss could build a mining camp in place of the airfield, with tall chimneys and, at the back of the picture, a school for Belgian engineers" (Bouissy, 1486).

15. *L'aria del continente* (1915), published under Nino Martoglio's name alone but actually a collaborative effort to which the Sicilian dialect actor, Angelo Musco, and Pirandello contributed, was perhaps the most successful farce of its time. It is a takeoff on the provincial's aspirations, doomed to failure, to share in a cosmopolitan way of life.

16. Emphasis on the importance of the "word" is pervasive in Pirandello's discussions of the staging of his works. Here is one instance, taken from the larger context of *Tonight We Improvise*: Pirandello is reported to have been particularly pleased with Reinhardt's production of his plays because, as a former actor, Reinhardt respected "the very essence of the word" (Bouissy, 1477).

17. First by Pirandello himself, at least according to Hinkfuss's interpretation after Sampognetta's scene (288).

18. Pirandello's reservations about the theater as a medium of communication underlie his entire theatrical production. In *Tonight We Improvise* the theme surfaces in the stage directions after the five scenes in the foyer when the narrative voice castigates the public for its "voracious gluttony" in preferring what are "extras" for "healthy nourishment" (268). As far as the relationship reader/spectator is concerned, the statement made by the playwright Camillo Antona-Traversi in Ugo Ojetti's series of interviews, *Alla scoperta dei letterati*, when Pirandello was just beginning to write, is significant: "The novel, being more extended and freer, is inevitably superior to the theatre. Since its public is not gathered together, the crowd does not disturb the spirit of the different individuals that compose it: the quiet reader, ready for his reading, is more receptive, more friendly, freer to understand and appreciate the artist."

19. The word is fraught with special meaning for anyone dealing with Pirandello, ever since he changed the title of his first three-act play, *Se non così . . .* (originally probably written in 1895–1889), to *La ragione degli altri*.

WORKS CITED

Adank, Mathias. *Luigi Pirandello e i suoi rapporti col mondo tedesco*. Berne: Aarau, 1948.

Alonge, Roberto. "Spostamenti progressivi della critica pirandelliana." *Pirandello. L'uomo lo scrittore il teatrante*. Eds. Fabio Battistini, Maria Grazia Gregori, and Mario Sculatti. Milan: Mazzotta, 1987. 134–39.

Atti del Congresso internazionale di studi pirandelliani. Pubblicazioni dell'Instituto di Studi Pirandelliani 2. Florence: Le Monnier, 1967.

Baratto, Mario. "Le Théâtre de Pirandello." *Réalisme et poésie au théâtre*. By Mario Baratto. Paris: Editions du Centre National de la recherche scientifique, 1960. 181–94.

Barberi Squarotti, Giorgio. "La trilogia pirandelliana e il rinnovamento del teatro." *Il teatro nel teatro di Pirandello*. Ed. Enzo Lauretta. Agrigento: Centro Nazionale di Studi Pirandelliani, 1977. 7–36.

Barbina, Alfredo. *Bibliografia della critica pirandelliana 1889–1961*. Pubblicazioni dell'Instituto di Studi Pirandelliani 3. Florence: Le Monnier, 1967.

Bassnett-McGuire, Susan. "Art and Life in Pirandello's *Questa sera si recita a soggetto*." *Drama and Mimesis*. Ed. James Redmond. Cambridge: Cambridge University Press, 1980. 81–102.

Bouissy, André. "Ce Soir on Improvise. Notice." *Théâtre complet*. By Luigi Pirandello. Eds. André Bouissy and Paul Renucci. Vol. 2. 1472–1513. Paris: Gallimard, 1985. 2 vols. 1977–1985.

Bragaglia, Leonardo. *Interpreti pirandelliani 1910–1969*. Rome: Trevi, 1969.

Büdel, Oscar. "Pirandello sulla scena tedesca." *Pirandello ieri e oggi*. Quaderni del Piccolo Teatro 1. Milan: 1961. 99–122.

Calendoli, Giovanni. "La trilogia e le esperienze europee d'avanguardia." *Il teatro nel teatro di Pirandello*. Ed. Enzo Lauretta. Agrigento: Centro Nazionale di Studi Pirandelliani, 1977. 207–21.

Cometa, Michele. *Il teatro di Pirandello in Germania*. Palmero: Novecento, 1986.

Donati, Corrado. *Bibliografia della critica pirandelliana 1962–1981*. Florence: Editrice La Ginestra, 1986.

Jansen, Steen. "L'unità della trilogia come unità di una ricerca continua." *Il teatro nel teatro in Pirandello*. Ed. Enzo Lauretta. Agrigento: Centro Nazionale di Studi Pirandelliani, 1977. 223–236.

———. "Struttura narrativa e struttura drammatica in 'Questa sera si recita a soggetto'." *Rivista italiana di drammaturgia* 2.6 (1977):55–59.

Lugnani, Lucio. "Teatro dello straniamento ed estraniazione del teatro in *Questa sera si recita a soggetto*." *Il teatro nel teatro di Pirandello*. Ed. Enzo Lauretta. Agrigento: Centro Nazionale di Studi Pirandelliani, 1977. 53–114.

Muecke, D. C. *Irony*. Critical Idiom Series 13. London: Methuen, 1970.

Ojetti, Ugo. *Alla scoperta dei Letterati*. 1895. Ed. P. Pancrazi. Florence: Le Monnier, 1946.

Pirandello, Luigi. " 'Appunti' editi dall'autore." *Saggi, poesie e scritti vari*. By Luigi Pirandello. Ed. Manlio Lo Vecchio-Musti. Milan: Mondadori, 1960. 1207–12.

———. "Leonora, addio!" *Novelle per un anno*. By Luigi Pirandello. Pref. Corrado Alvaro. Vol. 2. 569–76. Milan: Mondadori, 1957. 2 vols. 1956–1957.

———. "Questa sera si recita a soggetto." *Maschere nude*. By Luigi Pirandello. Vol. 1. 221–311. Milan: Mondadori, 1958. 2 vols.

———. *Tonight We Improvise*. Rev. and rewritten by Marta Abba. New York: Samuel French, Inc., 1960.

———. *Tonight We Improvise and "Leonora, Addio!"* Trans. J. Douglas Campbell and Leonard G. Sbrocchi. The Pirandello Society of Canada Series 1. Biblioteca di Quaderni d'Italianistica 3. 1987.

Ragusa, Olga. *Luigi Pirandello. An Approach to His Theatre*. Edinburgh: Edinburgh University Press, 1980.

———. "*Six Characters*, 1921–1925 and Beyond." *Pirandello, 1986*. Eds. Gian Paolo Biasin and Nicolas J. Perella. Rome: Bulzoni Editore, 1987. 19–30.

Tilgher, Adriano. *Studi sul teatro contemporaneo*. Rome: Libreria di Scienze e Lettere, 1922.

Vicentini, Claudio. "Dal 'teatro nel teatro' di Pirandello al teatro di guerriglia americano." *Il teatro nel teatro di Pirandello*. Ed. Enzo Lauretta. Agrigento: Centro Nazionale di Studi Pirandelliani, 1977. 237–51.

Part Four

PIRANDELLO'S INFLUENCE

18

A Hole Torn in a Paper Sky: Pirandello and Modern Drama

Martin Esslin

Jean Genet's *The Balcony* (1956) opens with a scene in which a richly robed bishop talks to two women, one of them scantily and the other most severely dressed. From the ecclesiastical elements in the set, from the unctuous language of the bishop, the audience is led to believe they are being shown a situation of some religious import. But suddenly the severely dressed older woman interrupts: time is up, she demands payment. The spectators realize that they are not seeing a bishop's palace but a brothel, in which customers can enact their erotic dreams in fancy dress. Today this kind of theatrical effect is rightly described in the critical jargon as "Pirandellian."

The most obvious parallel here is to Pirandello's *Henry IV* (1922): the stage setting—as well as the title—suggests a historical play. The set represents a medieval throne room peopled by characters in medieval costume. Soon, however, the audience is shocked to find that these characters use modern slang and make reference to twentieth-century conditions, until the entrance of people in modern dress shows us that in fact we are in the home of a madman who thinks he is a medieval emperor and who has the means to set up such a masquerade. Here as in *The Balcony* a fantasy situation is undercut by "reality." In his most famous play, almost contemporary with *Henry IV*, Pirandello proceeds in the reverse order—from reality to fantasy.

In *Six Characters in Search of An Author* (1921) the audience is made to assist at an actual rehearsal on the actual empty stage of the actual theater in which they are sitting, when this doubly "real" reality is invaded by one of fantasy: characters whom the author of the play has imagined but not brought to reality demand to be translated into a "theatrical" world. But here, we soon become aware, there are *three* layers of "reality" involved: the author's fantasy, the theater as a real entity, and the fantasy's demand to be "realized" as a play, which remains fiction but requires translation into performance by "real," flesh-and-blood actors. This constant undercutting of theatrical reality by the reality of our everyday life, and vice-versa, the showing up of everyday reality as another form of theater, role-playing, and pretense, is today the most obvious hallmark of the "Pirandellian." It has become one of the stock effects of modern drama from Genet to Anouilh, from Giraudoux to Peter Weiss of *Marat-Sade*. Yet Pirandello's use of the contrast between theatrical and extratheatrical reality is only one, though perhaps the most obvious, metaphor to give expression to his deeper concerns, his basic theme: the impossibility of ever arriving at any fixed and constantly valid verdict on any human situation, any human personality and character—in short, the problematic nature of human identity itself.

The theater, with its multiple layers of being—real human beings turning themselves into signs for fictional beings, which, yet, being "art" can claim a higher truth than any physical "reality"—preoccupied Pirandello's thought from the very beginning.

Long before he began to concentrate his efforts on the theater, Pirandello had shown himself fascinated by the theater as a metaphor for this, his basic preoccupation, the problem that has occupied philosophers ever since Plato's parable of the cave, the problem which German philosophy sums up in the rhyming formula: "Schein und Sein"—"Seeming and Being." In his early novel *Il fu Mattia Pascal* (1903), Pirandello's first real success as a writer, two of the characters are discussing an advertisement for a performance of a version of the *Elektra* of Sophocles by a marionette theater:

Now listen to the curious idea that's occurred to me: if at the climax of the play, just when the marionette who is playing Orestes is about to avenge his father's death and kill his mother and Aegisthus, suppose there were a little hole torn in the paper sky of the scenery. What would happen? Answer me that . . . Orestes would be terribly upset by that hole in the sky? . . . he would still feel his desire for vengeance, he would still want passionately to achieve it, but his eyes, at that point, would go straight to that hole, from which every kind of evil influence would then crowd the stage, and Orestes would feel suddenly helpless. In other words, Orestes would become Hamlet. There is the whole difference between ancient tragedy and modern, . . . believe me—a hole torn in a paper sky (148).

Orestes would become Hamlet because the hole in the paper sky would destroy his belief in the "reality" of the gods whose moral imperative he is about to obey. Yet Shakespeare's—and our—Hamlet still believes in the reality of the world around him, his "all too solid flesh." He merely doubts the reality of the moral imperative that demands revenge for murder. The marionette of Orestes who has become Hamlet through doubting the reality of his sky does not himself realize that he is a marionette, but the spectators of the puppet play know that. If Hamlet is a more dramatic character than Orestes, Pirandello's characters have entered another, even more "modern," phase of modernity. They—or at least the more insightful among them—know they are marionettes, that is: that their own reality as autonomous "characters" is most doubtful, that human identity, human selfhood, and autonomy—the ability to act freely—is itself more than problematic.

In one of his earliest successes as a playwright—*Il beretto a Sonagli* (Cap and Bells, 1916)—Pirandello makes his protagonist, Ciampa, say:

We are all only puppets . . . the divine spirit enters into us and becomes a puppet. A puppet, I—a puppet you, puppets everyone. . . . Moreover, everyone makes himself a puppet of his own accord: the puppet that he can be or that he is . . . (II 375).

The madman who thinks he is Henry IV has created himself as his own puppet in his own puppet play, and as long as he believes himself to be an emperor this is his "reality." Later, he reveals that he has in fact emerged from his madness, and that he has merely persisted in the masquerade out of laziness and disillusionment with the contemporary world. Here the character now knows himself to be a puppet of his own creation. And yet: is not the decision to remain in that position itself a symptom of a deranged, abnormal mind, one of which the character himself is again unaware?

Conversely, the Six Characters that have been created by an author's day-dreaming, as long as his consciousness is haunted by them, are his puppets. They have a greater reality than any of the humdrum actors trying to embody them. He has created those puppets, and yet those puppets have assumed an independent existence, even prior to the moment in which they have been written down in the text of a play, which, in any case, would assume a reality independent of the volition of its author, as contemporary post-structuralist theory rightly insists. There is thus an independent reality within the imagining, image-creating, mind. As soon as a thought, an image has been conceived, it is "in being" and can separate itself from the mind in which it has arisen. We generate our thoughts, yet our thoughts become independent agents that act on ourselves. Ultimately, therefore, all "reality" resides in the mind, but it is never fixed, always in flux. As long as the audience believes they are seeing a medieval throne room, that *is* reality for them until that reality is undercut by another. And all the while, of course, they know that they are sitting in a theater and have temporarily "suspended their disbelief."

The extreme case of this creation of reality through what the mind believes is madness. It is said that Pirandello experienced this situation through the insanity of his wife. Living with a person who suffers from intense delusions obviously is a prime example of the coexistence of multiple "realities," different world systems, within the same household. In *Così è (Se vi pare) (It Is So (If You Think So))* (1918) this thesis is demonstrated with classical simplicity. Two cases of strictly symmetrical, complementary delusions are confronted here, without the possibility of deciding which of them is the delusion and which the "reality."

But madness is merely the extreme case. At the other end of the spectrum is the theater with its manifest role-playing, with its openly displayed character of an illusion, an illusion within an illusion.

Between these extremes of the spectrum, between madness and play-acting, lies the everyday reality of "role-playing," the puppets playing the characters they themselves have created, knowing full well that these are roles but, when they are alone, able to discard those roles, assuming their real characters, which in turn are merely secondary roles. They are illusions of what they themselves want, or believe themselves, to be—roles as illusory as the publicly assumed ones, because they are made up of wishful thinking, self-delusion, and lack of self-knowledge.

Maschere nude—naked masks—Pirandello called the collected edition of his plays. "Maschere" in Italian not only denotes masks of cloth or wood that are worn by people who want to disguise themselves, but also the stereotypic characters of the *commedia dell'arte*: Harlequin and Columbine, Pantalone and Capitano, Dottore, Truffaldino, Brighella, and the rest. Take away these characters' masks and costumes and they will be naked, and yet they will still wear masks, the masks that conceal their real selves from themselves.

Thus, our existence is essentially one of multiple realities that mutually undercut and relativize each other. If the theater is a house of multiple illusions, so is the internal theater within ourselves: the roles we play in society toward others, and the roles we play toward ourselves within ourselves.

"Reality" thus appears a structure made up of innumerable layers of an onion, which when peeled away ultimately reveal a nothingness at its core. Or rather, each layer invalidates the next as well as the previous one. The sky we have taken for real is pierced to reveal another sky behind it, which in turn may well itself be pierced to reveal another, and so on, *ad infinitum*. "Reality" is what we think it to be, but the wise know that what we think must always be subjective rather than an objective reality, that in fact any "ultimate" reality, that realm of eternal ideas on which Plato founded the edifice of idealistic philosophy, must by definition ever remain outside the reach of human endeavor.

Thus, no "reality," no fact, experienced by the human mind can ever be fixed and immutable. Life for Pirandello is constant flux. The moment you try to capture a situation, a character, a fact, to say: "yes, that's it!", that very moment your statement turns into a falsehood, for life has passed on and the very fixedness of the statement itself already falsified it. Hence, it is futile ever to try to capture the essence of life in the eternally fixed form of "art."

This is the basic insight in Pirandello's most important theoretical statement, his essay on humor, *L'umorismo* (1908). At any given moment, in any situation, this fluidity of life creates the constant coexistence of contradictions within characters and situations. If it is so now, we already sense that it is also not so. If traditional artists therefore tried to distill from the confusions and trivialities of ordinary life an essential and lasting picture of eternal truth, the modern artist must be a "humorist" who always remains aware of the contradictions and oscillations of human situations and tries to convey them to his audience through constant reflection, through a constant undermining of certainties, so that every statement, every feeling is always accompanied by its "contrary like the body by its shadow" (*Umorismo* 160). Thus, Pirandello essentially saw himself as a "humorist" and his plays as basically comedic. However, that comedy arises from the shadow thrown by the body of events that are often tragic in nature. Therefore, Pirandello's theater is a *tragicomic* theater, one of the prime examples, one of the decisive embodiments, the most influential expressions of the fact that modern drama tends toward tragicomedy.

The puppet of Orestes in *Il fu Mattia Pascal* had become Hamlet when he saw the rent in the sky of his backdrop, but Hamlet himself was still a tragic figure in a play labeled "tragedy" by its author. The archetypal Pirandellian protagonist has become aware of the uncertainty not only of the moral law he is, or is not, obeying, but also of his own nature as a human being. The author of the play himself is also aware that what the protagonist feels subjectively is an illusion, shadowed by the futility of those feelings in a universe of constantly shifting "reality," so that the effect on the audience must be a mixture of the tragic and the comic. Pirandello—and that is one aspect of his immense importance for the development of modern drama—was one of the first to be wholly aware of the "Death of Tragedy" resulting from the decline of certainties about the world, human nature, and the position of humankind within the universe— the consequences, that is, of what Nietzsche called the "death of God." The naturalists, Ibsen, Hauptmann, Strindberg, still believed in the possibility of tragedy in modern drama. Pirandello and Chekhov are the two masters who realized that the tragic and the comic necessarily coexisted in a world bereft of moral certainties.

It is no coincidence that Samuel Beckett, already in his early essay on Proust, expresses views very similar to those of Pirandello about the impossibility of fixing life through art. He also maintains the constant coexistence of the tragic and the comic, notably in his famous analysis of the types of laughter in the novel *Watt*:

Of all the laughs that strictly speaking are not laughs, but modes of ululation, only three I think need detain us, I mean the bitter, the hollow and the mirthless. . . . The bitter laugh laughs at that which is not good, it is the ethical laugh. The hollow laugh laughs at what is not true, it is the intellectual laugh. . . . But the mirthless laugh is the dianoetic laugh. . . . It is the laugh of laughs, the *risus purus,* the laugh laughing at the laugh, the beholding, the saluting of the highest joke, in a word the laugh that laughs—silence please—at that which is unhappy (Beckett, 48).

The *risus purus,* the laugh that laughs at human unhappiness, is, according to Beckett, the "dianoetic" laugh. "Dianoia" is the term Aristotle uses for the moment of deep insight in Greek tragedy. Dianoetic laughter is tragicomic laughter. Thus, there is clearly a definite line of development from Pirandello to Beckett and Ionesco, the "theater of the absurd."

The connecting link between Pirandello and the French avant-garde of the period after the Second World War was provided by the Pitoëffs, that brilliant family of Russian emigré actors and directors who established Pirandello as one of the classics of the French stage in the 1920s. Antonin Artaud, whose influence on writers like Amadov, Ionesco, and Genet is generally acknowledged, was, for a time, a member of the Pitoëffs' ensemble. There can be little doubt that it was Pirandello who introduced some of the main themes and preoccupations of the theater of the absurd into French drama.

Among these themes the exploration of the problem of human identity is the most obvious. Yet if most of Pirandello's *oeuvre* developed that subject matter in plays that retained the outward realism of the well-made play, it was from his most daring experiment, the materializations of emanations of an author's inner world in *Six Characters* that the theater of the absurd took off. For much of that theater can be seen as a series of dramatizations of an "inner reality": the dreams, fantasies, and internal conflicts within the authors concerned. The characters in many of the plays of the dramatists of the absurd are often merely fantasies of their authors that have assumed autonomy and independence. The characters in a play like Ionesco's *The Chairs* merely dramatize, it may be argued, the conflict within their author, between his desire to bequeath the sum of his experience to an audience, and his consciousness, on the other hand, that he is incapable of ever clearly articulating it. Similarly, Beckett's *Endgame* might well be an image of the conflict within a single consciousness at the point of death and dissolution. These plays may thus be "monodramas." But even if one does not follow the literal interpretation of the term monodrama which this view represents, the freedom with which the authors' imaginations are unleashed in these plays, with a total disregard of any considerations of "realism," marks these dramas as "monodramatic"—in the sense that they are images of the fantasies and daydreams of their authors, wholly subjective emanations of a single mind, laying no claim whatever to any representation of an objective, external reality.

It is this monodramatic quality that marks the direct descent of the theater of the absurd from the Six Characters in Pirandello's mind that materialize during the rehearsal of another play. At a deeper level the absurdists follow Pirandello in making the presentation and exploration of the problem of human identity the central theme of their drama. Although much bolder in their formal technique, in their rejection of even the rudiments of photographic realism, Beckett and Ionesco circle the same subject matter—I and Not-I—in ever renewed guises. If one considers that both in Pirandello as in the absurdists this theme frequently takes the form of an exploration of states of mental alienation and madness, the close affinity between them becomes even more manifest.

Much of Pirandello's dramatic output, however, remained formally strictly realistic, following indeed at times the model of his fellow-Sicilian Giovanni Verga and his *verismo,* as well as that of his contemporaries in the Italian *teatro grottesco,* notably Luigi Chiarelli. The influence of this more traditional Pirandello proved equally strong, perhaps even stronger, on the somewhat more mainstream dramatists of the interwar and postwar periods in France and in Germany, where Max Reinhardt became his standard-bearer in the 1920s and until Hitler's advent to power in 1933.

In France it was Jean Anouilh who made the most effective and original use of Pirandellian devices. For example, in *Le rendezvous De Senlis* (1937), the hero engages a pair of actors to give his beloved the illusion that he has a solid family background, and *La grotte* (1961) shows us an author trying to write a play by producing the characters for us on the stage and trying them out in various situations. In the end the characters become autonomous enough to refuse to go along with their author's intentions.

Giraudoux's free use of Pirandellian theatrical devices in plays like *Ondine* (1939) and *Intermezzo* (1933), or his delicate treatment of the problematic nature of human identity in *Amphitryon 38* (1929) or Sartre's theater of philosophical discussion and demonstration equally testify to Pirandello's pervading influence. In the postwar German-language theater the Swiss playwrights Max Frisch and Friedrich Dürrenmatt use a wealth of openly Pirandellian devices as well as Pirandellian themes: Dürrenmatt's *The Visit* (1956) and his *Physicists* (1962) make masterly use of the Pirandellian notions of role-playing and madness. In plays like *Don Juan or the Love of Geometry* (1953) and *Biography: A Game* (1967) Frisch develops Pirandellian devices and notions to new extremes, Don Juan staging his descent into Hell in order to escape his reputation as a seducer of women, or, in the latter play, the hero rehearsing various different versions of his biography to find out where his life went wrong. Peter Weiss's *Marat/Sade* (1964) is another prime example of an abundance of Pirandellian techniques: theater within the theater performed, moreover, by madmen. Here the overlapping realities are no longer doubled, but tripled and quadrupled.

Another aspect of Pirandello's influence on modern drama concerns the decline of the theater's claim and aspiration to evoke in its audience an illusion of reality, a suspension of disbelief. Pirandello is one of the pioneers of today's anti-illusionist stage. Of course, Pirandello was by no means the first to create a meta-theatrical theater, a theater within the theater, a theater openly proclaiming its theatricality, its unreality. Theater within theater goes back to *Hamlet,* to Corneille's *L'Illusion Comique,* to the undercutting of theatrical reality in the work of such German romantics as Tieck who, in his *Der Gestiefelte Kater* (Puss in Boots, 1797) had the actors refuse to go on with a silly play, members of the audience arguing with them and the alarmed author, and so on. But Pirandello, more than any of his predecessors, made this meta-theatricality one of the major metaphors of modern drama. Beckett's characters frequently refer to their awareness of the presence of an audience and thus to the nonillusionistic nature of the proceedings they inhabit. In this they are following Pirandello who so radically exposed the inner mechanisms of an illusionistic theater in a play like *Questa sera si recita a soggetto* (*Tonight We Improvise*).

In an entirely different manner Pirandello's conviction that "reality" is never one-dimensional, that the true "humorist" sees not only one but always at least two aspects of reality, and that this is the source of the tragicomic nature of modern drama, emerges in Brecht's theories of the "Verfremdungs-Effekt" (strangemaking—often wrongly rendered as "alienation"—effect). It is precisely the dialectic between contradiction inherent in any given personality and situation that Brecht is concerned with, albeit for very different ends from those in which Pirandello and the absurdists were mainly interested. Brecht is concerned chiefly with the uncovering of *social* contradictions, but this treatment of characters split into two, as in *The Seven Deadly Sins, The Good Person of Setzuan, Mr. Puntila and His Servant Matti,* or in the division between Galileo the glutton and Galileo the sensualist of knowledge, in *The Life of Galileo,* or the mother as mother and the mother as businesswoman, in *Mother Courage,* which closely follows Pirandello's ideas of reality and its shadow in his essay on humor. Moreover, the open theatricality of Brecht's theater, which never denies its artifice and insists on the actor's retaining his private personality underneath his fictional character, owes a great deal to Pirandello's playfulness with the same contrast in plays like *Six Characters, Tonight We Improvise,* or *Ciascuno in suo modo* (*Each in His Own Way*).

Pirandello's influence in the English-speaking world has been less powerful and less direct, owing partly to the general resistance of the English-speaking theater to foreign influences and its notorious reluctance to present plays in translation. Moreover, Pirandello has been dogged by the scarcity of good relations, to some extent because he entrusted the translation rights to many of his plays to the woman friend of his latter years, Marta Abba, who was anything but a brilliant translator. As a result, quite a number of Pirandello's most interesting plays remain untranslated into English.

Yet Pirandello's techniques and ideas have penetrated into the English-language theater. A play like Thornton Wilder's *The Skin of Our Teeth* (1942) is a case in point. Wilder, of course, had traveled extensively in Central Europe and had been exposed to the theater of Berlin and Vienna in the 1920s. Indirectly, Pirandellian ideas have penetrated into the English-speaking world through the pervasive influence of Brecht and the absurdists, above all Beckett.

It can certainly be argued that the use of dream images, fantasy, and meta-theatrical devices in the work of English playwrights like Edward Bond (*Early Mourning, Lear*) or Tom Stoppard (*Jumpers, Travesties*) or American dramatists like Arthur Kopit (*Dad, Poor Dad* or *Indians*) and Sam Shepard (*Angel City* and many others of his plays) would not have been possible without the influence of Pirandello, however distant and mediated.

Pirandello is an intellectual playwright, and many of his dramas are largely discussions of philosophical problems. During his studies at the university of Bonn, Pirandello became immersed in the intellectual climate of post-Nietzschean German philosophy. His work thus reflects the *Zeitgeist*, the spirit of the times, which saw the demise of so many of the certainties and deep convictions of the Victorian-Wilhelminian age. It is surely no coincidence that ideas and techniques very similar to those of Pirandello's theater arose at the very same time in Eastern Europe, an area particularly open to ideas coming from Germany. The Russian playwright Nikolai Evreinov (1876–1953) actually put the inside of a single character's mind onto the stage in his monodrama *The Theater of the Soul* (English translation, 1915) in which we see, perched on the character's diaphragm (where the ancient Greeks situated the soul) his rational and his emotional selves struggling with each other to the death, that is, the character's suicide. In his theoretical works Evreinov repeatedly preached the theatricality of life, reality as a receding series of role-playings, and so forth. In Poland Stanislas Ignacy Witkiewicz (1885–1939) advocated a theater of pure form and pure fantasy, a wholly subjective distillation of dreams.

In the period after World War II, Witkiewicz's influence merged with that of the French avant-garde to produce a vigorous absurdist strain of drama, in the work of writers like Mrozek and Rozewicz in Poland, while in Czechoslovakia brilliant dissident writers like Havel and Kundera used Pirandellian and absurdist techniques to castigate the follies of the communist regimes in their countries in satirical fantasies so far removed from the daily "reality" that they could be represented as remote from direct political comment. Here, too, Pirandello's influence is indirectly present, together with that of the French absurdists, Witkiewicz, Brecht, and ultimately the satires of Swift or Hasek.

Pirandello, the playwright whose drama is so largely philosophical, has greatly enhanced the theater's claim that it can be more than a mere pastime and entertainment, and can serve rather as a vehicle of serious thought. In this respect, too, Pirandello's theater has a common aspect with Brecht's, who was also convinced that the theater could and should serve as an instrument of cognition, a place where the abstractions of theory could be tested and concretized through the individual experience of particular human beings. Such a theater requires authors who possess not only a formidable intellect, capable of the highest reaches of abstract thought, but also a strong, sensuous, imaginative nature able to imagine a wealth of concrete situations. Pirandello, far from being a dry-as-dust philosopher, also had immense emotional intensity and a strong, and earthy, sensuality, which, for example, emerges in his Sicilian folk comedies like *Liolà* or *L'uomo, La bestia e la virtù* (*Man, Beast, and Virtue*). It is this combination of human passion with deep intellectual penetration that makes the man who started out as a poet and storyteller, and has also left a vast body of novels and short-stories, one of the great dramatists of world literature.

WORKS CITED

Beckett, Samuel. *Watt*. New York: Grove Press, 1958.

Pirandello, Luigi. *Il beretto a sonagli* in *Maschere nude*. Milano: Mondadori, 1968.

———. *L'umorismo* in *Saggi, poesie, scritti varii*. Milano: Mondadori, 1965.

———. *The Late Mattia Pascal*. Translated by William Weaver. Garden City, N.Y.: Doubleday, 1964.

19

Pirandellian Humor and Modern French Drama

David A. Powell

Theater represents the third and last mode of Pirandello's artistic production. Having established himself as a writer of prose fiction and then of lyric poetry, the Sicilian turned, after the age of fifty, to a successful career in dramatic writing. International accolades made of him an important figure in European theater. But why link Pirandello to French theater, and to what French theater? What is the nature of the relationship?[1]

During the height of Pirandello's active and popular theatrical career in the 1920s and 1930s, there was almost always at least one of his works being produced in Paris. Alfred Mortier stated that Pirandello was sometimes playing at three theaters at once, an unprecedented accomplishment for a foreigner (Weiss, 9). In 1925, the year *Henry IV* opened in Paris, five Pirandello plays were being performed in the French capital (Bishop, 7). In addition, there were few national stars of the Paris stage at the time, and the theatergoing public welcomed new ideas. Paris, still recuperating from the devastation of World War I, was struggling to rid itself of empty reason and a false sense of order. Pirandello's dramatic presentation of life's absurdities served up to a willing audience exactly what they longed to hear and see. Georges Pitoëff's 1923 production of *Six Characters in Search of an Author* brought to the French public a much needed treatment of modern problems conceived in an innovative form. Because of the direction of Pitoëff and Charles Dullin and the brilliant translations of Benjamin Crémieux, Pirandello's rise in Paris between the wars could not fail.

There is no doubt that a certain *Zeitgeist* of resigned disgust with the modern world reigned from between the wars until well after World War II. And still, dramatic devices as well as themes of postwar France can be traced back to Pirandello's successes in the Paris of the 1920s and 1930s. So popular were many of Pirandello's techniques that a spate of copies flooded the Parisian stage, especially in the 1930s, reducing the author's art to a mechanical craft easy to replicate but devoid of any messages. "Pirandellisme" became a derogatory term during this period, whereas previously it had denoted the fine dramatic style of the playwright's innovations (Bishop, 51).[2]

Other playwrights used similar themes about the same time as Pirandello, which renders arguments of influence somewhat precarious. Wilder in America and Shaw in England display currents reminiscent of Pirandello, though less anguish-filled and more easily comical. Kafka and later Brecht show similar directions, though imbued with the weight of expressionism. The influence of Freud, who was publishing his findings on the human psyche at this time, can hardly be ignored. The grotesques and the futurists in Italy were beginning to present the meaningless of life on stage. Ibsen and Strindberg can also be said to have contributed to Pirandello's sense of the theatrical metaphor for life. Yet, the unmistakable presence of Pirandello in Paris for over fifteen years, both in French translation and in the original Italian performed by Pirandello's own troupe, must be considered an important element in the shifting of directions which the modern French theater undertook about the same time.

Pirandello's treatment of modern problems helped to assure his success at home and abroad. An anti-bourgeois tendency had already soured the Parisian public on the traditional, well-ordered play—"la pièce bien faite." Logical development in plot and characterization soon became the mark of the pretense and stagnation of the early Third Republic. With Alfred Jarry's earth-shattering "Mierdre!" (*Ubu roi,* 1888), the ideals of a bourgeois society no longer held any importance for the intellectual public, especially not for the theatergoing public. Beyond the realists' and the naturalists' search for the everyday and the banal, beyond the symbolists' attempt at a total art form, modern French theater after Pirandello aimed to return the individual to the center of the dramatic universe. The modern individual, unlike the romantic individual, finds himself inextricably attached to a society he neither esteems nor wants. Rather than the pains and pleasures of solitude, the modern hero, or anti-hero, examines the place of his perceptions and his responsibilities within a society he can no longer control or understand.

Pirandello's philosophy, which explains most of his dramatic themes and many of his theatrical innovations, can be found in his essay on humor. *L'umorismo,* originally published in 1908, contributes to our understanding of Pirandello's art as he applied it to the theater. A brief summary of the fundamental elements of Pirandello's thoughts on humor will make clear what will follow. The humorist does not write to make us laugh; this is the realm of the comic, who perceives something opposite to the norm. The humorist transcends this perception and feels the opposite from a deeper source that, for him, translates the anguish of life. This *sentimento del contrario* is best described in Pirandello's example of an old woman dressed up like a young girl. Laughing at her shows merely a perception of the opposite, which remains at the comic level. Humoristic reflection, an impulsive and spontaneous force that pierces superficial perception, may reveal that the woman is quite aware of, and displeased with, her state. She may persist in this action out of necessity, to hold her husband, for instance. Herein lies the feeling of the opposite which is Pirandello's humor (*On Humor*, 113).

Humor goes beyond contrasting ideals and reality, for the humorist's state of mind rejects ideals. This aspect perhaps best indicates how the humorist differs from the ironist. Irony, as a rhetorical figure, involves a deception, which runs contrary to the nature of humor. Rhetorical irony implies an apparent contradiction between denotative and connotative meaning. But the contradiction in humor lies at its essence. Romantic irony, after Tieck, comes closer to humor in its depiction of the ambiguity of reality, albeit more mordant than humoristic. Schlegel's irony, which reduces artistic matter to a perpetual parody wherein the author never loses his awareness of the unreality of his own creation, makes the ironist superior to his characters. It is in this aspect that humor differs radically from irony, for the humorist penetrates to the depths of his own being along with that of his characters.

Humor stands at the center of Pirandello's theater, a humor just as natural as it is philosophical and rhetorical. As much as Pirandello persisted in thinking his humor was spontaneous, it is self-aware and self-analyzing. Pirandello replaced the highly contorted rhetoric of the expressionists with a simpler, more natural speech. The characteristic ordinary aspect of his theater underscores the importance of life's banality. Pirandello's subtle rhetoric operates on two levels. First, using natural dialogue to express matters of significant personal importance blends the everyday of naturalism with the passion of expressionism. Exchanges that seem banal actually divulge an underlying anguish central to modern life. The second function of Pirandello's rhetoric follows logically. Listening to natural dialogue, the spectator is lulled into a sense of complacency, when suddenly the tone or subject of the script shifts almost imperceptibly and the spectator feels lost. The programmed loss of security duplicates an aspect of life's absurdity which Pirandello offers in several plays. Life is not only absurd, but we often accept its absurdities as "normal," only to be jolted into a moment of conscious anxiety and disgust from which we cannot escape.

The rhetoric of absurdity pervades all of Pirandello's theater. Not merely a stylistic device, it also supports one of the playwright's most common themes: the relativity of truth. Pirandello's first play to be produced in Paris, *Il piacere dell'onestà* (*The Pleasure of Honesty*) (1922), demonstrates the implications involved in confusing appearance and illusion. Ciampa's mistress, Agata, is pregnant. In order to preserve her respectability, Ciampa, who is already married, persuades his friend, Baldovino, to marry her. Baldovino decides the pleasure of honor cannot be ignored. Thus, he assumes the role that he had originally agreed only to seem to portray. To exaggerate the reversal of roles, he and Agata end up falling in love. Illusion therefore takes over reality instead of concealing it.

Così è (se vi pare) (Right You Are (If You Think So)) (1918) communicates its theme of the relativity of truth in the title. The whole town involves themselves in the search for the truth. Who is Signora Ponza? Digging up the past in an attempt to solve the mystery, the neighbors unearth more about themselves and each other than they would have liked to reveal, and all in vain, for they are no closer to knowing the truth. Only Laudisi, a character detached from the frenzy of discovering "the truth," can see and accept that Signora Ponza will be whoever she appears to be at any particular time and to whoever is regarding her at any particular time. Multiple truths need not cancel each other out.

Several French plays of the early 1950s convey a similar confusion of illusion and reality. As in Pirandello, these playwrights accept the relativity of truth and emphasize the coexistence of many truths and illusions. Ionesco portrays such a world in *La Cantatrice chauve (The Bald Soprano)* (1950). His parody of English life, using the caricatures of the "Assimil" language method familiar to all French people, ridicules the formulaic repetition of life's meaningless habits. As the Smiths recite to each other their evening's menu of fish and potatoes, the spectators wonder why they need to indulge in a litany about a meal that they have clearly just finished. The situation blurs even more at the arrival of unexpected guests, the Martins. Their conversation mimics the opening banter between strangers often found in language manuals. Mr. and Mrs. Martin soon discover they not only took the same train that day, but they also live at the same address and both have a daughter with one white and one red eye. Here we encounter the famous line, "Comme c'est curieux, comme c'est bizarre, quelle coïncidence!" (How odd, how strange, what a coincidence!), which promotes the false sense of life as a series of coincidences. The maid soon destroys any complacency when she informs the audience in an aside that Mr. Martin's daughter's left eye is red and the right one is white, whereas Mrs. Martin's daughter has the opposite configuration. How can we know the truth? The maid tells us, "Ne tâchons pas de le savoir. Laissons les choses comme elles sont." (Let's not try to find out. Leave things as they are.)

Adamov's *La Parodie* (1952) describes a similar routine existence that imitates life in a mechanical fashion, reminding the spectator a bit too much of his own daily habits. Both *La Cantatrice chauve* and *La Parodie* share a concern for the time of day, a futile attempt of man to dominate the passing of time. Yet, neither play represents time as we know it. The clock chimes thirteen times, for example, or the characters differ radically in their interpretation of what time it is. Our perception of reality is tested by an element we consider to be constant and exact.

En attendant Godot (Waiting for Godot) (1952) introduces another aspect of illusion, the illusion we create for ourselves in a vain attempt to give our lives meaning. Vladimir and Estragon struggle to construct a significant life while they await the arrival of Godot. Whether Godot be God or truth or simply meaning, he never comes, though his coming continues to be promised. Godot is illusion, Vladimir's and Estragon's lives are illusions, but they convince themselves so completely that the illusory end is worth the wait that illusion becomes their only reality. The theme comes from Pirandello, but the religious overtones are pure Beckett.

Camus' *Le Malentendu* (1944) recasts the situation of *Così è (se vi pare)* in terms of a murder mystery. The mystery here, however, is not who committed the murder but who is the murdered man. On the surface a simple case of mistaken identity, the play uses dramatic irony to tell the tragedy of a man returning home after twenty years of self-exile only to be killed for his money at the hands of his wife and mother. On still another level, Camus reveals, through the three characters' individual blindness, the illusion of happiness under which humanity struggles. Camus examined this struggle, which is itself the very meaning of life according to him, in his essay, *The Myth of Sisyphus* (1942). Absurdity carries a more systematized, philosophical explanation with Camus than with Pirandello, but the theme of individual perceptions that cannot be changed remains a strong bond between the French and the Italian playwrights.

As Pirandello's characters slip in and out of reality (or is illusion the base level from which they depart?), they begin to accept the coexistence of several realities. This recognition will eventually lead to their perception of several facets of their personalities, facets that, as Freud was then discovering, often hide from each other. Pirandello borrows the image of the mask to designate the most consistent, therefore the least "real," facet of one's personality. But for Pirandello, the mask represents a facade not for others, but for oneself. The mask is necessary in order to survive daily existence, in order to "save face" in one's own eyes. The horrible moment when the mask falls forces us to accept the gap that separates our own and others' perceptions of ourselves. The title *Maschere nude,* as Pirandello called the edition of his collected plays, describes the process many of his characters pass through, not always successfully.

Henry IV (1922) stands as the best example of Pirandello's plays on the multiplicity of personality. It is also his dramatic masterpiece. Placed in a politico-historical background which is rare for Pirandello, the play examines the mind's ability to choose fantasy over reality, at once understanding and ignoring the process one is undergoing. As humorist, Pirandello paints an intriguingly lucid confusion in the character of Henry IV. Costumed for a masquerade, Henry IV—who carries no other name throughout the play—falls from his horse and sustains a head injury. For twenty years he lives as though he were Henry IV of Germany. The Doctor develops an elaborate plan to cure Henry of his madness. The plan backfires, and Henry reveals that he had awakened from his confusion after twelve years, but he so enjoyed the eleventh-century surroundings his sister had lovingly provided, he preferred to continue that existence. So he had done for eight more years. Yet, he berates his former beloved for trying to appear younger than she is in a speech reminiscent of the famous passage from the essay on humor cited above. The Doctor's plan has jolted Henry into yet another realm of "reality" and he nearly reverts to his former, "mad" amnesia. At the end of Act II, Henry declares that acts, be they illusion or responsible actions, must be carried out strictly, as if they were true, "Because only in that way can truth be considered anything but a joke!" (Firth, 139; translation mine).

Henry kills the present lover of his beloved and immediately withdraws back into his fantasy world. Here ends the play. Pirandello has shown a Henry with several sides among which he can move, now, at will. The fantasy world presents no challenges. Everything has been done for him, and he has but to live out each day. But his principal reason for reverting to his life of illusion resides in the twelve years the surrounding world progressed and he stagnated. The others resumed their lives and changed, whereas he awakened the same as before. He felt out of place, out of tune.[3] The momentary lapse into the present is sparked mostly by his jealousy at being replaced by another lover. Once he has eliminated the usurper, he can quietly return to the calm of his illusions.

The hero of *Quando si è qualcuno (When One Is Somebody)* (1933) changes his identity and thus his life. A successful poet, ***—his only name, other than Maestro—has lost his inspiration. But the love for a young girl rejuvenates him. Posing as an Italo-American called Délago, he writes beautiful, modern verse. The hero now leads two opposing lives, for as Délago, he attracts a group of young admirers who repudiate the older style of poetry. He has also shunned his family for the sake of his youthful mistress. All is disclosed, and he must make a choice. Although he considers Délago's poetry more inspired and honest than his, he cannot continue to live the life of a youth and abandon his family. He thus rejects Délago, and with that rejection, his poetic dynamism disappears. Soon afterward, however, he is celebrated as a national poet and feels he is being classified as a national monument.

***'s story represents a complex twist of Pirandello's mask image. To all appearances, he would seem to have assumed another, a supplementary mask. Yet, he actually changes his life consciously and attempts a total change of identity. In the process of adding a mask, or changing masks, however, *** is forced to examine himself and to choose the life with the fewest masks. Would this decision have come so early if Délago's identity had not been exposed? It is uncharacteristic of Pirandello to leave anything to fate, and subtleties in Délago's character suggest that he subverted his own disguise. The existential perspective always surfaces in Pirandello's drama: we choose our own destiny, Pirandello's philosophy of "*construirsi*" (to construct oneself).

Dropping the mask, as I have stated, concerns revealing one's "true" identity to oneself as much as to others. Such is the subject of *Come tu mi vuoi (As You Desire Me)* (1930), which ends without any certainty as to the main character's identity. The Strange Lady is called alternately Signora Lucia Pieri, Elma, and Cia—the second is the name she assumed in Berlin as an exotic dancer· the first and third are the married and childhood names, respectively, of the missing

Italian woman she is thought to be. The missing person has been gone for ten years, since immediately after World War I. Her sister has had her declared legally dead in order to ensure the inheritance for her own daughter. Now ten years later, not only does everyone hesitate to recognize her, but the Strange Lady doubts her own identity. Another woman, the Demented Lady, surfaces from a hospital in Vienna. Is she not perhaps the missing one?

Proof of identity is the focal point of the game. The Strange Lady does resemble a portrait of the missing woman. Pirandello opposes art to life here as he has the Strange Lady challenge such a comparison: "I am Cia—I alone! I!—I!—not she (pointing to the portrait)" (*Come*, 145). The husband, Bruno, also admits to having searched for a hidden mole his wife had. The Strange Lady claims to have had it removed, though she expects no one to believe her. At the end of the play, the Demented Lady will be shown to have such a mole, though a different color and in a slightly different location.

In any case, the Strange Lady rejects the identity some contest and others doubt. She decides to return to Berlin to her career of revealing illusions through dance. In dropping the mask, she has found another one, the mask worn in an earlier life perhaps, or maybe a new one, donned to assume a new identity. The act of donning a mask creates as much suffering as that of removing one. Here, instead of the multiplicity of identities in *Henry IV*, Pirandello concentrates on the problems of trying to switch personalities in a willful change, a return to the past that discounts the passage of time and the non-static nature of life.

Ciascuno a suo modo (Each in His Own Way), (1924) exploits the superficial perception of the actress as the adventuress, the courtesan. Delia Morello must confront her own perception of herself after her ex-lover, the painter Giorgio Salvi, commits suicide. She explains that she broke up with him because he wanted her only for her body, not as a sexual but as an aesthetic object. Salvi regarded the relationship with complete selfishness, not only emotional but also physical selfishness. She examines herself in her mirror and is "horror-stricken at the pallor and at the coldness" and tries to explain the impression she gets "in the circle of that mirror, of her painted lips and her painted eyes!" (Bentley, 303). A friend suggests she cannot see herself as others do. Delia tries to understand why people only see the surface when they look at her: "I see them walk in front of me and they seem—well—to be dazzled by my eyes, by my lips, by my beauty, in short; but no one cares for me . . . no one cares for what most concerns me" (304). This scene of incomplete self-discovery demonstrates the pain of letting down the mask.

Huis clos (No Exit) (1944) will employ a similar device to portray self-examination. Sartre puts his three characters in a closed room where they must all learn to accept themselves. Estelle wonders whether she exists if she cannot see herself in a mirror, that is, as others see her. Inès, on the other hand, can always feel herself on the inside. She invites Estelle to use her eyes as a mirror. A high concentration of visual vocabulary fills the one-act play with the importance of looking and seeing.

Oreste, in Sartre's *Les Mouches* (1943), performs a much more courageous act. By killing Aegisthus and Clytemnestra, he avenges not the death but the unaccepted responsibility for the death of Agamemnon, as well as sets the example for having the conviction of one's actions. In the midst of a riotous crowd of Furies, Oreste takes on the collective guilt of his subjects, thus demasking them and leading them, like the pied piper, into an existence of commitment. A similar situation occurs in Sartre's *Le Diable et le bon dieu* (1951), where Goetz tries to force his fellow man to lower his mask, accept responsibility for his own actions, and abandon the false security of religion.

Adamov's *Le Professeur Taranne* (1953) presents a character reminiscent of Pirandello's *** in *Quando si è qualcuno*. Taranne is a university professor (we never know in what discipline) who has made a reputation by plagiarizing another professor's work. Eager to let down the mask and to assume the punishment for his deceit, he tries to get arrested, but no one is quite sure of his true identity. He is even mistaken for the professor whom he plagiarized! Finally, in a desperate attempt to reveal the truth, he stalks the beach naked. The map he holds up at the end of the play is completely grey. It fascinates him as he begins once again to undress. Adamov would seem to be adding to Pirandello's philosophy of the mask the necessity of these masks. We are, in fact, the ensemble of masks we wear; without the results of our creation, we are nothing.

Camus' *Caligula* (1945) comes close to *Henry IV* in terms of a strong central character who loses touch with the reality of those around him. His own reality crumbles, as did Henry's, when he realizes the sacrifice of his comrades and subjects in his behalf. As his illusions fall one by one, he retreats more and more into his fantasy until he can simply accept the absurdity of existence. Caligula, like Henry, is partly responsible for his own situation, but the realization of the responsibility only pushes them further from reality. Genet's *Les Bonnes* (1946) also portrays the reversal of roles that transforms illusion into reality. The transfer of personality, through the donning of clothes (masks) and role-playing, reveals the disintegration of individualism as a singleness and the coherence of several, intermeshing personalities.

In many of Pirandello's works, the stage plays a centralizing role as the locus of "the game," the illusion that a group of actors, in conjunction with the author and a director, present to an audience. The self-conscious attitude of theater as theater runs counter to the naturalists' goal of "a slice of life" and even reverses Ibsen's concept of removing the fourth wall. Pirandello's drama constitutes a comment on drama, especially in the three plays connected by the common use of the play-within-the-play: *Six Characters in Search of an Author, Each in His Own Way, Tonight We Improvise*. This meta-theatrical trilogy demonstrated innovations in the concept of the stage play that were to alter the French modern theater for years.

The device of the play-within-the-play was not new to Pirandello. Shakespeare used it in several of his comedies, and in the French tradition, Molière also used it in the famous *L'Impromptu de Versailles*. Pirandello's innovation consists in the overt disengagement of the "willing suspension of disbelief." He plays on the subtle shades of grey that constitute disbelief, or illusion, and he makes it the task of the very structure of drama, and therefore the function of the actors, to ask the question: what is real? Pirandello's humor is again at work here. As opposed to Shakespeare's framing device or Molière's parody, Pirandello puts theater in a position to look at itself and at the act of illusion, thus forcing the audience to look at life's illusions. While Shakespeare and Molière provide a valid observation of the discrepancy between theater and life, what in Pirandellian terms would be called an *avvertimento del contrario*, Pirandello attempts to make his spectators see and feel the gap from within the structure of the play, a *sentimento del contrario*.

Theatricality in *Six Characters* represents perhaps the single most famous device of Pirandello's drama. Six people, claiming to be the creation of an unknown playwright, interrupt other actors and demand the use of the stage for their own play. They explain their unique difficulty: the playwright was unable to finish the play, which left them incomplete as characters. As long as the play is unfinished, they are still alive, but unsatisfied. They want to reproduce the play as it stands, hoping an author will come forward to help them complete the play. The interplay between the Director, who claims these six people are mad, and the characters, who desperately need to play out their roles, offers an exhilarating view of the "life" that stands at the center of both plays. Spectators, so intrigued by the unresolved ending, beg for a denouement as much for the interior play as for the one they came to see. However, the two deaths at the end, as they are reenacted, cannot be easily assigned to reality or illusion. Pirandello has ingeniously demonstrated the relativity of truth in form and content.

Each in His Own Way uses another, similar device wherein the plot will be duplicated within the structure of the play. The audience is instructed on the program not to leave their seats at the first curtain because the actors will return to play the role of spectators discussing and repeating the action of the first act. This will happen twice. Pirandello sketches out these *intermezzi*, but they are meant to be largely improvised. The public receives further encouragement that the dramatic event is entirely unrehearsed and spontaneous by the announcement that the house manager cannot predict the total number of acts, depending on what might happen during the course of the performance. In fact, the "spectators" again revile the play and cause it to end "early," yet two "spectators" proceed to relive the roles of the romantic duo in the play.

Pirandello is playing here with the notion of art versus reality. His play is static and thus always at the mercy of a director, the actors and, to a certain extent, the public. More than just a denunciation of realist theater, *Each in His Own Way* asks the audience to consider their own complacency in accepting to sit in a comfortable seat and be entertained by a play unfolding nicely before them. The mere structure of *Each in His Own Way* communicates its theatricality and challenges the role of modern drama. This doubtless contributed to the play's success in French and many other languages, given that the structure has as much, if not more, influence on the public than the content.

Finally, *Tonight We Improvise* (1930) takes up again, this time more directly, the problems evoked by the theme of improvisation. The director, Doctor Hinkfuss, presents a story line by Pirandello that he wants the actors to follow. It is the story of a family destroyed by desire and jealousy. But the actors feel stifled by the ambiguity of the drama: they want either a more solid script or a freer improvisation. When Hinkfuss loses his authority, the actors take charge. But as the play ends, the spectators are not sure whether the final scenes were play-acting or the acting out of real-life relationships and emotions.

A three-level structure has been defined in these three metadramas: the audience, the characters, and, in between, the actors, who play both sides as well as the middle (Bentley, 21, 36, 38, 40). The public must become involved if only to engage in a more active intellectual and emotional participation in the dramatic experience. French surrealists made an attempt in this direction, though the radical and esoteric nature of the endeavor did not ultimately earn them a large public. However, in the 1940s and 1950s in Paris, several dramatists began to prod the audience into involvement through the structure of their plays and sometimes the restructuring of the actual theater building.

Antonin Artaud attempted a revolution in theatrical representation, largely based on ancient and Oriental drama told with an abundance of emotion and mysticism. His influence, not without noticeable ties to Pirandello, is best seen in Jean Genet. *Le Balcon* (1956) gives at once a metaphysical and a banal representation of the stage within the theater. The characters are clients of a meeting house for spontaneous trysts. They continually meet, couple, regroup, and delay departing on the balcony of this house. The balcony serves as a physical "stage," a locus set apart from the rest of the house, just as the house is set apart from the rest of society. On this balcony-stage, suspended above the main level of the house-stage, clients discuss their dissatisfaction with their lives in a language that ill suits a middle-class audience, therefore hoping to shock. Irma, the house Madame, ends the play by commanding a recasting: she faces the public and entreats them to fill the roles they have watched, if they dare.

The minimalist décor of Beckett's theater shows a modern reworking of Pirandello's theatricality. In *Fin de partie (End Game)* (1957), Beckett reduces the individuality of his characters by putting them into garbage cans. Instead of the Pirandellian device of enlarging the dramatic space, Beckett reduces it in an effort to make the locus of meaning and experience more concise and concentrated. The lack of a realistic décor brings the audience inevitably into the realm of the theater and thereby forces them to consider the reality of the illusion to which they are witness.

Ionesco's *Les Chaises* (1952) makes innovative use of stage space. While the old couple contemplate their lives, the room fills with chairs occupied by imaginary guests. Not only does the structure of the play parody the space of the theater—in this case the audience's space as well as the actors'—but it also projects the private life of the old couple into an illusory space filled with emptiness and imaginary people.

The French theater of the 1940s and 1950s cannot deny the heritage of Pirandello. Most modern French dramatists of this period admit to Pirandello's influence on their thinking. His influence continued to surface in the theater of the 1960s and the early 1970s, but by that time the typical traits of the author of *Six Characters* had become completely assimilated by the Parisian dramatic tradition and could no longer be so easily ascribed to Pirandello.

If we distinguish, in the modern French tradition, between existential theater and absurd theater by declaring Sartre, Camus, and Beauvoir more consciously intellectual than Ionesco, Beckett, and Adamov, we must also separate Pirandello from the French absurdists on the issue of the structuring of absurdity. Pirandello never claimed to systematize the absurdities of life. He is, in this sense, more postmodernist in his artistic approach to life than the French absurdists. Pirandello refused to represent life as if he understood it. His vision—and I purposely avoid the systematizing stigma of a concept such as "philosophy"—of the multiplicity of life's possibilities is entirely implicit, though entirely clear. The devices and innovations that make up the unique mark of Pirandello's theater are repeated in many of his plays, thereby becoming unmistakably his without recourse to a theoretical treatise.[4] In much the same way as his style comunicates absurdity, the repetition of subtle ideas becomes blatant. Hence, the repetition of language in the plays of the French tradition, those of Ionesco, Artaud, Audiberti, Vian, creates an unreal world that soon turns to nonsense, the absurd. In the words of the Stage Manager in *Six Characters*: "Pretence? Reality? To hell with it all!"

NOTES

1. I continue to employ the term *modern French drama,* expressly avoiding the pitfalls of more restrictive appellations, such as theater of the absurd, "le nouveau théâtre," existential theater, avant-garde theater, theater of revolt. I wish to designate by this umbrella term the theater concerned with innovations both in perceptions of the world and in devices for presenting the confused points of views without an unnatural attempt to resolve the conflict. While all French theater from World War I to the postmodernist period displays evidence of such a theatricality, most of my analysis will be directed at the Paris stage of the 1940s and early 1950s.

2. I have retained the French spelling of *pirandellisme* because it was principally in France that inferior copies of the playwright's style and themes surfaced and enjoyed a brief, box-office success. In Italy, *pirandellismo* remained a flattering epithet.

3. Pirandello uses the expression *"fuori di chiave"* in the essay *On Humor* to describe the "feeling of the opposite." He uses it again as the title of a collection of poetry, published in 1912.

4. Apart from applying the theory of humor indirectly to drama, another instance of Pirandello's theory of drama might be found in the preface to *Six Characters in Search of an Author*. Written in 1925, the short foreword acknowledges the fantasy in the author's

works and discusses the organic quality of most of the characters. The importance of the Father and the Stepdaughter in the fixity of art is made explicit.

WORKS CITED

Bentley, Eric, ed. *Naked Masks: Five Plays by Luigi Pirandello*. New York: E. P. Dutton, 1952.

Bishop, Thomas. *Pirandello and the French Theater*. New York: New York University Press, 1960.

Brustein, Robert. *The Theatre of Revolt: An Approach to the Modern Drama*. Boston: Little, Brown, 1964.

Esslin, Martin. *The Theatre of the Absurd*. Garden City, N.Y.: Anchor Books, 1969.

Firth, Felicity, ed. *Pirandello: Three Plays*. Manchester: Manchester University Press, 1969.

Giudice, Gaspare. *Pirandello: A Biography*. Trans. Alastair Hamilton. London: Oxford University Press, 1975.

Pirandello, Luigi. *Come tu mi vuoi*. Trans. Samuel Putnam. New York: Dutton, 1931.

———. *On Humor*. Trans. Antonio Illiano and Daniel Testa. Chapel Hill: University of North Carolina Press, 1960.

———. *L'Umorismo. Saggi, poesie, scritti varii*. Ed. Manlio Lo Vecchio Musti. Milan: Mondadori, 1960.

Pronko, Leonard Cabell. *Avant-Garde: The Experimental Theater in France*. Berkeley: University of California Press. 1962.

Starkie, Walter. *Luigi Pirandello: 1867–1936*. Berkeley: University of California Press, 1965.

Weiss, Auréliu. *Le Théâtre de Luigi Pirandello dans le mouvement dramatique contemporain*. Paris: Librairie 73, 1965.

20

Alter Egos: Clown Power and Enactment in Pirandello and Fo

Jana O'Keefe Bazzoni

The humorist does not recognize heroes, or rather he lets others represent them. For his part, he knows what a legend is and how it is created, what history is and how it is made: they are all compositions, more or less ideal; and the greater the pretense of reality, the more idealized they are. The humorist amuses himself by disassembling these compositions, although one cannot say that it is a pleasant amusement.

(Pirandello, *On Humor*)

My plays are provocations, like catalysts in a chemical solution. . . . I do the same thing as a clown. I just put some drops of absurdity in this calm and tranquil liquid which is society, and the reactions reveal things that were hidden before the absurdity brought them out into the open.

(Dario Fo)

"Manicomio! Buffone!"
(first night audience, *Six Characters In Search of an Author*)

In his own theoretical writings, especially in the 1908 essay *On Humor*, Pirandello was careful to distance himself from the comic writer whose interest focused on "the perception of the opposite" in contrast with the humorous writer who went beyond recognition to "the feeling of the opposite" (113). Yet his very first theatrical successes were written for Angelo Musco, the Sicilian actor described by Gaspare Giudice as "gesticulating and insisting," an invasive presence to whom Pirandello at first "felt completely alien" (106). Olga Ragusa notes that contemporary critics described Musco as "irresistible. He possesses the secret, which few have, of causing laughter. . . . He is all instinct, with his fiery eyes, his sun-burnt face, his devilish mischief, as colorful as an ancient mask." [Renato Simone]. "Most of the time he doesn't even have to say a word. . . . His legs speak for him . . . his shoulders . . . the folds of his suit . . . the brim of his hat" [Eugenio Cecchi] (69). Antonio Gramsci wrote of Musco: "his entire body becomes language, his whole body speaks" (322).

The description echoes back to those "ancient masks" and after them the *giullari* (jesters) and re-echoes from Musco's day to our own, including the film comedians Keaton and Chaplin and others, later comics such as Jacques Tati or the Italians Scarpetta, Edoardo, and Toto who through gesture and dress, needing little or no language, could bring an audience a mix of humor and pathos, comic parodies of political and social authorities, and a taste of pleasure at the at least temporary triumph of the little man, the underdog, over societal restraints and official repression and injustice.

The figure in contemporary Italian theater who best fits this description is Dario Fo: actor, archivist, activist, writer, designer, director, producer. Over the last thirty-five years, Fo's dramatic output has delighted, transformed, infuriated, astounded, and enraged. His work includes monologues and revue sketches dating from his early collaboration with Franco Parenti and continuing to the present, performed first on radio and later for live audiences and eventually on television; the 1950s absurdist one-act farces and *Comica finale,* based on nineteenth-century popular farces; the 1960s full-length farces, performed for mainstream audiences; the increasingly political post–1968 plays, sometimes based on actual, historical events; the recreated medieval texts of *Mistero buffo*; and the monologue plays, written with Franca Rame.[1]

When Fo began to work in the theater, he brought talents developed elsewhere which he was to use to great advantage: storytelling ability and a repertoire of stories overheard as a child which Fo had collected and adapted, an extraordinary ability to improvise and invent, and training in art and design. In *A Finger in the Eye* (1953), Fo worked with Jacques Lecoq, the French mime who had worked on the first Italian productions of Brecht's plays. Lecoq is credited with introducing Fo to mime and to certain vocal techniques that gave structure to his improvisations. Lecoq encouraged Fo to use his exaggerated body—long arms and legs, flat feet, long, "horselike" head and mouth, and uncoordinated body—to his advantage.[2] It is these traditional actor's techniques, in mime, improvisation, and voice, that the fool character so often at the heart of a Fo drama has borrowed to produce a uniquely effective impact on an audience.

Pirandello's acting was primarily confined to the private meetings with the actors to whom he read his new plays aloud and as a director in helping actors to realize his own work and that of other playwrights.[3] To his work in the theater he brought his own narratives, drawn from personal experience and imagination. As he was increasingly able to take part in the daily life of the theater, he adopted the theatrical sensibilities of those "theater professionals" he had once scorned ("Theatre and Literature," 1018).

Long before Pirandello began to write regularly for the theater, he had developed a way of seeing the world that relied on perception, reflection, and compassion. In *On Humor,* he wrote, "Every feeling, every thought, or every impulse that arises in the humorist immediately splits into its contrary: every affirmative into a negative, which finally ends up assuming the same value as the affirmative" (125). This "doubling," as he called it, caused the humorist writer to produce "works [that] are disorganized, disconnected, interrupted by constant digressions." These characteristics stemmed not "from the writer's eccentricities or personal whim" but were merely the result of the process of "active reflection, which evokes an association through contraries: in other words, the images, instead of being linked through similarity or juxtaposition, are presented in conflict. . . . Every genuine humorist is not only a poet, he is a critic as well, but—let us take note—a critic *sui generis,* a fantastical critic" (119). In his plays about the theater and in other of his dramas, wrote Nicola Chiaromonte, Pirandello discovered the value in replaying, repeating an acknowledged past act, a discovery rooted in Pirandello's "humorization" which Chiaromonte equates with Brecht's "distancing." "The concept of the stage action as repetition, re-enactment of an already accomplished fact (rather than simulation of a set of facts still in the course of happening) goes back to the very origins of the theatre" (31).

Pirandello and Fo are both heirs and admirers of the *commedia dell'arte* and of the earlier popular culture sources from which it drew. Pirandello, in his essay *Introduction to the Italian Theater,* faulted "learned professors of literary history" (*Introduction,* 16) who had not recognized the value of early devotional plays, written by "ingenuous poets" (15). In the same essay, Pirandello traces the evolution of the *commedia* masks from "those new, thoroughly human, and romantic adventures that already were being felt . . . among the common people . . . on a popular level" (20). In a tribute unusual for his day, Pirandello praised the actor-writers of the *commedia* such as Ruzante who knew "the pulse of the public" (23) and wrote "in the warm breath of the public" and who improvised their entertainments, "constantly revising" after trying "out on their audiences the effectiveness of certain flourishes" (24). Pirandello's championing of what he called the "riches" of the Italian theater legacy (27), as Olga Ragusa notes, gave "new dignity to the actor; the actor who is able to improvise is an author, that is a creative artist . . . " (72). Pirandello reached this position only through his work with modern-day counterparts of the *commedia,* especially actors like Musco, whose roots could still be traced back through the variety theater to *commedia* and popular farce and whose improvisations and revisions caused Pirandello difficulty but were openly acknowledged as genuine contributions to the success of the four plays he wrote for the actor.[4] Pirandello continued to enjoy a collaborative relationship with actors, particularly with Ruggero Ruggeri, Lamberto Picasso, and Marta Abba, and at the very end of his life, with Eduardo

DeFilippo. Significantly, he came at last full circle back to those popular roots through another actor, who like Musco, was linked with that great tradition.[5]

For his part, Dario Fo has remarked "the commedia dell'arte is the indispensable primer for studying what's effective on stage" and he, like Pirandello before him, has acknowledged Ruzante's importance to Italian theater history, calling him "the greatest theatrical writer that we have ever had in Italy" (Fo, Riverside Workshop, 8). He has taken up the challenge offered by Pirandello to take up "boldly with a revitalizing spirit" those "riches" of the early theater (*Introduction*, 27). Through *Mistero buffo*, Fo has introduced audiences to updated versions of medieval performance pieces and has continued the work of the *giullare*, the irreverent jester of the piazza. Both in *Mistero buffo* and in his many theater performances he and the groups he has been associated with have brought theatre to modern-day piazzas and to factories and other "found" spaces outside the boundaries of mainstream theater. Fo has found in the figure of the *giullare* a medieval alter ego capable of playing "as many as 15 characters" and has capitalized on the *giullare*'s "necessity of doing everything on his own" in many of the *Mistero buffo* texts (Mitchell, 23). In his research, adaptation, and performance of medieval texts, Fo has found evidence of the collaborative nature of the audience-actor relationship and of its effect: "even the most able inventions of the *giullare* required audience participation. The play of allusions and the collaboration of the audience who picked them up, redoubled the poetic and comic charge" (23).

Few parallels in the drama of Pirandello and Fo have thus far been drawn, perhaps because their considerable differences have obscured certain correspondences in their work. Recent writers, however, have considered the presence of similar motifs and devices in the work of each playwright. For example, both playwrights have separately been linked to the Carnival tradition. Elio Gianola, in *Pirandello la follia* (1983), compares Pirandello's poetics with Bakhtin's theories and asserts that the carnivalesque and the humorous are similar worldviews, although Pirandello specifically links his notion of humor to particular psychological conditions present in the humorist writer. In a 1987 article in *Modern Drama*, I traced carnival ritual elements as a recurring motif throughout Pirandello's drama. Martin Walsh examined carnivalesque elements in Fo's *We Won't Pay, We Won't Pay*, calling the play a "proletarian carnival" (211). Joel Schechter in *Durov's Pig*, his 1985 study of "clowns, politics and theatre," describes Fo as "a one-man carnival" whose ability to transform himself "fosters a comic, carnival vision of society in which (as Bakhtin said of Rabelais's carnivalesque world), people become interchangeable within their mass body" (154).

Fo, of course, is widely recognized as a playwright and performer whose work is aimed at raising political consciousness in its audience and achieving political and social change. Richard Sogliuzzo once referred to Fo as "Italy's foremost practitioner of AgitProp theatre" ("Puppets," 72). Numerous articles and essays since have focused on this aspect of his work, including Joel Schechter's recent chapter on Fo in *Durov's Pig,* his book on political clowning. Pirandello's work has most often been studied for its themes and techniques, while little emphasis has been placed on the sociological or political aspects of his work. Some writers, however, have made mention of social concerns that underlie his narrative and drama. Eric Bentley, in *The Playwright As Thinker,* recognized that Pirandello, like his contemporaries, "i grotteschi," utilized the mask and face "antithesis" in its "broader meaning of the social form, identified with tyranny, and the individual soul which it sought to crush" (150). Gramsci recognized Pirandello's social voice in his novels and plays set in Sicily, and this view has more recently been explored by several scholars whose work appears in the anthology *Pirandello dialettale* (1983).

In both playwrights, the notion of "the theater in the theater" is important, as are the related Pirandellian concerns of multiple identity, role-playing, reality versus illusion, and the relativity of truth.[6] Both Pirandello and Fo have frequently used a central fool or clown figure in their plays. As modern clowns, these central figures combine and transform the traditional properties and functions of the fool (country bumpkin, court jester, merrymaker, trickster, scourge, and scapegoat) in order to become Bakhtin's "constant accredited representatives of the carnival spirit out of carnival season" (8). These clown figures embody "special" abilities to transform themselves and to engage in role play with others, to present others. They recognize, accept, and even revel in this ability and provide a constant reminder of a theatrical presence in their very being. These figures use openly theatrical devices such as direct address, narrative commentary, and the deliberate acknowledgment of the action as enactment. They serve as critical commentators on the stage life being presented and by implication or specific reference on contemporary social and cultural life. On the significance of the clown figure, Fo has remarked:

Clowns concretize our obsessions, our fears, our desires. They act out our repressions and transgress our taboos. They laugh, they cry, they fall down, they jump up. They play out for us the absurdities of our life. They're also violent and cruel. It's the cruelty of clowns that appeals most to children. Clowns are grotesque blasphemers against our pieties. That's why we need them. They're our alter egos (*ART News* interview, 6).

A central clown figure and the use of Pirandellian motifs and devices related to identity appear to be important characteristics in the work of Pirandello and Fo, providing a meta-theatrical sensibility to the personal and social concerns which are the subject matter of the dramas. The examination of carnival elements in the plays of Pirandello and Fo has initiated a discussion of parallels in the work of the two playwrights. An analysis of the function and significance of the central clown character and Pirandellian motifs and theatrical devices in the plays offers an opportunity to explore correspondences and contrasts in the work of these playwrights.

William Willeford in a 1969 book, *The Fool and His Sceptor,* defines the fool/jester/clown figure: "The fool actor stands somewhere between the reality, possibly horrible, of idiocy or madness and its character as a show, something to be entertained by, and, if taken seriously, loved rather than despised" (10). Willeford notes that, although "clown" in modern times has been most closely identified with the circus, fool and clown "quite early became more or less synonymous" (12). I will use both terms and the allied term, jester, in this discussion interchangeably.[7]

Clowns may be exploited and treated as inferiors, as idiots. Or they may be adept at manipulating formal social codes and the social authorities. They may be naive, or knowing, or they may be sorrowing. They are elusive, hard to pin down, and they seem to have an uncanny ability to survive. The fool is catastrophic for order and always brings chaos, from which he himself may escape and even remain miraculously unaware of as he leaves ruin in his path. Or he may combine knowingness with fooling as do many characters in Pirandello and Fo. These central figures may often be outsiders, and they may demonstrate their difference from others through appearance, through speech and gesture, and through a heightened mental state. Clowns are meta-theatrical because they are generally aware of presenting themselves to the world as a part of a clown show, in some kind of mask. Clowns are actors and acknowledge this feature in themselves, and may induce this acknowledgment in others. As a meta-theatrical figure, the clown quite naturally uses costume, makeup and disguise, props, even scenery; the clown also uses rhetorical strategies such as monologue, dialogue, direct address or narration, polemic, and dramatic invention in shifting identities, improvised plots, and impromptu performances. Clowns may operate alone, or they may work in pairs or groups. Frequently, there is a straight man in the pair, and much of the action has to do with their crosstalk.

The clown's difference is frequently signaled by a physical deformity such as a limp or hump or an ungainly or grotesque face with one peculiar feature, or a body whose parts seems ungainly and out of control. The clown's wardrobe is often unconventional or at least slightly "wrong." Willeford contends that at the extreme, clown costume is made up of "chaotic and disproportionate elements" (15), which may or may not be reconciled with one another. Or the costume may be part of an obvious disguise, a see-through disguise much as in child's play. The costume may include animal references. These costumes are often accompanied by a prop of some sort, or by an object or related series of objects in the clown's environment. These objects might include sticks (derivations of the slapstick, perhaps), a cap with bells, mirrors, or other seeing derivations, such as spectacles.

The clown's speech may be babble, may be an extended turn, along with a partner, great quantities of unrelated talk, or it may be a prodigious display of oratory. Using his fool's license and his jester's reason, the clown may have great powers of persuasion, may act as pedant, lawyer, or judge, and may turn the tables on authority by showing superior knowledge of the "master's" field.

Or the fool may use exaggerated gesture or other physical display or silence as part of his show, as a substitute or corollary of speech (29).

Pirandellian characters who have clown attributes and functions appear in the Sicilian dialect plays written for Musco—*Think About It, Giacomino!*, *The Jar*, *Cap and Bells, Liolà*, as well as in plays such as *The License, The Pleasure of Honesty, The Rules of the Game, It Is So (If You Think So), Henry IV, Tonight We Improvise*, and *The Mountain Giants*. These clowning characters are Professor Toti, Zi Dima, Ciampa, Liolà, Chiarchiaro, Baldovino, Leone, Laudisi, perhaps the Ponza/Frola trio, "Henry," Hinkfuss, Sampognetta, Cotrone and his collaborators, and the traveling theater company headed by Ilse.

Here are some of the physical cues Pirandello gives us in this collection of characters: Zi Dima's hump which causes him to get stuck in the prized jar; his broken spectacles, held together by cord and carefully carried in a handkerchief, his magic pot of glue; Ciampa's long, threadbare coat, his "long mustaches and acute, mobile, slightly insane eyes," the pen, his signature object, behind his ear. Chiarchiaro, made up to look like a man with the Evil Eye: "a rough tangled beard; a pair of huge bone-rimmed spectacle . . . a glossy, mouse-colored suit that bulges out in every direction, and he carries a bamboo cane with a handle made of horn. His pace is funereal and at every heavy step he strikes the cane on the ground." Henry IV—"very pale. The hair on the back of his head is already grey; over the temples and forehead it appears blond, owing to its having been tinted in an evident and inexperienced fashion. On his cheek bones he has two small, doll-like dabs of color, that stand out prominently against the rest of his tragic pallor. He is wearing a penitent's sack over his regal habit, as at Canossa." And imagine grotesquely tiny Hinkfuss, with his wild clown's head of hair, Cotrone with his unkempt beard, his splayed feet, large oversized jacket and pants, his Turkish fez, surrounded by a gang of clowns of grotesque appearance.

Each of these characters treats us to clown speech in the way of extended address and intensive argument: Ciampa's "three keys"; Henry's improvisation on his historical namesake and lecturing of the false courtiers and visitors; Hinkfuss's direct address oratory to the audience and harangues to the actors; Laudisi's insistent baiting of the household. Clown-related manipulations include game-playing: Professor Toto, Leone, Laudisi, Zi Dima, Liolà, Henry; enactments: Ciampa, Chiarchiaro, Henry, Hinkfuss, Cotrone; argument: Toto, Chiarchiaro, Ciampa, Laudisi; tricks: Cotrone, Chiarchiaro, Henry, Liolà, Hinkfuss.

Clowns and clown "sight gags, songs and stunts" (Sogliuzzo, "Dario Fo," 72) have always been recognized as a hallmark of Fo's plays. Plays that use clowning figures include *A Finger in the Eye, Archangels Don't Play Pinball, Throw the Lady Out, Accidental Death of an Anarchist, We Won't Pay, We Won't Pay, About Face, The Sneering Opera*, and *Almost by Chance a Woman: Elizabeth*.

Clowning in Fo is physical and verbal: slapstick, *lazzi*, pratfalls, doubling, men playing women's roles. In addition to elements of the grotesque, Fo includes more of the purely comic. There are only flashes of depth in the characters; these are largely the surface characters of farce, playing on the situation more than on character. Clowning speech is a series of one-liners or a double clown act or the extended type of joke Fo refers to as *tormentone* (extended torment) in which a character unseats the power of authority by a series of small but insistent irritations and insults, a technique Fo has elaborated from its original form, attributed to Italian comedian Toto.[8]

Often in Fo's plays, clowning behavior centers primarily in a clown "innocent" who questions authority. One example is Lungo (Lucky) in *Archangels Don't Play Pinball*, the outsider in a gang of clowns. He's the butt of the gang's jokes, seems to be a simpleton, and has been damned with a silly name. This is probably the most sentimental of Fo's plays, but it has much clowning throughout the play, both physical and verbal: knockabouts, slapstick, various *lazzi*, such as chair passing, a fake doctor, men dressed as women, pratfalls, doubling. One actor takes on many roles and is continuously recognized in his transparent, clownish disguise. In *Archangels*, Lucky is a knave pretending to be a simpleton for his living. He is transformed through a dream in which he has to become a dog in order to regain status as a human.

A clown fall precipitates much of the action as it knocks out Lucky, whose dream becomes the stage action. Lucky, the apparent fool, is a trickster who earns his living by playing the patsy for his friends. Typically, he is physically different, with a disability that prevents him from being "a man." He calls himself a "poor man's Rigoletto," in acknowledgment of his role as a professional clown who alternates between fool and jester modes, using idiocy as a refuge and, ultimately, as a weapon. In the dream sequence, Lucky undergoes a journey. Through a series of exposure sequences, Lucky reveals the corruption of authority and the bureaucracy that serves authority. When he finds that a series of government clerks (the Act I friends wearing clown wigs) have staged their own rebellion against the "system" by deliberately altering records and that he has been given a new identity as a dog, he demands a license and begins to take charge, to fight back. Escaping from his dog's life, he steals a government official's trousers and his mistress (who is none other than the prostitute Angela with whom Lungo has fallen in love in Act I). Eventually, Lungo impersonates the official and runs away with the girl. The transformation, which occurs in the dream, carries over after Lungo's "awakening." Fo effects a crossover of dream and reality when Lungo and Angela recognize each other from the dream sequence. In this piece, Fo begins to differentiate one clown character who will be central to the play's action and in some cases will be transformed by it. Giovanni, in *We Won't Pay, We Won't Pay*, is another such transformed fool.

In *Accidental Death of an Anarchist*, the game is more focused, more violent, more palpably dangerous, and still more extravagantly clownesque. The central figure is a madman, who is a physical construction (he has a false eye, hand, and leg) with a series of false identities as his personal history. The Madman's constructed outer self suggests Pirandello's notion of *costruirsi* and bears a resemblance to Dürrenmatt's grotesque heroine in *The Visit*. During the course of the play, the madman/fool/suspect (brought in on charges of impersonating a psychiatrist) plays an Inspector and while maintaining that guise plays a Scientific Specialist, a Bishop, an anarchic Madman, a judge, and finally an unidentified character with a beard. Impersonating, making actor's choices, the Madman chooses for his Inspector's persona a "cold, detached commanding tone, monotonous voice, sad, somewhat nearsighted look, and a monocle." We see him choose the proper walk, a "wall-eyed look," the right voice and mannerism. To finish off his character, he costumes himself in the real Inspector's dark overcoat, hat, and briefcase (22–23). Later, this reveals a clown briefcase when, as judge, he withdraws from it a magnifying glass, tweezer, staples, judge's mallet, and a copy of the legal code (29). He makes disorder of the police office, with their complicity, for he has convinced them he is working on their behalf to get out the "real" story of an anarchist's accidental death, the story the police want told their way. Throughout, it is the Madman, an acknowledged "histromaniac" (11) with the need to role play, who directs the action, impersonating others together with the supporting cast of police officers to whom he suggests lines as might a prompter. As director, he asks his actors to replay their lines, gives them ideas for improvisations, and rehearses them through various "versions" of the story. He becomes, in effect, the *capocomico* in his own acting company with a supporting cast of the authorities Fo has written the play to indict.

The audience knows—or thinks it does—that the Madman is merely a fool, but his identity remains elusive and ambiguous, especially when the Madman reveals an expert's knowledge of bomb construction. Is the Madman an anarchist? Fo uses several alienation or distancing devices in the piece, including direct address and audience acknowledgment. But counter notes to this are struck by audience plants who act as government agents. The Madman warns the audience that these are just actors, but there are no doubt real government agents seated among them. Pirandello's theater plays anticipate Foian (and Brechtian) techniques used to keep the audience conscious of message. Countering the process of identification, Fo creates deliberate confusion between real life and stage illusion as the boundaries between stage and audience overlap and are transgressed, a technique he has also used on other occasions.[9]

In plays in which the fool/clown character dominates, there is a Carnival reversal of roles: the fool becomes leader, and there is an unmasking of social roles and theatrical subterfuge. The art of transformation is celebrated and empowered, self-transformation functions for the good of others and for the independence of the self, as a joke with a purpose: to amuse, to escape punishment, to escape reality, to trick death, to celebrate change and renewal. There are elements of shock and surprise, the unexpected unease of spectator; spectators are involved but may also be surprised and discomforted by not knowing everything, by being fooled. Rules are suspended or reinvented, roles are exchanged, disguises are multiple and appearance deceptive; gaming devices catch the audience up, may leave them breathless, and the games may turn serious.

Both Pirandello and Fo develop the clown figure in the course of their own development as playwrights. Early clown types tend to be undifferentiated, generic; they engage in more obviously physical and gratuitous kinds of comedy. Later clown figures are less "knowable" and effect more substantive action. They use tricks, games, and violence to expose individual and social fictions and crimes, and they may emerge as actors on behalf of others, as "authorized" (see Wilshire and Bakhtin). At times the clown's freedom to act comes through madness—the character portrayed may be a madman (sometimes in disguise as sane, or at least controlled; sometimes a confusion of madness and sanity) able to perform miracles of performance in an explosion of "sanity" and an exposure of social, personal, and political fraud and corruption. The fool becomes *the* voice crying out in the wild, and madman/fool, the crosser of boundaries both from real to surreal and from hell to paradise.

Pirandello's most sophisticated clown types are most effective, unsettling, and dangerous: Laudisi, Leone, "Enrico," Hinkfuss, Cotrone. These figures all have an undisclosed, tragic, or "entrapped" personal history. Yet whatever the degree of suffering they may be experiencing, they retain some control over their situation. As is true of carnival fools, these characters are allowed free reign; they are safe and simultaneously vulnerable; they take risks and may manipulate and even harm others in order to preserve their right to their peculiar kind of fool's freedom. Even as we feel compassion for these figures, as Pirandello intended, we also feel revulsion and fear; we do not dare to embrace these heroes as they retreat to their self-imposed isolation. They stand isolated, exposed, distanced, and yet strangely empowered.

As Fo develops the clown figures in his plays, they become increasingly "Brechtian" presenters. Their personal histories may be undisclosed, not internalized or made visible, or their identities may be patently false (as in the Madman), and what underlies the falsity is unrevealed. What matters is not the knowledge of their personal angst or tragic history but their function as social agents of exposure and judgment. Fo's clowns, such as the Madman in *Accidental Death* and the *giullare* Fo represents as he enacts *Mistero buffo*, assume other identities and represent other voices who question the status quo. They not only speak out but act as judges. As in Pirandello's theater plays, they are able to do this with fewer stage trappings, or with illusions exposed, for the focus is on the gap filler, the actor, who both fills and deliberately creates critical gaps in order to bring home the lesson more clearly. Barbara Babcock, in an article on ritual clowning, remarks: "The clown's performance . . . disrupts and interrupts customary frames and expected logic and syntax and creates a reflexive and ironic dialogue, an open space of questioning" (107).

In Fo's piece, "The Birth of the Giullare" from *Mistero buffo*, the *giullare* first calls his audience's attention to him, as though giving a *piazza* performance. After he tells the story of his sufferings, the piece ends with his being given the gift of a tongue. He is transformed by Jesus into a *giullare,* and as translator and performer Ron Jenkins points out: "As he viciously satirizes the landowner with a tongue that now has the power to cut like a knife, it slowly becomes apparent that the piece is ending where it had begun. The *giullare* is again shouting for the public's attention in the piazza, but now his actions resonate with indignation and the memory of the injustices he has suffered . . . as in all of Fo's work, the cadences of the comedy echo the rhythms of revolt" (14–15). As Jenkins remarks, the piece can be read as "a kind of self-reflective poetics on the art of the epic clown" (14). And we might add, Fo has brought his audience from the perception of the opposite to the feeling of the opposite and has aroused the stirrings of new understandings about the nature of the comic gift, its value, and its mandate as antiauthoritarian voice of the people.

Both Pirandello and Fo demonstrate their apparently innate affinity for what Leszek Kolakowski termed the "philosophy of the jester,"

a philosophy which in every epoch denounces as doubtful what appears as unshakeable; it points out the contradiction in what seems evident and incontestable; it ridicules common sense and reads sense into the absurd—in other words it undertakes the daily toil of the jester's profession along with the inevitable risk of appearing ludicrous (233).

Like those members of the first-night audience at Pirandello's *Six Characters in Search of an Author* who shouted "Manicomio! Buffone!" and like some of Fo's many critics, it is only natural that those at whom the jester points may deride and condemn or exile him when he goes too far, exposes too much. But for those of us whose voices are invoked in the jester's toil, let us celebrate the potential as well as the risk in the ludicrous and let us welcome and applaud the challenge of the jester's laughter.

Catharsis can be achieved only in a community as a result of a social ritual. It transcends the individual; it enlarges the individual. . . . It is the confrontation of a society with its gods and its devils (Fo, *ART News* interview, 6)

The Theater offers what might properly be called a public trial of human actions as they truly are, in that pure and everlasting reality which the imagination of poets creates as an example and a warning for our commonplace and confused natural life—a trial both free and human, which spurs the conscience of the judges themselves to an ever loftier and more rigorous moral life (Pirandello, *Introduction* 14).

NOTES

1. For an English-language survey of Fo's work through 1983, see Mitchell's *Dario Fo: People's Court Jester.* Mitchell's work also includes a selected bibliography of books and articles by and about Fo in both English and Italian.

2. This brief reference to Fo's work with Lecoq appears in the short article on Fo by Chiara Valentini in the *Enciclopedia internazionale di teatro.* On Fo's biography and

work, see Valentini, Binni, Meldolesi, Puppa (all in Italian) as well as Mitchell, Schechter, and Jenkins.

3. On Pirandello's acting abilities, as recounted by his contemporaries, see Sogliuzzo.

4. On Musco's career, see Sarah Zappulla Muscara's "Pirandello, Martoglio e Musco:sodalizi e baruffe" in *Pirandello dialettale*, 119–59.

5. For a description of this last collaborative effort, see Mignone's *Edoardo De Filippo*.

6. Albert Bermel notes that it was Pirandello who "gave new currency to the play within a play as conscientiously as Brecht did to the aside and the soliloquy" (338). Fo, of course, has combined Brechtian and Pirandellian techniques.

7. In the discussion of the clown or fool's characteristic attributes, I follow Willeford who attempts to see through "the fool show" to the nature of the fool, his properties, and effects.

8. Fo discusses Toto's comic technique in "Toto: The Violence of the Marionette and the Mask," in *Theater* (Summer/Fall 1987): 6–12.

9. One very effective use of this type of confounding of stage-life barriers occurred during performances of Fo's *The People's War in Chile*, when the audience was tricked into believing a coup d'etat was taking place in the theater. See Chiara Valentini's account of sample performances of the play in *Theater* (Summer/Fall 1983): 54.

WORKS CITED

Babcock, Barbara. "Arrange Me into Disorder: Fragments and Reflections on Ritual Clowning." *Rite, Drama, Festival, Spectacle*. Ed. John J. MacAloon. Philadelphia: ISHI, 1984.

Bakhtin, Mikhail. *Rabelais and His World*. Trans. Helen Iswolsky. Bloomington: Indiana University Press, 1984.

Bentley, Eric. *The Playwright As Thinker*. New York: Harcourt, Brace & World, 1967.

Bermel, Albert. *Farce*. New York: Simon and Schuster, 1982.

Binni, Lanfranco. *Attento te!* . . . Verona: Bertani, 1975.

Chiaromonte, Nicola. "Clothing the Naked." Trans. Mary McCarthy and Ronald Strom. *New York Review of Books* (February 10, 1975):30–31.

Fo, Dario. *Accidental Death of an Anarchist*. Trans. Suzanne Cowan. Adapted by Richard Nelson. New York: Samuel French, 1987.

———. *Archangels Don't Play Pinball*. London: Methuen Ltd., 1987.

———. "Dario Fo: Andiamo a Ridere." *ART News*. Interviewer Arthur Holmberg. Vol. 7, No. 4 (1987):1 & 6.

———. *Le commedie di Dario Fo*, Vol. 1–6. Torino: Einaudi, 1966–1988.

———. "Popular Culture," translated by Tony Mitchell. *Theater* 14, No. 3 (1983): 50–54.

———. "Toto: The Violence of the Marionette and the Mask." *Theater*, 18, No. 3 (1987): 6–12.

———. and Franca Rame. *Dario Fo and Franca Rame Theatre Workshops at Riverside Studios*. London: Red Notes, 1983.

———. *We Won't Pay! We Won't Pay!* Trans. R. G. Davis. New York: Samuel French, Inc., 1984.

Gianola, Elio. *Pirandello la follia*. Genoa: il Melangolo, 1983.

Giudice, Gaspare. *Pirandello*. Trans. Alastair Hamilton. London: Oxford University Press, 1975.

Gramsci, Antonio. *Letteratura e vita nazionale*. Turin: Einaudi, 1974.

Jenkins, Ron. "Clowns, Politics and Miracles." *American Theatre* 9, No. 3 (1986):11–17.

Kolakowski, Leszek. "The Priest and the Jester." *Dissent* 9 (1962):215–35.

Meldolesi, Claudio. *Su un comico in rivolta*. Roma: Bulzoni, 1978.

Mignone, Mario. *Eduardo De Filippo*. Boston: Twayne Publishing, 1984.

Mitchell, Tony. *Dario Fo: People's Court Jester*. London: Methuen Ltd., 1984.

O'Keefe Bazzoni, Jana. "The Carnival Motif in Pirandello's Drama." *Modern Drama* 30, No. 3 (1987):414–25.

Pirandello, Luigi. "Introduction to the Italian Theater." Trans. Anne Paolucci. *The Genius of the Italian Theater*. Ed. Eric Bentley. New York: New American Library, 1964. Now reprinted in *Review of National Literatures, Pirandello* 14 (1987): 11–30.

———. *Naked Masks, Five Plays*. Ed. Eric Bentley. New York: E. P. Dutton, 1952.

———. *On Humor*. Trans. Antonio Illiano and Daniel P. Testa. Chapel Hill: University of North Carolina Press, 1974.

———. *Pirandello's One Act Plays*. Trans. William Murray. New York: Samuel French, Inc., 1970.

———. *Sicilian Comedies*. Trans. Norman A. Bailey and Roger W. Oliver. New York: Performing Arts Journal Publications, 1983.

———. "Theatre and Literature." *Opere di Luigi Pirandello, 6: Saggi, poesie e scritti varii*. Milan: Mondadori Editore, 1960. 1018–1024.

Puppa, Paolo. *Il teatro di Dario Fo*. Venice: Marsilio, 1978.

Ragusa, Olga. *Pirandello*. Edinburgh: Edinburgh University Press, 1980.

Schechter, Joel, "Dario Fo: The Clown as Counter-Informer." *Durov's Pig*. New York: Theatre Communications Group, 1985. 142–47.

Sogliuzzo, Richard. "Dario Fo: Puppets for Proletarian Revolution." *The Drama Review* 16, No. 3 (1972):71–77.

———. *Luigi Pirandello, Director*. Metuchen, N.J., and London: Scarecrow Press, 1982.

Valentini, Chiara. "Dario Fo." *Enciclopedia internazionale di teatro*. Ed. Antonio Attisani. Milan. 1980.

Walsh, Martin W. "The Proletarian Carnival of Fo's *Non si paga! Non si paga!*." *Modern Drama* 27, No. 2 (1985):211–22.

Willeford, William. *The Fool and His Sceptor*. Evanston, Ill.: Northwestern University Press, 1969.

Wilshire, Bruce. *Role Playing and Identity*. Bloomington: Indiana University Press, 1982.

Zappulla Muscara, Sarah, ed. *Pirandello dialettale*. Palermo: G. B. Palumbo & Co., 1983.

Part Five

PIRANDELLO'S WORK IN PRODUCTION

21

Interviews with Robert Brustein and Sandro Sequi

John Louis DiGaetani

BRUSTEIN

Robert Brustein was a founding director of the Yale Repertory Theater and is the artistic director of the American Repertory Theater in Cambridge, Massachusetts. A professor of English at Harvard University, he is also director of Harvard's Loeb Drama Center. He has written nine books on the theater, the most recent being *Who Needs Theater* (1987), for which he won his second George Jean Nathan Award for dramatic criticism, and he also writes drama criticism for the *New Republic*. I spoke with Mr. Brustein in New York City in July 1988 while he was preparing his production of *Six Characters in Search of an Author* for the Joyce Theater as part of the New York International Festival of the Arts.

DiGaetani: Within the last few years you've directed *Six Characters in Search of an Author, Right You Are (If you Think You Are)*, and *Tonight We Improvise*. So you've had substantial experiences as a director of Pirandello. What do you feel are the main problems for the director in staging Pirandello for contemporary American audiences?

Brustein: I think the problems vary from play to play. In This theater plays, one has to find some way to adapt Pirandello's notion of the theater to the American notion of theater because they are different. In *Six Characters*, for example, I think credibility collapses if you do the play precisely the way it's written—involving an Italian company with the leading lady and the character actress, and all those generic types of an Italian theatre company of the 1920s. If you introduce those types rehearsing an Italian play, the audience won't believe they're entering a real rehearsal. So I felt that it was important to change the opening, the framework into which those characters walk, to something that an American can see as American, a play that an American theater company might actually be rehearsing. So in that case, it was our actual company playing under their own names, rehearsing a production of *Sganarelle* to play on an actual tour, rehearsing an actor, in this case Peter Gerety, into a part he has not yet played. So we have to rehearse him into the part. This is actually true; we were rehearsing him into a part of the play, which we're taking to Madrid in September. This is what we did with *Six Characters*. With *Tonight We Improvise* again the play is about a company, an Italian company, once again led by a Max Reinhardt-type director. The difference from *Six Characters* is that in this case the company is aware of the audience and playing before an audience, and improvising a play before an audience. And there once again, we felt it necessary to establish credibility; our company did it by improvising a play based on a Pirandello short story, and that's the way we advertised it. (*Tonight We Improvise* actually was based on a Pirandello short story, "*Leonora, Addio*.") After that, we adhered strictly to Pirandello's script, except adapting it to a situation which we think was more convincing to audiences. I didn't invent this; actually, Julian Beck invented it in his production of the play with the Living Theater in 1960. He was the director and was listed in the program as Julian Beck. Since I directed this production, I became the director, under my own name Bob Brustein, and there was a certain self-reflectiveness about the situation, but only in order to reinforce and underline the credibility of Pirandello in this setup, in order to have you believe that these actors are improvising this play, and ultimately they throw the director out of the play and go on to finish the scene.

DiGaetani: In other words, in some ways Pirandello's plays are dated?

Brustein: It's not that they're dated, it's that they are designed for another culture and another ambiance. He himself, in his article on the Italian theater, urged directors to adapt and modernize plays since the theater is a collaborative art; as long as you preserve the spirit of the play, then you are free to adapt the letter of the play. With *Right You Are*, the adaptation was probably more problematical, although I'll stand by it. In that case once again we are in an Italian setting, and I thought that play was sufficiently about a present problem of our own time, namely, the intrusion of private lives by public officials and the media, in particular prying reporters, that we changed the milieu of the play to a Cambridge suburb, set it in the living room of a newspaper reporter, and made Mr. Ponza into a character who had come from Kansas to Boston to take a job on the circulation department of a newspaper. It is *he* they are investigating, and prying into, as they pry into the privates lives of various politicians— as in the case of Joe Biden and Ted Kennedy. That was the change we made.

DiGaetani: What you're saying is that the plays need some adaptation so that the situations reflect contemporary American realities.

Brustein: In certain cases yes, and in certain cases no. I mean, there are plays of Pirandello's that I would never touch. I would simply leave them in their Italian settings. But these two plays need adaptation.

DiGaetani: You had mentioned improvisation. Of course, improvisation is one of Pirandello's major themes. There's a long tradition of Italian theater from *commedia dell'arte* improvising, and the comedies of Plautus and Terence earlier, all the way up to the present. Do you feel that this approach to theater demands a particular improvisational style, and how do you direct your actors and actresses to develop an improvisational style suitable to Pirandello?

Brustein: The ironic, paradoxical thing about Pirandello's approach to improvisation is that he writes out all the improvisations. In *Tonight We Improvise*, they are all written, and there seems to be no leeway for actors to improvise. So we felt it necessary to reestablish that latitude in that play, as well as in *Six Characters*. I wrote a fairly strict and relatively faithful adaptation, only making adjustments for the American-ness of the actors and the actresses, then let them proceed to improvise around their own characters. It's interesting what happens when you do this because I had one character in a Pirandello play who was showing up late. I had Harry Murphy play that character, and he protested, saying he is never late. So every move we made tried to reflect and reinforce Pirandello's point about the relationship between reality and illusion.

DiGaetani: But in terms of improvisation, is any necessary?

Brustein: It is necessary. For the same reasons that we adapted the play to an American company and an American environment, it is necessary in order to establish credibility, in order to create a situation which an audience will buy as a real improvisational performance. And I must say I'm very proud of our actors because they can give an appearance of extreme naturalness to written language, and as I told you, are now playing with a half improvised, half actually established script. But with the six characters themselves, the parts are fairly closed, and what the actors say should always be about the same. The hardest thing we have really is to get the Father to say exactly what he says to the Stepdaughter, and then to have the actor playing the Father try to imitate exactly what the Father is saying because an actor's tendency is always to change the lines. American actors never like to deal with lines as written. Even in Shakespeare, you find them changing lines; we had an actress in the company who almost totally revised her part in the script. It is a fact about American actors that they feel very central to any collaborative effort. They feel that they can always improve on any play-wright's work, making the language more amenable to what an actor says. So naturally, there is a lot of improvisation from that point of view. I think of Pirandello as the perfect playwright for those kinds of actors. He is a playwright for a Stanislavsky-trained actor. But he is a playwright for a Stanislavsky-trained actor who can also improvise, and of course Stanis-lavsky put a great deal of emphasis upon improvisation.

DiGaetani: How do you feel contemporary American audiences respond to Pi-randello?

Brustein: Well, so far they've loved him. We've run through a variety of re-actions. *Six Characters* seems to be universally admired, with tiny exceptions here and there. *Right You Are* split the critics right down the middle. We got two headline reviews: one said *"Right You Are* Is All Wrong," and the other was *"Right You Are* Is Right On the Mark." Underneath them we wrote *"Right You Are (If You Think You Are),"* which is our attitude towards the critics, that they too were entitled to think they were right. But as Pirandello pointed out, there is no absolute judgment to be made about anything in life. So, there was a divided reaction to the production, although our audiences seemed to like it very much. *Tonight We Improvise* was the most controversial of all. In a way I was most proud of that production because it did make the audience terribly uneasy, and at the same time very confused about what was actually real and what wasn't. Critics who hadn't read the play, for example, accused me of writing my own play, whereas I didn't deviate from Pirandello's lines at all except to adapt them to our own situation; it was all Pirandello from start to finish. So the critics were really crediting me with what Pirandello wrote, and of course since that director was such a fatuous fool, I had to do a little self-satire on myself, and they didn't get that at all. They didn't realize that there was self-mockery going on, that we were kidding our own penchant for experimentation, our own penchant for playing with plays—all those things that were criticized, were actually in the play as satire. Pirandello allows you to do that; he's wonderful.

DiGaetani: The audiences were largely positive in terms of accepting and en-joying what Pirandello was doing—over fifty years ago.

Brustein: I think audiences are really prepared for a lot of Pirandello. He is the only great, unexplored, unproduced playwright of our times, and it's time to do all his plays.

DiGaetani: How do you feel about translations currently available?

Brustein: Well, obviously I'm not very happy with the translations of the plays that I did, or else I would have used them. I don't know if you can do a good translation; someone associated with a company can do a good trans-lation for that company, for a particular theater program. Take *Each In His*

Own Way. How do you do that play unless you find a scandal in your own town and adapt the play to that scandal? We were thinking of doing that play and doing it around the Klaus von Bulow scandal, which took place in Newport, not far from Boston. And, in fact, a few of the principal players in that scandal actually lived in Boston—for example, Alan Dershowitz, who I actually called and asked if he wanted to be in that play, to be in the audience protesting what was going on on stage.

DiGaetani: What did he say?

Brustein: He was very happy to do it. I was thinking of getting Alexandra Isles, who is an actress, as you know, to play herself in the audience protesting the actress who was playing her. The trouble with that is you can only do it once. I mean, once you've done the play on opening night, it's over because the secret is out and it's no longer a surprise. But you have to do something with that play in order to make it work.

DiGaetani: What advice would you give other directors who share your enthusiasm for Pirandello and would like to do some of his plays?

Brustein: I think every director is going to approach Pirandello in his or her own way, and I wouldn't presume to give advice. All I know is what I need to do, what I feel I need to do, in each of the productions I did. Pirandello both encourages and stimulates a pluralism in theater because there can be dozens, hundreds, thousands of productions of *Six Characters*, and every one of them is going to be different. For example, this is what we do for the entrance of the Six Characters in our production: the loading door of the theater rises, and framed against a bright, white background these Six Characters stand swaying back and forth. They are seen through a scrim, which is actually the drop from *Sganarelle*, which the actors are rehearsing. The scrim goes transparent and we see the Characters through the scrim. The scrim is raised, and then they come to the stage and enact their scenes. At the very end of the play, after they've disappeared and the Director is left alone in a dark theater, instead of simply saying ''Reality or illusion! Who cares? Let's get out of here,'' the Director only asks that the lights be turned out, and the house goes dark. The Director then complains bitterly about the fact that he hasn't been left enough light to get off the stage, and suddenly through the scrim we see the loading door rise again and there are the Six Characters seen through the scrim, and the Director looks at them for about four or five seconds and suddenly all six fall forward on their faces—it's a cut out, polaroid photograph.

DiGaetani: Sounds fascinating.

Brustein: It always gets a gasp. Also, a mirror plays a very important part in this production. As you know, it plays a very important part in Pirandello's vision of the theater and his vision of life—*teatro del specchio*, he called it. In this production the Stepfather asks that the mirror be brought in to project the stage for the scene, and we bring in a large dance mirror because there's no other mirror around. So, it's generally brought in from the flies; it's used by the company for movement classes. And the Six Characters play their scene in front of the mirror. Even before they play their scene, the Stepfather conjures up Madame Pace, who in our production is Emilio Paz, a Hispanic pimp. The mirror becomes transparent and Paz is seen through the mirror. Everything is exactly duplicated in front of the mirror into the room we see behind the mirror, because a whole room has materialized behind the mirror. So where we had used a wooden bench for the couch, there is a real couch behind the mirror; and where there is a false rolling rack for the actors, there is now a genuine rolling rack; there's a window with the wind blowing through it. You see the real room behind the mirror, but it's exactly duplicated in front by props. And what's even more interesting is that this mirror is not only transparent, but it projects the images from in front of the mirror into the room. So when the Step-daughter sits down on the bench, she sits down with Paz, who is sitting on the couch, and her image is sitting on the couch with Paz. So when he smacks her in the face, you see his hand smack her face. This effect duplicates the notion of Pirandello's—the difference between the stage reality and the real reality. We have changed also the situation of the little girl dying in the fountain; people don't die in a fountain unless it's a huge fountain. We changed it to a pond, and the pond is simulated by a piece of blue plastic, which we actually used as a swimming pool in one of our other productions, *Lulu*. The piece of blue plastic is put on the stage and the little girl is put on the plastic, and then as the story is being told, we see the little girl's body descending and water bubbling up through the plastic. When the Stepdaughter picks her out of this, she is dripping wet. In another scene, the little boy is set behind the scrim, and the scrim goes transparent and, again, completely reflects and parallels what is on the stage. We've been using a kind of fake moon that comes from the flies, and all of that is paralleled by what looks like real birch trees, a real moon, and a painting that looks like a real pond. The boy is behind there next to the trees when he commits suicide.

DiGaetani: It must be very difficult, as the Director in the play itself says, to get child actors to do that kind of thing.

Brustein: I've had very good luck with that. We've had much younger children than Pirandello calls for, and they're marvelously poignant, tragic children. In *Tonight We Improvise* we used another Pirandellian trick. When Mommina sings to her children, we turned the children into twins, and then they were statues. These came up from the stage floor, sitting on chairs, all white, sitting together, exactly duplicated, and she sang to them, and then Mommina died. Suddenly the children's faces became animated and they began to speak.

DiGaetani: How did you do that?

Brustein: By motion picture, by a film which was projected on their faces, and they begin to speak and said: "Mommy, get up, we're frightened, get up, mommy, mommy." And then their faces went dark, and the family comes in, discovers Mommina's body, and then the director comes out and says, "It was all a trick, and thanks very much, and take a bow." But he can't get Mommina up because she's lying lifeless, and the director says, "Don't worry, she's playing out her role," and he takes a bow and walks off stage, and the audience sees these two statues just sitting there in their chairs. One of them gets up and takes a bow too, and walks off stage. What we did, behind the bow, was to bring the statue down through the traps, and replace it with the little girl in exactly the same position, and then she gets up and takes her bow, and Mommina's body is still lying there, and the audience does not know what to do. We had the fine documentary film director Frederick Wise televising the proceedings for a documentary he was doing. He goes up to televise the body at this point. The audience sits there. The screen comes down, which has been serving as a curtain, and the audience just doesn't know whether to leave or stay, and then two medics come in from the lobby with a gurney, saying "Please get out of the way, get out of the way." They come behind the screen and they put Mommina on the gurney, and then the audience at this point leaves, and as they leave there is an ambulance in the street with its lights on.

DiGaetani: Oh, terrific.

Brustein: And we were even giving out information, that she was in Mt. Auburn Hospital and doing well. So we carried Pirandello's idea as far as we could.

DiGaetani: Do you feel then that the main thing Pirandello's plays have to offer contemporary audiences is provocative ideas?

Brustein: Well, that certainly is one of the most extraordinary things he has to offer. He is the man who really explored the boundary lines separating life and the stage, and that's become very important to us today. It's very important to us today because the movies have effectively usurped and coopted reality. We don't need realism anymore. What we have to show is what the stage can do that films can't do, and Pirandello is the perfect playwright to demonstrate that. That is what he was concerned with all his life—not with simulating reality or having real doorknobs and real hot and cold running water on stage; he'd rather show you that the stage reality is not less real than the real reality; it is a parallel reality. That is a very important philosophical point, it's a very important religious point, it's a very important theatrical point, and it's an important social point. Pirandello on all these levels is preeminent.

DiGaetani: What, other than the ideas, do you think the plays have to offer us?

Brustein: Well, it's not just ideas but the fact that the ideas are embodied and clothed in human form. He enacts the ideas; he creates the dramatic action that makes them a living idea; he is very unlike Shaw, whom I think is an inferior playwright in his use of the stage and much less adventurous in his approach to theater. With all the humanity of his characters, Shaw never really shows us the tragic apparatus that proceeds from the ideas, and I think that's what Pirandello does. He sees both a tragic and a comic eventuality. Pirandello does not create great characters. One does not come away remembering a great character, except in a few plays. One comes away, when Pirandello is at his best, remembering a really original situation and a way of looking at life that one never thought of before—through the medium of human action.

DiGaetani: How do you feel about Pirandello's use of language?

Brustein: I think it's eloquent without being poetic. He's not really a poet. He's a dramatic poet, and I think his poetry resides in his structures and his concepts.

DiGaetani: Do you have any plans for future Pirandello productions?

Brustein: Well, I took a vow that I wouldn't do another Pirandello for at least six months. I think I'm going to let him rest for a while.

DiGaetani: What about *Henry IV*?

Brustein: That is certainly Pirandello's most powerful and best constructed play.

DiGaetani: But you better have an actor to play that role.

Brustein: You better have a great actor. And I have a great actor, but the trouble is getting his schedule free to do it.

DiGaetani: Have contemporary playwrights been influenced by Pirandello?

Brustein: Oh, I think every modern playwright remains under Pirandello's spell.

DiGaetani: Is a perfect Pirandello production possible?

Brustein: I believe firmly that there is no such thing as a definitive production. The next production is an answer to the previous production, or builds upon the previous production, and that is really what theatrical culture is about. Critics really send us in the wrong direction when they say, "This is the finest production of the play you'll ever see." It isn't and it shouldn't be. It is just an interpretation of the play, which will be answered in the next interpretation. And thank heaven that Pirandello, being the kind of playwright he is, allows for these various interpretations. Most living playwrights don't.

DiGaetani: You're right. There are good productions and not so good productions, but no definitive productions. A theatrical dialogue is created, and one production responds to another.

Brustein: Well, is there a definitive critical essay on a play? There is a critical essay, and then another critic comes along and says, "you're all wet, I think the play means *this*."

DiGaetani: Yes.

SEQUI

Sandro Sequi is most famous in the United States as a director of opera, primarily for his fine productions of the classics of the Italian lyric stage for the Metropolitan Opera in New York and the Lyric Opera in Chicago. He has been called Joan Sutherland's favorite director, and he has directed several notable American productions with that great singer, especially *Lucia di Lammermoor* and *La fille du Regiment*. But in Italy Mr. Sequi is more famous as a theater director, though the 1988 Rome Opera season began with his imaginative production of Mozart's *Il Re Pastore*. I spoke with Mr. Sequi in Rome in October of 1988 about his experiences directing Pirandello's plays.

DiGaetani: What was the most recent Pirandello production you have done here in Italy?

Sequi: Last season I did a production of *La vita che ti diedi* for the Teatro Stabile di Catania, a company known for its fine productions of Pirandello, a company which often tours with these productions throughout Italy and abroad.

DiGaetani: Yes, I saw their excellent production of Pirandello's *Il Berretto a sonagli* in New York last year.

Sequi: Since Pirandello was Sicilian, some of the Sicilian theater companies do the best productions of his plays. In any case, I did this production of *La vita che ti diedi* for the Teatro Stabile di Catania. The play itself is in many ways similar to one of Gabriele D'Annunzio's plays. Pirandello wrote the play for Eleanora Duse, but she was never able to appear in it—in fact, this greatest of Italian actresses never appeared in any of Pirandello's wonderful plays. Perhaps because *La vita che ti diedi* was written with Duse in mind for the lead role, there is a decadent quality to this play about the problems of maternity, especially the problems of a possessive, consuming maternity. Marta Abba eventually performed the role at the play's premiere.

DiGaetani: Have you done any other Pirandello productions before this one?

Sequi: I have also staged *Il giuoco delle parti* for the National Academy of Dramatic Art in Rome; that was one of my earliest productions, when I was just starting out as a director of theater.

DiGaetani: I know that you direct both opera and theater, but which do you prefer?

Sequi: Well, both are wonderful, but I prefer directing in the theater. Generally, you get better acting from actors than singers—to mention the obvious. Also, a director has more control in the theater. In opera, the conductor usually has more control because of his responsibility for the musical component of the performance.

DiGaetani: Are Pirandello's plays particularly difficult to do for contemporary Italian audiences? Are there any special problems for the director in staging Pirandello for modern audiences?

Sequi: Pirandello's plays are easy to do in Italy today. We have a great tradition of theater in Italy going back for centuries—back, in fact, to the ancient Roman theater. In addition, we also have a tradition of staging Luigi Pirandello's plays, an established tradition of Pirandello productions here. Pirandello himself, in fact, staged many of his own plays, and he himself did much to establish this wonderful tradition of Pirandello productions. Audiences here generally respond very well to him because, for one thing, he is now a classic, an established classic in the theater—like Shaw or Ibsen or Chekhov. But Italians sometimes feel that Pirandello is too cerebral, too intellectual. But when I direct Pirandello, I try to establish a mysterious, spiritual quality in the plays, which I believe is there in the text. There are a lot of similarities between the plays of Pirandello and D'Annunzio, and this mysterious, spiritual quality is one of them.

DiGaetani: But these two playwrights hated each other. Pirandello had nothing but contempt for D'Annunzio's work.

Sequi: That is true, but they were writing during the same time period, and there are some similarities of tone and theme in their plays.

DiGaetani: One of the great attractions for me in Pirandello's plays is the fascinating complexity of the major characters in most of his works. But why are the minor characters so often dull?

Sequi: Well, the lack of interest of many of the minor characters is due, I feel, to the way Italian theater was produced during Pirandello's lifetime. Before the modern period, Italian theatrical companies were formed around one or two great actors, there not being enough money left over to hire any other great actors. As a result, amateurish actors were generally used for minor roles, and Pirandello had to write plays for the Italian companies of his day.

DiGaetani: One of the great traditions in Italian theater is certainly *commedia dell'arte,* with its bands of players who traveled throughout Italy, and indeed throughout Europe, giving performances based on improvisation. Does the *commedia dell'arte* tradition operate significantly in Pirandello's plays?

Sequi: I don't feel that the *commedia dell'arte* tradition really exists in Pirandello's plays. He sometimes wrote about improvisation and the necessity for the actor to be able to improvise, but in point of fact, he wrote down all the lines in his plays. There is not much improvisation possible for actors when the lines of the play are written.

DiGaetani: Do young people in Italy respond well to Pirandello's plays?

Sequi: Young people seem to respond well to his plays. Pirandello's plays are often staged in Italy, and especially his more cerebral plays are especially popular.

DiGaetani: Are Pirandello's plays in any way dated?

Sequi: Sometimes the language in his plays is dated. After all, his plays were written over fifty years ago, and as a result his language reflects the Italian language of the 1920s and 1930s, and modern Italians often speak a different way, and with a different vocabulary. I saw a very interesting production of a Pirandello play in France last year, and hearing the play in contemporary French made me feel that we need to make his language more contemporary for modern Italian audiences.

DiGaetani: What about Pirandello's use of the Sicilian dialect in some of his Sicilian folk plays?

Sequi: I myself feel that there are really two Pirandellos. The first Pirandello is the great Pirandello, the great dramatist of ideas, the author of plays like *Six Characters in Search of an Author* and *Henry IV*. And this Pirandello ranks with the greatest of the modern European dramatists—people like Shaw, Ibsen, Chekhov, etc. But the second Pirandello is the Pirandello of the Sicilian folk plays, the author of plays like *Liolà, Il berretto a sonagli*, and *La giara*. This Pirandello seems like a very minor playwright to me. The first Pirandello is a great innovator and revolutionary of twentieth-century theater. But the second Pirandello is very much within a tradition of nineteenth-century Italian theater—a tradition that culminated with Giovanni Verga. This second Pirandello is a minor playwright in a provincial tradition of folk theater, and the concerns of this second-rate, minor Pirandello seem very distant from those of modern audiences.

DiGaetani: What does Pirandello offer modern audiences?

Sequi: Well, the first Pirandello, the great Pirandello offers modern audiences some wonderful characters and some wonderful ideas. The problem of identity and the modern problem of a lack of identity certainly remain major concerns for people. And because of a lack of identity, Pirandello also speaks of the impossibility of relationships—especially in plays like *Sei personaggi in cerca d'autore* and *Così è (se vi pare)*. In these plays Pirandello was really the first playwright to open a new path to a new kind of modern theater—in fact, a new form of theater. And in this sense, Pirandello is already a classic since he belongs to both the past and the present.

22

Pirandello, the Actor, and Performance

Estelle Aden

The paradox of situation and character in Pirandello's plays provides a dynamics that actors thrive on. There are the intricacies of concealment, illusions versus realities, the presentation of a mask, and the destruction of it, which create tensions and tempos. Pirandellian plays demand accomplished actors working with their equals. There is such substance in these works! The ensemble will reveal level upon level of intensity. Pirandello has given the actors a task of continual discovery. The plays continue to be theatrically exciting works because the "balance" and "build" of each scene develops into a living event. The sensitivity within the ensemble can be likened to a spider web, for the work must be even and continuous. The "center" must hold. This results from a process of working closely together and weaving the intricate connections and relationships between the spoken word, the unspoken text, and the physicality and nuances in the context of the play. The ensemble does not lose sight of the playwright's intention, which is shaped and determined anew in each production. There has to be a blending of technique, talent, and dramatic intelligence which lends cohesiveness to the stage work.

When a script is read, it is unrealized. Plays are meant to be played. When life is breathed into them, a remarkable transformation begins. An art form is begun in which the actors blend together the auditory and visual elements of theater. They liberate the life of the play and exchange ideas and emotions that resonate on stage and out into the audience.

The term *ensemble* has been used, and some working definition of an ensemble should be given: simply put, it is an organization of creative artists. The roster usually consists of an artistic director, actors, a dramaturg, directors, and a technical staff. Very often a particular philosophy of theater emerges. The set designers, lighting designers, and costumers are a strong creative force and work closely with the production concept of the director. This community of theater practitioners supports, creates, and carries through the vision of the play. All of this interaction and developmental work makes a theatrical statement.

Certainly, Pirandello's plays require this cohesive presentational approach. This takes time; there has to be a maturation period, and there is no substitute for it. From the first line readings and discussions to the opening performance, Pirandellian plays require all the actors have to give. The play itself would quickly expose an inexperienced actor. Each cast member is inhabiting the body and soul of his or her assigned character in the context of the play. Even when the movement is static, the concentration has energy. The audience can feel this energy as well as see it. Being a witness, they are emotionally involved, listening, judging, and being drawn into the action on stage. Pirandello's own view of his work on stage is reflected in this statement.

In the theatre the work of the author does not exist any longer. Thus, one might ask: "What is going on on the stage?" The answer is precisely "The stage creation made by the actor." The actor does the contrary of what the author has done. He translates again into life and movement that which the author has extracted from life, and gives it shape and form. The shape again becomes matter to which the actor gives dimension; his own shape, according to his own means, talent and sensitivity, through and by his body and his voice, becomes a creation quite apart from that of the playwright (Pirandello, "Playwright," 7).

The challenge and responsibility to the ensemble make the same demands of technical proficiency and dramatic skill as any work of Shakespeare, Shaw, and Ibsen. The actors must be linguistically adept, vocally flexible, and physically mobile. The pacing of the play requires a clear understanding of the play's concept from first to last. This understanding has to be mutual between the director and the cast. The actor has to get out of his own way to allow the character plenty of room to develop. Pirandello gives his actors so many options. The roles can be compared to mirrors that keep reflecting different images with infinite variety.

The two plays I will refer to from the actor's point of view are *It Is So! (If You Think So)* and *Six Characters in Search of an Author*. Both of these masterworks share a mystery and innovative quality. Actors relish working with these scripts because these plays present endless variation. *It Is So! (If You Think So)* has many traditional aspects to it. Written in 1918, it still has the mark of a well-made play with some important differences that continue to make the play theatrically exciting today. *Six Characters in Search of an Author*, written in 1921, continues to receive bold directorial treatment and captures its audience with the theatricality of text and staging.

Some problems for the actors are the profound questions that are raised and never resolved. The problems go well beyond the plot and continue to puzzle us, Pirandello's hallmark. Pirandello himself claims that he had made intellect a passion. The ensemble must communicate this notion. Pirandello is an actor's playwright because the speeches he gives his cast of players are wonderfully written. They are articulate and emotionally explosive at the same time. The opening scene in *It Is So! (If You Think So)* has Signora Agazzi setting out the problem to Laudisi. The characters are delineated very quickly. Laudisi is more than a witty fellow. He is the *raissoneur*-like character who ends the play saying, "and there, my friends, you have the truth. Are you satisfied?" No one is satisfied. It could very well be that all the others in the Agazzi parlor are regretting the effort they made to try to find the truth. It could be that many in the audience consider the solution is not solving the problem, an ending worthy of an Arlecchino in *commedia dell' arte*. There is a strong *commedia* influence in Pirandello, and yet the action leading up to it is heartwrenching.

Ponza and his mother-in-law, Signora Frola, are shaken with emotion and are supporting each other as they exit. And what a stage exit it is! Everyone on stage is affected by this exit, and they turn their attention to the daughter to find the truth. The moment is intense with expectation. And the answer is, "I am nobody." The solution to the problem simply vanishes. So Laudisi's curtain line underscores his contention from the very beginning. The traditional structure of the play expands, and new areas are opened when this character quips and questions the mirror image to disclose which of them is mad. He performs a *lazzi* and conveys the theme that exposed them all. "The truth! But it is already known: all that remains is the unmasking." The interpretation of this bravura role can vary from a cool intellectual to an Arlecchino. Not only do the actors have to be capable of wild swings of mood, but so does the audience. Consolation is the last thing they come to expect. Constant speculation on the probabilities is what we have. These persistent questions are set before the audience wrapped in intellectual packages. We are reminded of the Sicilian heritage that illuminates Pirandello's writing. Actors must embrace the passion, jealousy, love, arrogance, and revenge that smolder under intellectual tirades. The speeches disarm you emotionally, and then the audience is left to struggle with a conclusion. I consider the fluid line of focus in these speeches and confrontations a game that the ensemble and the audience are engaged in. Walter Kerr in a review in the *New York Times* in 1964 commented, "the deck has been honestly shuffled, then . . . dealing them faceless cards . . . " Although the play is set in a small provincial town in Italy, these "Faceless cards" are everywhere.

Pirandello gives his cast a cameo description of the characters. In this particular play there will be some consideration of the period. Details are important to Pirandello, who is a thorough man of the theater. Laudisi in Act One is attired in a semiformal street suit with black braid around the edges. He is on stage at the beginning and end of the play, very much like the Master of Ceremonies in

Cabaret. The "right look" for the actor is important since it makes a statement about him.

Pirandello defines Amalia Agazzi so that her dominance in her home is unmistakable—the self-satisfied matron with a sense of her importance. "She gives you to understand that if she had a free rein she would be quite capable of playing her own part in the world and, perhaps, do it better than Commendatore Agazzi." Dina, her daughter, is prattling away, and the two of them have a relationship that stands in sharp contrast to the tragic arrangement that Signora Frola has with her daughter. Although Amalia is advised to mind her own business, she commands the scene with confidence. Other characters make entrances into the Agazzi parlor, establishing the delicate network in the provincial town. Their personalities and relationship underscore the excitement of discovery about Ponza, his mother-in-law, and the daughter or wife. Pirandello's description of these personalities has charm and wit, and so should the presentation of these people. They must not be parodies. Both Signora Sirelli and Signora Cini are delineated with humor. Neither matron knows that she is funny. The humor of the scene is in the enjoyment of this group, and they are an easy mark for Laudisi. The pace of the scene builds to a point where the guests are completely baffled. Signora Cini finally says, "I give up! I give up! If we can't believe our eyes and feel with our fingers." Laudisi explains to her that she must understand. "All I'm saying is that you should show some respect for what other people see and feel, even though it be exactly opposite of what you see and feel."

The stage is set for Signora Frola to make her entrance and bring with her the sadness and the mystery of what is going on. Her gentleness will win over the group who now becomes totally confused by the pieces of the puzzle. How committed the strangers are to each other! How the story conflicts with impressions they are forming and reforming as they listen! There must be a quality of commitment on the part of the son-in-law and Signora Frola. Tempo is very important in a Pirandello play. The acting reflects these particular people who have known each other all their lives. They instinctively respond to one another. When this episode intrudes on their lives, they are vulnerable. They have a collective need to understand what these strangers are doing. Playing these scenes many times builds the freedom to respond to each other as close community participants in a dramatic moment. It has a touching and amusing effect on the audience. They are not up to the assignment they have given themselves. But then again, what is one to do? As Professor Paolucci says: "It's hard to say, after seeing a Pirandello play, just what this or that person really is: but we know quite well what he thinks, feels, suffers. We seem to be inside looking out" (12).

The set design's visual impact is instantaneous for an audience. For the actor the impact is just as great. The setting for *It Is So (If You Think So)* is a parlor in the Agazzi home. While the selection of furniture and other appointments to the room has limitless possibilities, it is still a box set. The three walls of the room represent the confining space in which the movements of the actors play out the action. How they sit, stand, and cross the stage from one side of the parlor to another defines their attitude and their relation to each other. The ensemble is capable of using the set to embellish their characterization. Some are comfortable. Some just don't belong there. There will be marked differences in the manner in which each character physicalizes a part. Not only are the large movements of entering the room and crossing from one side of the set to another, or sitting and rising to greet each other, individual, but the psychological gestures will define their place in the small provincial setting in which they play out their lives. Laudisi is different, and he will set himself apart by his gestures and wit and use of the mirror to extend the dimensions of the Agazzi home into an infinite place in the audience's imagination.

The rehearsal period will bring many innovations. Many stage gestures, line readings, and responses within the cast will be tried. Many rehearsals will be devoted to a short interval in an act. The entrances of Signora Frola and Ponza are carefully set by the text. The preparation of the actors before they set foot on the stage is important. When they are on stage, their presence has to support the introduction into the play that Pirandello has provided for them. For example, the entrance of Signora Nenni in Act II is a challenge. There cannot be a false note anywhere. Pirandello describes this woman this way: "She, too, is a bundle of concentrated curiosity, but of the sly, cautious type, ready to find something frightful under everything." All of these suggestions are important elements in setting the main action of the scene, which is made up of "beats" similar to musical notes in a score. In a Pirandello play each vignette has to be "in tune." Acting is physical work, and the action begins internally for the actor. The parts that Pirandello wrote for his cast are an actor's dream. The actor knows that the word comes after the emotion and thought. If Pirandello's words are to ring true, the imperative to say them must also be there. Doing a run-through of a scene and then an act and then the entire play will give the work continuity.

Technically, the company can do a great deal to support the actors in the process of discovery and realization. The set designers will recreate the living style of that time and place. The lighting designer, with the director, will light the stage and the individual players to set a mood. The costumes of that period will explain a great deal of the movement and pace of these people. For the actors the adaptation to period clothes is another facility they acquire. There is more distance between people because of the design and length of the women's dresses. There is a formality in their manner that must seem natural to them. Pirandello fully appreciated detail in production and preparation.

We have many accounts of how the playwright immersed himself in the design of costumes and the building of sets. Pirandello even "blocked" some of the scenes with the actors he was working with. Today most directors are recognized as the ultimate integrating force in a production. He or she accepts or rejects set design, lighting design, and acting interpretations to mold the production with a unified point of view. He or she delegates a great deal of the work involved in these areas since they are so highly specialized. It is rare that a director is also a playwright, although there are always exceptional talents who do accomplish this twin feat. Edward Albee wrote and directed a brilliant production of *Who's Afraid of Virginia Woolf*, starring Ben Gazarra and Colleen Dewhurst. Athol Fugard is another remarkable playwright who writes, directs, and acts in his works. This is rare, and Pirandello belongs to an elite group of multitalented theater people. One quality they all share is a particular vision of the play. Another is knowing what they want the actors to achieve.

In a Pirandello play an actor has so many options that the director may try many different approaches to the work in progress. After the audience has seen the play, other changes will often be made in movement and interpretation. With all the work that has gone before, the cast must be secure enough to allow for improvisation. That freedom is important. The ensemble working in close concert with each other can sense change and have the freedom to trust, even welcome, spontaneity. We are all redefined by spontaneity, and so are the characters in the play. Every cast at the outset of the rehearsal period is "outside" the play, just as the audience is. As the play becomes more secure, the actors have freedom to use their dramatic imagination. As Robert Brustein said: "The living nature of theatrical art is further exemplified by its immediacy . . . the drama takes place in the present with nothing separating the speaker from the speech" (123).

Having perfected the production to the point where it is stageworthy, the final test can begin. The audience is the witness and essential participant for the play to live. Without an audience, we have a run-through. Even a dress rehearsal is not a performance unless there is a dynamic response. Playing on stage often is as important as rehearsing often. By responding at different times to the scene, actors can slow it down or speed it up. An audience can even take a performance away from an inexperienced cast, the audience can take control. Certainly, with a Pirandello play the involvement should be complete. There is so much for the audience to resolve for themselves because emotions travel back and forth, reinforcing the action and events that are unfolding. The ensemble should know as one artistic unit how to embrace whatever response they get. The audience heightens the experience. Interrelationships and sensitivity expose the theme and focus of the play, and the audience as witness acts on one another. The laughter that occurs in *It Is So, If You Think So* balances the tragic moments: the shock and the final perplexing curtain line. By integrating the traditional with the comedic and the innovative, Pirandello has given world theater a play that is in repertory today.

The APA-Phoenix presented *It Is So, If You Think So*, using the translation *Right You Are If You Think So*, in two outstanding productions, both directed by Stephen Porter. The artistic director of the ensemble company was Ellis Rabb. Some of our finest actors and actresses were featured in these bravura roles— Nancy Marchand as Amalia and Joanna Roos as Signora Frola. In this 1964 production Sydney Walker portrayed Ponza. The company, which played in repertory, brought this play back in 1967 featuring Helen Hayes as Signora

Frola, Donald Moffat in the role of Laudisi, and Sydney Walker repeating the role of Ponza. Walter Kerr, commenting on the performances of Donald Moffat and Helen Hayes, wrote in his review: "they are players doing the work in question. They are first rate, and to watch them take center stage at the Lyceum is like stepping into a cool serene garden after a day of hard work. We are soothed and exhilarated in the same time" (34).

The innovations of *Six Characters in Search of an Author* are also startling. They take the audience by surprise, the cast is thrown off-balance, and the Six Characters are unsettling. As the play begins, the Company of actors makes no attempt to recognize the audience. By the manner in which the actors move and speak their lines, one gets the feeling that the audience has no business being there. They are in rehearsal, and rehearsals can be very complex. According to Peter Brook:

The quality of the work done in any rehearsal comes entirely from the creativity of the working climate—and creativity cannot be brought into being by explanations. The language of rehearsals is like life itself: it uses words, but also silences, stimuli, parody, laughter, unhappiness, despair, frankness and concealment, activity and slowness, clarity and chaos (77).

The stage in rehearsal, which is the performance in this play, is stripped, and the events and illusions will appear suddenly. The cast will improvise with all the dramatic imagination that their technique has given them. In many ways the play is a magic show and a ghost story, and nothing is fixed except the age of the Older Son. He is twenty-two. Time floats in space. Pirandello provides his ensemble with infinite possibilities so the play is pliable. In the American Repertory Theater production under the direction of Robert Brustein (1988), local color and comments indigenous to contemporary America were used, and the audience related to these working actors as part of the community. The play has a timelessness that helps the audience feel more comfortable since the cast ignores them until the arrival of the family.

That entrance has an eerie effect. At that point the working Company of actors joins the audience in their surprise at the intrusion of these "spectres." Until that frightening moment when they enter, the actors are working, moving in an environment they are comfortable in. The walls are brick, the radiators are exposed, the light is harsh. There are usually ropes and weights suspended in the wings and an occasional table and chair. The area is drab and barren, but it will shortly be transformed with theatricality and emotions. The actors will create the miracle with this Pirandellian approach to the stage. As Francis Fergusson said: "The most fertile property of Pirandello's dramaturgy is his use of the stage itself. By so boldly accepting it for what it is, he freed it from the demand which modern realism had made of it, that it be a literal copy of scenes off stage" (193).

Pirandello opened up the box set; in fact, he did away with it altogether. The stage becomes a place where anything can happen. The confrontations multiply as the Six Characters confront the actors and then each other. With all this confrontation, the actors of the company and the Six Characters have to be very careful to control the intensity of emotion and not have the scene gain too much momentum. They know how the play ends since they have lived and breathed the script for some time. They must allow the play to unfold at its own pace. The discovery that they make at the end of the play will gather cumulative impact if it is allowed to play itself out. The relationships the actors of the Company develop on stage are in striking contrast to those of the Six Characters. The actors are practitioners of illusions and they play their parts, but their manner changes when they are "out of character." The Six Characters are never "out of character" since they are the real characters. The Stepdaughter is unable to accept her role being taken over by an actress.

Stepdaughter: What? What? I, that woman there? (Bursts out laughing)

The Manager: What is there to laugh at?

Leading Lady: Nobody has ever dared to laugh at me.

Such elements of paradox occur in the scenes where actors are trying to act, and they are lacking in the credibility of the role in spite of their talented attempts.

There is opportunity after opportunity for acting cameos. The Father, who is the driving force of the family, is a dominant and outspoken person who relates much of the family's tragic plight. Yet, when he is directed by the Manager, the Father suddenly becomes awkward and unsure. His posture is tentative, and in an instant he looks like he had never been on stage. To watch Alvin Epstein act this moment out in the Brustein production (July 1988) is like watching someone going in and out of focus. It is a brilliant moment for the accomplished actor and underscores Pirandello's paradox of reality and illusion.

The sustained silence of the Mother and the Older Son is another test of an actor in performance. They are internalizing emotions that are strongly felt and communicated through their stance and gesture. These are difficult roles that test an actor because, when they speak, the inner life and passion of their emotions are condensed into the lines they speak. The Mother expresses her guilt, shame, and distress. She is the archetypal *mater dolorosa*. The Son is a mask of disdain filled with anger and loathing for the Father, his half-brother, his sisters, and even himself. Each of these characters has strong ties with the Father and the Stepdaughter, and their relationship with each other is another failed attempt to communicate. The Son will not have any part in this play, nor can he leave. There is a surreal feeling in these scenes as time goes forward and then back. The Stepdaughter is a schoolgirl, and then she is working at Madame Pace. There is an intense hatred for her Stepfather while she plays her scene, yet she pleads for her mother to intercede and stop the scene. It is as if she has multiple selves that are responding to the moment. The Stepdaughter is also compassionate to her mother, indignant at her Half-Brother, and incredulous that anyone could feel her grief and know how to play her part.

The improvisational elements in this play are an advantage to the cast of players. There are moments of personal freedom in the development of their roles because Pirandello gave the actors the freedom to show their creativity. There are many moments of laughter when the two groups of actors clash. The quiet competition between the Company of actors and the Six Characters finally causes an exchange when the Manager asks: "And where does all this take us anyway?"

Father: Oh nowhere! It's only to show you that if we (Six Characters) have no other reality beyond the illusion, you too must not count overmuch on your reality as you feel it today. Since like that of yesterday, it may prove an illusion for you tomorrow.

Pirandello has his actors questioning acting. The structure in an improvisation requires the keenest observation and listening to those involved. This facility to be alert to every possibility and to use what the other actor has given you to work with is a technique of its own. Dramatic shaping and communication are the bonds that the actors establish. Whether they are in the company of actors or one of the Six Characters, they must keep their relationships and interactions vibrating with energy and possibilities. The time warp is another consideration for the actors as they drift from present to past, from the reality of the theater to the illusion of the theater. Actors with a director who has a clear vision of the multiplicity of the work can pace these scenes effectively until the final cry of the Father that "this *is* reality."

These are bravura roles that must be coordinated to carry the impact of Pirandello's statement about realism in the theater and how restrictive it is. The parts are dramatically emphatic when spoken, acted, mimed, and improvised by an ensemble equal to the task. The empty space of the stage and areas of the orchestra are used. In some productions many areas of the stage are put to use. Bill Ball, as director of the American Conservatory Theater production of the play in 1963, used many areas of the theater. He was daring in his use of space. Whether a director uses the innovative approach or the proscenium stage approach, as in *It Is So, If You Think So,* there are demands for vocal technique from actors. Many speeches in Pirandello's plays are loaded with emotion, which creates tension throughout the body, particularly in the throat. How to release these emotions and have a voice left to perform with is where technique and training are essential to the professional actor. Tyrone Guthrie advised his players that it was not enough to "know what" the intention of the playwright and the motivation of the character was. The actors have to "know how" to communicate when the call from the stage manager goes out over the intercom system backstage, "Places Please."

And when the Manager decides to run through some of the scenes with the Father and Stepdaughter, the movement is not right. It is not true. It is not real.

That is the cry of the Six Characters. They enter on stage close to each other, mystery in their walk. The entrance is ethereal, but there is an unhealthy aura about them. The choreography that the group of six develop in rehearsing this entrance will make that first impact. They are phantoms with demands. Pirandello details that entrance. His direction indicates to the group that "they preserve something of the dream lightness in which they seem also suspended." The visual impact of their entrance creates a moment of mystery for the audience and the company of rehearsing actors. Everyone in the theater thinks, "What is this? Where did they come from?" For the Manager and working actors, the questions of what do these characters want and what are they doing here engage most of the play. The Six Characters are defined by their movements, but an integrated presence on stage gives the observer the sense that these are beings of a different quality. The Son is defiant, and that quality strengthens as the play progresses. The Mother is weighed down by shame and grief, and her lines are filled with weariness and despair. The Stepdaughter gives off sparks in her defiance of her fate and fury at her father. Each in turn plays an emotion and an attitude that is sustained throughout the play. Madame Pace, who materializes out of nowhere, has a persona that adds a different tone than the others in the group, but she is still one of the characters who wanders through a creative eternity looking for a resolution to existence.

During the last five minutes of the play, when the youngest children die, the cast of actors and the characters move as one. They are all engulfed with the action and the Manager asks, "Is he really wounded?" Everyone is rushing to aid the stricken family. "He's dead! dead!" The illusion becomes reality. The stage is peopled with a single group of actors, all of whom have been stunned by the events they have witnessed. The ensemble must drift into that sense of reality and out again. The characters have become the reality and the actors mere pretenders. The ensemble has to project the fluidity of this theme since it is central to the play.

The voice, movement, and study of the text are preparation for performance. There should be some mention of the mask that the actor wears. Whether the mask is makeup or any of the thousands of masks devised by various artists and cultures, each has a profound effect on the person who wears it. As the actor in this play approaches his role, the mask determines the visual and emotional life of the role. Pirandello writes of the masks we wear and the stripping away of the mask. As the ensemble prepares for presentation of a script of improvisation, the use of masks can open the actor to depths of understanding that were unknown to him. Pirandello himself entitled his play collection *Naked Masks*. Eric Bentley refers to that figure of speech "as a pointer": "As you know he called all his plays Naked Masks—not naked faces. Let your actors remember that. Naked Masks—a violent oxymoron indeed!"(6)

The last twenty-five years have seen some memorable productions of Pirandello's work throughout the world. The productions mentioned here were staged in New York City, but that by no means completes the list. Regional theaters throughout America keep these remarkable works in their repertory. Robert Brustein has directed both *It Is So (If You Think So)* and *Tonight We Improvise*. The production at the Joyce Theater in July 1988 included striking performances by Alvin Epstein as the Father, Patricia Gein as the Stepdaughter, and Patricia Smith as the Mother. What Brustein did shocked many critics. From the acting point of view, the most obvious was the introduction of Emilio Paz, as the pimp, in place of Madame Pace, the madam of the brothel. It was very effective. The explanation given was that there was a character actor who could do the part. William Harris used a Pirandello quote in his *New York Times* review of July 10, 1988:

The theater is not archaeology. Unwillingness to take up old works, to modernize and streamline them for fresh production, bespeaks indifference, not praiseworthy caution. The theatre welcomes such modernization and has profited by it . . . the original text remains intact for anyone who may want to reread it at home (5).

WORKS CITED

Bentley, Eric. *The Pirandello Commentaries*. Evanston, Ill.: Northwestern University Press, 1986.

Brook, Peter. *The Empty Space*. New York: Atheneum, 1968.

Brustein, Robert. *The Theatre of Revolt*. Boston: Little, Brown, 1960.

Fergusson, Francis. *The Idea of Theatre*. Princeton, N.J.: Princeton University Press, 1972.

Harris, William. "Brustein Confronts 'Six Characters'." Arts and Leisure Section. *New York Times*. July 10, 1988. 5–6.

Kerr, Walter. "A.P.A. Stages Pirandello's 'Right You Are'." *New York Times*, November 23, 1966: 34.

Paolucci, Anne. *From Tension to Tonic*. Carbondale Ill.: Southern Illinois University Press, 1974.

Pirandello, Luigi. *L'Umorismo*. Introduced, translated, and annotated by Antonio Illiano and Daniel P. Testa. Chapel Hill: University of North Carolina Press, 1974.

———. "Playwright and Actor." *Plays & Players* 7 (1960): 6–7.

23

Pirandello's Women on Stage: Theories and Techniques

Mimi Gisolfi D'Aponte

While current bibliography on the literary aspects of Luigi Pirandello's dramaturgy continues to be voluminous in the Western world today, little has been written about production.[1] This chapter focuses on the roles of several popular Pirandellian heroines from the viewpoint of contemporary American production, and examines the contiguous theories that may prove relevant to the stage life of these characters.

It might be well to begin with some sense of the playwright's personal views about women, and of his concerns about the production of his works. Biographer Gaspare Giudice points out Pirandello's "aversion for all the movements of female emancipation of the early twentieth century,"[2] and suggests that socially "he remained caught in a network of conformity which was far closer to atavistic Muslim-Catholic Sicily than to the conventions of contemporary Italy." Pirandello's own statements in his famous preface to *Six Characters in Search of an Author* offer more direct insight into his thinking regarding at least the mothering members of the species. Whereas the Father in the play agonizes visibly and at length about his own identity, the Mother, states Pirandello, is "perfectly organic. Indeed, her role of Mother does not of itself, in its natural essence, embrace mental activity. And she does not exist as a mind. She lives in an endless continuum of feeling."[3]

Biographical data about Pirandello's own relationships with women divide themselves naturally into the period of his married life and the period following his wife's retirement to a mental institution. His was an arranged marriage to a young woman from his hometown of Girgenti (Agrigento), Sicily. The drama of this union centers on her eventual mental illness. Biographers uniformly note the playwright's marital fidelity and his devotion to his wife's care and to that of their three small children when not at the Roman high school for girls where he made a modest living as a teacher. It is relevant to the question of creativity to realize that such a restricted life-style should have become the springboard for his playwriting, for it was to his writing that Pirandello retreated from his wife's madness. Following his recognition as a playwright, the great Roman actress Marta Abba became prominent in Pirandello's life, both personally and as the artist for whom he was to write many of his later plays.

Pirandello expressed his views about actors in the essay *Illustratori, attori e traduttori*[4] in which he implies that the illustrators, actors, and translators of his title are second-class artists. He notes that Benedetto Croce, in his *Estetica*, states that every translation must necessarily either diminish or damage the aesthetic form of the original. Pirandello not only assents to Croce's concept, but also expands it to apply to the work of illustrators and actors:

All three have before them a work of art already expressed, that is already conceptualized and executed by others, which the first must translate into another art; the second, into material action; the third, into another language. . . . What Croce says about translators . . . is true also for the illustrator and actor; likewise there are in all three cases diminution and damage.[5]

Thus, Pirandello, at least in 1908, considered stage production a form of translation, and while he uses adjectives such as "true" and "real" in reference to an original text, he resorts to "artificial" and "fictional" to describe stage life.[6] Of chronological interest to the contemporary theater historian is the fact that Pirandello's essay, essentially concerned with the relationship between performance and text, predates the seminal work of the Prague Linquistic Circle whose "Theses" of 1928 laid the foundations for the semiotic study of art (Carlson, 407).

Pirandello wrote over forty dramas, and in nearly half of these he created female protagonists. The choice of plays to be analyzed here from the viewpoints of both performance and text springs in part from their being fairly well known in English translation, and in greater part from the fact that each offers a different organizational role to its female protagonist or protagonists. Furthermore, the subject matter offered by these works may be said to have been strongly influenced both by Pirandello's wife and by Marta Abba, for madness within a family setting is germane to each and the quality of an artist's life provides a primary focus in three of the four texts. *It Is So! (If You Think So)* (1918), *Six Characters in Search of an Author* (1921), *To Clothe the Naked* (1923), and *As You Desire Me* (1930) also span the most creative playwriting years of Pirandello's life.[7]

The stage life of a play is generally created out of two "scripts"—the original text of the playwright and the "script" composed by actors in concert with a director. It is this second, "performance script" that is so elusive by nature and that was so feared by the novice playwright Pirandello as a potentially damaging translation. In order to bring specificity to such a performance script, it is necessary to examine the techniques by which it may be developed. Since mainstream twentieth-century American acting has incorporated the basic principles of the "Stanislavsky Method,"[8] refined and redeemed by nearly a half century of American production experience, it is appropriate to turn to the masters of such technique for methodology. Clearly representative both of the "Method" and of its "Americanization" are the works of two esteemed theater artists, Uta Hagen's *Respect for Acting* (1973) and Harold Clurman's *On Directing* (1972).

The essence of Uta Hagen's acting technique consists of finding, both through script study and through stage work with the director, the *action verbs* that motivate stage action and stage life, the verbs that make the character's words "work." During this process, the actor may break his part down into small sections or "beats," and choose a specific action verb for each beat. Miss Hagen searches first for her character's *objectives*, second for the *obstacles* in conflict with those *objectives*, and third for the *action verbs* that will overcome *obstacles* in order to achieve *objectives*. On the basis of these *action verbs*, the actor decides on an overall *action verb* that works as the spine of her character.[9]

The essence of Harold Clurman's directing technique consists of supervising the *spines* of the characters' parts, of analyzing the *beats* of the entire text, and of deciding somewhere along the path of rehearsal and private study, what will function as the *spine* of the play as a whole.[10]

It is of considerable theoretical interest that the vocabulary of these techniques, practiced and taught since the 1940s, demonstrates affinity with that of the Speech-Act theory presented by John L. Austin and John R. Searle in the 1960s and 1970s. In *Speech Acts* (1969), Searle works from the hypothesis that "speaking a language is performing Speech arts" (Searle, 16), and he elaborates on Austin's terms "illocutionary act" (which states, questions, commands, promises, or otherwise exists in the manner of speaking) and "perlocutionary act" (which persuades, frightens, or otherwise brings about an effect in the listener). In *Expression and Meaning* (1979), Searle elaborates on the differences between illocutionary acts and verbs and differentiates between those illocutionary verbs that have performative uses and those that do not (7). He also discusses "indirect speech acts" at length (30–36) and explores linguistically that territory which the actor knows so well—the labyrinth of multiple differences between a text's literal meanings and its implied meanings. It seems evident that the Clurman/ Hagen action verbs are, in Searle's speech-act theory, illocutionary verbs with performative uses. Notice also that the "spine" of the actor's character identifies underlying action and is often, in Searle's system, an indirect speech act.

What follows, then, are representative samples of performance scripting for four plays, prepared for the specific purpose of seeing what light these secondary texts may shed on the original question: the role of women in Pirandello's dramaturgy. The action verbs and the spines of the heroines are identified, as is the spine of each play.

In *It Is So! (If You Think So)* we find what Eric Bentley would term typically Pirandellian structure: "a center of suffering and a periphery of busybodies."[11] At this center we find a man and a woman, an unusual pair to be sure, since they are son-in-law and mother-in-law to one another, with the mysterious figure of their wife/daughter between them. If I undertake an analysis of Signora Frola's character, I identify these action verbs: *to convince* (the village busybodies of an acceptable family arrangement), *to explain* (her own strange behavior in not visiting her daughter), *to justify* (her son-in-law's role in keeping her daughter and herself apart), *to defend* (her own sanity), *to accuse* (unwillingly, her son-in-law of insanity regarding the identity of his wife), *to pretend* (to agree, before the assembled busybodies, to her son-in-law's version of reality). And if I must find a single verb with which to express the spine of this character, a verb on which all these other verbs depend, then I identify *to protect* (the reputation of Signor Ponza). Here is one of Signora Frola's most explicit monologues: she is addressing the village elders at the conclusion of Act I as she justifies her son-in-law's actions in order *to protect* his reputation.

You have noticed him, haven't you? Fine, strong looking man . . . violent . . . when he married my daughter he was seized with a veritable frenzy of love . . . he risked my little daughter's life almost, she was frail . . . they had to take his wife off in secret and shut her up in a sanatorium. And he came to think she was dead. Just imagine when we brought my daughter back to him—and a pretty thing she was to look at, too—he began to scream and say, no, no, no, she wasn't his wife, his wife was dead! He looked at her: No, no, no, not at all! She wasn't the woman! Imagine my dear friends, how terrible it all was. And do you know to get him to accept my daughter at all again, we were obliged to pretend having a second wedding! He is seized with a terrible fear, from time to time, that this little wife he loves may be taken from him again. So he keeps her locked up at home where he can have her all for himself. But he worships her—he worships her; and I am really quite convinced that my daughter is happy.[12]

Analysis of Signora Frola's role, as well as those of other leading characters in *It Is So*, leads me to select three major premises on which to build the stage action of the production. First, the sufferers at its core are each other's victims, as well as each other's protectors. The gigantic effort each makes to explain, to justify, to defend, to pretend, and to flee if need be in order to protect the other, achieves protection only at the cost of victimization. Second, all other energies in the play are directed at attempting to understand this protect/victimize relationship of the Frola/Ponza pair. Third, this attempt to understand backfires, thereby creating the spine of the play which Pirandello has basically stated in his title: *to deal with the enigma of truth by becoming its victim*.

The structure of *Six Characters*, like that of *It Is So*, is built around a trio of characters, again one man and two women. At its core is a deceptively normal-looking triangle with Father at its apex and with Mother and Stepdaughter at its two right angles. Together these three characters maintain a common victim/victimizer bonding similar to the Frola/Ponza relationship in *It Is So*. If I analyze the Mother's part from the actress's viewpoint, I identify the action verbs *to convince* (the Son that she deserves his respect, if not his love) and *to escape* (the dramatization of the painful parts of her family's tragedy). As Stepdaughter I find a greater choice of action verbs: *to justify* (her own position), *to avenge* (her life on the streets), *to escape* (being a noncharacter), *to convince* (the Manager to enact the Madame Pace scene), and *to accuse* (her father of moral blindness, her mother of naiveté, the Son of indifference, and the Boy of stupidity).

I choose for the spine of the Mother *to protect* (my children) and for the spine of the Stepdaughter *to establish guilt* (of the Father in this drama). Here, from Act II, is the Stepdaughter in a screaming explanation to the Manager of how she must act her own part in Madame Pace's brothel where she will meet her own Stepfather as a potential customer:

You can put me on as you like; it doesn't matter. Fully dressed, if you like—provided I have at least the arm bare; because, standing like this [She goes to the Father and leans her head on his breast.] with my head so, and my arms around his neck, I saw a vein pulsing in my arm here; and then, as if that live vein had awakened disgust in me, I closed my eyes like this, and let my head sink on his breast. [Turning to the Mother.] Cry out, Mother! Cry out! [Buries head in Father's breast, and with her shoulders raised as if to prevent her hearing the cry, adds in tones of intense emotion.] Cry out as you did then! (260–61)

In *Six Characters*, then, the victim/victimizer relationship under the guise of a be-protected/protect relationship exists in triangle form. Note that the triangle structure is accentuated by its parallel in the theater Company. Here the Manager with his Leading Lady and Ingenue alternately seem to protect one another from and expose one another to the needs, obsessions, and criticisms of these itinerate characters whom they try valiantly to understand. As in *It Is So*, Pirandello basically expresses the spine of the work through its title. *Six Characters in Search of an Author* translates easily for the director into *to give life to these characters*.

To Clothe the Naked starred Marta Abba and was the first of her many Pirandellian successes on the stage. The play provides a strong organizational contrast to both *It Is So* and *Six Characters*. There is a single individual in the play's central circle of suffering—the young Ersilia Drei. She functions as the center of the play's action, the human hub of a four-spoked wheel created by her four admirers and would-be benefactors. As the actress undertaking the role of Ersilia, I would find myself resorting to the following verbs: *to explain*, *to justify*, *to plead innocent*, *to convince*, *to accuse*, *to escape*, *to find refuge*, and *to die*. (Note that many of these verbs are identical with those of Signora Frola.) Ersilia finds herself in the dual role of victim and victimizer—with Signor Nota whose creative imagination she has roused, with Alfred Cantavale whose newspaper article bears terrible consequences, with Franco whose real love comes too late, and with Grotti whose attentions have led to an unintended crime of neglect. In accepting Nota's shelter Ersilia threatens it, in being the subject of Cantavale's article she causes a would-be suit against the newspaper, in arousing Franco's real love she jeopardizes both his social and professional position, and in attempting to clarify and clean up her relationship with Grotti she only succeeds in arousing his passion for her again. Listen to her attempt to protect herself from Grotti's accusations and continued pursuit:

> We're all scum! How can you stand there and blame it all on me? Is it my fault that I've never been strong enough to make anything of my life? . . . My God, nothing, ever . . . not even, I don't know, not even something so fragile that, if you dropped it, it would smash into a thousand pieces. But then at least you'd know by all those fragments that you once had something. . . . My whole life . . . one day after another . . . and no one I could ever call my own. . . . At the mercy of every chance event, of every whim . . . never left alone long enough even to take a deep breath . . . pushed and pulled this way and that . . . used and thrown away and never a moment, never a time when I could look up and say, "Wait! I'm also here!" [Suddenly turning on him like a whipped animal.] And now, what do you want from me? (52)

The director of *Naked* is again confronted with the need to dramatize an all-pervasive victim/victimizer relationship, one that radiates outward from Ersilia and extends to each of her male friends. Ersilia's spine becomes to *protect*—herself; the spine of each friend becomes *to protect*—Ersilia. Each admirer justifies his need to know more, to understand more about Ersilia's situation, with the idea that he may thus be better able to protect her. Thus, the spine of this play becomes *to deal with tragedy by protection which is victimization*, or as Pirandello puts it, to deal with tragedy of the naked personality with the clothing (or protection) of victimization.

As You Desire Me is by all critical accounts the most successful of Pirandello's later plays. Its heroine, the Unknown Woman, was played with great success not only by Marta Abba but also by Greta Garbo—the Garbo performance being in a 1932 film directed by Erich von Stroheim in Hollywood for Metro-Goldwyn-Mayer. If we imagine this play in iconographic terms, we see the Unknown Woman pulled backward by her present lover and life as a dance hall figure, while being pulled forward by the demands of one who claims to have been her husband in the past.

The principal action verbs of the Unknown Woman are these: *to understand* (the invitation of Boffi, her "husband's" friend, to return to her former life), and *to escape* (first, from her meaningless life with Salter and her frenetic existence as a sex object and, later, from the persona of "Cia" whom she has so successfully "become" for four months). The spine of the Unknown Woman's character lies in the reflexive verb *to free oneself*, for her need *to understand* and her overwhelming compulsion *to escape* the entanglements of two different lives reveal a deep-seated confusion concerning her own identity. Here is the protagonist as she reacts to the question of whether she wants "to return" to her "husband":

To flee from myself—yes, that I want; no longer to remember anything at all—to put my whole life behind me—here—look: this body—to be only this body—you say that it is hers? That I am like HER? I no longer feel myself, I don't want myself, I have nothing any longer and I don't even know myself. My heart beats and I don't know it; I breathe and I do not know it; I no longer know I am alive—a body, a body without a name, waiting for someone to come and take it! Very well; if he can re-create me—if he can give a soul again to this body, which is his, Cia's, let him take it—let him take it and fill it with his memories—a beautiful life—a beautiful life, a new life—Oh, I am in despair! (24–25)

In preparing to direct *As You Desire Me*, I find its spine to revolve around conflicting victim/victimizer relationships, for the Unknown Woman, first in her present life (which becomes her past) and in her future life (which was evolved from another's past). *As You Desire Me* is another way of saying, *It Is So, If You Think So . . .*

To summarize, then, what do these performance scripts offer by way of revealing underlying truths about Pirandellian heroines? Whether as part of a pair or standing alone, whether as part of a family triangle, or whether pulled in opposite directions by the members of two different "families," Pirandello's women are deeply involved *with men* in mutual protection relationships that evolve, through ineffectual attempts to understand their situations, into mutual victimization relationships. In acting vocabulary, therefore, the spine of the typical female protagonist from the drama of Pirandello is this: the desire *to protect*, undermined by the desire *to understand*, reduced to the unwanted need *to victimize*.

Turning from sample performance scripts back to comparison among primary texts, three conclusions may be drawn which elucidate the manner in which Pirandello places his female protagonists within the structure of his plays. First, in examining *It Is So*, *Six Characters*, *Naked*, and *As You Desire Me*, it becomes immediately obvious that *no* female character is given the task of the Chekovian/Pirandellian author-narrator, that person connected with the action but *not merely an actor within it*.[13] Such a character is endowed with sufficient objectivity about the action to become the link between the audience's sense of reality and the "madness" being perpetuated on stage. Indeed, in juxtaposition to this author-narrator type, who maintains a certain distance from the play's events, is the Pirandellian female lead—a woman who inevitably becomes fully involved, immersed really, in the action at hand. This limits, therefore, the multiplicity of stage realities open to female characters within Pirandello's dramaturgy.

A second conclusion, on the other hand, reveals Pirnadello's evenhandedness in assigning central roles (the intricacies of whose characters the reader/audience must study intimately during the course of three acts) to both men and women. Ersilia and the Unknown Woman, for example, are as surely the central subjects of *Naked* and *As You Desire Me* as is Henry in *Henry IV* or Angelo in *The Pleasure of Honesty*.

A third conclusion concerns the commonality of a dominant character trait

among Pirandello's heroes and heroines alike. A comparison of the driving
passions that possess the female protagonists presented in this chapter suggests
that pursuit of an elusive self-identity remains the playwright's primary subject—
whether embodied in the character of a man or a woman. From his original
Mattia Pascal to Pirandello's last powerful characterization, Cotrone in *The
Mountain Giants*, the question of "Who am I?" remains paramount in his
dramaturgy. Signora Frola and the mysterious Signora Ponza, the Stepdaughter
and her Mother, Ersilia, the Unknown Woman—all find themselves on the brink
of a disaster that stems from their inability to "lay hands on" the persons within
their physical selves. While supporting characters express confidence in their
abilities, they themselves are constantly tripped up by their frightening sense of
non-identity.

Signora Frola obliterates her own identity by permitting herself to be thought
of as mad. Speaking of her daughter to the representative village gossips, she
says:

It is hard on my poor girl. she has to pretend all along that she is not herself, but another,
his second wife; and I . . . oh, as for me, I have to pretend that I am mad when he's
around, my dear friends: but I'm glad to, I'm glad to really, so long as it does him some
good. (95)

Signora Frola, for all her seeming frailty, is one of those powerful dramatic
enigmas whose dual identity continues to puzzle the mind of the beholder long
after the performance of *It Is So*.

For the Stepdaughter, the spectre of hated non-identity is thrust on her by
illegitimacy. With great loathing she explains to the Manager why it is that she
detests her Half-Brother:

After what has taken place between him and me [indicates the Father with a horrible
wink,] I can't remain any longer in this society, to have to witness the anguish of this
mother here for that fool . . . [indicates the Son.] Look at him! Look at him! See how
indifferent, how frigid he is, because he is the legitimate son. He despises me, despises
him (Pointing to the Boy.), despises this baby here; because . . . we are bastards. [Goes
to the Mother and embraces her.] And he doesn't want to recognize her as his mother—
she who is the common mother of us all. He looks down upon her as if she were only
the mother of us three bastards. Wretch! [She says all this very rapidly, excitedly. At
the word "bastards" she raises her voice, and almost spits out the final "Wretch!"]
(220)

The indelible anger and pain which the Stepdaughter carries throughout *Six
Characters* is eased, one is led to believe, by the fact that she and her family
are finally, convulsively, able to act out their tale of anguish.

In the final soliloquy of *Naked*, Ersilia, as she lies dying, is obsessed with
physical appearance, with her non-costume at this moment seeming to symbolize
to all the world her life of non-identity:

I only wanted to make myself a decent little dress to die in. There, you see why I lied? That's the only reason, I swear it! My whole life I'd never been able to wear one, to make some sort of impression on anyone. It was always torn away from me by all the dogs—the dogs who waited for me everywhere, in every street—no dress that—and so I wanted one nice one—one beautiful one—to die in—the most beautiful of all—the one I'd dreamed of back there—a bridal gown—but only to die in, to die in, that's all—you see—a few tears shed over me, nothing more. Well I couldn't have it! Not even to die in! (75)

Ersilia epitomizes the woman who uses her powerlessness as a means of manipulating the powerful figures in her life—until this defense begins to backfire, and the only solution is self-destruction.

A climax of character occurs in *As You Desire Me* when the Unknown Woman's concern with one aspect of her physical appearance leads her to announce who she is *not*. Here she demands of her "husband," Boffi, that he understand his authorship of her present self:

Look at me! Right into my eyes—deep within them!—They have no longer seen for me, these eyes; they are no longer mine, not even to see myself! They have been like this— like this—in yours—always—so that there might be born in them, out of your eyes, my own image, as you were me! The image of all things, of all life, as you have seen it!— I came here; I gave myself to you utterly, utterly; I said to you: "Here I am, I am yours; there is nothing left in me of my own: Take me and make me AS YOU DESIRE ME!" 2 (54–55).

With "there is nothing left in me of my own," the Unknown Woman reveals her terrible truth: she has been reduced to being merely clay in the hands of other human beings.

Ultimately, each of these texts offers us the unique dramatic portrait of a woman who, for one reason or another, has given over her self-identity to a man in her life, whether son-in-law, father, lover, or husband. The terrible price paid for this loss of self-identity evolves into the need to victimize either herself or that man. Thus, primary text and performance script meet in that cycle common to the Pirandellian heroine—the desire to protect, undermined by the desire to understand, reduced to the unwanted need to victimize.

In the larger context of women bequeathed to Pirandello by virtue of Italian inherited dramaturgy, his female protagonists take a huge step forward. While the prototypical figures of Mother and Mary Magdelene remain recognizable through various transformations—medieval passion play, Renaissance Machiavellian drama, *commedia dell'arte*, Goldoni's comedy of manners, Verga's tragedy[14]—it is not until their embodiment in Pirandello's work that they achieve two distinctions simultaneously. The Pirandellian heroine (1) affects the action of the play in which she exists (as do the heroines of Machiavelli, *commedia*, Goldoni, and Verga) and (2) discusses and analyzes, *in public as well as in private*, the concerns of her life (as her predecessors in Italian drama do not).

Pirandello's women speak their minds—they express their hopes and concerns and disappointments to many people, often strangers. More often, they speak the truth as they see it, regardless of consequence. They are verbal women. The woman's image under Pirandello's tutelage grows in verbal freedom and verbal complexity, and this verbal complexity represents multidimensional characterization which is, I believe, Pirandello's contribution to this image.

Perhaps we might listen closely to what women critics are saying about Pirandello's characters, for while Eric Bentley, Richard Gilman, and Robert Brustein are firm admirers of Pirandello's genius, their conclusions point repeatedly to the pessimistic aspects of his work—to the dissolution of the ego, and the disintegrated personalities of his characters.[15] Indeed, Joseph Wood Krutch went so far as to say that, "Chekhov gets rid of plot and Pirandello gets rid of character."[16] Anne Paolucci, on the other hand, in the final chapter of *Pirandello's Theater: The Recovery of the Modern Stage for Dramatic Art*, suggests the enormous wealth of Pirandellian character creation as she concludes with a hypothetical repartee: " 'I'm nobody,' he [Pirandello] is saying. 'Are you nobody too?' And in a split second, one, a hundred, a hundred thousand figures come rushing into our consciousness, like characters who have found their author and their play" (145).

Bonnie Marranca, co-editor of *Performing Arts Journal* and author of several impressive volumes of theater criticism, offers a new voice concerning Pirandello's work. In *Theatrewritings* Ms. Marranca suggests that Pirandello's contribution to the theory of social psychology has been overlooked in favor of our interest in what his drama offers regarding individual psychology. We might do well, she suggests, to note that his "plays demonstrate the disappearance of the public realm as sole mediator of opinion and belief" (173).

The typical Pirandellian female protagonist is one whose ultimate stance is that of the victim/victimizer. One may choose to attribute this, in part at least, to the playwright's misogyny, suggested at the beginning of this chapter. One may also choose the more comprehensive view that Pirandello, in this instance as in many, was a theatrical seer, for he succeeded in creating women for the stage who, while not liberated, are crying out for liberation. These heroines are understood and interpreted today as complex, miltifaceted, verbal, intelligent, and passionate—very much women of the twentieth and, perhaps, twenty-first centuries.

NOTES

1. "A Listing of Recent Pirandello Bibliography," *The Pirandello Newsletter* 3:1 (Spring 1979): 3.

2. Gaspare Giudice, *Pirandello*, trans. Alastair Hamilton (London: Oxford University Press, 1975), 27.

3. Luigi Pirandello, Preface, *Six Characters in Search of an Author*, *Naked Masks*, ed. Eric Bentley (New York: E. P. Dutton, 1952), 230.

4. Luigi Pirandello, *Illustratori, attori e traduttori*, in *Saggi, poesie, scritti varii*. (Milan: Mondadori Editore, 1960), 209–24.

5. Pirandello, *Saggi*, author's translation.

6. Pirandello, *Saggi*, 218. This essay, written in 1908, predates Pirandello's active involvement in theater production by seventeen years. In 1925 he and eleven associates, among them writers, publishers, and designers, established the Teatro d'Arte in Rome. It flourished for three years, and Pirandello eventually directed there.

7. As Anne Paolucci notes in *Pirandello's Theater* (Southern Illinois University Press, 1974, 106), Pirandello's later plays possess a mythical aura that "tends to carry them beyond the traditional limits of art."

8. Constantin Stanislavsky, *An Actor Prepares*, trans. Elizabeth Reynolds Hapgood (New York: Theatre Arts, 1936). See especially "Action," 31–50 and "Units and Objectives," 174–90.

9. Uta Hagen, *Respect for Acting* (New York: Macmillan, 1973). Note especially "The Objectives," "The Obstacles," and "The Action," 174–90.

10. Harold Clurman, *On Directing* (New York: Macmillan, 1972). See, for example, "Pages from the director's script," 268–89.

11. Eric Bentley, *In Search of Theatre* (New York: Vintage Books, 1957), 288.

12. Luigi Pirandello, *It Is So (If You Think So!)*, *Naked Masks: Five Plays by Luigi Pirandello* (New York: E. P. Dutton, 1952), 94.

13. The obvious example of such a type is Laudisi in *It Is So*. The Manager in *Six Characters* also exemplifies the Pirandellian character who is somewhat apart from the action and therefore able to "explain" it to the audience.

14. See Fra Simone's *La passione di Gesu' Cristo* (di Revello) (1492), Machiavelli's *La mandragola* (1520), Leon Katz's play version of *The Three Cuckolds* (a sixteenth-century *commedia* scenario) (1958), Goldoni's *La Locandiera* (1745), and Verga's *La lupa* (1880).

15. See Eric Bentley's *The Playwright as Thinker* (New York: Harcourt Brace & World, 1967), 146–57 and *In Search of Theater* (New York: Vintage Books, 1957), 279–95; Richard Gilman's *The Making of Modern Drama* (New York: Farrar, Straus & Giroux, 1972), 281–317; Robert Brustein's *The Theatre of Revolt* (Boston: Little, Brown, 1962), 157–89.

16. Joseph Wood Krutch, *Modernism in Modern Drama* (Ithaca, N.Y.: Cornell University Press, 1953), 87.

WORKS CITED

Bentley, Eric. *In Search of Theatre*. New York: Vintage Books, 1957.
———. *The Playwright as Thinker*. New York: Harcourt Brace & World, 1967.
Brustein, Robert. *The Theater of Revolt*. Boston: Little, Brown, 1962.
Carlson, Marvin. *Theories of the Theatre*. Ithaca, N.Y.: Cornell University Press, 1984.
Clurman, Harold. *On Directing*. New York: Macmillan, 1972.
Gilman, Richard. *The Making of Modern Drama*. New York: Farrar, Straus & Giroux, 1972.
Giudice, Gaspare. *Pirandello*. Trans. Alastair Hamilton. London: Oxford University Press, 1975.
Goldoni, Carlo. *Mirandolina*. Trans. Lady Augusta Gregory. *The Classic Theatre*, Volume I: *Six Italian Plays*. Ed. Eric Bentley. New York: Doubleday & Co., 1958.

Hagen, Uta. *Respect for Acting*. New York: Macmillan, 1973.

Katz, Leon. *The Three Cuckolds*. New York: Applause Theatre Book Publishers, 1986.

Krutch, Joseph Wood. *Modernism in Modern Drama*. Ithaca, N.Y.: Cornell University Press, 1953.

Machiavelli, Niccolò. *La Mandragola*. Trans. Bruce Penman. *Five Italian Renaissance Comedies*. Ed. Bruce Penman. New York: Penguin, 1978.

Marranca, Bonnie. *Theatrewritings*. New York: Performing Arts Journal Publications, 1984.

Paolucci, Anne. *Pirandello's Theater: The Recovery of the Modern Stage for Dramatic Art*. Carbondale: Southern Illinois University Press, 1974.

Pirandello, Luigi. *As You Desire Me*. Trans. Marta Abba. New York: Samuel French, 1948.

———. *To Clothe the Naked and Two Other Plays*. Trans. William Murray. New York: E. P. Dutton, 1962.

———. *Illustratori, attori e traduttori*. In *Saggi, poesie, scritti varii*. Milano: Mondadori Editore, 1968.

———. *Naked Masks, Five Plays*. Ed. Eric Bentley. New York: E. P. Dutton, 1952.

Promis, Vincenzo, Ed. *La Passione di Gesù Cristo, rappresentazione sacra in Piemonte nel secolo XV*. Torino: Fratelli Bocca, 1888.

Searle, John R. *Expression and Meaning*. Cambridge: Cambridge University Press, 1979.

———. *Speech Acts: An Essay in the Philosophy of Languages*. Cambridge: University Press, 1969.

Stanislavsky, Constantin. *An Actor Prepares*. Trans. Elizabeth Reynolds Hapgood. New York: Theatre Arts, 1936.

Verga, Giovanni. *La lupa. Teatro di Giovanni Verga*. Milano: Mondadori Editore, 1960.

Part Six

PIRANDELLO'S NON-THEATRICAL WORKS

24

Pirandello as Novelist

Glauco Cambon

For a long time, Pirandello's name has been so tyrannically identified with theater that few among his devotees seem to be aware that he came to drama rather late, from an intensive career as a writer of fiction. Considering his many short stories and his seven novels, his contribution to fiction is indeed so rich that it deserves much closer examination than it generally receives. It is not to be dismissed as a mere prelude to the plays, never mind how often they superseded in the public's attention the sensitive short stories from which they had taken their thematic cue. Pirandello's experiments as a novelist, in particular, proved as searching as his more widely acknowledged theatrical ventures. Although I disagree with those nonconformist critics who downgrade the Pirandello of the plays in favor of Pirandello the narrative artist, I recognize in the narrative artist the same greatness that asserted itself on the stage. We would do well to remember in this regard that some of the best avant-garde fiction of this century evinced a strong dramatic bent—Joyce's *Ulysses* and Faulkner's *Absalom! Absalom!* providing clear examples. And it is precisely with these innovators, as well as with formally more conservative moderns like James, Gide, Svevo, and Mann, that Pirandello the novelist belongs.

The first two novels Pirandello wrote, *L'Esclusa* (*The Outcast*) and *Il turno* (*The Turn*), date from the early 1890s, even though they were published in the first decade of the present century. If they can hardly match the formal assurance

Source: First presented as a lecture at the Istituto Italiano di Cultura of New York City, 1985.

of their immediate successor, *Il fu Mattia Pascal* (*The Late Mattia Pascal*, 1904), they do present focal themes of Pirandello's art with poignancy that we cannot ignore. *Il Turno*, an expanded novella, is a Sicilian grotesque, a musical-chairs ballet of love, frustration, and jealousy. In Verga's naturalist vein, characters are seen as products of their environment, and the situation itself is capitalized to the point that what counts with the reader is not so much the study of regional mores as the utter absurdity of a human condition that is emphatically insular and therefore typical of whatever is eccentric, warped, and irrational in man.

L'Esclusa*, a very different kind of novel, still heavily indebted to Verga, explores the insular condition. Its point is not to show the predicament of those who are caught in it because they accept the insular code, but the contrary predicament of one who discovers the eccentricity of that code and, having rejected its constrictiveness, chooses her own solitude: to be in but not of the island. Marta Ayala, a blood cousin of such defiant bourgeois heroines as Ibsen's Nora of *A Doll's House* and Dreiser's *Sister Carrie*, finally interests us more as an individualization of consciousness than as a study in feminine emancipation, germane though that theme may have been to the era. What happens *in* Marta herself matters more than what happens *to* her. She meets her ordeals with a fighting spirit that becomes an ascetic type of compassion when she sees that the odds are too many. It was a felicitous touch on the author's part to have her yield once to her longtime suitor Gregorio Aliprandi only to part with him and then receive her distressed husband with a detached, if warm, understanding. She is no Bovary. That final scene in her mother-in-law's death chamber has flaws of execution and a certain melodramatic quality, yet it appropriately climaxes the firm linear design of the whole. Marta, the "outcast," has turned the tables against the community that cast her out, and is now ready to survive and forgive. She has accepted the absurdity of human mores, of existence itself, and this knowledge, which brands her as the black sheep, makes her immeasurably stronger than the congregated gossips and stuffed shirts, victims of a fossilized tradition, who persecuted her. She is an ancestor of Mrs. Ponza, a saint of the absurd. The structure of the whole narrative is linear and focuses on the heroine's development, unlike the functionally tortuous plottiness of *Il Turno*. *Il Turno* shows men as puppets of their sanctioned inhibitions and thus finds its proper climate in the grotesque, while *L'Esclusa*'s treatment of human absurdity verges on sublime compassion.

Respectively grotesque chorus and elegiac solo, these first two novels exhibit Pirandello's versatility, his experimental verve, though strictly within the naturalist mode he had inherited from his fellow-islanders Verga and Capuana and their French contemporaries. The third novel, *Il Fu Mattia Pascal*, goes beyond that mode in a way that places it alongside works like Gide's *L'Immoraliste*, Thomas Mann's *Tonio Kroeger* and *Felix Krull*, Italo Svevo's *La Coscienza di Zeno*, Henry James's *Stories of Artists and Writers* and, more distantly, Joyce's *Portrait of the Artist*. All these writers, each in his way, digested the naturalist experience, and sooner or later they came to terms with the problem of an individual consciousness alienated from its social matrix by the crying need for a freedom the social conventions would not allow. This theme of liberty through alienation (Joyce's and Mann's "silence, cunning, and exile") would be finally accessible to the artist, namely, to the man of imagination, the man who could virtually consummate experiences.

It was thus only logical that writers who had explored the jungle of social determinism in a naturalist key should come to focus on the *exceptional* consciousness, the consciousness that knew no bounds precisely because it suffered most from the actual limitations of social mores, laws, and institutions: the consciousness of the artist. Viewed in this light, the theme of the artist as variously treated in a kind of *Bildungsroman* literature at the turn of the century bespeaks soul-searching and not escape or narcissistic self-involvement on the part of the writers. The artist is a marked man; the artist is a scapegoat; he takes on himself the moral burden of a whole society, by examining himself in it and it through himself; Tonio Kroeger runs symbolically afoul of the law by being mistaken for a wanted criminal. But "criminality" (in the etymological sense of "separation," *crimen*, *cerno*) is the mark of so many of Mann's artist characters, from Kroeger to Krull, from Aschenbach to Leverkuehn, as well as of Gide's "immoralist" persona in quest of *disponibilité*, aesthetic and ethical freedom, that adding Mattia Pascal to the list is only an overdue recognition of fundamental affinities. Whether this involves labeling that phase of European fiction as "decadent" is an open question; we can certainly see it as the resurgence of an earlier romantic theme and attitude, the Promethean one (with spleen outweighing buoyancy), and drop the pejorative implications of the term *decadentism* to employ it in a purely descriptive, historical sense.

I refer to De Castris's brilliant analysis of *Il fu Mattia Pascal* for a closer look at that novel (which deservedly won Pirandello his first international recognition). I would also like to point out how it somehow synthesizes and transcends, through its freer form, *Il Turno*'s social grotesque and *L'Esclusa*'s individual elegy. In the new novel, all of society, not just Sicilian, is viewed as cramping, both because of its local mores in the Ligurian village and because it is based on institutionalized behavior. The attempt of the narrator persona to conquer freedom is doomed to failure, and Mattia Pascal eventually returns to his home village on the paradoxical condition of remaining cfficially "dead" and living on marginally, as a librarian holed up in a deconsecrated church, while the artist is born in him out of his acceptance-rejection. His autobiography is the book itself, and we extrapolate it into Pirandello's biography very easily. After all, he had written in *L'Esclusa* in his quasi-monastic refuge of Monte Cavo, in 1893, in external circumstances somewhat similar to those of Mattia (i.e., self-chosen isolation after a return to his native country from a foreign country). Mattia Pascal is in turn a fictional rebirth of Marta Ayala with the added ingredient of humor—a humor, to be sure, that never obliterates but rather enhances the elegiac sadness that is so deeply ingrained in our Sicilian introvert. Pirandello's essay on humor, *L'umorismo* (1908), is only the theoretical realization of the literary experience he had been progressively unfolding in book after book. He was, of course, a fond reader of Cervantes and Shakespeare.

Yet Pirandello's development as novelist (or as writer in general) is hardly linear. *Il fu Mattia Pascal* marks a bold thrust forward for Pirandello, a kind of symbolic self-definition in an artist who conquers his own inner freedom by recognizing his complicated estrangement from society, a society to which he is inextricably bound even though he is not really of it. The first-person narrative, which for other novelists represented the beginning of their career, was for Pirandello a calculated conquest. We see that, after the interlude of *Giustino Roncella nato Boggiólo* (*Her Husband*) and *I vecchi e i giovani* (*The Old and the Young*) dating from the immediate pre-World War I years, he returned to the autobiographic type of narrative mode with *Quaderni di Serafino Gubbio* (*Notebooks of Serafino Gubbio, Cameraman*) in 1916 and *Uno, nessuno e centomila* (*One, No one, and a Hundred Thousand*) in 1926. On the other hand, the "interlude" I am talking about is itself of major importance just because it somehow regresses to the pre-*Mattia Pascal* period, both thematically and stylistically. Stylistically, we have in *Giustino Roncella* and *I vecchi e i giovani* a return to the descriptive third-person narrative that was ideally suited to a detached exploration of society from a fairly deterministic viewpoint. Thematically, *Giustino Roncella* resumes, in ironic key, the cue of *L'Esclusa*, whereas *I vecchi e i giovani* comes to grips with the harrowing question of modern Sicily, that is, with the history of modern Italy, with the failure of its Resorgimento ideals, the drabness and hopelessness that followed the flash of Garibaldi's liberating sword. *Giustino Roncella* is the most sophisticated psychological novel Pirandello ever wrote, and the self-denying figure of the husband who sacrifices everything to his wife's artistic career even when she abandons him is hard to forget. He is a Don Quixote of marital love, and the scene of his child's death (an obvious improvement of the final scenes of *L'Esclusa*) is such an impressive example of funereal gaudiness, Sicilian baroque style, that I find it indispensable in the Pirandello canon. Still, this is a throwback from the new mode that *Mattia Pascal* had initiated.

So is, for that matter, the huge historical fresco of *I vecchi e i giovani*, something between a "generational" novel and a combined aftermath of Nievo's and Tolstoy's classics. Unlike *Il fu Mattia Pascal*, this book is far from effortless. It is so busy telling a story woven of multiple patterns that we are tempted to say of it: Good, a historical novel come too late. It is also unevenly written, marred by occasional clichés and melodrama. But its indwelling force, recurrent brilliance of characterization, and density of evoked atmosphere quite redeem its faults. Its primary importance lies in its having faced, as broadly and deeply as Pirandello could, the problem of history. It answers the question: What is Sicily? Therefore it also answer two other questions: Who is Pirandello? What made him possible? Because the Pirandellian consciousness, at variance with history, is the embodiment of Quixotic anachronism: it is Mauro Mortara and Cosmo Laurentano and his brother Ippolito, sage and madman, hero and crank.

The antihistorical bent of Pirandello's subsequent work finds its explanation in this novel. History has gone wrong in Sicily, and if in Sicily, then anywhere—in Rome, for instance. Sicily is to Pirandello what the South is to Faulkner and what Ireland is to Joyce: a hopeless case, a fierce love, and a hotbed of anachronistic dreamers. *Henry IV* will condemn history even while using it as a stage effect. *Così è se vi pare* will condemn the results and evidence of history in the document, which is lost and which anyway, being a mere public fetish, proves nothing about one's real identity.

With typical discontinuity, Pirandello jumps from an ostensibly traditional to an avant-garde novel with *I quaderni di Serafino Gubbio operatore* (*Shoot!*, 1916). Once again the choice of the first-person narrative form signals disruption of standard structures; it ties in with the unhistorical present of narration and with rhapsodic looseness. The Sicilian past was a kind of original sin; the rootless industrial present is a verification of that sin. The curse of history was one thing but the curse of the machine is even worse. Serafino Gubbio has no choice but to fix his alienation in the posture of the movie camera operator. At the end he is a mere recording consciousness, with no powers to alter the events he sees, with no resources except his compassion behind a mask of impassability. This novel explodes the novelistic form, and in some respects it parallels the stream-of-consciousness experiments of Joyce. In others it anticipates the "école du regard" of Robbe-Grillet and Serraute. The final sequence of the killing of the tiger is pure Faulkner, twenty years before the fact. These are no accidental coincidences. Pirandello's "demon of experiment" (to say it with the Father in *Six Characters*) was more restless than that of Thomas Mann or Henry James, and just as restless as that of Joyce. Like Joyce, in his own creative trajectory he consummated the fundamental experiences of nineteenth- and twentieth-century fiction, and having phylogenetically recapitulated the development of the novel, he "killed" it.

For nothing else would do. Likewise, he "killed" traditional drama with bombshells like *Six Characters, Henry IV, Tonight We Improvise*. The killing of a novel—a feat comparable to Joyce's in *Finnegans Wake*— is accomplished in *Quaderni di Serafino Gubbio* and, even more irrevocably, in *Uno, Nessuno e Centomila*. First-person narrative; unhistorical present; explosion of personal identity. Who am I? Vitangelo Moscarda? With my conspicuous nose? Well, I am going to find out. So will the others. I rid myself of conscience, conscience being the others in me. I refuse all masks. I can even essay the gratuitous act of murder—without actually consummating it. I am *other*, I have achieved the ultimate liberation of consciousness. I have killed history.

No name whatsoever. No remembrance today of yesterday's name; or of today's name, tomorrow. If the name is the thing; if a name is in us the concept of each thing placed outside ourselves; and without name there is no concept, and the thing remains in us as if blind, indistinct and indefinite; well, then, this name which I bore among men, let everyone engrave it, a funereal epitaph, on the forehead of the image with which I appeared to him, and peace be to it forevermore. . . . I am alive and I do not conclude. Life does not conclude. And life knows nothing of names. This tree, a quivering breath of new leaves. I am this tree. Tree, cloud; tomorrow, book or wind: the book I read, the wind I drink. All outside, a vagabond. (my translation)

That is to say, Pirandello achieves in *Uno, nessuno e centomila* his final deliverance from the nightmare of history, that history which had only led to the burden of insufferable limitation, Sicilian peculiarity, grotesque doom, the prison of the defined self; and he (or his persona, rather) exists in nonhistorical time, in perpetual ecstasy, in nothingness as no-thing, therefore all things, a cosmic all-inclusiveness. That seals his development, ever since he brooded on the doom of history and identity in the grotto at Monte Cavo, a latter-day hermit. Pirandello's antihistoricism and unworldliness are worthy of a monk. It all came out of Monte Cavo, and monastic life appeals to the 1925 persona, Moscarda. As a Sicilian, Pirandello could find no better way to go against the grain, to assert his separatism, to protest without committing himself to an ideology. It is in the sequence of the seven novels that this mystical iconoclasm is best outlined. Vitangelo Moscarda dies to the social and historical world to commune with the cosmos; he is Pirandello's innermost self and his fictional testament. It had taken a desperate thinker to weigh all of history and find it wanting.

25

Luigi Pirandello as Writer of Short Fiction and Novels

Douglas Radcliff-Umstead

Although Luigi Pirandello gained international fame as a powerfully innovative dramatist, he was an extremely prolific author of novels and short fiction. There is a strong line of continuity between the writer's narrative and stage works since both reflect his compassionate vision of human existence. Pirandello's best developed theoretical statements on life and literature can be found in his treatise *L'umorismo* (*On Humor*) of 1908. He distinguished humor from the comic, burlesque, ironical, satirical, and grotesque. For him humor did not exist as an attribute of any particular literary genre such as the comic epic poem; rather, it was a quality of expression that required the greatest possible linguistic freedom. In Cervantes' *Don Quixote* Pirandello recognized a masterpiece of humor in the pathetic contrast between the Don's grandiose dreams of chivalric glory and the wretchedness of his personal situation.

Pirandello points out two moments that create a humoristic situation: "the awareness of the contrary" and "the sentiment of the contrary." The awareness comes about when we recognize the ridiculous contrast between a grotesque situation (as when an elderly individual uses makeup and a wig to appear youthful) and the accepted image of proper makeup and attire. Reflection leads to the sentiment of the contrary on considering the individual's reasons for using cosmetics and a wig in order to hold onto the affections of a young lover or spouse. One of Pirandello's novellas, *Le dodici lettere* (*The twelve letters*, 1897), tells of a pathetic wife who deceives herself by thinking her seductive coiffure and smart clothes will prevent further infidelities by her philandering husband. Pirandello leads his readers to look beyond ridiculous appearances to pity an individual's anguish. In presenting his fictional characters, Pirandello as humorist always sought to reveal the self-contradicting situations into which life thrust its victims. The humor inspiring Pirandello's short fiction and novels unmasks the deceptions of private and public life to arrive at a sympathetic understanding of the human situation.[1]

THE SHORT FICTION

Before his death Pirandello hoped to write a novella for each day of the year and to gather them in the series *Novelle per un anno* (*Stories for a year*). By 1937, the year after the writer's death, fifteen volumes had appeared in print. In all the author succeeded in completing 233 tales. The earliest story dates from his seventeenth year, and the final surrealistic dream stories belong to the last five years of the writer's life. Before being included in volumes, many of the tales originally appeared on the story page of major daily Italian newspapers like Milan's *Corriere della sera* as well as the provincial *Giornale di Sicilia*. The writer directed his stories to a reading public of the professional and semi-professional middle class, for whom the novellas were intended as little mirrors of their aspirations and frustrations.

In composing his tales, Pirandello had behind him the long Italian narrative tradition of novelistic art that arose in the late thirteenth century and early attained near perfection with Boccaccio's *Decameron* of 1350. The stories tend to concentrate on a single central event that determines the course of the protagonist's life by exposing the main character's inner strengths or weaknesses. Pirandello had before him the recent literary experience of his fellow Sicilian writer Giovanni Verga (1840–1922), whose collections *Vita dei campi* (*Life of the Fields*, 1880) and *Novelle rusticane* (*Rustic Tales*, 1883) marked the shift of emphasis in the novella from exterior action and verbal witticism, as in Boccaccio's tales, to an examination of inner motivation and the influence of environment. Both Verga and his Sicilian compatriot Luigi Capuana (1839–1915) were associated with *verismo*, the literary school of regional realism that stressed fidelity to truth. Many of Pirandello's tales study the same insular Sicilian world as is depicted in the narrative works of Verga and Capuana. Despite the veristic aim to achieve objectivity, all three Sicilian authors display a fatalistic attitude that seems to be inherent to the novella and that distinguishes it from the regional short stories of other nations like Russia or the American South. The art of the novella lends itself to an irrational presentation of life, where chance or fate strikes the protagonist. With his humoristic vision Pirandello represented life as a cruel practical joke, and his tales are histories of the jests that mock his characters.

Neither in the early volumes nor in the definitive editions of the *Novelle per un anno* is any attempt made to place the tales in a frame story as occurs in the *Decameron*. Pirandello realized that in the twentieth century encircling the chaotic material of life in a harmonious frame would have been artistically false. Instead, his novellas should be experienced as isolated moments of intense agony or brutal irony as filtered through humorism. The wretched characters in the world of his tales appear as calculating peasants, hypocritical clergymen, disillusioned artists, game-playing entrepreneurs, lonely students, shrewd lawyers, disappointed war veterans, unfulfilled teachers, exploited sulfur miners, reactionary aristocrats, neglected wives, unloved children, and the elderly longing only to die. For the settings of his tales, Pirandello moved from the fetid peasant huts of his earliest veristic tales of Sicily to the swarming tenements of modern Rome in the stories of his midcareer to the apartments of black Harlem and Jewish Brooklyn in his final novellas. Quite often the scene takes place in a train compartment, usually second class, or a railroad station restaurant where the restless reach out in vain to each other. A large number of characters suffer from myopia, both physical and (by symbolic extension) spiritual, and are thereby hampered in their quest for self-realization. Whatever the social roles may be, wherever the tale is set, the characters frequently remain separate from each other. The stories can be classified according to certain predominating themes or situations; fables where animals stare with amazement at the inane rituals of human life; graveyard tales with obligatory scenes in cemeteries or at funerals; stories of nihilism that explode in violence; pictures of life's barrenness often ending in suicide; exposés of the falseness of bourgeois customs (especially in marriages); and visions of a super-reality transcending everyday experience.

Even in his earliest stories, Pirandello tended toward dramatic enactment of scene (Lubbock). Indirect discourse is almost totally missing as lively dialogue or interior monologue (in the first or third person) take its place. As some critics have pointed out (Zangrilli, 95–97), there exists in Pirandello's narrative writing an entire language of silence made up of nonverbal communication through gestures and expressions of the eyes as well as represented voice inflections. Syntax, the use of tenses, and the choice of verbal modes (particularly the subjunctive to express emotional expectations) all contribute to creating a language of deception, to oneself and others, that Pirandello's humoristic art unmasks.

Between 1894 and 1920, before the writer conceived the plan for the comprehensive *Novelle per un anno*, Pirandello published his stories in volumes with antithetical titles like *Amori senza amore* (*Loves Without Love*); *Beffe della morte e della vita* (*Jests of Death and Life*); *Quand' ero matto* (*When I Was Mad*); *Bianche e nere* (*White and Black*); *Erma bifronte* (*The Two-faced Herm*); *La Vita nuda* (*Naked Life*); *Terzetti* (*Tercets*); *Le due maschere* (*The Two Masks*); *La Trappola* (*The Trap*); *Erba del nostro orto* (*Grass from Our Garden*); *E domani, lunedì* (*And Tomorrow, Monday*); *Un cavallo nella luna* (*A Horse in the Moon*); *Berecche e la guerra* (*Berecche and the War*); and *Il carnevale dei morti* (*The Carnival of the Dead*). On opening any of these volumes, the reader soon discovers that death plays a role in about two-thirds of the stories (Janner, 85). Pirandello's obsession with death differs from the nightmare tales of Poe, Heine, and Maupassant as the Sicilian author focused on the empty rituals and the often pompous settings associated with death. While for a few of the characters in the novellas a tomb may provide a consoling sense of permanence, in many cases the grave fails to testify to enduring sentiments of attachment and comforting eternal rest. Death often occurs on an August afternoon as the result of a heat stroke when the African scirocco wind blows across the blazing fields of Sicily or the burning concrete streets of Rome. A recurring situation in the tales is that of the death watch where relatives and acquaintances gather at the home of a moribund person to wait out the final hours. Although the certainty of dying may offer release from the pain of living, the realization of immediate fatality can intensify the awareness of life.

Two tales that strikingly illustrate Pirandello's novelistic art are "Il Viaggio" ("The Journey," 1910) and "Felicità" ("Happiness," 1911). A critical analysis of each story will reveal the writer's investigation of a subterranean world of human anguish and expectation. Adriana Braggi, the protagonist of "Il Viaggio," begins to reawaken to her instinctual longing for life and love at the very time she receives a sentence of death from cancer of the lung. This tale reflects the influence of *verismo* on Pirandello as the author takes pains during the first two pages to detail the monotonous mode of life within the environment of a small town (called, pejoratively with the diminutive suffix, a "*cittaduzza*") in the interior of Sicily. The heroine appears to be an unconscious prisoner of time-honored custom in the narrow community where women lead a claustrophobic existence, usually leaving their homes only once a week to attend Sunday mass. In that rigid society women do not function as persons in their own right but merely as extensions of their husbands' being. The fashionable gowns and jewels, ordered from Palermo or Catania, that the women wear on their weekly expedition to church are intended to impress the townspeople with the prosperity of the husbands. Throughout the opening passages, the tense that predominates is the imperfect ("she used to go out," "she used to dress," "they used to see each other") to indicate the eternal monotony and unchanging character of village life. Upon describing the region's drought-ridden conditions the author establishes a leitmotif for the story:

In all the houses, even in the few lordly ones, water was lacking; in the vast courtyards, as at the end of streets, there were old cisterns at the mercy of the heavens; but even in winter it rarely rained . . . (*Novelle per un anno*, II, 440).

This story's inner structure is based on the principle of water as the source of life and death, such as the French phenomenologist Gaston Bachelard has traced in his text *Water and Dreams*. As the tale's title suggests, this is the story of a journey that the heroine will make to escape that land of drought and life-denying inflexible customs. Throughout Pirandello's novellas, the journey motif marks the attempt to discover a hitherto repressed reality.

Before her departure from the village Adriana Braggi lived in a state of unawareness, unquestioningly obeying social demands for proper behavior. Her brief marriage of four years had been a silent and voluntary martyrdom of fidelity without love for a tyrannically jealous husband. What Pirandello emphasizes is that almost all the women in that empty provincial world suffer the identical fate as Adriana, except that they are never called to a journey of self-knowledge. Along with the aridity of their existence there is an atmosphere of oppressive silence that seems to annihilate the passing of time itself within the imprisoning walls of their homes "where time seemed to stagnate in a silence of death" (II, 441). After her husband's death, Adriana continues the routine of a provincial homemaker, staying on in the same house with her two sons, her mother, and her brother-in-law Cesare who according to village custom is the actual master of the home. It never occurs to her to deviate from time-honored custom or to rebel against a stultifying existence of being buried alive. Pirandello does not intervene directly into the tale; instead of commenting, he allows thoughts and events to take place as in a natural process. Indirect free style conveys how the death of Adriana's mother causes her to acknowledge the loss of her youth at age thirty-five. Premature old age, a drying up of vital energies, appears to be the inevitable destiny of those who accept provincial life.

Adriana's routine of living according to the village code is interrupted when she has to seek medical consultation and travels with her brother-in-law to Palermo. Away from the little town's suffocating environment, Adriana changes her apparel and her coiffure, as if she were starting a new life. The scene where she stands before a mirror and shows her new traveling outfit to her teenaged sons and astonished brother-in-law is an example of Pirandello's art of dramatic enactment: all four individuals take part in an experience of discovery, wherein Adriana realizes that she has not withered away in her silent widowhood. Although her new outfit is black for mourning, its elegance makes everyone aware of the youthful vitality previously submerged under the melancholy mask of provincial existence. Through brief snatches of dialogue Pirandello allows the scene to unfold for the reader as if it were a stage performance.

This tale of Adriana's journey is one of overcoming barriers. The first barrier is passed as Adriana leaves on her first train trip and watches the narrow houses of her arid village disappear from the window of her coach. She is leaving behind a life of unconscious captivity to village tradition. With the train trip all the solidity of life vanishes, a solidity which a writer like Verga saw symbolized by the domestic hearth but which Pirandello viewed as an illusion. After a medical specialist in the island's capital city pronounces a fatal diagnosis, Adriana refuses to succumb to the lethargy that had earlier oppressed her. As she stands by the Fountain of Hercules in Palermo's public garden, the widow undergoes a mystical experience on beholding the jets of water spraying over the statue of the demigod. The joy of a seemingly endless moment permits the woman to dominate the dread of death and for the first time in her life she opens her being to all the elusive magic of rich sensations: the brilliant colors of the capital city's streets at sunset, the exciting commotion of crowds of shoppers, and at the fountain a voluptuous feeling of eternity. At last, as life and death confront each other in her consciousness, Adriana ends her stagnation.

Rather than allow Adriana to return to the slow death of living in the village, Cesare takes her with him to Naples. Crossing the sea to reach the continent marks the passing of the second barrier, for the widow, with the primitive insular mentality of Sicilians, feels that the trip across the water must signify a turning point in her life. In Naples a mere touch of each other's arm as they promenade on the street one night suffices to reveal to Adriana and Cesare the affection which earlier they would never have acknowledged. Previously, the two were "masked" to each other and to the world of their home village, but now the certainty of death permits them to violate a traditional way of life which both had accepted without question. Adriana can cross the barriers of social taboos to discover the freedom of surrender to rapture. Transgression follows naturally upon reawakening.

With the collapse of moral strictures Adriana starts out on what will be both a journey of Eros and Thanatos for her—"a journey of love toward death" (II, 445). Pirandello deliberately brings his tale to a swift close to represent the heroine's frenetic journey through Rome, Florence, and Milan in a delirium of passion, where every moment becomes more precious than the one before since it might be the last the lovers will share. At Venice, the city most symbolic of decay and death, Adriana spends a day of velvet voluptuousness: the velvet of gondolas which, however, reminds her of the velvet lining of coffins. No longer able to elude the mirror image of death on her face, Adriana passes the ultimate barrier by poisoning herself. Her love for Cesare could never know the disenchantment that usually follows the rapture of passion in Pirandellian tales. From the imprisonment of life in a Sicilian village, Adriana has moved to the final confinement of death to end her journey of self-discovery. Water dominates throughout the tale: the arid village where rainfall seems like a holiday, mystical rebirth at the Palermo fountain, the liberation of the steamer trip, the dreamlike vision of Venice emerging proud and melancholy from its ever silent lagoons. The passionate journey to the source of life in water frees Pirandello's heroine from entrapment but ironically leads her to the surrender of death.

According to Pirandello, a sensual and sentimental relationship between a man and a woman can never end in enduring happiness. Instead, one of the few sources of lasting contentment, Pirandello suggests, is maternal love when it is permitted to blossom. The story "Felicità" illustrates how the satisfaction of the maternal instinct enables a woman to withstand social humiliation and poverty. This tale also demonstrates Pirandello's art of contrasting sadness with warmth and intimacy. It, too, is a story of barriers, in this instance, the barriers that the characters raise to isolate themselves from each other. The story opens in a zone of nearly explosive tension: at Palermo in the town palace of Duke Gaspare Grisanti, whose last hope for financial salvation has vanished after his only son deserted a wealthy wife to run off with an actress. An air of decay hangs over the gloomy rooms of the palace, made all the more oppressive by the stuffy odor of old furniture. Pirandello makes the tense atmosphere an almost tactile experience where a violent electric charge seems about to burst forth from every familiar object. All her childhood the duke's daughter Elisabetta lived in the palace's shadows, knowing her father did not love her because her lack of beauty would not attract a rich match to restore the family fortune. When Elisabetta asks for her father's consent to wed a tutor (a man from a far inferior social class), the duke agrees to the shameful marriage but banishes her forever from the palace. This tale then is concerned with the distances that people build between themselves. Pirandello portrays in spatial terms the spirit of exclusion that leads the duke to separate others (including his own child) from his aristocratic presence. Consequently, the son-in-law can enter the palace only by the servants' staircase to collect the meager checks granted to him in place of a dowry. Since the duke never intends to look at Elisabetta again, he arranges for his wife to meet her in a rented carriage. Here the author emphasizes how some individuals stubbornly attempt to manipulate reality, to the point of determining the space others can occupy and share with each other.

After Elisabetta's husband deserts her and flees Sicily to avoid prosecution for theft, the young woman rises above misery to radiant joy when she gives birth to a boy. She does not seek reconciliation with the duke, who continues to make his pompous daily appearance in public riding through the streets in a coach attended by footmen in perukes and livery. She has already established a humble "*casetta*" ("the little house"—the diminutive stresses both the impoverishment and the warm intimacy of the home), feeling no need to return to the palace's melancholy darkness. Mother and child can live at the outskirts of town, near a countryside of cheerful sunlight and fragrant flowers. The tale closes with Elisabetta's resolute dismissal of her mother's hope that the duke might relent and readmit his daughter and grandson to the palace. For in the little house a sense of sunny openness predominates, in contrast to the palace's dark constriction. As the story's title indicates, Elisabetta has created her own corner of happiness, such as Bachelard studies in his treatise *The Poetics of Space*. With a strength of will Pirandello thought unique to mothers, Elisabetta can bear exclusion from her aristocratic heritage because the truly vital identity she has discovered in maternity allows her to construct a zone of private contentment. Motherhood can then offer a release from the anguish of living.[2]

Throughout his novellas Luigi Pirandello examined individual cases of the failure or success of his fictional characters to reach an accord with life. Adriana Braggi of "Il Viaggio" discovers renewal and annihilation simultaneously, while Elisabetta Grisanti finds liberation in banishment. In his short fiction the writer explored situations of distress and alienation in a naturally condensed literary form. But in order to view his fictional characters across the expanse of society with its restricting codes and hypocritical compromises, the author had to turn to the breadth offered by the novel.

THE NOVELS

The Outcast (L'Esclusa)

Ostracism without just cause is the motivating situation of Pirandello's first novel, *L'Esclusa*, of 1894. An accusation of adultery results in banishment for the novel's heroine Marta Ayala from her hometown in Sicily, even though she was guilty merely of exchanging letters with her ardent admirer, the lawyer and parliamentary deputy Gregorio Alvignani. This novel is essentially about the violence that communities inflict on their victims. Sicilian society, as represented in this work, is an example of what Henri Bergson in his book *Laughter* (1956) calls a place of "habit, ritual bondage, and arbitrary laws." Marta Ayala does not choose her solitude since isolation is society's punishment for her supposed transgressions. Upon receiving Alvignani's letters her vanity had led her on the dangerous, though fully innocent, course that destroyed her marriage and the position of her family in society.

In this novel Pirandello presents a text of feminist investigation into the restrictions that society imposes on women. Like some of the adolescent heroines of Pirandello's tales, Marta was forced by her parents to leave school at age sixteen to make a socially advantageous union with a stranger, well-to-do Rocco Pentagora. Marta had planned a career of her own as a teacher, but her desire for independence is fated always to be undermined by others: her parents, her husband, her tyrannical father-in-law, her neighbors, and after her exile, the school authorities and her teaching colleagues. Pirandello goes beyond probing the problem of a woman imprisoned in a male-dominated world and demonstrates the emptiness of the romantic myth of individual autonomy. Society does not permit individuals to forge independent identities. Marta Ayala could not assume any role for herself except as daughter, wife, and outcast: the excluded one.

Pirandello's treatment of space in this earliest of his extended narrative writings reveals that already in the 1890s he had begun the task of humoristic deconstruction which would be completed in his stage works. Unlike Verga and Capuana, Pirandello rejected the fundamental constructs of Sicily's provincial world. Even though both Verga and Capuana wrote tales of adultery, respectively, in "Cavalleria rusticana" ("Rustic chivalry") and "Ribrezzo" ("Disgust"), still they accepted the Sicilian honor code as a necessary means to preserve one's dignity in social relationships, though they deplored its cruelty and inflexibility.The ceremony of the duel between the wronged husband and the offending male, that results in the death of the lover Turiddu in "Cavalleria rusticana," appears as little more than a farce in *L'Esclusa* where Rocco challenges Gregorio to a contest that leaves the husband with a scar across his left cheek. Pirandello sought to expose the absurdity of social codes. He rejected the positivistic faith of his era in the ability to establish an absolute and verifiable truth through documents, as when Rocco tried to prove his wife's infidelity with the letters Marta received from her admirer. Instead of portraying firm codes and concrete truths, Pirandello pointed out narrowminded prejudices.

Buildings are an example of the ideal constructions people erect and furnish to give meaning to their lives and to gain the respect of others. A home can function as a public mask whose façade displays what the owner wants to show to the world. In Verga's novels, such as his masterwork *I Malavoglia* (*The House by the Medlar Tree*, 1881), the home is the most sacred of all precincts whose loss must occasion years of toil. But throughout *L'Esclusa* Pirandello illustrates that buildings represent the attempts of his characters to patch up the crumbling structures of their existence. The power of past tradition and the tyrannical authority of the father-figure in Sicilian society are all expressed in the oppressive mass of the house that Marta's father-in-law Antonio Pentagoro constructed like a tower, story by story. A moldy odor pervades the building that could never know happiness with its suffocatingly low ceilings and yellowed walls; the lack of domestic harmony is emphasized by the long lines of unmatching chairs. Embarrassed silences alternate with the explosive outbursts of Pentagoro, whose wife betrayed him with a lover. Yet in that house Rocco feels a sense of freedom from marital responsibilities, which he rejects after casting Marta from their luxuriously furnished new home. By returning to his father's house, Rocco voluntarily surrenders to the weight of the past, which reclaims him with the family's curse of conjugal infidelity. Distrust and superstition emanate from the poisonous atmosphere of the Pentagoro homes.

Love was also a stranger at the house of Marta's father, Francesco Ayala, who would fly into a violent rage even when someone accidentally broke a small and insignificant object like a bottle—as if the offender were trying to undermine his prestige as head of the household and as man of authority in town. Pirandello's characters do not experience the object-malady that characterizes the protagonists of later novels like Antoine Roquentin in Jean-Paul Sartre's *La Nausée* (*Nausea*, 1983) and Dino in Alberto Moravia's *La Noia* (*The Empty Canvas*, 1960). Whereas the antiheroes of Sartre and Moravia feel unable to relate to physical objects, Pirandello's characters often long to possess the solidity and apparent permanence of inanimate objects. Pirandellian alienation does not arise from the nauseous sense of separation from a world of physical objects as befalls Roquentin and Dino, but from a melancholy awareness of isolation. Marta Ayala can spend hours staring at familiar objects like armchairs, both to understand the feeling of identity they give her and to appreciate the meaning of their separate inanimate existence. In his home, with all its objects, Francesco Ayala sought to create his own realm that others would acknowledge as his claim to their respect. Once that respect is withdrawn because of the scandal over Marta's alleged infidelity, Francesco reveals his true indifference to material possessions by retreating to a single room of his home, which he makes his refuge. After his death, Marta has to assist a process-server in making an inventory of the house and its belongings for an auction to settle the family's debts. Unlike the central situation in *I Malavoglia*, there will be no battle for the family to regain their home of disgrace.

Three bright rooms in an apartment where Marta, her sister Maria, and their mother move after the auction attest to the heroine's brave attempt to triumph over local prejudices by passing the examination to become a schoolteacher. After community pressure drives her away from town, Marta and her family take an apartment in Palermo where she has received a new teaching appointment. In many of Pirandello's works, the characters select certain sites to live because of their important associations with events in the past: Francesco Ayala once fought as a Garibaldian volunteer on the very street in the island's capital where the family locate their new home. In the apartment's cheerful rooms Mother Ayala and Maria restore a semblance of meaningful order to their lives, but Marta continues to feel excluded from the happiness her family has regained through her labor. Although the Palermo school building with its elegant class-room pleases her, she comes to regard the teachers' reading-room as a place of ambush where her amorous male colleagues compete for her attention. Only one building in Palermo seems to welcome her: a villa with a spacious courtyard where flocks of doves seek refuge. In that tastefully furnished villa, where death and unhappiness would appear to be impossible, Gregorio Alvingnani has found refuge from the political tempests in Rome. Yet there in that charming dwelling Marta comes to know the disenchantment of a purely sensual relationship after she and Alvignani make a reality of the adulterous relationship that others had earlier attributed to them. Their infidelity occurs in a typically Pirandellian humoristic situation: when Rocco accused her of faithlessness, she was innocent. Forced away from her home community, Marta Ayala takes revenge in the capital by forming precisely that illicit relationship.

Pirandello's descriptions of buildings and landscapes contribute to an under-standing of character. An empty street usually symbolizes a sense of loss for characters who are suddenly without direction. Nighttime and its quiet create an impression of dream, where the moonlight fails to console human despair. Rain-fall parallels the turmoil in the hearts of the characters. Most of the novel's minor characters are realized on the level of the "*macchietta*," a boldly drawn sketch presenting an eccentric type as in a caricature. One secondary figure whose grotesque characterization transcends the "*macchietta*" is Marta's col-league Matteo Falcone, teacher of design. Physically deformed by his club feet, the art instructor admires Marta as the incarnation of the beauty he has always worshiped. Falcone's domestic life could be staged as an absurdist drama by Ionesco, for his insane mother and aunt fill their home to the rafters with unused furniture and reject him as an absolute stranger. After Marta turns down Matteo's furious declaration of love on a rain-swept street, the design instructor, on seeing beauty forever denied to him, loses his sanity. Pirandello's art does not work sadistically to distort character; instead, the writer portrays how life has twisted his characters to become caricatures of human beings.

In most nineteenth-century novels of adultery, the errant wife perishes: Madame Bovary takes arsenic in desperation over her debts; Anna Karenina hurls herself on railroad tracks after romance has turned to scorn; Effi Briest, the title character in Theodor Fontane's novel of 1895, dies of tuber-culosis, reunited at last with her parents but irreconcilably cut off from her vindictive husband and the daughter who is a stranger to her; Edna Pontel-lier in Kate Chopin's *The Awakening* (1899) drowns herself to escape the imprisonment of her own female biology. In contrast to all these heroines, Marta Ayala was blameless when she fell from respectable society. When

Rocco's mother dies in a wretched Palermo apartment one night after a violent thunder storm, Marta and her husband are prepared to put aside the turbulent past and renew their marriage. Pregnant with a child by her lover Alvignani, Marta shows her final willingness to participate in a counterfeit and hypocritical society since she will be returning to the closed space of her native town to resume her place as Signora Pentagora. Although the idea of suicide did tempt Marta, self-inflicted death would simply have justified the ostracism imposed by her community. Ironically, she was cast out when she was innocent and then readmitted with Rocco's fervent entreaties after she became guilty of the original charge of adultery. Marta's attempt to achieve economic and social independence on her own initiative meets frustration as she has to reach an accommodation with social custom. The Marta, Rocco, and Gregorio triangle does not conform to the usual adulterous triad, but instead reflects the writer's belief that even the most intimate persons can never communicate with each other. In *L'Esclusa* Pirandello the humorist has exposed a society of conventional bonds that forever inhibit loving tenderness.

The Turn (Il Turno)

In Pirandello's first novel society appears as an oppressive force. In his second novel, however, *Il Turno* of 1895, the community in the city of Girgenti (present-day Agrigento in Sicily), serves as a critical conscience to condemn a marriage forced on a young woman, Stellina Ravì, to the elderly but wealthy Don Diego Alcozer at the insistence of the girl's economically ambitious father Marcantonio. When Stellina resists the match despite Diego's daily gifts of expensive jewels (souvenirs of his first four wives, all deceased), her father places her in solitary confinement with just bread and water until she consents to the wedding. Later by chance Stellina meets the aggressive and astute lawyer Ciro Coppa, who successfully argues the annulment of the marriage and then weds her himself. Her second marriage turns into the typical nightmare of enslavement to an almost insanely jealous husband, but her marital imprisonment comes to a swift end after Ciro dies of a stroke. She finally marries a young, attractive aristocrat, Pepè Alletto, who would have been her father's original choice except for the nobleman's impoverishment; but at last the attorney's estate will provide for the young couple's future.

With its choreographic treatment of literary time as a continual carousel of aspirations and frustrations, *Il Turno* is an example of late nineteenth-century decadentism in the mode of Arthur Schnitzler's Viennese drama *Reigen* (*La Ronde*) of 1896–1897. In these works Schnitzler and Pirandello present life's routines as a merry-go-round in which one obsession leads to another connecting obsession in a circle of frenzied pursuits.[3] In this Sicilian novel Don Diego ends up marrying six times while Stellina enters into three marriages as both old age and youth play a round of recurring matrimony. As in Pirandello's novellas death takes the part of a jester in two parallel death watch sequences, one early in the narrative and the second near its end. When Don Diego contracts pneumonia after being drenched by a shower at a picnic, Stellina, her father, and Pepè Alletto hold a vigil of hope and remorse by the elderly man's bedside in their contradictory desire to see him die and their guilt at wishing for his demise. Whereas the old man survives his crisis, the energetic and athletic Ciro Coppa will later expire at the second watch held by the identical trio. The three marvel over the capriciousness of fate that spares an old man so that he can wed again but claims another individual at the seeming height of his vigor. The occurrence of the two death watches results from the novel's circular structure which makes of the work a dance not of love but of delusions.

In this third-person narrative, Pirandello achieved the veristic goal of objectivity by virtually disappearing from the text. As a humorist, Pirandello subjects his characters to a thorough exposé, uncovering the self-deceit behind their well-reasoned arguments. Ravì, Alcozer, and Coppa constantly feel the presence of the disapproving community when they make repeated efforts to explain themselves before their many accusers. In Marcantonio's conversations and monologues the key word is "*Ragioniamo,*" with the double meaning of "Let's talk things over" and "Let's reason things out." Because of Pirandello's humoristic vision, none of the arguments persuades.

Throughout the novel the characters remain on the level of the "*macchietta*" since they are all puppets of fate. Marcantonio Ravì falls victim not to greed but to logic as he plans for his daughter's future happiness and financial security, even if he has to treat her as a slave to achieve his aim. Don Diego emerges as a decadent twilight character involving himself in an endless succession of marriages: he attempts to cheat time by surrounding himself with youth as he adroitly plays one rival against another for the attentions of his latest wife. Stellina proves to be the opposite of Marta Ayala, for her whole being consists in her appearance for others. Pirandello did not give us a detailed physical portrait of Stellina as he customarily does with most of his characters, because she is a malleable creature in the hands of the men around her. Pepè Alletto demonstrates La Rochefoucauld's maxim that some persons would never fall in love unless others planted the idea of love in their minds. The young aristocrat was never interested in Stellina until Marcantonio implored him to wait patiently for his turn. Although Pepè attributes his poverty to the lack of opportunities in Girgenti for an enterprising individual to establish himself, the effete youth is not the victim of a stifling provincial environment but a plaything in the designs of others. The most self-assertive of all the characters is Ciro Coppa, who as an attorney represents the new Sicilian professional middle class that Verga scarcely alludes to in his writings: Coppa uses law not to defend family honor, but as a weapon of conflict in an increasingly complex society. Although Coppa yearns to be free of others, he becomes a slave to his self-doubts, insecurities, and domestic jealousy. All the characters of *Il Turno* wear themselves out by running the round of hopes and disappointments in this narrative of decadent obsession.

The Late Mattia Pascal (Il fu Mattia Pascal)

Pirandello's third novel *Il fu Mattia Pascal* brought him national and even European recognition following its publication in 1904. Eventually, its storyline would inspire three motion pictures. Basically, the novel falls into three broad divisions to relate the failed attempt of the title protagonist to escape living in society. The opening section, comprising the first seven chapters, deals with Mattia Pascal's youth of indolence and irresponsibility, his bad marriage, and the decline of his family's fortune. The sixth and seventh chapters provide a transition toward this antihero's metamorphosis into the unattached traveler Adriano Meis. Chapter Six moves from the backwater stagnation of Mattia's hometown Miragno in Liguria to the exciting prospects of the gambling casino at Monte Carlo where the protagonist wins a small fortune at roulette. The seventh chapter is pivotal: there Pascal learns of his supposed death by drowning and decides to discard his conventional identity as an impoverished town librarian and seek a new identity outside the bounds of normal society. From the eighth through the sixteenth chapters, the antihero poses as the autonomous Adriano Meis, only to discover the limitations of his nonlife as a shadow creature of imagination. A fictitious life like that of Adriana Meis requires a fictitious death— by feigning to have jumped from a Roman bridge into the Tiber to mark the close of the second division. A movielike change in tempo from slow motion to accelerated action occurs through the final division's seventeenth and eighteenth chapters as the protagonist returns home to resume his old identity as Mattia Pascal only to discover that his "widow" during the two-year interval has remarried and has had a child by her new husband. While Mattia's mere physical presence in town invalidates his wife's second marriage, the antihero withdraws to the civic library where he will spend his time writing the memoirs that are the text of this novel.

This work's first-person narration creates the impression of an autobiographical confession, thereby making this book a fictitious successor to the long-established Western tradition of confessional literature which goes back to Saint Augustine. The narrator-protagonist is forever explaining his unconventional behavior. His assertions are quickly followed by his humoristic logic which at once dismantles his statements. Showing all life in society to be lacking in substance, Pascal chooses isolation. Here the technique of first-person interior monologue advances Pirandello's investigation into life's provisional forms. Significantly, the author was later to dedicate his treatise *L'Umorismo* to "Mattia Pascal the librarian."

Much of this novel's popular success (which accounts for its numerous adaptations for the screen; see Jackson, 17–21) derives from its escapist story of evasion from life's responsibilities, offering readers the vicarious adventures of a fugitive from life who must continually adjust his new identity to radically changing circumstances. But Pirandello also created a profound study, showing us the impossibility of forging a life that is entirely independent of the feelings of other persons and modern societal institutions. One critic called this novel the "triumph of the civil state" (Croce, 6:352) because of the way the modern totalitarian (but not dictatorial) government successfully intrudes into the lives of the most elusive individuals. In his impersonation as Adriano Meis, the protagonist cannot deposit his roulette winnings in a bank or invest them on the stock market because he would have to show positive identification. He cannot even own a puppy, buy a house, marry the woman with whom he falls in love (Adriana Paleari, the daughter of his landlord at a Roman boardinghouse), or report to the police the theft of a large portion of his money. If it had not been for Western Europe's politically relaxed conditions in the early twentieth century, "Adriano Meis" could not have traveled throughout Italy and into the Rhine Valley without producing a state identity card or a passport at border crossings or when checking into hotels. Precisely because of his extralegal status, Adriano Meis must abandon the gentle and vulnerable young woman to whom he imprudently declared his love with a kiss as his illicit presence can only wreak havoc on her life. Through carefully limited focus and the forever questioning technique of interior monologue, Pirandello exposes the existences of Mattia Pascal and Adriano Meis in order to determine the tormenting reasons why the protagonist has to undergo two fictitious deaths and return to the nonlife of retreat at a dilapidated library.

All the futility and ignorance of Miragno finds its concrete symbol in the Boccamazza Library which none of the townspeople frequents. In that crumbling edifice, Mattia Pascal discovers that a great deal of his work consists in chasing away the rats that devour the mildewed, disintegrating volumes. Housed in a deconsecrated church, the library is a shrine to absurdity where anyone who works there eventually yields to its deadening immobility. Since libraries are places where people ought to read books and periodicals, Pascal's predecessor as librarian assumed the task of reading as a moral and intellectual obligation. It was in part because Miragno's library was threatening to turn him into another slave to its dust-covered shelves that Mattia Pascal yearned to flee from that monument of meaningless routine where he was buried alive. The fundamental bleakness of this Pirandellian novel arises from Mattia's feeling that he has to go back to that library after his return to town and to assist his successor in cataloguing the books no one would care to read. Since the antihero intends to bequeath his memoirs to the library, it is obvious that the message of his three existences is to be entombed in a building that stores useless and unwanted information.

In this novel Pirandello employs a technique of restricted vision similar to the device of limited vision which Joseph Conrad used in his novels and short stories. On the night that Adriano Meis first encounters the man who will later rob him of much of his Monte Carlo winnings, the entire scene is relayed by what Meis can hear and see through the shutters over the window of his rented room at the

Paleari boardinghouse. Tones of voice and gestures—like someone touching the shoulder of the enigmatic visitor to the *pensione*—reveal to the protagonist the power that the stranger exerts over the roominghouse dwellers. This method of constructing characterization through suspense-filled degrees of limited point of vision is reinforced by Mattia Pascal's physically distorted eyesight. (He has a cockeye that asserts its independence even at times of greatest stress.) As Adriano Meis, he will undergo an eye operation that requires him to remain in a darkened room for forty days. There he will learn to observe persons by relying on nonvisual impressions that ultimately prove more trustworthy than the images he later perceives in full light. Before his flight, Mattia Pascal was spiritually blind to the inner character of the persons around him who swindled him of his estate and treated him as a dunce. The protagonist's experiences as Adriano Meis, more than surgical intervention, permit him to see through limited perceptions the whole truth of persons and situations.

Critics generally regard *Il fu Mattia Pascal* as the "point of arrival" where Pirandello became "Pirandellian" by working out the tragic dichotomy between an individual's longing for complete freedom and the forms of life that society imposed on him. To create the transformation from Mattia Pascal to Adriano Meis, the writer anticipated other authors like André Gide in rebelling against the psychological determinism and character consistency that prevailed among *fin-de-siècle* novelists in Europe. Both Pirandello and Gide tried to reproduce life's unpredictability with its tempestuous surprises. Like the main character Michel in Gide's *The Immoralist*, Adriano Meis learns that it is easy to free oneself but that to be free is extremely difficult. Just as Gide's Michel has his beard shaved off so that his altered appearance will reveal the authentic personality that manifested itself after a close contact with death, so too does Pirandello's protagonist have his beard trimmed. But in the context of the Italian novel the antihero does not react to his changed appearance with joy at the rebirth of his spirit. Instead Meis recoils with horror before the image that his barber holds up to his gaze in a hand mirror. Pirandello's antihero will never succeed in "seeing his way through" to establishing an existence independent of persons and social institutions. Coming to know only a poor counterfeit of freedom, the protagonist retreats to an existence as a shadow haunting an unused library. Through his story of the different lives of the late Mattia Pascal, the narrator affirms that to dwell within society is to sustain a forever self-renewing fiction.

The Old and the Young (I vecchi e i giovani)

Disillusionment with the new Italy of 1860–1870, produced by the movement for unification and independence is the pervasive theme of the novel *I vecchi e i giovani* (1909). The period represented in the text is 1892 to 1894, the time of a scandal in the Bank of Rome and an insurrection of Sicilian socialist trade unions. All the enthusiasm and spirit of sacrifice that made possible Italy's liberation from foreign domination vanished amidst corruption and compromise:

the "bankruptcy of patriotism" engulfing the former heroes of the older generation and the youth of the united country.

Sicily and Rome are the two poles around which Pirandello structures this novel of desperate oppositions. The setting for Part One is Sicily, the province of Girgenti where sulfur mining has virtually destroyed the agriculture that had sustained the area since ancient times. Rome, the embodiment of the new nation, is the scene for the opening of the novel's second part with its picture of an aristocracy devoted to hedonistic pursuits and a parliamentary leadership devoted to their own enrichment. With the rebellion of the Sicilian trade unions, the action shifts back to the island where government troops savagely suppress the insurrection. The patriotic dream of founding a kingdom of justice and greatness degenerates into a reign of brutality where all hope for the present and future dies.

Out of the past loom two apparent models of heroic self-sacrifice: General Gerlando Laurentano and Stefano Auriti. Because of his opposition to the Bourbon monarchs of southern Italy, in 1848 General Laurentano went into exile in Malta, where his later suicide seemed to be a positive act of rebellion against reactionary authority. But in Pirandello's humoristic spirit of the contrary, it appears that Laurentano never fought for a united Italy; instead, he suffered banishment for advocating Sicilian independence from the Bourbon regime. In that same year of revolution, 1848, the general also lost his daughter Caterina to the Italian patriot Stefano Auriti, who took her to share his own exile in Turin for his efforts to have Sicily united to a liberated Italian nation. Then in 1860 as one of Garibaldi's Thousand Soldiers, Stefano Auriti died as a martyr at the battle of Milazzo in Sicily. Despite their deaths long before the start of the novel, Laurentano and Auriti continue to influence the thoughts and actions of their sons and grandsons. The general's son Prince Ippolito would become a pro-Bourbon reactionary supporting royal restoration decades after Sicily's annexation by Italy, while the prince's son Lando would express his need for autonomy by becoming a militant socialist revolutionary. Roberto Auriti continues to live in the shadow of his father's martyrdom, and his nephew Antonio Del Re grows to despise the parliamentary democracy that betrayed the heroic death of Stefano Auriti. In the embattled situations of the Laurentino and Auriti families, Pirandello studies the tensions that tear apart individuals and classes in modern-day Italy under the Savoys.

Ironically, the true ruler of Girgentian society in this novel is neither an aristocrat nor a former war hero. Through control of the sulfur industry, the financier Flaminio Salvo has become the determining force in Girgenti. Salvo is both the sustaining and denying figure in the community; his denial can bring about starvation as he closes down the sulfur mines to manipulate the mineral's international price. The terms Salvo uses to describe himself are the reverse, however, of a dynamic entrepreneur: *"sazio"* (sated), *"stanco"* (tired), and *"nausea"* in visceral scorn for the servile persons around him whom he arrogantly handles like a master puppeteer. But in his domestic life Salvo has met defeat: his wife is insane, his son died in adolescence, and his daughter Dianella lives on the edge of lunacy. In the course of the novel Salvo victimizes both his daughter (shattering her delicate sanity) and his ward Aurelio Costa. Fifteen years before the novel's start, Costa as a boy rescued the banker from drowning; Salvo took the child into his home and financed his education to become chief engineer of the sulfur mines. As surrogate son, Costa would end as a sacrificial victim, the scapegoat for Salvo before the explosive anger of striking sulfur miners who dismember and set the youth's remains aflame. Costa's nearly ritualistic death will mark the destruction of hope for Italy's future. The Salvo household is a place of entrapment where the sole escape is through insanity, the route that Dianella takes after the death of her beloved Costa.

While Salvo represents Sicily's bourgeois-dominated present, Ippolito Laurentano upholds the island's aristocratic traditions. Ippolito remains voluntarily absent in time and space, exiling himself to an estate where he has bound himself to the past by maintaining an honor guard of twenty-five men dressed in Bourbon uniforms like marching icons of delusions of past grandeur. But this living anachronism is not such a slave to past pageantry that he cannot decisively influence the current political scene. From his retreat Ippolito conspires with the local bishop and the leaders of the clerical party to defeat the electoral campaign of the central government in Rome. Above all else the prince desires to hold back time to delay what he recognizes to be his unavoidable appointment with death.

Along with the representatives of the generation of the "old" are characters who are of middle age but whose allegiance ties them to the warriors of the struggle for national unity. Roberto Auriti has never outgrown the childhood glory of having been the youngest soldier in Garibaldi's army; he was twelve at the time of the battle of Milazzo. Because of his boyhood exploits, the government in Rome nominates him as Girgenti's parliamentary representative. Roberto, however, does not even receive his mother's vote since she sees him as the puppet of a debased regime. After his arrest in the bank scandal for having signed IOUs to cover loans for his political patron Corrado Selmi, the one-time hero loses his most precious possession—the reputation he won on the battlefield.

Two Girgentian outcasts of the older generation, Luca Lizio and Nocio Pigna, are known contemptuously as "Propaganda and Co." for their work as organizers of socialist trade unions. The duo operate through political slogans and abstract dogma that they do not fully comprehend. Ironically, both survive by exploiting others: Pigna's seven daughters take in sewing to support their father, and Lizio manipulates people's sympathy over the suicide deaths of his father and brother. Pigna and Lizio are priests of a new religion that in the novel appears to be as empty and formal as traditional Christian religion. The two propagandists never succeed in re-educating and reforming a society that refuses to see in them anything other than a pathetic spectacle of individual dishonor and incompetence.

Pirandello's portrayal of the young overwhelmingly shows victims and frustrated rebels with no way of constructively expressing resentment over the treachery of their parents' generation. Aurelio Costa's exceptional qualities never emerge as a force to change Girgentian society; with his lower class background as the son of a sulfur miner and as recipient of a university education, he might have been able to mediate between labor and management. Many of the young are continually tempted to madness and acts of aggression. Antonio Del Re exhibits the explosive fury of late adolescence that cannot find constructive outlets for psychosexual energies. After withdrawing from classes at the University of Rome, Antonio contemplates a sensationalistic act of violence like dropping a homemade bomb from the gallery of the House of Deputies. Instead, Del Re attacks the deputy Corrado Selmi with a dagger at the very moment that that scandal-ridden politician is dying from self-inflicted poisoning. Like a naughty child, Antonio has to return to Sicily to the grieving company of his widowed mother and grandmother.

Only one youth has the will and the means to rebel on a grand social scale: Prince Lando Laurentano. Lando's vision of Italy's future goes beyond class struggle and proletarian revolution (Dombroski, 68). On his Sicilian estates the young prince has enacted reforms to distribute land fairly, found rural schools, and publish a weekly newspaper. But returning to Sicily to participate in an insurrection he knows is doomed to failure, the prince will follow his grand-father's example by seeking exile. Before his departure from his native island, Lando gains a final insight into history as a play of illusions.

The women in this novel are creatures of absence. Salvo's wife hovers in a twilight world of insanity that allows her more freedom than most Sicilian women can enjoy. Donna Caterina Laurentano Auriti, of her own choosing, leads a life of mortification in Girgenti's slums, recognizing the futility of her youthful sacrifices to unite a country whose government yielded to corruption. The novel's supreme feminist is Celsina Pigna, who refuses to accept femininity as a sign of social enslavement. An honors graduate of a technical institute for men, Celsina arrives in Rome as Girgenti's socialist representative at a national con-vention, but she soon joins the bohemian circle around Roberto Auriti in the hope of pursuing an operatic career. Pirandello intentionally leaves Celsina's story incomplete to hold out some vague hope for the future.

As a major novel of Sicilian history, *I vecchi e i giovani* must be classed with two other works that study the social and political upheaval following the fall of the Bourbon regime in 1860: *I vicerè* (*The Viceroys*, 1894) by Federico de Robertis and *Il gattopardo* (*The Leopard*, 1958) by Giuseppe Tomasi di Lam-pedusa. All three novels present a princely family that has to come to terms with the ascendancy of the crass middle-class entrepreneurs to take political control of Sicily. Each of the novels highlights death: that of individuals and also of an entire aristocratic class. Pirandello represents the passing of a myth of national glory.

Her Husband (Suo marito)

Soon after the novel *Suo marito* appeared in print in 1911, Pirandello yielded to pressure and had the work withdrawn from circulation: It was embarrassingly obvious that he had based his study of the career of a young author being managed by her ambitious husband on that of the Sardinian writer Grazia Deledda (1871–1936). Pirandello began to revise the book twenty years later under the new title *Giustino Roncella nato Boggiolo* (*Giustino Roncella, né Boggiolo*), but it was left half finished at the time of his death in 1936. Written in the third person, *Suo marito* has a purposely narrow concentration: it is the story of a marriage that collapses under the stress of a change from a traditional life in the provinces to a sophisticated life-style in Rome. Each chapter's subject is clearly announced by a title like "Fly Away," and the novelist never strays from the focus of interest in the various scenes of the chapters. Occasionally, when the author's direct comment intrudes into a sequence, objective representation recedes before a satirical portrait of a petty Roman elite reduced to unflattering caricatures. Even in his most superficially comic scenes, the writer makes his readers aware of a perilous sense of loss that pervades the entire novel.

The language in *Suo marito* becomes narcissistic; the discourse of Roman salon society, sprinkled with French phrases and the names of famous foreign writers and composers, is imposed on the Tarantine writer Silvia Roncella after her arrival in the capital. Silvia learns from an American journalist that words are an economic commodity since her stories and plays will be purchased at so many dollars per word. Throughout the sections of the novel that occur in a Piedmontese mountain village, the area's French-like dialect is used to suggest the exotic quality of the region where Silvia is exiled. Above all in this novel, language blocks rather than advances communication, for neither Silvia Roncella nor her husband Giustino Boggiolo succeed in communicating with each other. Boggiolo never speaks of his need to affirm his own self-sufficiency before the world that applauds Silvia's literary creations, and his wife equally fails to let Giustino know how degraded she feels by his commercial exploitation of her work. In whatever dialect language is conveyed here, it obstructs meaning.

Rome provides the setting for a large part of this narrative. Pirandello portrays the city as a metropolis whose inhabitants are without deep roots. Members of the Roman literary salons could just as easily be living in Paris, London, or St. Petersburg. The pretentious characters who frequent those salons resemble the malicious habitués of artistic circles in Chekhov's story "The Grasshoppers": pedants and dilettantes. For two chapters the setting moves to the village of Cargiore in Piedmont, Giustino's homeland. After the birth of a son, Silvia has to spend months convalescing in that mountain valley town where despite her loneliness she writes poems and stories about the moon-lit valley and its snow-capped peaks. But she also comes to associate the village with death as both her uncle and her son die there along with the hope of her continuing her marriage with Giustino. Nowhere in this novel is there an idyllic retreat.

Pirandello's portrait of Boggiolo is ambiguous: the character can be viewed as an insensitive exploiter of his wife's talents (making her a writing machine) or as a self-sacrificing martyr to her literary ambitions. There exists a profound cultural difference between the spouses: Silvia adheres to a strict provincial view of a husband as the individual who provides for his family, while Giustino reflects a flexible urban attitude that permits him to resign from his civil service post and dedicate himself to promoting his wife's career. Eventually, the husband begins to thrust his wife into the background as he demands public recognition for his entrepreneurship as her public relations manager. After Silvia breaks with him, Boggiolo ends as one of the most pathetic of Pirandello's protagonists— without a career, a nonentity in his home village away from the excitement of Rome.

This novel has attracted the attention of biographers and critics (see Nardelli and Janner) because of an episode detailing the relationship between the older writer Maurizio Gueli and his insanely jealous and tyrannical mistress Livia Frezzi. Pirandello admittedly based this relationship on his own unhappy marriage to a mentally disturbed woman who constantly accused him of forming romantic liaisons with younger women. Through the eyes of his mistress Gueli is forced to see within himself the existence of another personality: instead of the austere persona that he presents to the world, there is Frezzi's image of a man who lives only to indulge his vanity. The Gueli episode illustrates Pirandello's interest in multiple personalities.

This novel as a story of alienation anticipates Alberto Moravia's *Gli Indifferenti* (*The Indifferent Ones*) of 1929. Just as Moravia's hero Michele sees himself as an indifferent puppet moving automatically along the rain-swept streets of Rome, so the heroine of *Suo marito* is a sensitive, creative individual who almost perishes from the cultural shock of leaving her provincial life for the bewildering society of the new Rome that by the final decade of the nineteenth century emerged as the center of Italian political and intellectual life. Pirandello explored how the move to the Roman metropolis with its literary coteries could exercise a devastating impact on an impressionable newcomer. As both titles of the novel indicate, however, the true protagonist is not the wife but her husband.

Shoot! (Si gira!)

First published in 1915 under the title *Si gira!* (*Shoot!*), ten years later the text appeared as *Quaderni di Serafino Gubbio Operatore* (*Journals of Serafino Gubbio, Cameraman*) to stress the importance of the first-person narrator recording his impressions of Rome and its movie industry. The narrator Serafino Gubbio experiences a psychic crisis when he refuses to accept the role of automaton that comes from his profession as a movie studio cameraman during the era of silent films. Like film clips, the scattered passages of Gubbio's various journals make this work almost an essay-novel on the relationship of humanity with machines. The novel's fragmentary form attests to the difficulty of trying to order life coherently, as Gubbio produces retrospective accounts of anguished situations from his past.

Despite his avowed intention to remain neutral, the narrator does not maintain the impassive "I am a camera" attitude which Christopher Isherwood aspired to in his *Berlin Stories*. Certain passages, as when the novel's cameraman remembers a countryside villa near Sorrento and its beloved inhabitants, recall

Marcel Proust's techniques in *Remembrance of Things Past* to recapture lost time. Olfactory, visual, and auditory elements work together as the vanished past surges back to present time: the fragrance of flowers, the aroma of coffee, the color of wallpaper.

As a novel about the vain intentions of the motion picture industry, this work stands with Nathanael West's *The Day of the Locust* (1939) and F. Scott Fitzgerald's *The Last Tycoon* (1941) for its merciless revelation of a dream factory producing distorted images to beguile the minds of the masses. In *Si gira!* life resembles a cheap, sensationalistic movie in which everyone plays a vapid role. The world presented here is that of the Roman movie studio Kosmograph where giggling starlets dash in and out in limousines provided by the studio. Serious actors from the stage prostitute themselves for high salaries, while famous writers entreat disinterested directors to consider their sketches for scripts that might introduce depth to films. Pirandello accurately describes the period when the emphasis of Italian movie industry was changing from historical costume epic to bourgeois drama. Kosmograph recalls the actual studios that caused their backruptcy through an expensive star system centered on screen sirens. In the novel the actress Varia Nestoroff is the typical diva who humiliates other actors and directors, while her co-star Baron Nuti comes from the class of aristocrats who in real-life Italy paid for the privilege to play members of their decadent social group in movies. Serafino Gubbio sees La Nestoroff as a *femme fatale* who has always ruined the lives of the men who worshiped her beauty. For this actress the movies offer grotesque images of herself, yet she fails to find her identity.

The violence of "real-life" emotions explodes when Baron Nuti shoots La Nestoroff to death during the filming of a scene of a jungle hunt where he is supposed to kill a tiger that instead leaps on him. Standing in the cage to "shoot" the sequence with his camera, Gubbio persists in cranking the handle on his camera even as the animal starts to stalk him—until a shot from outside the cage fells the beast. Although royalties from the tiger sequence will enrich Serafino, the shock of witnessing and filming Nuti's death permanently deprives him of his voice. Having become part of the process of making silent movies, Gubbio will continue his career as a silent cameraman.

Three key terms predominate in this novel of spiritual desolation: "*grottesco*" to show how the industrial age has left humans as grotesque beings; "*silenzio*" for the silence between persons that prevents all communication; and "*ombra*" understood as "shadow," "ghost," or "phantom" since individuals of flesh and blood are reduced to insubstantial shadow-like figures flickering on a movie screen. The characters populating this novel appear to be cruelly deformed by life's circumstances, which frustrate their aspirations.

One, None and a Hundred Thousand
(*Uno, nessuno e centomila*)

In his last novel *Uno, nessuno e centomila* (1925–1926), Pirandello completed a process of novelistic deconstruction that he had initiated in *Il fu Mattia Pascal*.

In its apparent formlessness, this work anticipates by more than a quarter century the "new novel" which writers like Alain Robbe-Grillet, Michel Butor, Nathalie Sarraute, and Anaïs Nin advocated in the 1950s and early 1960s. The authors would attempt to destroy the traditional novel to make a fresh departure for new explorations, feeling that the public was wary of the old-fashioned omniscient novelist claiming to be fully knowledgeable about what occurred in the minds of his characters. Instead of outmoded papier-mâché characters, there would be an indefinable anonymous *I* engaging in continuous dialogue with dreamlike figures who frequently reflected the narrator. With his final novel, Pirandello was already exploring the world of subconversation that a later generation of experimentalist authors would investigate.

This novel is largely an unending monologue by Vitangelo Moscarda, delivering an interior discourse of inner selves struggling against each other according to the conflicting identities that everyone else imposes on the narrator. Once again the technique is first person, like a diary without date headings. Moscarda tries to relate the story of his rapid disillusionment with his privileged existence, his period of extended distress, and his eventual liberation. Every veristic concern about rendering concrete details of outer reality has disappeared from the text. The characters are not a collection of colorful "*macchiette*" but presences that impinge on the narrator's identity. Only those salient details of interior and exterior distance that form part of the narrator's inner mood of anger, curiosity, or irony are recorded in his reflections: the fierce wind, the rotting garbage in alleys, the grimness of his family's bank. The novel's stylistic movement is an inward one through the narrator's steadily disintegrating personality.

Throughout this work, the reader "listens" to the voice of Vitangelo Moscarda's dissolving consciousness. It unfolds like a mathematical demonstration in eight stages or books to illustrate the multiplicity of the human personality as one being, nobody, or a hundred thousand beings. Each book marks a definite step in Moscarda's disintegration and nearly pantheistic fusion with the cosmos. In Book I, when Moscarda was twenty-eight, his wife Dida remarked one day as he stood by the mirror that his nose sagged to the right. That astonishing discovery of his physical defect forced Vitangelo to realize how everyone else pictured him far differently than he had imagined himself. During Book II the narrator comes to understand how his wife has replaced him with a marionette husband named Gengé whom she regards as a harmless imbecile. Book III begins with his declaring he will carry out a relentless campaign of mad acts to eliminate those hundred thousand Moscardas that others have fashioned; Vitangelo has to admit that the general public considers him a "usurer" because his father was a banker who charged excessively high interest rates. But by the final page of Book IV an angered public has substituted the epithet "usurer" with "madman" on account of Moscarda's contradictory acts of cruelty and generosity. Throughout Book V the protagonist continues the strategic attacks on his images as indifferent businessman and innocuous husband as he undermines his financial interests and his marriage. Although Moscarda in the sixth book considers other possible social roles in a variety of professions, he rejects them all as imprisoning his personality. By the final two books, Vitangelo completes his mission of rational and social suicide: first, he nearly dies from a gunshot wound inflicted on him by a young woman driven to insanity by the seductive logic of his arguments about identity; then he saves himself from being committed to a mental asylum by turning his estate over to ecclesiastical authorities to build a hospice where he will be the first person to seek refuge. Freed from constricting social roles, the narrator can spend his days rapturously contemplating nature, of which he now feels an integral part.

Because of the novel's prevailing ambiguity, we can judge it as either the story of increasing self-awareness or as the story of the development of madness. The reader may well wonder to what extent Moscarda has genuinely liberated himself from compromise. Although he claims to worship God as that feeling within himself of self-respect which every individual should defend from the mockery of others, he has allied himself with the bishop who expects persons to erect buildings to the honor of that "other God from without" Who does not dwell in a blade of grass or the azure of the sky. Even if the narrator at the end considers himself nameless, others continue to call him Moscardo the madman. But for Pirandello the way of salvation is frequently that of madness that carries his protagonists away from the hypocrisies of everyday reality. The narrator has become a "nobody" (*nessuno*), not as earlier when others robbed him of his identity, but because he has succeeded in abandoning every form of conventional identification.

With this last novel Pirandello has arranged a collage of pseudo-autobiographical fragments whose pattern traces an individual's alienation and disintegration. Here the writer unmasks the hidden man and exposes the disorder of his inner world. Through the seemingly incongruous collage patterns of his last novel, Pirandello recaptures the pure relativity of the self.

CRITICAL REACTION TO PIRANDELLO'S NOVELS

Pirandello's writings received serious critical attention after the controversial premiere of his play *Sei personaggi in cerca d'autore* (*Six Characters in Search of an Author*, 1921), and for decades interest in the dramas overshadowed studies of the novels. Until the writer's death in 1936, most of the essays dedicated to his literary compositions appeared as journalistic reviews and followed two opposing attitudes: the verists (led by Capuana) and the experimentalists (like Massimo Bontempelli, the novelist and dramatist) who expressed admiration for Pirandello's depth of observation into the human heart, as countered by the philosopher-critic Benedetto Croce and his disciples who rejected Pirandello's "cerebral humorism" as being neither poetry nor philosophy. A schematic approach to all his writings, based on Hegelian antitheses such as life versus form, came to predominate critical thought on Pirandellianism through the influence of Adriano Tilgher's treatise *Studi sul teatro contemporaneo* of 1923. Already by 1926 Walter Starkie in his book *Luigi Pirandello* (later revised in 1937 and 1967) placed the author in a European context, dedicating an entire chapter to the novellas and the novels as probing studies of present-day psychological torment. After the author's death, critical attention moved from journalistic reviews to full-scale essay investigations such as Salvatore Francesco Romano's "La poesia del racconto pirandelliano" ("The Poetry of the Pirandellian Tale") of 1938 which showed how the writer transcended naturalism into a study of human obsessions. By 1948 Arminio Janner in his book *Luigi Pirandello* produced a predominantly psychological and thematic text stressing the writer's preoccupation with the agony of life and the fatal insistence on death. The Marxist critic Giuseppe Petronio distinguished in his book *Pirandello novelliere e la crisi del realismo* (*Pirandello the Writer of Novelle and the Crisis of Realism*, 1950) between the peasant tales, the stories of city life, the ideological tales, and the surrealistic stories—stressing the enduring importance of the sociologically penetrating peasant stories. Attention to the vocabulary and syntax of the short fiction is evident in Benvenuto Terracini's "Le *'Novelle per un anno'* di Luigi Pirandello," of 1966.

In 1967, the centenary of Pirandello's birth, numerous scholarly journals devoted entire editions to essays on his works such as Zina Tillona's article on death in the short fiction which appeared in *Forum Italicum*. That same year also saw publication of Sarah D'Alberti's *Pirandello romanziere*, the revisionist text that reestablished the writer's significance as a novelist. Although Allen McCormick denied that narrative importance to the author in his essay of 1969, "Luigi Pirandello: Major Writer, Minor Novelist," subsequent studies have reaffirmed Pirandello's value as a novelist. In 1984, Giovanni Bussino brought out his translation, with a critical introduction, of *Tales of Madness* to emphasize the author's portrayals of insanity. As the fiftieth anniversary of Pirandello's death arrived in 1986, worldwide conferences on his writings once again pointed out the continuing legacy of his narrative work in equal importance with his plays.[4]

NOTES

1. The text of *L'Umorismo* can be found in *Saggi, Poesie, Scritti varii*.

2. Terror of sexual intimacy and resultant pregnancy can drive some Pirandellian heroines to suicide, as with Eleonora Bandi in the story "Scialle nero" ("The Black Shawl").

3. The English translation of this novel bears the title *The Merry-Go-Round of Love*, trans. Frances Keene (New York: New American Library, 1964).

4. Zangrilli, *L'Arte novellistica di Pirandello*, prefaces his thoroughly well-argued analyses of key Pirandellian tales with an introduction on the critical fortune of the novellas, 14–61.

WORKS CITED

Bachelard, Gaston. *The Poetics of Space*. Trans. Maria Jolas. New York: Orion, 1964.
———. *Water and Dreams*. Trans. Edith Farrell. Dallas: Pegasus Foundation, 1983.
Bergson, Henri. *Laughter* in *The Meanings of Comedy*, ed. by Wylie Sypher. Garden City, N.Y.: Doubleday, 1956.
Croce, Benedetto. "Luigi Pirandello." *Letteratura della nuova Italia*. Bari: Laterza, 1974. 6:335–52.
D'Alberti, Sarah. *Pirandello romanziere*. Palermo: Flaccovio, 1967.
Dombroski, Robert. *Le totalità dell'artificio: ideologia e forma nel romanzo di Pirandello*. Padua: Liviana, 1978.
Jackson, Giovanna. "Ambiguities or Adaptations: *Il fu Mattia Pascal* Revisited." *Transformations: From Literature to Film*. Ed. D. Radcliff-Umstead. Kent: Kent State University, 1987. 16–24.
Janner, Arminio. *Luigi Pirandello*. Florence: La Nuova Italia, 1948.
Lauretta, Enzo. Ed. *Il Romanzo di Pirandello*. Palermo: Palumbo, 1976.
Lubbock, Percy. *The Craft of Fiction*. New York: Viking Press, 1957.
McCormick, Allen. "Luigi Pirandello: Major Writer, Minor Novelist." *From "Verismo" to Experimentalism*. Bloomington: Indiana University Press, 1969. 61–80.
Nardelli, Federico Vittore. *Vita segreta di Pirandello*. Rome: Bianco, 1962.
Petronio, Giuseppe. *Pirandello novelliere e la crisi del realismo*. Lucca: Lucentia, 1950.
Pirandello, Luigi. *Novelle per un anno*. 2 vols. Milan: Mondadori, 1957.
———. *Saggi, Poesie, Scritti varii*. Milan: Mondadori, 1973.
———. *Tales of Madness*. Trans. Giovanni Bussino. Brookline Village, Mass.: Dante University of America, 1984.
———. *Tutti i romanzi*. 2 vols. Milan: Mondadori, 1979.
Radcliff-Umstead, Douglas. *The Mirror of Our Anguish, A Study of Luigi Pirandello's Narrative Writings*. Cranbury, N.J.: Fairleigh Dickinson University Press, 1978.
Romano, Salvatore Francesco. "La poesia del racconto pirandelliano." *Dialettica della letteratura contemporanea*. Palermo-Milan: Sandron, 1938. 38–51.
Starkie, Walter. *Luigi Pirandello 1867–1936*. Berkeley: University of California Press, 1967.
Terracini, Benevenuto. "Le '*Novelle per un anno*' di Luigi Pirandello." *Analisi stilistica. Teoria, storia, problemi*. Milan: Feltrinelli, 1966. 283–395.
Tilgher, Adriano. "Il teatro di Luigi Pirandello." *Studi sul teatro contemporaneo*. Rome: Libreria di scienza e di lettere, 1923. 157–218.
Tillona, Zina. "La morte nelle novelle di Pirandello." *Forum Italicum* 1 (1967): 279–88.
Zangrilli, Franco. *L'Arte novellistica di Pirandello*. Ravenna: Longo, 1983.

26

Philosophical Humor and Narrative Subtext in Pirandello's Novels

Robert S. Dombroski

In marked contrast to naturalistic realism, the collective aim of Pirandello's novels is not to represent or describe human, social, and political realities. The truth of a certain society at a certain level of development can no doubt be deduced from the author's choice of plots and settings, not to mention certain character types that carry the burden of their upbringing and socialization. But from a narrative standpoint, the procedures used to confirm the validity of the story can be seen as raw materials that constitute a realistic assumption or precondition on which Pirandello inscribes a symbolic text. His stories manipulate commonplace situations and highlight improbable events and eccentric personalities for the purpose of creating apprehension and anxiety about modern life. Above all, the fiction describes the uncertain status of knowledge and individuality.

The following discussion of Pirandello's novels focuses on the process whereby realistic hypotheses about the problematic nature of life are rewritten in terms that deny the human subject all purposive intervention into a society of his or her own making.[1] Through a narrative technique that distances the negative effects of realistic portrayal by means of humor and paradox, Pirandello attacks the rigid structure of literary naturalism, unmasking its conventions and inadequacies.

On the surface, Pirandello's first novel *L'Esclusa* (1894, *The Outcast*, 1935) depicts the social milieu in a way that is consistent with the general poetics of *verismo*. It presents situations and events that exemplify the positive concept of a universe governed by necessity and by a "struggle for life" in the Darwinian sense. For example, all the males in the Pentagora family believe they are destined to be betrayed by their wives. Also, as fate seems to dictate, after the death of the father, the financial and social decline of the Ayala family is inevitable. The novel's plot depicts the protagonist's fatal subjection to her environment. Marta Ayala cannot rebel against the tyranny of a closed, semi-feudal society that rejects her when she is faithful to her husband and, paradoxically, accepts her when she in fact commits the very adultery for which she was originally an outcast. Her eventual pregnancy illustrates the naturalistic norm that, once defamed, a woman has no hope of salvation. She must necessarily conform to the role society has forced her to play.

But from the standpoint of narrative form, we notice in the way the facts of the story are related a divergence from the essentially horizontal line of narration typical of verist or naturalistic composition. Keeping within the boundaries of verisimilitude, Pirandello creates the exceptional circumstances of Marta's exclusion from society, presenting them in two stages. He begins by referring to the discovery of Rocco, her husband, of a letter that will cause him to suspect her honesty. We learn of the circumstances of Rocco's discovery later in the story. At an even later time come the intimate reasons for the mishap, projected by the narrator into the mind of the heroine.

Whatever sense of moral indignation, surprise, or disbelief such a situation might evoke, it is evident that our reception of the facts necessitates a double mental operation. First, we must reorder the various moments of Rocco's fateful discovery in a causal sequence. On the one hand, we have: (1) Marta's loneliness and her husband's inability to understand her; (2) the exchange of letters with her suitor, Alvignani; (3) Marta's compromising response when faced with Rocco's discovery of the letter; and (4) her being driven from home by her husband. We must also account for why Rocco reacts the way he does: (1) his knowledge of the Pentagora's fate as cuckolds; (2) his childhood traumas; (3) his finding the letter. We must also interpret the context and circumstances from which these facts emerge. By isolating and separating chronologically two equally pathetic experiences, Pirandello makes the reader focus on the vague substance of the narrative and consider the ambiguous motivation concealed within the action. In other words, to understand such a stylized conflict, we must assume that it contains a "deeper meaning," and to penetrate that meaning requires use of an interpretive code different from that provided in the narration. For example, we may offer a psychological explanation and consider the justification that Marta gives to her letter-writing as a sign of repressed sexual desires that, in the exchange with Alvignani, take on the form of an intellectual or literary seduction. Or we could interpret, from a sociolinguistic standpoint, the entire situation as an index of the acutely equivocal character of the written word, as symbolized by the letter. But whatever formula is used to explain the facts on which Pirandello bases his story, whatever hidden motivation is revealed, the openly exaggerated quality of the predicament forces the reader to seek meaning beyond the logical development of events.

The same notable degree of stylization is present in the action. Rocco's discovery of the letter generates a rapidly developed series of events that modify the conditions linking Marta to her past: mainly, the sudden death of her father, caused by the dishonor he suffered on account of her and the death of her child at birth. These events lead to the heroine's illusion of beginning a new life as a schoolteacher. But in order to keep her job, Marta is forced to consummate her relationship with Alvignani and becomes his mistress. All this prepares us for the final, paradoxical reconciliation with her husband.

To understand better the situations and characters thus far described, it will be useful to consider briefly Pirandello's notion of "humorism." For Pirandello, the illusions on which social life depends are obstacles to the free expression of human feelings and emotions. To recognize incongruity and to reflect upon it humoristically liberates us, albeit momentarily, from the social masks or mechanisms that entrap or imprison human individuality. This, in a word, is the aesthetic function of philosophical humor. Through humor, we regain contact, as Pirandello himself states, with "a reality different from what we normally perceive, a reality beyond human perception, outside the boundaries set by human reason" (*L'Umorismo*, 152).

In *L'Esclusa*, Pirandello deconstructs the various unities regulating the mechanism of social norms on which the story is constructed by making *prominent* things deemed strange or abnormal. Let us take as a significant example the reconciliation between Marta and Rocco at the deathbed of Rocco's mother. Through the dying woman's presence, husband and wife are in fact reunited, but in a way that causes the reader to reflect humoristically on tragic irony and paradox. The mediating presence of the mother, both as dying and as deceased, provides us not only with a realistic occasion for the couple's final encounter, but also with a means for understanding a relationship experienced at once as need, possession, desire, and death. The love-death dualism is then superseded by the image of a tragic and passionate gesture projected against the vision of the mother's corpse:

Weakened by grief, he tottered under the weight and nearly fell with her. But he made a furious effort, clenching his teeth, and shaking his head desperately, his features working under strain. Just at that moment his eyes fell on his mother's face, uncovered as Marta had left it, his mother there on her deathbed, between four yellow candles. It was as though death had paused to look at him. Mastering the shudder his wife's body, much as he desired it, inspired in him, he pressed her close against his breast, and his eyes on his mother's face, he stammered in sudden terror: "She is looking . . . my mother is looking. I forgive . . . I forgive . . . Stay here . . . stay! . . . We'll keep watch together. . . ." (*The Outcast*, 334)

Here Pirandello has us dwell not only on the tragedy of his characters, but on their parody and caricature as well. The whole scene produces a grotesque perspective, typical of humoristic decomposition, aimed at destroying every exaggeration of naturalistic form.

The humoristic form of *L'Esclusa* may also be located at different points in the development of the plot. It appears, for example, in the episode describing the simultaneous deaths of Marta's father and newborn child, where the sound of grief suffered in the Ayala house blends into the clamorous shouts of Alvignani's political supporters. Another perhaps more transparent example of philosophical humor is the scene where Rocco is being taught the stances and moves to use in his duel with Alvignani. The reader is made witness to the "ridiculous leaps of the fantastically distended shadows those two duelists made, so frantically lunging at one another in the dead of night" (*The Outcast*, 23).

Not infrequently the characters themselves are aware of having gone beyond the mechanical schema of form. Antonio Pentagora, for instance, resigned to his role as a cuckold, detaches himself from his part with the consciousness of an actor playing a role. And the novel's most complex figure, its Pirandellian character par excellence, Luca Blandino, fulfills in the course of the story two contrasting roles: Rocco's "godfather" in the duel with Alvignani, and Alvignani's faithful counsel.

The humoristic perspective taken in *L'Esclusa* indicates Pirandello's position on the problem of the relationship of art and society. In order that humorism be operative, there must exist a *form*. For Pirandello, this *form* is social life in general, seen negatively as "mechanical" and "inauthentic." The various components of social life that were the substance of nineteenth-century fiction become in Pirandello's first novel the negative term of his narrative dialectic, which he deconstructs through humor and paradox.

Turning now to Pirandello's second novel, *Il fu Mattia Pascal* (1904, *The Late Mattia Pascal*, 1923), considered by many his greatest novel, we see right from the start that the protagonist presents the reader with a kind of epistemological principle: "One of the few things, in fact about the only thing, I was sure of was my name: Mattia Pascal. Of this I took full advantage also." With such a declaration, the reader is immediately estranged from a realistic situation recognizable in the setting, as in *L'Esclusa*, and, therefore, from any direct participation in the events about to be recounted.

The role of the humorist is now being played by the protagonist who comments on the incongruous circumstances of his life. Moreover, in order for his humorism to triumph, Mattia Pascal must become invulnerable. His invulnerability is constantly marked out by brilliant displays of Pirandellian paradox, of which the story is a formidable example. A man believed to be dead, when he reappears alive, fails to be readmitted to family and society because for them he is truly "dead."

Upon closer inspection, however, the novel reminds one more of a joke than a humoristic experience in the strict sense, because the narrator actually creates, rather than discovers, the comic and humoristic elements of his story. The polemic object of this rather tendentious joke is the authority of rational knowledge. The joke goes something like this: A young gentleman, Mattia Pascal, made half crazy by an oppressive marriage and by the death of both his newborn twins and his mother, leaves his home in search of diversion. While he is away he learns that people think he is dead, and, exploiting these circumstances, he sets out to make a new life for himself by taking on a new identity. Then, when he realizes that his new life is just as debilitating as the old one, he feigns suicide and, equipped again with his original identity, returns home to find out that his wife has married his best friend. He requests no justification but only asks to be left in peace. The joke concludes with a kind of double punch line. First, replying to the opinion that it is impossible to live outside the laws that we have created for ourselves and because of which we are ourselves, Mattia retorts that he hasn't in any way regularized his life in relation to law and that his wife is now Pomino's and that he really can't say who he is. Then, to conclude with a practical example, the protagonist, while bringing flowers to his own gravesite, is asked his name by a passerby. Mattia tells him that he is the "late Mattia Pascal."

Solidly positioned behind the protective screen of humor, Mattia Pascal tells his story. His father was a sea captain who invested his gambling fortunes in real estate, thus making it possible for his family to live comfortably from the earnings derived from the property. The inheritance, however, was put in the hands of a fraudulent administrator by the name of Malagna, who in short order brings the family to bankruptcy. Mattia reacts to Malagna's economic aggression by fathering the children of Romilda (Malagna's niece) and the child of Malagna's second wife, Olivia. At the same time Mattia is subject to the financial shrewdness of Romilda who, knowing that she is carrying Mattia's child, lies with her uncle who now believes that he will finally have his much desired heir. Mattia ends up marrying Romilda in order to ensure financial gain. It is an oppressive and economically disastrous marriage, made ultimately intolerable by the death of his daughters. Now on the brink of madness, Mattia finds a potentially magical solution to his woes in the form of the *roulette*, the goddess of Fortune, that helps him overcome his depression.

As in *L'Esclusa*, Pirandello's philosophical humor becomes a particularly effective means of contesting the materialist and positivist culture at the basis of literary naturalism. In the first novel, the reader is made to experience the protagonists' fears and anxieties as signs of the individual's loss of control over reality. In *Il fu Mattia Pascal*, alienation is taken for granted. The specific contents of Mattia's desperate life are, in fact, neutralized and replaced by a general aesthetic content. With Mattia's eccentric story, the novel seeks to point out the possibility of our attaining, beyond the natural, social, and economic confines of human life, a new coherence and stability in creativity or, as Mattia would have it, in the ingenious resurrection of human ruins. In this light, *Il fu Mattia Pascal* is best defended against critics like Giacomo De Benedetti, who accuses Pirandello of treating superficially the problem of human identity,[2] and like Roberto Alonge, for whom the novel demonstrates the impossibility of a petty bourgeois individual to be anything other than a petty bourgeois (154). It would be hard to deny that Mattia is unknowable as a character because his acts are wholly gratuitous. He is indeed an abstraction. But precisely on account of his devalued status, we are in a position to understand the meaning Pirandello has given him. Mattia, after all, is eminently knowable—not as a character who typifies a historical or social milieu, but rather as a character who both speaks for and personifies Pirandello's aesthetics of humorism.

In this light, the seemingly arbitrary digression on Copernicus which we find at the beginning of the novel, where Mattia accuses the astronomer of having ruined humankind beyond repair, acquires a deeper significance. No doubt to extract man from the center of the universe destroys his illusion of supremacy, but now that he has become one among many elements in a complex system of relationships, and cognizant as he is of his new status, he is capable of avenging his fate by becoming the supreme organizer of those relationships. He is now the mind that measures, composes, and decomposes in order to form altogether new totalities. He has become the craftsman of a new relational reality in the very same way as is Mattia Pascal of his own life.

In terms of the story, *Il fu Mattia Pascal* presents two interpretative hypotheses: (1) a romantic hypothesis in which Pirandello juxtaposes matter and spirit, reason and passion, money and love, in order to portray the fall of common man into materialism's diabolical trap; (2) a naturalistic hypothesis that exploits Mattia's strange case history in order to highlight the infallible determinism of society's institutions. However, in order to transcend the themes of alienation and determinism, Pirandello neutralizes these contents or storylines by casting them within the context of an elaborate joke. In doing so, he exposes the inadequacies of the realist structuring of experience, while at the same time highlighting the power of human fantasy and creativity. For the romantic and naturalist traditions, the exceptional or eccentric personality supported contentions about the nature of social reality. In *Il fu Mattia Pascal* the protagonist's strange life, to the extent that it is like a joke, takes on characteristics that are above all metaphysical. The novel's humoristic treatment of society's insufficiencies elicits in the reader a sense of the insufficiency of rational thought processes in expressing the nature of human existence. The novel, therefore, suggests new cognitive possibilities. The humoristic pleasure we derive from Mattia's final words is nothing but the effect of a new harmony found amid the dissonance of human experience.

With *Il fu Mattia Pascal* Pirandello displays his credentials as a literary modernist. In contrast to *L'Esclusa*, the novel becomes its own object, finding its justification in the faith it shows in its own artistic capacity. Its form repudiates radically both literary naturalism and philosophical realism; it exalts creative freedom and, therefore, both the mystical and intellectual character of literary practice. The novel becomes its own symbol, a work that reflects only the mental processes responsible for its creation.

Compared to *Il fu Mattia Pascal*, Pirandello's historical novel, *I vecchi e i giovani* (1913, *The Old and the Young*, 1928)[3] appears to mark a regression in the development of his narrative art. Its principal fault is seen to consist in the absence of focus and the preponderance of unconnected, dispersive elements.

On the one hand, the novel depicts chaos, desolation, and paradox as signs of the failure of Risorgimento ideals. The novel provides accurate documentation of the political and social problems that beset Italy at the turn of the century: the aristocracy's extreme devotion to feudal values as a means of containing the economic ambitions of the bourgeoisie; the seditious potential of the peasantry; the patriotic alliance of aristocracy and bourgeoisie and their failure to incorporate the lower classes into the process of unification; the North's outright colonization of the South through the imposition of inordinate tariffs and taxes; the centralized government in Rome, which provided a never-ending source of corruption; the peasantry's incapacity for self-government, its ignorance and riotousness. The novel attempts to demonstrate that history is but a series of contradictory and inconclusive events in which only the morally inferior, who can readily adapt to forever changing circumstances, will achieve success.

On the other hand, this disharmony contains a principle of existential unity that absorbs the discordant social and political interests in a new, nonrational synthesis. The character of Lando Laurentano illustrates best the meaning and function of the "existential" in the novel. His characterization underlines the synthetic force of existentially rooted ways of looking at life, according to which thought and objectivity are devalued in favor of an active, enterprising human essence. Lando is genetically a political animal, but not by virtue of any concept of human gregariousness or social contract. Pirandello verifies his political being in terms of suppressed existential needs that become the ultimate force behind his actions. Rational knowledge of political relationships and conditions are subjected to the vital forces of movement and turmoil, which in the author's view are the real forces of history. Lando's politicization, his alliance with the Sicilian popular movement, and the actual reforms he enacts on his estates appear as an obligation of "existence" deriving from the universal mandate of suppressed life forces. Although the character's commitment to pressing social questions is subsequently justified in political language, the justification comes after the fact.

The relationship between being and action, as outlined in Pirandello's description of Lando, provides a model of experience that governs the created history embodied in the narration. The form of *I vecchi e i giovani* may be formulated in terms of "existence" as a concept of some mysterious, chaotic force in the world. "Existence" distinguishes the novel from other Italian historical narratives, such as those based on the structural principles of Providence (*I promessi sposi*), reason and common sense (*Le confessioni d'un Italiano*), or contradiction (*I Viceré*). In Pirandello's work, the traditional conflict between the ideal, represented in various ways by the aristocracy, and the machinations of vulgar compromise, dictated by human ambition and corruption, gives way to the determining role played by existence in the story.

The story of *I vecchi e i giovani* is contained between two relatively independent spheres of action. The first centers on the political defeat of Roberto Auriti, a character of noble heritage who is unable to overcome the pressures of class-oriented politics and falls prey to corruption, which eventually leads to his arrest. The second is the complex, intrigue-filled account of the social and political ambitions of Flamminio Salvo. With the objective in mind of marrying his daughter Dianella to Lando Laurentano, Salvo successfully prepares the way by arranging a marriage between his sister Adelaide and the aged Ippolito Laurentano, Lando's uncle. Now the only obstacle is Aurelio Costa, manager of the sulphur mine owned by Salvo's client Ignazio Capolino, Dianella's suitor. Salvo arranges the journey of Capolino's wife, Isabella, from Rome to Sicily in the company of Costa, thus disposing of the last encumbrance to his plan. At this point in the narration, the two parallel stories meet with abrupt, unforeseen resolutions. Roberto Auriti is imprisoned for his involvement in the bank scandals, and Aurelio and Isabella are killed during a peasant revolt. Costa's death causes the psychosis of Dianella, who can no longer marry Lando. Now, Lando becomes the story's chief element, because his presence and actions unwittingly bring about the major transitions in the narrative.

Lando's interclass mobility depends in the last analysis on the existential foundations of his political character: his potential ability to belong to everyone by virtue of his vitality. In him, the traditional class demarcations and limitations are absorbed in an "existence" that motivates and is the final arbiter of action. If it is true, as criticism has often claimed, that the novel's different story lines cannot be unified through the reciprocal interaction of characters and that Lando himself, though dominant, does not succeed in bringing together the many divergent parts of the narrative, it is precisely at the level of irrational, existential needs and impulses that the disparate elements of the story coalesce.

As in *L'Esclusa*, the realistic hypothesis of social conflict is undercut by a narrative of "existence." The difference between the two novels in this respect lies in the distinctively passive and defensive character of "existence" in *L'Esclusa*, in contrast to its optimistically active quality in *I vecchi e i giovani*. With greater complexity than in *L'Esclusa*, the disintegration of human life projects its own resolution in the atemporality of nature or in the mystery of the universe. Dianella, for instance, whose madness radically determines the story's outcome, at the slightest contact with harsh reality escapes into the solace and harmony of nature:

She perceived, in that mysterious, disturbing intimacy with unpeopled nature, the slightest movements, the faintest sounds, the vague rustle of the leaves, the hum of insects; and ceased to feel that she was living only for herself; she lived for an instant, unconscious and yet alertly wondering, with the earth, as though her soul had been diffused among and confused with all these country things (202).

If seen against the background of the historical novel in Italy, *I vecchi i e giovani* ultimately defeats all of its author's aspirations to historical synthesis because the realities it narrates remain formally incommensurable. Coherence is functionally severed from discord, history from existence. The consonance achieved through the creativity of Mattia Pascal is forever lost in the vast, but crowded, space of lived history.

In the three novels discussed above, alienation is a starting point and a necessary historical condition that cannot be defeated but only transcended through the artful invention of a creative individual. The question of the effect of alienation on art itself is addressed in the novel *Suo marito* (1911, *Her Husband*).

The main theme of *Suo marito* is the helplessness of the creative individual before the products of her art. Pirandello believed that art in modern society had been reduced to merchandise, governed by the economic laws of supply and demand. To dramatize the conflict between art as human creativity and its devaluation as a product to be bought and sold, the author presents us with the heroine, Sylvia, a writer who embodies the same passionate and tragic attributes of her art. At the same time, however, the novel focuses on Sylvia's husband, Giustino, who strives to transform his wife's art into commercial products. The novel's message issues from the juxtaposition of creation to production and from the ideological charge that these two elements contain.

In the character of Sylvia, Pirandello presents a model of problematic femininity. Like Marta and Dianella before her, Sylvia fears her own nature and the terror that introspection elicits. She counters the effects of an alienated daily existence with realities that defy the limits of reason. Thus, she fights against abstractness and against the human impoverishment caused by the commercialization of art at the expense of its creator.

In *Suo marito* Pirandello attempts to reformulate the new relationship that has been established between individuals and daily life in the world of monopoly capitalism. According to market principles, the more the product becomes detached from its producer, the more it gains in value. Objects can actually enter into new relationships with each other and even with the person who has produced them. The displacement of certain relationships from the person to the object creates the illusion that the inanimate thing is a live organism, endowed with powers and needs of its own. Such a mutation of values is seen in the episode where melancholic Sylvia contemplates the objects around her:

Often, while meditating, it occurred to her to focus on some object and study its minute characteristics, as if she were interested in it; the eyes of her body were concentrated on that sole object, almost as if to ward off all distractions in order to help the mind's eyes in their meditation. But slowly that object made a strange impression on her; it began to live for itself, as if suddenly it became aware of all the peculiarities she discovered, and it detached itself from its relationship to her and to other surrounding objects.[4]

Her sense of the illusory reality of things is inextricably linked to such a displacement of relationships, so that looking outside of herself into the world of material objects does nothing but heighten her anxiety and desperation. Sylvia's existential dilemma consists in preferring things over individuals. But for fear of the emptiness caused by giving life to objects, she is forced to look within herself for help and is terrified by what she finds.

Giustino, by contrast, has no problem either with his identity or with the quality of his daily existence. He is capable of following his wife's art, the now anthropomorphized object, into the marketplace, in much the same way that he is a spectator at the theater. The theater in the novel becomes a mirror of alienation in the sense that Giustino, while attending his wife's plays, believes that the only reality is the product, not its author, nor the players, nor the public. Giustino thus becomes a kind of appendage of the literary product he has transformed into merchandise.

The displaced relationship of subject and object gives way to an exchange of functions or roles between art and nature. Sylvia's entire story is based on the metaphor of giving birth. She conceives and gives birth to works of art in the same way she conceives and gives birth to a child. It is clear, however, that such a confusion is not Sylvia's, but Giustino's. It stems from his appropriation of her art, which is now his creation, his giving birth, which for him is greater than the natural birth of their child and quite different from the triumph of his wife's art.

Yet Giustino is not merely a negative term in a dialectic of true and false values. He acquires a certain moral stature as a dramatic character by virtue of his capacity for self-deception. His drama consists in believing that he, as manager of his wife's art, is actually engaged in a creative activity qualitatively greater and more lasting than his wife's art. Compared to Sylvia's practical orientation toward her art, Giustino's mental disposition is largely theoretical: he sees art as a miracle, a phenomenon without either cause or effect, an object existing in itself and for itself, and not connected in the least to its original author. His abstractness and alienation are so accentuated that not even at the death of his newly born child—a moment of the highest emotional tension—is he able to free himself from the mind-set that separates him radically from nature. In fact, he cannot express himself in any language other than that of his profession, and before his son's coffin he still behaves like the great impresario he is:

Here he is! Here is our little angel! See how beautiful he looks among so many flowers. These are life's tragedies, my dear sir, tragedies that take hold of us. . . . There is no need to look for life's tragedies always on far away islands among savages! I say this for the public, you know? You journalists go and explain it clearly to the public that today a writer can conceive of a brutal tragedy that everyone immediately likes because it is new; tomorrow, she herself, the writer, she can be gripped by one of these tragedies of life that tears to pieces a poor child and the hearts of a mother and father, do you understand? (*Suo marito*, 866–67)

With *Suo marito* Pirandello attempts to respond to the complex question of the authenticity of a work of art in a society that produces for commercial gain. This historical situation is contained in the absolute inability of the protagonists to communicate with one another at an intimate level, an inability that makes the resolution of the conflict virtually impossible according to traditional realistic standards.

Instead, the novel's plot remains a dynamically constructed hypothesis that, in order to acquire meaning, must become an alienated object, just like the characters. The novel's highly stylized subject matter testifies to Pirandello's pessimism in regard to a historical solution to the problem of dehumanization. As a result, the theme of alienation is reset in a grotesque perspective, whereby the historical drama becomes a paradox and so acquires a genuine abstractness.

From the standpoint of form, the transition from *Suo marito* to *I quaderni di Serafino Gubbio operatore* (1916, *Shoot: The Notebooks of Serafino Gubbio Cinematograph Operator*, 1926), marks a definite change in narrative perspective. Here Pirandello adopts the concept of alienation, not only as a theme, but also as a structural principle. The novel becomes a diary, composed by a passive cameraman, a hand that turns the crank, nicknamed "Si gira" to denote his mechanical function. The more proficiency Serafino Gubbio attains as cameraman and the more overwhelming the alienating world of objects appears, the more impoverished he becomes and the less capable he is of taking possession of the reality around him. He has given the machine his powers of appropriation, thus renouncing all creative activity.

As a kind of existential therapy, Serafino composes his notebooks: "Through writing I satisfy the powerful need to vent my rage, and, thus, I vindicate many people like me who have been sentenced to being nothing else but a 'hand that turns the crank' " (8). Now the passive character of the camera belongs to him; the notes he composes, however, will be no less approximate and alien than the camera's renderings of experience. But, at the same time, the neutral voracity of his new objectivizing perspective allows him to capture the vital flux of life that the mechanism tries in vain to efface. In this way, rather banal stories of love and suicide are means of avenging nature and vitality, the forces that modern industrial society endeavors to tame and program. For Serafino writing becomes a means of taking possession of oneself, while, at the same time, objectivizing and reintegrating a human substance that history has deformed.

Within the recesses of the Kosmograph movie studio, Serafino Gubbio develops his awareness of the negative effects that the film industry exerts on human life. By taking the movie camera as metaphor, he depicts a technological inferno, inhabited by a mechanical monster responsible for the protagonist's automatism:

Long live the Machine that mechanizes life! Do you still retain, gentlemen, a little sound, a little heart and a little mind? Give them, give them over to the greedy machines, which are waiting for them! You shall see and hear the sort of product, the exquisite stupidities they will manage to extract from them (*Shoot*, 9)

All the life that the machines have devoured with the voracity of animals gnawed by a tapeworm, is turned out here, in the large underground rooms, their darkness barely broken by dim red lamps, which strike a sinister blood-red gleam from the enormous dishes prepared for the developing bath (84–85).

The theoretical components of this polemic are the demystification of the myth of velocity and the triumph of the machine, which for Pirandello is the main cause of human madness. Serafino thus presents a portrait of humanity made utterly desperate by the products of industrial civilization.

Juxtaposed to such a miserable fate is nature and an idyllic past, experienced abstractly as a poetic ideal. In fact, the entire narrative revolves around the conflict between natural and mechanical vitality. The natural is represented by the dynamic instincts of the actress Varia Nestoroff, who is forced to work in the artificial and mechanical world of film, and also by the instincts of a tiger who, like Miss Nestoroff, acts according to his animal nature. The mechanical counterpart of natural vitality is the movie camera, the other voracious beast that in its rage seeks to consume all that is natural. The conflict reaches its high point in the work's final pages, when Serafino's passive hand records the terrifying scene of the tiger clawing to death the film's leading man:

Turn the handle; I have turned it. I have kept my word: to the end. But the vengeance that I sought to accomplish upon the obligation imposed on me, as the slave of the machine, to serve up life to my machine as food, life has chosen to turn back upon me. Very good. No one henceforward can deny that I have now arrived at perfection. As an operator I am now, truly, perfect. About a month after the appalling disaster which is still being discussed everywhere, I bring these notes to an end (326).

The central idea of Serafino's Notebooks is that, in the modern world, the control we exercise over the work-process through machinery undergoes a radical transformation: the mechanism becomes the principal means of controlling production and, as such, it curbs human creativity. All of Notebook One, in fact, describes the effects of such a transformation. In the hospice for mendicants, Serafino meets the individual who symbolizes the miserable fate to which progress has condemned humanity. He appears among other patients, holding a violin under his arm and, like Serafino, he is passive and mute, having relinquished his creative impulses to the power of technology.

Ironically, Pirandello judges as absolute and necessary those same historical forces on which the social organization and the ideological systems he renounces depend. If, on the one hand, he denounces bourgeois technology (its commercialization of human emotion as well as the optimism of its industrial rhetoric), on the other he provides no solution to the problem. This is so because, like the futurists who, by contrast, revered the machine, Pirandello too saw technology not as a mediating factor in human relations, but as their efficient cause, an absolute beyond which it was impossible to move. Yet, however flawed his critique of industrial civilization may be, it nevertheless represents the problem of alienation in a most concrete way. Through his portrayal of Serafino's total estrangement from reality, Pirandello contests the social division of labor that has historically been conditioned by automation. It is in this sense that the *Quaderni* reflects social reality and takes on an historically coherent dimension.

By general consensus, Pirandello's last novel, *Uno, nessuno e centomila* (1926, *One, None and a Hundred Thousand*, 1933)[5] is the work of prose fiction that best presents the problem of human identity as developed in his plays. The novel is recounted in the first person by its principle character, Vitangelo Moscarda, whose story begins when his wife casually observes that his nose appears somewhat tilted. This apparently banal, innocent, and playful observation throws Moscarda headlong into a complex existential predicament: what is "oneself" if that "self" lives continually at the mercy of the "other." The story Moscarda tells revolves around a fundamental principle: the position of the subject as the object of analysis and the ongoing process of verifying the radically divergent relationship between the narrative "I" and the Other—the "you" whom Moscarda continually addresses. But it is equally important to note that the gaze of the Other that Moscarda solicits is a sign of his need to be the center of attention, to be thus in control by placing his "self" in a tactical position. At the same time, however, his desire to dominate the Other is charged with guilt and anxiety, which explains the comic distance he seeks. We can assume that Moscarda's predicament derives from his inability to gain a clear sense of his own identity. Therefore, to be aware of himself and to know that others are aware of his existence are ways of defending himself against the dangers of being self-less.

Moscarda's obsession to know himself objectively shows that his ego has become an invisible and transcendent entity, knowable only to itself. His being in the world does not confirm a definite presence of self, for his "self" does not reside in his body. Instead, like a spectral entity, it exists divided or dissociated from him, present everywhere but nowhere in particular. Moscarda's dilemma is that his reality depends on the possibility of being seen and recognized by the other, while it is precisely the other whom he sees as an insurmountable threat to his identity.

Instead of being resolved, Moscarda's existential dilemma is aptly transcended in the condition of pure subjectivity attained at the novel's end. Moscarda's self has now become everything and exists beyond space and time. It speaks the paradoxical language of a schizoid fantasy, according to which living is tantamount to self-annihilation:

No name. No memory today of yesterday's name; of today's name tomorrow. If the name is the thing, if the name in us is the concept of everything that is situated outside of us, and without a name there is no concept, and the thing remains blindly indistinct and undefined within us, very well, then, let everyone take that name which I once bore and engrave it as an epitaph on the brow of that image of me that they beheld; let them have it there in peace and not speak of it again. For a name is no more than that, an epitaph. Something befitting the dead. One who has reached a conclusion. I am alive, and I reach no conclusion. Life knows no conclusion. Nor does it know anything of names. This tree, the tremulous breathing of new leaves, I am this tree. Tree, cloud;

tomorrow, book or breeze: the book that I read, the breeze that I drink in. Living wholly without, a vagabond (266–67).

By losing his specific identity in nature, Moscarda no doubt loses the "self" that had been endangered by the scrutiny of others. Thus, paradoxically, he avoids "nonbeing" by ceasing "to be." But like his tragic companion Henry IV, who also pretends to be mad, Moscarda discovers that true deception consists in the act of pretense and that in effect he has fallen into that very condition against which he has sought to safeguard himself. In fact, that condition was inevitable from the very moment he renounced seeing himself objectively. If nonbeing is equal to being, the desire for total liberty beyond society leads Moscarda paradoxically to renounce freedom altogether and to live an indefinite existence within the empty world of fantasy.

In sum, *Uno, nessuno e centomila* is the story of Pirandello's encounter with "nonbeing," represented as the loss or abandonment of the synthetic unity of the self and of the relativity of existence. Moscarda's experience is based on the conviction that to live means, necessarily, to pretend or to play a part. In it we find the basis of Pirandello's plays and of the dilemma of life versus form in which the plays find their philosophical support. Pirandello's diverse characters all endeavor to convince themselves of the reality of this or that thing or event. Their way of winning the battle with the Other is forever to attempt an ultimate fiction in order to avoid facing the ultimate truth about themselves.

As we have seen in our brief survey, Pirandello's work as a novelist enabled him to attempt to solve the mysteries and contradictions associated with "being-in-the-world." With his last novel, *Uno, nessuno e centomila*, the epistemological certainty in which all narration is grounded is displaced. The speaking "I" becomes the critical agent of interrogation that questions the presumption of its own being. It is not altogether clear if Pirandello's negation of the possibility of knowledge of the subject was designed to reestablish its primacy and independence by dramatizing its will to live despite its own existential precariousness. Seen in a more contemporary context, his overriding goal might have been to leave his readers suspended within an abyss of uncertainty. In any case, what cannot be denied is that Pirandello believed the human being to contain an infinite collection of possible roles.

NOTES

1. The only book-length study of Pirandello's fiction available in English is Douglas Radcliff-Umstead's *The Mirror of Anguish: A Study of Luigi Pirandello's Narrative Writings*. In Italian, see Enzo Lauretta, ed., *Il romanzo di Pirandello*, which contains important essays by A. Leone de Castris, N. Borsellino, N. Tedesco, G. Mazzacurati, G. Andersson, and R. Barilli; Robert S. Dombroski, *Le totalità dell'artificio: ideologia e forma nel romanzo di Pirandello*; Corrado Donati, *La solitudine allo specchio*; Giancarlo Mazzacurati, *Pirandello nel romanzo europeo*.

2. According to De Benedetti, Mattia poses an absurd predicament: he wants to become

a person outside the social context of concrete human relations, while at the same time returning to the very society from which he fled.

3. For a complete discussion in English of *I vecchi e i giovani*, see Robert S. Dombroski, "The Form of Chaos," 85–113.

4. *Suo marito*, 641 (translation mine).

5. On *Uno, nessuno e centomila*, see Gian-Paolo Biasin, "Moscarda's Mirror"; Gregory Lucente, "Non Conclude: Narrative Self-Consciousness and the Voice of Creation."

WORKS CITED

Alonge, Roberto. *Pirandello tra realismo e mistificazione*. Napoli: Guida, 1972.

Biasin, Gian-Paolo. *Literary Diseases: Theme and Metaphor in the Italian Novel*. Austin: University of Texas Press, 1975.

De Benedetti, Giacomo. *Il romanzo del Novecento*. Milano: Feltrinelli, 1971.

Dombroski, Robert S. "The Form of Chaos in Pirandello's *I vecchi e i giovani*." *Yale Italian Studies* 2 (1978): 85–113.

―――. *Le totalità dell'artificio: ideologia e forma nel romanzo di Pirandello*. Padova: Liviana, 1978.

Lauretta, Enzo. *Il romanzo di Pirandello*. Palermo: Palumbo, 1976.

Lucente, Gregory. *Beautiful Fables: Self-Consciousness in Italian Narrative from Manzoni to Calvino*. Baltimore: Johns Hopkins University Press, 1986.

Mazzacurati, Giancarlo. *Pirandello nel romanzo europeo*. Bologna: Il Mulino, 1987.

Pirandello, Luigi. *The Late Mattia Pascal*. Trans. A. Livingston. New York: E. P. Dutton, 1923.

―――. *The Old and the Young*. Trans. C. K. Scott-Moncrieff. New York: E. P. Dutton, 1928.

―――. *One, None, and a Hundred Thousand*. Trans. Samuel Putnam. New York: E. P. Dutton, 1933.

―――. *The Outcast*. Trans. L. Ongley. New York: E. P. Dutton, 1935.

―――. *Shoot: The Notebooks of Serafino Gubbio, Cinematograph Operator*. Trans. C. K. Scott-Moncrieff. New York: E. P. Dutton, 1926.

―――. *Suo marito* in *Tutti i romanzi*. Giovanni Macchia, ed. Milano: Mondadori, 1973.

―――. *L'Umorismo* in *Saggi, Poesie, Scritti varii*. Manlio Lo Vecchio-Musti, ed. Milano: Mondadori, 1960.

Radcliff-Umstead, Douglas. *The Mirror of Anguish: A Study of Luigi Pirandello's Narrative Writings*. Rutherford, N.J.: Fairleigh Dickinson University Press, 1978.

27

Nature as Structural-Stylistic Motive in *Novelle per un Anno*

Maria Rosaria Vitti-Alexander

In the preface to *Six Characters in Search of an Author*,[1] Pirandello calls himself a philosophical writer because he aims to give his "figure, vicende, paesaggi" (characters, vicissitudes, landscapes) a universal value, a "patricolare senso della vita" (a particular sense of life). Driven by a "profondo bisogno spirituale" (a profound spiritual need), he continually probes, dissects, and analyzes everything, be it man, vicissitude, or nature.

This chapter shows how nature in the Pirandellian short stories does not stand alone, for a "paesaggio" (landscape) is not presented "per il solo gusto di descriverlo" (for the simple reason of a mere description). Rather, it acts within the limits of narration, as a structural motive, almost always a catalyst for the action of the characters. In several short stories, the character finds the only possibility of development—that is, escaping his present predicament—through a specific reference to nature. In other stories, nature becomes an important tool for emphasizing the characters, and in so doing, clarifies and completes their personalities. This completion is sometimes achieved by focusing on various aspects of the character's personality and at other times through a humoristic opposition to nature itself.

This use of landscape is particularly effective because of the characteristics of the short story genre. By definition the short story must keep within a limited narrative space and make maximum use of its content by concentrating on a close sequence of events. Because Pirandello's focus is on his preoccupation with man and his ensnarement in the incongruous ways of life, everything else, including nature, becomes subjected to this central focus. By nature I mean the natural elements around us, such as the sky, the sea, and the earth, which can be either experienced first hand or filtered through the imagination of the artist.

In the preface to *Novelle per un anno*,[2] Corrado Alvaro, close to Pirandello through many years of friendship, talks of the man Pirandello—of his ways of living, seeing, and understanding things. For Alvaro, Pirandello was a lover of humankind, an indefatigable observer of the infinite meanderings of the human mind, one who ''lasciava parlare e ascoltava'' (would let others talk while he listened) (I, 26). Alvaro also recounts that Pirandello, after having visited much of the world, remembered only people from these trips, rarely the things he saw:

Non lo sentii mai parlare di mobili, di oggetti, di decorazioni, ma molto di uomini, dal fondo di tutte le città che aveva vedute, e come seguitando ad aver da fare con essi, contrastarvi, accordarsi, inveire (I, 15–16).

I never heard him speak of furnishings, of objects, of decorations, but a lot of men, from the background of all the cities he had seen, and as if continuing to have to deal with them, oppose them, agree with them, inveigh at them.

Even the memories of his son Stefano emphasize this aspect of the writer's interest—that desire to know, penetrate, and understand the human mind, paying little attention, so it seems, to the outside world. Stefano recounts that his father would remain taciturn during parties and reunions, only to return to his study and recall precise and revealing details about all those present.

This curiosity about man, whom Pirandello thought both simple and complex, comprehensible and incomprehensible, has always been at the center of his interest and the focal point of his writings. In all his works, the main focus is always on the character of man, humoristically Pirandellian, because

il giudizio che dava sugli uomini glielo dettava il momento, la circostanza, l'umore; e non era mai definitivo. A un giorno di distanza diceva l'opposto (I, 16).

the judgment he would give on men was dictated to him by the moment, the circumstance, the mood; and it was never final. A day later he would say the opposite.

A glance at Pirandello's writings reveals this insatiable preoccupation with man and the workings of his mind. In the later preface to *Il fu Mattia Pascal*, Pirandello himself acknowledges this penchant when he says that the humorist goes out and looks for specimens with a wooden leg, or a glass eye, because for him man is not an abstraction or a type, but an individual with faults, shortcomings, and imperfections. His last novel, *Uno, nessuno e centomila* (*One, None and a Hundred Thousand*), is about a dissolution of personality which the reader follows through the mentality of the main character. The play *Trovarsi* is built entirely on the mental anguish of the protagonist who finally realizes the double aspect of human experience.

Pirandello's own personal life played an important part in his disposition toward the workings of the mind. From 1903 until 1913, Pirandello lived with a mentally ill wife, always feeling himself divided into two—the man he thought he was and the man his wife saw. Later, these tormented years gave birth to many works that focus on man and his psyche—*Diana e la Tuda*; *Cap and Bells*; *Her Husband, Shoot,* to mention a few. Pirandello felt his southern origin might also account for his preoccupation with the dialectics of the mind; in the short story "Il Professor Terremoto" one of his characters reminds us that:

Sono così tormentosamente dialettici questi nostri bravi confratelli meridionali. Affondano nel loro spasimo, a scavarlo fino in fondo, la saettella di trapano del loro raziocinio, e frù e frù e frù, non la smettono più (I, 608).

They are so tormentingly dialectical these good Southern brethren of ours. They drive the point of the drill of reason deep into their sorrow to dig to the very bottom, and they go and go and go at it without ever stopping.

Given the extensive collection *Novelle per un anno*, I will limit myself here to only a few short stories as examples. The short story "Fuga" is a beautiful example of nature determining the action of the character. In this story the natural elements of the outside world push the main character, Bareggi, to accomplish his escape from his personal world. Nature offers him the only possibility of development. Bareggi is locked in by an oppressive world of stressful work and by an impossible family life caused by the presence of three women dependent on him economically and psychologically. Nature provides him with the stimulus and resolve to act against his circumstances. Note how the dim light of a rural world incites him to flee his unsustainable situation:

appena nelle nari avverti il fresco odore fermentoso d'un bel fascio di fieno nella rete e il puzzo caprigno del cappotto del lattajo . . . : gli odori della campagna lontana, che immaginò subito, laggiù, laggiù, oltre la barriera nomentana, oltre Casal dei Pazzi, immensa, smemorata e liberatrice (I, 1261).

as soon as his nostrils caught the fresh, fermenting odor of a nice bundle of hay in the feedbag and the stench of goats on the milkman's coat . . . : the smells of the distant countryside, which he imagined immediately, over there, over there, behind the barrier of the Nomentana, behind Casal dei pazzi, immense, forgetful, and liberating.

A rural odor and the presence of a country object excite the character's imagination and compel him to escape the asphyxiating, immediate reality. Arriving home from work tired, suffering from nephritis, and harassed by the thought of his daughters and wife, Bareggi seizes a horse-drawn milkman's cart parked outside a home and scurries into the country:

Volò Ponte Nomentano, volò Casal dei Pazzi, e via, via, via, nella campagna aperta, che già s'indovinana nella nebbia (I, 1263).

Ponte Nomentano flew by, Casal dei Pazzi flew by, and on and on into the open countryside, which was dimly visible through the fog.

  Bareggi's escape is accomplished through a tumultuous crescendo of sounds
and through continuous references to the outside world. The horse's neighs are
echoed by the tremendous noise of the cans and the jugs in the cart which
"doveva sembrare una tempestà quel carretto in fuga con tutti quegli arnesi che,
traballando, s'urtavano" (it must have seemed a racket, that cart in flight with
all those tools which, bumping, hit one another). Above it all rises Bareggi's
voice, accompanying "la pazza corsa" (the mad flight) with long, repeated
laughs; "rideva il signor Bareggi, pur nel terrore . . . rideva di quel terrore; . . . E
rideva,
rideva, . . . " (He was laughing, Signor Bareggi, even in his fear . . . he was
laughing at his own fear; . . . and he kept on laughing and laughing . . .) At the
same time there is the constant reference to the fog which "si faceva sempre
più fitta col calar della sera" (was becoming always ever more heavy with the
approaching nightfall), and "che gli impediva di veder perfino le lampade elet-
triche" (which prevented him from seeing even the electric lamps). The fog
both heightens the sensation of the flight toward an "immensa," "smemorata,"
and therefore "liberatrice" countryside, and displays the symbiosis between the
confused psychological state of the character, who runs away unconscious of
where he is going and of what is happening to him, and the landscape which,
wrapped in a cotton-wool cloud, hides the reality of things. His unconsciousness
is reaffirmed by the fact that the horse, not he himself, is the agent of the mad
escape. It is only the horse and the empty milk wagon that the reader sees at
the end of the story. What has become of Bareggi the reader is never told:

Quando il cavallo si fermò davanti al rustico casalino, col carretto sconquassato e senza
più né bidone né un orcio, era già sera chiusa (I, 1263).

When the horse stopped in front of the rustic farmhouse, with the ruined cart, but with
neither the milk can nor the pitcher, it was already late night.

  As Bareggi's unconscious mental state is evidenced by a sharp, dense, and
assailing fog that wraps and hides the world, the meticulous and repetitive
presentation of aspects of nature emphasize the conscious decision Matteo Sinagra reaches in "Da sé." In this short story, the fusion between character and
landscape is continued and amplified, so that nature becomes an absolute and
the character's state of mind is explained and understood through the repeated
lists of natural elements.
  Matteo Sinagra, having lost all confidence in himself after experiencing a
bankruptcy, and feeling "dead" for all practical purposes, decides to resolve
his miserable existence by taking his own life. Not having money for his funeral,
Sinagra decides to walk himself to the graveyard, as a "corpse" walking to his
own funeral. It is during this walk that Sinagra, a dead-man-alive, as he calls

himself, experiences quite a different world around him, now that he is detached from his own subjective conceptions. In his condition as a "living corpse" he observes the world for the first and last time. The nature he sees is the everyday elements: trees, rocks, clouds, flowers, the sea, and the mountains. But the presentation of these elements illustrates the character's new perspective. The character himself has changed. Mundane aspects of the surrounding world reveal themselves to him from a different perspective because they were seen with different eyes. As a dead person, Sinagra is amazed by a world he had never seen before. With newfound innocence, he rediscovers known aspects of nature that his mundane familiarity with nature had taught him to neglect:

Gli alberi . . . o guarda! erano così gli alberi? E quei monti laggiù . . . perché? quei monti azzurri, con quelle nuvole bianche sopra . . . Le nuvole . . . che cose strane! . . . E là, in fondo, il mare . . . Era così? Quello, il mare? (II, 652)

The trees . . . oh look! Were the trees like this? And those mountains down there . . . why? Those blue mountains, with those white clouds on top . . . Clouds . . . what strange things! . . . And there, at the bottom of the sea . . . It was like this? That, the sea?

In the position of a corpse walking himself to his grave, Sinagra's condition becomes as absolute as the nature he focuses on; because nature is seen through a fresh and unbiased perspective, it becomes an object that exists in itself.

The symbiosis between nature and character finds an ulterior and more complex application in "Un cavallo sulla luna," where the characters' personalities are presented and developed through a humoristic opposition to nature. In this short story the narrator utilizes nature for a double purpose; he uses it to show the symbiosis of the characters' souls with the rural world, and he exploits it to focus on the characters' humoristic differences. Nino Berardi, an older man of noble Sicilian descent, has married a young, naive northern girl. They have chosen to spend their honeymoon in an old family house located in the Sicilian countryside. The short story opens with the rural landscape of an arid and dry farmland:

Di settembre, su quell'altipiano d'aride argille azzurre, . . . la campagna già riarsa dalle rabbie dei lunghi soli estivi, era triste: ancor tutta irta di stoppie annerite, con radi mandorli e qualche ceppo centenario d'olivo saraceno qua e là (II, 79).

In September, on that plain of arid, blue clay, . . . the countryside, already parched by the rage of the long summer sun was gloomy: yet all was bristling with blackened stubbles, with a few almond trees and some centennial Saracen olive trees here and there.

The landscape so particularly introduced does not exist per se but is instead employed mystically as an explicative mirror of the protagonist's mental state. It is through the exterior representation of nature that the character's internal parching thirst finds its expression. The "campagna riarsa dalla rabbia dei lunghi soli estivi'' (the countryside, parched by the rage of the long summer suns) mirrors Nino's

volto infocato, che guardava qua e là coi piccoli occhi neri, lustri, da pazzo, e non intendeva più nulla, e non mangiava e non beveva e diventava di punto in punto più pavonazzo, quasi nero (II, 79).

excited face, that looked here and there with small glowing black eyes, those of a madman, and he was no longer hearing anything, and was not eating and not drinking and was becoming from moment to moment more purple, almost black.

Nino is not a groom capable of understanding "la giovanissima sposa . . . una vera bambina ancora, fresca, aliena'' (the very young bride . . . truly a little girl still, fresh, aloof), but rather a mature man who burns with desire for "una bambina.''
    The humoristic employment of the natural aspects of the countryside becomes evident when applied to the other character, Ida:

Ida dietro le spesse siepi . . . sentiva, invece, correndo, come strillavano gaje al sole le calandre, e come, nell'afa dei piani, nel silenzio attonito, sonava da lontane aje, auguroso, il canto di qualche gallo; si sentiva investire, ogni tanto, dal fresco respiro refrigerante che veniva dal mare prossimo (II, 81).

Ida, as she ran, heard how gaily the wood-larks sang in the sun, from behind the thick hedges . . . she heard also, in the sultriness of the plain, and in the astonished silence, the crow of cocks, full of prophecy from distant barnyards; she felt assailed now and then by the fresh, cool breath coming from the nearby sea.

While for Nino the narrator uses nature to describe his uncontrollable passion, for the innocent Ida that same nature reflects her gentleness and docility. Ida sees neither aridity nor rage, only peace. While the dense, pungent, heavy breath of nature is truly a detailed visual and olfactory representation of the man's burning sexual desire, nature also signifies Ida's innocence. It is only at the closing of the short story, when she panics at seeing her husband dying, that the surroundings become the operating motive of Ida's escape. The countryside is hostile now, with a large, menacing moon, which

sorgeva lenta da quel mare giallo di stoppie. E, nera, in quell'enorme disco di rame vaporoso, la testa inteschiata di quel cavallo . . . mentre i corvi, facendo la ruota, gracchiavano alti nel cielo . . . (II, 83).

was rising slowly from that yellow sea of stubbles. And, black, against that enormous vapory copper disk, the skull-like head of that horse . . . while the crows, circling above, croaked, high in the sky . . .

Ida wants to flee and calls for the father "a gran voce il padre, il padre che se la portasse via . . . via, via, via" (in a loud voice to her father, her father to take her away . . . away, away, away) (II,84).

The presence of landscape in Pirandello's narrative has been studied at length.[3] Yet the operating function of nature in relation to the protagonist has been ignored. In many cases nature acts as a determining aspect of Pirandello's narrative because the final action of the protagonist—even though precarious—finds expression and explanation in the only landscape description present. Such short stories are usually narrations of human misery (such as a tormented life or a boring or insufficient job), which are almost totally deprived of landscapes but always end with an image of nature or a simple reference to it. In many cases the image and reference are short and incisive because they are symbolically tied to the main character of the story. It is, in fact, this mention of the outside world that offers the character the only possibility of development, of freeing himself from his world.

An example is the short story "La distruzione dell'uomo," where Pirandello presents the complex and totally absorbing existential suffering of a man. Petix, the main character, can neither accept nor explain humanity's insistence on procreation, even when it means raising children in poverty. Petix's atrocious suffering is dissected and analyzed thoroughly. The world that obssesses him, and in which he is condemned to live, is populated by the poor, who in Petix's eyes are completely lacking in dignity and decorum. While the object of study in this short story is the misery of this world, and the nausea that Petix feels toward it, Pirandello provides the only possibility of action through the landscape descriptions, and thereby allows Petix to escape the hated world of procreation.

Signora Porrella, a forty-seven-year-old woman, is pregnant for the sixteenth time in her life and completely unconscious of her repulsively deformed body. She comes to symbolize, for Petix, the world of his suffering. At the end of her ninth month, Signora Porrella, accompanied by her husband, takes daily walks through the city toward a river nearby where she stops to rest on a rock by the river bank. The river, the only reference to nature in this otherwise totally closed and inescapable world of mental suffering, provides Petix with the only way to carry out his revenge. One day Petix, provoked to the limits by the strolling couple,

non disse nulla; e tutto si svolse in un attimo, quasi quietamente. Come la donna s'accostò al pietrone per mettervisi a sedere egli l'afferrò per un braccio e la trasse con uno strappo fino all'orlo delle acque straripate; là le diede uno spintone e la mandò ad annegare nel fiume (I, 904).

said nothing; and everything happened in an instant, almost quietly. As the woman came close to the big stone to begin to sit down, he seized her by the arm and with one tug dragged her to the edge of the flooding river; there he gave her a strong shove and sent her to drown in the river.

That landscape, seemingly introduced by chance, is an integral part of the motive
for Petix's homicidal act, the only action that the narrator provides for him to
free himself of this woman who symbolizes, with her pregnancy, the world of
bestial procreation that he so despises. The river, so opportunely introduced in
the narration, offers him the way to freedom. The presence of the water, the big
rock on the river bank, Petix's shove, and the death of the woman are all fused
in the short but necessary description of the natural landscape. Petix's violence
to the woman, impetuous and without escape, mirrors the violence of the turbulent
current that inexorably drags away the body of the victim.

Nature can also be used to continue a character's life, as in the case of the
short story "La morte addosso." The protagonist, condemned by a mortal illness,
knows he cannot escape his cruel fate. Death tells him, after having put "un
fiore in bocca," a cancerous growth on his lip, that "ripasserò tra otto o dieci
mesi!" (I will be back within eight or ten months) (I, 950). The only action the
narrator assigns him is to wait until death returns. But as in the previous story,
the escape comes from nature. One night the dying character meets a man who
is waiting in a train station for the next train. The two spend the night speaking
together and in the morning, before the casual companion of a night leaves to
return to the country, the dying man turns to him and asks him to help him find
a way to escape his death and so continue to live:

E mi faccia un piacere, domattina, quando arriverà. . . . All'alba, lei può far la strada a
piedi. Il primo cespuglietto d'erba su la sponda. Ne conti i fili per me. Quanti fili saranno,
tanti giorni ancora io vivrò. Ma lo scelga bello grosso, mi raccomando. Buona notte,
caro signore (I, 951).

Do me a favor. Tomorrow morning, when you get back. . . . At dawn, you can make the
rest of your journey on foot. The first small tuft of grass by the roadside. Count the
number of blades for me. The number of those blades will be the number of days that I
have yet to live. But, I implore you, choose a nice, big tuft. Good-night, dear signore!

Again in this short story it is a glimpse of landscape, of nature, that widens the
perspective of the protagonist and offers him a means to escape death. A "ces-
puglio campestre," a tuft of grass, in a faraway place will be the character's
lifeline.

The landscape description also stimulates the character's imagination to the
point where his fantasy actually becomes reality. This is the case in "Rimedio:
la geografia," whose character, desperate because of his family condition, a
dying mother, a wife with whom he cannot communicate, and a meager family
budget, finds an escape by wandering through the pages of his daughter's atlas.
The character's wanderings around the globe are not only mental flights, but
they become for him real escapes from which he returns with an impression so
concrete and tangible that his nostrils still sense "il tanfo caldo e grasso del
letame nelle grandi stalle" (I, 227) (the warm and heavy stench of the manure

in the big stables). The mental flights are real enough to cause the character to contrast them to the sad reality of his household.

Even though the landscape presented here is not real but imagined, it equally carries out its function for the character. When his wife becomes intolerable and begins to request things he cannot provide, he immediately replaces her with the image of a place, Lapland, where conjugal conduct is different because

I Lapponi, . . . sudici cani, cara mia! . . . Ti basti sapere che, mentr'io ti tengo così cara, essi tengono così poco alla fedeltà coniugale, che offrono la moglie e le figliuole al primo forestiero che capita. Per conto mio, cara puoi star sicura: non son tentato per nulla, cara, a profittarne (I, 228).

The Laplanders, dirty dogs, my dear! . . . It is enough for you to know that, while I am so fond of you, they are so little interested in conjugal fidelity, to offer the wife and their daughters to the first foreigner who comes by. As for me, dear, you can be sure I am not at all tempted, dear, to take advantage of that.

The wife can neither follow him in his mental escape from the immediate reality, nor can she understand his humoristic answer:

Ma che diavolo dici? Sei pazzo? Io ti sto domandando. . . . Sì, cara. Tu mi stai domandando, non dico di no. Ma che triste paese, la Lapponia! (I, 229)

But what in the world are you saying? Are you crazy? I am asking you. . . .
Yes, dear. You are asking me, I am not denying it. But what a sad country Lapland is!

As Corrado Alvaro reminds us in his preface: ''gli uomini lo interessavano . . . nessun ricordo di paese, molti sugli uomini'' (men interested him . . . not one remembrance of a country, many of the men) (I, 26). Yet it would be unjust to say that Pirandello was insensitive to nature and that he felt detached from it. For Pirandello nature provides the vehicle through which he develops his characters. Even in those short stories where it is man, as character, who dominates, nature is never absent but is represented symbiotically by the character himself. Pirandello's memories of people he met during his frequent trips around the world and of his countrymen, that ''contrastarvi, accordarsi, inveire con essi'' (to oppose them, agree with them, inveigh at them), is all transformed in a remembrance dense as a landscape. Unfailingly, the reader leaves the Pirandellian short stories with a vision of nature, a smell of earth, and an indelible feeling of landscape because it is part of the subconscious of the characters themselves.

In many Pirandellian short stories nature is a function of human thought—not as a direct representation but mirrored. Although the short story ''La giara'' takes place in the countryside, among olive groves and planted fields, there is not one direct description of the landscape itself. We do not see the bountiful olive trees, but we know of their presence through the voice of the narrator who instead describes an ''annata buona,'' a good harvest year, and lined-up jars ready to be filled with oil. Such an indirect presentation of nature continues throughout the story. It is men working, the coming and going of the olive pickers and the mule-drivers who ''con le mule cariche di concime da depositare a mucchi su la costa per la favata della nuova stagione'' (with the mules loaded with manure to deposit on the slope by the field where he was going to sow beans next year) (II, 272), which suggest an image of a rural Sicilian countryside. A description of the olive groves, of the fields to be cultivated, does not interest the narrator. More important are the thoughts of the characters toward the groves and the countryside. The result is a fusion, a symbiosis between men and nature, that does not allow us to see one without the other. An old peasant is therefore seen as a tree, ''vecchio sbilenco, dalle giunture storpie e nodose, come un ceppo antico d'olivo saraceno'' (a misshapen old man, crippled and gnarled, just like an ancient Saracen olive tree) (II, 273).

In ''Notte'' we see the casual encounter of two wretched individuals, an unhappily married man and a young widow. While waiting for their train, the two spend the night on a deserted beach, sharing their miseries and sorrows. But in a moment of silence the two become aware of the nature in front of them, and through nature their individual sufferings take on a universal meaning, an existential suffering shared by all humankind:

di tutti gli esseri e di tutte le cose, . . . di tutta la vita che non può sapere perché si debba nascere, perché si debba amare, perché si debba morire (I, 526).

of all the human beings and of the things, . . . of all life which cannot know why one should be born, should love, or should die.

At dawn the two are ready to resume their journey and to continue with their own miserable existence; but now they have learned to find in the surrounding nature a consoling force for their unhappy lives.

Because of Pirandello's predilection for short stories, and his lifelong writing of them, he has been called Boccaccio's successor in the tradition of Italian short prose writing.[4] Indeed, like Boccaccio, Pirandello has found in this literary genre a most suitable mode of narration. But while Boccaccio often describes nature, landscape, and the environment, Pirandello makes character prevalent over landscape. In his essay L'umorismo[5] Pirandello says:

Dopo aver considerato il cielo, il clima, il sole, la società, i costumi, i pregiudizzi, ecc., non dobbiamo forse appuntar lo sguardo sui singoli individui e domandarci che cosa siano divenuti in ciascuno di essi questi elementi, secondo lo speciale organamento psichico, la combinazione originaria, unica, che costituisce questo o quell'individuo? Dove uno s'abbandona, l'altro si rivolta; dove uno piange, l'altro ride; e ci può esser sempre qualcuno che ride e piange a un tempo. Del mondo che lo circonda, l'uomo, in questo o in quel tempo, non vede se non ciò che lo interessa; fin dall'infanzia, senza neppur sospettarlo, egli fa una scelta d'elementi e li accetta e accoglie in sé; e questi elementi, più tardi, sotto l'azione del sentimento, s'agiteranno per combinarsi nei modi più svariati.

After having considered the sky, the climate, the sun, society, customs, prejudices, etc., don't we really have to turn our gaze to the single individuals and ask ourselves what these elements have become in each one of them, according to the special psychic organism, the original, unique combination, which constitutes this or that individual? Where one lets himself go, the other rebels; where one cries, the other smiles; and there can always be someone who laughs and cries at the same time. Of the world which surrounds him, man, in this or in that time, sees only what interests him: since childhood, without even suspecting it, he chooses elements, accepts them, and makes them his own; these elements, later, under the action of feeling, will be stirred to combine themselves in the most varied ways.

With regard to the relationship between Pirandello and nature, Corrado Alvaro says that "Pirandello transferì ogni sentimento della natura in una legge fatale del cuore e dei sensi, . . . '' (I, 38), (Pirandello transferred every feeling for nature into a fatal law of the heart and the senses, . . .).[6] But such a transference must not be seen as the author's insensitivity to the natural world;[7] it must be seen, rather, as a will to see and understand nature through its relationship with humankind, because

l'arte è la natura stessa, ma proseguente l'opera sua nello spirito umano. E da questo appunto deriva l'amore dell'artista per la natura: egli si riconosce in essa, e al contatto di lei assume coscienza del proprio genio.

art is nature itself, but continuing its work in the human spirit. In fact, from this derives the artist's love for nature: he recognizes himself in her, and through this contact with her he assumes consciousness of his own genius.[8]

NOTES

1. Luigi Pirandello, *Maschere Nude* (Milano: Mondadori, 1958), 1. Vol. I., 58.
2. Luigi Pirandello, *Novelle per un Anno*, edited by Corrado Alvaro (Milano: Mondadori, 1978), I, II. Hereafter the page number in the text will refer to this edition.
3. Among the few critics who have dealt at some depth with landscape in Pirandello's works is Franco Zangrilli. He has treated the employment of landscape both in Pirandello's poetry and his prose. Zangrilli correctly points out that in both genres Pirandellian landscape has a representative structural function and that it is not at all a mere decorative presence. In the treatment of poetry, consult "La funzione del paesaggio nella poesia di Pirandello" in *Review of National Literature: Pirandello*, Vol. 14, 93–122. For the prose, see "La funzione del paesaggio nella novellistica pirandelliana" in *Le novelle di Pirandello: Atti del 6 convegno internazionale di studi pirandelliani raccolti e ordinati da Stefano Milioto* (Agrigento: Sarcuto, 1980), 129–65. Among other critics who have written on Pirandello's use of landscape are Enzo Lauretta, "I luoghi e il tempo delle memorie nel romanzo pirandelliano" in *Il romanzo di Pirandello*, edited by Enzo Lauretta (Palermo: Palumbo, 1976), 271–93, and Benvenuto Terracini, "*Le novelle per un anno* di Luigi

Pirandello" in *Analisi, stilistica, teoria, storia, problemi* (Milano: Feltrinelli, 1975), 309–10.
   4. See Oscar Büdel, *Pirandello* (London: Bowes and Bowes, 1966). Büdel had mentioned that the short story genre starting from Boccaccio seems to have been the narrative genre most favored by Pirandello, thus placing him in a long tradition. Therefore, a Pirandello "boccaccesco" must be understood only in the form and not in the content.
   5. Pirandello, *Saggi, poesie e scritti varii*, a cura di Manlio LoVecchio-Musti (Milano: Mondadori, 1960), 29.
   6. Corrado Alvaro is among those Pirandellian scholars who deny that Pirandello used nature as a literary tool. For Alvaro, Pirandello remains indifferent, detached, and uninterested in the natural world. From this perspective Alvaro observes a virtual absence of landscape in Pirandello's works.
   7. Among the better known critics who have seen in Pirandello an insensitivity, a detachment, a distance toward nature, see Gaspare Giudice, "Pirandello in Sicilia: I paesi dell'infanzia" in *Belfagor*, 15, 3 (May 31, 1960), and also *Luigi Pirandello* (Torino: UTET, 1963); Luigi Russo, "Pirandello e la provincia metafisica" in *Belfagor*, 15, 4 (July 31, 1960).
   8. Pirandello, *Saggi, poesie e scritti varii*, 1221.

WORKS CITED

Büdel, Oscar. *Pirandello*. London: Bowes and Bowes, 1966.
Giudice, Gaspare. "Pirandello in Sicilia: I paesi dell'infanzia." *Belfagor*, 15, 3 (May 31, 1960).
Lauretta, Enzo. *Il romanzo di Pirandello*. Palermo: Palumbo, 1976.
Pirandello, Luigi. *Maschere Nude*. Milano: Mondadori, 1958, Vol. 1.
———. *Novelle per un Anno*. Milano: Mondadori, 1978, Vol. 1, 2.
———. *Saggi, poesie e scritti varii*. Milano: Mondadori, 1960.
Russo, Luigi. "Pirandello e la provincia metafisica." *Belfagor*, 15, 4 (July 31, 1960).
Terracini, Benvenuto. *Analisi, stilistica, teoria, storia, problemi*. Milano: Feltrinelli, 1975.
Zangrilli, Franco. "La funzione del paesaggio nella poesia di Pirandello." *Review of National Literature: Pirandello*, 14, 1987.
———. "La funzione del paesaggio nella novellistica pirandelliana." *Le novelle di Pirandello: Atti del 6 convegno internazionale di studi pirandelliani raccolti e ordinati da Stefano Milioto*. Agrigento: Sarcuto, 1980.

Appendix A

Three Poems by Luigi Pirandello

Introduced and Translated by John Louis DiGaetani

The manuscripts for these three poems are located at the Biblioteca Nazionale Centrale in Rome. The poems were published during Pirandello's lifetime and are reprinted in *Opere di Luigi Pirandello: Saggi, Poesie e Scritti Varii* (Vol. 6), published by Mondadori, 1960. I am presenting the texts as they appear in the Biblioteca Nazionale Centrale along with my very free translations.

Roma—January 6, 1900

Le pagliuzze e gli stracci della via
esposti alla mercè di chi cammina
ànno anch'essi nel mondo
il lor breve momento d'allegeria:
viene un soffio di vento e li molina
come bambini che fan girotondo.

Rome—January 6, 1900 (Epiphany)

The straws and rags of the road,
at the mercy of travelers,
also have in this world
their brief moment of happiness:
a slight wind comes and moves them
like children playing ring round the rosy.

Come muore

Ecco, a un mandorlo appende
il suo mantel di neve
l'Inverno che già muore.
Il mantel bianco e lieve
su i rami si rapprende
ed ogni grumo é un fiore.

Steso del tronco al piede
guarda l'Inverno in su
con occhi acquosi, intento.
Farfalle o fior? Non vede
il suo mantello. Più
s'adira, soffia: il vento

è solo un debil fiato,
agita i fiori appena . . .
E un'altra un'altra pena
la sorte gli riserba:
muor tutto fili d'erba!
il crin, la barba: un prato . . .

Dying

There on an almond tree
Winter, already dying, hangs
his mantle of snow.
The light, bright mantle
thickens on the branches
and every clump is a flower.

From his trunk to his feet
Winter watches intently,
with watery eyes.
Butterfly or flower? He does not see
his mantle. The angrier
he gets, the more he huffs,

Winter now is only a weak breath.
It barely stirs the hanging flowers . . .
And yet another pain
Fate reserves for him:
He dies into blades of grass!
His hair, his beard: a meadow . . .

Le Nubi e la Luna

La nuvolaglia va stracca, raminga,
e or si sparpaglia ed ora si raduna,
quasi un soffio aspettando che la spinga
a far del bene altrove. Tutta bruna
d'acqua la terra e paga s'addormenta,
e vien dal colle su grande, la Luna.
Sale pian piano, come diva intenta
a vigilare, e a sè le nubi chiama.
Or questa or quella le si appresta lenta,
prende consiglio, si dirada, sciama
al Lume, si raddensa, s'allontana . . .
Che mai la Luna con le nubi trama?
Quatta musando se ne sta la rana.
Forse ha compreso ch'ora qui ripiove?
Salta in un borro la d'acqua piovana.

Ma van le nubi a far del bene altrove.

The Clouds and the Moon

The storm clouds move lazily, they wander,
now scattering and now gathering together,
as if waiting for a slight wind to nudge them
to bring rain elsewhere. Brown from the rain,
the Land, satiated, sleeps,
and from beyond the hill a large Moon rises.
It rises very slowly, like a goddess intent
to rule, and she calls the clouds to her.
Now this one and then that one slowly come to her;
Seeking direction, they condense, they swarm
to the Light, thickening, moving apart . . .
What are the Moon and clouds planning?
The frog is quietly musing.
Maybe he knows it will rain soon?
The frog jumps into a ditch of rain water.

But the clouds wander elsewhere.

Appendix B

A Production History of *Six Characters in Search of an Author* and *Henry IV*

Jana O'Keefe Bazzoni

Six Characters and *Henry IV* have had a number of important productions all over the world since their first performances in Italy in 1921 and 1922, respectively. This production history begins with premiere productions of both plays in Italy and the United States, as well as in France, England, and Germany. In the selected listing that follows I have included productions in Italy, the United States, and Great Britain which were of particular significance often because of the introduction of a new translation or adaptation or the distinguished acting company and/or director associated with the production.

PREMIERE PRODUCTIONS OF *SIX CHARACTERS IN SEARCH OF AN AUTHOR*

Italy: *Sei personaggi in cerca d'autore*

1921   Rome, Teatro Valle, Compagnia Niccodemi
                Milan, Teatro Manzoni
                Director: Dario Niccodemi
                Actors: Vera Vergani, Luigi Almirante

England: *Six Characters in Search of an Author*

1922   London, Kingsway Theatre, London Stage Society
                Translator: Edward Storer (Private Production)

United States: *Six Characters in Search of an Author*

1922   New York, Princess Theatre
                Translator: Edward Storer
                Producer/Director: Brock Pemberton
                Actors: Moffat Johnston, Florence Eldridge, Margaret Wycherly

France: *Six Personnages en Quête d'Auteur*

1923   Paris, Théâtre des Champs Elysees, Pitoëff Co.
                Translator: Benjamin Cremieux
                Director: Georges Pitoëff
                Actors: Ludmilla and Georges Pitoëff

Germany: *Sechs Personen Suchen einen Autor*

1924   Berlin, Komödie Theater
                Translator: Hans Feist
                Director: Max Reinhardt

A CHRONOLOGICAL HISTORY OF SELECTED PRODUCTIONS OF *SIX CHARACTERS IN SEARCH OF AN AUTHOR* IN ITALY, THE UNITED STATES, AND GREAT BRITAIN

1923   New York, Forty Fourth Street Theatre
                Producer/Director: Brock Pemberton
1925   Rome, Teatro Odescalchi, Compagnia del Teatro d'Arte
                European tour
                Revised edition
                Director: Luigi Pirandello
                Actors: Lamberto Picasso, Marta Abba
1926   Tour of Italy, Georges and Ludmilla Pitoëff
1928   London, Arts Theatre (Public Production)
                Translator: Edward Storer
1932   London, Westminster Theatre
                Translator: H. K. Ayliff
                Director: Tyrone Guthrie
                Cast included Flora Robson as the Stepdaughter

1940	San Francisco, Geary Theatre
	Revival of Reinhardt adapation entitled "At Your Service"
	English Adaptation by Karla Martell
1946	Rome, Teatro Quirino
	Director: Orazio Costa
1949	Rome, Piccolo Teatro
	Director: Orazio Costa
1950	Leeds, Riley-Smith Theatre
	Translator: Frederick May
1950	Mt. Holyoke College (Mass.), Dramatic Club
	Adaptation: Denis Johnston
	Director: Denis Johnston
1953	Milan, Il Piccolo Teatro
	Director: Giorgio Strehler
1955	New York, Phoenix Theatre
	Adaptation: Tyrone Guthrie and Michael Wager (based on a translation by Frank Tauritz)
	Director: Tyrone Guthrie
	Actors: Kurt Kasznar, Natalie Schaffer, Frances Bethencourt, Whitfield Connor, Betty Lou Holland
1959	New York, City Center Theater, City Center Opera Co.
	Operatic Version
	Music: Hugo Weisgall
	Libretto: Denis Johnson
	Director: William Ball
1959	Bloomington (Ind.), Indiana University Theater
	Translator: Lander MacClintock (based on 1925 Pirandello text)
	Director: William E. Kinzer
1961	Washington, D.C., Arena Stage
	Translator: Paul Avila Mayer
	Director: Zelda Fichandler
1961	Houston, Alley Theatre
	Adaptation: Paul Avila Mayer
	Director: Nina Vance
1961	Los Angeles, University of California (UCLA)
	Director: John Houseman
	Actors: Joseph Wiseman, Joanne Linville, Katharine Bard, Larry Gates
1962	Milwaukee (Wis.), Fred Miller Theater

Adaptation: Paul Avila Mayer

Director: William Ball

Actors: Jacqueline Brookes, Richard Dysart, Michael O'Sullivan, Will Geer

1963   New York, Martinique Theatre

Adaptation: Paul Avila Mayer

Director: William Ball

Actors: Jacqueline Brookes, Richard Dysart, Michael O'Sullivan

1963   Tour in Eastern Europe, La Compagnia dei Giovanni

Director: Giorgio De Lullo

Actors: Rosella Falk, Romolo Valli, Ferruccio De Ceresa

1963   Princeton, N.J., McCarter Theatre

Adaptation: Paul Avila Mayer

Actors: Franklin Cover, Irene Baird

1964   London, Mayfair Theatre

Adaptation: Paul Avila Mayer

Director: William Ball

Actors: Ralph Richardson, Barbara Jefford

1964   Rome, Teatro Quirino, La Compagnia dei Giovanni

Director: Giorgio De Lullo

1965   London, Aldwych Theatre, La Compagnia dei Giovanni

Director: Giorgio De Lullo

1967   Williamstown (Mass.), Adams Memorial Theater

Director: Olympia Dukakis

1969   New York, Brooklyn College

Translation: Eric Bentley

1976   Los Angeles, Hollywood Television Theater

Adaptation: Paul Avila Mayer

Director: Stacy Keach

Actors: John Houseman, Andy Griffith, Beverly Todd

1979   London, Greenwich Theatre

Translation: John Linstrum

1979   Rome, Teatro Eliseo

Director: Giancarlo Cobelli

1983   Rome, Teatro Mobile

Director: Giuseppe Patroni Griffi

1984   Cambridge (Mass.), American Repertory Theatre

Adaptation: Robert Brustein

Director: Robert Brustein
Actors: Robert Stattel, Lise Hilboldt, Linda Lavin, Jeremy Geidt
1985 New York, Jean Cocteau Repertory Company
Adaptation: David Caldwell
Director: Daniel Irvine
1986 Louisville (Ky.), Actors Theater of Louisville
Adaptation: Paul Avila Mayer
Further Adaptation: Jon Jory
Director: Jon Jory
Actors: Lisbeth Mackay, Jonathan Bolt
1987 London, Olivier Theatre, National Theatre
Adaptation: Nicholas Wright
Director: Michael Rudman
1988 New York, Joyce Theatre, American Repertory Theatre Company
Adaptation: Robert Brustein
Director: Robert Brustein
Actors: Alvin Epstein, Pamela Gien, Jeremy Geidt, Priscilla Smith
1988 Washington, D.C., Arena Stage
Translator: Robert Cornthwaite
Producer: Zelda Fichandler
Director: Liviu Ciulei

PREMIERE PRODUCTIONS OF *HENRY IV*

Italy: *Enrico IV*

1922 Milan, Teatro Manzoni, Compagnia Ruggeri–Borelli–Talli
Enrico: Ruggero Ruggeri

United States: *The Living Mask*

1924 New York, Forty-Fourth Street Theater
Producer: Brock Pemberton
Translator: Arthur Livingston
Sets: Robert Edmund Jones
Enrico: Arnold Korff

England: *Henry IV*

1924   Cambridge (Eng.), New Theatre, Cambridge Amateur Dramatic Club
                    Translator: Edward Storer
                    Set Design and Costumes: Cecil Beaton
                    All Male Cast, including Cecil Beaton as Matilda

France: *Henri IV*

1925   Monte Carlo, Teatro di Monte Carlo Pitoëff Company
                    Paris, Théâtre des Arts
                    Translator: Benjamin Cremieux
                    Director: Georges Pitoëff
                    Enrico: Georges Pitoëff

Germany: *Die Lebende Maske* (The Living Mask)

1925   Hamburg, Thalia Theater
                    Translator: Hans Feist
                    Director: Alexander Moissi

A CHRONOLOGICAL HISTORY OF SELECTED PRODUCTIONS OF *HENRY IV* IN ITALY, THE UNITED STATES, AND GREAT BRITAIN

1925   Rome, Teatro Odescalchi, Teatro d'Arte Company
                    Director: Luigi Pirandello
                    Enrico: Ruggero Ruggeri (London and Paris) and Lamberto Picasso
                       (Germany)
1926   Tour of Italy, Georges and Ludmilla Pitoëff Company
1929   London Queen's Theatre
                    Title: "The Mock Emperor"
                    Translator: Edward Storer
1935   Berkeley (Calif.), Wheeler Auditorium
                    Translator: Edward Storer
1943   Rome, Minerva Films
                    Film Adaptation: Giorgio Pastina, Fabrizio Sarazoni, Stefano Landi
                       [Pirandello's son], and Vittore Brancati
                    Director: Giorgio Pastina

	Enrico: Osvaldo Valenti
1944	Rome, Compagnia Memo Benassi
	Enrico: Memo Benassi
1947	New York, New York Public Library
	Adaptation: John Reich
	Enrico: Herbert Berghof
1950	Sea Cliff (N.Y.), Sea Cliff Summer Theater
	Title: "Barefoot at Canossa"
	Adaptation: John Reich
1953	Leeds, Riley-Smith Theatre
	Translator: Frederick May
1954	Rome, Compagnia del Teatro Pirandello
	Director: Lamberto Picasso
1956	Dublin, Dublin Gate Theatre
	Translator: Michael MacLiammoir
1958	Naples, Teatro Stabile
	Director: Orazio Costa
1958	Philadelphia, Erlanger Theater
	Adaptation: John Reich
	Director: Billy Matthews
	Enrico: Burgess Meredith
	Matilda: Alida Valli
	Dr. Genoni: Barnard Hughes
1959	London, New World Theatre Play Series, BBC-TV
	Television Adaptation of Storer Translation
	Producer: John Harrison
	Enrico: Paul Scofield
1960	Chicago, Goodman Theatre
	Adaptation: John Reich
	Director: John Reich
	Enrico: Ivor Harries
1963	Glasgow, Citizens Theatre
	Enrico: Albert Finney
1963–1964	Washington, D.C., Arena Stage
	Adaptation: John Reich
	Directors: Zelda Fichandler with Herbert Berghof
	Enrico: Herbert Berghof
	Frida: Joan Van Ark

Belcredi: Ray Reinhardt

Fino: Rene Auberjonois

1964   Turin, Teatro Stabile

Director: Jose Quaglio

1964   Chicago, Harper Theater

Translator: Eric Bentley

Director: Gene Frankel

Enrico: Alvin Epstein

1968   New Haven, Yale School of Drama Repertory Company

English version: Eric Bentley

Director: Carl Weber

Enrico: Kenneth Haigh

Dr. Genoni: Michael Lombard

Frida: Kathleen Widdoes

Landolf: Anthony Holland

1968   Venice, Compagnia del Teatro di Ankara

Director: Maurizio Scaparro

1972   Turin, Teatro Stabile

Television Adaptation

Director: Tino Buazzelli

1973   New York, Ethel Barrymore Theater

Adaptation: Stephen Rich, Rex Harrison, and Clifford Williams

Director: Clifford Williams

Enrico: Rex Harrison

Matilda: Eileen Herlie

Dr. Genoni: David Hurst

Belcredi: James Donald, Paul Hecht

1974   Providence (R.I.), Trinity Square Repertory

Title: "The Emperor Henry"

Translator: Eric Bentley

Director: Brooks Jones

Enrico: Richard Kneeland

Belcredi: Richard Kavanaugh

1974   London, Her Majesty's Theatre

Translator: Stephen Rich

Enrico: Rex Harrison

1977   Rome, Teatro Eliseo

Director: Giorgio De Lullo

                    Enrico: Romolo Valli
1984   Rome, Film Adaptation
                    Director: Marco Bellocchio
                    Enrico: Marcello Mastroianni
                    Matilda/Frida: Claudia Cardinale
1988   Washington, D.C., Kreeger Theater
                    Translation: Robert Cornthwaite
                    Director: Mel Shapiro and Zelda Fichandler
1989   New York, Roundabout Theatre
                    Translation: Robert Cornthwaite
                    Director: J. Ranelli
                    Enrico: Paul Hecht
1990   London, Wyndham's Theatre
                    Translation: John Wardle and Robert Rietty
                    Director: Val May
                    Enrico: Richard Harris
                    Matilda: Isla Blair

SOURCES

Battistini, Fabio, "Cronologia delle messinscene in Italia 1910–1986." *Pirandello: l'uomo, lo scrittore, il teatrante*. Rome: Mazzotta, 1987.

O'Keefe Bazzoni, Jana. "Pirandello on the American Stage: Translations and Adaptations of *Six Characters in Search of an Author*," part of a work in progress delivered at the 1986 Convention of the American Association of Teachers of Italian.

Pirandello, Luigi. *Opere*, VI (*Saggi, poesie e scritte varii*). Manlio Lo Vecchio-Musti, ed. Milan: Mondadori, 1965.

Shipley, Joseph T. *The Crown Guide to the World's Great Plays*. New York: Crown Publishers, 1984.

Theatre Collection of the New York Public Library at Lincoln Center: Library Collection Clippings, Programs and Photograph Files as well as Scrapbooks from the Pemberton Collection.

Appendix C

A List of Pirandello's Publications

POETRY

Mal Giocondo. Palermo, 1889.

Pasqua di gea. Milan, 1891.

Pier gudrò. Rome, 1894.

Elegie renane. Rome, 1895.

Elegie romane. Legorn, 1896 (a translation of Goethe's *Roman Elegies*).

Zampogna. Rome, 1901.

Scamandro. Rome, 1909 (verse play).

Fuori di chiave. Genoa, 1912.

CRITICISM

"Laute und Lautenwickelung der Mundart von Girgenti." Halle, 1891. (Pirandello's dissertation.)

Arte e scienza. Rome, 1908.

L'umorismo. Lanciano, 1908; second edition, Florence, 1920.

MAJOR SHORT STORIES

Amori Senza Amore. Rome, 1894.

Beffe della morte e della vita. Florence, 1902.

Quand' ero Matto. Turin, 1902.

Beffe della morte e della vita. Seconda serie. Florence, 1903.

Bianche e nere. Turin, 1904.

Erma bifronte. Milan, 1906.

La vita nuda. Milan, 1910.

Terzetti. Milan, 1912.

Le due maschere. Florence, 1914.

La trappola. Milan, 1915.

Erba del nostro orto. Milan, 1915.

E domani, lunedi. Milan, 1917.

Un cavallo nella luna. Milan, 1918.

Berecche e la guerra. Milan, 1919.

Il carnevale dei morti. Florence, 1919.

Pirandello rearranged his stories into the fifteen-volume work entitled *Novelle per un Anno.*

NOVELS

L'esclusa. 1901 (written in 1894).

Il turno. 1902.

Il fu Mattia Pascal. 1904.

I vecchi e i giovani. 1909.

Suo marito. 1911.

Si gira. . . . 1915 (later published with the title *Quaderni di Serafino Gubbio, operatore.*)

Uno, nessuno e centomila. 1925.

MAJOR PLAYS

(with year of publication)

La morsa. 1898.

Lumie di Sicilia. 1911.

Il dovere del medico. 1912.

Liolà. 1917.

Pensaci, Giacomino! 1917.

Il berretto a sonagli. 1918.

Il piacere dell'onestà. 1918.

La patente, 1918.

Così è (se vi pare). 1918.

Ma non è una cosa seria, 1919.

Il giuoco delle parti, 1919.

Tutto per bene. 1920.

La ragione degli altri. 1921.

Come prima, meglio di prima. 1921.

L'innesto. 1921.

Sei personaggi in cerca d'autore. 1921.

Enrico IV. 1922.

L'uomo, la bestia, e la virtù. 1922.

La signora Morli, una e due. 1922.

Vestire gli ignudi. 1923.

La vita che ti diedi. 1924.

Ciascuno a duo modo. 1924.

Sagra del signore della nave. 1924.

La giara. 1925.

L'altro figlio. 1925.

Cece. 1926.

All'uscita. 1926.

L'imbecille. 1926.

L'uomo da fiore in bocca. 1926.

Diana e la tuda. 1927.

L'amica delle mogli. 1927.

La nuova colonia. 1928.

O di uno o di nessuno. 1929.

Lazzaro. 1929.

Sogno (ma forse no). 1929.

Come tu mi vuoi. 1930.

Questa sera si recita a soggetto. 1930.

Trovarsi. 1932.

Quando si è qualcuno. 1933.

Non si sa come. 1935.

Bellavita. 1937.

La favola del figlio cambiato. 1938.

I giganti della montagna. 1938.

Appendix D

A Pirandello Bibliography

Mimi Gisolfi D'Aponte

ARCHIVES THAT CONTAIN PIRANDELLO MANUSCRIPTS

United States

Houghton Library, Harvard University (Cambridge, Mass.).
Library of Congress (Washington, D.C.).
Theater Collection, New York Public Library (New York City).

Italy

Biblioteca Nazionale Centrale (Rome).
Biblioteca Teatrale di Burcardo (Rome).
Guido Salvini Collection, Museo degli Attori (Genoa).
Istituto Pirandelliani (Rome).
Mondadori Editore Press (Milan).

Great Britain

Enthoven Collection, Victoria and Albert Museum (London).

CLASSIC ITALIAN BIBLIOGRAPHIES OF PIRANDELLO'S WORK

Barbina, Alfredo. *Bibliografia della critica pirandelliana 1889–1961*. Pubblicazione dell'Istituto di Studi Pirandelliani, 3. Florence: Le Monnier, 1967.
Donati, C. *La solitudine allo specchio: Luigi Pirandello*. Roma: Lucarini, 1980.

Lo Vecchio-Musti, Manlio. *Bibliografia di Pirandello*, 2. ed. rifusae e aggiornata. Milan:
   A. Mondadori, 1952.
Zappulla Muscara, Sarah, ed. *Pirandello Dialettale*. Palermo: G. B. Palumbo, 1983.

PRIMARY SOURCES: ORIGINAL WORKS

Pirandello, Luigi. *Saggi, poesie, scritti varii*. Ed. Manlio Lo Vecchio–Musti. Milan:
   Mondadori, 1960.
———. *Opere di Luigi Pirandello*. 6 vols. Milan: Mondadori, 1967.
———. *Tutti i romanzi*. Ed. Macchia. Milan: Mondadori, 1973.
———. *Tutti i romanzi*. Ed. Macchia and Costanzo, 4th ed. Milan: Mondadori, 1981.
———. *Lettere da Bonn: 1889–1891*. Rome: Bulzoni, 1984.
———. *Il berretto a sonagli, La giara, Il Piacere dell'onestà*. Ed. Simioni. Milan:
   Mondadori, 1989.

EXCERPTS FROM THE F. MAY "SELECT BIBLIOGRAPHY"

At the suggestion of Eric Bentley, whose advice in compiling this Pirandello bibliography
is gratefully acknowledged, the following excerpts from the considerable bibliographical
information included in Frederick May's *Short Stories* (Oxford University Press, 1965)
are published here. We have retained May's format for his entries; asterisks indicate the
studies he recommended most highly.

Select Bibliography

Giovanna Abete, *Il vero volto di Luigi Pirandello*. Roma, A. B. E. T. E. 1961.
*Corrado Alvaro, 'Prefazione' to Vol. I of the *Novelle per un anno*. Milano-Verona,
   Mondadori. 1965.
Luigi Baccolo, *Luigi Pirandello*. Torino, Bocca. 1949.
*Sandro D'Amico, edited a group of 'Lettere ai famigliari' in *Terzo programma*, n. 3,
   1961; and the first of the *Quaderni del Piccolo Teatro*. Milano, 1961: *Pirandello
   ieri e oggi*.
*Arcangelo Leone de Castris, *Storia di Pirandello*. Bari, Laterza. 1962.
*Gaspare Giudice, *Luigi Pirandello*. Torino, U. T. E. T. 1963.
Arminio Janner, *Luigi Pirandello*. Firenze, La nuova Italia. 1948.
Frances Keene, "Introduction" to the Lily Duplaix translations. New York, Simon and
   Schuster. 1959.
Federico Vittore Nardelli, *L'uomo segreto*. Milano-Verona, Mondadori. 1944.
Ferdinando Pasini, *Luigi Pirandello (come mi pare)*. Trieste, La vedetta italiana. 1927.
Luigi Russo, *Il noviziato letterario di Luigi Pirandello*. Pisa, Il paesaggio. 1947.
———. 'Pirandello e la provincia metafisica.' Melfagor, XV. 1960, pp. 389–401.
*Leonardo Sciascia. 'Pirandello' in his *Pirandello e la Sicilia*. Caltanissetta-Roma, Scias-
   cia. 1961, pp. 7–124.
Walter Starkie. *Luigi Pirandello*. London, Murray. 1937.
Aldo Vallone, *Profilo di Pirandello*. Roma, Edizioni di *Dialoghi*. 1962.
Domenico Vittorini, *The Drama of Luigi Pirandello*. New York, Dover. 1957.

J. H. Whitfield, in his *Short History of Italian Literature*. London, Penguin, 1960, is acute and stimulating in his comments on Pirandello.

Nella Zoja, *Luigi Pirandello*. Brescia, Morcelliana. 1948.

Pirandello's Stories in Chronological Order

1884	Capannetta
1894.	I galletti del bottaio. La signorina. L'onda. L'amica delle mogli. *Concorso per referendario al Consiglio di Stato.*
1895.	In corpore vili. Il 'no' di Anna. Dialoghi I: Nostra moglie. *Pallottoline.*
1896.	Sole e ombra. Chi fui? Visitare gl'infermi. Sogno di Natale.
1897.	Le dodici lettere. Dialghi II: L'accordo. La paura. Le tre carissime. Vexilla Regis . . . Il giaradinetto lassu. Acqua e li.
1898.	La scelta. Se . . . Padron Dio.
1899.	Dono della Vergine Maria. La maestrina Boccarme.
1900.	Lumie di Sicilia. Prima notte. Le levata del sole. *Un altra allodola. Un invito a tavola. Scialle nero.* Alberi cittadini.
1901.	Nenia. Prudenza. Notizie del mondo. Il vecchio dio. Con altri occhi. E due! Marsina stretta. Lontano. Gioventu. *La paura del sonno. Quand'ero matto. Il valor civile.* Il 'fumo'.
1902.	La berretta di Padova. Il figlio cambiato. Tanino e Tanotto. Alla zappa! Amicissimi. Il corvo di Mizzaro/Come gemelle. *Il vitalizio. La signora Speranza.*
1903.	Il marito di mia moglie. La balia. Il ventaglino. Il tabernacolo. La disdetta di Pitagora. *Formalita.*
1904.	Nel segno. La veglia. Sua Maesta. La buon anima. Le Medaglie. Una voce. La Mosca. La fedelta del cane. Fuoco alla paglia.
1905.	L'esesia catara. L'altro figlio. Senza malizia. La casa del Granella. Tirocinio. Pallino e Mimi. Va bene. Le sorprese della scienza. Acqua amara. In silenzio. *Lo scaldino. Il sonno del vecchio.*
1906.	L'uscita del vedovo. Tutto per bene. La toccatina. Tra due ombre.
1907.	Dal naso al cielo. Un cavallo nella luna. Volare. La cassa riposta. La vita nuda.
1908.	La guardaroba dell'eloquenza. Due letti a due. *Di guardia. Il dovere del medico.*
1909.	Stefano Giogli, Uno e due. Difesa del Meola. Mondo di carta. La giara. L'illustre estinto. Il lume dell'alta casa. L'ombrello. Non e una cosa seria. *Distrazione. Pari.*
1910.	L'uccello impagliato. Musica vecchia. Benedizione. Pensaci, Giacomino! Il professor Terremoto. Lo spirito maligno. La lega disciolta. Leviamoci questo pensiero. Lo storno e l'Angelo Centuno. Leonora, addio! Il viaggio. La morta e la viva. Paura d'esser felice. *Ignare.*

1911.	Felicita. Zafferanetta/L'uomo solo. La patente. I fortunati. Il libretto rosso. La tragedia d'un personaggio. 'Ho tante cose da dirvi....' Canta l'Epistola. *Richiamo all'obbligo.*
1912.	I nostri ricordi. Risposta. L'avemaria di Bobbio. Certi obblighi. Nene e Nini. La trappola. Superior stabat lupus. Il coppo. La verita. Notte. Maestro Amore. Chi la paga. L'imbecille. Tu ridi. I due compari. Ciaula scopre la luna. *Nel dubbio. La corona. La librazione del re.*
1913.	Il bottone della palandrana. La veste lunga. Requiem aeternam dona eis, Domine! La vendetta del cane. Quando s'e capito il giuoco. Tutt'e tre. L'abito nuovo. Nel gorgo. La Madonnini. Male di luna. La rallegrata. Rondone e Rondinella. Da se. Il capretto nero. I pensionati della memoria. *I tre pensieri della sbiobina. Candelora. L'ombra del rimorso.*
1914.	Il treno ha fischiato...Zia Mivhelina. Sopra e sotto. Filo d'aria. Un matrimonio ideale. Un ritratto. Servitu. Berecche e la guerra. La realta del sogno. La rosa. *O di uno di nessuno. Visto che non piove....* Mentre il cuore soffriva. Zuccarello, distinto melodista. La fede.
1915.	Colloqui coi personaggi I e II. Il signore della nave. *Nell'albergo e morto un tale. Romolo. La mano del malato povero. La signora Frola e il signor Ponza, suo genero.*
1916.	La camera in attesa. Piuma. Donna Mimma. La carriola. *Frammento di cronaca di Marco Leccio.*
1917.	Il gatto, un cardellino e le stelle.
1918.	La maschera dimenticata. La cattura. *Quando si comprende. La morte addosso. Un 'goj'.*
1919.	Ieri e oggi. Il pipistrello.
1920.	Pena di vivere cosi.
1921.	La distruzione dell'uomo. *Rimedio: la geografia.*
1922.	*Niente.*
1923.	Fuga. Ritorno. Un po' di vino.
1924.	Resto mortali. Sedile sotto un vecchio cipresso.
1926.	Puberta. *Guardando una stampa.*
1927.	*Spunta un giorno.*
1931.	Uno di piú. Soffio.
1932.	Lucilla. Cinci.
1933.	Sgombero.
1934.	I piedi sull'erba. Di sera, un geranio. Un'idea. C'e qualcuno che ride.
1935.	Visita. La prova. La casa dell'agonia. Fortuna d'esser cavallo. Una sfida.
1936.	Il chiodo. Vittoria delle formiche. La tartaruga. Una giornata. Effetti d'un sogno interrotto. Il buon cuore.

Note: May listed these stories by their final titles.

The Stories and the Plays. (A note of the relationships between the stories and the plays.)

	PLAY	DRAWING ON THE STORIES
1898.	La morsa	La paura (1897)
1910.	Lumie di Sicilia	Lumie di Sicilia (1900)
1911.	Il dovere del medico	Il dovere del medico (?1908)
1916.	Pensaci, Giacomino!	Pensaci, Giacomino! (1910)
1917.	Il berretta a sonagli	Certi obblighi, La verita
	La giara	La giara (1909)
	La patente	La patente (1911)
	Cosi e (se vi pare)	La signora Frola e il signor Ponza, suo genero (1915)
	Il piacere dell'onesta	Tirocinio (1905)
1918.	Ma non e una cosa seria	La signora Speranza (?1902)
		Non e una cosa seria (1909)
	Il giuoco delle parti	Quando s'e capito il giuoco (1913)
1919.	L'uomo, la bestia e la virtu	Richiamo all'obbligo (?1911)
	Tutto per bene	Tutto per bene (1906)
1920.	La signora Morli, una e due	Stefano Geogli, uno e due (1909)
	Come prima, meglio di prima	La veglia (1904)
1921.	Sei personaggi in cerca d'autore	La tragedia d'un personaggio (1911), Colloqui coi personaggi (1915)
1922.	L'imbecile	L'imbecile (1912)
1923.	L'uomo dal fiore in bocca	La morte addoso (?1918)
	La vita che ti diedi	I pensionati della memoria (?1913), La camera in attesa (1916)
	L'altro figlio	L'altro figlio (1905)
1924.	Sagra del Signore della Nave	Il Signore della Nave (?1915)
1927.	Bellavita	L'ombra del rimorso (?1913)
	L'amica delle mogli	L'amica delle mogli (?1894)
1928.	O di uno o di nessuno	O di uno o di nessuno (?1914)
1929.	Questa sera si recita a soggetto	Leonora, addio! (1910)
1933.	La favola del figlio cambiato	Il figlio cambiato (1902)

1934.	Non si sa come	Nel gorgo (1913), La realta del
		sogno (1914), Cinci (1932)
	May notes that:	

1921.   *Enrico IV* draws upon Fileno's notion of the inverted telescope, as it is put forth in "La tragedia d'un personaggio."

1924.   *Ciascuno a suo modo* absorbs an episode in the novel *Si gira . . .* (1914–15)

1933.   *Quando si e qualcuno* is in many ways a rifacimento of the novel *Il fu Mattia Pascal* (1904).

Pirandello's Works Other Than The Short Stories (Principal Works).

Poetry
1. *Mal giocondo*. Palaremo, Clausen, 1889.
2. *Pasqua di Gea*. Milano, Galli, 1891.
3. *Pièr Gudrò*. Roma, Voghera, 1894.
4. *Elegie renane*. Roma, Unione cooperative editrice, 1895.
5. *Elegie romane*—a translation of the poems by Goethe—Livorno, Giusti, 1896.
6. *Zampogna*. Roma, Societa editrice Dante Alighieri, 1901.
7. *Scamandro* (a verse play). Roma, Tipografia 'Roma' (Armani e Stein), 1909.
8. Fuori di chiavi. Genoa, Formiggini, 1912.

Essays

9. *Laute und Lautenwickelung der Mundart von Girgenti*. Halle a.S., Druck der Buchdruckerei des Waisenhauses, 1891.
10. *Arte e scienza*. Roma, Modes, 1908.
11. *L'umorismo*. Lanciano, Carabba, 1908. A new and extended edition is: Firenze, Battistelli, 1920.
12. *Saggi, a cura di* Manlio Lo Vecchio-Musti. Milano-Verona, Mandadori, 1939. (In addition to Nos. 9 and 10 there is a useful gathering in of materials from periodicals, etc. The work on Verga and Dante is especially valuable.)

Novels

13. *L'esclusa*. Roma, *La tribuna*, June-August, 1901.
14. *Il turno*. Catania, Giannota, 1902.
15. *Il fu Mattia Pascal*. Roma, *Nuova antologia*, April-June, 1904.
16. *Suo marito*. Firenze, Quattrini, 1911. (The 2nd edition—with a substantially revised first part—is published in the 1941 *Tutti i romanzi* put out by Mondadori (Milano-Verona). It has the new title *Giustino Roncella nato Boggiolo*.)
17. *I vecchi e i giovani*. Roma, *Rassengna contemporanea*, January-November 1909. (It was thoroughly reworked for the 1931 edition put out by Mondadori (Milano-Verona)).

18. *Si gira* . . . Roma, *Nuova antologia*, June-August 1915. (It gained the new title *Quaderni di Serafino Gubbio operatore* for the Bemporad (Firenze) presentation of 1925.)

19. *Uno, nessuno e centomila*. Milano, *La fiera letteraria*, 1925–26.

Plays

Where a play was performed in a year earlier than that in which it was published the date is signalized thus: (P. 1910)

20. *L'epilogo*. Roma, *Ariel*, 20 March, 1898. (The final title is *La morsa*.)

21. *Lumie di Sicilia*. Roma, *Nuova antologia*, 16 March 1911. (P. 1910)

22. *Il dovere del medico*. Roma, *Noi e il mondo*, January 1912.

23. *Cece*. Milano, *La lettura*, October 1913.

24. *Se non cosi*. Roma, *Nuova antologia*, January 1916. (P. 1915) (Its final title is *Laragione degli altri*. It was written in 1899.)

25. *All'uscita*. Roma, *Nuova antologia*, 1 November 1916.

26. *Pensaci, Giacomino!*. Roma, *Noi e il mondo*, 1 April–1 June 1917. (P. 1916.)

27. *Liolà*. Roma, Formiggini, 1917. (Both Sicilian and Italian texts.) (P. 1916.)

28. *Cosi e (se vi pare)*. Roma, *Nuova antologia*, 1–16 January 1918. (P. 1917.)

29. *La patente*. Roma, *Rivista d'Italia*, 31 January 1918.

30. *Il piacere dell'onesta*. Roma. *Noi e il mondo*, 1 February–1 March 1918. (P. 1917.)

31. *Il beretto a sonagli*. Roma, *Noi e il mondo*, 1 August–1 September 1918. (P. 1917.)

32. *Il giuco delle parti*. Roma, *Nuova antologia*, 1–16 January 1919. (P. 1918.)

33. *L'uomo, la bestia, e la virtu*. Milano, Comoedia, 10 September 1919.

34. *Ma non e una cosa seria*. Milano, Treves, 1919. (As part of Vol. II of the first collection of *Maschere nude*.) (P. 1918.)

From now on, where a Roman numeral precedes the title of the play, the text belongs to the second series of *Maschere nude*.

35. I. *Tutto per bene*. Firenze, Bemporad, 1920.

36. II. *Come prima, meglio di prima*, Firenze, Bemporad, 1921. (P. 1920).

37. III. *Sei personnagi in cerca d'autore*. Firenze, Bemporad, 1921. (The IVth edition, 1925, is very important, for the play was recast and given a valuable preface.)

38. *L'innesto*. Milano, Treves, 1921. (As part of Vol. IV of the first collection of the *Maschere nude*.) (P. 1919).

39. *'A vilanza* (in collaboration with Nino Martoglio). Cantania, Giannotta, 1922. (In Sicilian. Part of Vol. VII of Martoglio's *Teatro dialettale siciliano*.) (P. 1917)

40. *Cappiddazzu paga tuttu* (in collaboration with Nino Martoglio). Catania, Giannotta, 1922. (In Sicilian. The rest of VII—see No. 39.)

41. *Enrico IV*. Firenze, Bemporad, 1922.

42. VI. *La signora Morli, une e due*. Firenze, Bemporad, 1922. (P. 1920.)

43. VII. *Vestire gli ignudi*. Firenze, Bemporad, 1923. (P. 1922.)

44. VIII. *La vita che ti diedi*. Firenze, Bemporad, 1924. (P. 1923.)

45. IX. *Ciascuno a suo modo*. Firenze, Bemporad, 1924.

46. *Sagra del Signore della nave*. Milano, *Il convegno*, 30 September 1924.

47. *L'altro figlio*. Firenze, Bemporad, 1925. (As part of Vol. XII of the second series of *Maschere nude*.) (P. 1923.)

48. *La giara*. Firenze, Bemporad, 1925. (As No. 47.) (P. 1917—in Sicilian.)

49. *L'imbecile*. Firenze, Bemporad, 1926. (As part of Vol. XIX of the second series of *Maschere nude*.) (P. 1922.)

50. *L'uomo dal fiore in bocca*. Firenze, Bemporad, 1926. (As part of Vol. XX in the second series of *Maschere nude*.) (P. 1923.)

51. XXI. *Diana e la tuda*. Firenze, Bemporad, 1927. (P. 1926–in German.)

52. XXII. *L'amica delle mogli*. Firenze, Bemporad, 1927.

53. XXIII. *La nouva colonia*. Firenze, Bemporad, 1928.

54. *Bellavita*. Milano, *Il secolo XX*, July 1928. (P. 1927.)

55. XXV. *O di uno o di nessuno*. Firenze, Bemporad, 1929.

56. XXVI. *Lazzaro*. Milano-Verona, Mondadori, 1929.

57. *Sogno (ma forse no)*. Milano, *La lettura*, October 1929.

58. XXVII. *Questa sera si recita a soggetto*. Milano-Verona, Mondadori, 1930.

59. XXVIII. *Come tu mi vuoi*. Milano-Verona, Mondadori, 1930.

60. XXIX. *Trovarsi*. Milano-Verona, Mondadori, 1932.

61. XXX. *Quando si e qualcuno*. Milano-Verona, Mondadori, 1933.

62. *La favola del figlio cambiato*. Milano, Ricordi, 1933. (As the libretto for Malipiero's opera.)

63. XXXI. *Non si sa come*. Milano-Verona, Mondadori, 1935.

64. *I giganti della montagna*. Milano-Verona, Mondadori, 1938. (As part of the Xth volume of the third series of *Maschere nude*. Parts of the play had appeared in periodicals from 1931 on.) (P. 1937.)

A translation

65. '*Il ciclope*: THE CYCLOPS of Euripides. Only the first scenes were published (*Messaggero della Domenica*, 13 November 1918). The translation was produced in 1919.

Scenari

66. *La salamandra*, a pantomime, Milano-Verona, Mondadori, 1960. (In *Saggi, poesie, scritti varii*, pp. 1145–50.) (P. 1928.)

67. *Sei personaggi in cerca d'autore* (in collaboration with Adolf Lantz), published as a *film-novelle*, Berlin, Hobbing, 1929. (In German.)

TRANSLATIONS OF WORKS BY PIRANDELLO INTO ENGLISH

Pirandello, Luigi. *The Late Mattia Pascal*. Trans. Livingston. New York: E. P. Dutton, 1923.

————. *Each in His Own Way and Two Other Plays* (*The Pleasure of Honesty and Naked*). Trans. with a note by Livingston. New York: E. P. Dutton, 1923.

————. *Three Plays* (contains *Six Characters in Search of an Author, Henry IV*, trans. Storer, and *Right You Are*. Trans. Livingston). New York: E. P. Dutton, 1923.

————. "Pirandello Confesses . . . Why and How He Wrote *Six Characters in Search of an Author*," Trans. Ongley. *Virginia Quarterly Review* April (1925):36–52.

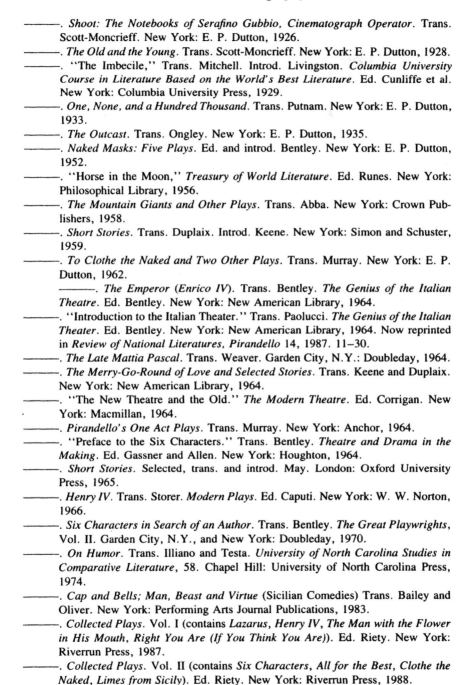

———. *Shoot: The Notebooks of Serafino Gubbio, Cinematograph Operator*. Trans. Scott-Moncrieff. New York: E. P. Dutton, 1926.

———. *The Old and the Young*. Trans. Scott-Moncrieff. New York: E. P. Dutton, 1928.

———. "The Imbecile," Trans. Mitchell. Introd. Livingston. *Columbia University Course in Literature Based on the World's Best Literature*. Ed. Cunliffe et al. New York: Columbia University Press, 1929.

———. *One, None, and a Hundred Thousand*. Trans. Putnam. New York: E. P. Dutton, 1933.

———. *The Outcast*. Trans. Ongley. New York: E. P. Dutton, 1935.

———. *Naked Masks: Five Plays*. Ed. and introd. Bentley. New York: E. P. Dutton, 1952.

———. "Horse in the Moon," *Treasury of World Literature*. Ed. Runes. New York: Philosophical Library, 1956.

———. *The Mountain Giants and Other Plays*. Trans. Abba. New York: Crown Publishers, 1958.

———. *Short Stories*. Trans. Duplaix. Introd. Keene. New York: Simon and Schuster, 1959.

———. *To Clothe the Naked and Two Other Plays*. Trans. Murray. New York: E. P. Dutton, 1962.

———. *The Emperor (Enrico IV)*. Trans. Bentley. *The Genius of the Italian Theatre*. Ed. Bentley. New York: New American Library, 1964.

———. "Introduction to the Italian Theater." Trans. Paolucci. *The Genius of the Italian Theater*. Ed. Bentley. New York: New American Library, 1964. Now reprinted in *Review of National Literatures, Pirandello* 14, 1987. 11–30.

———. *The Late Mattia Pascal*. Trans. Weaver. Garden City, N.Y.: Doubleday, 1964.

———. *The Merry-Go-Round of Love and Selected Stories*. Trans. Keene and Duplaix. New York: New American Library, 1964.

———. "The New Theatre and the Old." *The Modern Theatre*. Ed. Corrigan. New York: Macmillan, 1964.

———. *Pirandello's One Act Plays*. Trans. Murray. New York: Anchor, 1964.

———. "Preface to the Six Characters." Trans. Bentley. *Theatre and Drama in the Making*. Ed. Gassner and Allen. New York: Houghton, 1964.

———. *Short Stories*. Selected, trans. and introd. May. London: Oxford University Press, 1965.

———. *Henry IV*. Trans. Storer. *Modern Plays*. Ed. Caputi. New York: W. W. Norton, 1966.

———. *Six Characters in Search of an Author*. Trans. Bentley. *The Great Playwrights*, Vol. II. Garden City, N.Y., and New York: Doubleday, 1970.

———. *On Humor*. Trans. Illiano and Testa. *University of North Carolina Studies in Comparative Literature*, 58. Chapel Hill: University of North Carolina Press, 1974.

———. *Cap and Bells; Man, Beast and Virtue* (Sicilian Comedies) Trans. Bailey and Oliver. New York: Performing Arts Journal Publications, 1983.

———. *Collected Plays*. Vol. I (contains *Lazarus, Henry IV, The Man with the Flower in His Mouth, Right You Are (If You Think You Are)*). Ed. Riety. New York: Riverrun Press, 1987.

———. *Collected Plays*. Vol. II (contains *Six Characters, All for the Best, Clothe the Naked, Limes from Sicily*). Ed. Riety. New York: Riverrun Press, 1988.

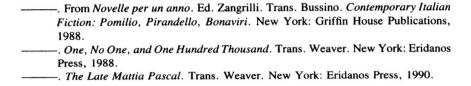

———. From *Novelle per un anno*. Ed. Zangrilli. Trans. Bussino. *Contemporary Italian Fiction: Pomilio, Pirandello, Bonaviri*. New York: Griffin House Publications, 1988.

———. *One, No One, and One Hundred Thousand*. Trans. Weaver. New York: Eridanos Press, 1988.

———. *The Late Mattia Pascal*. Trans. Weaver. New York: Eridanos Press, 1990.

SECONDARY SOURCES: BOOKS

Alberti, A. C., ed. *Il teatro nel fascismo: Pirandello e Bragaglia: documenti inediti negli archivi italiani*. Rome: Bulzoni, 1981.

Alonge, Roberto. *Pirandello tra realismo e mistificazione*. Naples: Guida, 1972.

———, and Roberto Tessari. *Immagine del teatro contemporaneo*. Naples: Guida, 1970.

Anderson, Gösta. *Arte e teoria: Studi sulla poetica del Giovane Pirandello*. Stockholm: Almquist and Wiksell, 1971.

Articoli, Umberto, and Francesco Bartoli. *Il ritmo e la voce: alle sorgente del teatro della crudeltà*. Brescia: Shakespeare and Co., 1984.

Aste, Mario. *La narrativa di Luigi Pirandello: dalle novelle al romanzo "Uno, Nessuno e Centamila."* Madrid: Studia Humanitatis, 1979.

Barbina, Alfredo. *La Biblioteca di Luigi Pirandello*. Rome: Bulzoni, 1980.

Barilli, Renato. *Pirandello: una rivoluzione culturale*. Milan: Mursia, 1986.

———. *La linea Svevo-Pirandello*. Milan: Mursia, 1972.

Barzini, Luigi. *The Italians*. New York: Atheneum, 1964.

Bassnett-McGuire, Susan. *Luigi Pirandello*. New York: Grove Press, 1983.

Bentley, Eric. *The Genius of the Italian Theatre*. New York: New American Library, 1964.

———. *The Life of the Drama*. New York: Atheneum, 1967.

———. *The Theory of the Modern Stage*. Middlesex and Baltimore: Penguin Books, 1976.

———. *The Pirandello Commentaries*. Evanston, Ill.: Northwestern University Press, 1986.

Bermel, Albert. *Contradictory Characters: An Interpretation of the Modern Theatre*. New York: E. P. Dutton, 1973.

Biasin, Gian Paolo, and Nicholas J. Perella, eds. *Pirandello 1986: Atti del Simposio internazionale (Universita di California, Berkeley, 13–15 Marzo 1986)*. Rome: Bulzoni, 1987.

Bishop, Thomas. *Pirandello and the French Theatre*. New York: New York University Press, 1960.

Bloom, Harold, ed. *Luigi Pirandello*. New York: Chelsea House, 1989.

Borsellino, Nino. *Ritratto di Pirandello*. Rome: Bari Laterza, 1983.

Bragaglia, Leonardo. *Interpreti pirandelliani*. Rome: Trevi, 1969.

Brustein, Robert. *The Theater of Revolt: An Approach to the Modern Drama*. Boston: Little, Brown, 1964.

Büdel, Oscar. *Pirandello*. New York: Hillary House, 1969.

Calendoli, Giovanni. *Il grido di Laconte: tre saggi sul teatro*. Venice: Rebellato, 1982.

Cambon, Glauco, ed. *Pirandello: A Collection of Critical Essays*. Englewood Cliffs, N.J.: Prentice-Hall, 1967.

Cantoro, Umberto. *Luigi Pirandello e il problema della personalità*. Bologna: Nicola Ugo Gallo, 1954.

Caputi, Anthony. *Pirandello and the Crisis of Modern Consciousness*. Urbana and Chicago: University of Illinois Press, 1988.

Catalano, Ettore. *Il contesto teatrale: richerche sulle condizione teatrale meridionale*. Bari: Levante, 1982.

Comes, Salvatore. *Scrittori in cattedra: Ferrari, Capuana, Pirandello, Bertocchi*. Florence: Olschki, 1976.

Cometa, Michele. *Il Teatro di Pirandello in Germania*. Palermo: Noveciento, 1986.

Corsinovi, Graziella. *Pirandello e l'espressionismo*. Genova: Tilgher, 1979.

D'Amico, Alessandro, and Allesandro Tinterri. *Pirandello capocomici*. Palermo: Salerio, 1987.

De Castris, Arcangelo Leone. *Storia di Pirandello*. Bari: Editori Laterza, 1986.

Dombroski, Robert S. *Le totalità dell'artificio: Ideologia e forma nel romanzo di Pirandello*. Padova: Liviana, 1971.

Ferrante, Luigi. *Pirandello*. Florence: Parenti, 1958.

Ferrario, E. *L'occhio di Mattia Pascal: poetica e estetica in Pirandello*. Rome: Bulzoni, 1978.

Gilman, Richard. *The Making of the Modern Drama*. New York: Farrar, Straus and Giroux, 1974.

Gioanola, Elio. *Pirandello: la follia*. Genova: Il melangolo, 1983.

Giudice, Gaspare. *Pirandello: A Biography*. Trans. A. Hamilton. London: Oxford University Press, 1975.

Illiano, Antonio. *Introduzione all critica Pirandelliana*. Verona: Fiorini, 1976.

———. *Metapsichica e letteratura in Pirandello*. Agrigento: Vallecchi, 1982.

Janner, Arminio. *Luigi Pirandello*. Firenze: La Nuova Italia, 1948.

Krutch, Joseph Wood. "Pirandello and the Dissolution of the Ego." *"Modernism" in Modern Drama, A Definition and an Estimate*. Ithaca, N.Y.: Cornell University Press, 1953. Pp. 65–87.

Lauretta, Enzo. *Il romanzo di Pirandello*. Palermo: Palumbo, 1976.

Licastro, Emanuele. *Luigi Pirandello: Dalle novelle alle commedie*. Preface by Giorgio Barberi Squarotti. Verona: Fiorini, 1974.

Lindauer, Martin S. *The Psychological Study of Literature: Limitations, Possibilities and Accomplishments*. Chicago: Nelson-Hall, 1975.

Lucas, Frank L. *The Drama of Chekhov, Synge, Yeats and Pirandello*. London: Cassell, 1963.

Lucente, Gregory. *Beautiful Fables: Self-Consciousness in Italian Narrative from Manzoni to Calvino*. Baltimore: Johns Hopkins University Press, 1986.

Luciani, Vincent. *A Concise History of the Italian Theatre*. New York: Vanni, 1961.

Lugnani, Lucio. *Pirandello: letteratura e teatro*. Florence: La Nuova Italia, 1970.

Macchia, Giovanni. *Pirandello o la stanza della tortura*. Milan: Mondadori, 1981.

Mathews, Godfrey W. *Pirandello: A Study in the Psychology of the Modern Stage*. Liverpool: Bryant, 1928.

Matthaei, Renate. *Luigi Pirandello*. Trans. S. and E. Young. New York: Frederick Ungar Publishing Co., 1973.

Mazzacurati, Giancarlo. *Pirandello nel romanzo europeo*. Bologna: Il Mulino, 1987.

Mignone, Mario, ed. *Pirandello in America*. Rome: Bulzoni, 1988.

Milioto, Stefano, and Enzo Scriano. *Pirandello e la cultura del suo tempo*. Centro Nazionale Studi Pirandelliani. Milan: Mursia, 1984.

Miller, Karl. *Doubles: Studies in Literary History*. Oxford: Clarendon Press, 1985.

Nardelli, Frederico V. *Vita segreta di Pirandello*. Rome: Vito Bianco, 1962.

Newberry, Wilma. *The Pirandellian Mode in Spanish Literature*. Albany, N.Y.: SUNY Press, 1973.

Oliver, Roger W. *Dreams of Passion: The Theater of Luigi Pirandello*. New York: New York University Press, 1979.

Padellaro, Giuseppe. *Trittico siciliano: Verga, Pirandello, Quasimodo*. Milan: Rizzoli Editore, 1969.

Paolucci, Anne. *Pirandello's Theater: The Recovery of the Stage for Modern Art*. Carbondale: Southern Illinois University Press, 1974.

Pirouè, Georges. *Pirandello*. Trans. Zaccaria. Palermo: Sellerio, 1977.

Pronko, Leonard Cabell. *Avant-Garde: The Experimental Theater in France*. Berkeley: University of California Press, 1962.

Puppa, Paolo. *Dalle parti di Pirandello*. Rome: Bulzoni, 1987.

Radcliff-Umstead, Douglas. *The Mirror of Our Anguish: A Study of Luigi Pirandello's Narrative Writings*. Rutherford, N.J.: Fairleigh Dickenson University Press, 1978.

Ragusa, Olga. *Pirandello: An Approach to His Theatre*. Edinburgh: Edinburgh University Press, 1980.

Ridenti, Liuco. *Teatro italiano fra due guerre: 1915–1940*. Genoa: Dellacasa, 1968.

Sciacca, M. F. *L'Estetismo, Kirkegaard, Pirandello*. Milano: Marzorati, 1974.

Sciascia, Leonardo. *Pirandello e la Sicilia*. Caltanissetta-Roma: Salvatore Sciascia, 1968.

Starkie, Walter. *Luigi Pirandello*. 3rd ed. revised. Berkeley: University of California Press, 1965.

Steiner, George. *The Death of Tragedy*. New York: Alfred A. Knopf, 1961.

Tamberini, Carlo. *Pirandello nel 'Teatro che C'Era'*. Rome: Bulzoni, 1982.

Virdia, Ferndinando. *Invito alla lettura di Luigi Pirandello*. Milan: Mursia, 1975.

Weiss, Auréliu. *Le Théatre de Luigi Pirandello dans le Mouvement Dramatique Contemporain*. Paris: Librarie 73, 1965.

Zangrilli, Franco. *L'Arte Novellistica di Pirandello*. Ravenna: Longo, 1983.

———. "Max Frisch's *Stiller* und Luigi Pirandello's *Mattia Paschal*: Die Odysse zu dich Selbst, *Frisch: Kritik-Thesen-Analysen*, ed. Manfred Jurgesen. Bern: Franche, 1977.

———. *Pirandello in Guanti Gialli*. Rome: Scascia, 1983.

Zappala Muscarda, Sarah, ed. *Pirandello Dialettale*. Palermo: G. B. Pabembo, 1983.

SECONDARY SOURCES: ARTICLES

Alonge, Roberto. "Madri, puttane, schiave sessuali e uomini soli." *Studi pirandelliani, dal teṣto al sottotesto*. Bologna: Pitagora (1986):90–110.

———. "La riscoperta di Pirandello sulle scenè italiane nel secondo dopoguerra." *Quaderni di teatro* 34. Florence (April 1986):102–18.

———. "Subalternità e masochismo della donna nell 'ultimo theatro Pirandelliano'." *Struttura e ideologia nel teatro italiano fra '500 e '900*. Torino: Stampatori (1978):200–33.

Angelini, Franca. "Pirandello e Sartre." *Pirandello e la cultura del suo tempo*. Milano: Mursia (1984):273–84.

Anschutz, G. "Masks: Their Use by O'Neill and Pirandello." *Drama* (April 1927):201–202.

Asor Rosa, Alberto. "Pirandello fra soggettivismo e oggettivismo." *Pirandello Saggista.* Palermo: Palumbo (1982):11–21.

Bander, Robert. "Pulcinella, Pirandello and Other Influences on De Filippo's Dramaturgy." *Italian Quarterly* 12.46 (Fall 1968):39–72.

Baratto, Mario. "Le Thèâtre de Pirandello." *Realisme et Poèsie au Thèâtre.* Paris: Editions du Centre National de la Recherche Scientifique (1960): 181–94.

Barberi Squorotti, Giorgio. "La trilogia Pirandelliana e il rinnovamento del teatro." *Il teatro nel teatro di Pirandello.* Ed. Enzo Lauretta. Agrigento: Centro Nazionale di Studi Pirandelliani (1977):7–36.

Bassnett-McGuire, Susan. "Art and Life in Pirandello's *Questa sera si recita a soggetto.*" *Drama and Mimesis.* Ed. James Redmond. Cambridge: Cambridge University Press (1980):81–102.

Bentley, Eric. "Pirandello's Joy and Torment." *In Search of Theater.* New York: Vintage Books (1959):279–95.

Bonora, Ettore. "Pirandello studioso di Dante." *Pirandello saggista.* n.d.:89–102.

Borrello, Oreste. "Il pensiero estetico di Pirandello." *Letterature moderne* 11 (1961):634–53.

Brunettas, Gian Piero. "La conquista dell'impero dei sogni: D'Anunzio e Pirandello." *Annali d'Italianistica* 6 (1988):38–65.

Buck, Philo Melvin, Jr. "Futility in Masquerade: L. Pirandello." *Directions in Contemporary Literature.* London: Oxford University Press (1942):79–100.

Büdel, Oscar. "Pirandello Sulla Scena Tedesca." *Pirandello ieri e oggi.* Quaderni del Piccolo Teatro 1: Milan (1961):99–102.

Calendoli, Giovanni. "Dai futuristi a Pirandello attraverso il grottesco." *Sipario* 260 (December 1967):14–16.

———. "La trilogia e le esperienze europee d'avanguardia." *Il teatro nel teatro di Pirandello.* Ed. Enzo Lauretta. Agrigento: Centro Nazionale di Studi Pirandelliani (1977):207–21.

Campailla, Sergio. "Il verismo e Pirandello." *Pirandello e la cultura del suo tempo.* Milan: Mursia (1984):87–102.

Carotenuto, Aldo. "La personalita e lo psicodramma." *Atti dello Psicodramma* 8.6 (1983):76–90.

Caserta, Ernesto G. "Croce, Pirandello e il concetto di umorismo." *Canadian Journal of Italian Studies* 6.22–23 (1983):103–10.

Cassinasco, Maura. "Osservazioni sulle stesure di l'esclusa Pirandelliana." *Rassegna della letteratura Italiana* (1976):400–23.

Chandler, Frank Wadleigh. "Philosophic Pirandello." *Modern Continental Playwrights.* New York: Harper (1931):573–95.

Cincotta, Strong M. "L'esistenzialismo nelle novelle di Pirandello." *Le novelle di Pirandello.* Atti del 6 Convegno di Studi Pirandelliani. Agrigento: Edizioni del Centro Nazionale di Studi Pirandelliani (1980):103–17.

Cometa, Michele. "Pirandello e Lipps: Due lettre psicologiche dell'umorismo." *Pirandello e la cultura del suo tempo.* Milan: Mursia (1984):303–26.

Costa, Gustavo. "Pirandello e la filosofia." *Pirandello 1986: Atti del Simposio internazionale.* Eds. Biasin and Perella. Rome: Bulzoni (1987):149–64.

————. "Self and Representation in Pirandello's *Henry IV*." *Modern Language Studies*
11.3 Fall (1981):16–24.

Croce, Benedetto. "Luigi Pirandello." *La letteratura Italiana* 4. Bari: Laterza
(1963):326–33.

Cudini, Piero. "Pirandello e Croce: a proposito di Dante." *Pirandello saggista*, n.d.:103–
14.

D'Angeli, Concetta. "Il turno, prima indicazione del distacco di Pirandello dal verismo."
Paragone 310 (1976):51–65.

De Bosio, Gianfranco. "Maschera, speccio di vita." Eds. Sartori and Lanata. *Arte della
maschera nella commedia dell'arte*. Florence: Casa Usher (1984):159–162.

della Fazia, A. M. "Pirandello and His French Echo Anouilh." *Modern Drama* 6
(1964):346–67.

della Terza, Dante. "Luigi Pirandello e la ricerca della distanza umoristica." *Studi in
memoria di Luigi Russo*. Pisa: Nistri-Lischi (1974):405–22.

Dombroski, Robert S. "Pirandello e Freud: le dimensioni conoscitive dell'umorismo."
Pirandello Saggista. Palermo: Palumbo (1982):59–67.

————. "The Form of Chaos in Pirandello's *I vecchi e i giovani*." *Yale Italian Studies*
2 (1976):85–113.

Donati, Corrado. "Rito e conflittualità sociale in Pirandello." *Studi Urbanati di Storia:
Filosofia e Letteratura* 48 (1974):103–14.

Fazio Allmayer, Vito. "Il problema Pirandello." *Belfagor* 12.1 January (1957):18–34.

Fido, Franco. "Una novella 'Siciliana' di Pirandello e i suoi rapporti col verismo." *Atti
del Congresso Internazionale di Studi Pirandelliani* 2–5. Le Monnier (1961):553–
58.

Freedman, M. "Moral Perspective in Pirandello." *Modern Drama* 4 (1964):368–77.

Gaggi, Silvio. "Pirandello and Antilogic." *South Atlantic Bulletin* 41.2 (1976):112–16.

Gardair, Jean-Michel. "Pirandello e il suo doppio." *L'Evento Teatrale: Sezione "Saggi"*
3. Ed. Giulio Ferroni. Rome: Edizioni Abete (1977).

Germano, Joseph E. "La forza drammatica di *Cosi è (se vi pare)*." *Forum Italicum* 11
(1977):184–91.

Gramsci, Antonio. "The Theater of Pirandello." *Praxis* 3 (1950):30–37.

Guglielmino, Salvatore. "Retroterra e implicazioni del saggio su L'umorismo." *Pirandello e la cultura del suo tempo*. Milan: Mursia (1984):143–55.

Hamilton, Clayton Meeker. "L. Pirandello and Maurice Maeterlinck." *Conversations
on Contemporary Drama*. New York: Macmillan (1924):150–74.

Heffner, H. C. "Pirandello and the Nature of Man." *Tulane Drama Review* I.3 (June
1957):23–40.

Herman, William. "Pirandello and Possibility." *Tulane Drama Review* 10 (Spring
1966):91–111.

Hudecek, Vaclav. "On *Henry IV*." *ITI World Theatre* 16.4 (1967):1–10.

Hutchinson, P. "Wit and Wisdom in Pirandello, Italy's Winner of the Nobel Prize for
1934." *New York Times* (November 1934):25.

Illiano, Antonio. "Pirandello in England and the United States: A Chronological List of
Criticism." *Bulletin of New York Public Library* 71 (1967):105–30.

————. "Pirandello and Theosophy." *Modern Drama* 20 (1977):341–51.

Kelly, A. "Una rivaluazione della maternità nelle protagoniste Pirandelliane." *Le Ragioni
Critiche* 6.21 (1976):169–75.

Kernan, Alvin B. "Truth and the Dramatic Mode in the Modern Theater: Chekhov, Pirandello and Williams." *Modern Drama* 1 (1958):101–14.

Kligerman, Charles. "A Psychoanalytic Study of Pirandello's *Six Characters in Search of an Author.*" *Journal of the American Psychoanalytic Association* 10 (1961):731–44.

Knowlton, E. C. "Metaphysics and Pirandello." *South Atlantic Quarterly* (January 1935):42–59.

König de Estrada, Vera. "La Primera Novela de Pirandello y la Poetica de la Renunciaciòn." *Kàñina* 1.1 (1977):159–66.

Kowzan, T. "Wyspianski-Apollinaire-Pirandello-Maiakovski: Etude Comparative sur l'Illusion Thèâtrale." *Revue de Littèrature Comparèe* 50 (1976):184–97.

LeRoux, Monique. "De la Sicilianitè: Sciascia Lecteur de Pirandello." *Revue de Litterature Comparee* 2 (April-June 1985):171–78.

Lewis, Alan. "The Relativity of Truth—Pirandello." *The Contemporary Theatre: The Significant Playwrights of Our Time.* New York: Crown (1962):127–45.

Licastro, Emanuele. "Luigi Pirandello, statico dinamico," *L'Osservatore Politico Letterario* (Milano) 19.2 (1974):47–56.

———. "La funzionalita del cerebralismo: da *La camera in attesa* a *La vita che ti diedi,*" *Italica* 51 (1974):236–248.

———. "The Anti-theatre in Pirandello: *The Man with the Flower in His Mouth,*" *Romance Notes* 15 (1974):513–515.

———. "Pirandello: Conversation with Sicily." *Canadian Journal of Italian Studies* 6.22–23 (1983):52–59.

Macchia, Giovanni. "Luigi Pirandello." *Storia della Letteratura Italiana.* Eds. Cecchi and Sapegno. *Il Novacento* 9. Milan: Garzanti (1969):439–92.

Mariani, Umberto C. "Pirandello e il futurisimo." *NEMLA* 10 (1986):18–37.

———. "Liolà: Beyond Naturalism." *Review of National Literatures* 14 (1987):160–90.

Marranca, Bonnie. "Pirandello: A Work in Progress." *Performing Arts Journal* 7.2 (1983):7–28.

Mauri Paolo. "Cosi nacque *Il fu Mattia.*" *Republica* 5 (December 1986):24–25.

May, F. "Three Major Symbols in Four Plays by Pirandello." *Modern Drama* 6.4 (1964):78–96.

McDonald, David. "Derrida and Pirandello: A Post-Structuralist Analysis of *Six Characters in Search of an Author.*" *Modern Drama* 20 (1977):421–36.

Melcher, E. "Pirandellism of Jean Genet." *French Review* 36.1 (October 1962):32–36.

Miller, H. "Actor Looks at Pirandello." *Canadian Forum* (November 1931):78–79.

Montante, M. "The Woman in the Plays of Luigi Pirandello and Paul Claudel." *Claudel Studies* 8.2 (1980):38–47.

Moore, M. J. "Sicily in the *Novelle* of Pirandello." *Modern Language Review* 40 (July 1945):174–79.

Moses, Gavriel. "Film Theory as a Literary Genre in Pirandello and the Film Novel." *Annali d'Italianistica* 6 (1988):18–37.

Nathan, George Jean. "Pirandello." *The Magic Mirror: Selected Writings on the Theatre.* New York: Alfred A. Knopf (1960):186–88.

Nelson, Robert James. "Pirandello," *Play Within a Play: The Dramatist's Conception of His Art: Shakespeare to Anouilh.* New Haven: Yale University Press, 1958.

Newberry, W. "Echegaray and Pirandello." *PMLA* 81.1 (1966):123–29.

————. "Influence of Pirandello in Two Plays of Manuel and Antonio Machado." *Hispania* 48. May (1965):255–60.

Nicholosi, Francesco. "Su i vecchi e i giovani di Pirandello." *Le Ragioni Critiche* 6 (1976):n.p.

O'Keefe Bazzoni, Jana. "The Carnival Motif in Pirandello's Drama." *Modern Drama* 30.3 (1987):414–25.

————. "Seeing Double: Pirandello and His Audience." *Review of National Literatures* 14 (1987):31–46.

Oldcorn, Anthony. "Pirandello o del candore?" *Modern Language Notes* 91.1 (1976):139–49.

Pacifici, Sergio. "Pirandello, L.," *A Guide to Contemporary Italian Literature: From Futurism to Neorealism.* Cleveland: World Publishers (1962):213–16.

Palmer, John Leslie. "L. Pirandello and the Enigma of Personality." *Studies in the Contemporary Theatre.* Boston: Little, Brown (1927):45–64.

Paolucci, Anne. "Comedy and Paradox in Pirandello's Plays (An Hegelian Perspective)." *Modern Drama* 20 (1977):321–40.

Perloff, Eveline, and Clerge, Claude. "Theatre et la Folie." *Comedie-Francoise* 108 (April 1982):22–27.

Phelps, Ruth Shepard. "Pirandello's Plays." *Italian Silhouettes.* New York: Alfred A. Knopf (1924):116–41.

Poggioli, R. "Pirandello in Retrospect." *Italian Quarterly* 4 (1958):19–47.

PSA (The New Official Publication of the Pirandello Society of America) 1 (1985), 2 (1986), 3 (1987).

Puppa, Paolo. "Rossi di San Secondo e Pirandello: la cultura dei morti." *Quaderni di Teatro* 5.18 (1982):106–20.

Ragusa, Olga. "Pirandello's Teatro d'Arte and a New Look at His Fascism." *Italica* (Summer 1978):236–53.

Reifield, Beatrice Ann. "A Theory of Tragicomedy in Modern Drama," *Dissertation Abstracts International*, no. 37, 1976.

Rey, John B. "Pirandello's Last Play: Some Notes on *The Mountain Giants.*" *Modern Drama* 20 (1977):413–20.

Roda, Frederic. "Ritorno a Pirandello." *Els Gegants de la Muntayna.* Barcelona: Edicions Robrenyo (1983):5–8.

Rosenberg, M. "Pirandello's Mirror." *Modern Drama* 6.4 (1964):331–45.

Russo, Luigi. "Pirandello e la Psicanalisi." *Pirandello e la cultura del suo tempo.* Ed. Milito and Scrivano. Milano: Mursia (1984):31–54.

Savage, E. B. "Masks and Mummeries in Enrico IV and Caligula." *Modern Drama* 6.4 (1964):397–401.

Sawecka, Halina. "L'opposition Pirandellienne Forme-Vie et al Dialectique Sartrienne être-pairaître." *Pirandello: poetica e presenza.* Ed. Giovanelli. Rome: Bulzoni (1987):291–304.

Schulz-Buschhaus, Ulrich. "L'umorismo: L'anti-retorica e l'anti-sintesi di un secondo realismo." *Pirandello saggista.* n.d.:77–86.

Scherer, J. "Marivaux and Pirandello." *Modern Drama* 1.1 (1958):10–14.

Scully, Frank. "L. Pirandello." *Rogues' Gallery: Profiles of My Eminent Contemporaries.* Hollywood: Murray and Gee (1943):82–93.

Sinicropi, Giovanni. "The Metaphysical Dimension and Pirandello's Theatre." *Modern Drama* 20 (1977):353–80.

Sogliuzzo, Richard A. "The Uses of the Mask in *The Great God Brown* and *Six Characters.*" *Educational Theatre Journal* 18.3 (1966):224–29.

Spizzo, Jean. "Pirandello: théâtre du reflet, théâtre du conflit." *Lectures pirandelliennes.* Centre de recherche de l'Université de Paris VIII—Vincennes (Groupe "Culturelles, idéologies et sociétés des XIXe et XXe siècles." Section Italien II. Abbeville: Paillart (1978):175–232.

Squarzina, Luigi. "Directing Pirandello Today: An Interview with Gino Rizzo." *Tulane Drama Review* 10 (Spring 1966):76–85.

Stella, Vittorio. "Pirandello e la filosofia italiana." *Pirandello e la cultura del suo tempo.* Milan: Mursia (1984):5–30.

Stone, Jennifer. "Beyond Desire: A Critique of Susan Sontag's Production of Pirandello's *Come tu mi vuoi.*" *Yearbook of the British Pirandello Society* 1 (1981):19–25.

Storer, E. "Grotesques of Pirandello." *Forum* (October 1921):271–81.

Styan, John L. "Manipulating the Characters: 'Arms and the Man', 'A Midsummer Night's Dream', 'Six Characters in Search of an Author.' " *The Elements of Drama.* Cambridge: Cambridge University Press (1960):63–88.

Thomas, Johannes. "Il pensiero tedesco degli anni 20." *Pirandello e la Germania.* Palermo: Palumbo (1984):

Tilgher, Adriano. "Il teatro di Luigi Pirandello." *Studi sul Teatro Contemporaneo.* Rome: Libreria di Scienza e di Lettere (1923):157–218.

Tillona, Zina. "La morte nelle novelle di Pirandello." *Forum Italicum* 1 (1967):279–88.

Verdone, Mario. "Teatro Pirandelliano e futurismo." *Teatro Contemporaneo* 2.4 (1983):113–125.

Vincentini, Claudio. "Pirandello, Stanislavsky, Brecht, and the 'Opposition Principle'." *Modern Drama* 20 (1977):381–92.

Vowels, R. "Existentialism and Dramatic Form." *Educational Theatre Journal* (October 1953):215–20.

Whitfield, J. H. "Pirandello and T. S. Eliot: An Essay in Counterpoint." *English Miscellany* 9 (1962):329–57.

Williams, Raymond. "L. Pirandello." *Drama from Ibsen to Eliot.* London: Chatto and Windus (1952):185–95.

Young, Stark. "Pirandello's Commedia (*Right You Are If You Think You Are*)." *Immortal Shadows: A Book of Dramatic Criticism.* New York: Scribner's (1948):84–87.

Zangrilli, Franco. "La funzione del paessaggio nella poesia di Pirandello." *Review of National Literature: Pirandello* 14 (1987):93–122.

———. "Motivi Pirandelliani nel primo pomilio." *NEMLA* 10 (1986):117–31.

SECONDARY SOURCES: DISSERTATIONS

Asciutto, Joseph Louis. "The Sicilian Microcosm as Reflected in the Early Works of Pirandello." University of Southern California, 1977.

Bindert, Kathleen Rita. " 'Ethos' A Mask: A Study of Character in the Plays of Pirandello." Northwestern University, 1975.

Campo, Michael R. "The Influence of Luigi Pirandello on the Italian Dramatic Literature." Johns Hopkins University, 1954.

Canale-Parola, Thelma S. "The Proem in Pirandello's Short Stories." University of Illinois, 1962.

Chinotti, Louis Lawrence. "Luigi Pirandello and the Play Within the Novella." Harvard
    University, 1971.
Faustini, Giuseppi. "Luigi Pirandello: A Critical Study and a Contribution to His Bib-
    liography with Appendix." Harvard University, 1982.
Gattnig, Charles J. "Pirandello, Umorismo and Beckett." Southern Illinois University,
    1967.
Hodess, Kenneth M. "In Search of the Divided Self." City University of New York,
    1978.
O'Keefe Bazzoni, Georgiana. "Avant-Garde Italian Drama: Futurists, I Grotteschi and
    Pirandello." City University of New York, 1983.
Suboczewski, Irene. "The Figure of the Artist in Modern Drama from Ibsen to Piran-
    dello." University of Maryland, 1970.
Timm, Neil Herman. "A Comparative Study of Pirandello, Yeats and Brecht: The Mask
    as a Paradigm for Modern Theater." Columbia University, 1973.
Zeller-Cambon, Marlis. "Max Frisch und Luigi Pirandello: Eine Untersuchung zur The-
    matischen und Stilistischen Affinitat iher Romane." Bryn Mawr College, 1976.

SECONDARY SOURCES: BOOKS AND YEARBOOKS
DEVOTED TO PIRANDELLIAN STUDIES

"Yearbook of the British Pirandello Society," University of Warwick, Coventry, En-
    gland. First published 1981; annual.
"PSA: The New Official Publication of the Pirandello Society of America," St. John's
    University, New York. First published 1985; annual.
"Pirandellian Studies," University of Nebraska-Lincoln, Nebraska. First published 1985;
    irregular.

PIRANDELLO WORKS IN PRINT IN ENGLISH

Works by Pirandello Listed in *Books in Print* as of 1989.

Better Think Twice about It: And Twelve Other Stories. (Short Story Index Reprint Ser.)
    Repr. of 1934 ed. Ayer Co. Pubs.
Cap and Bells. 1974. Maryland.
The Late Mattia Pascal. 1987. Hippocrene Bks.
The Late Mattia Pascal. Weaver, William, tr. from Ital. 1988. Eridanos Pr.
Naked Masks: Five Plays, Bentley, Eric, ed. Incl. *It Is So If You Think So*; *Henry Fourth*;
    Six Characters in Search of an Author; *Each in His Own Way*; *Liolà*. 1957. pap.
    Dutton.
Novelle per un Anno. McCormick, C. A., ed. 1988. pap. St. Martin.
One, None & a Hundred-Thousand. Putnam, S., tr. 1983. Repr. of 1933 ed. Fertig.
One, None & a Hundred-Thousand. Weaver, William, tr. 1989. Eridanos Pub.
Pirandello Plays: Volume I. Includes *Henry IV*; *Right You Are*; *Lazarus*; *The Man with
    the Flower in His Mouth.* 1986. Riverrun NY.
Pirandello Plays: Volume II. Includes *Six Characters in Search of an Author*; *All For
    the Best*; *The Limes of Sicily*; *Clothe the Naked.* Bullock, et al. tr. 1989. pap.
    Riverrun, NY.

Shoot! (Si Gira) The Notebooks of Serafino Gubbio, Cinematograph Operator. Moncreiff, C. K., tr. 1975. Repr. of 1926 ed. Fertig.
Sicilian Comedies. 1983. PAJ Pubns.
Tales of Madness. Bussino, Giovanni R., tr. 1984. Dante U Amer.
Tales of Suicide. Bussino, Giovanni R., tr. 1988. Dante U Amer.
Three Plays: 'Enrico IV,' 'Sei personaggi in cerca d'autore,' 'La giara' Firth, F., ed. 1988. St. Martin.

Works Listed in the Samuel French, Inc. *Basic Catalogue of Plays and Supplement* as of 1990.

As You Desire Me, trans. Marta Abba.
Cap and Bells, trans. Norman A. Bailey (in *Sicilian Comedies*).
Diana and Tuda, trans. Marta Abba.
Each in His Own Way, trans. Arthur Livingston (in *Naked Masks*).
Emperor Henry IV, trans. Edward Storer (in *Naked Masks*), Robert Cornthwaite.
It Is So! If You Think So, trans. Arthur Livingston (in *Naked Masks*).
The Jar, trans. William Murray (in *Pirandello's One-Act Plays*).
Liola, trans. Eric Bentley, and Geraldo Guerrieri (in *Naked Masks*).
The Man With the Flower in His Mouth, trans. William Murray (in *Pirandello's One-Act Plays*); Eric Bentley (ms.).
No One Knows How, trans. Marta Abba.
Right You Are If You Think You Are, trans. Eric Bentley (in ms.).
The Rules of the Game, trans. William Murray.
Six Characters in Search of An Author, trans. Edward Storer (in *Naked Masks*), Eric Bentley, Denis Johnston (libretto of an opera version), Paul Avila Mayer, Frederick May, Robert Cornthwaite.
To Clothe the Naked, trans. William Murray.
To Find Oneself, trans. Marta Abba.
Tonight We Improvise, trans. Marta Abba.
When One Is Somebody, trans. Marta Abba.
The Wives' Friend, trans. Marta Abba.

Index

About the Contributors

ESTELLE ADEN is a professor in the Drama Department at Hofstra University. Professor Aden teaches classes in acting, improvisation, and voice for the actor. She has participated in the Pirandello Conference at Hofstra University and has written and lectured on the topics of communication and acting.

ANNA BALAKIAN is a past chairperson of the Department of Comparative Literature at New York University. She is the author of *Literary Origins of Surrealism, Surrealism: The Road to the Absolute, The Symbolist Movement: A Critical Appraisal, André Breton: Magus of Surrealism*, and most recently served as editor and collaborator to a collective volume, *Symbolism in the Literature of European Languages*. Her numerous articles include studies in poetics and theoretical criticism.

SUSAN BASSNETT is a professor in the Comparative Literature Department at the University of Warwick in England. She has written two books on Luigi Pirandello. She has also written *Sylvia Plath, Elizabeth I*, and *The Actress in Her Time: Bernhardt, Terry, Duse* and numerous articles in the fields of theater studies, translation studies, and women's studies.

ANGELA BELLI is a comparatist, with a primary interest in modern drama. Her current projects focus on the relations between literature and medicine, specifically as they are reflected on the contemporary stage. She has written on current dilemmas in the field of medical ethics as perceived by the creators of such celebrated plays as *Whose Life Is It Anyway?, The Elephant Man*, and *As Is*. Her articles have appeared in *Literature and Medicine, Medical Heritage*, and *The Journal of Medical Humanities and Bioethics*.

ERIC BENTLEY's most recent book is *The Pirandello Commentaries*. He has also written *The Playwright as Thinker* and edited *Naked Masks: Five Plays by Luigi Pirandello* and *The Theory of the Modern Stage*, plus numerous other books and articles on drama. He is currently most busy as a playwright, having written a modern adaptation of Pirandello's *Henry IV* entitled *H for Hamlet*. He has also written the plays *A Time to Live, A Time to Die, The Red, White and Black, The Kleist Variations*, and *Lord Alfred's Lover*.

GEORGE BERNSTEIN is a professor in the Education Department of Montclair State College in New Jersey. He specializes in the philosophy of education. He has published articles on the French novelist George Sand, on the Italian political thinker Antonio Gramsci, and on the Brazilian educator Paulo Freire.

DANIELA BINI is an assistant professor at the University of Texas at Austin in the Comparative Literature Department. She is the author of *A Fragrance from the Desert: Poetry and Philosophy in Giacomo Leopardi* and various articles on nineteenth- and twentieth-century literature and philosophy. Her present project is a study of Carlo Michelstaedter, a philosopher, poet, and painter.

VINCENZO BOLLETTINO is a professor of Italian, Spanish, and Comparative Literature at Montclair State College. He has published *The Narrative of Gabriel García Marques, Rememorando Sin Tiempo* (a collection of his own poetry) and *The Life of Dante*. He has published scholarly articles on Latin American and Italian literature.

GLAUCO CAMBON unfortunately did not live to see the completion of this volume. He had been a professor of Italian at the University of Connecticut. He edited a famous anthology of essays on Pirandello for the Twentieth Century Views series of Prentice-Hall. He also wrote numerous articles on Italian literature, especially the history of Italian drama.

GUSTAVO COSTA is professor and chairman of the Department of Italian at the University of California, Berkeley. He is the author of numerous scholarly books and articles on various aspects of Italian literature from Dante to Pirandello. He has received fellowships from various institutions, including the John Simon Guggenheim Foundation, and has taught at universities in Italy and America.

MIMI GISOLFI D'APONTE is professor of theater at the City University of New York Graduate School and University Center, as well as at Baruch College where she chairs the Speech Department. Her writing has appeared in *Centerpoint, Commonweal, Communication Education, Educational Theatre Journal, Italica, Modern Drama, Other Stages, Performing Arts Journal*, and *The Drama Review*. She and her husband Nello D'Aponte have translated Andrea Perrucci's *La Cantata dei Pastori* as *Shepherd's Song*. Her book on Italian ritual theater, *Teatro Religioso e Rituale Della Penisola Sorrentina e la Costiera Amalfitana*, has been published by Studia Humanitatis Press.

JOHN LOUIS DIGAETANI is a professor in the English Department at Hofstra

University, where he specializes in modern drama. He has written *Richard Wagner and the Modern British Novel*, a study of Wagner's influence on five modern novelists. He has also edited a collection of essays on Wagner's Ring Cycle called *Penetrating Wagner's Ring, An Anthology*. He has written an introduction to opera, *An Invitation to the Opera*, an analysis of Puccini's operas, *Puccini the Thinker*, and translations of three plays by Carlo Gozzi (Greenwood Press). He has specialized in the connections between the arts, especially in theater and opera.

ROBERT S. DOMBROSKI has taught at the University of Chicago and, since 1971, at the University of Connecticut where he is professor of Italian and chairman of the Comparative Literature Program. He is the author of numerous articles on modern Italian literature, including books on Manzoni, Pirandello, Gadda, and Antonio Gramsci. He is currently writing a book on the figure of the intellectual in modern Italian fiction.

MARTIN ESSLIN is a professor of drama at Stanford University. He was head of BBC Radio Drama from 1963 to 1977 and is the author of numerous books, including *Brecht—A Choice of Evils*, *The Theatre of the Absurd*, *Antonin Artaud* in the Modern Masters series, *Pinter—The Playwright*, *The Age of Television*, and most recently, *The Field of Drama—How the Signs of Drama Create Meaning on Stage and Screen*. He has also published numerous articles on modern drama.

GASPARE GIUDICE has written the standard biography of Pirandello. Entitled *Luigi Pirandello Biografia*, it appeared in Italy in 1963 and was published in a fine English translation by Alastair Hamilton in 1975. He has also written on Pirandello for such journals as *Belfagor* and *Paragone*. He was born in Rome and currently writes and lives in Naples.

ANTONIO ILLIANO is a professor of Italian at the University of North Carolina, Chapel Hill. His numerous writings on Italian drama include *Metapsichica e Letteratura in Pirandello* (1982). He has also written on Manzoni's narrative technique and on other aspects of modern Italian literature from Alfieri to Calvino. He is currently working on a study of medieval Italian literature; he is also the editor for the forthcoming *Dictionary of Literary Biography*.

EMANUELE LICASTRO is a professor of Italian at the State University of New York at Buffalo. He is the author of *Luigi Pirandello: Dalle Novelle alle Commedia* (1974), *Ugo Betti: an Introduction* (1985), and various articles on Italian literature.

JENNIFER LORCH, graduate in Italian at the University of Leeds, U.K., has been a professor at the University College of North Wales, Leeds, and Sydney.

She is currently a lecturer in the Italian Department at the University of Warwick. Her published writings include an annotated edition of a *Sacra Rappresentazione* and articles on Pirandello. She is currently completing a book on Mary Wollstonecraft. She is also editor of the *Yearbook of the British Pirandello Society.*

UMBERTO MARIANI is a professor of Italian at Rutgers University, where he also edits *The Italian Quarterly.* He has published and lectured extensively on Pirandello as well as on nineteenth- and twentieth-century Italian and American literature.

JANA O'KEEFE BAZZONI is assistant professor of speech at Baruch College of the City University of New York. She has published articles on Pirandello and other figures in modern drama in *Modern Drama, Review of National Literatures, Performing Arts Journal, PSA, Sipario,* and *Ridotto.* Her research interests include Italian futurism, contemporary Italian drama, and contemporary American productions of Pirandello's plays.

DAVID A. POWELL is an assistant professor of French at Hofstra University. He has published articles on George Sand in *George Sand Studies, Le Bulletin des Amis de George Sand,* and *Nineteenth Century French Studies.* He wrote the Twayne volume on George Sand and is currently working on a book on music and Sand. Dr. Powell is also the author of an article on the musical functions in the poetry of Pirandello.

MATTHEW N. PROSER is a professor of English at the University of Connecticut. His research interests include modern Italian and English drama, and he has published articles in this field in *Modern Drama* and other scholarly journals.

DOUGLAS RADCLIFF-UMSTEAD is a professor in the Department of Romance Languages and Literatures at Kent State University. Among his scholarly books are *The Mirror of our Anguish, A Study of the Narrative Writings of Luigi Pirandello; The Exile into Eternity, A Study of the Narrative Writings of Giorgio Bassani; Carnival Comedy and Sacred Play: The Renaissance Dramas of Giovanmaria Cecchi; Ugo Foscolo, A Biographical and Critical Study;* and *The Birth of Modern Comedy in Renaissance Italy.* He has published articles on Italian literature in *Italica, Yale French Studies, Onoma, The Canadian Journal of Italian Studies,* and he is editor-in-chief of *Italian Culture.* Dr. Radcliff-Umstead has also won the John Simon Guggenheim and National Endowment for the Humanities fellowships.

OLGA RAGUSA is Da Ponte Professor of Italian and chairperson of the Italian Department at Columbia University. Her publications on Pirandello include: *Luigi Pirandello* and *Pirandello: An Approach to his Theater.* Her essays on

Pirandello have appeared in *From Petrarch to Pirandello, The Two Hesperias, Pirandello 1986, European Writers: The Twentieth Century, Encyclopedia of World Literature in the 20th Century, The Dictionary of Italian Literature*, and *The Columbia Dictionary of Modern European Literature*, in addition to other scholarly journals.

MAURICE VALENCY has been professor of modern drama at Columbia University and dean of the drama division of the Juilliard School. He has written books on the theater of Ibsen, Chekhov, Strindberg, and Shaw. His most recent book is *The End of the World: An Introduction to Contemporary Drama*. In addition, he has written numerous books and articles on modern drama and Pirandello.

MARIA ROSARIA VITTI-ALEXANDER teaches Italian at the University of Michigan in Ann Arbor. She has written on Pirandello's fiction and theater and on Italian women writers of the twentieth century. Among her current projects is a series of articles on Italian women writers from the turn of the century to the present. She is also director of the University of Michigan's Florence Program.

MARY ANN FRESE WITT is professor in the Department of Foreign Languages and Literatures at North Carolina State University. She has published essays on various modern writers including Kafka, Camus, Sartre, Genet, Ionesco, and Buzzati as well as Pirandello. Her *Existential Prisons* is concerned primarily with Malraux, Camus, Sartre, and Genet. She is also the author of a textbook, *The Humanities: Cultural Roots and Continuities*.